Internet: The Complete Reference, Second Edition

About the Authors

Margaret Levine Young is the best-selling author (with various coauthors) of over two dozen books, including *The Internet For Dummies* and *Windows XP: The Complete Reference* (with her brother, John Levine). She holds a B.A. in computer science from Yale University and has two children. You can find out more at her web site, **net.gurus.com**.

Doug Muder has contributed to several books about computers and the Internet, including *Windows XP: The Complete Reference*. He is the author of numerous research papers in geometry and information theory and holds a Ph.D. in mathematics from the University of Chicago. Doug lives with his wife, Deborah Bodeau, in Nashua, New Hampshire and amuses himself by playing with other people's children, writing fiction, and dabbling in all forms of mysticism.

Dave Kay is a writer; former engineer; and aspiring artist, naturalist, and wildlife tracker. His business, BrightLeaf Communications, provides marketing communications services for high technology companies. His books include several titles in John Wiley & Sons' (formerly Hungry Minds') *...For Dummies* series, including, most recently, *Paint Shop Pro™ 7 For Dummies*.

Kathy Warfel is a technical writer who has been teaching people how to use computers and writing about computers for the past 15 years. She holds a B.S. in journalism from the University of Colorado and hopes one day to own a small-town online newspaper.

Alison Barrows is the author of several computer books, including John Wiley & Sons' (formerly Hungry Minds') *Dummies 101: 1-2-3 97*, *Dummies 101: WordPerfect 8*, and *Access 97 For Dummies Quick Reference*. She teaches and consults about the Internet in the Boston area.

William Steinmetz was the man who bought computer books for Borders and Waldenbooks for seven years before he decided it was time to go out and write his own. He lives in Cleveland and is geeky.

Although frequently lauded as the inventor of duct tape, **Gila Jones** is better known to her friends as a jackal of all trades. She has been putting people together with computers for more than 30 years and has previously written for private publication and *Computer Reseller News*. An avid do-it-yourselfer and fiber artist, Gila holds an M.B.A. in Information Systems Management from Northeastern University and lives in San Juan Capistrano, California with her partner and two sons.

Internet:
The Complete Reference,
Second Edition

Margaret Levine Young

McGraw-Hill/Osborne

New York Chicago San Francisco
Lisbon London Madrid Mexico City
Milan New Delhi San Juan
Seoul Singapore Sydney Toronto

McGraw-Hill/Osborne
2600 Tenth Street
Berkeley, California 94710
U.S.A.

To arrange bulk purchase discounts for sales promotions, premiums, or fund-raisers, please contact **McGraw-Hill**/Osborne at the above address. For information on translations or book distributors outside the U.S.A., please see the International Contact Information page immediately following the index of this book.

Internet: The Complete Reference, Second Edition

1234567890 DOC DOC 0198765432

ISBN 0-07-219415-4

Publisher	**Copy Editor**
Brandon A. Nordin	Jan Jue
Vice President & Associate Publisher	**Proofreaders**
Scott Rogers	Paul Medoff, Linda Medoff
Acquisitions Editor	**Indexer**
Megg Morin	Valerie Perry
Project Editor	**Computer Designers**
Laura Stone	Lucie Ericksen, Tabitha M. Cagan
Acquisitions Coordinator	**Illustrators**
Tana Allen	Michael Mueller, Lyssa Wald
Technical Editor	**Series Design**
Will Kelly	Peter F. Hancik

This book was composed with Corel VENTURA™ Publisher.

This book is dedicated to
Dionir Souza Gomes Young and Jordan Marten Young, Sr.
on the 50th anniversary of their marriage.

Contents at a Glance

Contents

Part I

Connecting to the Internet

Part II

Exchanging E-mail

Part III

Chatting and Conferencing on the Internet

13 Internet Relay Chat (IRC)

Part IV

Viewing the World Wide Web

Part V
Creating and Maintaining Web Sites

Part VI

File Transfer and Downloading

Acknowledgments

The authors would like to thank Megg Morin, Scott Rogers, Tana Allen, Laura Stone, Jan Jue, Paul and Linda Medoff, Valerie Perry, Lyssa Wald, Michael Mueller, the entire Production team, and many others at McGraw-Hill/Osborne for making this book happen.

We also thank Simon St. Laurent for the write-up about XML in Chapter 17; Deborah Shadowitz for GoLive information in Chapter 25 (you can find out more about her coverage of GoLive at **www.shadovitz.com/writing**); Will Kelly for his insightful technical editing; and John Levine, for general technical information.

Margy would also like to thank Shoreham Internet of Shoreham, Vermont for their fabulous DSL service; Jordan Young for making all our computers work; and John Levine for hosting the web site for this book.

Introduction

The Internet has grown explosively over the last ten years, with increases in the number of users, the amount of information that it makes available, and the number of different programs you can use. If you're a serious Internet user—relying on e-mail for business and personal communications and the Web for news and entertainment—you've probably run into snags and questions that basic Internet books don't answer. This book can help you with the complexity of the Internet and solve these snags. It covers the most important aspects of the Internet, skipping the basics, with clear instructions for how to get the most out of the Net.

Who Is This Book For?

This book is for anyone who uses the Internet and wants to know more. You might have one of the following questions, for example:

- What do I need to reconfigure if I switch from dial-up to a DSL connection?
- Should I prevent my browser from storing cookies on my hard disk? How can I look at the cookies that my browser has already stored on my system?
- How can I minimize my chances of getting a virus?

- What's the best search engine?
- How do I register a domain name and set up my own web site?
- How can I deal with the increasing number of e-mail messages I get each day?
- Can I run my own e-mail discussion list?
- Is it safe to try peer-to-peer file-sharing services like KaZaA and Morpheus?
- Is voice conferencing over the Internet hard to set up? Is it expensive?

This book answers all of these questions and thousands more. It describes programs for Windows XP, Windows 2000, Windows ME, Macintoshes, and UNIX, and covers how to configure your e-mail program and web browser, connect your home network to share one Internet connection, and much more.

In this book, the authors assume that you know how to use your computer—whether it's Windows, a Mac, or UNIX. We also assume that you know the basics of the Internet, including how to send and receive e-mail and browse the Web.

Note   *If you want an introduction to the Internet (or you think someone you know needs one), get* How to Do Everything with the Internet *by Dennis Jones (McGraw-Hill/ Osborne, 2000) or* The Internet For Dummies, 8th Edition *by John R. Levine and Margaret Levine Young (John Wiley & Sons [formerly Hungry Minds], 2002).*

What's in This Book?

This book is divided into six parts.

Part I: Connecting to the Internet

Part I describes the components of the Internet—hosts, domains, Internet services, and how computers and LANs can connect to the Internet.

Chapter 1 covers Internet concepts, including the new Internet domains. If you want to register your own domain (or you've wondered how the domain naming system works), it's covered in Chapter 2. Chapter 3 contains the instructions you need to configure your computer to connect to an Internet account, including DSL and cable Internet accounts. If you want to connect an entire local area network (LAN) to the Internet as an intranet, read Chapter 4.

Part II: Exchanging E-mail

The most widely used Internet service is e-mail. It's worth learning the advanced features of your e-mail program so you don't have to spend as much time keeping up with your messages.

Chapter 5 covers basic e-mail concepts like attachments, formatting, and netiquette. Configuration commands for the most popular e-mail programs—Outlook, Outlook Express, Netscape Messenger, Netscape Mail, Eudora, and web-based mail—are described in Chapter 6, including reading and sending mail from multiple accounts and with multiple addresses. If you've had trouble sending or receiving files by e-mail, read Chapter 7 to learn about file attachments. Chapter 8 has instructions for handling the increasing amount of e-mail many people receive, including how to configure your e-mail program to presort your incoming messages and how to deal with spam.

Part III: Chatting and Conferencing on the Internet

Instant messaging, chat rooms, and other person-to-person Internet programs are incredibly popular. This part of the book describes the various Internet services that allow groups of people to communicate over the Internet.

Chapter 9 provides an overview of ways you can use the Internet for conferencing and chatting. In Chapter 10, you learn how to participant in e-mail mailing lists and set up your own mailing lists. If you want to read or post to Usenet newsgroups, read Chapter 11 for the basic concepts and Chapter 12 for how to use the most popular Usenet newsreading programs. Chapter 13 is an introduction to the world of Internet Relay Chat (IRC), the Internet's original real-time chat network. If you use AOL Instant Messenger or another IM program (or you're ready to try one), check out Chapter 14. Chapter 15 describes web-based discussions, including how to set up your own. For voice and video conferencing, look at Chapter 16.

Part IV: Viewing the World Wide Web

Everyone can use a browser, but not everyone knows how to configure browsers to make web-surfing fast and efficient. Part IV describes how to take advantage of the possibilities of the Web.

Chapter 17 gives you an overview of the Web's components, including plug-ins and ActiveX controls. To configure your browser to display the toolbars and buttons you really use and to install plug-ins for interactive web sites, see Chapter 18. Chapter 19 covers the ways you can set up your browser to make it easy to return to your favorite web sites. If you are concerned about privacy and security, see Chapter 20. Chapter 21 lists the best web search engines and directories and how to use them. In Chapter 22, you learn how to find and play Internet-based audio and video.

Part V: Creating and Maintaining Web Sites

If you or your organization want to provide information over the Web, you need to plan, design, create, test, and maintain a web site. Part V tells you how.

Chapter 23 covers the concepts of web site creation, including HTML, web site design, and programs for creating pages. In Chapter 24, you learn how to create Web pages using a text editor, inserting the necessary HTML codes yourself. Chapter 25 describes the best and most popular web page editing programs: Dreamweaver, GoLive, Netscape Composer, and FrontPage. To create or edit graphics files to enliven your web pages, read Chapter 26; and if you want your Web site to include audio clips, take a look at Chapter 27. For more advanced sites, Chapter 28 contains an overview of interactive and database-driven web site design, including CGI, JavaScript, PHP,

Active Server Pages, and ColdFusion. Chapter 29 describes how to use cascading style sheets to make your web site better looking and easier to maintain and how to add message boards, news feeds, and other features without programming.

Once you have created and tested your web site on your own computer, Chapter 30 describes how to upload it to a web server so that the rest of the world can see it, too. To analyze how people find your site and increase the number of visitors you receive, see the tips in Chapter 31. In Chapter 32, you can find out how to turn your web site into a retail store.

Part VI: File Transfer and Downloading

Whether you have created a web page and need to upload it to your web server or you've heard about a program that you can get from a web-based shareware library, sooner or later you'll need to upload or download files. Chapter 33 has an overview of FTP (file transfer protocol) concepts and step-by-step instructions for using FTP programs. It also describes how to use telnet and ssh to log into web servers to manage the files in your web site. In Chapter 34, you learn what to do with the files you have downloaded, including how to install programs.

Conventions Used in This Book

This book uses several icons to highlight special advice:

   A handy way to make the Internet work for you.

   An observation that gives you insight into the way the Internet works.

   Something to watch out for so you don't have to learn the hard way.

When you see instructions to choose commands from a menu, the parts of the command are separated by vertical bars (|). For example, "choose Tools | Internet Options" means to choose Tools from the menu bar and then choose Internet Options from the Tools menu that appears. If the command begins with "Start |," click the Start button on the Windows Taskbar as the first step. Unless otherwise noted, all the instructions in this book are for Windows XP. If you need more information about using Windows, refer to *Windows XP: The Complete Reference*, *Windows Millennium Edition: The Complete Reference*, and *Windows 98: The Complete Reference* (all published by McGraw-Hill/Osborne).

To find out which button is which on the toolbar of most programs, move the mouse pointer to the button and wait a few seconds without clicking. Most programs display a little box, or tooltip, *with the name of the button.*

Contacting the Authors

This book isn't just a book—it's a Web site, too. For updated information about the Internet, use your browser to see our Web site at **net.gurus.com/nettcr2**. While you're there, you can tell us what you thought of the book, or you can let us know by writing to us at **nettcr2@gurus.com**. Please don't ask us a lot of questions about the Internet, though—we're too busy updating this book and writing new ones to provide a lot free e-mail consulting. With luck, you'll find some answers at the book's web site.

The
Complete
Reference

Internet

Part I

Connecting to the Internet

The
Complete
Reference

Internet

Chapter 1

Internet Connection Concepts

Y ou're already on the Internet—or you would never have decided to tackle an 800-page book about it. However, to use the Internet effectively, it helps to learn how it works. This chapter looks under the hood and describes how the Internet connects millions of computers that share a communications protocol (TCP/IP) and a system of addresses and names (the domain naming system). We also talk about the types of Internet connections (from dial-up to DSL to satellite) that you can use, along with Internet-related security concerns such as passwords, viruses, and firewalls.

The rest of the chapters in Part I describe other Internet connection topics. Chapter 2 explains how domain names work (and how you can register your own), Chapter 3 contains configuration instructions for dial-up and broadband Internet accounts, and Chapter 4 tells you how to connect a LAN to the Internet to create your own intranet.

Internet Communications Protocols

Computers connected to the Internet communicate by using the *Internet Protocol (IP)*, which slices information into *packets* (chunks of data to be transmitted separately) and routes them to their destination. Because the Internet was designed to operate even during a war, it uses *dynamic routing*, so that even if one part of the network is knocked out, packets can be rerouted around the problem. Warfare hasn't been a problem for Internet communications (yet), but dynamic rerouting helps the Internet deal with other types of equipment failures. Along with IP, most computers on the Internet communicate with *Transmission Control Protocol (TCP)*, and the combination is called *TCP/IP*.

Before Windows 95, Windows users had to get a separate TCP/IP communications program, and several free and commercial programs were available. All versions of Windows starting with Windows 95 come with TCP/IP connection software called Dial-Up Networking. A similar standard exists for the Macintosh: MacTCP. MacOS 7.6.1 or later come with MacTCP-compatible Internet connection software. In 7.1.1 through 9.2, it's called Open Transport/PPP or Apple Remote Access. In Mac OS X, Internet connection software is built right into the underlying UNIX operating system.

Internet Hosts

Each computer on the Internet is called a *host computer* or *host*. The computers on the Internet—and there are now millions of Internet hosts—are connected by cables, phone lines, and satellite connections. They include large mainframe computers, smaller minicomputers, and personal computers. When your PC or Mac dials into an Internet account, your computer is an Internet host, too.

Internet Protocol (IP) Addresses

Each host computer on the Internet has a unique number, called its *IP address*. IP addresses are in the format *xxx.xxx.xxx.xxx*, where each *xxx* is a number from 0 to 255. IP addresses identify the host computers, so that packets of information reach the correct computer. You may have to type IP addresses when you configure your computer for connection to the Internet.

If you connect to the Internet by using a dial-up account, your Internet service provider (ISP) assigns your computer an IP address each time that you connect. This system enables your ISP to get along with fewer IP addresses, because it needs only enough IP addresses for the number of users who are connected simultaneously (as opposed to assigning a permanent IP address to each customer of the ISP). If you use a high-speed DSL or cable Internet account, you may have a *static* (unchanging) IP address, or your ISP may assign you an address each time you connect. Static IP addresses get rarer every year and usually cost extra.

Computers on a local area network (LAN) usually have IP addresses that are reserved for use on LANs rather than on the Internet itself. These addresses are usually in the range 192.168.*x.x* or 169.254.*x.x*. A server on the LAN usually assigns them: the most common IP assignment server is called *DHCP (Dynamic Host Configuration Protocol)*. For more information about IP addresses on LANs, see Chapter 4.

On Windows XP systems, you can find out your computer's IP address by choosing Start | Control Panel | Network Connections to see your Internet and LAN connections. Right-click your Internet or LAN connection, choose Status from the menu that appears, and click the Support tab. You see a window like this:

*If your computer connects to the Internet through a LAN, this IP address is probably not the one that appears on the Internet. (LAN-connected computers have LAN-only IP addresses.) To find out your IP address according to the Internet, go to **www.whatsmyipaddress.com**.*

Domain and Host Names

So that people don't have to remember strings of numbers, host computers also have names. The name of each host computer consists of a series of words separated by dots. The last part of the domain name is called the *top-level domain (TLD)*. The TLDs of three or more letters are used mainly in the United States and indicate the type of organization that owns the domain. The original seven three-letter TLDs are the following:

com	Originally for commercial organizations, but now used by individuals, government agencies, and nonprofits as well
net	Internet service providers and other network-related companies
org	Noncommercial (often nonprofit) organizations
gov	U.S. government agencies
mil	U.S. military
edu	Educational domains
int	International organizations like NATO and the International Red Cross

More three-or-more-letter TLDs are coming into use, such as these:

aero	Airlines
arpa	Internet infrastructure (named after the U.S. government agency that originally created the Internet)
biz	Businesses
coop	Cooperatives
info	Anyone
museum	Museum
name	Individuals

Two-letter TLDs indicate the country in which the organization that owns the computer is located. U.S. organizations can register domains that end with **us**. Canadian organizations, for instance, usually have the TLD **ca**. You can find the full list of geographic TLDs on the Web at **net.gurus.com/countries**. A few countries are taking advantage of their two-letter TLDs (like **tv** for Tuvalu, **am** for Armenia, and **fm** for the Federation of Micronesia) to make some money on domain registrations: see the next chapter for details. The most recent two-letter TLD is **eu** for the European Union, added in mid-2002.

The last two parts of a host computer name constitute the *domain*. The second-to-last part of the name (the *second-level domain*) is chosen by the organization that owns the computer and is usually some variant of the organization's name. For example, computers at the U.S. president's offices at the White House have the domain **whitehouse.gov**.

Computers at Yale University have names that end with **yale.edu** because Yale is an educational institution. Computers at the McGraw-Hill publishing company are named with the domain **mcgraw-hill.com**.

Because most organizations own more than one computer on the Internet, most host computer names have at least one more part, preceding the domain name and called a *third-level domain* (or sometimes a *subdomain*). This additional part (or parts) is assigned by the organization itself. For example, the **gurus.com** domain (which is owned by one of the authors of this book) has several host names, including **www.gurus.com** (the main web site), **net.gurus.com** (the Internet Gurus web site), and **wine.gurus.com** (the web site of the Society of Wine Educators). By far, the most widely used addition to domain names is *www*, because it is frequently used for an organization's web server (the computer that stores web pages). Some organizations name their computers using stars, planets, animals, or other themes, so don't be surprised if e-mail from Middlebury College comes from **panther.middlebury.edu**.

Capitalization doesn't matter in host names. **Gurus.Com** and **gurus.com** are both valid forms of the same name. Host names usually appear in lowercase.

One host computer can have many different names. For example, many ISPs also offer *domain hosting,* which means that they allow your domain name to be applied to one of their host computers. Domain hosting enables you to have your own domain name, even if you don't have a host computer. See Chapter 2 for information on how to register a domain name.

*Technically, **gurus.com** and **net.gurus.com** are both domains. However, most Internet users refer to second-level domains (like **gurus.com**) as "domains" and third-level (or more) domains (like **net.gurus.com**) as "subdomains."*

Servers and Clients

Many of the host computers on the Internet offer services to other computers on the Internet. For example, your ISP probably has a host computer that handles your incoming and outgoing mail. Computers that provide services for other computers to use are called *servers.* The software run by server computers to provide services is called *server software.*

Conversely, many of the computers on the Internet use servers to get information. For example, when your computer dials into an Internet account, your e-mail program downloads your incoming messages from your ISP's mail server. Programs that ask servers for services are called *clients.* Your e-mail program is more properly called an *e-mail client.*

Here are some types of servers and clients that you may encounter:

■ **Mail servers** handle incoming and outgoing e-mail. Specifically, *Post Office Protocol (POP* or *POP3)* and *IMAP (Internet Message Access Protocol)* servers store incoming e-mail, whereas *Simple Mail Transfer Protocol (SMTP)* servers relay outgoing e-mail. *Mail clients* get incoming messages from, and send outgoing messages to, a mail server, and enable you to read, write, save, and print messages. See Part II for how to use e-mail clients.

- **Web servers** store web pages and transmit them in response to requests from *web clients*, which are usually called *browsers*. See Part IV for details about browsers and Part V for how to create web pages and store them on web servers.

- **FTP servers** store files that you can transfer to or from your computer if you have an *FTP client*. See Chapter 33 for how to use FTP.

- **News servers** store Usenet newsgroup articles that you can read and send if you have a *news client* or *newsreader*. See Chapters 11 and 12 for how to use newsreaders.

- **IRC servers** act as a switchboard for Internet Relay Chat (IRC) channels. To participate, you use an *IRC client*. See Chapter 13 for how to use IRC.

Ports and Port Numbers

One host computer can run more than one server program. For example, a small ISP might have one computer running a POP server, SMTP server, web server, and news server. To keep requests for information straight, each type of server responds to packets sent to specific *ports* (input for a specific Internet service). Ports are numbered, and standard port numbers used throughout the Internet. You almost never need to type port numbers, but here are some widely used port numbers in case you do:

Port Number	Internet Service
21	FTP (file transfer)
23	Telnet (remote login)
25	SMTP (mail relaying)
80	World Wide Web
110	POP3 (storage of incoming mail)
194 (as well as 6667 and many others)	IRC (online chat)
532	Usenet newsgroups (discussion groups)

 For a complete listing of port numbers, see the IANA web site at www.iana.org/assignments/port-numbers.

The Domain Name System and DNS Servers

You use one other type of Internet server almost every time that you request information from an Internet host. A *Domain Name System (DNS)* server translates between the numeric IP addresses that identify each host computer on the Internet and the corresponding domain names. People prefer to use host names because they are easier to type and remember, but actual Internet communications use the numeric addresses. For example, if your browser requests a web page from the Yahoo! web site, which has the host

Connection Speeds

Everybody wants more speed. The moment that you get it, all the Internet content providers clog up the pipes with video and audio, applets, and animation. So it's hard to generalize about how much speed is enough. It's a moving target. It's also a matter of individual preference and the size of your pocketbook. However, if you regularly do large downloads—such as software upgrades—you may be interested in the following comparison:

Modem Speed	Time to Download a 10MB File
28.8 Kbps	46 minutes
56 Kbps	24 minutes
128 Kbps	10 minutes
1.544 Mbps	52 seconds
4 Mbps	20 seconds

Don't neglect your need for *upstream* speed, either. When you e-mail files, publish a web page, or have a video conference, you're sending data. If you set up a computer as a server and make information on it available to others, upstream speed *really* matters.

name **www.yahoo.com**, a DNS server translates that name to 204.71.200.69, one of Yahoo's web servers, and then sends the request to that IP address. Chapter 2 describes in more detail how the Domain Name System works.

Your ISP provides a DNS server to handle domain name translations. If the DNS server isn't working properly, or you have configured your computer with the wrong IP address for the DNS server, your computer can't find any of the computers on the Internet that you specify by host name. It has no way to translate host names to IP addresses. You may see error messages such as "Unable to locate host" or "Server does not have a DNS entry." (Contact your ISP to fix the problem, or consult Chapter 3.)

Types of Internet Connections

To connect to the Internet, you connect your computer to a computer that is on the Internet, usually one run by an ISP. You can connect your computer by using a dial-up phone line, which is how most home users connected to the Internet during the 1990s. If you need to connect at higher speeds than a regular phone line allows, you can get a high-speed phone line, assuming that your phone company offers them. You may have three options, depending on what your phone company offers: DSL, ISDN, or a leased line (such as a T1).

If your cable TV company offers an Internet service, you can connect your computer to the Internet by using a cable TV connection. Rural users may consider installing a satellite dish for Internet connections, whereas urban users may have access to a wireless connection. In offices, most computers connect via a local area network (LAN), and many homes are beginning to connect their computers into Internet-connected LANs, too.

 High-speed Internet connections, including DSL, ISDN, leased lines, cable Internet, and satellite, are all called broadband *connections.*

The following sections describe each type of connection, and Chapter 3 contains information about how to set up and configure these connections.

Dial-Up Connections

A dial-up connection to the Internet works over an ordinary phone line. Dial-up connections use the *Point-to-Point Protocol (PPP)* and are also called *PPP accounts.* Early dial-up connections used older protocols (SLIP and CSLIP), but these protocols are no longer used.

To use a dial-up account, you need a modem. (To distinguish dial-up modems from newer, high-speed modems, they are also called *analog modems* or *dial-up modems.*) Most computers come with an internal modem—check the back of the computer for a phone jack (RJ-11 jack). Most ISPs support modems at speeds of 28.8 kilobits per second (Kbps) and 56 Kbps. You connect only when you want to use Internet services and disconnect (hang up) when you are done.

To connect, you need a PPP-compatible communications program, such as Dial-Up Networking, which comes with all versions of Windows since Windows 95. This program dials the phone by using your modem, connects to your ISP, logs into your account by using your user name and password, and then establishes a PPP connection, thus connecting your computer to the Internet. While connected, you can use a variety of programs to read your e-mail, browse the Web, and access other information from the Internet. When you are done, you use your communications program to disconnect from your Internet account. (See Chapter 3 for how to set up and configure a dial-up connection.)

DSL Connections

Digital Subscriber Line (DSL) is a family of all-digital, high-speed lines that use your normal phone wires with special modems on either end. Most DSL lines are actually *ADSL (Asymmetric Digital Subscriber Line).* ADSL is optimized for the way many people use the Internet: more downloads than uploads. The line is *asymmetric,* because it has more capacity for data received by your computer (such as graphics, video, audio, and software upgrades) than for data that you send (such as e-mail and browser commands).

Configurations and prices vary depending on your phone company. The *downstream bandwidth* (data transfer speed from the Internet to your computer) can range from

UNIX Shell Accounts

Before the advent of dial-up PPP accounts, most Internet accounts were text-only *UNIX shell accounts*, and these accounts are still available from a few ISPs. You run a *terminal-emulation program* (a program that pretends that your PC is a computer terminal) on your PC to connect to an Internet host computer—Windows comes with HyperTerminal, a good terminal emulation program. Most Internet hosts run UNIX, a powerful but frequently confusing operating system, and you have to type UNIX commands to use a UNIX shell account. To send and receive e-mail or browse the Web, you run text-only programs, such as Pine (the most popular UNIX e-mail program) and Lynx (the most widely used UNIX web browser). When you use a UNIX shell account, you don't see graphics or use a mouse, and you can't easily store information on your own computer. For information about how to give commands once you are connected to a UNIX shell account, see the section in Chapter 33 that covers logging into a Web or FTP server. The web site **net.gurus.com/shell** describes how to use Pine and Lynx.

384 Kbps to 8 megabits per second (Mbps). The *upstream bandwidth* (speed from your computer to the Internet) can range from 90 Kbps to 768 Kbps. In real life, however, speeds are usually much lower and depend on the distance between you and the phone company's Central Office (CO) or wherever the DSL modem at their end is located.

With a DSL line, you can connect your computer to the Internet and talk on the phone at the same time on the same phone line. This feature means that if you currently have two phone lines, one for voice and one for Internet, you can get rid of one of them. However, the speed of your Internet connection may drop while you are talking on the phone.

Costs for DSL lines are higher than for regular phone lines, averaging $50 per month. There's usually a sign-up fee of several hundred dollars. The price for the Internet connection is generally a flat rate, but you are usually charged extra for voice calls, including local calls.

You can order a DSL line through your ISP or directly from your phone company— talk to both before you place your order. Availability depends on your location; DSL lines can't be more than 18,000 feet (5,460 meters) from the phone company's central office (or switching point for your exchange).

The phone company or ISP usually provides the DSL modem, which must match the DSL modem installed at their end. Because there are several competing DSL modem standards, not all DSL modems work with all DSL lines. If you already have a DSL modem, check with your phone company to find out whether you can save some money by using your own modem.

DSL modems usually connect to your computer through an *Ethernet* or other network card in your computer. If you don't have one, add another $20 (for a desktop computer) or $50 (for a laptop) to your cost. Many newer computers come with built-in

Ethernet jacks, which look like oversized phone jacks. Some DSL modems connect to a USB port, although these modems limit your connection speed. If you plan to use a phone or fax machine on your ADSL line, make sure the modem has a phone jack. If possible, choose a model with a built-in telephone filter.

When you sign up for a DSL line, the phone company (or other DSL provider) comes to your location, installs the DSL modem, and configures your computer to use it. Some DSL lines are configured so that you are always connected—no more logging in. Others use *PPPoE (PPP over Ethernet)* to pretend that you are still dialing in, so you still have to log in, too.

 *ADSL is just one of a family of DSL products on the drawing board. See the ADSL Forum (**www.adsl.com**), DSL Reports (**www.dslreports.com**), and TeleChoice's xDSL site (**www.xdsl.com**) for more background.*

ISDN Connections

Integrated Services Digital Network (ISDN) lines are also available from many local telephone companies. ISDN is an upgraded phone line that can be used for faster Internet access and for regular voice calls. Using one line, you can talk on the phone while you're surfing the Web. Like DSL, ISDN is all digital, which means that data doesn't have to be converted to an *analog signal* (that funny noise you hear modems make) for transmission.

The ISDN service intended for residential use is *Basic Rate Interface (BRI)*. On one ISDN line, BRI provides two 64-Kbps channels, or *B channels,* and one 16-Kbps channel, or *D channel*. The D channel is mostly used for signaling—for instance, to indicate that the line is busy. The B channels are where the action is. When the two B channels are combined, you have a 128-Kbps line to the Internet. That's roughly twice the speed of the fastest analog modem, 56 Kbps. If you want to talk on the phone or send a fax, your Internet access drops down to one 64-Kbps B channel, while the other B channel is used for voice. Integrated Services Digital Network (ISDN) lines, like DSL lines, are all-digital, high-speed phone lines that provide a faster way to connect to the Internet.

To connect your computer to an ISDN line, you need an *ISDN adapter,* which is like a modem. Your phone company or ISP usually provides the ISDN adapter as part of the sign-up fee. ISDN adapters may be internal or external: external adapters usually connect to your computer's serial port, which, until recently, was limited to a top speed of 115.2 Kbps. (Newer serial interfaces have faster chips.) Internal adapters bypass any serial port bottleneck, so you can get a full 128 Kbps out of your ISDN line.

The cost of an ISDN line usually depends on the number of minutes of use. It may also depend on time of day, with higher rates for business hours. The cost of Internet service accessed through ISDN also goes up with use. A typical ISDN package gives you a certain number of minutes per month "free," included in a base rate. Additional use is charged per minute. *If* you can stay within the base rate guidelines, you can get an ISDN line plus ISP access for about $60 per month. Look at your past usage patterns to see whether that's a realistic figure for you. (For most heavy Internet users, it's not.)

Clearly, ISDN is not intended to be left on all day. (DSL and cable modem service are.) However, with a new type of ISDN service, you'll never have to dial up again: *Always On/Dynamic ISDN (AO/DI)* uses the D channel to provide a constant 9.6-Kbps connection to the Internet. E-mail is delivered, chat pals can find you, and your stock ticker stays up to date. When you need more capacity, AO/DI switches over to one or two of the B channels. If you are considering ISDN, ask whether AO/DI is available for your line— and compare its price.

An ISDN line shouldn't be the only phone line in your house. Your regular analog phone will work only if it's connected through the ISDN terminal adapter. If the power were to go out in an emergency, the adapter couldn't power the phone, and you couldn't make or receive any calls. Be sure to keep a regular analog line. The phone system can power a corded phone even if the rest of the power in your house is out. (DSL lines don't have this problem. Phones can be plugged in directly to the line and draw their power from it.)

To order an ISDN line, contact your phone company or ISP (better yet, contact both). The phone company usually provides the ISDN adapter, installs it at your site, and configures your computer to use the connection.

If you're going to use a phone or fax machine on your ISDN line, make sure that your adapter has at least one analog phone jack on it. You plug in your existing equipment to the adapter. Also, check to see whether the adapter has full *ringing support*. That is, when a phone call comes in, does the phone actually ring, or do you just get some flashing lights on the front of the adapter? Flashing lights are easy to miss when you're busy poring over your computer screen.

 DSL is the most common in the United States; ISDN is widely used in Europe.

Leased Lines

If you (or more likely, your corporation) need to transfer very large amounts of data or run Internet server software, contact your telephone company for a *leased line,* the same type of phone line that organizations use to connect corporate offices. Leased lines come in various speeds, including *T1* (1.5 megabits per second, or enough for 24 voice channels) and *T3* (44 megabits per second, enough for 672 voice channels). If you don't need quite that much speed, you can ask for a *fractional-T1* (half or a quarter the speed of a T1 line). You also need to contact your ISP for a leased-line account, which costs more (usually a lot more) than a DSL or ISDN account. Unless you have a huge amount of data to transfer, or you want to provide Internet services that your DSL or cable company don't allow over their lines, stick with DSL or cable Internet (or in Europe, ISDN).

Cable TV Internet Connections

Cable modem service is the competitive threat that's caused phone companies to accelerate their ADSL efforts. The same network that brings you dozens of TV channels can now bring you millions of web sites. The problem is that the cable network was designed to move information in one direction, from the broadcaster to you. Downstream speeds are impressive—the line can theoretically bring you data as fast as 30 Mbps, much faster than your computer can handle it—but upstream speed depends on line quality. Large cable companies are spending money to upgrade their networks to *hybrid fiber-coaxial (HFC)* to better handle two-way traffic. Smaller providers can't afford the upgrade, so they have you use a phone line at 28.8 Kbps for upstream data.

From a large company with an HFC network, expect downstream speeds of 1 to 2 Mbps or more, and upstream speeds between 500 Kbps and 1 Mbps. These numbers aren't exact, because you share digital cable capacity with your neighbors. If more of them are online, you compete with them for bandwidth.

Note   *Some major ISPs and online services, like EarthLink and AOL, are making deals with cable TV companies to provide cable Internet access. If you use AOL or a national ISP, check whether they offer cable access.*

See **www.cablemodeminfo.com** for in-depth coverage of cable modem issues, as well as DSL resources.

Satellite Internet Connections

Digital Satellite Systems (DSS), or direct broadcast satellite, lets you get Internet information by satellite. Two companies currently offer this service in the United States: Hughes DirecPC or DIRECWAY (**www.direcpc.com** or **www.direcway.com**) and Microsoft/Radio Shack's StarBand (**www.starband.com**). To connect, you use a 24-inch antenna, a coaxial cable, a PC adapter card, and Windows-based software. With early satellite systems, you received data from the Internet at a high speed via the satellite, but to send data to the Internet, you needed a dial-up connection and an ISP. (DirecPC still offers this option.) StarBand and DirecPC's Two-Way System enable a connection that doesn't use a phone line at all, with uploads and downloads by satellite. With StarBand, you can use the same satellite dish to get DISH Network television.

Setup can be difficult, and pricing has been controversial. (How much you pay used to depend on how much data you downloaded.) An installer comes to position the satellite dish, which needs an unobstructed view of the southern sky, and to connect the dish to your computer's USB or Ethernet jack. Installation costs about $200, with additional equipment fees of up to $400. Download speeds can be as high as 500 Mbps, although there is a slight delay before the data begins flowing, which can affect highly interactive Internet applications like games.

Tip   *If you can get DSL, ISDN, or cable Internet, connection will be simpler than with a satellite dish. However, if your phone and cable companies don't offer high-speed Internet connections, satellite may be your best alternative.*

Online Services

An *online service* is a commercial service that enables you to connect to and access its proprietary information system. Most online services also provide an Internet connection, e-mail, the World Wide Web, and, sometimes, other Internet services. Online services usually require special programs to connect to and use your account.

The three most popular online services are the following:

- **America Online** (AOL, at **www.aol.com**) is the world's most popular online service, with a wide range of AOL-only chat rooms. To connect to AOL, read AOL e-mail, browse the Web, and access other AOL servers, you use AOL's proprietary program. AOL doesn't provide a POP (mail) server, so you must read your AOL mail by using the AOL software, by accessing AOL's web site, or by using Netscape 6's Mail program. (AOL owns Netscape.) You can call AOL in the United States at 800-827-6364.

- **CompuServe** (at **www.compuserve.com**) is one of the oldest online services, with an excellent selection of proprietary technical- and business-oriented discussion groups. AOL purchased CompuServe, so the two services may merge. CompuServe has access phone numbers in dozens of countries. To connect to CompuServe and access its services, you use CompuServe's proprietary program. You can call CompuServe in the United States at 800-336-6823.

- **Microsoft Network** (MSN, at **www.msn.com**) is Microsoft's online service. You connect to MSN by using Dial-Up Networking, send and receive e-mail by using Outlook or Outlook Express, and browse the Web by using Internet Explorer. You can call MSN in the United States at 800-386-5550.

Other online services exist, but they aren't nearly as popular as these three. Some computers come equipped with sign-up software for some online services: because Microsoft owns MSN, it bundles MSN sign-ups with all recent versions of Windows.

Wireless Internet Connections

In a few urban areas, you can use *wireless* Internet access. To set it up, you attach a radio modem, about the size of a deck of cards, to your laptop. Wireless service (also called *WAP*, or *Wireless Application Protocol*) made its debut at analog speeds (28.8 Kbps), but it is being upgraded to 128 Kbps, which is faster than dial-up but slower than most DSL. As of 2002, few companies offer wireless Internet access, but availability may expand.

Another way to connect to the Internet via wireless is by using a digital cell phone that includes Internet connectivity. Because these devices have tiny screens, limited keyboards, no mouse, and slow connection rates, Internet content must be tailored to them and is usually limited to text. Check with your cell phone company to find out whether they offer cellular Internet access.

Some ISPs offer wireless connections to *personal data assistants (PDAs)* such as the BlackBerry, Palm, Compaq iPaq, or HandSpring Visor. These small devices have small screens, but you can use them to read your e-mail and browse the Web. Like cell phones, PDAs require web content to be tailored to their small screens and their slow connection rates. Check with your local ISPs to find out what they offer.

Connecting Local Area Networks to the Internet

Homes or organizations that have many PCs can connect the computers in a network and then connect that network to the Internet. This method is more efficient than connecting each PC to the Internet by using its own modem and phone line. Colleges, universities, and large corporations have used the Internet this way for a decade, and smaller offices and even homes increasingly do, too. Chapter 4 describes how it works.

Internet Service Providers (ISPs)

An *Internet service provider (ISP)* is an organization that provides Internet accounts, whether dial-in, DSL, ISDN, cable, satellite, or wireless. Thousands of ISPs exist in the United States, including dozens of ISPs with dial-up access phone numbers throughout the country, and many with phone numbers in limited regions. For example, EarthLink (**www.earthlink.com**) has access phone numbers in all major U.S. cities, whereas

How Do You Connect When You're Away?

Do you use the Internet when you travel? If your laptop has a high-speed connection at home, what happens when you take it elsewhere? You're unlikely to find DSL, ISDN, or cable modem access, although some business-oriented hotels offer high-speed access through an Ethernet jack (the same one you usually use to connect to a DSL, ISDN, or cable modem). Otherwise, you need to use your analog modem.

The issue is having an ISP that supports both your dial-up access and high-speed access. You'd think that getting dial-up access wouldn't be a problem if you sign up for a DSL or ISDN account; chances are good that your ISP is either a branch of the local phone company or an independent ISP that has provided dial-up access for years. However, many ISPs have separated their DSL and dial-up divisions and don't offer a package rate for both. And if you have a cable modem package, dial-up access to the cable company ISP is expensive—if it's provided at all.

One solution is to keep your current ISP for dial-up access. Some ISPs offer lower monthly rates for a limited number of hours of usage. Be sure to choose a dial-up ISP with phone numbers everywhere you plan to travel.

Shoreham Internet (**www.shoreham.net**) has phone numbers only in central Vermont, but provides local access from towns that EarthLink doesn't reach. Large ISPs provide both dial-up and DSL or ISDN connections.

 If the ISP doesn't have an access phone number that is a local phone call for you, you can spend more on long-distance charges than on your Internet account. Check with your phone company before you run up a horrendous phone bill.

In addition to connecting you to the Internet, here are some other features that your Internet account may provide:

- **E-mail mailboxes**   Your account almost certainly comes with at least one e-mail mailbox on a POP or IMAP server (described in Chapter 5). Many ISPs provide more than one mailbox, so that each member of your family can read his or her mail separately, either as part of the cost of the account or for an extra fee.

- **Web server space**   Most Internet accounts include a modest amount of disk space (perhaps 10MB) on a web server, so that you can make your own web pages accessible to the Internet. If you need more space, you can usually buy more for a small monthly fee.

- **Domain hosting**   If you want your own domain name (refer to "Domain and Host Names," earlier in this chapter), most ISPs can host your domain, so that e-mail to the domain lands in your mailbox, and web addresses in your domain refer to pages that you store on your ISP's web server.

If you plan to create a large web site or one that requires a secure server, shopping cart application, CGI scripts, or other advanced web server options, consider storing your web site on a web-hosting service rather than on your ISP's server (see Chapter 23).

To find ISPs that have local phone numbers in your area, try The List (**thelist.internet.com**), which lists over 5,000 ISPs by state or province, country, or area code. For each ISP, you see the area code(s) that it serves, the modem speeds that it supports, the address of the ISP's web site, its fees, and its sales telephone number. For other pointers about choosing an ISP, see our web site at **net.gurus.com/isp**.

Security Issues on the Internet

The Internet was not designed to be secure. Security wasn't built into the design (neither was billing), so as the Internet has become widely used by the public, many security issues have arisen, including viruses, cookies, and firewalls.

For information on web-based security issues, such as cookies and web filtering, see Chapter 20.

Protecting Your Computer from Viruses

A *virus* is a self-replicating program, frequently with destructive side effects. Viruses that spread via e-mail attachments are called *worms.* When the Internet was young (ten years ago), viruses were spread only in programs that were downloaded from FTP servers or passed around on floppy disks. Now your computer can catch a virus from an infected e-mail message, too.

Viruses can't travel in plain text, like e-mail messages. They contain programming, so they need to be in binary (nontext) files. You can receive a virus as an e-mail attachment or in a file you download. Document and spreadsheet files can contain viruses, too— *macro viruses* are viruses that make use of a word processor's or spreadsheet program's ability to execute instructions (macros), as well as to display a file.

Always run a virus-checking program on all computers that connect to the Internet. For the most complete virus checking, obtain commercial virus-checking software such as McAfee VirusScan (**www.mcafee.com**) or Norton Anti-Virus (**www.symantec.com/ product**). Don't just install the program; you also need to sign up to receive updates as new viruses appear. (Your software license may come with the first year's subscription free.)

Although virus-checking software cannot guarantee that it will find a virus that it is not specifically aware of, the better software contains heuristic capability that will alert you to files it deems suspicious. That can become annoying fast if the program is too conservatively designed, though, because a paranoid virus checker finds nearly everything suspicious.

Commercial virus-checking software does its job at various times, depending upon how you set it up—when you start your computer, at a particular time (such as every Friday), or continuously in the background. When it runs in the background, it checks whenever you download files through a specified browser or e-mail program or when you attempt to move them to a specified safe zone of your computer. You can determine how the software does its job when you install it or by setting your preferences from the program window when the program is running.

If a virus arrives attached to an e-mail message, your virus-checker should pop up a message asking what you want to do. You usually have the option of deleting the entire attachment, deleting the virus from the attachment but saving the rest of the file, or keeping the file in "quarantine" until you deal with it later.

Background virus checking has good and bad points. It is safest if you are forgetful and is convenient if you download often. Background checking also provides the best protection against the subtle (and rare) viruses that arrive, not as files, but as infections of your computer's memory that can travel through your web browser. In some instances, however, background checking can slow down your system, cause conflict with other background programs, or cause other erratic behavior. Background checking may also not guard against viruses that arrive through Internet tools that are not specifically checked by the software. For instance, your virus scanner may check only files that arrive through Netscape Navigator, and not check files that arrive through Microsoft Internet Explorer or an FTP client program. If you download programs (as described in Chapter 34), run your antivirus software manually after downloading files.

> *Until you can buy a good virus scanner, a decent (and free) online scanner can be found at **www.antivirus.com/pc-cillin**. However, this online scanner only works when you connect to it, and it does not check e-mail viruses for you.*

You can't catch a computer virus by reading the text of an e-mail message; you need to open (run) the attached virus program to infect your system. Some e-mail programs automatically "preview" e-mail attachments, which infects your computer automatically. Chapter 8 contains instructions for turning off e-mail program options that increase your risk of virus infection.

Protecting Your Computer from Intruders with Firewalls

A *firewall* is a program that controls what information passes from one network to another. You can use a firewall between your PC and the Internet to stop outsiders from getting access to your PC via the Internet.

How Firewalls Work

Each packet on the Internet is addressed to a specific port number (described in the section "Ports and Port Numbers" earlier in this chapter), and you can control access by port. As a general rule, most people use only a few ports for Internet communication: port 21 (for FTP, or file transfer), port 25 (for outgoing e-mail), port 80 (for web pages), and port 110 (for incoming e-mail). If your computer is on a local area network, it may use port 139 for file and printer sharing. You do *not* want outsiders to be able to use this port, so you may want to block anyone on the Internet from accessing port 139.

A firewall controls which ports are open, refusing to respond to packets addressed to other ports. Some firewalls enable you to specify what types of packets can cross the firewall—for example, requests for web pages might be allowed outgoing, but not incoming.

Some firewalls control only incoming information. For example, Windows ME and XP come with the Internet Connection Firewall (ICF), described in Chapter 3. ICF prevents some types of incoming Internet traffic based on the port number, so that hackers can't detect that your computer is there, much less access its files.

However, with the advent of *Trojan horse* programs, you also need to worry about outgoing Internet traffic. A Trojan horse is a program that installs itself on your computer (usually arriving as a virus). It then sends packets out from your computer, with information about your files or what you have been typing lately (including passwords). A Trojan horse program can allow hackers to log onto your computer and run programs on it, send e-mail (usually spam) through your computer, or cause your computer to participate in a *denial-of-service attack,* in which many computers simultaneously bombard an Internet server with thousands of requests for information, overloading the server.

A good firewall program monitors both incoming and outgoing packets and makes sure that outgoing packets come from a program that you know about. If it doesn't recognize a program, it alerts you and asks what to do, as shown here:

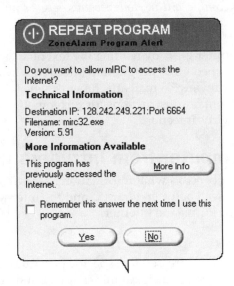

You can run a firewall program on your computer or on a router or hub that stands between your computer and the Internet. For example, if your computer connects to the Internet through a local area network, the LAN's hub or router can run a firewall program to provide protection to the whole LAN.

Popular Firewall Programs

Popular firewall programs that you can run on your PC include ZoneLabs ZoneAlarm (**www.zonelabs.com**), BlackIce PC Protection (**www.iss.net**), McAfee Firewall (**www. mcafee-at-home.com**), and Norton Personal Firewall (**www.symantec.com/product**). ZoneAlarm has a version that is free for individuals and nonprofit corporations—try it if you're not yet using a firewall.

*For Macs, the most popular firewall program is Norton Anti-Virus, which runs on OS 8 and later, including OS X. OS X has a built-in firewall. You can also download BrickHouse from **securemac.com/brickhouse.php** for a $25 shareware fee, to make OS X's built-in firewall more user friendly.*

Microsoft's Internet Connection Firewall

Windows XP comes with the Internet Connection Firewall, a firewall program that protects your incoming, but not outgoing, Internet traffic. You configure the Internet Connection Firewall when you create a dial-up connection, as described in Chapter 3. Your only configuration option is to turn the firewall on or off—there are no other settings.

Testing Your Firewall

A firewall is no good if you don't test that it's working. To test your firewall, follow these steps:

1. Go to the Gibson Research Corporation's web site at **grc.com** and follow the links to the Shields Up pages.

2. Download the free IP Agent program (it's small—only 16Kb) and run it. The program displays your computer's IP address, like this:

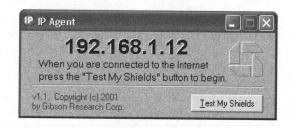

3. Click the Test My Shields button. A web page appears with the results of the test, telling you how well your firewall is working.

4. To test whether your firewall monitors outgoing packets, download the free LeakTest program from the Shields Up site (at **grc.com/lt/leaktest.htm**) and run it. The program is tiny (25Kb) and downloads in an instant.

5. Click the Test For Leaks button. LeakTest tries to connect to the Shields Up site (using the FTP file transfer port), and your firewall program should alert you. If your firewall doesn't say anything, it's not effectively monitoring outgoing packets; a new and unknown program (LeakTest) is sending packets out from your computer, and your firewall should complain.

For more information on firewalls, see Steve Gibson's Shields Up web site at **grc.com/su-firewalls.htm**, or the How Firewalls Work page at **www.howstuffworks.com/ firewall.htm**.

Virtual Private Networks

Many large organizations have LANs that enable people within the organization to share files. Although the LAN is connected to the Internet, most organizations install a firewall to block Internet users from accessing information on the LAN. However, what if you work for such an organization and you are on a business trip? You can connect to the Internet through an Internet provider, but how can you access your organization's LAN?

Virtual Private Networking (*VPN*) provides a way for an authorized computer on the Internet to *tunnel* through a firewall and connect to a computer on a LAN. When you are on the road and you need to connect to a computer at your office, VPN is the way to make the connection.

To connect to a LAN through a firewall, the firewall must support *Point-to-Point Tunneling Protocol* (*PPTP*), which lets VPN connect you through the firewall. Your organization's LAN administrator sets up a *VPN server*, the program on the LAN that provides PPTP. Both the *VPN client* (the computer making the connection) and the VPN server must have Internet connections. See the section on connecting to an organization's LAN using VPN in Chapter 3 for how to configure your computer to make the connection.

Choosing Passwords

On the Internet, you need a password for your account (to get connected), a password for your e-mail mailbox (which may be the same as your connection password), and passwords for the many web sites with which you do business. What kind of passwords should you choose? A good password is easy to remember and hard to guess. It's hard to find a password that has both properties. A very simple, easy-to-remember password (such as the name of the street that you live on, for example) is also easy for someone else to figure out. A really difficult password (a random collection of letters and numbers, such as "ER3k76tB") will probably keep out almost anyone—including you, perhaps.

Writing down your password solves some problems, but creates others. If you travel with a laptop and keep a file named Passwd.txt, then anyone who steals your laptop can get into your accounts. Using the same password for all of your accounts saves wear-and-tear on your memory, but it's dangerous. If you tell someone how to use your *Wall Street Journal* account to read the news, the same password provides access to your brokerage account. In a nightmare scenario, someone could establish an attractive web site and ask people to register, simply to collect their favorite passwords and break into other accounts that they have.

You shouldn't let security issues keep you from using the Internet, but you should remain just paranoid enough to take a few precautions, such as the following:

- *Have a different password for each kind of account.* If you're the kind of person who likes to sign up for free things, you could easily wind up registering at dozens of web sites. Don't try to create and remember a different password for each one. Choose three or four passwords at different levels of difficulty, and use the same password for all accounts of the same type.

- *Vary the difficulty of the passwords depending on what you're trying to protect.* Some passwords are more for the web site's protection than for yours. For example, if someone could guess your ESPN password, he or she could pretend to be you and read the members-only parts of the ESPN web site without paying the subscription fee. That would annoy ESPN a lot more than it would annoy you. A password such as "LetMeIn" might be sufficient.

On the other hand, if you have an account with a retailer, and the retailer keeps your credit card number on file, someone who guesses your password can buy products with your credit card. Someone who guesses your online banking password may be able to write checks. Someone who guesses your online brokerage account password can buy and sell stocks for you. These accounts need very strong p`asswords.

Some passwords protect your private information. The password on an e-mail account, for example, prevents someone else from reading your e-mail and sending out messages that appear to be from you. Would that be a huge disaster, or merely a nuisance? Choose your password accordingly.

- *If you're protecting anything important, don't use any English word or common name.* Passwords are stored in an encrypted form that is very difficult to decrypt. However, password-cracking programs work by running through a large number of guesses, encrypting the guesses, and checking to see whether the encryption matches the encrypted password. Such a program can run through all the words in a dictionary within hours.

- *Use your brain sludge.* If you can't use words or names, where are you going to get all of these passwords, especially the difficult ones? And how are you going to remember them? The best passwords take advantage of what humorist Dave Barry calls "brain sludge"—all those useless odds and ends that stick in your memory for no good reason. Maybe you still remember the phone number of a high school girlfriend. She doesn't live there anymore and maybe you wouldn't call her if she did, but that number is taking up space in your head. Use it in a password. Let the guy who steals your laptop try to figure that one out.

- *Use acronyms.* You can make up a lot of easy-to-remember but hard-to-guess passwords by taking the first letter from each word of a memorable phrase. Nathan Hale's famous "I regret that I have but one life to give for my country" produces "IRTIHB1LTGFMC." The famous Richard M. Nixon quote "I am not a crook" could give you the password "rmnimnac." They look like random strings of characters, but they aren't. Best of all is an acronym based on a quotation that isn't even famous; maybe it's just something that your Aunt Betty used to say all the time.

- *Stick a number in, spell it wrong (or backwards), or glue a few words together.* A friend used to use friends' names spelled backward, with a digit in the middle (like "nas3uS").

- *Don't write down passwords, write down hints.* If you need to write something down, all you need is a hint that will activate the appropriate brain sludge. The notation "AOL-Tracy" might be enough to remind you that your America Online password has something to do with that high school girlfriend. Jotting down "watergate" or "Hale" might be all you need to remember the Nixon or Nathan Hale passwords.

Chapter 2

How the Domain Name System Works

When you make contact with any of the millions of computers on the Internet using a name like **gurus.com**, you're using the *Domain Name System (DNS)*. This chapter looks first at the way that DNS works and then at the practical issues involved in registering your own domain name. (Chapter 1 describes domains, host names, and IP addresses.)

How Domains Are Organized

The DNS is a very large distributed database that translates host names (like **gurus.com**) into IP addresses (like 23.45.67.89) and other information. DNS names are organized into a tree, as in Figure 2-1. All names start at the *root*, above the set of top-level domains. The root is considered to be at the right end of the name. In a domain name like **www.example.net**, **net** is a first-level name within the root, **example** is a second-level name within **net**, and **www** is a third-level name within **example**. The **example.net** domain contains another third-level domain called **fox.trot**. The tree can extend to any number of levels, but in practice is rarely more than four or five levels deep.

The DNS root has a small set of *top-level domains (TLDs)* that rarely changes. They are listed in Chapter 1, and currently include **aero**, **arpa**, **biz**, **com**, **coop**, **edu**, **gov**, **info**, **int**, **mil**, **museum**, **name**, **net**, and **org**, along with over 100 two-letter country-name TLDs.

Technically, all top-level domains work the same, although the rules and prices for registering domain names in them vary greatly. (See the section "Registering a Domain Name" later in this chapter for more information.)

Domain Records, Zones, Delegation, and Servers

Domain data is stored in a set of *records*. There are many types of records, each storing a specific type of information about the domain. For example, the record that says that a name like **www.example.net** has an IP address like 10.23.45.67 is called an *A (Address) record*. The names and details of all of the record types are beyond the scope of this chapter, but we'll mention some of the most common ones here.

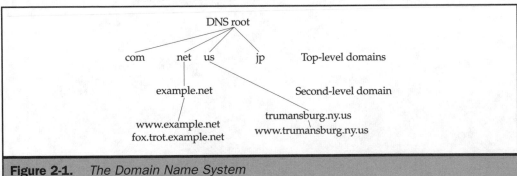

Figure 2-1.   *The Domain Name System*

Storing all of the DNS data in one place would be a logistical nightmare—what if the computer that stored it were to go down, or lose connection with the rest of the Internet? Instead, the DNS is divided up into subtrees called *zones*. Each zone contains the records for a bunch of domains. Large domains (like **ibm.com**) may be stored as many zones (for example, one for **austin.ibm.com** and one for **armonk.ibm.com**), so that the network administrators in different places can update the records for the computers in their domains. Smaller domains (like **gurus.com**) may be stored in one zone. Records are divided into zones purely for administrative convenience, and the most Internet users never notice which domain information is stored in which zone.

Different zones are stored on various computers called *name servers*. Most zones have at least two redundant name servers; a few (such as the extremely busy **com** zone) have a dozen. A single name server can handle DNS for many zones. The servers for the **gurus.com** zone, where this book's web site resides, handle over 1,800 zones, and some large commercial web hosts handle over a million. The *root zone* resides on a set of agreed-upon servers dispersed around the world. The root zone contains *NS (Name Server) records* for each TLD.

For instance, for **www.example.net**, the root zone contains NS records that identify **net** as a separate zone. The NS records *delegate* that zone to the name servers for that zone. The servers for the **net** zone in turn contain NS records that delegate the **example.net** zone, which contain the A record and other information for **www.example.net**. Although it's possible to start a new zone at each level of the tree, it's not necessary. If **example.net** had computers named after great dances, such as **fox.trot.example.net**, that information could and probably would be in the **example.net** zone. In Figure 2-1, each line indicates a new zone. The name at the top of the line is the name of the zone whose contents are at the bottom of the line.

If every computer on the Internet had to go through the complete lookup process every time a program were to use a domain name, the DNS would be impossibly overloaded. To avoid this problem, computers *cache* (store) domain information that they look up so that if it's needed again, it can be quickly retrieved. Each computer on the Internet that uses DNS has a small cache of its own. Most networks provide *cache servers* that handle DNS lookups for all of the computers on the network. This greatly improves performance for two reasons. First, all the computers on the network share the cache server's relatively large cache. (The cache server on our small network stores 20MB of DNS data, and larger network caches store far more.) Second, the cache server is on the same network as the client computers, so the time it takes a client to contact the cache server is short.

DNS and E-mail

For most Net services, including web, FTP, various kinds of chat, and instant messages, a client program looks up the IP address (A record) of the web, FTP, chat, or other server and connects to that address. E-mail works a little differently, using a two-step scheme. To send a piece of e-mail to, say, **nettcr2@gurus.com**, the sending program first looks for *mail exchanger (MX) records* for **gurus.com** in the DNS. Each MX record contains a host name of an incoming mail server and a numeric *preference value.* If there are several MX records for **gurus.com**, the sender starts with the record of the numerically smallest preference, looks up the host name in that record, and tries to contact that mail host. If it can, it delivers the mail there. If not, it tries the next higher preference. This system permits backup mail servers to receive mail if the regular server is unavailable. A domain can have multiple mail servers with the same preference, in which case clients choose one at random for load balancing.

Reverse DNS

Another feature that DNS provides in a slightly confusing way is *reverse DNS (rDNS).* *Forward DNS* is the familiar A record that turns a host name like **net.gurus.com** (our web site) into IP address 208.31.42.79. Reverse DNS lets you start with the IP address and find a corresponding host name.

Every IP address has a corresponding *rDNS name.* To get the rDNS name, reverse the order of the components in the IP address, and then add **in-addr.arpa**. Thus, the rDNS name for 208.31.42.79 would be 79.42.31.208.**in-addr.arpa**. When a program looks up the rDNS name, the usual result is a *PTR (pointer) record* with the domain name corresponding to that IP.

Note	*The forward and reverse DNS don't always correspond. It's entirely possible to misconfigure a network's rDNS so that forward and reverse don't match or to omit rDNS completely. Whenever you look up rDNS data, you should always look up the resulting name and make sure you get back the IP you started with. If not, the rDNS is untrustworthy.*

Server Software

For many years, the only DNS server software in wide use was the Berkeley Internet Name Daemon (BIND), which runs on UNIX and UNIX-like systems including Linux. Now many other programs are available (we like djbdns, written by a brilliant math professor in Chicago), but BIND remains the favorite. Windows 2000 and XP also have an optional DNS server component that works but that doesn't support the heavy loads that BIND does. (The F root server, for example, is a pair of UNIX boxes that handles 272 million queries per day.)

Registering a Domain Name

During the dot.com bubble, people were creating and trading domains with wild abandon. The frenzy has abated somewhat, but it still can be useful and fun to get a domain of your own. To do so:

1. Find an available name that you want.

2. Find a provider (possibly your own ISP) to host the mailboxes, web site, or whatever else you want to put there.

3. Find a registrar and register the domain.

What Types of Domains Are Available?

Currently the DNS roots have over 250 TLDs that permit some kind of domain registration. We divide them into four categories: generic, country, vanity, and specialized.

Generic Domains

Generic domains permit anyone from any part of the world to register. For each of these types of domains, the URL in the following list is for the organization that registers them:

- **com, org, and net**   These familiar domains are still the most popular. Anyone can register in any of them. (Contrary to rumor, **org** has never been restricted to nonprofits, although it's often used by them.) The **com** domain is extremely cluttered, with all the short and obvious domains long gone, so it can be difficult to find an available name that you want (**www.crsnic.net**).

- **biz**   This is an alternative to **com** that opened in 2001. In theory it's for businesses, but in practice anyone can register (**www.nic.biz**).

- **info**   This new TLD opened in 2001. Anyone can register (**www.nic.info**).

- **name**   This is for people's names, like **john.smith.name**; it opened in early 2002 (**www.nic.name**).

All of the generic domains offer registrations through third-party registrars, of which there are many.

Country Domains

Every country and country-like piece of land in the world, including many that are completely uninhabited, has a two-letter domain that with one exception matches the two-letter country code kept in a master list by the ISO, the International Organization for Standardization. (The one exception is Britain, which is **gb** in the ISO list, but **uk** on the Internet.) There's a reasonably up-to-date list of country domain managers at the Internet Assigned Numbers Authority (IANA, a long-time technical coordinator for Internet names and numbers) at **www.iana.org/cctld/cctld-whois.htm**.

Registration rules vary greatly from country to country. The **us** domain has traditionally been highly decentralized, permitting registration only by city or government agencies, such as **www.trumansburg.ny.us** for a community web page for Trumansburg, New York. In late 2001, management of the **us** domain was transferred to Neulevel, who also runs the new **biz** domain; see their web site at **www.neustar.us** for details.

In Canada, registrations are handled via resellers by an organization called the Canadian Internet Registration Authority (CIRA) at **www.cira.ca**. Registrations are supposed to be available only to people and organizations with a Canadian presence. Some domains are directly in **ca**, like **abc.ca**, others are by province or city like **abc.on.ca** or **abc.toronto.on.ca**.

In Britain, registrations are handled by a co-op called Nominet, to which all British ISPs belong, so your ISP usually handles registrations. Registrations are usually in **co.uk**, like **abc.co.uk**. As of January 2002, you could register personal domains in **me.uk**.

For other countries, see the IANA list.

Vanity Domains

The political process of creating new generic domains took many years. During that time, several small countries, starting with Tonga, turned their domains into generic "vanity domains" by permitting anyone to register for a price. Current vanity domains include

- **to** Tonga (**www.nic.to**)
- **nu** Niue, (**www.nic.nu**)
- **cc** Cocos or Keeling Islands (**www.nic.cc**)
- **ws** Western Samoa (**www.nic.ws**)
- **cx** Christmas Island (**www.nic.cx**)
- **tv** Tuvalu (**www.tv**)
- **hm** Heard and McDonald Islands (**www.registry.hm**)

All are small islands in the Pacific Ocean, for which selling Internet domain names has turned into a cash windfall.

There are also domains that are trying to appeal to specialized groups:

- **am and fm** These are for Armenia and the Federated States of Micronesia. Each offers a special deal to AM and FM radio stations, respectively, at **www.dot.am** and **www.dot.fm**.
- **md** This is for Moldova in Eastern Europe, which is trying to sign up doctors for a "medical" domain at **www.register.md**.
- **tm** This is for Turkmenistan, which is trying to be a domain for trademark owners (**www.nic.tm**).

With the advent of more generic domains, there's little reason to use a vanity country domain unless you can come up with a really clever name. To find out how to register, see the IANA list at **www.iana.org/cctld/cctld-whois.htm**.

Specialized Domains

The DNS has always had a few domains that are restricted to particular kinds of organizations. If you don't qualify, you can't get in.

- **edu**   This is nominally for four-year degree-granting colleges and universities, although a few other kinds of schools have snuck in over the years, and two-year colleges will soon be officially admitted (**www.educause.edu**).

- **gov**   This was originally for any kind of government in the United States. New registrations are limited to the federal government.

- **mil**   This is for the U.S. military. Don't even think of trying to sneak in.

- **int**   This is for international treaty organizations like the Red Cross (**redcross.int**) and European Union (**eu.int**).

- **arpa**   This is for Internet infrastructure information, primarily the in-addr reverse DNS discussed earlier.

In 2001, several new specialized domains were opened, although all are starting up quite slowly.

- **aero**   This is for the airline industry. It may be limited to airlines, although the rules aren't very clear yet (**www.nic.aero**).

- **museum**   This is for museums (**www.nic.museum**).

- **coop**   This is for cooperatives (**www.nic.coop**).

- **pro**   This is for professionals. The rules were not defined, and registration was not open as of mid-2002 (**www.registrypro.com**).

Using WHOIS

Looking for an available domain can be a challenge because often you can't easily tell what domains are in use and what domains are available. Each domain registrar is supposed to provide a service called WHOIS, listing contact information for all of its domains. We like the combined WHOIS server at **www.geektools.com**. On the Geektools home page, click the small "whois" link near the upper right, which brings you to a page that does an admirable job of figuring out the appropriate WHOIS server for any possible domain, querying that server, and reporting the result. If it can't find a domain, you can try to register it.

For many years, the master WHOIS server for **com**, **org**, and **net** was run by Network Solutions (NSI), and some older WHOIS programs automatically use that server. Don't trust the results from NSI's server because it only has authoritative information for domains registered through NSI, and not for any of the dozens of other registrars.

Preparing to Set Up Your Domain

Once you find a domain name that's available and that you like, you need to arrange for someone to provide the web, mail, or other services for your domain, as well as to provide the domain name servers for your domain's DNS zone. The first place to ask is your ISP. If your ISP can't or won't provide the service at an acceptable price, hundreds of web hosting companies are on the Internet, with prices starting as low as $10 a month, depending on the kind and scale of services they provide. No matter who hosts your domain, you need to get the names of the domain servers to use from them.

Choosing a Registrar

Finally, you're ready to register your domain. Assuming you're registering in one of the generic domains or other domains handled through third-party registrars, you need to choose a registrar. There are hundreds of registrars, again with widely varying prices and services. All registrars accept registrations and updates through web forms with payment by credit card. If you later become dissatisfied with the registrar you're using, you can transfer your domain to another registrar, so the choice of registrar is not particularly critical.

If your ISP or web hosting company acts as a registrar (especially if they resell registration service from the oddly named but extremely competent TUCOWS/Opensrs), you might as well use them. Otherwise, here are a few registrars with which we've had good luck:

- **www.gandi.net**   French registrar specializing in noncommercial domains
- **www.joker.com**   German general-purpose registrar
- **www.godaddy.com**   Low-cost registrar also offering web and e-mail hosting

*For many years the only registrar for **com**, **org**, and **net** was Network Solutions, now owned by VeriSign. Despite their experience, due to a combination of high prices and less than stellar service, we don't suggest you use them.*

Registering a domain involves choosing the name, then putting in the contact information. Each domain has three contacts: the domain's owner (who legally owns the domain), the technical contact (whom to contact with technical problems, usually the ISP or hosting company), and the billing contact (who pays for the domain). You also enter the names of the domain servers to use and payment information.

If you use a third party to register your domain, be sure you are listed as the owner. If the third party lists themselves as owner, they own the domain, not you, and you have no recourse if you later want to host your domain elsewhere.

Once your domain is registered, the domain takes between 12 and 24 hours to appear in the DNS, at which point the domain is "live," and your web pages and e-mail will work using that domain.

The
Complete
Reference

Chapter 3

Configuring Your
Internet Connection

Anyone who tackles as large a book as this one has already been using the Internet for a while, so you already know how to get connected. However, you may be thinking about switching to a faster connection, or you may need to know more about your connection options, like autodialing when you go offline or turning on a firewall to protect your computer from intruders.

This chapter describes your configuration options if you use Windows XP, 2000, Me, or 98, or Mac OS 9 or OS X. We describe both dial-up and broadband (that is, cable Internet or DSL) connections, as well as ISDN connections (which are widely used in Europe). If you need to connect to your organization's LAN over the Internet, we describe how to use VPN, too.

Note	*If you want to connect a LAN to the Internet, so that a group of computers can share one Internet connection, flip forward to Chapter 4. Read this chapter if one computer on the LAN will serve as a "gateway," connecting the LAN to the Internet.*

Configuring Your Broadband Connection

Broadband connections (DSL and cable Internet) are usually configured by the installer who hooks up your DSL or cable modem. Alternatively, your ISP may send you a kit with instructions to follow. Unfortunately, standards are still emerging in both cable and DSL equipment, so we can't tell you how to configure your configuration. Some DSL and cable Internet providers use the networking features built into Windows and the Mac, whereas others supply software to make the connection.

DSL providers differ by how much of the time you are connected, and how your ISP assigns your computer an IP address. The two methods are Dynamic Host Configuration Protocol (DHCP) and PPP over Ethernet (PPPoE):

- **DHCP (Dynamic Host Configuration Protocol)**   Your computer is online all the time, with a numeric IP address assigned to you by your ISP's DHCP server (a server computer that issues IP addresses as needed). You log in with a user name and password only in the rare instance that you lose connectivity.

- **PPPoE (PPP over Ethernet)**   Your computer must log on each time you want to use the Internet, as if you were dialing in. Once you log in, your ISP issues your computer a numeric IP address that works until you log out (or the connection times out).

Which method you use depends on your DSL provider; you don't get to choose.

When you sign up for a DSL connection, your phone company may give the *Virtual Path Identifier/Virtual Channel Identifier (VPI/VCI)* for your modem. These are two numbers that identify the hardware in your DSL modem (for example, 0/35). If you have a problem with your DSL connection and call for technical support, you may need to type these numbers into a configuration window.

Configuring a Broadband Connection from Windows XP

If your ISP hasn't given you other information, you can try setting up a connection to your cable or DSL modem by running the New Connection Wizard. Choose Start | Control Panel | Network Connections to display the Network Connections window. Click Create A New Connection in the task pane on the left side of the window, or choose File | New Connection from the menu. Answer the wizard's questions as follows:

- **Network Connection Type**   Choose Connect To The Internet.
- **Getting Ready**   Choose Set Up My Connection Manually.
- **Internet Connection**   Choose one of the broadband options, based on whether your DSL or cable Internet provider uses PPPoE or "always on" (DHCP).
- **Remaining questions**   Answer the remaining questions using the information your ISP provided.

If your DSL or cable connection uses Windows networking, rather than a separate program that the ISP provides, you can see your DSL configuration by choosing Start | My Network Places, clicking View Network Connections in the Task pane, right-clicking your DSL or cable connection, and choosing Properties. When you see the Properties dialog box, click Internet Protocol (TCP/IP) and click the Properties button to see the configuration for the connection. Don't change the settings without information from your phone company, cable company, or ISP.

 On the Properties dialog box for the DSL or cable connection, make sure that neither the Client For Microsoft Networks nor the File And Printer Sharing For Microsoft Networks check box is selected. If they are, deselect them—otherwise, you may be giving other people on the Internet access to your files and printer!

Enabling the Internet Connection Firewall in Windows XP

The Internet Connection Firewall (ICF) controls what ports are open, refusing to respond to packets addressed to other ports. We recommend that you enable the Internet Connection Firewall on all your Internet connections. Follow these steps:

1. Open the Network Connections window (choose Start | Control Panel | Network And Internet Connections | Network Connections).
2. Click the Internet connection.
3. Click Change Settings Of This Connection in the Network Tasks listed in the Task pane. You see the Properties dialog box for the Internet connection.
4. Click the Advanced tab. You see the Internet Connection Firewall and Internet Connection Sharing settings.
5. Select the Protect My Computer And Network By Limiting Or Preventing Access To This Computer From The Network check box.
6. Click OK to put the changes into effect.

Configuring a Broadband Connection from Windows 2000, Me, and 98

If your ISP hasn't given you other information, and the connection uses "always on" (DHCP) rather than PPPoE (as described earlier in this chapter), you can try setting up a connection to your cable or DSL modem by running the Internet Connection Wizard. In Windows 2000 or Me, choose Start | Programs | Accessories | Communications | Internet Connection Wizard, and answer the wizard's questions as follows:

- Choose I Connect Through A Local Area Network (LAN).
- Deselect Automatic Discovery Of A Proxy Server. (This option is for local area networks, not broadband connections.)
- Answer the remaining questions with the information your ISP provided.

Configuring TCP/IP in Windows 2000

Windows 2000 configures your computer's Ethernet (network) adapter for an Internet connection using TCP/IP. If you need to configure the TCP/IP connection, follow these steps:

1. Choose Start | Settings | Network And Dial-Up Connections. You see the Network And Dial-Up Connections window.

2. Right-click the Local Area Connection icon, and choose Properties from the menu that appears. You see the Local Area Connections Properties dialog box:

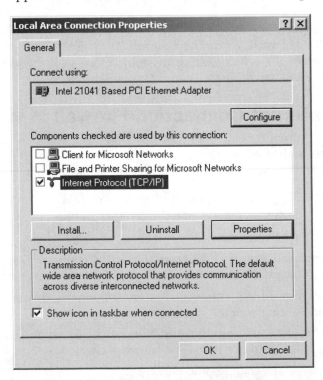

3. In the list of components used by the connection, make sure that only the Internet Protocol (TCP/IP) check box is selected. Deselect the check boxes for all the other protocols.

4. With Internet Protocol (TCP/IP) selected, click the Properties button. You see the Internet Protocol (TCP/IP) Properties dialog box:

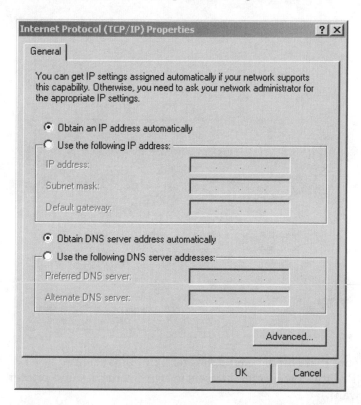

5. If your ISP uses DHCP to assign IP addresses, make sure that Obtain An IP Address Automatically is selected. Check with your ISP before making any other changes.

6. Click the Advanced button to display the Advanced TCP/IP Settings dialog box. Click the WINS tab, shown here:

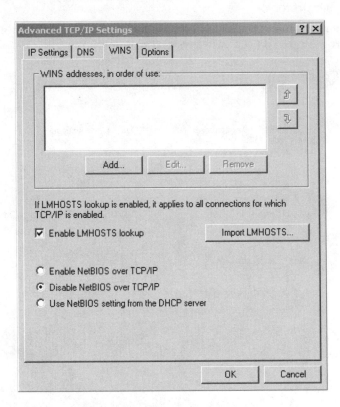

7. Make sure that Disable NetBIOS Over TCP/IP is selected. (Net BIOS Over TCP/IP allows other Internet users to share your files and printer, which you don't want.)

8. Click OK to close the open dialog boxes.

Configuring TCP/IP in Windows Me/98

To install and configure TCP/IP manually, follow these steps:

1. Choose Start | Settings | Control Panel, and run the Network program (or right-click My Network Places on the desktop and choose Properties). On the Network dialog box that appears, click the Configuration tab if it's not already selected, as shown in Figure 3-1.

2. If the list of installed components includes TCP/IP bound to your network interface card (for example, "TCP/IP -> LinkSys EtherFast 10/100"), TCP/IP is already installed. Skip to step 5.

3. To install TCP/IP, click the Add button, select Protocol, and click the Add button again. You see the Select Network Protocol dialog box:

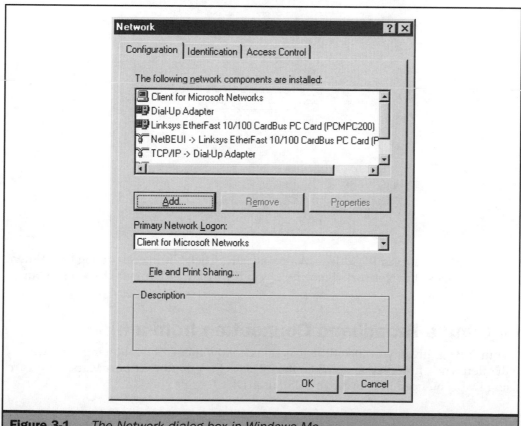

Figure 3-1.   *The Network dialog box in Windows Me*

4. If more than one manufacturer is listed, click Microsoft. Select TCP/IP in the Network Protocols box and click OK. You return to the Network dialog box.

5. On the list of installed network components, select the binding of TCP/IP to your network interface card (for example, "TCP/IP -> LinkSys EtherFast 10/100").

6. Click Properties. You see the TCP/IP Properties dialog box shown next. Click the IP Address tab if it's not already selected.

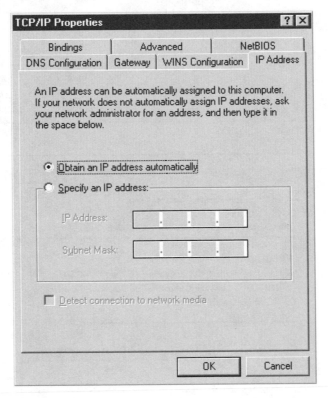

7. Click Obtain An IP Address Automatically. Click OK in each dialog box. When you close the Network dialog box, Windows may prompt you to restart your computer.

Configuring a Broadband Connection from a Mac

If your ISP has given you specific instructions, follow them. The following procedures will often work, however, even when the ISP says they do not support Macs. If you are using DSL, you need to know if your ISP uses DHCP or PPPoE.

Configuring a Broadband Connection from OS-X

Select Apple System Preferences | Network | TCP and make the following selections:

- **Connect Via** Ethernet
- **Configure** DHCP Server or PPP (for PPPoE providers)

If you selected PPP, click the PPPoE tab and enter your user name and password there. Leave everything else blank. Then make sure your cable or DSL modem is on and connected and reboot your Mac.

Configuring a Broadband Connection from OS 9

If your DSL provider uses PPPoE, you need to download a PPPoE client such as MacPoet (**www.finepoint.com/macpoet/macpoet-content.html**) or EnterNet (**www.efficient.com/products/enternet.html**); ask your ISP how to get a copy of one of these programs. Then Select Apple | Control Panels | TCP and make the following selections:

- **Connect Via** Ethernet
- **Configure** DHCP Server or PPP (for PPPoE providers)

Leave everything else blank. Then make sure your cable or DSL modem is on and connected and reboot your Mac.

Configuring Your Dial-Up Connection

When you configure your computer to connect to the computer or edit your connection configuration, you need to know some technical information about your Internet account, which your ISP should supply. Table 3-1 shows the technical information you need to know about your dial-up account.

Item	Description
Access number	Phone number your computer's modem dials to connect to the Internet (for example, 555-1234)
User name	Account name to enter when logging in, identifying you to the ISP (for example, jsmith)
Password	Password that verifies that you are the person with this user name (for example, Sword3fish)
Connection name	Name you want to give to the icon for this connection (for example, EarthLink NYC)

Table 3-1. *Information About a Dial-Up Account*

Configuring Dial-Up Connections in Windows XP/2000

Like previous versions of Windows, Windows XP and 2000 come with dial-up connections built in. To see your existing Internet and LAN connections in Windows XP, choose Start | Control Panel and click the Network Connections icon to display the Network Connections window, shown in Figure 3-2. (You might think to click the Internet Options icon instead, but the dialog box that this icon displays pertains mainly to Internet Explorer rather than connecting to the Internet.) In Windows 2000, choose Start | Settings | Network And Dial-Up Connections to display the Network And Dial-Up Connections window, which works similarly.

The Network Connections window lists every way that your computer connects to other computers: LAN, cable Internet, and DSL connections are listed in the LAN Or High-Speed Internet section, and dial-up connections (including ISDN connections) are listed in the Dial-Up section. You can right-click a connection in the Network Connections window and choose Properties from the menu that appears to see or change the properties for that LAN or Internet connection.

You can also display the Network Connections window in Windows XP by choosing Start | Connect To | Show All Connections (if Connect To appears on your Start menu)

Figure 3-2. *The Network Connections window shows both Internet and LAN connections in Windows XP.*

or by choosing Start | All Programs | Accessories | Communications | Network Connections.

Creating Dial-Up Connections in Windows XP

To create a new dial-up connection, run the New Connection Wizard. It starts automatically when you run an Internet application (such as Internet Explorer or Outlook Express) with no Internet connection configured. You can also start the New Connection Wizard by clicking Create A New Connection in the Task pane of the Network Connections window or by choosing Start | All Programs | Accessories | Communications | New Connection Wizard.

To set up a dial-up connection, answer the wizard's questions as follows, using information from Table 3-1:

- **Network Connection Type**   Choose Connect To The Internet.

- **Getting Ready**   Choose Set Up My Connection Manually.

- **Internet Connection**   Choose the type of phone line (or cable Internet connection) you use.

- **ISP Name**   Type the name that you want to use for this connection. It doesn't have to be your ISP's name—it's the name that Windows assigns to the connection icon in the Network Connections window.

- **Phone Number**   Type your ISP's access phone number.

- **Internet Account Information**   Type the user name and password for the account (your ISP provides this information).

- **Use This Account Name And Password When Anyone Connects To The Internet From This Computer**   If you want all user accounts on your computer to be able to use this Internet account, leave this check box selected.

- **Make This The Default Internet Connection**   If you want to use this network connection to connect to the Internet whenever you run an Internet program and you're not already online, leave this check box selected.

- **Turn On Internet Connection Firewall For This Connection**   Unless you have a specific program (for example, a chat program or interactive game) that doesn't work through a firewall, leave this check box selected. See Chapter 1 for information about firewalls.

- **Add A Shortcut To This Connection To My Desktop**   A shortcut to your ISP connection used to be handy, but no longer. Now Windows can connect to your account automatically when you run your browser, e-mail program, or other Internet program, so you rarely need to start your Internet connection yourself.

The Wizard creates a new icon in the Network Connections window, and you see the Connect window.

> **Note**   *Previous versions of Windows came with the Internet Connection Wizard, which has been replaced with the New Connection Wizard. If the Internet Connection Wizard is still lurking on your system (for example, if you upgraded from Windows Me/9x), close this Wizard if it runs, and use the New Connection Wizard instead. The only time we find the Internet Connection Wizard useful is when Outlook Express runs it to set up your e-mail account.*

Creating Dial-Up Connections in Windows 2000

To set up a dial-up connection, choose Start | Programs | Accessories | Communications | Internet Connection Wizard. The Windows 2000 wizard works like the Windows Me and 98 wizards, which are described in the section "Creating Dial-Up Connections in Windows Me/98" later in this chapter.

Changing the Settings for a Dial-Up Networking Connection in Windows XP/2000

To configure a network connection or change an existing connection's configuration, open the Network Connections window by choosing Start | Control Panel | Network Connections or by clicking View Network Connections from the Task pane of the My Network Places window. Right-click the icon for the connection and choose Properties from the menu that appears, or select the connection icon and choose File | Properties. Either way, you see the Properties dialog box for the network connection. Different types of connections display different properties dialog boxes. Figure 3-3 shows one for a dial-up connection, and Table 3-2 lists dial-up connection properties. The dialog box in Windows 2000 is almost identical, except that the Advanced tab is called the Sharing tab, and it doesn't include the Internet Connection Firewall.

Tab in Properties Dialog Box	Setting	Description
General	Connect Using	Specifies which modem to use to connect. Click the Configure button to check or change the configuration of the modem.
General	Phone Number	Specifies the phone number your computer dials to connect to the account. Click the Alternates button to enter additional phone numbers.

Table 3-2.   *Dial-Up Connection Settings in Windows XP and 2000*

Tab in Properties Dialog Box	Setting	Description
General	Use Dialing Rules	Specifies whether to follow Windows' dialog rules for the dialing location to determine whether to dial 1, the area code, or other digits before the actual phone number. Click the Dialing Rules button to define rules and locations.
General	Show Icon In Notification Area When Connected	Specifies whether to display an icon at the right end of the taskbar. You can click the icon to see the status of the connection.
General	All Devices Dial The Same Number	Appears only for multilink connections (which use multiple phone lines for the connection). Specifies whether the same phone number is dialed when additional phone lines are used for this connection.
Options	Display Progress While Connecting	Specifies whether to display the Connection dialog box, which shows whether Windows is dialing or verifying your user name and password before the connection is made.
Options	Prompt For Name And Password, Certificate, Etc.	Specifies whether to display a dialog box that prompts for your user name and password (or other security information if your account requires it) before connecting.
Options	Include Windows Logon Domain	Specifies that if the preceding check box is selected, Windows also prompts for your logon domain. This setting isn't used by most ISPs.
Options	Prompt For Phone Number	Specifies whether to include the phone number in the Connect dialog box displayed before connecting to the account. This setting allows you to check or change the phone number each time you dial the account.
Options	Redial Attempts	Specifies how many times Windows redials the connection if it can't connect.
Options	Time Between Redial Attempts	Specifies how long Windows waits before dialing again.
Options	Idle Time Before Hanging Up	Specifies whether Windows disconnects if the connection is idle for a specified length of time. Choose Never to disable autodisconnect.

Table 3-2.   *Dial-Up Connection Settings in Windows XP and 2000* (continued)

Tab in Properties Dialog Box	Setting	Description
Options	Redial If Line Is Dropped	Specifies whether Windows reconnects if the connection is lost (for example, if the ISP hangs up).
Options	X.25	Displays the X.25 Logon Settings dialog box, in which you specify the X.25 network provider and the X.121 address of the server to which you are connecting.
Security	Validate My Identity As Follows	Specifies how your ISP determines who you are. For most ISPs, choose Allow Unsecured Password (that is, passwords are sent unencrypted). For corporate networks, you may need to choose Require Secured Password or Use Smart Card.
Security	Automatically Use My Windows Logon Name And Password (And Domain If Any)	Specifies what user name and password to use (available only if you set the preceding setting to Require Selected Password or Use Smart Card). Usually not selected for Internet accounts.
Security	Require Data Encryption (Disconnect If None)	Specifies that the computer to which you are connecting must support encryption for all information transmitted and to disconnect otherwise (available only if you set the preceding setting to Require Selected Password or Use Smart Card). This setting is rarely used.
Security	Advanced (Custom Settings)	Click the Settings button to display the Advanced Security Settings dialog box, on which you can specify EAP (Extensible Authentication Protocol) or other advanced protocols if your ISP supports them.
Security	Show Terminal Window	Specifies whether to display a terminal window that shows the interaction between the network connection and the account while the logon script is running. During debugging, select this setting so you can see the terminal window.
Security	Run Script	Specifies the name of the file containing the logon script for this connection. Click Edit to edit a script file or Browse to select an existing file.

Table 3-2.   *Dial-Up Connection Settings in Windows XP and 2000* (continued)

Tab in Properties Dialog Box	Setting	Description
Networking	Type Of Dial-Up Server I Am Calling	Specifies the type of account; all ISPs now provide PPP. Click Settings to display the PPP Settings dialog box, in which you can choose whether to use LCP (Link Control Protocol) extensions, which are not supported by older PPP accounts; whether to enable software compression, which enables most PPP accounts to speed up throughput; and whether to use multilink (multiple phone lines for one connection).
Networking	This Connection Uses The Following Items	Specifies how to communicate over the network. Choose Internet Protocol (TCP/IP) and QoS Packet Scheduler.
Advanced/Sharing	Protect My Computer And Network By Limiting Or Preventing Access To This Computer From The Internet	(Windows XP only) Specifies whether to use the Internet Connection Firewall when connected. We recommend that you select this option if it has been disabled. See Chapter 1 for information about firewalls.
Advanced/Sharing	Allow Other Network Users To Connect Through This Computer's Internet Connection	Specifies whether to run Internet Connection Sharing on this PC, allowing other computers on the LAN to access the Internet through your connection. See Chapter 4.

Table 3-2. *Dial-Up Connection Settings in Windows XP and 2000* (continued)

You can set a few more items by clicking the Configure button on the General tab of the Properties dialog box for the connection: you'll see the Modem Configuration dialog box.

 We recommend enabling the Internet Connection Firewall by selecting its check box on the Advanced tab of the Local Area Connection Properties dialog box in Windows XP.

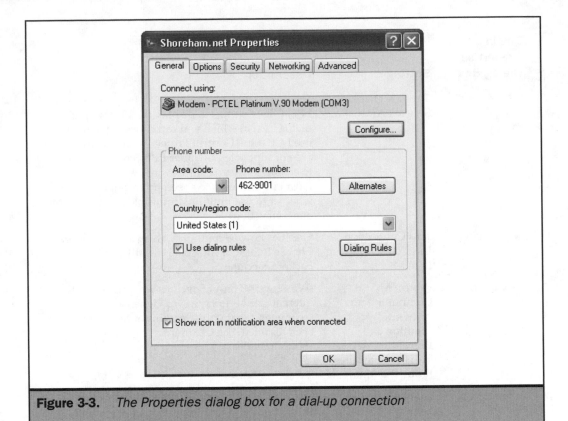

Figure 3-3.   *The Properties dialog box for a dial-up connection*

Caution   *Make sure that file and printer sharing are not enabled for your Internet connection, unless you want to allow everyone on the Internet to access the files on your computer. On the Networking tab of the Properties dialog box for your Internet connection, make sure that the check boxes are not selected for these two components:*

- *File And Printer Sharing For Microsoft Networks*
- *Client For Microsoft Networks*

Configuring TCP/IP Settings for an Internet Account in Windows XP/2000

For a connection to an Internet account, you may also need to configure the TCP/IP protocol. On the Properties dialog box for the connection, click the Networking tab, select Internet Protocol (TCP/IP) in the list of components, and then click the Properties button. You see the Internet Protocol (TCP/IP) Properties dialog box, shown here:

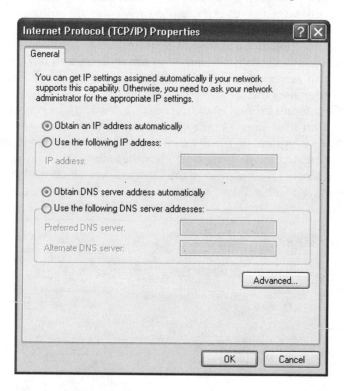

The dialog box includes these entries:

- **Your IP Address**   Ten years ago, when you signed up for an Internet account, your ISP assigned you a static IP address—an IP address that never changed. Now, almost all ISPs assign you a temporary IP address when you connect, so choose Obtain An IP Address Automatically, unless your ISP has given you a static IP address (unlikely).

- **DNS Server Address**   Until a few years ago, you needed to choose Use The Following DNS Server Addresses and to type in the addresses. Now most ISPs can tell Windows the DNS addresses when you connect, so choose Obtain DNS Server Address Automatically unless your ISP tells you otherwise.

Note   *For more settings, click the Advanced button to see the Advanced TCP/IP Settings dialog box. Few ISPs require you to change these settings.*

Setting Additional Dial-Up Options in Windows XP/2000

You might think all the properties of a dial-up connection would appear on the connection's Properties dialog box, but they don't. Most of the settings on the (ill-named) Internet Properties dialog box pertain to Internet Explorer, rather than to your Internet connection, but a few additional settings appear on its Connections tab. (This dialog box is called *Internet Options* in some places and *Internet Properties* in others, even in the same version of Windows.) All versions of Windows from XP to 98 use this peculiar arrangement.

To display the Internet Properties dialog box, choose Start | Control Panel (in Windows XP) or Start | Settings | Control Panel (in Windows 2000/Me/98). Run the Internet Options program. Figure 3-4 shows the Connections tab of the Internet Properties (or Internet Options) dialog box. The other tabs of this dialog box apply to Internet Explorer. Most of the settings on the Connections tab control your Internet connection, as shown in Table 3-3.

Figure 3-4.   *The Connections tab of the Internet Properties (or Internet Options) dialog box in Windows XP/2000*

CONNECTING TO
THE INTERNET

Setting	Description
Dial-Up Settings	Lists your Dial-Up Networking connections, so you can enable those to use, disable those not to use, and set the default connection. In Windows XP, this box also lists your VPN connections.
Never Dial A Connection, Dial Whenever A Network Connection Is Not Present, And Always Dial My Default Connection	Specify what Windows does when a program tries to connect to the Internet (for example, an e-mail program tries to connect to a mail server, or a browser tries to retrieve a web page).
Current Default	Displays the name of the connection Windows uses unless you specify another connection. To change the default, select a connection from the Dial-Up Settings list, and click the Set Default button.
Perform System Security Check Before Dialing	(Windows Me only) Before connecting to the Internet, checks whether your network settings might let others read or change files on your computer.

Table 3-3.   *Connection-Related Settings on the Internet Properties Dialog Box in Windows XP/2000/Me/98*

Click the Setup or Add button to run a wizard to create a new connection. The Remove button deletes the selected dial-up connection. The Settings button displays a Settings dialog box (shown in Figure 3-5) that contains settings for the selected connection: you see the same settings that appear on the Properties dialog box for the connection, but arranged differently. A few items on the Settings dialog box pertain to connecting to the Internet over a LAN. (In Windows Me, none of the settings related to dial-up connections.)

Other Dial-Up Connection Settings in Windows XP

Two other settings are available for dial-up connections, although not usually used for regular Internet accounts:

■ **Autodial**   Windows automatically dials an Internet connection if you are not connected to the Internet and you ask for Internet information (for example, you run your browser or e-mail program, or click a web address in a document). You can turn autodial off, or control which dialing locations it

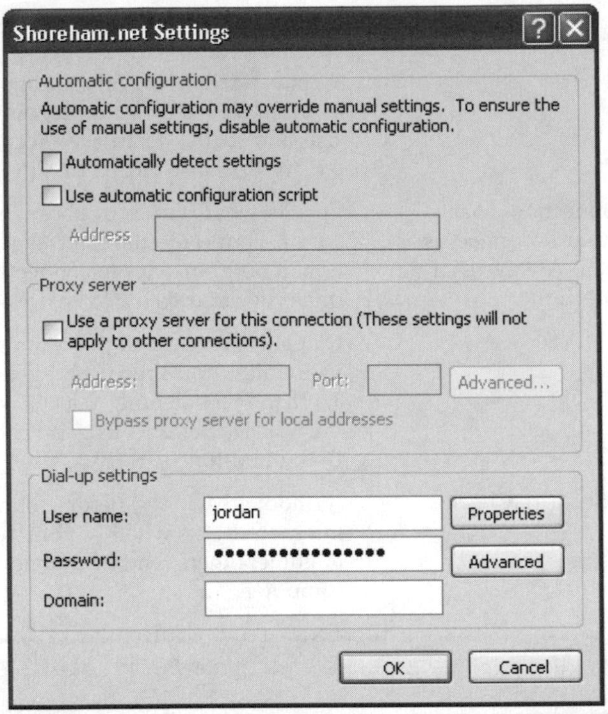

Figure 3-5. *Settings dialog box for a dial-up connection in Windows XP*

works from, by choosing Advanced | Dial-Up Preferences from the Network Connections window menu bar. Click the Autodial tab if it's not already selected, and choose which dialing locations from which you want Windows to autodial.

■ **Callback** Some Internet hosts offer to call you back to continue the connection. Callbacks ensure that you are who you say you are (or at least that you are at the phone number that you're supposed to be at). If an Internet host offers to call you back, Windows usually displays a dialog box that asks whether you want to do so, but you can configure how Windows responds to the offer. Choose Advanced | Dial-Up Preferences from the Network Connections window menu bar and click the Callback tab.

Streamlining Your Internet Connection in Windows XP/2000

Your Internet connection uses the TCP/IP protocol, and you can disable any other protocols that your computer supports. You can speed up the process of connecting to your ISP and make sure that your computer isn't open to intruders by following these steps:

1. Display the Network Connections or Network And Dial-Up Connections window.

2. Right-click the connection you use to connect to your ISP. Choose Properties from the shortcut menu that appears. You see the Properties dialog box for the connection.

3. Click the Networking tab. If NetBEUI or IPX/SPX appears among the installed components, make sure that its check box is cleared.

4. On the Networking tab, deselect the File And Printer Sharing For Microsoft Networks check box and the Client For Microsoft Networks check box. These are not needed (or wanted!) on dial-up Internet connections.

5. Click the Options tab. Deselect the Include Windows Logon Domain check box, unless your computer is on a domain-based LAN. (Check with your LAN administrator.)

6. Click OK.

7. Connect to your ISP to make sure that changing these settings doesn't prevent you from connecting. (If so, repeat the steps and reverse your changes.)

Connecting and Displaying Your Connection Status in Windows XP/2000

To connect to your Internet account, double-click the dial-up connection icon in the Network Connections (or Network And Dial-Up Connections) window. While you are connected, the dial-up connection icon—two overlapping computer screens—may appear in the notification area at the right end of the taskbar. (It appears if you have selected the Show Icon In Notification Area When Connected check box on the General tab of the Properties dialog box for the connection.) Move the mouse pointer to the icon (without clicking) to see the name of the connection, your connection speed, and how many bytes have been sent and received. Click the icon to see more details, as shown here:

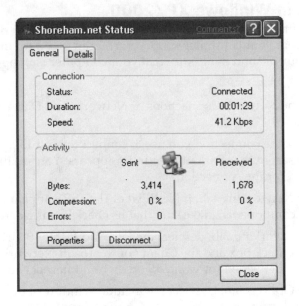

Click the Details tab on the status dialog box to see the modem name, connection type, IP address, and other information.

You can disconnect your Internet connection in several ways:

- If a dial-up connection icon appears in the notification area of the taskbar, right-click it and choose Disconnect from the menu that appears.

- Click the dial-up connection icon in the notification area to display the status dialog box for the connection and click the Disconnect button.

- Choose Start | Connect To and choose the dial-up connection to display its status dialog box. Click Disconnect.

Connecting and Disconnecting Automatically in Windows XP/2000

What happens if you aren't connected to the Internet and you tell your e-mail program to fetch your mail or you ask your browser to display a web page? Windows can dial up and connect to your Internet account automatically when you request Internet-based information.

To set Windows to connect automatically, follow these steps:

1. Choose Start | Control Panel | Network And Internet Connections | Internet Options (or choose Tools | Internet Options from Internet Explorer) to display the Internet Properties (or Internet Options) dialog box, shown in Figure 3-4

earlier in this chapter. (In Windows 2000, choose Start | Settings | Control Panel and run the Internet Options program.)

2. Click the Connections tab and make sure the Always Dial My Default Connection setting is selected. (If your computer is sometimes connected to the Internet over a LAN, choose Dial Whenever A Network Connection Is Not Present instead.)

3. Click the dial-up connection you want to use and then click the Set Default button to make this connection the one Windows will use.

4. With the dial-up connection still selected, click Settings to display the settings dialog box for the connection. (See Figure 3-4 earlier in this chapter.)

5. In the Dial-Up Settings part of the dialog box, type your user name and password.

6. Click the Advanced button to display the Advanced Dial-Up dialog box, shown here:

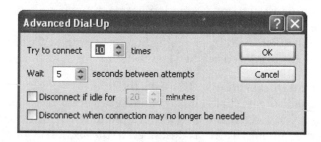

7. Set the number of times to try to connect, how long to wait between dialing attempts, whether to disconnect if the Internet connection has been idle, and whether to disconnect when the program that originally triggered the connection exits.

8. Click OK to dismiss the Advanced Dial-Up dialog box and OK again to dismiss the Internet Properties dialog box.

When you use an Internet program and Windows detects you are asking for information from the Internet, Windows dials your default connection. You don't see anything at all if you have configured the connection not to display the progress of the connection (using the Display Progress While Connecting check box on the Options tab of the Properties dialog box). If the connection is configured to display its progress, you see the Connecting dialog box.

Configuring Dial-Up Connections in Windows Me/98

Windows Me and 98 come with Dial-Up Networking (DUN) for use with dial-in connections. These Windows versions (and Windows 2000) use similar components and commands for dial-up connections.

Windows Me/98 Dial-Up Components

To connect to a dial-up Internet account with Windows Me or 98, you use Dial-Up Networking, which dials the phone and communicates with an Internet PPP, CSLIP, or SLIP account via TCP/IP. To use Dial-Up Networking, you create a *Dial-Up Networking connection*, a file with all the settings required to connect to an Internet account. You can have several Dial-Up Networking connections on one computer. For example, your laptop might have one connection for the local Internet service provider (ISP) that you use every day and another connection for the national Internet provider you use when you travel.

You also use the Dial-Up Adapter, the network driver that Dial-Up Networking uses to connect to the Internet. To check whether the Dial-Up Adapter and the TCP/IP protocol are already installed on your computer, choose Start | Settings | Control Panel and run the Network program to display the Network dialog box, shown in Figure 3-1 earlier in this chapter. Click the Configuration tab if it is not already selected. You should see at least two entries, Dial-Up Adapter and TCP/IP -> Dial-Up Adapter. Click Add to install them if they don't appear. (Choose Protocol, Microsoft, and TCP/IP in the dialog boxes you see.)

The Control Panel (displayed by choosing Start | Settings | Control Panel) includes two icons that you may need to use when connecting your system to the Internet:

- **Internet or Internet Options**   Displays the Internet Properties dialog box. Most of the tabs in this dialog box contain settings for the Internet Explorer browser, but you can use the Connections tab to tell Windows to connect to the Internet automatically, as described in the section "Connecting and Disconnecting Manually and Automatically in Windows Me/98" later in this chapter. You can choose Tools | Internet Options in Internet Explorer to display the same dialog box, but with the title Internet Options.

- **Modems**   Displays the Modems Properties dialog box, which you use when configuring your modem for a dial-up connection. With luck, Windows configured your modem automatically when it detected the modem. If not, double-clicking the Modems icon in the Control Panel runs a wizard that configures your modem.

Creating Dial-Up Connections in Windows Me/98

To create a new Dial-Up Networking connection to an Internet provider, you can use the Internet Connection Wizard to create a Dial-Up Networking connection. The Wizard can help you to sign up for a new Internet account or to configure your computer to work with an existing account.

You can start the Wizard by choosing Start | Programs | Accessories | Communications | Internet Connection Wizard or Start | Programs | Internet Explorer |

Connection Wizard. The Internet Connection Wizard differs slightly depending on the version of Windows. You see several choices:

- Sign up for a new Internet account and configure Dial-Up Networking to connect to it. We don't recommend this option because the wizard lists only ISPs that have signed up with Microsoft's referral program.

- Transfer an existing account to this computer. If your ISP supports the wizard's autoconfiguration feature (not all do), the wizard can set up a Dial-Up Networking connection for your ISP. Choose this option only if your ISP told you to do so.

- Set up Dial-Up Networking manually to connect to an existing account. We recommend this option.

You should usually choose the manual configuration option, entering the information about your ISP and account. (See Table 3-1 earlier in this chapter for a list of the information about your account.) The wizard also offers to configure Outlook Express as your e-mail program. (See Chapter 6 for information about Outlook Express.) The wizard may prompt you to insert the Windows CD-ROM for additional program components.

Note *If the wizard asks whether you want to set up a "white pages" directory service (Lightweight Directory Assistance Protocol [LDAP]) for this account, answer No. (A few accounts include an LDAP server that acts as a centralized directory of names and e-mail addresses.)*

If you want to create a new Dial-Up Networking connection without any help from a Wizard, run the Make New Connection Wizard instead. Choose Start | Programs | Accessories | Communications | Dial-Up Networking to see the Dial-Up Networking window. Run the Make New Connection icon. The Make New Connection Wizard asks what you want to call the connection and what phone number to dial to connect to the account. Next, the wizard creates a new icon in your Dial-Up Networking window. Unless you are dialing into an ISP with the very latest autoconfiguration systems, you probably still need to configure some settings; see the next section for how to enter the rest of the settings yourself.

Changing the Settings for a Dial-Up Networking Connection in Windows Me/98

To work with Dial-Up Networking—to create a new connection, connect to the Internet, edit the settings for an existing connection, or get rid of a connection—open the Dial-Up Networking window, shown in Figure 3-6. (Your window may be

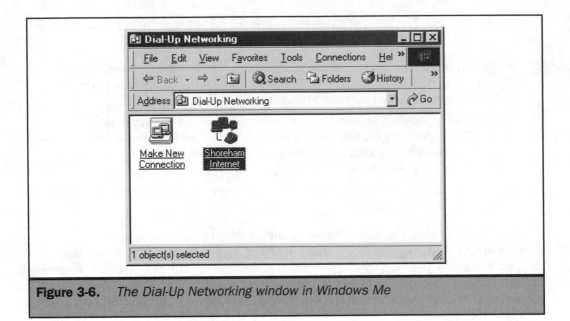

Figure 3-6.   *The Dial-Up Networking window in Windows Me*

configured to look different.) To open it, choose Start | Programs | Accessories | Communications | Dial-Up Networking. If you don't have any connections, Windows runs the Internet Connection Wizard rather than displaying the window. You can also see the contents of the Dial-Up Networking window by using Windows Explorer. At the bottom of the folder tree, Dial-Up Networking is listed as a subfolder of Control Panel or My Computer.

To configure a Dial-Up Networking connection or to change an existing connection's configuration, right-click the icon for the connection in the Dial-Up Networking window, and choose Properties from the menu that appears. Alternatively, select the connection icon and choose File | Properties from the Dial-Up Networking menu bar. Either way, you see the Properties dialog box for the Dial-Up Networking connection (see Figure 3-7); the name of the dialog box depends on the name that you gave the connection. Table 3-4 lists the properties for a Dial-Up Networking connection in Windows Me; Windows 98's settings are similar.

The Options tab of the modem Properties dialog box contains additional settings about the connection. To display this tab, click the Configure button on the General tab of the Properties dialog box for the connection and then click the Options tab. Strangely, these settings don't appear when you display the modem Properties dialog box from the Control Panel. The additional settings are listed in Table 3-5.

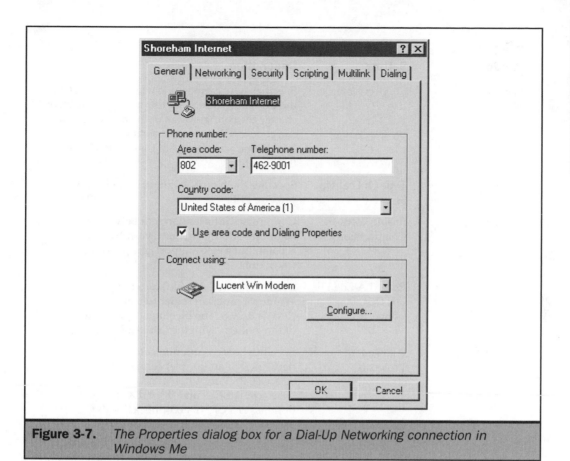

Figure 3-7.   *The Properties dialog box for a Dial-Up Networking connection in Windows Me*

Tab in Properties Window	Setting	Description
General	Phone Number	Specifies the phone number your computer dials to connect to the account. Composed of the area code, telephone number, and country code. (You choose from a list of countries.)

Table 3-4.   *Properties of a Dial-Up Networking Connection in Windows Me*

Tab in Properties Window	Setting	Description
General	Connect Using	Specifies which modem to use to connect. Click the Configure button by this setting to check or change the configuration of the modem. You can choose VPN. (See the section "Connecting to an Organization's LAN Using VPN" later in this chapter.)
Networking	Type Of Dial-Up Server	Specifies the type of account; all ISPs now provide PPP.
Networking	Enable Software Compression	Compresses information sent between this computer and the account; your Internet account must also support compression (most do).
Networking	Record A Log File For This Connection	Logs events in a text file stored in your Windows program folder (usually C:\Windows). The filename is the name of the modem, with the extension .log.
Networking	Allowed Network Protocols	Specifies how to communicate over the network. For an Internet connection, select TCP/IP for Internet accounts, and deselect NetBEUI and IPX/SPX. To set options for TCP/IP accounts, click the TCP/IP Settings button.
Security	Authentication	Specifies the user name and password to use when you connect to the account. The Domain box is usually left blank.
Security	Connect Automatically	Specifies that when you open the Dial-Up Networking connection, Windows connects automatically. Save Password must also be selected on the Dial-Up Connection dialog box when you connect manually.
Security	Log On To Network	Tells Dial-Up Networking to log onto the account by using your Windows user name and password. Usually not selected for Internet accounts.

Table 3-4. *Properties of a Dial-Up Networking Connection in Windows Me* (continued)

Tab in Properties Window	Setting	Description
Security	Require Encrypted Password	Encrypts your password before sending it to your Internet account when logging on. Your Internet account must support password encryption (most don't).
Security	Require Data Encryption	Encrypts data to and from your ISP. (We've never seen this setting used.)
Scripting	Script File	Specifies the name of the file containing the logon script for this connection. Click Edit to edit a script file or Browse to select an existing file.
Scripting	Step Through Script	Runs the logon script for this connection.
Scripting	Start Terminal Screen Minimized	Minimizes the terminal window that shows the interaction between the Dial-Up Networking connection and the account while the logon script is running. During debugging, deselect this setting so you can see the terminal window.
Multilink	Do Not Use Additional Devices	Specifies this connection uses only one device to connect.
Multilink	Use Additional Devices	Specifies this connection uses more than one device to connect (for example, two modems and two phone lines). The large box below this setting lists the additional devices used by this connection, and the Add, Remove, and Edit buttons let you add, delete, or change devices on the list.
Dialing	This Is The Default Internet Connection	Specifies that if you have more than one Dial-Up Networking connection, this connection is the one to dial automatically. When this is selected, you can choose whether Windows dials your Internet account when an Internet program (like an e-mail program or browser) needs to connect.
Dialing	Redial Settings	Specifies how many times Dial-Up Networking dials the connection if it can't connect (default is ten times) and how long to wait between attempts (default is five seconds).

Table 3-4. *Properties of a Dial-Up Networking Connection in Windows Me* (continued)

Tab in Properties Window	Setting	Description
Dialing	Enable Idle Disconnect	Specifies Windows disconnect if the Internet connection is idle for a specified length of time. (The default is 20 minutes.) Windows considers the connection idle if it is used no more than the specified connection speed.
Dialing	Don't Prompt Before Disconnecting	Specifies whether Windows asks before disconnecting an idle Internet connection.
Dialing	Disconnect When Connection May Not Be Needed	Specifies whether Windows disconnects the Internet connection when you close the program that initiated the connection. (For example, if a request from a browser caused Dial-Up Networking to log on, exiting the browser can cause Windows to disconnect.)

Table 3-4. *Properties of a Dial-Up Networking Connection in Windows Me* (continued)

Setting	Description
Bring Up Terminal Window Before Dialing	Displays a terminal window before dialing, which you can use to type modem commands and see the results. (Refer to your modem's manual for the commands it understands.)
Bring Up Terminal Window After Dialing	Displays a terminal window after dialing, which you can use to type commands and see the results.
Operator Assisted Or Manual Dial	Prompts you to dial the phone yourself, for situations where you need to speak to an operator. When you are connected, click the Connect button and hang up your phone.
Wait For Credit Card Tone: ___ Seconds	Specifies the number of seconds to wait for a tone when you are using a telephone credit card.
Display Modem Status	Displays a status window indicating the progress of your phone connection.

Table 3-5. *Settings on the Options Tab of the Modem Properties Dialog Box in Windows Me*

For most dial-up Internet accounts, you can leave almost all of these settings alone. Just check the phone number and modem on the General tab and the type of connection and network protocols on the Server Types tab.

 If you don't expect to connect to a particular account in the future, you can delete its connection from the Dial-Up Networking window by selecting the icon for the connection and pressing DELETE. Be sure to delete any shortcuts to the connection, too.

Configuring TCP/IP Settings for an Internet Account in Windows Me/98

You may also need to configure the TCP/IP protocol, although the default settings work fine for most Internet accounts. On the Properties dialog box for the connection, click the Server Types tab, select TCP/IP as an allowed network protocol, and then click the TCP/IP Settings button. You see the TCP/IP Settings dialog box, shown in Figure 3-8. Table 3-6 shows the settings on the TCP/IP Settings dialog box in Windows Me. Contact your ISP for the settings and addresses to enter.

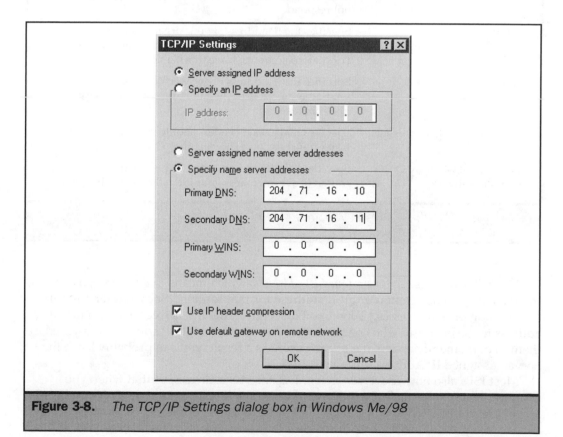

Figure 3-8.   *The TCP/IP Settings dialog box in Windows Me/98*

Setting	Description
Server Assigned IP Address	Specifies that your ISP assigns an IP address to your computer when you log on. (Most ISP accounts do this.)
Specify An IP Address	Indicates that your computer has a permanently assigned IP address, which you specify in the IP Address setting.
IP Address	Specifies your permanently assigned IP address.
Server Assigned Name Server Addresses	Specifies that your ISP assigns domain name servers to your computer when you log on. (Most ISP accounts do this.)
Specify Name Server Addresses	Indicates that you have entered primary and secondary domain name server IP addresses in the next two settings.
Primary DNS	Specifies the IP address of your ISP's domain name server.
Secondary DNS	Specifies the IP address of another domain name server that your account can use when the primary DNS does not respond.
Primary WINS	Specifies the IP address of your organization's WINS (Microsoft's Windows Internet Naming Service) server. For dial-up accounts, leave this blank.
Secondary WINS	Specifies the IP address of another WINS server that your account can use when the primary WINS server does not respond.
Use IP Header Compression	Specifies that packet headers should be compressed for faster transmission. (The default is On.)
Use Default Gateway On Remote Network	Specifies how IP packets to the rest of the Internet are routed (leave on, unless your ISP tells you to change it).

Table 3-6.   *TCP/IP Settings in Windows Me/98*

Most ISPs now use *server-assigned IP addresses*, which means that when you connect, the ISP assigns your computer an IP address for that session. (See Chapter 1 for an explanation of IP addresses.) When you disconnect, the ISP is free to assign that IP address to the next user who connects. Few ISPs have enough IP addresses assigned to them to permanently assign one to each user. As a result, you can probably leave the Server Assigned IP Address setting selected.

Most ISPs also now use *server-assigned name server addresses*, so that when you connect, the ISP informs Dial-Up Networking of the IP addresses to use for your DNS server (described in Chapter 2). If your ISP assigns these addresses, you can leave the Server Assigned Name Server Addresses setting selected, too. However, if your ISP gave you the IP address of its domain name servers, you need to enter them. Select

Specify Name Server Addresses and enter the IP addresses in the Primary DNS and Secondary DNS settings.

Some ISPs (not many) also provide WINS (Microsoft's Windows Internet Naming Service) servers, which provide other name lookups. If your computer is connected to a large corporate system via a LAN or by dialing in, your connection may use WINS to manage network parameters automatically. Your computer contacts the WINS server, either at boot time (if you connect via a LAN) or when you dial up, to get its own configuration information.

Setting Additional Dial-Up Networking Options in Windows Me/98

You might think that all the properties of a Dial-Up Networking connection appear on the connection's Properties dialog box (shown back in Figure 3-7), but they don't. Most of the settings on the Internet Options or Internet Properties dialog box pertain to Internet Explorer rather than to your Internet connection, but a few additional settings appear on its Connections tab. To display the Internet Options or Internet Properties dialog box, choose Start | Settings | Control Panel and run the Internet Options or Internet program. Alternatively, run Internet Explorer and choose Tools | Options, Tools | Internet Options, or View | Internet Options.

See the section "Setting Additional Dial-Up Options in Windows XP/2000" earlier in this chapter for how to set the options on this dialog box.

Other Dial-Up Networking Settings in Windows Me

In Windows Me, when you display the Dial-Up Networking window (shown in Figure 3-6) by choosing Start | Settings | Dial-Up Networking, the menu bar contains a new command, Connections. Choose Connections | Settings to display the Dial-Up Networking dialog box, which contains settings that affect all Dial-Up Networking connections:

- **Show An Icon On Taskbar After Connected**   This displays the Dial-Up Networking icon on the taskbar. This icon provides a convenient way to monitor or hang up your connection.

- **Show A Confirmation Dialog After Connected**   Deselect this check box so you don't have to see a confirmation dialog box each time you connect.

- **Disable Sending Of LAN Manager Passwords**   For backward compatibility with Windows NT, this specifies that passwords not be sent over the LAN in plain text (unencrypted), for better security.

- **Require Secure VPN Connections**   If you use Virtual Private Networking (VPN) to connect to your organization's intranet, this specifies that secure (encrypted) connections be used. See the section "Connecting to an Organization's LAN Using VPN" later in this chapter.

- **Only Accept 128 Bit Encryption (When Required)**   When connecting to secure web servers, this rejects encryption lower than 128 bits.

Connecting and Disconnecting Manually and Automatically in Windows Me/98

To connect to the Internet using a Dial-Up Networking connection, double-click the connection's icon. If a shortcut for the connection appears on your desktop, you can double-click it instead. To disconnect your Internet connection, double-click the Dial-Up Networking icon in the system tray. You see the Connected dialog box. Click Disconnect. Another way to hang up is to right-click the Dial-Up Networking icon on the system tray and choose Disconnect from the menu that appears.

If you are connected to your Internet account and don't use it for a while (usually 20 minutes), Windows or your ISP may disconnect you automatically. You may see a dialog box saying that you have been disconnected and asking whether you'd like to reconnect.

You can configure Windows to dial your Internet connection whenever a program (like your browser or e-mail program) calls for a connection. The process is different for Windows Me and Windows 98.

Windows Me   To set Windows Me to connect automatically, follow these steps:

1. Choose Start | Settings | Control Panel and run the Internet or Internet Options program to display the Internet Properties dialog box. Click the Connections tab and make sure the Always Dial My Default Connection setting is selected.

2. Click the Dial-Up Networking connection you want to use and then click the Set Default button to make this connection the one Windows will use.

3. Click OK to dismiss the Internet Properties dialog box.

4. Choose Start | Settings | Dial-Up Networking to display the Dial-Up Networking window, right-click the same connection you chose in step 2, and choose Properties from the shortcut menu that appears. The properties dialog box for the connection appears.

5. Click the Security tab (shown in Figure 3-9) and type your user name and password into the boxes, if they don't already appear. Select the Connect Automatically check box.

6. Click the Dialing tab (shown in Figure 3-10). Set the options to dial your default connection and tell Windows how many times to try and how long to wait between attempts (if your ISP's line is busy, for example). If you want Windows to disconnect automatically after a period of inactivity, choose the Disconnect If Idle For ___ Minutes check box and type the number of minutes.

7. Click OK to dismiss the Properties dialog box for the connection.

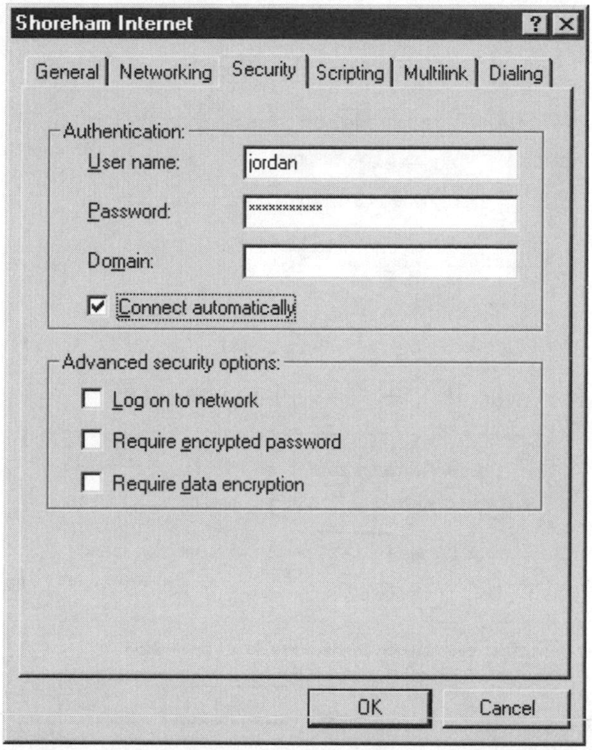

Figure 3-9.   *Providing the information Windows Me needs to log onto your Internet account automatically*

Windows 98   To set Windows 98 to connect automatically, follow these steps:

1. Choose Start | Settings | Control Panel and run the Internet program. Click the Connection tab on the Internet Properties dialog box, and make sure that the Connect To The Internet Using A Modem setting is selected.

2. Click the Settings button to display the Dial-Up Settings dialog box.

3. In the first box, choose the Dial-Up Networking connection that you want to use when connecting automatically to the Internet.

4. Set the other options to tell Windows how many times to try to make a connection and how long to wait between attempts (if your ISP's line is busy, for example). Also, type your user name and password. If you want Windows to disconnect automatically after a period of inactivity, choose the Disconnect If Idle For ___ Minutes check box and type the number of minutes.

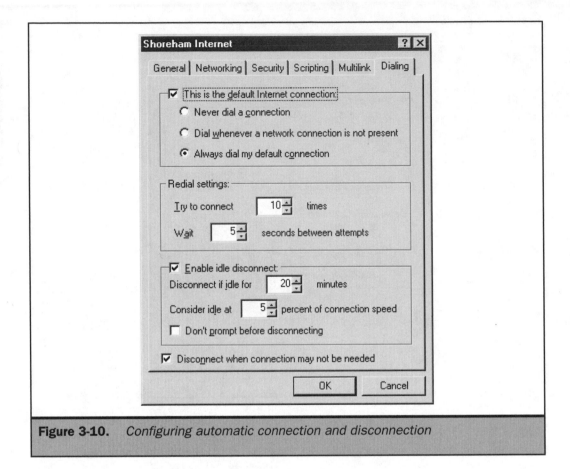

Figure 3-10. Configuring automatic connection and disconnection

5. Click OK to dismiss the Dial-Up Settings dialog box and then click OK again to dismiss the Internet Properties dialog box.

Tip *The first time that you run an Internet client program—such as a browser or e-mail program—and you aren't connected to the Internet, Windows may display the Internet Autodial window, which asks a series of questions to configure the same options that appear in the Dial-Up Settings dialog box.*

When You Connect Automatically When you use an Internet program and Windows detects that you are asking for information from the Internet, you see the Connect To dialog box. Type your Internet user name and password. If you aren't worried about anyone else using your computer to connect to your Internet account, select the Save Password setting. If you want Windows to connect automatically (without requiring you to click anything) whenever you request information from the Internet, select the Connect Automatically setting.

Configuring Dial-Up Connections on Macs

When you purchase a new Mac or install an operating system upgrade, Apple's Setup Assistant asks for basic information needed to configure your Mac. The assistant takes you through the steps needed to connect to the Internet.

Configuring Your Mac with the Internet Setup Assistant

When you see Apple's Internet Setup Assistant, follow these steps:

1. When the Internet Setup Assistant asks if you already have an ISP, select I'll Use My Existing Internet Service. Otherwise (if you don't have an ISP), Apple can recommend one.

2. When the Assistant asks how you connect to the Internet, select Modem. Next, the Assistant asks for your modem settings.

3. Most newer Macs have a built-in modem; leave the Apple Internal 56K Modem setting selected. For older Macs, select the type of modem you are using from the pull-down list, and then select which port it is plugged into. (The modem port on pre-USB Macs has an icon of a telephone handset next to it.)

4. The Internet Setup Assistant asks for ISP configuration information, including

   - **ISP Access Phone Number**   Include the area code if needed to dial a local number.

   - **Dialing Prefix To Obtain An Outside Line**   Enter the number (for example, 9) if needed. Otherwise, leave blank.

   - **Call Waiting**   Select Yes if you need to disable call waiting when dialing.

   - **User Name**   Type your login name for your ISP account.

   - **Password**   Type your ISP account password if you want your Mac to remember your password. If you do not enter your password, your Mac prompts you to enter it each time you connect.

   - **Domain Servers And Domain Name**   Your ISP should have given you this information. Type it exactly as your ISP specified.

5. The Internet Setup Assistant asks for your e-mail account information. (See Chapter 5 for more information about e-mail accounts.) Enter this information:

   - **E-mail Address**

- **E-mail Password**   If you leave this blank, the Mac prompts you for it each time you get your mail.
- **E-mail POP Account And SMTP Host**   Your ISP should have provided this information.

When you finish, the Internet Setup Assistant makes the necessary configuration changes for you.

Configuring Dial-Up Connections in Mac OS X

You can configure your dial-up connection yourself if you need to make changes after the Internet Setup Assistant runs. Follow these steps:

1. *Choose Apple | System Preferences | Network to display the Network dialog box.*

2. In the Location pull-down menu, select Automatic.

3. In the Configure pull-down menu, select Internal Modem. Almost all Macs that can run OS X include a built-in modem.

4. Click the TCP/IP tab. In the Configure pull-down menu, select Using PPP.

5. If your ISP has given you a domain name server address (for example, 192.168.0.0) and name (for example, **earthlink.net**), enter them in the Domain Name Servers field and Search Domains field, respectively.

6. Click the PPP tab. In the Service provider field, type the name of your ISP.

7. In the Telephone Number field, type the phone number of your ISP. Include any extra digits that you need to dial, such as *70 to disable call waiting.

8. In the Account Name field, enter your user name.

9. In the Password field, type your password. You can click the Save Password box, but if you do, anyone who has physical access to your machine will be able to log onto your Internet account.

10. Click the Save button.

11. From the Finder, select Go | Applications and double-click the Internet Connect icon.

12. Wait impatiently while the two modems introduce each other and become acquainted.

Your Mac is connected to the Internet. You are ready to run your e-mail program, browser, or other Internet client program.

To connect the next time, just choose Go | Applications and double-click Internet Connect.

Configuring Dial-Up Connections in Mac System 8.5 through 9.2

1. Choose Apple | Control Panels | Modem to display the Modem dialog box:

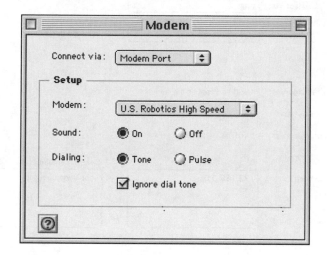

2. In the Modem pull-down menu, select the model of your modem. Most new Macs come with a built-in modem, and Apple Internal 56K appears as the default.

3. If you have an older Mac, use the Connect Via pull-down menu to select the serial port that your modem is plugged into. (The modem port has a telephone handset icon next to it. You can also use the printer port, which has a document icon next to it.)

4. Turn the sound on or off as you prefer.

5. Unless your phone system accepts only pulse dialing, leave Dialing set to Tone.

6. The Ignore Dial Tone setting is helpful if your phone uses an unusual beeping or dial tone to indicate that you have a message waiting. The modem will not dial if it doesn't detect a dial tone on your phone line, unless you check Ignore Dial Tone.

7. Close the Modem dialog box and save your changes.

8. Choose Apple | Control Panels | TCP/IP to display the TCP/IP (Default) dialog box:

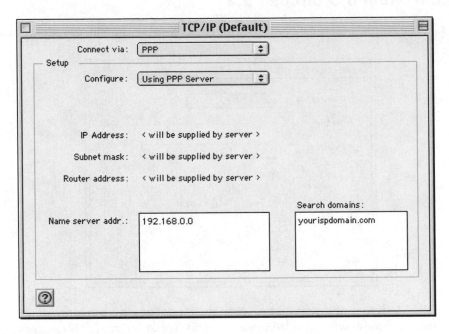

9. On the Connect Via pull-down menu, choose PPP.

10. On the Configure pull-down menu, choose Using PPP Server.

11. In the Name Server Addr field, type the IP address of your ISP's domain name server (DNS), for example, 192.168.0.1. Ask your ISP for this information.

12. In the Search Domains field, type your ISP's domain name (for example, this is **earthlink.net** for the EarthLink ISP).

13. Close the TCP/IP dialog box and save your changes.

14. Choose Apple | Control Panels | Remote Access to display the Remote Access dialog box:

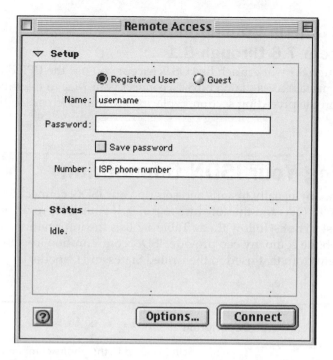

15. Click the Options button and click the Connections tab in the Options dialog box. Turn off the Prompt Every 5 Minutes To Maintain Connection setting and the Disconnect If Idle For More Than 10 Minutes setting, so that your Mac doesn't nag you constantly to hang up.

16. Choose OK to return to the Remote Access dialog box.

17. In the Name field, type your user name.

18. In the Password field, type your password. You can click the Save Password box, but if you do, anyone who has physical access to your machine will be able to log onto your Internet account.

19. In the Number field, type the phone number of your ISP. Include any extra digits that you need to dial, such as *70 to disable call waiting.

20. Click the Connect button.

21. Wait impatiently while the two modems introduce each other and become acquainted.

Your Mac is connected to the Internet. You are ready to run your e-mail program, browser, or other Internet client program.

To connect the next time, choose Apple | Control Panels | Remote Access and click Connect.

Configuring Dial-Up Connections in Mac System 7.6 through 8.1

Systems 7.6 through 8.1 work much like OS 9, except you use the PPP dialog box instead of the Remote Access dialog box. To connect your Mac to the Internet, follow the instructions in the preceding section, replacing "Remote Access" with "PPP" throughout.

Configuring Your ISDN Connection

Your phone company usually installs and sets up your ISDN connection, including a Terminal Adapter (TA) and the software to run it. If your ISP provides you with configuration instructions, follow them. Table 3-7 lists the information about ISDN lines that your phone company can provide. ISDN configuration information in Europe is different from that used in the United States and Canada.

Item	Description
Switch Type	Type of switch installed in the phone company's office. Your Terminal Adapter must be compatible with the switch.
Terminal Adapter (TA)	Modem-like device that connects your computer to the ISDN phone line.
Phone Number	Number assigned by the phone computer to your ISDN line. Your ISDN line may have one or two phone numbers.
Service Profile Identifiers (SPIDs)	Codes that identify your ISDN line to the phone company equipment. Typically, you have two SPIDs, one for each B channel. They look like phone numbers plus extra digits that are specific to the switch type. For example, one of your B channels may have the phone number (925) 555-3434 and the SPID 92555534340101. SPIDs are generally used only in the United States and Canada.
Multi-Subscriber Numbers (MSNs)	Phone number(s) of your ISDN line for European ISDN (DSS1), which allows multiple phone numbers on an ISDN line. Enter only the MSN(s) you actually intend to use with your computer—the MSNs you want your computer to accept calls for and the MSN to which you want outgoing calls billed.

Table 3-7. *Information About an ISDN Account*

Item	Description
B Channel Rate	64 Kbps or 56 Kbps.
User Name	Account name to enter when logging in, identifying you to the ISP.
Password	Password that verifies that you are the person with this user name.

Table 3-7.   *Information About an ISDN Account* (continued)

Configuring Your ISDN Connection in Windows XP/2000

When you or an installer has installed your terminal adapter, Windows should detect the new hardware and run the Add Hardware Wizard automatically. If it doesn't, choose Start | Control Panel (Start | Settings | Control Panel in Windows 2000), run the Printers And Other Hardware program, and choose Add Hardware from the See Also list. If the wizard doesn't detect the ISDN adapter, choose Add A New Device.

When Windows has installed the drivers for the ISDN adapter, you (or your telephone installer) configure Windows to use it. The Add Hardware Wizard usually displays a dialog box asking for configuration information: if it doesn't, choose Start | Control Panel | Printers And Other Hardware and choose System to display the System Properties dialog box. Click the Hardware tab and click the Device Manager button. (You can also see the Device Manager from the Computer Management window.) Your ISDN adapter appears in Modems if it is external or in Network Adapters if it is internal. Right-click the ISDN adapter and choose Properties from the menu that appears. Click the ISDN tab and select the Switch type or D-channel protocol your phone company uses. (Ask your phone company for this information.) Then click the Configure button and enter the requested information. (See Table 3-7.)

| **Tip** | *You must be logged on using an administrator account to configure your ISDN adapter.* |

Windows XP uses dial-up connections for ISDN lines. To create a dial-up connection, start the New Connection Wizard by clicking Create A New Connection in the Task pane of the Network Connections window or by choosing Start | All Programs | Accessories | Communications | New Connection Wizard. Answer the wizard's questions as follows:

■ **Network Connection Type**   Choose Connect To The Internet.

■ **Getting Ready** Choose Set Up My Connection Manually.

■ **Internet Connection** Choose Connect Using A Dial-Up Modem.

■ **Devices** Windows shows a list of available devices that contains the individual ISDN channels of your ISDN adapter, as well as an entry named All Available ISDN Lines Multi-linked, which is selected by default. Keep this selection if you want to bundle both channels of your ISDN line (for 128-Kbps speed), or clear it and select only one of the channels if you always want to connect with a single channel at 56/64 Kbps.

The Wizard creates the dial-up connection for the ISDN line. Now you can configure the ISDN line type to use. Follow these steps:

1. Right-click the dial-up connection icon in the Network Connections window. Choose Properties from the menu that appears. You see the Properties dialog box for the ISDN connection.

2. On the General tab, select the ISDN channel that you want to configure. Click the Configure button to display the ISDN Configuration dialog box.

3. Set the Line Type, Negotiate Line Type, and other settings according to the instructions you receive from your phone company or ISP.

> **Tip** *Some phone companies charge "data" calls by the minute, whereas "voice" calls are free. For that reason, some ISPs allow you to connect with the "56K Voice" line type, which disguises the connection as a "voice" call to the phone company. This method is called* Data Over Voice (DOV).

If you create a multilinked ISDN connection that bundles both of your ISDN channels, you can also configure the bundling. Click the Options tab of your dial-up connection's Properties dialog box and select the bundling behavior under Multiple Devices:

■ **Dial Only First Available Device** This uses only the first free ISDN channel and leaves the other one available so you can still make or receive phone calls.

■ **Dial All Devices** This creates a "static" 128-Kbps connection that uses both ISDN channels all of the time.

■ **Dial Devices Only As Needed** This allows dynamic use of the ISDN channels, which you can configure by clicking the Configure button. With this setting, Windows initially uses only one ISDN channel and starts using the second one when you fully exploit the bandwidth of this channel for an extended period (for example, when you start downloading a big file). When the download is finished, Windows automatically disconnects the second ISDN channel again.

(Thanks to Robert Schlabbach for these instructions.)

Configuring Your ISDN Connection in Windows Me/98

In Windows Me/98, you can run the ISDN Configuration Wizard to set up a connection. Choose Start | Programs | Accessories | Communications | ISDN Configuration Wizard. Enter the information about your ISDN line.

Note *The wizard appears only if your computer has an ISDN adapter installed.*

Connecting to an Organization's LAN Using VPN

Virtual Private Networking (VPN) allows a computer to connect to a corporate LAN over the Internet. (See the section on virtual private networks in Chapter 1.)

To connect to an existing VPN server, you don't have to worry about configuring the server. Contact your organization's system administrator to find out the host name or numeric IP address of the VPN server. However, if you are creating both the VPN client and the server, then you need to configure the server.

Note *The VPN server must have a routable IP address—that is, it must be directly on the Internet. If the computer you want to connect to shares an Internet connection, it is not accessible using VPN. Computers inside a firewall on a company LAN and those otherwise sharing an Internet connection (using ICS, for instance) do not have routable IP addresses.*

Connecting via VPN to or from Windows XP

Windows XP includes both a VPN client and a VPN server.

Configuring the VPN Client in Windows XP

Follow these steps for creating a VPN connection on the client computer over the Internet:

1. Connect to the Internet.
2. Open the Network Connections window by choosing Start | Control Panel | Network Connections.
3. Click Create A New Connection in the Network Tasks part of the Task pane to run the New Connection Wizard. Click Next to move from window to window.
4. Select Connect To The Network At My Workplace. Click Next.
5. Select Virtual Private Network Connection. Click Next.
6. Type a name for the connection in the Company Name box (like "VPN" or the name of your organization or the location of the VPN server). Click Next.
7. In the Public Network window, specify which Internet connection to use to connect to the Internet. If you'd prefer to make the Internet connection yourself,

rather than allowing the VPN connection to initiate a connection, choose Do Not Dial The Initial Connection. Click Next.

8. In the VPN Server Selection window, type the host name or numeric IP address of the VPN server (for example, **pptp.microsoft.com**). If you are connecting to an organization, get this information from your organization's system administrator.

Note   *To find out a computer's IP address, right-click the Internet connection in the Network Connections window, choose Status from the shortcut menu, and click the Details tab. The following blocks of IP addresses are reserved and not used on the Internet, so a computer with one of these numbers cannot be used in VPN: 10.0.0.0 through 10.255.255.255, 172.16.0.0 through 172.31.255.255, and 192.168.0.0 through 192.168.255.255.*

9. You see a window confirming that you have created a VPN connection. Choose whether you want to add a shortcut for the connection to the desktop. Click Finish.

The VPN connection appears in a new Virtual Private Network section of the Network Connections window.

Now, when you want to connect to your VPN, open the VPN connection you just created. It connects to the Internet through the connection you specified in step 7 (unless you told it you wanted to make the connection yourself) and then connects to the VPN through the Internet.

Note   *If your VPN server has a dial-up connection to the Internet, it may be issued a new IP address each session by its ISP. If so, you'll have to adjust the address on the VPN properties dialog box of the client computer before each connection.*

Configuring the VPN Server in Windows XP

To configure a computer to accept VPN connections, you must have an Incoming Connections icon in the Network Connections window. If you already have this icon, double-click it to display the Incoming Connections Properties dialog box. Check that the Virtual Private Network option is selected (Allow Others To Make Private Connections To My Computer By Tunneling Through The Internet Or Other Network).

Note   *Windows XP includes VPN server software that can accept only one incoming connection at a time. If you need more than one simultaneous VPN connection to your server, upgrade to Windows .NET Server.*

If you do not have the Incoming Connections icon, follow these steps to create it and configure your computer to accept incoming VPN connections.

1. Open the Network Connections window by choosing Start | Control Panel | Network Connections.

2. Click Create A New Connection to start the New Connection Wizard.

3. Select Set Up An Advanced Connection and click Next.

4. Select Accept Incoming Connections and click Next.

5. The Devices For Incoming Connections dialog box doesn't include an option for the Internet, which is the actual device you'll be using. Deselect all modems and ports and click Next.

6. Select Allow Virtual Private Connections. Click Next.

7. Select the users you want to allow to connect. Click Next.

8. Deselect any protocols that you don't want used. Generally, no change to this page is necessary as long as TCP/IP is one of the selected protocols. Click Next.

9. Click Finish. An icon called Incoming Connections is created in your Network Connections window. If you already have an Incoming Connections icon, its properties are changed to support VPN.

Once you configure a computer as a VPN server, be sure to read the section "VPN Security Issues in Windows XP" that's coming right up.

Configuring a VPN Connection in Windows XP

You can display and change the settings for your VPN or incoming connection. In the Network Connections window, right-click the VPN or incoming connection and choose Properties from the menu that appears. The properties for clients and servers are different—the Properties dialog box for a VPN client connection is shown in Figure 3-11.

On the General tab, you can change the host name or IP address of your company's VPN server or the Internet connection to use. The Advanced tab allows you to enable the Internet Connection Firewall, and to share the VPN connection.

The properties for the VPN server allow you to make changes to the options you selected with the New Connection Wizard. You can turn VPN on or off, display an icon in the notification area of the taskbar, and add and remove allowed users.

VPN Security Issues in Windows XP

When a computer is configured as a server that accepts dial-in or VPN connections, it is open to abuse by unauthorized users. Damage can include reading and destroying files on shared drives, as well as introducing viruses.

Be sure to disable Incoming Connections when you don't expect any. Here's how:

1. Open the Network Connections window by choosing Start | Control Panel | Network Connections.

2. Double-click the Incoming Connections icon to display the Incoming Connections Properties dialog box.

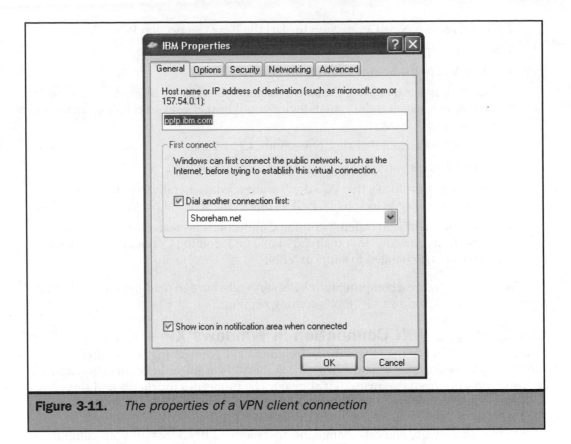

Figure 3-11. *The properties of a VPN client connection*

3. Deselect the modem in the Devices box to disable Dial-Up Networking and deselect the Virtual Private Network option to disable VPN.

4. Click OK.

Repeat the same steps, but select the modem, to turn Dial-Up Networking and VPN back on when you plan to use your computer as a server. Because networking does you no good when it's turned off, take some additional prudent security measures for the times you need it enabled:

- Keep your modem's phone number a closely guarded secret.
- Use passwords and change them regularly.
- Consider using the callback feature.

If your computer is a remote access server, you have the option of enabling *callback*. When callback is enabled, the caller logs in. Then, if login is accepted, the server disconnects and calls the client back.

Enable the callback feature by following these steps:

1. In the Network Connections window, click the Incoming Connections icon to display the Incoming Connections Properties dialog box.

2. Click the Users tab.

3. Select the user for whom you want to enable callback. Click Properties.

4. Click the Callback tab.

5. Choose either to Allow The Caller To Set The Callback Number or to Always Use The Following Callback Number. (Enter the number with any additional digits, such as 9, to get an outside line.)

6. Click OK.

Connecting via VPN from Windows 2000/Me/98

Windows 2000, Me, and 98 come with a VPN client so you can connect into your organization's VPN server. Windows 2000 also comes with VPN server software.

To connect to your organization's LAN, you use two Internet connections from your computer. One connection—a Dial-Up Networking connection for a dial-up account or a network connection for a DSL or cable Internet account—connects your computer to the Internet. A second connection, which is always a Dial-Up Networking connection (even though it doesn't actually dial up anything), "tunnels" through the Internet and your organization's firewall to connect to your LAN.

 VPN is not automatically installed when you install Windows Me or 98. If it is not installed, choose Start | Settings | Control Panel, double-click the Add/Remove Programs icon, click the Windows Setup tab, choose Communications from the list of components, click Details, and select Virtual Private Networking from among the Communications options. You might need to insert your Windows CD-ROM.

Once you have configured your computer to connect to a dial-up or broadband Internet account and tested the connection, you are ready to create the Dial-Up Networking connection for VPN.

Creating a VPN Connection in Windows 2000

Follow these steps for using VPN Dial-Up Networking to connect to a LAN through a firewall:

1. Choose Start | Settings | Network And Dial-Up Connections.

2. Run the Make New Connection icon. The Network Connection Wizard runs.

3. Choose Dial-Up To Private Network Through The Internet. Click Next.

4. When the wizard asks about your "public network" (Internet) connection, specify how your computer connects to the Internet. If you connect using broadband, choose Do Not Dial The Initial Connection. Click Next.

5. Specify the host name or IP address of the VPN server to which you want to connect (for example, **pptp.gurus.com**). If your system administrator gives you the IP Address of the server, you can type that instead. Click Next.

6. Specify whether you want this VPN connection to be available for all users of this computer or just you. (If you want to log into a Windows domain when you connect to your organization's VPN server, choose All Users.) Click Next.

7. Specify a name for the Dial-Up Networking connection. Click Finish.

Creating a VPN Connection in Windows Me/98

Follow these steps for using VPN Dial-Up Networking to connect to a LAN through a firewall:

1. In Windows Me, choose Start | Settings | Control Panel and click the Dial-Up Networking icon to display the Dial-Up Networking window. In Windows 98, choose Start | Programs | Accessories | Communications | Dial-Up Networking.

2. Click the Make New Connection icon. ·

3. In the Make New Connection window, type a name for the connection (like "VPN" or the name of your organization) in the top box. Set the Select A Device box to Microsoft VPN Adapter. Click the Next button.

4. In the Host Name Or IP Address box, type the host name of your organization's VPN server (for example, **pptp.gurus.com**). If your system administrator gives you the IP Address of the server, you can type that instead. Click Next.

5. You see a window confirming that you have created a Dial-Up Networking connection. Click Finish.

Making the VPN Connection

Now, when you want to connect to your private network, connect to the Internet through your ISP and then connect to the private network through the Dial-Up Networking connection you just created.

If you have trouble with your VPN connection, right-click the Dial-Up Networking icon, choose Properties, and check the connection's settings. Check with your organization's LAN administrator for the correct settings.

> **Tip**
>
> *Some ISPs offer PPTP services that let you connect to your private network by using one Dial-Up Networking connection. If your Internet provider does offer these services, ask your ISP what to type in the User Name box in the Dial-Up Networking Connect To dialog box. You may need to type an entry in the format* name@companyname.com, *rather than your usual user name. When you use this special user name, you connect both to the Internet and to your private network.*

Configuring Windows 2000's VPN Server

If you want another computer (perhaps your own laptop, when you are on the road) to be able to connect to your computer, you can enable Windows 2000's built-in VPN Server. Follow these steps:

1. Choose Start | Settings | Network And Dial-Up Connections.

2. Run the Make New Connection program. The Network Connection Wizard starts and asks a series of questions. Click Next to move from screen to screen.

3. Choose Accept Incoming Connections.

4. Choose the modem (or network connection, for broadband Internet connections) you use to connect to the Internet.

5. Choose Allow Virtual Private Connections.

6. Choose which users can connect via VPN. Don't choose Guest because this might open a security hole.

> **Note** *You must be logged in as an administrator to configure the VPN server.*

Connecting via VPN from a Mac

Several VPN clients are available for the Mac, including Cisco VPN, PGP, and PiePants. See **www.macwindows.com/VPN.html** for more information on these products.

Displaying Your IP Address

Sometimes you need to know your computer's IP address. If you are running a web server or FTP server on your own computer and other people need to know your address so that they can connect to your server, you tell them your IP address. (Few PCs have host names.)

Most versions of Windows come with a DOS program called *Ipconfig* that displays your IP address. Open a DOS window by choosing Start | All Programs | Accessories | Command Prompt (in Windows XP/2000), Start | Programs | Accessories | MS-DOS Prompt (in Windows Me), or Start | Programs | MS-DOS Prompt (in Windows 98). Then, type **ipconfig** and press ENTER. You see something like this:

```
Ethernet adapter Local Area Connection:
        Connection-specific DNS Suffix  . :
        IP Address. . . . . . . . . . . . : 192.168.1.16
        Subnet Mask . . . . . . . . . . . : 255.255.255.0
        Default Gateway . . . . . . . . . : 192.168.1.1
```

In Windows XP, there's another way. Display the Network Connections window by choosing Start | Control Panel | Network Connections. Select the connection and click View Status Of This Connection in the Network Tasks section of the Task pane. You see the status dialog box for the connection. Click the Details or Support tab.

Windows Me and Windows 98 have a graphics program called *Winipcfg* that displays your IP connection information in a window. Choose Start | Run, type **winipcfg** in the Open window, press ENTER, and click the More Info button in the window that appears.

Macintosh users can select the TCP/IP control panel or run the Apple System Profiler to see this information.

Testing Your Connection with Ping and Traceroute

After dialing a Dial-Up Networking connection, you can use the Ping program to test whether packets of information can make the round-trip from your computer, out over the Internet to another computer, and back to your computer. You can use the Traceroute or Tracert program to check which route the packets take to get from your computer to another computer. You can use the Netstat program to find out which computers your computer is talking to.

 Note   *Mac OS X users can execute the UNIX ping command from a Terminal window. Mac OS 9 users can download the freeware programs WhatRoute or OTTool from www.macorchard.com.*

Pinging Another Computer

Sending a small text packet on a round-trip is called *pinging,* and you can use a Ping program to send one. Windows XP, 2000, Me, and 98 come with a Ping program.

To run Ping in Windows, open a DOS window by choosing Start | All Programs | Accessories | Command Prompt (in Windows XP/2000), Start | Programs | Accessories | MS-DOS Prompt (in Windows Me), or Start | Programs | MS-DOS Prompt (in Windows 98). Then, type the Ping command:

```
ping system
```

Replace *system* with either the numeric IP address or the host name of the computer that you want to ping. Choose any Internet host computer that you are sure is up and running, such as your ISP's mail server, and then press ENTER.

 Tip   *To see a listing of all the command-line options for the Ping program, type **ping /?** at the DOS prompt.*

For example, you can ping the Yahoo web server (a web search engine and directory) by typing

```
ping www.yahoo.com
```

Ping sends out four test packets (pings) and reports how long the packets take to get to Yahoo's computer and back to yours, like this:

```
 Command Prompt                                                    - □ ×

C:\Documents and Settings\Margy>ping www.yahoo.com

Pinging www.yahoo.akadns.net [64.58.76.177] with 32 bytes of data:

Reply from 64.58.76.177: bytes=32 time=78ms TTL=241
Reply from 64.58.76.177: bytes=32 time=78ms TTL=241
Reply from 64.58.76.177: bytes=32 time=77ms TTL=241
Reply from 64.58.76.177: bytes=32 time=98ms TTL=241

Ping statistics for 64.58.76.177:
    Packets: Sent = 4, Received = 4, Lost = 0 (0% loss),
Approximate round trip times in milli-seconds:
    Minimum = 77ms, Maximum = 98ms, Average = 82ms

C:\Documents and Settings\Margy>_
```

For each packet, you see how long the round-trip takes in milliseconds, as well as summary information about all four packets' trips.

 *First try Ping with a numeric IP address, to see whether packets get out to the Internet and back. (To find a working numeric IP address, use Ping from another computer using a host name, and note the IP address that Ping displays for that host computer.) Then try Ping with a host name, such as **www.yahoo.com** or **net.gurus.com**, to see whether you successfully contact your DNS to convert the name into an IP address. If the first test works and the second doesn't, your connection isn't set up properly to contact a DNS server.*

Tracing Packets over the Internet

Packets of information don't usually go directly from one computer to another computer over the Internet. Instead, they are involved in a huge game of "whisper-down-the-lane," in which packets are passed from computer to computer until they reach their destination. If your data seems to be moving slowly, you can use the Tracert (short for "trace route") program to follow your packets across the Internet, from your computer to an Internet host that you frequently use. The technique that Tracert uses doesn't always work, so it's quite possible that running Tracert to a remote computer can fail, even though the computer is working and accessible.

Windows XP, 2000, Me, and 98 come with a Tracert program. To run Tracert, open a DOS window by choosing Start | All Programs | Accessories | Command Prompt (in Windows XP/2000), Start | Programs | Accessories | MS-DOS Prompt (in Windows Me), or Start | Programs | MS-DOS Prompt (in Windows 98). Then type the Tracert command:

```
tracert system
```

Replace *system* with either the numeric IP address or the Internet name of the computer to which you want to trace the route and then press ENTER.

 To see a listing of all the command-line options for the Tracert program, type **tracert** *at the DOS prompt, with no address.*

For example, you can trace the route of packets from your computer to the Internet Gurus web site at **net.gurus.com** by typing

```
tracert net.gurus.com
```

You see a listing like this:

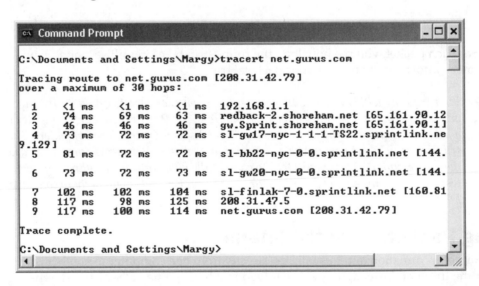

The listing shows the route that the packets took from your computer to the specified host. (Sometimes, Tracert reports a different host name from the one that you specified, which means that the host has more than one name.) For each *hop* (stage of the route), Tracert sends out three packets and reports the time that each packet takes to reach that far. It also reports the name and numeric IP address of the host.

Displaying Internet Connections Using Netstat

Netstat is a Windows network diagnostic program that you can use for any TCP/IP connection—Internet connections or LANs. You can run Netstat to see which computers your computer is connected to over the Internet—not the ISP to which you dial in, but other Internet hosts to or from which you are transferring information. Netstat comes with Windows XP, 2000, Me, and 98.

To run Netstat, open a DOS window by choosing Start | All Programs | Accessories | Command Prompt (in Windows XP/2000), Start | Programs | Accessories | MS-DOS Prompt (in Windows Me), or Start | Programs | MS-DOS Prompt (in Windows 98). Then, type **netstat** and press ENTER. You see a listing of the Internet connections that are currently running, like this:

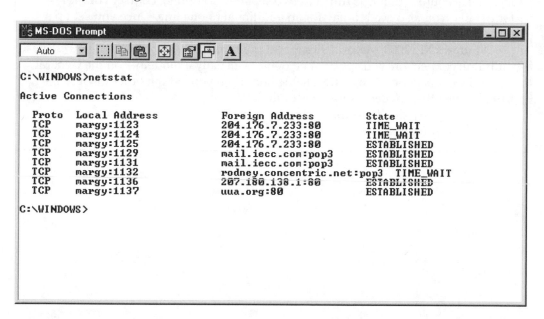

This example shows that the computer is connected to the host **mail.iecc.com** for POP (picking up incoming mail). The computer is also connected to **uua.org**, probably to receive web pages. (The *80* at the end of the address signifies the port commonly used for web page retrieval.)

  *To see a listing of all the command-line options for the Netstat program, type **netstat /h** at the DOS prompt.*

Combining Two Phone Lines into a Multilink Connection

Multilink enables your computer to use multiple modems and phone lines (usually two modems and two phone lines) for a single Internet connection to increase the effective connection speed (throughput). For example, you can use two 56-Kbps modems together to simulate a 108-Kbps connection to the Internet. Data flows through both modems and both phone lines for a single connection.

Your ISP must support multilink connections for you to use such a connection because the ISP's hardware and software must be able to combine the packets of information from the two phone lines into one Internet connection. Multilink connections, where they're available, usually cost more than a regular dial-up Internet account (but not as much as two separate accounts); contact your ISP for details. You also need to pay for an additional phone line. Once you set up a multilink connection, it works just like a regular Internet connection, but faster.

Windows XP, 2000, Me, and 98 support multilink connections. When you create a multilink connection, you specify one device—usually a modem—on the General tab of the connection's Properties dialog box. Then you list the other device(s)— usually one other modem—on the Multilink tab.

Generally, we don't recommend using multilink if high-speed connections are available in your area.

The Complete Reference

Internet

Chapter 4

Connecting Your LAN to the Internet

The Internet isn't the only computer network: private computer networks have existed for years. Most organizations have *local area networks (LANs)*, networks of computers connected by cables, usually in one building or campus, that allow their computers to share files, printers, e-mail, and other resources. LANs have become so easy to set up that most small offices and many homes have them.

When your computers are connected by a LAN, there's no point connecting each computer individually to the Internet. Instead, you can connect one computer to the Internet, and this computer serves as a *gateway* between the LAN and the Internet. All the computers can send and receive e-mail and browse the Web at the same time, although the traffic slows down if lots of people are sharing a slow phone line.

This chapter describes how to connect a LAN (for example, networked computers at home or in a small office) to the Internet using Internet Connection Sharing, which is included with Windows XP, 2000, and Me. If your home or small office has more than one computer, you should definitely consider connecting them into a LAN and sharing one Internet connection.

What Is an Intranet?

As the Internet became more popular, organizations began offering Internet-like services on their internal LANs, and the *intranet* was born. An *intranet* is a private network (usually a LAN, but it may be larger) that uses TCP/IP and other Internet standard protocols.

Because it uses TCP/IP (which is described in Chapter 1), an intranet can support TCP/IP-based protocols, such as HTTP (the protocol that web browsers use to talk to web servers), and SMTP and POP (the protocols that e-mail client programs use to send and receive mail). An intranet can run web servers, web clients, mail servers, and mail clients—it can work like a small, private Internet. Like the Internet, most intranets also carry lots of e-mail traffic: all those paper memos that used to float around large organizations have largely been replaced by e-mail messages. Intranets enable organizations to set up web sites and online discussion groups for their staff, invisible to the outside world. Home networks don't usually turn into intranets because home users don't need to use their LAN for e-mail and web pages within the home; instead, the LAN is used primarily to share files, printers, and the Internet connection.

Intranets vs. LANs

An intranet starts with a LAN and adds Internet protocol services. What's the advantage of running Internet protocols on your LAN? Some LANs have their own transport protocols: NetBEUI (from Microsoft) and IPX/SPX (from Novell) are both commonly used LAN communications protocols. These protocols do a good job for file sharing and printer sharing on a LAN, but they aren't Internet-compatible, and they don't support web browsers and web servers. Fortunately, you don't have to choose between a LAN communication protocol and TCP/IP. In most cases, you can run both simultaneously—the computers on your network use a LAN protocol, such as NetBEUI or IPX/SPX, to share files or send information to a shared printer and use TCP/IP to request web pages.

 The issue of TCP/IP vs. LAN protocols is disappearing, as most LANs of any size convert to TCP/IP. Microsoft is phasing out the NetBEUI protocol in favor of TCP/IP.

An intranet can be three networked computers, a LAN of 200 computers in a building, or six large LANs interconnected as a *wide area network* (*WAN*). You can also create an *extranet,* an intranet that allows people to connect into the network over the Internet. For example, if your organization sends salespeople out into the field, they could connect to the Internet and then use extranet features to connect to your organization's intranet. Organizations can allow their business partners (like suppliers and customers) to access their extranet, too.

On the other hand, if all you need is for everyone on your LAN to be able to view a private set of web pages, you need neither an intranet nor a web server. By using the File | Open command of almost any browser, you can view web pages stored on any hard disk that is accessible over the network. Instead of using web server URLs that start with *http://*, you can specify the hard disk and path name of the web page to display by using file URLs that start with *file:///* (yes, that's three slashes). For example, you can make an internal home page for your small organization, store it on a hard disk that is accessible from all the computers on the LAN, and set it as the home page of your users' browsers.

What Can You Do with an Internet-Connected LAN?

Connecting your LAN to the Internet can enable all the computers on your LAN to access the Internet with only one Internet account and one phone line. Now that most LANs are switching to TCP/IP as the LAN protocol, sharing an Internet connection is easy.

What Can You Do with a Home Network?

Many homes now have more than one computer and can benefit from connecting them into a LAN. For example, you can move your home calendar into a calendar program like Lotus Organizer that you can access from all the computers on a LAN. Put a computer in the kitchen, and updates to the LAN-based calendar are available on all your computers, as well as for synchronization with your Palm or Visor personal data assistant (PDA).

Connecting a home network to the Internet also saves on phone lines and family strife. Rather than having to take turns using the Internet to check your e-mail or surf the web, everyone can use the Internet at the same time with a shared Internet connection. That computer in the kitchen can display the local paper's weather web page when you're not using the calendar program.

When you get a new computer, consider putting the computer you just replaced in the kitchen or playroom and connecting it to your LAN. Even older computers do a fine job of running e-mail programs and web browsers.

What Can You Do with an Intranet?

An intranet adds Internet-like services to your LAN. Many organizations, especially those with large existing computer systems, have lots of information that is hard to get at. The intranet can change all that, by using Internet tools. Here are some ideas for ways that your organization—large or small—can use an intranet.

- **E-mail within the organization and to and from the Internet**   People can use one e-mail program to exchange mail both with other intranet users and with the Internet.

- **Private discussion groups**   Using a mailing list manager (described in Chapter 10) or a news server (described in Chapter 11) accessible only to people in your organization, you can set up mailing lists or newsgroups to encourage people to share information within departments or across the organization. Alternatively, you can use web-based message boards, which are discussed in Chapter 15.

- **Private web sites**   Each department in your organization can create a web site that is accessible only to people on the intranet. Instead of circulating memos and handbooks, information can go on these web sites. For example, the marketing department can post information about products, including upcoming release dates, how products are targeted, and other information that isn't appropriate for a public site on the Internet-based web. By using the intranet instead of printing on paper, it's economical to publish large documents and documents that change frequently.

- **Access to databases**   If your organization has information in databases, you can convert the data to web pages so that everyone on the intranet can see it. For example, a nonprofit organization might have a database containing all of its fundraising and membership information. By using a program that can display database information as web pages and enter information from web page forms into the database, all the people at the organization can see, and even update, selected information from the database by using only a web browser. Naturally, the program would need to limit who could see and change particular information in the database.

- **Teleconferencing**   Rather than spend big bucks on video teleconferencing systems, think about using your intranet (and the Internet), instead. If your organization has offices in several locations, you can use the Internet for online chats with text, voice, shared whiteboards, and even limited video. (See Chapter 16 for a description of Internet-based conferencing.)

Components of a LAN

This section presents the hardware that makes up a LAN. This chapter doesn't include specific instructions for how to set up a LAN because the instructions depend on which operating system(s) you are using. Instead, we list the components you'll need and how they work when you connect the LAN to the Internet.

For information about setting up a LAN, see Windows XP: The Complete Reference *(by John Levine and Margaret Levine Young),* Windows Me: The Complete Reference *(by the same authors),* Windows 98: The Complete Reference *(by the same authors),* Mac OS X: The Complete Reference *(by Jesse Feiler), or* Mac OS 9: The Complete Reference *(by Gene Steinberg). All these books are published by Osborne/McGraw-Hill.*

Workstations and Client Software

Most of the computers that are connected together by a LAN are *workstations*—computers that are used directly by people. A workstation can be almost any computer—a PC running Windows, a Macintosh, or a computer running UNIX. One LAN can combine different types of workstations. For the LAN to share an Internet connection, each workstation's operating system must be able to support TCP/IP: Windows 95 and later, Macs, and UNIX have TCP/IP networking built in. These operating systems also support file and printer sharing on the LAN.

In addition to other application programs, workstations run *client programs*, software that provides the user with access to network servers. Workstations might run e-mail clients (such as Outlook Express, Eudora, or Netscape Messenger) and web browsers. In fact, workstations can run any standard Internet client programs to access both LAN and Internet services.

Servers and Operating Systems

Most LANs—except the smallest networks—include computers that are not used directly by people. Instead, these servers provide services to the LAN. For example, a *file server* stores files to be shared by users on the network, a *print server* controls a printer that network users can print on, a *web server* provides web pages, and a *mail server* controls incoming and/or outgoing mail messages.

If you are connecting a small LAN to the Internet, you don't need a server. A workstation can act as the gateway computer, or you can use a router (a separate box) as the gateway.

Like a workstation, a server can be almost any computer. Servers can run Windows .NET Server, Windows 2000, Windows NT, UNIX, Linux, or a network-specific operating system such as Novell NetWare.

Servers also run *server software,* such as web server software, mail server software, or a mailing list manager. Many server programs run on UNIX or Linux, some on Windows .NET Server, 2000, and NT, and a few on Macs. If you have a UNIX or Linux server, you can run lots of freeware and shareware server programs that are used on Internet host computers (for example, the Apache web server and standard UNIX mail programs such as sendmail). Windows .NET, 2000, and NT servers come with a web server (Microsoft Internet Information Services).

A LAN turns into an intranet when you run servers that provide information to the people on the LAN. For lists of server software that runs on UNIX, Windows, and other platforms, visit the ServerWatch web site at **serverwatch.internet.com**. This site includes listings of web servers, e-mail servers, chat servers, mailing list servers, and other types of servers.

Network Cards, Cabling, and Hubs

A critical component of any LAN is the cabling and other hardware that connect the computers together. The most widely used method for connecting computers to a LAN is called *Ethernet.* Most Ethernet networks use a *hub* or *switch* as the center of a star, with a cable between the hub or switch and each computer, as shown in Figure 4-1. Switches are faster (and more expensive) than hubs because they have built-in processing that sends information more directly to the computer to which it is addressed. Hubs and switches come in 4-port, 8-port, and 16-port configurations. Larger LANs use multiple hubs or switches, cabled together.

LANs usually use Category-5 (Cat-5) cable, which contains four twisted pairs of wires. The connectors at the ends of Cat-5 tables are called *RJ-45 jacks,* which look like large U.S.-style phone connectors. To connect the cable to the computers, each workstation and server needs an Ethernet *network adapter,* which is either an adapter card that installs in a desktop computer or laptop base station, or a PC card that installs in a laptop. Many computers come with network adapters built in.

Wireless LANs avoid cabling altogether. In a wireless LAN, one computer has an *access point,* a box with a small radio antenna that acts as the hub of the LAN. The rest of the computers have *wireless LAN adapters* that connect by radio to the access point. You can combine wireless and cabled LANs. Set up a regular LAN for all the computers to which you can run cables, attach a wireless access point to one of them, and install wireless LAN adapters on the rest of the computers.

Assigning IP Addresses to Computers on the LAN

When you use TCP/IP on a LAN (as on the Internet), each computer has a unique IP address, as shown in Figure 4-1. On a LAN, computers usually use "private" or LAN-only IP addresses that are not used on the Internet. Several ranges of IP addresses have been set aside for LAN use. The most commonly used private IP addresses are in the format 192.168.0.*xxx*, where *xxx* is a number from 1 to 253. If one computer on the

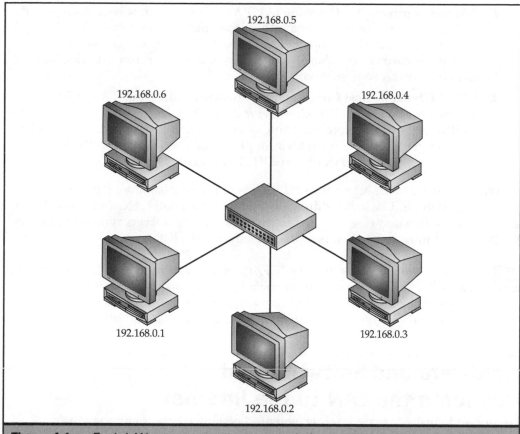

192.168.0.5

192.168.0.6

192.168.0.4

192.168.0.1

192.168.0.3

192.168.0.2

Figure 4-1.   *Each LAN computer connects to a hub or switch and has a separate IP address.*

LAN connects to the Internet, that computer has the address 192.168.0.1, and the rest of the computers have addresses from 192.168.0.2 up to 192.168.0.253.

How are IP addresses assigned? Your LAN can use one of three methods:

■ **Static IP addressing**   You can assign the IP addresses yourself, using addresses in the format 192.168.0.*xxx*. You need to keep track of which addresses you've assigned, so that you don't give two computers the same address. Another problem is that Windows' Internet Connection Sharing program (described in the section "Connecting a LAN to the Internet Using Internet Connection Sharing (ICS)" later in this chapter) doesn't work with static IP addressing.

- **Automatic private IP addressing (APIPA)**   This Windows system assigns IP addresses to the computers on a LAN automatically (called *dynamic addressing*) when the computer boots up or connects to the LAN. The addresses are in the format 169.254.*xxx.xxx,* where each *xxx* can be a number from 1 to 253. You can't use APIPA addresses with ICS, either.

- **DHCP (Dynamic Host Configuration Protocol) addressing**   A *DHCP server* is software that assigns IP addresses for the LAN. Like APIPA, DHCP assigns an IP address to your computer automatically, but it is designed to work with much larger LANs. ICS includes a simple DHCP server. Microsoft's TCP/IP networking systems generally use DHCP addressing.

When setting up a LAN that uses TCP/IP, you must choose among these IP addressing methods. Use static addressing only for very small LANs (with fewer than ten computers) that don't use ICS. If your network includes servers running Windows XP, 2000, NT, Linux, or UNIX, it probably already uses DHCP.

> **Note**   *If your computer has more than one TCP/IP connection, it needs more than one IP address. For example, your computer might have a network interface card that connects it to the LAN and another card that connects to a DSL modem that connects to the Internet. Each network interface card has one TCP/IP address.*

Hardware and Software that Connects the LAN to the Internet

To connect your LAN to the Internet, you need one Internet account, a gateway between the LAN and the Internet, and TCP/IP installed on each computer.

The Internet Connection

To connect your LAN to the Internet, you need an Internet service provider (ISP), described in Chapter 1. All the computers on the LAN connect to the Internet via this connection, so that each computer doesn't need its own modem, phone line, and account.

For a small network, a DSL or cable Internet connection will suffice; just sign up for a regular Internet account. Note that most DSL and cable Internet accounts prohibit you from running server software that offers services to the Internet because it might create too much traffic on the line.

If you are connecting a large LAN to the Internet and you anticipate more traffic than a DSL or cable Internet line can carry, contact ISPs in your area to discuss what kind of connection you need, depending on the size of your LAN, the types of services that you plan to provide to the LAN and the Internet, and the amount of data that you expect to transfer between the LAN and Internet.

The Gateway

The device or program that connects your LAN to the Internet acts as a *gateway*, passing messages between the computers on the LAN and computers on the Internet, and possibly controlling what types of information can pass.

 Even though DSL and cable Internet connections use the same cabling as a LAN (RJ-45 Cat-5 cable), don't plug the DSL or cable Internet cable into your LAN's hub or switch. The DSL or cable Internet must connect to a PC or router so that you have a gateway between the Internet and the LAN. (Connecting the modem to the hub is possible, but tricky and prone to error.)

What a Gateway Does

An Internet gateway can perform the following tasks:

- **Translating between the IP address on the LAN and the IP addresses on the Internet**   Computers on a LAN usually use private, LAN-only IP addresses, frequently assigned by a DHCP server on the LAN. Computers on the Internet use publicly visible IP addresses that are usually assigned by your ISP. A gateway accepts packets (messages) from the LAN, strips off the private IP address, substitutes its own ISP-supplied IP address, and passes the packet along to the Internet. When replies return, the gateway passes the replies back to the computer that made the request. To the rest of the Internet, all packets from the LAN appear to be from the gateway, so no information leaks out about the individual systems on your LAN. This service is called *Network Address Translation (NAT)*. All gateways to networks that use private addresses must perform this task.

- **Controlling the types of information that can flow between the Internet and your LAN**   The gateway, for example, can prevent telnet sessions (remote terminal sessions, described in Chapter 33) from coming in from the Internet or prevent chat sessions from going in either direction between the LAN and the Internet.

- **Caching**   The gateway can store information that has been requested from the Internet so that if a user requests the same information, the gateway can provide it without having to get it from the Internet again.

- **Logging usage of the Internet**   The gateway can log all packets that pass between the LAN and the Internet so you can have a record of who has access to your LAN from the Internet and what Internet services your LAN users have used.

Some gateway software (like ICS) provides only address translation. Other gateway programs, called *proxy servers*, provide address translation, caching, and logging. If the proxy server also provides security, controlling what information can pass between the LAN and the Internet, it's called a *firewall* (described in Chapter 1).

Devices That Can Act as Gateways

Three kinds of devices are commonly used as gateways, connecting LANs to the Internet:

- **Routers**   A "black box" that connects your LAN hub or switch to a phone line (dial-up, ISDN line, DSL line, or cable modem connection). Firewall software is built into the router. All you have to do is cable it to your LAN hub, connect your phone line or cable modem, plug it into power, and your LAN is on the Internet. Routers can be the simplest and most effective way to connect your LAN to the Internet. You connect your Internet connection (phone line or cable Internet cable) to the router and run a LAN cable from the router to your hub or switch.

- **UNIX or Linux systems**   Because the Internet was built on UNIX systems, lots of excellent TCP/IP communication software comes with most UNIX and Linux systems. Many "black box" routers are actually computers running UNIX or Linux, but you can set up your own for less money. You can run a wide variety of firewall software, as well as web server, POP (e-mail) server, or other Internet server software on the UNIX or Linux system. The UNIX or Linux system needs two connections: an Internet connection (phone line or cable Internet cable) and a LAN connection (cable to the LAN's hub or switch).

- **Windows systems running proxy server software**   A Windows XP, Me, 98, 2000, or NT 4 system can act as a router, running a gateway program. The Windows system connects to the Internet over a phone line or cable connection, and the gateway program provides the IP address translation. Windows XP comes with Internet Connection Sharing, which is easy to install and set up. Several Windows-based proxy server programs have been available for years, including SyGate (**www.sygate.com**), WinGate (**wingate.deerfield.com**), and WinProxy (**www.winproxy.com**). You install the proxy server program on the computer that is connected to the Internet and install a matching client program on each of the other computers on the LAN.

| Tip |

*Test the security of your LAN's Internet connection by going to Gibson Research Corporation's web site at **grc.com**. Follow the links to their Shields UP! service, which can check how vulnerable your computer is to attack or data theft from the Internet.*

Connecting a LAN to the Internet
Using Internet Connection Sharing (ICS)

If you have a small Windows-based LAN—up to ten computers in a home office or small business—you can share one Internet connection by using Internet Connection Sharing (ICS), which is built into Windows XP, 2000 (Server and Professional), and Me. (If you use an earlier version of Windows, you can use another Internet-sharing product, such as those listed in the previous section.) ICS allows all the users on a LAN to share one computer's Internet connection. The system running ICS—*the ICS server*—has two connections: one to the LAN (using a network interface card) and the other to the Internet (using a modem for dial-up or another network interface card or USB port for DSL or cable Internet connection). Figure 4-2 shows a LAN that uses ICS to share an Internet connection.

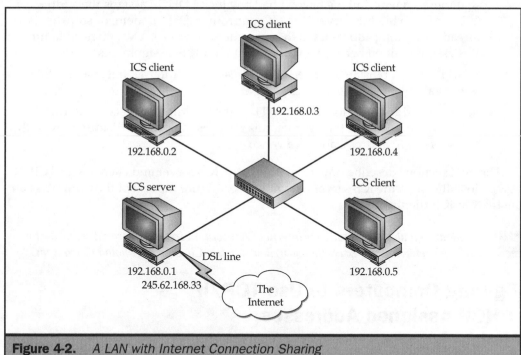

Figure 4-2. *A LAN with Internet Connection Sharing*

The rest of the computers on the LAN are *ICS clients.* These computers can run any version of Windows, UNIX, or the Mac OS, as long as they can communicate via TCP/IP. When any user on the LAN tries to communicate with the Internet—for example, by running a web browser or clicking the Check Mail button in an e-mail program—the request is routed to ICS. ICS connects to the Internet (if it is not already connected) and sends the request out to the Internet. When information comes from the Internet, ICS routes the information to the computer that requested it. ICS also serves as a proxy server, providing a firewall between your LAN and the Internet.

ICS Components

ICS includes these components:

- **DHCP Allocator**   Assigns IP addresses to ICS client computers on the LAN in the format 192.168.0.*xxx.* You can't use static IP addressing. (Microsoft claims that there's a way, but we haven't had any luck.) DHCP assigns the address 192.168.0.1 to the ICS server itself. If your router, DSL modem, or software is already assigning addresses to the computers on your LAN, you need to turn this assignment off because it will conflict with ICS' assignments.

- **DNS Proxy**   Translates between IP addresses and Internet host names (like **www.yahoo.com**) using your ISP's DNS server.

- **Network Address Translation (NAT)**   When passing packets of information between the LAN and the Internet, this replaces the private IP address with the ICS server's IP address, and vice versa.

The next sections describe how to configure the ICS server and clients with TCP/IP, how to install ICS on the ICS server, and how to configure the rest of the computers on the LAN at ICS clients.

 Windows XP also comes with an Internet Connection Firewall to provide security for any Internet connection, whether shared or not. See Chapter 3 for how to turn it on.

Configuring Computers to Use TCP/IP and DHCP-Assigned Addresses

Both the ICS server and ICS clients must communicate over the LAN using TCP/IP, the Internet's communication protocol. If your LAN uses another protocol for file and printer sharing, you can leave this other protocol in place, and add TCP/IP.

In addition, for ICS to work, ICS clients must use dynamically assigned IP addresses, which ICS assigns.

Configuring Windows XP to Use TCP/IP

Windows XP comes with TCP/IP preinstalled, and the Network Setup Wizard configures it to use dynamically assigned addresses.

To check that TCP/IP is still installed, choose Start | Control Panel | Network And Internet Connections | Network Connections to display the Network Connections window. Right-click your Local Area Connection and choose Properties from the menu that appears to display the Properties dialog box for the LAN connection. On the General tab, check that Internet Protocol (TCP/IP) appears and is selected so that your computer can communicate via TCP/IP on the LAN. If the TCP/IP entries don't appear, install TCP/IP by clicking the Install button, choosing Protocol, clicking the Add button, choosing TCP/IP from the list of network protocols, and clicking OK. Also make sure that the QoS Packet Scheduler appears and is selected.

Make sure that your computer is configured to get its IP address from the DHCP server that runs on the ICS server. On the General tab of the Local Area Connections Properties dialog box, click Internet Protocol (TCP/IP) on the list of installed components, and click the Properties button to display the Internet Protocol (TCP/IP) Properties dialog box. On the General tab, select Obtain An IP Address Automatically and Obtain DNS Server Address Automatically.

Configuring Windows 2000 to Use TCP/IP

Windows 2000 also comes with TCP/IP installed, but you can check its configuration. Choose Start | Settings | Network And Dial-Up Connections. Choose the Local Area Connection and click Properties to display the Properties dialog box for your LAN connection. If the Components Checked Are Used By This Connection box doesn't include TCP/IP, you need to install it. Click Install, choose Protocol, click Add, choose Internet Protocol (TCP/IP), and click OK.

TCP/IP in Windows 2000 is usually configured for dynamic IP addressing (which is what ICS requires), but you can check your computer. In the Properties dialog box for your LAN connection, choose Internet Protocol (TCP/IP) from the list of components and click Properties. You see the Internet Protocol (TCP/IP) Properties dialog box. Choose Obtain An IP Address Automatically.

Configuring Windows Me and 98 to Use TCP/IP

Here's how to install TCP/IP with dynamically assigned addresses in Windows Me and Window 98.

1. Open the Network dialog box by right-clicking the My Network Places or Network Neighborhood icon on the desktop and choosing Properties from the shortcut menu. Alternatively, choose Start | Settings | Control Panel and open the Network icon. Click the Configuration tab if it's not already selected. The Network dialog box is shown in Figure 4-3.

2. If the list of installed components includes TCP/IP bound to your network interface card (for example, "TCP/IP -> LinkSys EtherFast 10/100"), TCP/IP is already installed. Skip to step 5.

3. To install TCP/IP, click the Add button, select Protocol, and click the Add button again. You see the Select Network Protocol dialog box:

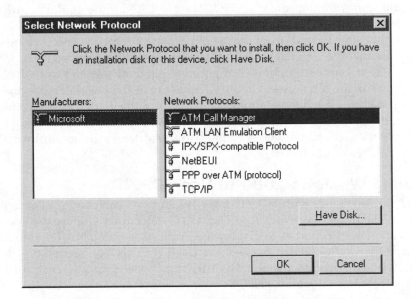

4. If more than one manufacturer is listed, click Microsoft. Select TCP/IP in the Network Protocols box and click OK. You return to the Network dialog box.

5. On the list of installed network components, select the binding of TCP/IP to your network interface card (for example, "TCP/IP -> LinkSys EtherFast 10/100").

6. Click Properties. You see the TCP/IP Properties dialog box shown next. Click the IP Address tab if it's not already selected.

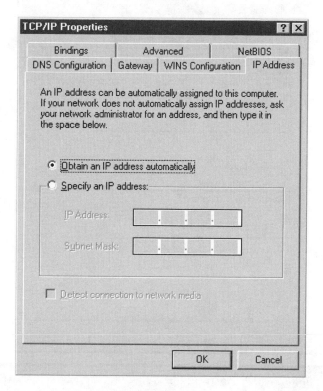

7. To use DHCP, click Obtain An IP Address Automatically. Windows will get IP addresses from the ICS server.

8. Click OK in each dialog box.

When you close the Network dialog box, Windows may prompt you to restart your computer.

To check your settings, Windows Me and 98 come with an IP Configuration program that can display your computer's IP address and other TCP/IP settings. To run IP Configuration, choose Start | Run, type **winipcfg** in the Open box, and click OK. You see the IP Configuration window. Click the More Info button to expand the IP Configuration window so it looks like Figure 4-4. If your computer has more than

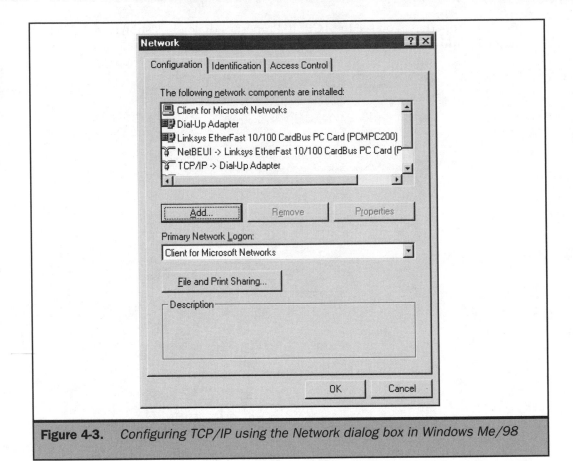

Figure 4-3.   *Configuring TCP/IP using the Network dialog box in Windows Me/98*

one network adapter configured to use TCP/IP, click the down-arrow at the right end of the box displaying the adapter name and choose another adapter. The settings in the lower part of the dialog box change to the settings you chose.

    If you have trouble with the IP addresses on the LAN, use the Networking (TCP/IP) Troubleshooter. Choose Start | Help, click Troubleshooting in the Help And Support window, click Home Networking & Network Problems, and click Networking (TCP/IP) Troubleshooter.

Configuring Macs to Use TCP/IP

Macs usually have TCP/IP installed, but you can look at the TCP/IP control panel to make sure. Set the Configure setting to DHCP Server to tell the Mac to get its IP address from the DHCP server included in ICS.

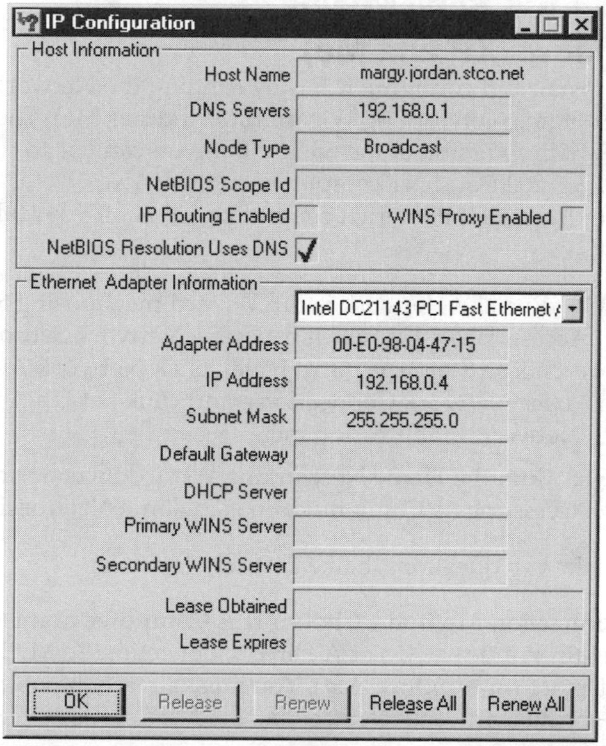

Figure 4-4. *Checking your computer's IP address and other TCP/IP settings*

Installing ICS on the ICS Server
in Windows XP, 2000, or Me

One computer on your LAN, the ICS server, runs the ICS program. This computer must connect to the Internet—make sure that you have this Internet connection working first. The ICS server must run Windows XP, Me, or 2000 because these are the versions of Windows that come with ICS.

Note *The wizard can't set up your computer as an ICS server if it's not connected to the Internet or to a LAN. It also doesn't work if another computer is already acting as the Internet gateway for the LAN, running a DHCP server, or using the IP address 192.168.0.1.*

Configuring the ICS Server Using a Wizard (Windows XP and Me)

The easiest way to install and configure ICS is by running the Network Setup Wizard (in Windows XP) or Home Networking Wizard (in Windows Me). The Wizard can create a floppy disk with a version of the wizard that you can use to configure the other Windows Me, 9x, 2000, and NT computers on the LAN.

On the computer that has the Internet connection, close all your other programs and run the wizard:

- **Windows XP**   Run the Network Setup Wizard by choosing Start | All Programs | Accessories | Communications | Network Setup Wizard. Alternatively, choose Start | Control Panel, click Network And Internet Connections, click Network Connections, and click Set Up A Home Or Small Office Network in the Task pane.

- **Windows Me**   Run the Home Networking Wizard by choosing Start | Programs | Accessories | Communications | Home Networking Wizard.

As the wizard asks you questions, make these choices:

- **Internet Connection Method**   Choose This Computer Connects Directly To The Internet (in Windows XP) or A Direct Connection To My ISP Using The Following Device (in Windows Me). You must already have created a dial-up, DSL, ISDN, or cable Internet connection.

- **Select Your Internet Connection**   The wizard displays a list of the connections (both Internet and LAN connections) on your computer. Choose the connection to the Internet, as shown here (in Windows XP):

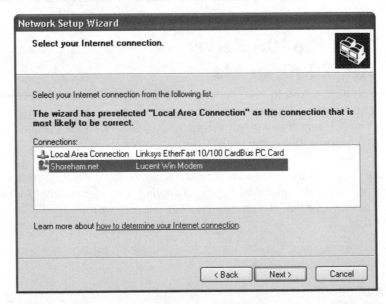

- **Computer Name**   Type a description of your computer in the Computer Description box and a unique name for your computer in the Computer Name box. The boxes may already be filled in if you entered this information when you installed Windows or when you set up your LAN.

- **Workgroup Name**   In the Workgroup Name box, type the name of your workgroup (for workgroup-based networks). The workgroup name must match the workgroup name of the other computers on the LAN.

- **Sharing Files and Printers (Windows Me only)**   Select the files and printers to share with other people on the LAN. This setting has nothing to do with ICS, but it's part of the Home Networking Wizard's list of questions.

- **You're Almost Done/Setup Disk**   If you haven't already set up your LAN, you need to configure each other computer on the LAN to work with the settings you've just installed. (That is, your ICS server computer is the DHCP server that hands out IP addresses, as well as being the Internet gateway.) You can choose to create a floppy disk with a wizard you can run on the other computers on your LAN. (If the other computers on the LAN run Windows XP, you can run the Network Setup Wizard instead.)

The wizard may restart your computer when it is finished.

Configuring the ICS Server Manually in Windows XP

If your LAN and Internet connections both work, you can turn on Internet Connection Sharing by hand. On the computer that has the Internet connection, follow these steps:

1. Open the Network Connections window. (Choose Start | Control Panel | Network And Internet Connections | Network Connections.)

2. Click the Internet connection (not the LAN connection).

3. Click Change Settings Of This Connection in the Network Tasks listed in the Task pane (or right-click the connection and choose Properties from the menu that appears). You see the Properties dialog box for the Internet connection.

4. Click the Advanced tab. You see the Internet Connection Firewall and Internet Connection Sharing settings, shown in Figure 4-5. The settings are as follows:

   - **Protect My Computer And Network By Limiting Or Preventing Access To This Computer From The Internet**   Select this check box to turn on the Internet Connection Firewall, which we highly recommend for all Internet connections.

   - **Allow Other Network Users To Connect Through This Computer's Internet Connection**   Select this check box to turn on ICS, or clear the check box to turn ICS off.

   - **Establish A Dial-Up Connection Whenever A Computer On My Network Attempts To Access The Internet**   Select this check box to enable dial-on-demand.

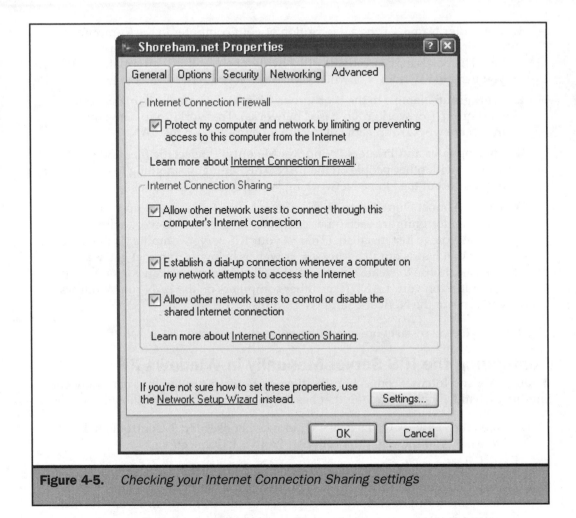

Figure 4-5.   *Checking your Internet Connection Sharing settings*

■ **Allow Other Network Users To Control Or Disable The Shared Internet Connection**   Select this check box to allow other people on the LAN to disconnect the Internet connection (hang up) or reconnect (if dial-on-demand is turned off).

5. Click OK to put the changes into effect.

Configuring the ICS Server Manually in Windows 2000

Windows 2000 doesn't come with a wizard to configure ICS for you. To configure ICS by hand, follow these steps:

1. Choose Start | Settings | Network And Dial-Up Connections. Right-click your Internet connection and choose Properties from the menu that appears.

2. Click the Internet Connection Sharing tab. Select the Enable Internet Connection Sharing For This Connection check box to turn on ICS. If you use a dial-up connection, select the Enable On-Demand Dialing check box so that ICS can dial the phone when any ICS client needs to connect to the Internet.

3. Click the Networking tab and make sure that only the Internet Protocol (TCP/IP) component is selected. No other LAN protocol works with the Internet, so none should be used with ICS.

4. If you have a dial-up connection, click the Options tab and configure your connection as to when and how often to redial.

5. Click OK. Windows warns you that your IP address is changing to 192.168.0.1, which is the address that the ICS server always assigns itself.

6. Right-click My Computer and choose Manage to display the Computer Management window. Click Services And Applications and then Services. You see a list of services that includes the Remote Access Auto Connection Manager, which controls whether Windows will connect to the Internet automatically.

7. Right-click this service and choose Start from the menu that appears. Right-click again and choose Properties to display the Remote Access Auto Connection Manager Properties dialog box. Set the Startup Type to Automatic and click OK.

Configuring the ICS Server Manually in Windows Me

In Windows Me, you can check your ICS server settings by following these steps:

1. Choose Start | Settings | Control Panel and run the Internet Options program to display the Internet Properties dialog box.

2. Click the Connections tab of the Internet Properties dialog box and click the Sharing button to see the Internet Connection Sharing dialog box. You see the Internet Connection Sharing dialog box, shown in Figure 4-6.

3. Check the Internet Connection Sharing settings as follows:

   ■ **Enable Internet Connection Sharing**   Clear this check box if you want to turn ICS off temporarily.

   ■ **Show Icon In Taskbar**   Select this check box if you want the ICS icon to appear on the system tray section of the taskbar. See "Using Internet Connection Sharing" later in this chapter for how to use the ICS icon to monitor ICS activities on the LAN.

   ■ **Connect To The Internet Using**   Select the network adapter with which you connect to the Internet. For dial-up Internet accounts, choose Dial-Up Adapter. For DSL or cable Internet accounts, choose the network interface card that connects to your DSL or cable modem.

   ■ **Connect To My Home Network Using**   Select the network interface card that attaches your computer to the LAN.

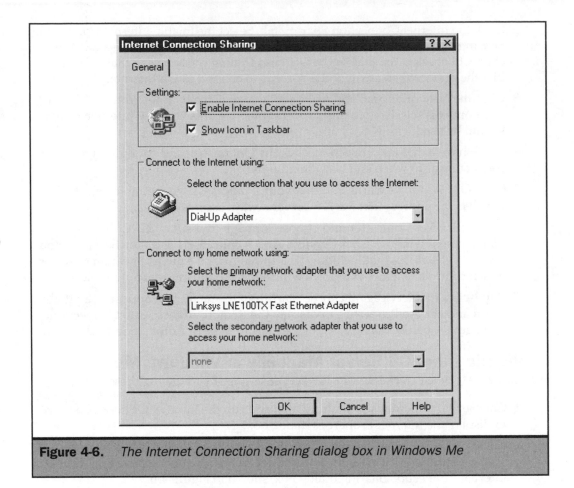

Figure 4-6.   *The Internet Connection Sharing dialog box in Windows Me*

4. Close the Internet Connection Sharing dialog box to return to the Internet Properties dialog box.

5. Click the LAN Settings button on the Internet Properties dialog box to see the Local Area Network (LAN) Settings dialog box. These are settings you might need to use if you connect to the Internet using a proxy server other than ICS. For ICS, select Automatically Detect Settings and leave the rest of the settings deselected.

You can also check that the ICS networking components are installed. In the Control Panel, run the Network icon. You should see installed components that look like the following. (Items in italics don't appear exactly as shown on your list of installed components; substitute the name of the appropriate network interface card.)

- Client For Microsoft Networks
- Dial-Up Adapter or *<network interface card for connection to a DSL or cable Internet account>*
- Internet Connection Sharing adapter
- *<Network interface card for connection to the LAN>*
- Internet Connection Sharing (protocol) -> Dial-Up Adapter or *<network card for Internet>*
- Internet Connection Sharing (protocol) -> Internet Connection Sharing
- Internet Connection Sharing (protocol) -> *<network card for LAN>*
- TCP/IP (Home) -> *<network card for LAN>*
- TCP/IP (Shared) -> Dial-Up Adapter or *<network card for Internet>*
- TCP/IP -> Internet Connection Sharing

You may also see File And Printer Sharing For Microsoft Networks entries for file sharing on the LAN.

| Note | *If other network protocols are installed (like NetBEUI or IPX/SPX), you may see additional protocols bound to Internet Connection Sharing, like "NetBEUI -> Internet Connection Sharing" or "IPX/SPX -> Internet Connection Sharing." Delete those protocols unless your LAN requires them because Internet Connection Sharing works only with TCP/IP. If NetBEUI or IPX/SPX is bound to the Dial-Up Adapter, delete those entries, too.* |

If the TCP/IP entries don't appear or don't include "(Home)" for the LAN network adapter and "(Shared)" for the connection to the Internet, ICS isn't installed properly, and you need to uninstall and reinstall it.

Testing the ICS Server

To test whether your computer is working as the ICS server, try connecting to the Internet from the ICS server—you should connect as if ICS weren't installed. Browsing, e-mail, and other Internet services should be unaffected. Right-click the Local Area Network connection in the Network Connections window and choose Status to see whether the LAN is working and confirm that your IP address is 192.168.0.1.

Make sure that the Internet connection works. To test it, connect to the Internet and browse the Web or send and receive e-mail.

If you use a dial-up line, make sure that the ICS server is set to connect to the Internet whenever it receives a request to connect. Set your Internet options to dial the Internet on demand:

- **Windows XP**   Choose Start | Control Panel | Network And Internet Connections and click Internet Options to display the Internet Properties dialog box. Click the Connections tab and choose Always Dial My Default Connection so that Windows can connect to the Internet on demand. Click the Settings button and make sure that your user name and password are entered so that the ICS server can connect to the Internet without waiting for you to type this information.

- **Windows 2000**   Choose Start | Settings | Network And Dial-Up Connections. Right-click your Internet connection and choose Properties from the menu that appears. Select the Enable On-Demand Dialing check box so that ICS can dial the phone when any ICS client needs to connect to the Internet.

- **Windows Me**   Choose Start | Settings | Control Panel and run the Internet Options program to display the Internet Properties dialog box. Click the Connections tab and choose Always Dial My Default Connection so that Windows can connect to the Internet on demand. Click the default connection and click the Settings button to display the Settings dialog box for the connection. The user name and password should appear. (You supplied these when you ran the Home Networking Wizard to install ICS.) Edit them if they have changed or are wrong. The Automatic Configuration and Proxy Server settings are used if your computer is on a LAN with another computer running a proxy server other than ICS. None of these settings should be selected.

Tip   *If you ran the Network Setup Wizard or Home Networking Wizard, take a look at its log file, which lists the actions that the wizard took when installing and configuring your LAN and ICS, including searching your system for networking components and deciding which to use. Open the Nsw.log file (in Windows XP) or the Icssetup.log file (in Windows Me), which is stored in your C:\Windows folder (or whatever folder Windows is installed in).*

Configuring the ICS Clients

You must configure each of the *ICS clients*—the other computers that share the ICS connection to the Internet. If you installed the ICS server using the Network Setup

Wizard or Home Networking Wizard and you chose to create a setup disk, you have a floppy disk that contains a version of the wizard program with which you can configure the ICS clients. The wizard configures computers running Windows XP, Me, 9*x*, 2000, or NT 4. For ICS clients running Windows XP, you can run the Network Setup Wizard that is part of Windows.

When you configure a computer as an ICS client, you add TCP/IP as a network protocol if it's not already installed and set the computer to get its IP address from a DHCP server (the one that is running on the ICS server as part of ICS).

Configuring an ICS Client Manually

The ICS client needs to use TCP/IP and receive its IP address from ICS. See the section "Configuring Computers to Use TCP/IP and DHCP-Assigned Addresses" earlier in this chapter for how to configure these settings by hand.

Configuring an ICS Client with the Network Setup Wizard

To configure a Windows XP, Me, 9*x*, 2000, and NT computer as an ICS client, insert the floppy disk that the Network Setup Wizard or Home Networking Wizard created, choose Start | Run, type **a:setup**, and click Open. If your computer runs Windows XP, choose Start | All Programs | Accessories | Communications | Network Setup Wizard.

As the wizard asks you questions, make these choices:

- **Internet Connection Method**   Select This Computer Connects To The Internet Through Another Computer On My Network Or Through A Residential Gateway (if this option appears). Alternatively, select A Connection To Another Computer On My Home Network That Provides Direct Access To My Internet Service Provider (ISP).

- **Computer Name**   Type a unique name for your computer and a description. (This description doesn't have to be unique and appears only in the My Network Places or Network Neighborhood window.)

- **Network Name**   Type the name for your workgroup. Use the same workgroup name you entered for the ICS server.

- **Sharing Files and Printers (Windows Me only)**   The wizard created by Windows Me asks about the folders and printers to share with other people on the LAN. This question has nothing to do with ICS.

■ When you click Next, the wizard confirms your settings, like this:

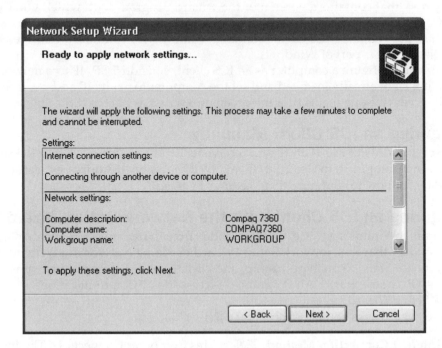

■ **You're Almost Done/Setup Disk**   After the wizard installs your settings, it offers to create a setup disk. Choose Yes only if you don't already have one.

The wizard may restart your computer when it finishes.

Testing Your Internet Connection from an ICS Client

When you ask a browser or other Internet program to display a web page or send or receive e-mail on an ICS client computer, Windows passes your Internet request along to the ICS server, which connects to the Internet on your behalf. If the ICS server was already logged into the Internet, you should see your web page or e-mail right away; if the ICS server has to connect, there's the usual delay in logging in. Once the ICS server and clients are configured correctly, users on all ICS servers and clients can use the Internet connection simultaneously.

To test your connection from an ICS server, try these actions:

■ Run a web browser and try to display a web page.

■ Run the Ping program (described in Chapter 3) and try to ping the ICS server at 192.168.0.1. If that works, try pinging a computer on the Internet, like **www.yahoo.com**.

Here are ways you can troubleshoot ICS.

Check that TCP/IP is installed on the ICS client and that the computer gets its IP address dynamically from the ICS server.   See the section "Configuring Computers to Use TCP/IP and DHCP-Assigned Addresses" earlier in this chapter.

Check the TCP/IP Settings on the ICS client.   In Windows XP, you can check the TCP/IP settings on the ICS client by opening the Network Connections window, right-clicking the Local Area Connection, and choosing Status from the menu that appears. Click the Support tab, shown here:

The settings should be the same as those in this illustration, except for the IP Address, which may end with a number other than 2.

In Windows 2000, choose Start | Run, type **cmd** in the Open box, and click OK to open a DOS command window. Type **ipconfig** and press ENTER to run the Ipconfig program. You see a listing like this:

```
Ethernet adapter Local Area Connection:

        Connection-specific DNS Suffix  . :
        IP Address. . . . . . . . . . . . : 192.168.1.16
        Subnet Mask . . . . . . . . . . . : 255.255.255.0
        Default Gateway . . . . . . . . . : 192.168.1.1
```

In Windows Me, choose Start | Run, type **winipcfg** in the Open box, and click OK to run the Winipcfg program. Click the More Info button. Set the box at the top of the Ethernet Adapter Information section to the network interface card to which your LAN is connected. The IP Address should be in the format 192.168.0.*xxx*, where *xxx* is a number other than 1 (because the ICS server is always 192.168.0.1). The DNS Servers, Default Gateway, and DHCP Server boxes should all be 192.168.0.1—the ICS server performs all those functions. IP Routing Enabled should not be selected.

Check to see that the ICS client is not configured to connect to the Internet directly. In Windows XP and Me, you can tell Windows to connect over the LAN and not directly. The Connections table of the Internet Properties box contains the settings that control whether Windows tries to connect directly rather than over the LAN and ICS. In Windows XP, choose Start | Control Panel, click Network And Internet Options, and click Internet Options. In Windows Me/98, choose Start | Settings | Control Panel and run the Internet Options program.

On the Connections tab of the Internet Properties dialog box, select either Never Dial A Connection or Dial Whenever A Network Connection Is Not Present. (If no connections appear in the Dial-Up And Virtual Private Network Settings box, the Never Dial A Connection setting is gray, but it's still selected.) In Windows 98, choose Connect To The Internet Using A Local Area Network.

Check the LAN settings. In Windows XP and Me, click the LAN Settings button on the Connections tab of the Internet Properties dialog box to display the Local Area Network (LAN) Settings dialog box, shown here:

These are settings you might need to use if you connect to the Internet using a proxy server other than ICS. None of the check boxes should be selected, unless your LAN administrator specifies otherwise.

Using Internet Connection Sharing

Once you've configured the ICS server and the ICS clients, ICS is easy to use. From either the server or a client, run a web browser, e-mail program, or other program that works with the Internet. When the program sends information to or requests information from the Internet, the ICS server connects to the Internet to provide the Internet connection.

To see how many people are sharing the Internet connection on the ICS server, double-click the ICS icon on the notification area or system tray (right end) of the taskbar (or click it and choose Status from the menu that appears). A small dialog box pops up, telling you how many computers are sharing the connection, including the ICS server itself.

If you can't get connected to the Internet from an ICS client computer, here are some things to try:

- Give the ICS server time to connect to the Internet, especially if it uses a dial-up phone line. The program on the ICS client may time out before the ICS server gets connected to your Internet account and ICS passes your request along.

- If you have restarted the ICS server since you restarted the ICS client, restart the client.

- Test your Internet connection from the ICS server (as described in "Testing the ICS Server" earlier in this chapter) and test your LAN connection from an ICS client (as described in "Testing Your Internet Connection from an ICS Client" earlier in this chapter).

- Run the Internet Connection Sharing Troubleshooter on the ICS server and at least one ICS client. In Windows XP and 2000, choose Start | Help And Support to display the Help And Support Center window, click Fixing A Problem, click Networking Problems, and click Internet Connection Sharing Troubleshooter. In Windows Me, choose Start | Help, click Troubleshooting, click Home Networking & Network Problems, and click Internet Connection Sharing Troubleshooter.

The
Complete
Reference

Internet

Part II

Exchanging E-mail

Chapter 5

E-mail Concepts

Most people love e-mail. It's nonintrusive—your correspondents can read and answer your e-mail when they have the time to do it. It's quick—far quicker than the U.S. Postal Service's "snail mail." For people who are logged on at work all day, e-mail can be almost instantaneous. It's free—once you've paid for your computer and Internet account. However, e-mail has its drawbacks, too: because e-mail is more casual than a letter or a memo, some people write things in an e-mail that they would never write in a regular letter. Also, lacking the nuances of face-to-face or phone conversation, an e-mail message can be misunderstood.

This chapter explains e-mail concepts, and the rest of the chapters in this part can help you with the technical side of communicating. For information about junk mail and how to control it, see Chapter 8.

Note   *This book discusses Internet e-mail. You may also get mail on an internal network, such as within your office or online service, but that isn't necessarily Internet e-mail—some offices use internal mail that works a little differently than Internet mail. However, most of what you learn about e-mail in this section of the book also applies to local mail within your office or online service. Also, more and more offices are switching to standard Internet mail services.*

How Do You Get Your E-mail?

You receive Internet e-mail when it's sent to your unique e-mail address. E-mail messages are passed through the Internet by using a protocol called *Simple Mail Transfer Protocol (SMTP)*. SMTP is understood by all e-mail applications that package your Internet e-mail message for sending and by all the computers (servers) that pass the message along its route.

Receiving Incoming Messages

How you collect and read your e-mail depends on how you're linked to the Internet. Most people don't have a computer that is always connected to the Internet—instead, they dial in when they want to do Internet stuff (including picking up and sending e-mail). Then they disconnect when they're done. Because e-mail can arrive at any time, you need an e-mail *mailbox* that resides on a *mail server*, a computer that is permanently connected to the Internet (barring unforeseen problems) and that is set up to handle your incoming e-mail. Like your postal service mailbox, the mail server is able to accept e-mail at any time and store it until you delete it. Depending on the type of connection that you have, you may download e-mail from the mail server to your computer, or you may read your e-mail while it sits on the mail server.

Even if your computer is always connected (using a DSL or cable Internet connection), your messages are usually still stored in a mailbox on a mail server. You can configure your e-mail program to fetch your messages automatically—for example, once an hour.

Mail servers receive and store e-mail messages in mailboxes by using a protocol called *Post Office Protocol (POP)* or *POP3* (the current version of POP is version 3) or *IMAP (Internet Message Access Protocol)*. IMAP is an emerging standard that improves on POP servers by allowing you to keep your mail on the server rather than on your own computer, so you can read your mail from any computer.

To read your e-mail, you need a *mail client* or e-mail application such as Outlook Express, Netscape Mail, Netscape Messenger, or Eudora. A *client* application works in concert with a *server*—in the case of e-mail, a mail server collects your e-mail, and your mail client enables you to read it.

If you have POP mail, you need a POP mail client that copies your mail from the mail server to your local computer. If you have an IMAP server, the mail stays on the remote server. You use your mail client to read it and do all your mail manipulations (such as filing messages in folders and deleting them). The advantage of IMAP is that if you use different computers, you don't end up with a different set of messages on each computer—your e-mail client simply reads what is on the IMAP server.

The most common mail clients—such as Microsoft Outlook, Outlook Express, Netscape Messenger, Netscape Mail, and Eudora—support both POP and IMAP. This book describes Outlook Express 6.0, Outlook 2002, Netscape Messenger 4.7, Netscape Mail (or more properly, Netscape Mail And Newsgroups) 6.2, and Eudora 5.1.

AOL uses IMAP, but prevents all e-mail programs except Netscape 6 Mail from accessing its mail servers. If you have an AOL account, you can read your mail with the AOL program, Netscape Mail (version 6 or later), or AOL's web site.

Sending Outgoing Messages

You write e-mail messages on your own computer by using your e-mail application. Then, you transfer the messages to an *SMTP server*—a mail server that accepts outgoing e-mail. Your Internet service provider (ISP) probably runs both an SMTP server and a POP or IMAP server for its customers; the SMTP server that takes care of sending your e-mail messages may be a different server than the POP or IMAP server that collects your e-mail.

EXCHANGING E-MAIL

Ways of Accessing E-mail

There are various ways to access your e-mail:

- You may use a mail client, such as Eudora, Outlook, Outlook Express, Netscape Mail, Netscape Messenger, or any one of the other popular packages that downloads your incoming messages from the POP server to your computer and uploads your outgoing messages to the SMTP server. This may occur through a *local area network (LAN)* or through a dial-up, DSL, ISDN, or cable connection. These programs are described in Chapter 6, including how to send, receive, reply to, forward, save, and print messages.

- You may use a web-based e-mail service. These web sites are described in the section "Web-Based E-mail," later in this chapter.

- You may use an online service, such as America Online, which has its own e-mail program.

- You may get your e-mail through a LAN, a common system at large organizations. If your organization has some sort of Internet connection, e-mail arrives in the company's POP or IMAP server. You then read your e-mail either on the server, using an e-mail application, or on your own computer, by downloading your e-mail from the server through the LAN by using an e-mail application. Your company may use a POP server, IMAP server, or some kind of proprietary protocol (for instance, Lotus' Notes or Microsoft's Exchange, which are not POP compatible). See Chapter 4 for more information about accessing the Internet over a LAN.

E-mail Addressing

Internet e-mail addresses look like **sneezy@grimm.com** and consist of two parts joined by @ (the "at" sign):

- **User name**   User names can contain characters other than letters—they can contain numbers, underscores, periods, and some other special characters. They can't contain commas, spaces, or parentheses.

- **Host or domain name**   The host name provides the Internet location of the mailbox, usually the name of a company or Internet service. The host name may include a period and a subdomain name, for example, **grimm.tales.com**. For more about host names, see Chapter 1.

| Tip | *The e-mail address to write to with comments about this book is **nettcr2@gurus.com**.* |

Here are some other points about addresses:

- Capitalization usually isn't important in e-mail addresses (that is, they are *case insensitive*). For example, **NetTCR2@Gurus.Com** works just the same as **nettcr2@gurus.com**. Of course, if you're sure that you have the right address, but you're getting error messages, you may want to try different capitalization—some mail servers pay attention to user name capitalization.

- E-mail addresses do not have punctuation marks (such as square brackets or quotes) around them. You may see e-mail addresses displayed with extra punctuation, but when you send a message to the e-mail address, make sure to remove the extra characters. When an e-mail address appears at the end of a sentence, the period is not part of the address!

- E-mail addresses do not have spaces in them. You will sometimes see e-mail addresses with spaces in e-mails and on bulletin boards. You need to take the spaces out in order to use the address to send e-mail. The spaces are added to foil address-harvesting programs that search the Web for addresses to which to send spam.

- Most e-mail programs allow you to type angle brackets (<>) around e-mail addresses. You can also precede an e-mail address with the person's name in quotes. For example, the address for this book might appear like this:

  "Internet Complete Reference book" <nettcr2@gurus.com>

Local vs. Internet Addresses

The standard e-mail addresses just explained may not apply when you send e-mail within an organization. Your *inhouse* (and that may mean within your company or within your online service) addresses may not look at all like the ones explained here. For example, when sending messages from one AOL account to another, you can include spaces in the person's AOL screen (user) name and omit the "@aol.com" (for instance, "Jane Smith" rather than "JaneSmith@aol.com"). If you are sending e-mail through the Internet, you *do* need to use an address that follows the naming conventions outlined here. When an AOL user sends a message outside AOL to the Internet, the address must be a valid Internet address, with an @.

Message Headers

Every e-mail message sent starts with *headers*—lines of text that tell you about the message. The headers are like the envelope for the message and include the addresses of the recipient and the sender. If you want to know more about where an e-mail came from, looking at headers can be useful.

Your e-mail package may not automatically show you all message headers—headers make the message look messy. (See Chapter 6 for how to display the complete headers in several popular e-mail applications.)

Each header consists of the type of header, a colon, and the content of the header. For example, the header that shows who the message is addressed to consists of "To:" followed by one or more e-mail addresses. Headers that start with X are always optional headers, and many e-mail applications ignore them.

Table 5-1 lists the standard headers that almost every e-mail message includes, along with some common additional headers. Here is a sample of the complete headers for a message:

```
Delivered-To: nettcr2@gurus.com
Received: from smtp.america.net (199.170.121.14) by ivan.iecc.com
    with SMTP; 10 Sep 2002 03:41:55 -0000
Received: from PentiumPro (max1-40.shoreham.net [208.144.253.42])
    by smtp.america.net (8.9.1/8.8.7) with SMTP id XAA23871; Wed,
    9 Sep 2002 23:41:20 -0400 (EDT)
Message-Id: <3.0.32.19980909223739.008be480@mail.gurus.com>
X-Sender: nettcr2@mail.gurus.com
X-Mailer: Windows Eudora Pro Version 3.0 (32)
Date: Wed, 09 Sep 2002 23:41:47 -0400
To: santa@northpole.com
From: Internet Complete Reference Authors <nettcr@gurus.com>
Subject: Re: Low hits on Web site
Cc: info@mcgraw-hill.com
Mime-Version: 1.0
Content-Type: text/plain; charset="us-ascii"
X-UIDL: 68193b0f0132f554cd78c0ae2372eac0
```

EXCHANGING E-MAIL

Header Type	Description
Date	The date and time the message was sent, according to the sender's computer.
To	The e-mail address(es) of the primary recipient(s) of the message. The "To" line may also contain names.
From	Who the message is from.
Subject	What the message is about—according to the sender.
Cc	Additional recipient(s) of the message. ("Cc" is an abbreviation for "carbon copy," a term that is outdated but still in use.)
Reply-To or Return-Path	Your e-mail application automatically uses this address when you reply to the message.
Received	Contains information from each host service that relayed the message.
Message-ID	The unique ID that identifies this message (generally not useful).
X-Sender	Adds a layer of authentication to the message by identifying the sender.
X-Mailer	The application used to compose the message. (Not all e-mail applications add this header to messages.)
Mime-Version	The version of MIME (Multipurpose Internet Mail Extensions) used. MIME is used for attachments and for HTML-formatted messages. (See section "Formatted E-mail" later in this chapter for more about MIME.)
Content-Type	The MIME data format used. Frequently, the data format is text/plain with some further information to identify the text type.
Lines	Number of lines of text in the message.
X-UIDL	A unique identifier added by some POP e-mail applications to identify messages that have been downloaded.

Table 5-1.   *E-mail Message Headers*

Downloading E-mail

Your e-mail accumulates on a POP or IMAP server (usually on a server at your ISP), and your e-mail application downloads the messages to your computer, so that you can read them. You have the following options:

■ You can usually work either offline or online. If you have a dial-up connection to the Internet, you can compose your messages before you dial in, queuing them in your e-mail program. Once you are connected to the Internet, you can send them.

■ You can choose either to leave downloaded messages on the server or to delete them from the server. For example, if you are testing a new e-mail program or using a friend's e-mail program to check your messages, you might want to leave your messages on the server so that you can download them again to the e-mail program you usually use. Most e-mail programs include settings that control whether downloaded message are deleted from the server.

Working Offline

Most POP e-mail clients allow you to work offline, which can be a real moneysaver if your ISP charges by the minute, if you connect via a long-distance call, or if you are away from a connection (for example, working while on an airplane). Working *offline* means that you read your e-mail by doing the following:

1. Connect to the Internet.

2. Download your e-mail.

3. Disconnect from the Internet.

4. Read your e-mail, delete messages you don't want to keep, compose replies, and write new messages. You can perform these tasks while you're not actually connected to the Internet—anywhere that you can use your laptop.

5. When you are ready, connect to the Internet.

6. Send your new messages and download any new messages that may have arrived.

7. Disconnect from the Internet.

IMAP mail generally stays on the server and you use your e-mail client to read it there, so the process for working on IMAP e-mail offline is different. Check the instructions for your e-mail client, but generally you need to download e-mail folders from your IMAP server to your local computer. You periodically synchronize your computer with the server so that the messages in each place are the same. If you download IMAP e-mail often, you are using IMAP mail like POP mail.

Most of the time that you spend doing e-mail consists of reading and writing messages—you don't actually need to be connected to the Internet to perform those tasks. Working offline may be as simple as following the preceding steps, or you may have to give your e-mail application a command to let it know when you're online and offline. Try disconnecting from the Internet and working in your e-mail application. (See Chapter 6 for the commands for working offline with several popular e-mail applications.)

Deleting Messages from the Server

If a POP server stores your messages until you download them, your e-mail program usually deletes them from the POP server after downloading. Your e-mail application may have a setting that enables you to choose whether to delete the e-mail from the server and, if so, when to delete it. The people who maintain your POP server would greatly appreciate it if you would delete your e-mail—in fact, they have every right to insist on it. Otherwise, your mailbox will balloon to an enormous size. Some ISPs limit the size of your mailbox. However, if your e-mail application supports it, you may want to leave your e-mail on the server for a day or two after you pick it up, so that if anything goes wrong, you can get the message again. See Chapter 6 for details on how to tell several popular e-mail applications when to delete your messages from the POP server.

Note   *If you have e-mail on an IMAP server, e-mail you delete is automatically deleted on the server.*

E-mail Netiquette

E-mail provides a medium to send casual messages quickly. This makes e-mail tremendously useful—but it can also make it annoying or worse. For instance, although sending a short request is easy, it is also easy for that request to sound brusque or even rude. It is usually worthwhile to spend an extra minute or so to write your message in a way that softens the request and doesn't raise the bristles of the recipient.

Netiquette is the term used for etiquette on the Internet—it is a set of suggestions intended to make the Internet community a more pleasant place. This section includes some netiquette guidelines for e-mail; you may see other guidelines that agree or disagree with these. Use your own judgment in deciding how to comport yourself online. Consider how you would feel being on the receiving end of any e-mail that you send, and remember that you are usually writing to a human being, not to a machine.

If you have some e-mail habits that don't align with the following suggestions, you should reconsider your e-mail habits. Although these rules are not enforceable, hanging out on the Internet is much more pleasant for everyone if e-mail doesn't anger or annoy anyone needlessly.

To practice good netiquette, *Netizens* (Internet users) should follow these guidelines:

■ *Think twice before sending an emotional message.* The speed and ease of e-mail enable you to jot and send a quick emotional reply to a message. Once you click Send, it's gone—not like a letter that sits in the mailbox for a while—and you may regret it. So, consider letting emotional messages sit a while before you send them—at least overnight, and sometimes longer.

■ *Use the subject line well.* It's a help to you and your recipient if the subject line tells you both what the message is about. If you store messages, you'll appreciate them having a useful subject line when you go looking for them again.

■ *Don't flame. Flaming* is the Internet term for sending messages that contain little information and much vitriol and abuse. Flaming is all too rampant on the Internet, especially in some newsgroups. Messages that are abusive or defamatory are not fun to read or receive.

■ *Check spelling and punctuation.* These don't need to be perfect, but don't annoy your friends and colleagues with funny punctuation, such as messages that are only punctuated with hyphens and ellipses. And make sure that no word is spelled so badly that the recipient has to guess what you mean. If your e-mail application has a spell checker, use it. E-mail is a casual form of communication, but it shouldn't be a sloppy one!

■ *Watch the sarcasm.* Sarcasm isn't always easy to identify without seeing the facial expressions or hearing tone of voice. Using smileys (described in the next section) may help to let people know that you're only kidding, but when in doubt, leave it out.

■ *Don't send e-mail to people who don't want it.* Lots of people break this rule—including the people who send messages that advertise software that can be used to send e-mail to millions of people. Sending unwanted e-mail is rude, and it costs money to the people who provide Internet resources at minimal cost. Even if you regularly forward jokes or information to a small list of friends, you should check in with your list recipients every now and then to offer them the chance to be removed from your list.

■ *Don't overquote, especially on mailing lists.* Most e-mail applications include the text of the message you're replying to. You should edit that original message to contain only the necessary information. This is especially important if you are sending a message to a newsgroup or mailing list, so that people don't have to see the same text over and over again in every response to a post. Deleting unrelated text is vital if you receive mailing lists in *digests* (daily collections of many messages), so that you don't send the entire digest in your response.

- *Don't use all capitals or any other weird formatting.* A message in all caps looks like shouting and is much more difficult to read than using mixed-case (upper- and lowercase) text. You can use caps to highlight certain words, but you can also enclose words with asterisks or underscores to emphasize them.

- *Send e-mail that everyone can read.* If you're not sure whether your recipients can read formatted text, send plain text. It's annoying not to be able to read a message, or to have to ignore all the HTML codes to read the text of the message. Don't send attached files unless you have asked the recipient whether they want and can deal with the file. Don't send attached files to mailing lists at all (unless the list has a policy that welcomes attachments).

- *Don't plagiarize.* Most people don't quote text without attribution to the author in a regular letter; the same applies to e-mail. The author of an e-mail message retains the copyright to the e-mail message. Just because something is posted on the Internet does not mean that the text is in the public domain.

- *Don't pretend you're someone else.* Using a pen name is okay if you don't want people to know who you are, but don't misrepresent yourself and pretend to be someone you aren't. Misleading people is at best impolite, and at worst illegal.

- *Don't send frivolous messages.* If you don't have anything to say, don't say it! This rule applies threefold on mailing lists.

- *Remember the law.* Laws about defamation, copyright, obscenity, fraudulent misrepresentation, freedom of information, and wrongful discrimination in written communication apply to e-mail messages also. If you have a concern about an unsolicited commercial e-mail message, forward it to the U.S. Federal Trade Commission (FTC) at **uce@ftc.gov**.

- *Don't forward chain letters and other junk e-mail.* These schemes are almost always illegal, and they annoy people because they fill up e-mail mailboxes. Included in this category are bogus virus warnings—if you see a virus warning that looks authentic, *check it out before you send it on to all of your friends!* Most virus warnings are hoaxes. See the sidebar in this chapter entitled "Messages Never to Forward," for more information.

Caution   *As good as e-mail is, you should never consider it confidential. Although e-mail is rarely hijacked through technical means, it is extremely easy and often tempting to forward a message—even (and maybe especially) one that the sender has asked you to keep confidential. So, never assume that only the people you send a message to will read it.*

EXCHANGING E-MAIL

Messages Never to Forward

Many e-mail messages that are forwarded around the Internet in good faith are actually hoaxes. Sending these messages is unnecessary and fills people's e-mail boxes. Often, well-connected *Internauts* (Internet users) receive these messages over and over, necessitating many clicks of the Delete button. Many computer hoaxes tell you not to open an e-mail with a certain name. In general, you cannot infect your computer with a virus just by opening an e-mail. In any case, if you use the Internet much, you should install a good virus protection program and update it regularly with the latest virus definitions (see the section "Avoiding Viruses" later in this chapter). You should also check the web site of the manufacturer of your e-mail client and browser, to see whether any security issues have been found and whether an update of the software has been released to fix them. E-mail clients that handle Java are at special risk.

You can check out a virus warning at **hoaxbusters.ciac.org/**, a U.S. government site that has a good list of virus and other e-mail hoaxes. Another good place to check to see whether a forwarded message is real is **www.snopes.com**, the Urban Legends Reference Pages. For information on real viruses, check out the Virus Information Library at **vil.nai.com/vil**.

The following are some examples of e-mail hoaxes. Please don't forward any of these, and verify any others before forwarding them:

- **Letters that tell you to "send this to everyone you know"**   Chain letters that claim to help you make money are always pyramid schemes and are almost always illegal.

- **SULFNBK.exe virus**   This is an old hoax—don't follow its directions, which instruct you to delete a file that is part of Windows. Ditto for the Good Times virus; there's no such thing.

- **Virus warnings in general**   New viruses come along every month or two, and the disruption is compounded if everyone receives dozens of warnings from their friends and coworkers.

- **Disney giveaway**   Disney is not tracking e-mail and giving away vacations or money. Ditto for Bill Gates.

Using Abbreviations, Emoticons, and Smileys

For better or worse, some users of e-mail tend to enjoy shortcuts, including what have become known as *emoticons* (including smileys) and abbreviations of frequently used terms.

Smileys and Emoticons

Smileys are punctuation used to portray faces or other pictures. For instance, :-) is the standard smiley face—tip your head to the left to see the face. The standard use of a smiley is to indicate a joke when the text might not show that the author is kidding. People use a whole range of smileys and other *emoticons* (icons used to indicate emotion, which is usually lacking in written communication). Some of the most common emoticons are listed at **net.gurus.com/smileys.html**.

Abbreviations Used in E-mail

Like any group of people, e-mail users have made up abbreviations to save themselves time and to confuse new folks. Frequently used abbreviations in e-mail, as well as in newsgroups, mailing lists, and online chat sessions, include the following:

BTW	By the way
FAQ	Frequently asked questions (Many lists and topics have a list of frequently asked questions—and answers—that they refer you to.)
FWIW	For what it's worth
FYI	For your information
IMHO	In my humble opinion
IMNSHO	In my not so humble opinion
NRN	No response necessary
LOL	Laughing out loud
OTOH	On the other hand
ROTFL	Rolling on the floor, laughing
TIA	Thanks in advance

You can find a far-too-complete list of abbreviations at *BABEL: A Glossary of Computer Oriented Abbreviations and Acronyms*, at **www.geocities.com/ikind_babel/babel/babel.html**.

Formatted E-mail

Five years ago, e-mail consisted solely of text characters, and the only way to send someone a formatted document was to send it as an attachment (as described in Chapter 7). Now, if both your and your recipient's e-mail support it, you can send formatted e-mail. However, that's a pretty big "if." Older e-mail packages don't support formatted e-mail. At best, your recipients will see the text of the message without the fancy formatting. At worst, they'll see all the codes that your e-mail package inserts to format the text, and they'll have to struggle to read the actual text. Formatted e-mail is also more likely to pass on a computer virus. Many readers just press DELETE when they receive e-mail with formatting tags.

Formatted e-mail is likely to become more and more common, so you might as well know something about it. Currently, formatted e-mail comes in the following flavors:

- **HTML**   This is formatted with HTML tags, just like web pages. HTML formatting can include text formatting, numbering, bullets, alignment, horizontal lines, backgrounds, hyperlinks, and HTML styles. HTML-formatted e-mail is actually sent using the MIME protocol.

- **Rich Text Format**   This is an older format that can be read by most word processing applications. (Documents in this format are also called RTF files.) Rich text formatting can include text formatting, bullets, and alignment.

- **MIME (Multipurpose Internet Mail Extensions)**   This is formatting created just for e-mail. MIME is also used for attachments (described in Chapter 7). Formatting can include text formatting, pictures, video, sound, and probably more. To a computer, MIME looks like plain text—to you, it looks like a lot of funny characters. A single MIME message can contain plain text as well as all the fancy formatting and extra stuff.

All of these formats require that the recipient's e-mail application be capable of handling them. Chapter 6 describes how to send formatted e-mail by using some popular e-mail programs.

Attaching Files to Messages

The ability to send attachments was a great stride in the development of e-mail. It made collaboration on work over the Internet possible. By attaching files to e-mail, you can exchange documents for revision, pass on spreadsheets for data entry, or send a presentation for review. Of course, you can also attach electronic pictures, sounds, or movies—anything that can be put in file form.

Attaching files to e-mail messages is described in detail in Chapter 7.

Web-Based E-mail

Web-based e-mail provides both advantages and disadvantages. The main advantage is that if you can access the Web, you can read your e-mail. You don't have to be at your own computer to access your e-mail application (although you may need an up-to-date version of your browser software). In addition, most web-based e-mail is free.

On the downside, because it's free, you have to look at a lot of ads (someone has to pay for the service), and when you sign up, you are usually asked for personal information, so that specific ads can be selected for you. You are likely to have strict limits placed on the amount of storage available for saved e-mail messages, and the web pages have fewer features than an e-mail program like Outlook Express. Also, security is not as good as with regular e-mail. However, for many people, the advantages outweigh the disadvantages.

Even if you don't use web-based e-mail all the time, you may find it useful when you're out of the office. Some people who have a business e-mail address at work use web-based e-mail for their personal e-mail.

You can read two kinds of messages on the Web:

■ **Messages sent to a web-only account**   For example, the Yahoo Mail web site at **mail.yahoo.com** lets you sign up for a free e-mail mailbox, with a user name that you pick. Your address is *username@yahoo.com*. You can read messages sent to your Yahoo Mail address at the Yahoo Mail web site or with an e-mail application.

■ **Messages stored in your POP mailbox**   Some web sites allow you to enter the name of your POP server (the Internet host computer on which your mailbox is stored), your user name, and your password. The site then retrieves the messages from your mailbox and displays them on a web page, enabling you to read and respond to them. This service means that you can check your e-mail anytime that you have access to the Web—you don't need access to your regular e-mail application. For example, once you have a free Yahoo Mail account, you can use it to check any account for which the mailbox is stored on a POP server.

If you're choosing a web-based e-mail service, study at the possibilities. (Use your favorite search engine to search for "Web-based e-mail" or "free e-mail.") Consider the following when looking for a package to meets your needs:

■ *Does it handle attachments?* If it doesn't handle both MIME and uuencoded attachments, find out which format you need by asking the people that you exchange attachments with which format their e-mail application supports.

■ *Is it free?* If so, can you tolerate the ads? If not, is the cost reasonable?

■ *Has it been in business long?* E-mail services do go out of business, so select one in the same way that you select any other service. If your e-mail service disappears, it takes your e-mail address (and possibly any messages waiting for you) with it.

■ *Does it provide the features you need?* For instance, do you want to be able to forward your e-mail to another e-mail address or to check the spelling in your messages? Can you file messages in folders to keep them organized? Can you filter messages as they arrive?

■ *How much space does it give you?* Most web-based e-mail accounts limit the size of your folders.

■ *Does it support formatted messages?* Some web-based e-mail sites support HTML or other types of formatted messages.

■ *Is it easy to use?* For instance, can you easily find your address book and figure out how to do all the common e-mail tasks?

■ *How fast is it?* How long does it take the page to load on your system? How long does it take for a message to be delivered or received?

You can find a list of free e-mail services at **email.about.com** (click the Free Email link). Alternatively, start at Yahoo (**www.yahoo.com**) and click Business And Economy | Business To Business | Communications And Networking | Internet And World Wide Web | Email Providers | Free Email. You may want to look at the following:

■ **Microsoft's Hotmail (www.hotmail.com)**   This provides both free e-mail accounts and access to your POP mailbox. However, you can create Hotmail only on the Web or with Outlook Express or Outlook.

■ **Yahoo Mail (mail.yahoo.com)**   This comes from a well-respected web portal company, provides free e-mail accounts, and also lets you read your POP mailbox. You can read your Yahoo Mail with most e-mail programs, although Yahoo has started charging $30 per year for this service because it allows you to avoid seeing the ads on their web site.

■ **Mail.com (www.mail.com)**   This offers both free e-mail and forwarding. It also owns 100 domain names, so you may be able to get an e-mail address such as *yourname*@**engineer.com**.

Truly Free E-mail

Juno (**www.juno.com**) provides free e-mail, even if you don't have an Internet connection—all you need is a modem. In the United States, you can call 1-800-654-JUNO for free software. However, you don't get web or other Internet access, just a limited e-mail account.

Free ISPs exist, although many have gone out of business (or started charging a fee) in the last few years. Take a look at NetZero (**www.netzero.com**) and Access-4-Free (**www.Access-4-Free.com**). ClickHereFree (**www.clickherefree.com**) maintains a list of free ISPs, many of which have phone numbers only in limited geographical areas.

In return for a free account, you usually have to give something up. Free ISPs and e-mail providers may ask for lots of personal information so that they can display ads that are targeted at your demographics and your interests. Free ISPs may also require you to use a special browser that displays additional ads.

Web e-mail is less secure than using a POP e-mail client, mainly because someone can click the Back button on your browser to read your e-mail. Someone even cleverer can read any e-mail that the browser has stored in cache. To prevent this, you should, at the very least, log out of the e-mail page and close your browser. For a greater degree of security, also empty the browser cache as described in Chapter 18.

Mail Away from Home

When you're away from your computer, you may still be able to read your e-mail, even if you don't regularly use a web-based e-mail service (described in the preceding section). You may be able to dial into your e-mail provider or use a web-based service.

If you use e-mail as part of your job and you travel on business, your e-mail administrator may have created a way for you to get your e-mail when you're out of the office. You should check with him or her before you try to figure out the methods described here. Your organization may provide a remote-connection product such as Reach Out Remote to dial into your office LAN to access its resources—including e-mail.

Dialing or Telnetting In

Even if you usually download e-mail to your computer, you may also be able to telnet into the mail server to read your e-mail when you're not at your computer, but do have access to someone else's computer. When you telnet in, you connect to the Internet and then use a telnet program to connect to your company's computer over the Internet. If your company's computer allows you to telnet in, you may be able to use a UNIX mail program like Pine or Elm. Check out Chapter 33 for more information on telnet and its secure equivalent, ssh. For instructions on Pine, a widely used UNIX mail program, see the web site **net.gurus.com/shell/pine.phtml**.

Reading Your E-mail on the Web

You may be able to use web-based e-mail on occasion, even if you don't use it regularly. Mail.com (**www.mail.com**), Yahoo Mail (**mail.yahoo.com**), and Hotmail (**www.hotmail.com**) all allow you to pick up e-mail that is on a POP mail server. If you don't use your web-based e-mail account for months at a time, be warned that the account may be canceled—but signing up for a new one is quick and easy.

If your office uses Microsoft's Exchange Server for e-mail, you may be able to access your e-mail on the company server through the Web. This service, which converts e-mail into web pages, is built into Microsoft Exchange Server 5.5, but some additional installation is necessary. (The server must be running Microsoft's web server.) Check with your e-mail administrator to see if this service is available.

Mail Forwarding

If you have found that your e-mail address changes frequently, you may benefit from an e-mail forwarding service. These services enable you to give out one e-mail address and then forward your e-mail from that address to whatever e-mail address is most convenient for you to access. To find an e-mail forwarding service, use your favorite search engine to search for "e-mail forwarding." Among the best known are Pobox (**www.pobox.com**), Onebox (**www.onebox.com**), and Bigfoot (**www.bigfoot.com**). You can find a list of forwarding services at **email.about.com/cs/emailforwarders**. Many organizations such as universities and professional associations now offer this service for alumni and members, and some free web-based e-mail providers also offer forwarding for a small fee.

Avoiding Viruses

Viruses spread via e-mail are a real danger in today's Internet world. Although it's true that many e-mail virus warnings are hoaxes, viruses certainly exist, and some viruses can do significant damage. It is worth some cost and effort to avoid them.

Tip   *The simplest way to avoid viruses is to avoid using the e-mail programs that most viruses target: Microsoft Outlook and Outlook Express. See Chapter 6 for information about other e-mail programs.*

Viruses cannot be contained in a purely text-based message. A virus must be an executable file (usually with the extension .exe or .com) attached to a message—however, file extensions can be hidden or disguised. The biggest danger is opening an infected attachment; it's good policy to always use your virus checker before opening an attachment. Simply saving an infected file will not infect your computer, but it's safer still to permanently delete the message and the attachment. (Don't let it sit in your Deleted folder.)

Tip   *To ensure that you know the real file extensions of files that you receive, tell Windows to display file extensions. If you use Windows XP, run Windows Explorer or My Computer, choose Tools | Folder Options, click the View tab, and clear the Hide Extensions For Known File Types check box.*

Some antivirus software, such as Norton AntiVirus (**enterprisesecurity.symantec.com/ products**), McAfee VirusScan (**www.mcafee.com**), and MailDefense (**www.indefense.com**), scans downloading e-mail for viruses (if you configure the software to do so). Antivirus software usually also scans a file as you open it. However, to be safe, and especially if e-mail is not automatically scanned, you may wish to manually scan attached files: save the file to your hard drive, right-click it, and choose to scan it with your virus checker. Some viruses infect files and can be cleaned by antivirus software, whereas other files need to be deleted. If you get a virus, your antivirus software will tell you what needs to be done. It's important to frequently update your virus checker with new virus definitions (available from the antivirus software manufacturer).

Your computer can also be infected with a virus if your e-mail software allows scripts to run in e-mail messages. Disable JavaScript and ActiveX execution in your e-mail program. (See Chapter 8 for instructions.) Viruses can also spread via macros in Microsoft Word or Microsoft Excel files. Be sure that you obtain from your software vendors all the recommend patches needed to avoid viruses. Patches are nearly always available on the manufacturer's web site. For information on viruses, check out the Virus Information Library at **vil.nai.com/vil**.

Note *E-mail isn't the only way to get a virus. You can infect your computer with a virus by downloading and running an infected file or by copying and running an infected file from a floppy disk or from a local area network.*

EXCHANGING E-MAIL

Chapter 6

Configuring Your E-mail Program

B y now, you probably know how to create, read, reply to, forward, print, and throw away messages. In fact, your e-mail program is probably one of the Internet programs that you use the most. However, most people don't know how to get the most out of their e-mail program by configuring it for the way they work, using shortcut commands and other tricks.

This chapter describes the most widely used e-mail clients: Eudora, Outlook 2002, Outlook Express, Netscape Messenger (part of Netscape Communicator 4.7), and Netscape Mail (part of Netscape 6, and formally called Netscape Mail & Newsgroups), which are available in Mac and Windows versions. (Outlook is available only for Windows.) This chapter describes AOL, Yahoo Mail, and Hotmail, too. If you use AOL, you can read your mail by using AOL program or by visiting the AOL web site; Hotmail and Yahoo Mail users can read and send mail from these services' web sites.

Our instructions describe these programs running under Windows XP, but other Windows and Mac users should be able to follow along. The basic e-mail commands are in tables because you probably already know them. This chapter concentrates on commands that you might not know. The first section covers some general definitions and should help you no matter which e-mail program you're using. Then skip forward to read about the e-mail program you use. Be sure to read the rest of the chapters in this part of the book, too, if you want to know more about sending and receiving attachments (Chapter 7), fighting spam, and presorting your messages by topic or sender (both in Chapter 8). Outlook and Outlook Express users should also read the section in Chapter 8 on preventing (or discouraging) viruses.

E-mail Configuration Concepts

You can configure your e-mail program to work with one or many e-mail addresses, for one or several people. With some e-mail programs, you can set options that add signatures to your messages, store form letters for messages you send often, and create folders so you can file your messages by topic or sender.

Configuring a New E-mail Program

When you install and configure an e-mail application, the program always asks you for some basic information, including what mail servers you use to receive and send messages. The terms may change slightly, but the program needs to know the following:

- Your name. (This is the name that will appear in the From line in messages that you send.)

- Your e-mail address.

- Your login name (the name you use to log into your e-mail provider).

- The incoming mail server on which your e-mail sits until you collect it. (Check with your ISP—but if your e-mail address is **alison@tiac.net**, for example, the server is probably tiac.net.)

■ The type of incoming mail server, usually POP (Post Office Protocol), POP3 (POP version 3), or IMAP (Internet Message Access Protocol), as described in Chapter 5.

■ The outgoing mail server (Simple Mail Transfer Protocol or SMTP server) to which you send your outgoing e-mail. (Some e-mail applications assume that your incoming and outgoing mail servers are on the same computer, so they don't ask this question.)

The setup process may ask you whether you want to store your password on your computer (so you don't have to type it each time the e-mail program logs into the mail server). Choose to save your password only if your computer is relatively secure—otherwise, anyone can sit down at your computer and send e-mail using your name.

The setup process may also ask whether you want this e-mail program to be your default e-mail program. The default e-mail program is the one that springs into action when you click a mailto link on a web page (that is, a link that contains an e-mail address), or otherwise initiate an e-mail message without first opening the e-mail program. If this is the only e-mail program that you are using, then by all means make it the default program. If you are just trying it out, you probably want to continue using your other program as the default e-mail application.

Switching to Another E-mail Program

If you are switching e-mail programs, several useful options may be available in the programs that you're switching from and to, such as the following:

■ If you're just trying out an e-mail program or using a computer that you don't normally use to check e-mail, look for the option that allows you *not* to delete e-mail on your incoming mail server. By not deleting your e-mail, when you go back to your regular computer or regular e-mail program, you can get all of your messages.

■ Changing e-mail programs can be a pain if you have lots of saved messages in different folders. Some e-mail programs can convert folders and messages from other programs—use the export command from one program and an import command from the other.

■ As a last resort, some e-mail programs offer a redirect command, which allows you to forward a message while retaining the original sender. For example, if you receive a message that should really have gone to someone else, you can redirect the message to the appropriate recipient. If the e-mail program from which you are switching has the redirect feature, you can redirect the messages in your inbox or other folders to yourself, send them, and then receive them again with your new e-mail program.

| Tip | *In general, changing your e-mail program (say, from Outlook to Eudora) has no effect on your e-mail address. The exception is if you are switching to or from AOL or a web-based mailbox like Hotmail, which store your messages on its own proprietary servers.* |

Using Multiple E-mail Addresses

Some e-mail programs can work with multiple e-mail addresses (accounts) and multiple users, including

- Features that support multiple e-mail addresses for one user
- Features that support totally separate sets of mailboxes for different users

Multiple E-mail Addresses for One Person

If you receive a lot of e-mail, you may find that filtering your incoming mail (described in Chapter 8) is not enough to keep it organized. You may need more than one e-mail account, so that you can use different accounts for different purposes. If you have more than one professional persona—say, you're a yoga teacher and a technical writer—you may want to have different addresses for each business card. For instance, your yoga teacher card might use the address **yogaprof@gurus.com**, whereas your technical writer card might use the address **writestuff@iecc.com**. Then, when you get e-mail asking for your services, you know immediately from the address that is used which service the writer needs. If you participate in e-mail mailing lists, you may use one address for newsgroups and mailing lists—and you can expect to receive some spam to that address. Additionally, you might want an address that you keep almost completely private and use only for correspondence with friends. With luck, you can keep that address spam-free.

Some e-mail programs (including Outlook, Outlook Express, Eudora, Netscape Messenger, and Netscape Mail) support multiple e-mail accounts, enabling you to pick up mail from two, three, or more e-mail addresses. Some (like AOL) do not; however, if the program supports separate mailboxes for separate people, you can set up the e-mail program as if you were creating accounts for different people, assigning them account names instead of user names.

If you use multiple e-mail accounts as a way of keeping your types of messages separate, you can use filters to sort your messages into folders based on which messages were sent to which address. (See Chapter 8.)

Multiple People Sharing One Computer

You may also have multiple accounts to manage because you have more than one person using the same e-mail program on the same computer. You can store the messages, signature, stationery, and saved messages for each person in a separate folder.

Many programs refer to the process of setting up the program for multiple users on the same computer as *creating profiles*. Each user has his or her own set of mailboxes and preferences, and usually can't even tell that someone else has been using the same program to send and receive e-mail. However, profiles often provide little security. In other words, you have to trust that the other users won't use your profile to enter the program and read your mail.

Sending and Receiving E-mail When You're on the Road

If you take a laptop with you when you travel, you can connect to the Internet and read your mail. You can connect to the Internet via a dial-up modem and phone line. (If your ISP has phone numbers where you travel, you can avoid a long-distance call; but even if you have to call long-distance to your home area, you can probably send and receive your e-mail messages in just a few minutes, hang up, and read your messages offline, as described in Chapter 5.) Alternatively, you may be able to connect through a high-speed connection at an office or business-oriented hotel. A few Internet users may have wireless connections that work away from home.

Once you are on the Net, you can read and send mail in two ways: using your e-mail program or using a web-based mail service.

Using Your E-mail Program When You're on the Road

Regardless of how you are connected to the Internet, you can pick up your e-mail just as you always do, using your e-mail program. The e-mail program retrieves your messages from your POP or IMAP server, regardless of how you are connected to the Internet.

However, when you send messages via another Internet connection, your ISP may (should!) refuse to accept messages from you. To avoid being used by spammers for mail distribution, most ISPs close their SMTP servers to all computers that aren't connected using that ISP. To send mail, find out the SMTP server name of the ISP that you are using, and configure your e-mail program to send via that server. (Instructions for each popular e-mail program are included in this chapter.)

For example, if you usually connect using EarthLink and send messages via their **smtp.earthlink.com** mail server, you'll run into trouble when you connect through the LAN at an office or hotel that uses another ISP. If you are at an office, find out what SMTP server user computers in that office use; if you are at a hotel or Internet café, find the instructions for sending mail.

Pegasus, a Free E-mail Program

Pegasus is a full-featured, widely used e-mail program that has been around for years. It was written in 1990 by a New Zealander named David Harris, who continues to upgrade and support it. Unlike many other e-mail programs, Pegasus sends and retrieves e-mail in the background—in other words, you can continue to read and create e-mail messages at the same time as Pegasus is sending or retrieving messages. Pegasus supports signatures and stationery, has extensive filtering features, and is available for all versions of Windows, DOS, and the Mac.

You can download Pegasus at **www.pmail.com**. Pegasus is free, but the developer requests that you pay for the manuals if you want to support the continuing development of the program.

Using Web-Based Mail When You're on the Road

Some ISPs provide a web-based interface for your e-mail. When you're away, you can go to the ISP's web site and follow the links to read your mail. If your ISP doesn't provide a web interface for your mail, and if your mail is stored on a POP server (rather than on an IMAP server), you can still read mail sent to your own address through a web-based mail service like Hotmail or Yahoo Mail. Configure Yahoo Mail, Hotmail, or another web-based mail service to display the messages from your POP server.

If your mail resides on an IMAP server, you can't pick it up with most web-based services. However, Mail2Web (**www.mail2web.com**) is a web-based e-mail program you can use to read mail on an IMAP server. Unlike Yahoo Mail and Hotmail, Mail2Web doesn't provide you with a mailbox; instead, it provides you access to your POP or IMAP mailbox via a web interface, regardless of how you are connected to the Internet.

Generally, it's more convenient to check your regular e-mail mailbox (using Yahoo Mail, Hotmail, or Mail2Web) than asking people to write to you at a Hotmail or Yahoo Mail address. Advantages include not having to tell everyone to switch *back* to your regular address when you return from your trip and not missing messages from people who didn't hear that you were away.

Even if we don't plan to deal with all our e-mail addresses when we are on a trip, we like to check our messages, if only to delete the spam and reply to the few truly urgent messages. This reduces the depressing number of messages waiting when we get home.

Other Configuration Options

Other options that you can configure in most e-mail programs are

- **Virus prevention**   You can configure your e-mail program to prevent (or inhibit) your e-mail program from allowing your computer to get infected by e-mail-borne viruses and to prevent it from passing viruses along to the people in your address book. This is especially important if you use Outlook or Outlook Express, which most viruses target. See the section on preventing virus infection in Chapter 8.

- **Folders**   Most e-mail programs have an *Inbox,* one of several *folders* that display message summaries. They usually have folders for outgoing mail and deleted messages, too. You can create your own folders so you can sort your mail by sender, topic, customer, project, or whatever way makes sense to you. See Chapter 8 for more information.

- **Folder windows**   Normally, your Inbox and other mail folders display a list of your messages with the name of the sender, the subject of the message, and a date stamp. Some programs allow you to add different columns to the folder list or to delete columns that you don't care about. Most programs also enable you to sort messages in a folder—often, you can sort messages by clicking the header that you want to sort by. For instance, if you want to sort by sender, click the header for the From or Sender column. If that doesn't work, look for a menu command that allows you to sort messages. You may also want to change column widths from their default values. For instance, if you can see only the first names of the people who send you e-mail, you may want to make the From column wider. In most programs, to change column widths, you move the mouse pointer to the right side of the column header and then click-and-drag the divider to the left or right to make the column narrower or wider.

- **Toolbar**   Some e-mail programs enable you to change the buttons on the toolbar to include the tasks that you perform most often. You can also remove buttons that you never use. Check in the section later in this chapter about your e-mail program for the program's configuration command.

- **Signatures**   Your name, e-mail address, and other identifying information should appear at the end of each e-mail message you send. To save having to type this information at the end of each message, many e-mail programs allow you to create a *signature*, that is, a file containing the list to be appended to each outgoing message. Signatures generally should be limited to four lines, so your regular correspondents don't have to see a long signature each time they receive a message from you. Include your name, e-mail address, and the organization (if any) you represent. You don't have to include your postal mailing address or phone number because people who see your signature are more likely to contact you by e-mail. You can include a cute or informative tag line, but keep it short.

- **Stationery**   If you send certain messages over and over with minor variations, check whether your e-mail program lets you define *stationery*—e-mail form letters. Some e-mail programs let you save *stationery files* with the headers and text you want to include in your frequently sent messages. To compose a message using stationery, you choose the name of the stationery file. You can then edit the message to insert information tailored to the recipient. You may also find it useful to store in draft form a message that you want to reuse often. Don't forget about copy-and-paste (CTRL-C and CTRL-V in most Windows programs) to copy text from one place to another—in some cases, this may be the easiest way to send a form letter.

The rest of this chapter describes how to configure and use the advanced features of the most popular e-mail programs.

Pine

If you use a Linux or UNIX system and prefer a text-based e-mail program, use Pine. It's easy to learn, with clear, simple menus. Try typing **pine** at the UNIX shell prompt—the program will probably run because many systems come with it.

Pine is a text-only program that is easy to use; it displays menus from which you choose commands by pressing single letters. You can also use Pine to read Usenet newsgroups (described in Chapter 11).

Pine can't display formatted e-mail, but you can file your messages in folders, create signatures, and deal with attached files. On most systems, it's faster than any graphics-based e-mail program! See **net.gurus.com/shell/pine.phtml** for how to use Pine.

Outlook 2002 and Outlook Express

Outlook and Outlook Express are Microsoft's major entries into the e-mail market. In fact, Outlook does much more than e-mail—it also has calendars, tracks contacts, and more. Neither is available for Windows 3.1 or the Mac.

Outlook 2002 comes with Microsoft Office XP and is also available to purchase and download at **www.microsoft.com/outlook**. (For instructions on downloading and installing programs from the Web, see Chapter 34.) It's more than an e-mail program: it includes an address book, calendar, to-do list, and other features.

If you prefer an e-mail program that has fewer features and uses fewer computer resources, you may want to consider Outlook Express, which comes with all versions of Windows since Windows 98, as well as with many versions of Internet Explorer. If you have Windows but an Outlook Express icon doesn't appear in the Quick Launch section of your taskbar (the small icons next to the Start button), choose Start | Control Panel, run Add Or Remove Programs, click the Add/Remove Windows Components icon, and select Microsoft Outlook Express from the list of Windows components. If it doesn't appear, you can download it from **www.microsoft.com/windows/ie/downloads**.

This section describes Outlook 2002, but most of the instructions also work for Outlook Express, although often you'll find that you can skip a step or two. Figure 6-1 shows a typical Outlook 2002 window, and Figure 6-2 shows Outlook Express 6. Table 6-1 lists the common Outlook and Outlook Express commands.

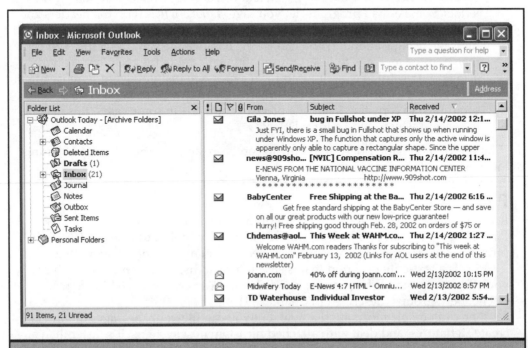

Figure 6-1. *Outlook and Outlook Express 2002*

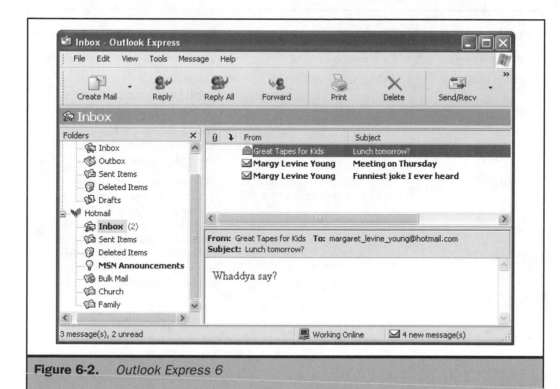

Figure 6-2.   *Outlook Express 6*

Task	Command	Notes
Create new message	New or Create Mail button or CTRL-N	Send the message by clicking the Send button.
Check e-mail	Send And Receive button or CTRL-M	You can also choose Tools | Send And Receive | Internet Mail. When new e-mail arrives, you see an envelope icon on your taskbar.
Check e-mail automatically	Tools | Options, click Mail Setup, and click the Send/Receive button In Outlook Express: Tools | Options and click the General tab	Type a number in the setting named Schedule An Automatic Send/Receive Every X Minutes. In Outlook Express, the setting is called Check For New Messages Every X Minute(s).

Table 6-1.   *Basic Outlook and Outlook Express 2002 Commands*

Task	Command	Notes
Print message	Print button or CTRL-P	You can also choose File | Print.
Delete message	Delete button or DELETE	The message moves to the Trash folder.
Forward message	Forward button or CTRL-F	You can also choose Action | Forward from the menu (Compose | Forward in Outlook Express).
Reply to message	Reply or Reply To All button, or CTRL-R or CTRL-SHIFT-R	You can also choose Action | Reply or Action | Reply To All (Compose | Reply To Author and Compose | Reply To All in Outlook Express). Reply To All (CTRL-SHIFT-R) addresses the reply to everyone who received the original message.
Check spelling	Tools | Spelling or F7	
Turn on spell checking	Tools | Options and click the Spelling tab	On the Spelling tab, select the Always Check Spelling Before Sending option.
Display address book	Address Book button	You can display addresses from Contacts by choosing Contacts in the Show Names From The drop-down list.
Save address	New Entry button on the Address Book toolbar	It's the first button.
Save address from current message	Right-click the address and choose Add To Personal Address Book	
Create new mailbox or folder	File | Folder | New Folder or CTRL-SHIFT-E	First, select the folder in which you want the new folder to be stored. You see the Create New Folder dialog box.
Move message to folder	Right-click the message, choose Move To Folder, and select the folder	You can also drag the message to the folder.

Table 6-1.   *Basic Outlook 2002 and Outlook Express Commands* (continued)

Task	Command	Notes
Create signature (or form letter)	Tools │ Options, click the Mail Format tab, and click the Signatures button at the bottom of the page In Outlook Express: click the Signatures tab	Click New, name the signature, choose how to create the signature, and click Next. Type your signature and click Finish. In the Options dialog box, choose signatures for new messages, replies, and forwards.
Append signature to message	Insert │ Signature	To add a signature to all messages, choose Tools │ Options, click the Mail Format tab, and choose signatures at the bottom of the dialog box.
Leave mail on server	Tools │ E-Mail Accounts and choose View Or Change Existing E-Mail Accounts In Outlook Express: Tools │ Accounts	Then click Next. Select the account and click Change. Click More Settings, click the Advanced tab, and select Leave A Copy Of Messages On Server. In Outlook Express, choose Tools │ Accounts, select the account, and click Properties. Click the Advanced tab, and select Leave A Copy Of Messages On Server.
Find message	View │ Find or View │ Advanced Find	
Change configuration settings	Tools │ E-Mail Accounts, Internet Mail, Properties button In Outlook Express: Tools │ Accounts, Mail tab; click the e-mail account you want to change; and click Properties	

Table 6-1.   *Basic Outlook 2002 Commands* (continued)

Configuring Outlook

The first time you open Outlook, a wizard guides you through setting up your account. You can import Internet e-mail account settings from Outlook Express, Eudora, or Netscape.

If you ever need to change these settings in Outlook, choose Tools | E-Mail Accounts from the menu, select Internet Mail, and click the Properties button. In Outlook Express, choose Tools | Accounts, click the Mail tab, click the e-mail account you want to change, and click Properties.

Configuring Outlook Express for Hotmail

If you have a Hotmail account, you can configure Outlook Express so that you can read your e-mail. Add a new account by using Tools | Accounts, clicking the Mail tab, and clicking Add to add an account. Specify that your incoming server is HTTP, and choose Hotmail from the list of providers. (If you type a Hotmail address as your e-mail address, the program displays these settings automatically.)

Using Outlook Express to read your Hotmail account allows you to collect your e-mail and then read it offline, as well as giving you access to Outlook Express' mail-sorting and other features.

Configuring Outlook Express for Multiple E-mail Addresses

You can configure Outlook Express to send and receive mail from more than one e-mail account, but it's not designed to allow multiple users to read e-mail separately. You *can* set up an account for each person to collect all the mail into Outlook Express and then set up filters to sort it out, but nothing stops one person from reading another person's messages. Other e-mail programs handle this situation better.

To set up e-mail accounts, one for each e-mail address you use, choose Tools | Accounts to display the Internet Accounts dialog box. Click the Mail tab to see a list of mail accounts. To configure Outlook Express to work with a new e-mail account, choose Add | Mail to run the Internet Connection Wizard. The wizard asks questions about your name, your e-mail address, and the names of the incoming (POP) and outgoing (SMTP) mail servers. If you want to make changes to an existing account, select it and click Properties.

Configuring Outlook for Multiple Users

Outlook supports multiple profiles and multiple e-mail accounts. Profiles are designed for different people using e-mail on the same computer (although you may find a different use for them). To set up multiple Profiles, use the Windows Control Panel rather than Outlook. Choose Start | Control Panel (or Start | Settings | Control Panel in older versions of Windows) to display the Control Panel, and then open the Mail program. (First, you may need to display the Control Panel in Classic View.) Mail appears in the Control Panel only if Outlook is installed. In the Mail window, click Show Profiles.

To create a new profile, click the Add button. Depending on which Microsoft software you have installed, the Microsoft Outlook Setup Wizard may run, or you may see another series of dialog boxes. Either way, choose to create an Internet e-mail service or profile, and enter the following information:

- **Profile name**   A short name or nickname for the profile—it appears in a drop-down list when Outlook is opened.

- **Mail Account Properties**   The name that you want to call the service and the information needed to set up the e-mail account. To display the Mail Account Properties dialog box, you may need to click the Setup Mail Account button. Be sure to click the Servers tab and the Connection tab to fill in the information requested there, also. The Advanced settings generally do not have to be changed. Click the OK button to close the Properties dialog box for the mail service.

Choose whether you want to be asked which profile to use or you want Outlook to always open with a default profile. If you always open a default profile, you can switch profiles by editing the profile settings using Control Panel. If you will be using alternate profiles with any frequency, choose to be asked which profile to use.

Configuring Outlook 2002 for Multiple E-mail Addresses

If you have multiple e-mail addresses, you need multiple *services* in your profile. Each service contains settings for one address. To add a service, choose Tools | E-Mail Accounts to display the E-Mail Accounts Wizard. Choose Add A New E-Mail Account, and provide the necessary information about the e-mail account that you're adding to the profile.

After you define multiple services, you can send and receive mail for all accounts (services) by clicking the Send And Receive button on the toolbar.

Formatting E-Mail

Outlook supports four message formats: HTML, Microsoft Outlook Rich Text Format (RTF), Plain Text, and Microsoft Word. When you reply to a message, Outlook automatically uses the same format as the message that you received. If you exchange mail with people who have a variety of e-mail programs, not all of which may support formatting, you should set the format of your outgoing mail to Plain Text. To choose the default mail format, choose Tools | Options to display the Options dialog box, and then click the Mail Format tab. The mail format that you select affects the formatting options that you see in the message composition window.

Outlook Express supports only HTML formatting. To control whether you send formatted messages, choose Tools | Options to display the Options dialog box, and then click the Send tab.

Both Outlook and Outlook Express have a stationery feature, but it is meant to allow you to add color and images and set fonts for your messages rather than to create form letters. Outlook's stationery feature has some limitations—for example, you must use HTML to create messages. People with e-mail programs that can't display formatted e-mail messages don't see your nice-looking formatting or they see lots of formatting codes. Choose Tools | Stationery to format your messages with the standard "stationery" (formats) that comes with the program.

You can use Microsoft Word as your e-mail editor when you use Outlook (not Outlook Express). Using Word enables you to take advantage of Word's automatic spell-checking and formatting features. (A recipient must have Outlook or another e-mail program that reads rich text e-mail messages to see the formatting.) To use Word as your editor, choose Tools | Options from the menu, click the Mail Format tab, and then select the Use Microsoft Word To Edit E-Mail Messages option.

If you want to see all the headings for an incoming message, including formatting information, choose View | Options. For only the headings, you can choose View | Message Header.

Sending Form Letters Using Signatures

To create form letters, you use Outlook's signature feature. Choose Tools | Options, click the Mail Format tab, and click the Signatures button at the bottom of the page. Click New, name the signature, and type the content of your form letter as the signature. Make sure that you don't set the form letter as your default signature, or all your messages will contain the form letter text.

To use the form letter text in a message, open a new message, click the Signature button on the toolbar or choose Insert | Signature, and then select the signature that contains the text of your message. You can edit the message before you send it if you like.

If you use Word as your Outlook e-mail editor, then you can use Word features such as templates and Mail Merge to create e-mail messages.

Eudora

Eudora is a popular e-mail program available from QUALCOMM. In the past, Eudora came in two versions: Pro and Lite. Now Eudora is available in three modes: Sponsored, Paid, and Light. The Sponsored version has all the features, but also displays ads. In Paid mode, Eudora has all the features with no ads, but is not free. Eudora Light has fewer features and no ads. Windows, Mac, web-based, and Palm OS versions of Eudora are available. This section describes the current version of Eudora (version 5.1). You can get Eudora from QUALCOMM'S web site at **eudora.qualcomm.com**.

Figure 6-3 shows a typical Eudora window. Table 6-2 lists the common Eudora commands.

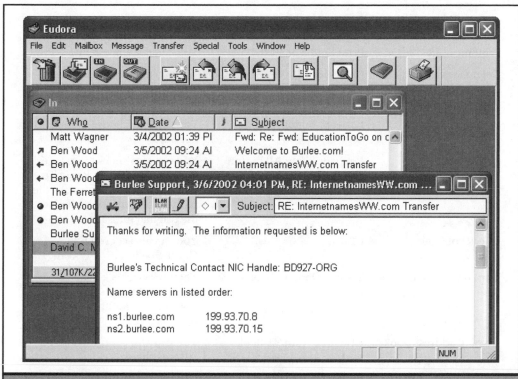

Figure 6-3.   *The Eudora window with the In mail folder and an incoming message open*

Task	Command	Notes
Create new message	New Message button	Use TAB to move between lines. Click the Queue button (or Send button, depending upon how Eudora is configured) to send the message.
Check e-mail	Check Mail button or CTRL-M	You can also choose File | Check Mail.
Check e-mail automatically	Tools | Options, Checking Mail category	Change the Check For Mail Every *X* Minutes setting.

Table 6-2.   *Basic Eudora Commands*

Task	Command	Notes
Print message	Print button or CTRL-P	You can also choose File | Print.
Delete message	DELETE or CTRL-D	You can also click the Delete Message(s) button. The message moves to the Trash folder.
Forward message	Forward button	You can also choose Message | Forward.
Reply to message	Reply or Reply All button or CTRL-R	You can also choose Message | Reply or Message | Reply To All. Reply To All addresses the reply to everyone who received the original message.
Check spelling	CTRL-6	You can also choose Edit | Check Spelling.
Turn on spell checking	Tools | Options, Spell Checking category	Then select Check When Message Queued/Sent. You may also find the additional spelling options useful.
Display address book	CTRL-L or Address Book button	You can also choose Tools | Address Book.
Save address	In the Address Book window, click New	Click the New button on the Address Book window, provide a nickname, and click OK. Type the address in the Addresses tab of the Address Book.
Save address from current message	Special | Make Address Book Entry or CTRL-K	You see the Address Book with the new entry.
Create new mailbox or folder	Mailbox | New	Use the Make It A Folder check box to create a folder (which can hold a group of mailboxes) rather than a mailbox.
Move message to folder	Transfer | *folder name*	You can also drag the message to the folder.
Create signature	Tools | Signatures	You can also click the Signatures tab if it appears. To create additional signatures, right-click the Signature tab and choose New.

Table 6-2. *Basic Eudora Commands* (continued)

Task	Command	Notes
Append signature to message	Signature drop-down list on the message toolbar, then choose a signature	To add a signature to all messages, choose Tools | Options from the menu, click the Sending Mail icon, and choose a signature from the Default Signature drop-down list.
Leave mail on server	Tools | Options, Incoming Mail category	Choose Tools | Options, choose the Incoming Mail category, and select the Leave Mail On Server option.
Create stationery	File | Save As Stationery	Create a message. Before sending, choose File | Save As Stationery, and specify a filename. Stationery files have the extension *.sta* and are usually stored in the Stationery folder in the Eudora program folder.
Create new message using stationery	Message | New Message With	Choose Message | New Message With, and choose from the list of existing stationery files.
Find message	Edit | Find | Find Messages or CTRL-F	In the Find Messages dialog box, choose where to look (headers, text, or anywhere), how to look, what to look for (a word or phrase), and which mailboxes to look in.
Change configuration settings	Tools | Options	In the Options dialog box, click a category (scroll down for more), and set the options that appear.

Table 6-2.   *Basic Eudora Commands* (continued)

Configuring Eudora

The first time that you run Eudora, the New Account Wizard guides you through setting up your account. If you are upgrading, install the program to the same directory to see all your mail and to reuse your settings. If you are switching programs and you currently have an e-mail application set up on your computer that uses the same e-mail account that you want to use with Eudora, you can use the New Account Wizard's Import Settings option. Eudora can import settings from Outlook, Outlook

Express, and Netscape Messenger 4.*x* and higher. If you haven't used your e-mail account from the computer that you're working on, choose the New Account Wizard's Create A Brand New E-Mail Account setting. You also have the option of getting settings from an ACAP server, or exiting the wizard and typing in your settings in the Options dialog box (Tools | Options).

If you ever need to change your configuration settings, choose Tools | Options from the menu. In the Options dialog box, click each category in the Category box to see the myriad options you can set, including Fonts (to control what fonts Eudora uses when displaying and printing messages) and Internet Dialup (to tell Eudora to dial the Internet automatically to send and receive mail).

> **Tip** *Right-click a blank part of the toolbar to change which buttons appear.*

Configuring Eudora for Multiple Users

If more than one person uses your computer, you can configure Eudora to maintain a separate mailbox folder for each person. Eudora's program files are stored in one folder (usually C:\Program Files\Eudora or C:\Program Files\Qualcomm\Eudora), but the mailboxes, address book, and other information can be stored in a separate folder. Eudora creates a file called Eudora.ini for each user, with information about that person's configuration.

To create a separate Eudora.ini file, mailboxes, address book, and other configuration files for a new user, follow these steps:

1. Create a new folder on your computer using Windows Explorer.

2. Create a new shortcut to Eudora on your Windows desktop by right-clicking the desktop and choosing New | Shortcut.

3. For the location of the item (program), specify the Eudora program file (Eudora.exe), which is usually in C:\Program Files\Eudora or C:\Program Files\Qualcomm\Eudora.

4. For the name of the shortcut, type whatever name you want associated with the new icon you are creating (for example, **Fred's Mail**).

5. Right-click the new icon and choose Properties from the menu that appears. In the Properties dialog box that appears, click the Shortcut tab if it's not already selected.

6. Click in the Target box, which contains the pathname to the Eudora program file (Eudora.exe); the pathname is enclosed in quotes if it contains any spaces. At the end of the entry, add the pathname to the folder you created in step 1. If the pathname to the folder contains spaces, enclose it in quotes. For example, if you created a folder called C:\Fred's Mail, edit the Target setting to read

   ```
   "C:\Program Files\Eudora\Eudora.exe" "C:\Fred's Mail"
   ```

7. Click OK to save the changes to the shortcut.

When you run the new shortcut, Eudora creates new configuration files in the new folder and runs the New Account Wizard.

 Alternatively, you can copy an existing Eudora shortcut, and modify its name and Target setting. Copy and paste a shortcut by selecting it and pressing CTRL-C and CTRL-V. Modify its properties by right-clicking the shortcut and choosing Properties from the menu that appears.

Configuring Eudora for Multiple E-mail Addresses

Eudora allows you to manage multiple e-mail accounts by using *personalities*. You can define different personalities to send and receive-mail from different e-mail addresses. However, all the mail that you receive goes to your In mailbox, so if you want to keep the mail separate, you have to create filters that will funnel the mail sent to a particular address to a mailbox that you create for that purpose. (See Chapter 8 for how to set up filters.)

To create or modify personalities, display the Personalities pane either by choosing Tools | Personalities or by clicking the Personalities tab (if it appears). The Personalities pane looks like this:

To create a new personality to send or receive mail from another address, start the New Account Wizard by right-clicking the white space on the Personalities pane and choosing New from the shortcut menu. The wizard asks you for all the information that Eudora needs to retrieve and send mail from the account: the name for the personality (what you see on the Personalities tab), your name (the name that will appear on messages that you send), the address for the account, the logon name for the account, the incoming mail server, the type of incoming server (POP or IMAP), and the outgoing (SMTP) server. As with the initial Eudora setup, you can import the information from an existing Outlook or Netscape account.

To edit a personality, right-click the personality name in the Personalities pane, and choose Properties from the shortcut menu. You can then change any of the settings in the Account Settings dialog box, shown in Figure 6-4.

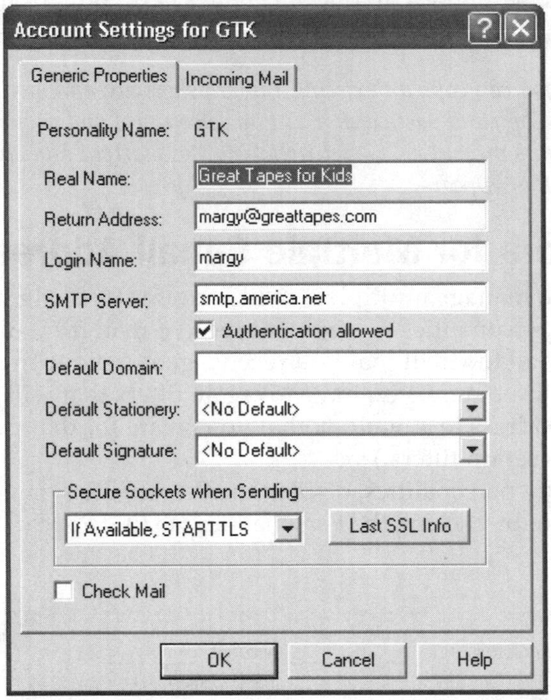

Figure 6-4.   *Editing a personality in Eudora*

When you send e-mail, Eudora uses the Dominant personality. If you want to use a different personality to send a message, either select the personality in the Personalities pane and press ENTER, or right-click the personality name and choose Message | New Message As. Alternatively, press SHIFT while you click the New Message button on the toolbar: when Eudora displays the Message Options dialog box, choose the personality and click OK. When you are composing a message, you can change which personality it will come from by clicking the From header button and choosing from the list that appears.

To reply to a message by using an account other than the account the message was sent to, right-click the message, choose Change Personality, and choose the personality that you want to use. Then reply to the message as usual—the address in the From header will be the address of the personality that you selected.

Formatting E-mail

Eudora provides many text-formatting options on the message composition window's toolbar, including font; font size; bold; italic; underline; color; indent; bullets; hyperlinks;

and left, center, or right alignment. However, because you can't control the default font used by the recipient's e-mail program, you can't totally control the look of the message. (You can change the default fonts for your own copy of Eudora by choosing Tools | Options to display the Options dialog box and then clicking the Fonts category.)

Before sending formatted e-mail, ask the recipient whether her e-mail program can handle formatting. Never post formatted e-mail to mailing lists.

You can turn on or off formatting options. If you don't see the formatting buttons on the message composition toolbar, you can turn them on by choosing Tools | Options to display the Options dialog box, and then choosing Styled Text options.

If you want to see all the headings for an incoming message, including formatting information, click the Blah Blah Blah button on the message window's toolbar.

Sending Form Letters Using Eudora Stationery

Eudora enables you to create form letters using *stationery*. If you write a message that you realize you might want to use again later, save it as stationery by choosing File | Save As Stationery when the message is open. To send another message using the same stationery (that is, the same subject and text that you saved), choose Message | New Message With, and choose from your existing stationery files. You can reply to a message with stationery by choosing Message | Reply With.

Eudora even enables you to send a reply automatically to a message that you filter using a particular stationery. For example, you can send an automated reply (stored as stationery) to all messages with the text "catalog request" in the subject line. To send replies automatically, use the filter feature described in Chapter 8.

If you are going to use stationery to reply to messages, you may want to leave the subject line blank. Then your reply will have the same subject line as the original message. If you type a subject line in your stationery and then use the stationery to reply to a message, the subject line will appear like this:

```
Subject of stationery (was RE: Subject of original message)
```

You also can choose default stationery to use for every new message; select Tools | Options to display the Options dialog box, click Composing Mail in the Category list, and set the Default Stationery option.

Netscape Mail

Netscape Mail (or more properly, Netscape Mail & Newsgroups) is the e-mail client that is part of Netscape 6. The program is available for free from Netscape at **www.netscape.com/computing/download**, as well as from TUCOWS (**www.tucows.com**) and other sites. This section describes version 6.2, which is also available for the Mac.

If you use the Netscape browser to access the Web, you may want to use Mail to send and receive e-mail. In addition, Netscape Mail is the only e-mail program that works with AOL mail.

To open Mail, choose Start | All Programs | Netscape | Mail (in Windows XP). If you are using Netscape to browse the Web, choose Tasks | Mail & Newsgroups (or press CTRL-2), or click the Mail & Newsgroups (envelope) icon located on the Netscape Component Bar, which may appear at the bottom of the Netscape window. Messenger and the Netscape Component Bar are shown in Figure 6-5. Table 6-3 lists the common Netscape Mail commands.

Note   *Netscape 6 Mail doesn't include a stationery feature for sending form letters.*

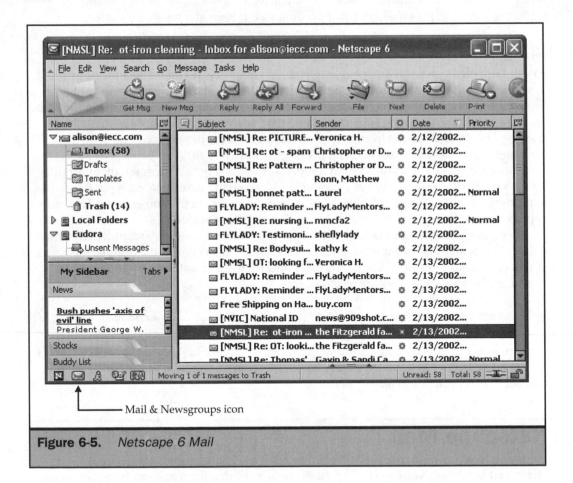

Mail & Newsgroups icon

Figure 6-5.   *Netscape 6 Mail*

Task	Command	Notes
Create message	New Msg button or CTRL-M	Send the message by clicking the Send button on the message window toolbar.
Check e-mail	Get Msg button or CTRL-T	You can also choose File | Get New Messages.
Check mail automatically	Edit | Mail & Newsgroups Account Settings	In the Mail & Newsgroups Account Settings dialog box, choose your e-mail account and click Server Settings. Select the Check For New Messages Every *xx* Minutes check box, and type the frequency (in minutes).
Print message	Print button or CTRL-P	You can also choose File | Print.
Delete message	Delete button or DELETE	The message moves to the Trash folder.
Forward message	Forward button or CTRL-L	You can also choose Message | Forward.
Reply to message	Reply or Reply All button, or CTRL-R or CTRL-SHIFT-R	You can also choose Message | Reply or Message | Reply To All. Reply To All (CTRL-SHIFT-R) addresses the reply to everyone who received the original message.
Check spelling	Spelling button on the message toolbar	
Turn on spell checking	Edit | Preferences, Mail & Newsgroups category, Message Composition category	Select the Check Spelling Before Sending check box.
Display address book	Tasks | Address Book or CTRL-5	
Save address	In the Address Book window, click the New Card button	Type the address and name, and click OK to save.

Table 6-3.   *Basic Netscape Mail Commands*

Task	Command	Notes
Save address from current message	Right-click sender's address and choose Add Sender To Address Book	Mail displays the New Card dialog box for each address that it adds to the Address Book. Accept all the entries by clicking OK, or correct or add to the information before clicking OK.
Create new mailbox or folder	Right-click folder list and choose New Folder	Type a name for the folder in the Name text box, and select a folder from the Create As A Subfolder Of option.
Move message to folder	Message | Move Message | *folder name*	You can also drag the message information to the folder—or right-click the message, choose Move Message, and select the folder from the folder list.
Create signature	Create text file containing text of signature (use Notepad or another text editor). Choose Edit | Mail & Newsgroups Account Settings, choose mail account	Select the Attach This Signature check box. Click the Choose button to its right, and browse to the text file with your signature.
Add signature to message		Your signature appears on all messages. Delete it manually if you don't want it on a particular message.
Leave mail on server	Choose Edit | Mail & Newsgroups Account Settings, choose mail account, and click Server Settings	Select the Leave Messages On Server check box.
Find message	Search | Search Messages	Specify which folders to search, what parts of messages to search, and what text to search for.
Change configuration settings	Edit | Mail & Newsgroups Account Settings	Choose the mail account from the list. Double-click to display categories below it. Settings appear to the right.

Table 6-3. *Basic Netscape Mail Commands* (continued)

Configuring Netscape Mail

The first time you run Netscape Mail, it asks whether you want to activate special features, which include creating a new Netscape.net e-mail address for you. If you want to use Netscape Mail with an existing e-mail account, click Cancel to skip activation. It will also ask whether you want to make Netscape your default browser.

Once you get past the opening screens, the Account Wizard runs to get information about your e-mail account. If you ever need to change these settings, choose Edit | Mail & Newsgroups Account Settings from the menu. You see the Mail & Newsgroups Account Settings dialog box shown in Figure 6-6. Choose the mail account from the list on the left side of the Mail & Newsgroup Account Settings dialog box. Double-click the mail account name to display the categories below it. The settings in that category appear to the right.

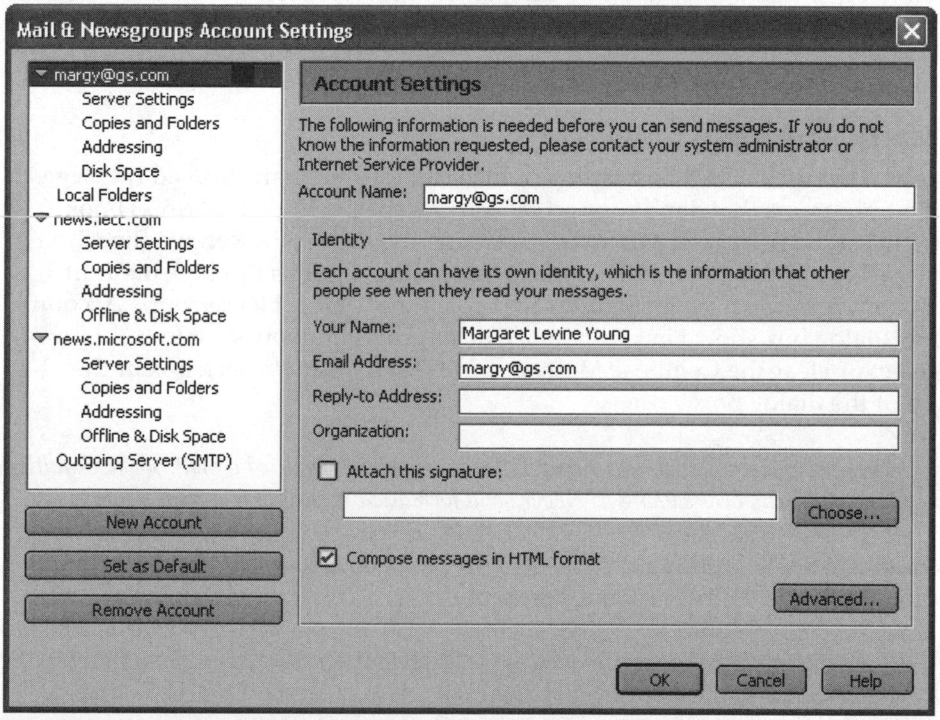

Figure 6-6.   *Configuring Netscape Mail*

Configuring Netscape Mail for Multiple Users

Netscape Mail allows you to set up multiple user profiles. Separate profiles enable different users to use one copy of Mail (actually, one copy of the whole Communicator program) and have their own mailboxes, personal settings (including Navigator bookmarks), and preferences. When you open Mail using your profile, it looks as though you are the only person who uses it—you see only your mail and folders. Profiles are not password-protected, however, and therefore aren't really private. Each profile can use only one e-mail account, but one person can use different profiles to collect mail from different accounts.

See the section on sharing Navigator with other users in Chapter 18 for directions on how to create and use a new user profile.

Configuring Netscape Mail for Multiple E-mail Addresses

If you use more than one e-mail address, you can configure Netscape Mail to pick up mail from all of them. Choose Edit | Mail & Newsgroups Account Settings, and click the New Account button. The Account Wizard asks for the type of account, name, and mail servers.

Formatting E-Mail

Netscape Mail uses HTML formatting, which can result in hard-to-read messages in e-mail programs that don't support it. You can specify in your address book always to send a person HTML text by selecting the Prefers To Receive Rich Text (HTML) Mail option. You can also choose formatting options by choosing Edit | Mail & Newsgroups Account Settings to display the Mail & Newsgroups Account Settings dialog box shown in Figure 6-6. Click the account you want to configure, and select or clear the Compose Messages In HTML Format check box at the bottom of the dialog box.

Many people have e-mail programs that can't display formatted e-mail, so check with your correspondents before using it. Never send formatted messages to e-mail mailing lists.

When you are composing a message, you can choose to send it as plain text by choosing Options | Format | Plain Text Only.

To see the complete headers for a message, display the message and choose View | Page Source or press CTRL-U.

Netscape Messenger

Netscape Messenger is the e-mail client that is packaged with Netscape Communicator 4.*x*. The program is available for free from Netscape at **home.netscape.com/computing/**

download (click the Other Netscape Products link for this version), as well as from TUCOWS (**www.tucows.com**) and other sites. This section describes version 4.7, which is also available for the Mac. If you use Netscape Navigator 4.7 (the browser that comes with the Netscape Communicator suite) to access the Web, you may want to use Messenger to send and receive e-mail. We find it to be more stable than Netscape 6.

   To open Netscape Messenger, choose Start | All Programs | Netscape Communicator | Netscape Messenger. If you are already browsing the Web with Netscape Navigator, choose Communicator | Messenger from the menu, or click the Inbox icon located on the Netscape Component Bar or at the bottom of the Navigator window. Netscape Messenger is shown in Figure 6-7. Table 6-4 lists the common Netscape Messenger commands.

 Netscape Messenger doesn't include a stationery feature for sending form letters.

Configuring Netscape Messenger

The first time you open Netscape Messenger, it asks whether you want to make Messenger your default e-mail application. If you're just trying it out, answer No; otherwise, answer Yes.

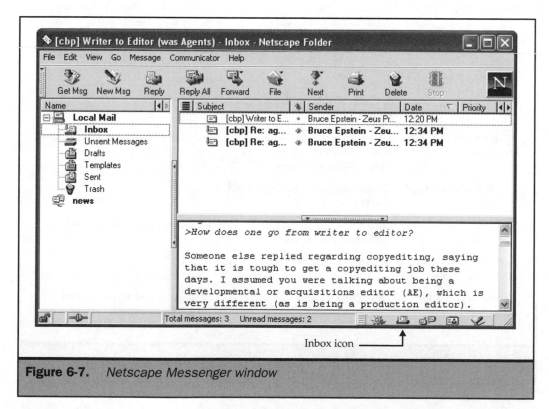

Inbox icon

Figure 6-7.   *Netscape Messenger window*

Task	Command	Notes
Create new message	New Msg button or CTRL-M	Send the message by clicking the Send button on the message window toolbar.
Check e-mail	Get Msg button or CTRL-T	You can also select File I Get New Messages.
Check e-mail automatically	Edit I Preferences, Mail & Newsgroups category, Mail Servers subcategory	Choose the mail server from the Incoming Mail Servers list and click Edit. On the General tab, select Check For Mail Every xx Minutes, and type the frequency (in minutes) to check the mail.
Print message	Print button or CTRL-P	You can also choose File I Print.
Delete message	Delete button or DELETE	The message moves to the Trash folder.
Forward message	Forward button or CTRL-L	You can also choose Message I Forward.
Reply to message	Reply or Reply All button, or CTRL-R or CTRL-SHIFT-R	You can also choose Message I Reply or Message I Reply To All. Reply To All (CTRL-SHIFT-R) addresses the reply to everyone who received the original message.
Check spelling	Spelling button on the message toolbar	
Turn on spell checking	Edit I Preferences, Mail & Newsgroups category, Messages subcategory	Select the Spell Check Messages Before Sending check box.
Display address book	Communicator I Address Book or CTRL-SHIFT-2	
Save address	New Card button on the Address Book toolbar	Or choose File I New Card.
Save address from current message	Message I Add Sender To Address Book	
Create new mailbox or folder	File I New Folder	Specify the folder name and which folder should contain it. (Local Mail is the default.)

Table 6-4.   *Basic Netscape Messenger Commands*

Task	Command	Notes
Move message to folder	Message | Move Message | *folder name*	
Create signature	Create text file containing text of signature. (Use Notepad or another text editor.) Edit | Preferences, Mail & Newsgroups category, Identity subcategory	Click the Choose button to the right of the Signature File box to specify the text file containing the signature.
Add signature to message		Your signature appears on all messages. Delete it manually if you don't want it on a particular message.
Leave mail on server	Edit | Preferences, Mail & Newsgroups category, Mail Servers subcategory	Select the mail server in the Incoming Mail Servers list, click Edit, click the POP tab in the Mail Server Properties dialog box, and choose the Leave Messages On Server check box.
Find message	Edit | Search Messages	Specify which mailbox to search, what part of the messages to search, and what to search for.
Change configuration settings	Edit | Preferences, Mail & Newsgroups category	Mail & Newsgroups has many subcategories. Click one to see its settings.

Table 6-4.   *Basic Netscape Messenger Commands* (continued)

Netscape Messenger does not immediately open a configuration wizard when you first run it, unlike many other e-mail applications. To configure Netscape Messenger to pick up and send e-mail, follow these steps:

1. Choose Edit | Preferences from the menu. You see the Preferences dialog box.

2. Select Mail & Newsgroups and Mail Servers in the Category list. The Incoming Mail Servers box lists each POP or IMAP mail server on which you have a mailbox.

3. Click a mail server and click the Edit button in the Incoming Mail Servers box. (Or click Add if no servers are listed.) You see the Mail Server Properties dialog box.

4. Enter the name of the server on which your e-mail is stored.

5. Select the server type—POP3 (POP) or IMAP. Currently, most e-mail accounts are POP3.

6. Type your user name (the name you use to log in when you access your mail server).

7. If you want Netscape Messenger to remember your password, select the Remember Password check box. If you want it to pick up e-mail automatically every few minutes, select the Check For Mail Every *xx* Minutes check box and enter a number of minutes.

8. Click OK to save your incoming mail server settings.

9. In the Preferences dialog box, type the name of your outgoing mail server in the Outgoing Mail (SMTP) Server box.

10. Click the Identity subcategory.

11. Fill in Your Name and E-Mail Address. The other settings on this page are optional.

12. Click OK to close the Preferences dialog box.

Configuring Netscape Messenger for Multiple Users

Like Netscape 6 Mail, Netscape Messenger allows you to set up multiple user profiles, one profile for each person's mailboxes, personal settings (including Navigator bookmarks), and preferences. See the section on sharing Navigator with other users in Chapter 18 for directions on how to create and use a new user profile.

Configuring Netscape Messenger for Multiple E-mail Addresses

Netscape Messenger allows you to check one POP3 server or multiple IMAP servers. Follow the instructions in the section "Configuring Netscape Messenger," earlier in this chapter, to configure the program for additional e-mail addresses. In step 3, click Add.

Formatting E-Mail

Netscape enables you to format your outgoing messages, although not everyone has an e-mail program that can display formatted messages correctly. To control whether you send plain text or formatted messages, choose Edit | Preferences and click the Formatting subcategory of the Mail & Newsgroups category. You can choose whether to format new messages, and how to format replies based on whether the message to which you are replying is formatted.

To send a plain text message, just don't apply any formatting!

 To see the complete headers for a message, display the message and choose View | Page Source or press CTRL-U.

America Online (AOL)

America Online is a popular online service because many people find that the easiest way to get online is to use one of the armload of free AOL CD-ROMs that they have received by mail or found inserted into magazines. Using AOL saves you the hassle of choosing an ISP—it makes information relatively easy to find, and it has a well-attended array of chat rooms. AOL includes e-mail as part of its service: you can exchange e-mail with other AOL users or anyone with an Internet address. This section describes version 7.0 of AOL's software—if you don't have it, you can download it from **www.aol.com**. Table 6-5 lists the common AOL commands.

Note   *AOL 7.0 doesn't include a stationery feature for creating form letters.*

Task	Command	Notes
Create message	Write button on the main toolbar or in the Mail Center window	Send the message by clicking the Send Now button. If you are offline, click Send Later to store the message to be sent the next time Automatic AOL goes online.
Check e-mail	Read button or CTRL-R	You can also click the You Have Mail button in the Welcome window or choose Mail Center | Read Mail.
Print message	Print button	
Delete message	Delete button or DELETE	
Forward message	Forward button	Open the message first.
Reply to message	Reply or Reply All button	Open the message first.
Check spelling	CTRL-=	You can also choose Edit | Spell Check.
Turn on spell checking	My AOL | Preferences, click Mail, select Perform A Spell Check Before Sending Mail	To disable automatic spell-checking for one message, hold down CTRL while you click the Send button.
Display address book	Address Book button	You can also choose Mail | Address Book.

Table 6-5.   *Basic AOL Mail Commands*

Task	Command	Notes
Save address from current message	Add Address button	You can also right-click an address in a message and choose Add To Address Book.
Create new folder	Save To Filing Cabinet button, choose Create Folder	
Move message to folder	Save To Filing Cabinet button	
Create signature	Mail	Mail Signatures, Create	Type the signature text in the box. Set the default to On or Off, depending on whether you want most messages to include the signature.
Change configuration settings	Mail	Mail Center	

Table 6-5.   *Basic AOL Mail Commands* (continued)

You can also read and send AOL mail by using a web browser, at **www.aol.com**. AOL displays web pages that look and work very much like AOL's software.

 AOL's mail features are much more limited than those of the e-mail client programs described in this chapter. For example, AOL doesn't provide stationery or message filtering into folders.

Configuring AOL

After you install the AOL software, you don't have to configure it to get your e-mail. Because AOL doesn't offer a POP mail server, you can't use Outlook, Outlook Express, Eudora, or other e-mail programs to read your AOL mail. However, now that AOL owns Netscape, they've included AOL support in Netscape 6 Mail; see the next section for instructions.

 You can change your AOL mail settings by choosing Mail | Mail Center when you are online.

Configuring Netscape 6 Mail to Work with Your AOL Account

Netscape Mail (that is, Netscape Mail & Newsgroups in Netscape version 6.*x*) is the only e-mail program that works with your AOL account. AOL provides a special IMAP server that talks only to Netscape Mail.

To configure Netscape Mail to receive and send messages from your AOL account, choose Edit | Mail & Newsgroups Accounts Settings, click New Account, and choose AOL Account from the New Account Setup window. The Account Wizard asks for your name and AOL screen name and sets up a mail account for AOL.

Configuring AOL to Pick Up Your Mail Automatically

You can set up AOL to connect, go online, collect your e-mail, send any messages that you've composed, and sign off, so that you can read and write your e-mail offline. This system, which is called *Automatic AOL* or *Flashsessions*, is useful if you have to make a long-distance call to connect to AOL or if you have chosen an AOL billing plan for which you pay by the hour to connect. To set up Automatic AOL (whether you are online or offline), choose Mail | Automatic AOL, which displays the Automatic AOL Walk-Through window. Answer the questions that appear, and then choose the screen names for which you want to collect e-mail messages. If you want Automatic AOL to collect your messages automatically (for example, at 2:30 each morning), it asks what days and what time you want it to run. You can change your Automatic AOL configuration any time by choosing Mail | Automatic AOL again: click Schedule Automatic AOL in the window that appears if you want to change its schedule.

After you configure Automatic AOL, you can tell AOL to connect and send/receive messages by choosing Mail | Automatic AOL.

Configuring AOL for Multiple Users

Once you sign up for an AOL account, your Internet address is your screen name (without the spaces) with *@aol.com* tacked onto the end. If you create additional screen names (each AOL account can have up to seven), each screen name has its own mailbox and its own Internet address.

AOL allows each account to have up to seven *screen names*. AOL's intention is to provide family access, so that each family member has his or her own screen name. However, you may use screen names for different people or for different personas (for example, one screen name for personal mail and another for business mail). Each screen name has its own e-mail address. In addition, each screen name has its own password, which provides some privacy. However, if you are logged on using the *master* screen name, you can change the settings for other screen names. The primary (master) screen name cannot be changed, but you can change the names of the other screen names whenever you wish.

Create a new screen name by logging onto AOL using your primary screen name. Go to the keyword NAMES, and double-click Create A Screen Name. If you have seven screen names already, you have to delete one before you can create a new one. When AOL suggests a screen name for you, you do not have to accept it—keep trying if you don't like the suggested name. Provide a password for the screen name because each screen name has a separate password.

Formatting E-mail

You can format a message by using the formatting buttons on the message window toolbar. However, only other AOL users will be able to see your formatting.

 *You can't send formatted messages from the **www.aol.com** web site. In fact, you may want to send messages from the web site whenever you need to send plain text messages (for example, when you are posting to an e-mail mailing list).*

Yahoo Mail

Yahoo Mail (**mail.yahoo.com**) is a web-based mail service that provides you with an e-mail address and a web-based interface to receive and send mail. Yahoo Mail is versatile, though, because in addition to being a web-based e-mail, you can use the web interface to read a POP mail account, and you can choose to read your Yahoo mail with a POP client like Outlook, Eudora, or Netscape Mail. However, for these services, you need to agree to "accept special offers in your mailbox"—that is, advertising e-mails.

To set up Yahoo Mail, go to **mail.yahoo.com** and sign up for a Yahoo ID and password. Once you have a Yahoo ID, you have a Yahoo mailbox (at ***your-yahoo-id*@yahoo.com**), a web site (at **geocities.com/***your-yahoo-id***), a sign-in for Yahoo Messenger (the instant messaging, voice, and video conferencing program described in Chapters 14 and 16), an account for bidding on Yahoo Auctions, and other benefits.

Table 6-6 shows the common commands in Yahoo Mail. Because Yahoo Mail is a web site, though, these commands may have changed since this book was written—web sites can be redesigned more quickly than software is updated. As of mid-2002, Yahoo Mail doesn't include stationery (used for sending form letters). There's also no way to search the messages in your mail folders for a specific word, phrase, or name.

Task	Command	Notes
Create new message	Compose (link at left of web page)	Click Send to send the message.
Check e-mail	Check Mail (link at left of web page)	When you log in, Yahoo checks for new mail.
Read message	Check Mail to see message list, click the message subject	Click Prev or Next to see other messages, or Inbox to see the message list again.
Print message	Print button on the browser toolbar	You can also choose File | Print on the browser menu.
Delete message	Delete button (when you are looking at a message)	When you are looking at the message list, select the message's check box, and then click Delete.
Forward message	Forward button	Open the message first.
Reply to message	Reply or Reply All button	Open the message first.
Check spelling	Spell Check button	
Display address book	Addresses (link at left of web page)	
Save address	Addresses, New Contact button	
Save address from current message	Add To Address Book button	
Create new folder	Folders (link at left of web page), type folder name in Create A Personal Folder box, Create Folder button	Display a message, Click Move, and type a name for the folder. Click OK to create the folder.
Move message to folder	Click Choose Folder drop-down list, choose folder name, click Move button	Alternatively, from the message list, select the messages to move (by selecting their check boxes), click the Choose Folder drop-down list and select the folder, and click the Move button.

Table 6-6.   *Basic Yahoo Mail Commands*

Task	Command	Notes
Create signature	Options (link at left of web page), Signature	Type the signature text and click Save. Optionally, select the Add Signature To All Messages check box.
Append signature to message	Use Signature check box at bottom of composition page	Also choose Plain Text or HTML for the format of the signature.
Leave mail on server		Messages stay on the Yahoo Mail server until you delete them.
Change configuration settings	Options (link at left of web page)	Then choose Account Information, Mail Preferences, Signature, Vacation Response, Block Addresses, Check Other (POP) Mail, Filters, POP Access & Forwarding, Voicemail, Subscriptions, Premium Services, or Yahoo Delivers.

Table 6-6. *Basic Yahoo Mail Commands* (continued)

Reading Yahoo Mail with Another E-Mail Program

To check your Yahoo Mail with a POP client, you need to sign up for Yahoo Delivers, Yahoo's opt-in advertising and newsletter service. Follow these steps:

1. Click the Options link on the left side of the Yahoo Mail page, and then click POP Access & Forwarding.

2. Answer the questions to sign up for the ads and newsletters you are willing to accept. Click Finish.

3. Choose Web And POP Access to set up your Yahoo Mail account to be accessible from other e-mail programs. (Don't choose Forwarding, which forwards your e-mail to another account.) Click Submit.

4. As Yahoo suggests, print the next page because it contains the names of Yahoo's POP and SMTP servers, which you'll need when you configure your e-mail program to work with your Yahoo Mail account. As of mid-2002, Yahoo's POP server is **pop.mail.yahoo.com**, and their SMTP server is **smtp.mail.yahoo.com**, but these servers may change.

5. Configure your e-mail program to retrieve mail from your Yahoo mailbox. Instructions for Outlook Express, Outlook, Eudora, Netscape Mail, and Netscape Messenger are included earlier in this chapter.

Configuring Yahoo Mail to Display Mail from Other Accounts

You can also use Yahoo Mail to access other e-mail mailboxes. For example, if you travel, you might want to set up your Yahoo Mail account so that you can check your e-mail from any computer with a web browser, via the Yahoo Mail web site.

> **Note**   *Yahoo Mail can access POP mailboxes, but not IMAP mailboxes.*

To configure Yahoo Mail to display mail from your other accounts (up to three), click the Options (at the left side of the Yahoo Mail web pages) and click Check Other (POP) Mail. Click the Add Mail Server button, and fill out the form with you mail server, user name, and password. If you want to leave your mail messages on the POP server so that they will still be there when you get back from your trip, select the Leave Mail On POP Server check box. If you want to delete messages you've dealt with in Yahoo Mail so they aren't waiting for you later, clear the check box. You can choose a color indicator so you can tell which messages in your Yahoo Mail inbox arrived from this mailbox.

Hotmail

Hotmail (**www.hotmail.com**) is Microsoft's web-based mail service. It's similar to Yahoo Mail. However, it requires you to sign up for a Microsoft .NET Passport, which some people would rather not do because of privacy and security concerns (see the section about .NET Passport in Chapter 18). A useful feature of Hotmail is that you can read its messages from Outlook Express. (See the section "Configuring Outlook Express for Hotmail" earlier in this chapter.) You can't read Hotmail messages with any other e-mail program. (Microsoft owns Hotmail and Outlook Express, and can keep the interface proprietary.)

To set up Hotmail, go to **www.hotmail.com** and sign up for a Hotmail account. Table 6-7 shows the common commands in Hotmail. However, the Hotmail web site may have changed since this book was written. As of mid-2002, Hotmail doesn't include stationery (used for sending form letters). There's also no way to search the messages in your mail folders for a specific word, phrase, or name.

Task	Command	Notes
Create new message	Compose tab	Click Send when you have addressed and written your message.
Check e-mail	Inbox tab	
Read message	Click the name or address of the sender	
Print message	Click Printer Friendly Version link, then click Print button on browser toolbar	You can also choose File | Print on browser menu or press CTRL-P.
Delete message	Delete button (when displaying message)	From the inbox or other folder, select the check box by the message(s) to delete and click the Delete button. Moves message to the Trash Can folder.
Forward message	Forward button	Display the message first.
Reply to message	Reply or Reply All button	Reply All addresses the reply to all the recipients of the original message.
Check spelling	Tools drop-down list (above text box when composing a message), Spell Check	
Display address book	Address Book tab	
Save address	Create New button on Address Book page	Each address has a Quickname (nickname).
Save address from current message	Save Address(es) button	Confirm the information and click OK.
Create new folder	Create Folder button	
Move message to folder	Put In Folder drop-down list	

Table 6-7.   *Basic Hotmail Commands*

Task	Command	Notes
Create signature	Options (link to the right of Address Book tab), Signature (under Additional Options)	Type the text in the box and click OK.
Append signature to message		Your signature is added to all messages you send. You can delete it when composing a message.
Leave mail on server		Messages stay on the Hotmail server until you delete them.
Change configuration settings	Options (link to the right of Address Book tab)	Choose links in the Mail Handling and Additional Options columns to configure your e-mail account.

Table 6-7.   *Basic Hotmail Commands* (continued)

You can sort the messages in your inbox (or any folder) by sender, subject, date, or size: click the From, Subject, Date, or Size column heading. Click Options (to the right of the Address Book tab), and then Mail Display Settings (in the Additional Options column) to set the number of messages per web page and other display options.

Configuring Hotmail to Display Mail from Other Accounts

You can also use Hotmail to access other e-mail mailboxes. When you are on the road without a computer, you can configure your Hotmail account so that you can check your e-mail from any computer with a web browser, via the Hotmail web site. You can configure Hotmail to display mail from up to five mail accounts.

Note	*Hotmail can access POP mailboxes, but not IMAP mailboxes.*

To tell Hotmail about your other e-mail accounts, click the Options link to the right of the Address Book tab. Click the POP Mail Retrieval Settings link in the Additional

Options column. Then type your POP server (incoming mail server), user name, and password, and click OK at the bottom of the page. You can also choose an indicator (icon) for the account, so that mail coming through this account appears with a color-coded icon in your inbox. If you want to look at the messages in your POP mailbox without deleting the messages (so that you can retrieve them later with your regular e-mail program), select the Leave Messages On POP Server check box.

The
Complete
Reference

Chapter 7

Sending and Receiving Files by E-mail

Attaching files to an e-mail message is the easiest way to exchange files with someone—assuming that you don't both have access to the same hard drive over a local area network (LAN). Sending files via e-mail is quicker and cheaper than shipping floppy disks, Zip disks, or CDs, and it enables you to send files that might not fit on one floppy disk. By attaching files to an e-mail message, you can do such things as exchange documents for revision, pass on spreadsheets for data entry, or send a presentation for review. Of course, you can also attach electronic pictures, sounds, movies, or anything else that can be stored in a file.

This chapter contains general information about e-mail attachments, followed by specific instructions for the most popular e-mail programs. For information about what to do with files that you receive, including how to uncompress ZIP files and how to protect your computer from viruses, see Chapter 34. See Chapter 5 for information about the e-mail programs and web-based e-mail accounts described here.

 If the file that you want to send contains only text, you can avoid attaching the file entirely. Instead, you can use cut-and-paste to copy the text into the body of your message. Depending on which word processing program you are copying from and which e-mail program you use, the text may arrive in your message with formatting intact.

General Information About Attachments

The Internet e-mail system was designed to transmit only text and thus can't handle *binary* (nontext) files such as graphics, audio, and programs. An *attachment* is a file that has been encoded as text so that it can be included in an e-mail message. The following are the three common ways to encode e-mail attachments:

- **MIME**   Multipurpose Internet Mail Extension is the standard method.
- **Uuencoding**   This is the old standard, and the only method supported by some older e-mail applications.
- **BinHex**   This is used by some Mac e-mail programs.

You usually don't need to know what type of encoding you're using because your e-mail application takes care of encoding and decoding messages. However, if you have trouble exchanging attachments with someone else, you may want to find out what type of encoding their e-mail application supports and make sure that you are using the same method. Try MIME first—it's the most commonly used encoding method.

Sending Attachments

To send a file by e-mail, you create a message to which you can attach the file. Address the message as usual and type a subject. You can also type text in the body of the message. Then attach the file by choosing a menu command or by clicking a toolbar button (depending on which e-mail program you use). Some e-mail applications support dragging-and-dropping the file that you want to attach—drag it from Windows Explorer or a folder window to the open message.

You may have to rearrange windows so that you can see both the folder window and the message window. You can also drag a file to the taskbar button for the message and hold it there until the message window opens.

Some mail systems choke on large files, so you may need to compress them (using a program such as WinZip or ZipMagic, as described in Chapter 34) before sending them as an attachment. Sending and downloading large attachments can take a while, so you'll save both yourself and the recipient time if you make the file smaller by compressing it. Before you "zip" a file, make sure that your recipient has the software and the know-how to unzip it.

Before you send an attachment with an e-mail message, consider these guidelines:

- Determine whether the person receiving the attachment has an e-mail program that can receive the file, and whether the person has the correct application needed to open or view the file. If necessary, send a message first (without the attachment) to ask.

- When you send a file, type an explanation in the body of the message to tell the recipient why you are sending the attachment and what it is.

- Send only solicited attachments. This advice applies to mail in general, but it certainly goes for attachments, which can fill up a hard drive and take time to download.

- Don't send attachments to newsgroups and mailing lists unless the newsgroup or mailing list explicitly encourages attachments (for example, in a newsgroup for people exchanging pictures of fractals).

If you have trouble sending or receiving attachments (which may happen with a particular recipient), you may want to use File Transfer Protocol (FTP) instead. Find an FTP site that you can both access, and upload your file to the FTP site, so that your recipient can then download it. FTP is covered in detail in Chapter 33.

Receiving Attachments

Different e-mail applications handle attachments differently. Most store the attachment in the mail message. You need to open the message and then open or save the attachment before you can do anything else with it. When you delete a message with an attachment stored with it, you also delete the attachment. To be able to use the attachment later, you need to save the attachment.

Other applications (notably Eudora) automatically save the attachment to a folder that you specify. If you are using one of these applications, you don't even need to open the message to use the attachment—you can open the attachment right from the folder where it is saved. You can choose whether deleting a message also deletes the files that were attached to that message.

Save attachments that you need rather than saving them with the message. Most people delete e-mail messages with abandon and may accidentally delete a message with a needed attachment. If you are done with an attachment, delete it to save disk space.

Outlook 2002 and Outlook Express

Outlook 2002 and Outlook Express 6 can handle MIME and uuencoded attachments. The commands for sending and receiving attachments differ slightly between Outlook 2002 and Outlook Express. Both programs also have a mechanism, called *linking files,* for sending files to other people on your local area network.

Sending an Attached File

The easiest way to attach a file to a message is to open a new message and drag the file to the message window. If you prefer to use a dialog box, open a new message and click the Insert File button on the message window toolbar (it looks like a paper clip) to display the Insert File dialog box. Alternatively, choose Insert | File (in Outlook 2002) or Insert | File Attachment (in Outlook Express) to display the Insert File dialog box. Double-click the file that you want to attach to the message and send the message as usual.

Linking a File (for LAN Users Only)

An alternative to sending a file with a message is to *link* the file to the message. A linked message is not included in the message, so it doesn't take up hard disk space. Instead, double-clicking the icon for a linked file opens a file in a specified location. Linking is useful when you are sending a large file to a number of people, but it only works when all the recipients have access to a network drive or some other shared resource where you can store the file that you want them to have. In this case, linking a file is more efficient than attaching a file. However, linking doesn't work for sending files over the Internet.

To link a file, follow the steps for attaching a file. On the Insert File dialog box, click the Make a Shortcut To This File button. This options works only if you have the proper access permissions for the file or folder and if your LAN allows this function.

Receiving an Attached File

When you receive a message with an attachment, the message information appears with a paper-clip icon. To access the attachment, open the message. In both versions of Outlook, attachments appear in the last line of the message header as icons. Open the attachment by double-clicking the icon for the attached file in the message. To save the attachment without opening it, right-click the icon and choose Save As from the shortcut menu. Edit the file and folder names, if necessary, and click OK. Alternatively, you can save the file after you open it, by using the program that opened the file.

Caution   *Because Outlook 2002 and Outlook Express store attachments with the messages to which they are attached, deleting the message also deletes the attachment unless you have saved it in a separate file.*

Attachment Options

By default, Outlook 2002 and Outlook Express use MIME when sending attachments. If you need to send a uuencoded attachment, or need to be sure which kind of attachment you're sending, you can check the program's attachment options.

In Outlook 2002, follow these steps:

1. Choose Tools | Options to display the Options dialog box.
2. Click the Mail Format tab.
3. Click the Internet Format button.
4. Look at the last check box, Encode Attachments In UUENCODE Format When Sending A Plain Text Message. If it's selected, then attachments to text messages are uuencoded, and attachments to formatted messages are MIME. If it isn't selected, all attachments use MIME.

In Outlook Express, follow these steps:

1. Choose Tools | Options to display the Options dialog box.
2. Click the Send tab. Your Mail Sending Format should normally be set to Plain Text, so that recipients whose e-mail applications do not support HTML can easily read your message.
3. Click the Settings button next to the Plain Text option to see the Plain Text Options dialog box. The encoding method is set in the Message Format section of the dialog box.

Eudora

Eudora Version 5.1 handles all three kinds of attachments.

Sending an Attached File

You can attach a file to a message by using drag-and-drop (dragging a file from Windows Explorer or a folder window to the Eudora message window), by clicking the Attach File button on the toolbar, or by pressing CTRL-H. Choose the type of encoding on the toolbar (the third drop-down list)—MIME is the default choice and should work most of the time.

Tip   *If you click the Attach File button or press CTRL-H, Eudora creates a blank e-mail message and opens the Attach File dialog box in one step.*

Receiving an Attached File

When a message has an attachment, the filenames appear at the bottom of the message, as shown in Figure 7-1.

When Eudora downloads messages, it puts any attachments in the folder that you specify in the Options dialog box (see the next section). To find out where the file is, open the message and position the cursor over the filename. Eudora displays the path and filename on the status line (at the bottom of the Eudora window). You can right-click the filename to open it, save it, copy it, or delete it.

The easiest way to open an attachment is to click the file icon in the message. You can open the file even if you see a message telling you that the attachment may have executable content; this message gives you a chance to not open a file that may be infected with a virus. Once you know where the file is, you may prefer to open it another way, such as from Windows Explorer or from the application that you'll use to read the file.

When you decide to keep an attachment, move the file out of your attachments folder into a more appropriate folder. Periodically delete files from the attachments directory so that you don't fill up your hard drive. Be sure to delete any executable files you receive from strangers because they may contain viruses.

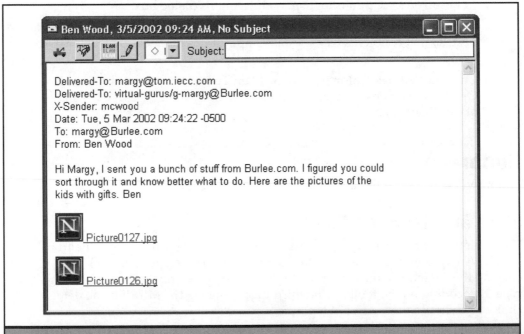

Figure 7-1. *Eudora displays the filenames when a message contains attachments.*

Attachment Options

Choose Tools | Options and then click the Attachments icon to see options for sending and receiving attachments (see Figure 7-2). These options include the default encoding method to use when sending attachments and the folder in which Eudora stores incoming attachments. You can also choose to delete attachments automatically when you delete the message to which they were attached.

Netscape Messenger and Netscape Mail

Netscape Messenger (which comes with the Netscape Communicator 4.*x* suite of programs) and Netscape Mail (or more properly, Netscape Mail & Newsgroups, which comes with Netscape 6) use MIME encoding for attachments. This section describes Netscape Messenger 4.7 and Netscape Mail 6.2.

Sending an Attached File

As with many other e-mail programs, the easiest way to attach a file to a Netscape Messenger or Netscape Mail message is to open a new message and drag the file to the message window. However, in Netscape Mail, you need to drag the message to the Attachments box that appears to the right of the addressing information. (If you drag a

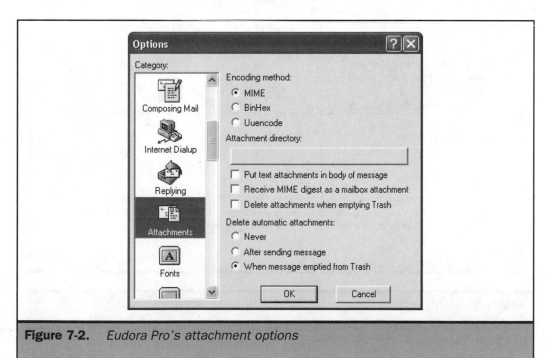

Figure 7-2.   *Eudora Pro's attachment options*

file to the message area of a message window, you create a web link to the file, which may be useful if the recipient has access to that location.) In Netscape Messenger, drag the file to the headers section of the Composition window.

If you prefer to use a dialog box in Netscape Mail, open a new message and click the Attach button on the message window toolbar (it looks like a paper clip) to display the Enter File To Attach dialog box. In Netscape Messenger, click the Attach button on the Composition window toolbar and choose File from the menu that appears.

Receiving an Attached File

Netscape shows which messages have attachments, but the indicator is hard to see: the message icon, which usually looks like an envelope, has a small paper-clip icon on it. To view the attachment, first open the message. Attachment information appears as shown in Figure 7-3: icons for the attachments appear in the Attachments box at the upper right.

To open or save an attached file, double-click the icon. You see a dialog box asking whether you want to open or save the file.

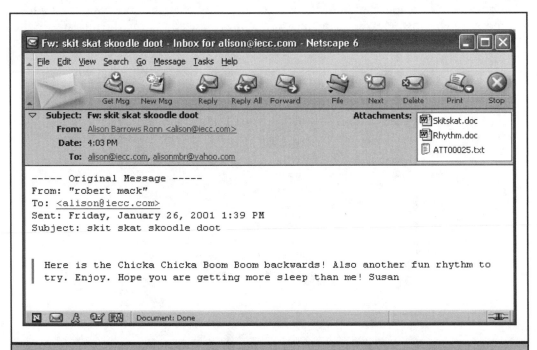

Figure 7-3. Attachments are listed in the Attachments box next to the message headers.

America Online (AOL)

AOL sends and receives MIME attachments. This section describes AOL 7.

Sending an Attached File

To attach a file to a message, click the Attachments button at the bottom of the Write Mail window. AOL displays the Attachments dialog box. Click the Attach button to choose a file. Select the file and click Open. Click OK to return to the Write Mail window.

Receiving an Attached File

AOL gives you a very subtle indication that a message has an attachment: the message icon appears as an envelope with a disk behind it rather than as a simple envelope. When you open the message, you see the Download button at the bottom of the message window (shown in Figure 7-4). Click the Download button to see the Download Now and Download Later options. Choose Download Now to save the file to the folder that you select; the Download Manager window lets you choose where to save the file. Click Save to begin downloading, and then click OK when AOL informs you that the file has arrived.

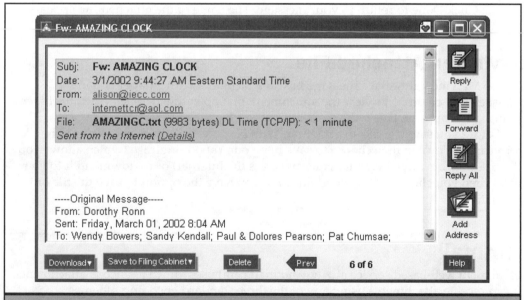

Figure 7-4. *Click Download in AOL's message window to download an attached file.*

If you are working offline or you'd rather not download the attached file now, click Download and choose the Download Later option to add the file to the Download Manager. When you close AOL, you will be prompted to download files in the Download Manager.

Yahoo Mail

Yahoo Mail (a web-based service at **mail.yahoo.com**) uses MIME encoding for attachments. It can receive attachments using any of the three standard encoding schemes.

Sending an Attached File

To attach a file to a Yahoo Mail message, start at the **mail.yahoo.com** web site, and log in with your Yahoo ID and password. Click Compose to start a message, and click the Add/Delete Attachments link below the message box. You'll see a window with three steps to attach a file:

1. Click the Browse button to find the file you want to attach.

2. Click Attach File to attach the file to the message. The file appears in the small table, as shown in Figure 7-5.

3. Click Done to return to your message. The name of the attached file appears next to the Attached heading below the message box.

Receiving an Attached File

Yahoo Mail indicates that a message has an attachment with a paper clip in the message size column. To view the attachment, first open the message. The attachment information appears below the message text in a big box.

Before you save the file, use the Scan With Norton AntiVirus link to check the file for viruses. You can then choose to save it to your Yahoo Briefcase (which allows you to access it from anywhere that you can access the Internet) or to download it to your PC. When you click the Download File link, you have the option to save the file or to open it.

Hotmail

Hotmail (a web-based service at **www.hotmail.com**) uses MIME to encode attachments. It can receive attachments using any of the three standard encoding schemes.

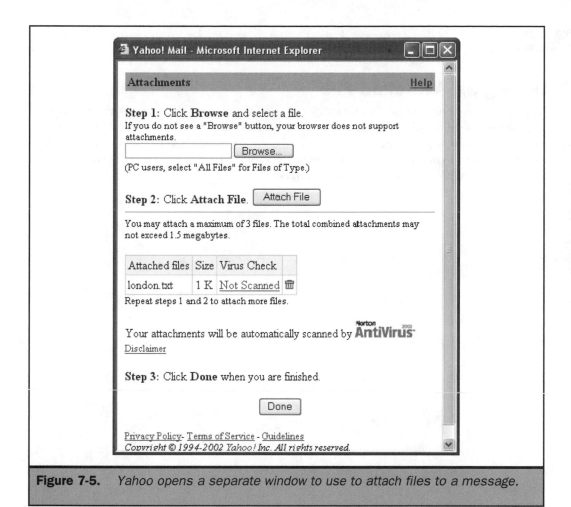

Figure 7-5.   *Yahoo opens a separate window to use to attach files to a message.*

Sending an Attached File

To attach a file to a Hotmail message, start at the **www.hotmail.com** web site, and log in with your Hotmail user name and password. Click Compose to start a message, and click the Add/Edit Attachments button. Then click the Browse button to find the file you want to attach. Click the Attach button. The filename appears in the Attachments box. Click OK.

If you need to send large attachments, you may need to sign up and pay for a Hotmail account with high limits for file transfer and storage.

Receiving an Attached File

You can tell when an incoming message contains an attachment because an envelope appears to the left of the sender's name on the list of your new messages. When you open the message, the filename appears on the Attachments line in the headers. Click the filename to download it to your computer; Hotmail scans the file for viruses and displays a Download File button for you to click.

Internet

Chapter 8

Fighting Spam, Sorting Mail, and Avoiding E-mail Viruses

Although e-mail provides a wonderful new means of communication for many people, it also provides an additional distraction in busy lives. E-mail may be an integral part of your day, but you may also find that you spend far too much time sorting through your messages. Some of that e-mail overload may be from mailing lists that you've signed up for, some may be humor forwarded by friends, and some may be unsolicited offers from people you've never heard of—*spam*. *Filtering*, sorting your mail into various mailboxes or folders as it arrives, can alleviate all of these problems, including throwing away unwanted e-mail.

This chapter discusses spam—why you get it, how to avoid it, and what to do when you do get it. We also explain filtering and the steps that are required to set up filtering in Outlook Express, Outlook, Eudora, Netscape Mail, Messenger, America Online, Yahoo Mail, and Hotmail. For more information about these programs, see Chapter 6.

Another danger of e-mail is that an e-mail-borne virus will infect your computer. This chapter also suggests ways to configure your e-mail program to minimize the risk of catching a virus from an e-mail message.

Controlling E-mail Volume and Reducing Spam

Spam is the term that Internet users apply to *unsolicited commercial e-mail (UCE)* or *unsolicited bulk e-mail (UBE)*. You receive spam because the sender has obtained your e-mail address, either from a mailing list or newsgroup or directly from you on a web site. Your address may be in one or more of the lists of e-mail addresses that are available for sale. If you use a large mail provider like Hotmail, AOL, Yahoo, or EarthLink, you may also get spam from *dictionary attacks* in which spammers try to guess user e-mail addresses—spammers don't care if they send out messages to 99 nonexistent addresses if one message gets to a valid address.

 To avoid getting spam from dictionary attacks, choose an unusual user name when you set up an e-mail mailbox. Pick a longish user name, and don't just pad it out with numbers; for example, use ArnoldRnld, not Arnold145.

What Can You Do About Spam?

Once spam starts landing in your inbox, it's hard to stop the flood. The best thing to do is to limit who can find your e-mail address before they have it. The following are a few ways to prevent spammers from getting your primary e-mail address:

■ Set up several e-mail accounts and use them selectively. (AOL lets you do this easily, and free e-mail services are another way to get alternate e-mail addresses.) For instance, have a separate e-mail address that you use when you join a mailing list and when you fill out forms on web sites. Separate addresses allow you to filter messages easily.

■ Some ISPs permit you to have several addresses like **joe-thislist@example.com** and **joe-thatlist@example.com** (if your address is **joe@example.com**). If your ISP allows this, you can use these addresses to track how spammers got your address.

■ If you type your e-mail address in a web form, look carefully for an option to opt out of mailings. Many "opt in" mailing lists claim to include only people who signed up to receive ads by mail, but actually contain people who didn't notice a tiny check box on a form they filled out.

■ Consider an e-mail account with an ISP that uses a mail filtering service such as Brightmail or Postini. These services filter out spam before it gets to your inbox. You can't sign up for these spam-filtering services directly; your ISP must subscribe to them.

■ Don't answer messages that look as though they were sent by mistake—they may be a way to find valid e-mail addresses for spamming. Once you reply, you let the senders know that they have found a valid address.

■ Don't bother "unsubscribing" from any service that sends you messages unless you originally subscribed to the service. Rather than taking your name off the list, the senders may keep you on the list. In fact, your e-mail address becomes more valuable to spammers when they receive a removal request from you because you've just confirmed that your e-mail address is valid. Exceptions are messages from mailing lists to which you actually subscribed or messages from organizations from which you specifically requested information or ordered products.

Once spam lands in your inbox, you need to deal with it. Here are some options:

■ Use the DELETE key often. This is our number one tip for spam control—once spam lands in your inbox, just delete it. In fact, this may be the most efficient way to deal with spam. Don't spend time on messages that you're not interested in. You don't actually have to open every e-mail that lands in your inbox—you can usually identify spam from the subject line.

■ Create filters that automatically delete spam messages. (Make sure that your filter matches only spam because you'll never see these messages!) Look at the headers and contents of the spam you receive to identify domains or other identifying features used only by spammers. You won't be able to block all spam this way, but you can reduce the amount that lands in your inbox.

■ Unless your friends or colleagues use the Bcc (blind carbon copy) header, automatically delete messages that contain your address on the Bcc line because this technique is frequently used by spammers.

EXCHANGING E-MAIL

Don't contribute to the spam problem by forwarding unwanted messages or by sending your own messages to many recipients. If you pass along messages regularly, periodically check whether the recipients on your list still want to receive your messages. Never pass on warnings to lists of people—they are rarely true, and everyone has usually already received ten copies from other people anyway. If you must, be sure to check that warnings are legitimate first at one of the many sites that lists hoaxes (such as www.snopes.com).

Stopping Spammers

You can do several things to reduce spam, but none of them is completely effective. If you feel strongly about spam, you may want to spend time researching where it comes from and sending messages to the appropriate system administrators. If you complain to the sender's system administrator or postmaster, he or she may close the spammer's account. Be aware, though, that not all system administrators care that their domain is being used to send spam.

If you want to get more involved, many web sites are available that discuss spam and what to do about it. Start with these sites:

- **www.cauce.org**   Coalition Against Unsolicited Commercial E-Mail (CAUCE).
- **www.abuse.net**   Network Abuse Clearinghouse.
- **spam.abuse.net**   Promote Responsible Net Commerce.
- **www.spamcop.net**   Spamcop helps you report spam to the appropriate ISP.
- **www.spamcon.org**   Spamcon Foundation.

Reporting Scams

If you are the victim of an e-mail scam and you are in the United States, file a complaint with the Federal Trade Commission (FTC). The FTC is a government agency whose purpose includes the following:

The Commission works to enhance the smooth operation of the marketplace by eliminating acts or practices that are unfair or deceptive. In general, the Commission's efforts are directed toward stopping actions that threaten consumers' opportunities to exercise informed choice.

Report scams that appear illegal (such as pyramid schemes, not just annoying e-mail) by using the complaint form that you can find at **www.ftc.gov** (click File A Complaint Online). Alternatively, forward the messages to **uce@ftc.gov**; this address collects spam statistics. They've already amassed a database of 8.5 million spam messages and take in an additional 10,000 each day. The FTC is also happy to get copies of all your spam at **uce@ftc.gov**, although they won't do anything with it immediately.

Avoiding Sending Spam

If you have a business, you may want to advertise your wares on the Internet. Bulk e-mail packages are available that make it very easy to send an e-mail to hundreds or thousands of people. You may find the ability to so easily access so many people very tempting, but sending mail of this type, which is unsolicited bulk e-mail, has its problems. The most important issues relating to unsolicited bulk e-mail are that it is not well received, and it may result in your ISP fining you or closing your account.

Renting a mailing list and sending unsolicited e-mail to thousands of unsuspecting users doesn't work, ruins the reputation of your company, and may cost you in fines, a lost Internet account, or legal problems. Don't do it!

Defining E-mail Abuse

Most people on the Internet believe that sending bulk unsolicited e-mail messages, even those that are basically advertisements similar to those that are delivered to you through the U.S. Postal Service, is abuse of the e-mail system. Bulk e-mail seems to be identical to bulk postal mail, but there is one important difference—when you send postal mail, you pay for the service; when you send bulk e-mail, the people who own the servers that handle the mail you send pay for the service.

Although much e-mail is unsolicited, unsolicited e-mail is not in itself abuse of the system. However, sending unsolicited mail to numerous people or sending numerous unsolicited mail messages to one address is considered to be abuse.

People may solicit e-mail, either knowingly or unknowingly, if they do any of the following:

- Subscribe to a mailing list
- Request information or opinions from a mailing list or newsgroup
- Send e-mail to an address to get more information
- Provide an e-mail address on a web site that explicitly states that the address will be used to send you information

You are not necessarily soliciting e-mail simply by providing your e-mail address to someone else, whether it is via a personal note, chat, message board, newsgroup, mailing list, or purchase of a product.

What Are the Legal Issues?

Currently, no federal law bans unsolicited e-mail. In fact, many people are concerned that laws prohibiting "junk" e-mail could negatively affect free speech and the free flow of information on the Internet. However, other laws may apply, and other factors may dampen your enthusiasm about sending bulk mail:

- Your ISP almost certainly prohibits sending unsolicited bulk e-mail; in the United States, all ISPs do because they all depend on a small number of backbones, all of which have no-UBE policies. If you send UBE, you will certainly be warned, and most likely have your account canceled with a charge for the ISP's cleanup costs. Most e-mail headers contain information that allows ISPs to trace your message back to your account, even if you forge the From and Reply-To addresses.

- Some laws already apply to e-mail. For instance, if you send e-mail that meets the legal definition of harassment, you could be sued under harassment laws. A few states prohibit UBCE (that is, commercial UBE) altogether. See **www.spamlaws.com** for the status of anti-spam laws in your state.

- Some states have a "truth in headers" law that makes it illegal to forge header information in an e-mail, such as who the message is from. Fraudulent e-mail offers are within the jurisdiction of the Federal Trade Commission.

- Many spammers don't include their real return address, so that they don't receive bounced messages from bad e-mail addresses to which they send spam. As a result, the holder of the return address that the spammer inserted (or the postmaster of that domain) ends up receiving hundreds or thousands of bounced messages—along with messages of complaint—for messages sent by someone else. Legislation has been proposed that prohibits sending spam using a fraudulent return address.

When Bulk Mail Isn't Spam

Not all bulk mail is spam, however. If you write a newsletter and ask people to subscribe, e-mailing your newsletter to your subscribers isn't spam. In fact, e-mail newsletters can be a very effective way to market products to your existing customers and to get the word out to members of organizations. Just make sure that the recipients signed up to receive what you are sending and that you provide a clear method for subscribers to remove themselves.

 *The authors of this book publish e-mail newsletters on a number of Internet-related topics; visit the Internet Gurus web site at **net.gurus.com** to subscribe.*

The Advantages of Filtering E-mail

Filtering is not always a surefire way to get rid of unwanted mail, but it can help. All the major e-mail packages allow you to filter incoming messages—if yours doesn't, you might want to find one that does, especially if you have a high volume of e-mail.

How Filtering Works

When you set up a filter in your e-mail program, the program moves messages from your inbox to a designated folder as soon they are received. This process enables you to focus on the mail in your inbox when time is tight and to leave the filtered mail in other folders for when you have more time. Alternatively, you may choose to target high-priority e-mail and filter it into another folder, which you attend to first.

Filtering works by looking at the contents of the message. Normally, you tell your e-mail application to look at the contents of the message and to do something with the message based on what it finds. You may choose to look at the headers, such as who the message is to or from, or what the subject line is. Alternatively, you may want to look at specific words in the message. For instance, you may want to filter all messages written to a particular mailing list and have them stored in a folder that you've created for that mailing list. In addition, you may want to create another filter that moves to a Humor folder all mail from friends who pass along jokes that they've heard. You could even ask your friends to put the word "humor" on the subject line, so that you can easily filter the messages and not miss any personal notes.

To filter mail, you need to create some criterion or rule—if the message matches the criterion or rule, then the e-mail application does whatever you specify with the message. It may put it in a folder, flag it in some way, or delete it. What a filter can do with a message depends on the application, but all applications that support filters can at least put the message in a folder that you specify.

Devising a rule to sort messages that always come from the same place or that are always addressed to the same address usually is easy. For instance, you can easily sort messages from a mailing list or from a small group of people (say, the eight colleagues working with you on a particular project). However, sorting junk mail (unsolicited marketing messages) out of your inbox is considerably more difficult because you have to devise a rule that sorts only junk mail and not the mail that you actually want to read.

Filtering Mailing List Messages

The usual way to sort messages sent from a mailing list is to use the "To" address. Because messages sent to a mailing list are always sent to the same e-mail address, you can use that address to define your criteria. For instance, if the address for the mailing list is **click-L@ListService.net**, you can specify that all mail you receive that has **click-L@ListService.net** in the To line should be moved to a folder that you've created to hold mail from that mailing list.

Filtering Spam

Unfortunately, spam doesn't come from easily identifiable addresses or come tagged with a "spam" keyword in their subject lines. However, filtering messages that include sexual body parts and phrases like "Accept Credit Cards" or "Lose Weight" catches a fair amount of spam. You can filter messages directly into your Trash folder, or you can filter it into a Spam or Bulk Mail folder that you can scan through by eye from time to time, to make sure that no personal messages were caught by mistake.

We recommend that you save your spam for a couple of days and then create filters based on sender addresses or subject lines that the spam has in common. Here are some ideas for identifying spam using filters:

- **Identifying spam by addresses in the headers**   Some domains are used as From or Reply-to addresses by spammers, including **public.com**, **listme.com**, and **uplinkpro.com**. (The owners of these domains aren't necessarily to blame—spammers may forge these addresses.) "Friend@" is unlikely to be part of the address of anyone you know. Look for addresses (or parts of addresses) that frequently appear in the headers of spam you receive, and filter messages that contain these addresses into the trash.

Note   *Identifying spam by address doesn't work as well as it used to because spammers have gotten more sophisticated about hiding their addresses and usually make up a new address for each spam attack. Some spam is even sent with the recipient's address on the From line.*

- **Identifying spam by subject**   We trash messages with subject lines that contain body part names, drug names, "adult webcam," "best cartridge prices," "stealth mass mailer," "stop losing sales," "accept all major credit cards," "get out of debt," "financial security," "home based business opportunities," and "free credit report." Make up your own list based on the spam you receive.

Replying to Messages Automatically with Mailbots

An *autoreply* or *mailbot* is an automatic response to an e-mail. An autoreply may save you the time of sending a personal e-mail, or it may let the sender know why you aren't responding, and thus save you from receiving additional messages from that sender. Depending on the package that you use, you may be able to send autoreply messages that meet certain criteria, or you may have to send an autoreply to all received messages. If you can't choose which messages to autoreply to, then the feature is useful only if you are going to be out of the office or in some other situation in which you want to reply with the same message to everyone who sends you an e-mail.

You can configure Eudora to send replies automatically by creating a filter that identifies the messages to which you want to reply and that triggers the "action" of replying with a predefined stationery file (form letter). Outlook Express works the same way: you create a rule that matches the messages to which you want to reply and store your form letter reply as an EML file. If you use Outlook with Exchange (usually in an office setting), you can send autoreplies and use filters to send responses to messages that meet criteria you set. If you use Outlook at home and don't use Exchange, this function isn't available. Netscape Mail and Netscape Navigator don't include a feature to do autoreplies. Yahoo Mail includes a Vacation Response feature, which can autoreply to messages from specific domains. Many domains host autoreply messages for their mailboxes.

A word of warning: A mailbot can get into an endless loop if it replies to another mailbot, and the mailboxes of everyone involved can fill up quickly with megabytes of garbage. Use autoreply features with caution. Besides, we find it annoying to receive multiple "Joe is out of the office until the 16th" messages, especially when they are triggered by postings to a mailing list that Joe is on.

Virus Security Issues

Originally, e-mail couldn't carry viruses because it contained only plain text, not executable programs. However, once people developed ways to attach files to e-mail and to format messages with HTML, e-mail became the most common way for viruses to spread. See the sections on avoiding viruses in Chapters 1 and 5 for information about e-mail-borne viruses.

Because Outlook (which comes with Microsoft Office) and Outlook Express (which comes with Windows) are so widely used, they are the targets of most e-mail-borne viruses. (That's why we prefer to use another e-mail program—Eudora.) If you use Outlook or Outlook Express, be sure to install all of Microsoft's security patches. Here's where to find them:

- Starting at Microsoft's Product Support Center FAQs page (**support.microsoft.com/ faqs**), choose the version of Outlook or Outlook Express that you use, and look for articles about security issues.

- For critical updates to Outlook Express (and Internet Explorer, with which it is bundled), you can also start at **www.microsoft.com/windows/ie/downloads/ critical**.

- If you use Outlook (which is part of Microsoft Office), be sure to install Microsoft's Service Pack updates, which are at **support.microsoft.com/highlights/ offxpset.asp**.

- If you use Office XP, download the Service Pack 1 update from **office .microsoft.com/downloads/2002/oxpsp1.aspx**.

You may also want to learn about the virus-protection features of these programs because they may occasionally get in the way of sending or receiving files—we describe them in the sections "Configuring Outlook 2002 Against Viruses" and "Configuring Outlook Express Against Viruses" later in this chapter. Because e-mail messages can contain HTML formatting (that is, the same codes that appear in web pages), take a look at Chapter 20 to learn more about the security threats that can arrive in e-mail.

Other e-mail programs can catch and spread viruses, too. See the sections "Avoiding Viruses with Eudora" and "Avoiding Viruses with Netscape Mail and Netscape Messenger" later in this chapter. Some web-based e-mail systems, including Yahoo Mail and Hotmail, offer free virus-scanning for files you download—a great service.

Filtering Mail, Deleting Spam, and Defending Against Viruses in Outlook 2002

Outlook 2002 comes with Office XP and includes sophisticated filtering features. You create a filter by using the Rules Wizard. In addition to regular filters, Outlook also has a feature to find and filter junk e-mail. (See the following section for information about Outlook Express.)

Filtering Messages in Outlook 2002

Before you create filters, make the folders into which you want to sort your messages. To create a folder, select the folder in which you want the new folder to be stored. Then choose File | Folder | New Folder or press CTRL-SHIFT-E.

To create a filter, use Outlook's Rules Wizard. Start it by displaying any mail folder and choosing Tools | Rules Wizard from the menu. The Rules Wizard lists all the rules that you currently have defined. You can turn off a rule by clicking it to remove the check mark.

The easiest way to create a new rule is to find a message that meets your criteria and to create a new rule based on that message. Here's how to do it:

1. Open the message.

2. Choose Actions | Create Rule from the message window menu to see the Rules Wizard. Answer its questions and click Next to move from screen to screen.

3. Select the aspect(s) of the message that you want to use to create the rule. For instance, you may want to filter all messages from this person or to this distribution list. Click the box next to your selection(s) so that a check mark appears. The selection(s) appears in the Rule Description box at the bottom of the dialog box.

4. You can edit the underlined text of any rules that you selected in the last step by clicking the text.

5. Next, the Rules Wizard asks you what you want to do with the messages that the rule finds. Frequently, you'll want to move the message to a specific folder—to do so, select the first option, Move It To The Inbox Folder, and then edit the folder name. You can select more than one option.

6. Edit any underlined text, as necessary. For instance, you may want to edit the name of the folder to which the message is sent or copied. When you click a folder name to edit it, Outlook displays a list of existing folders—you can pick from the list or create a new folder.

7. Next, the wizard allows you to select exceptions to the rule.

8. The last step asks you to name the rule and gives you a last chance to make changes to the rule that you've defined. You can change any of the underlined items by clicking them, as shown here:

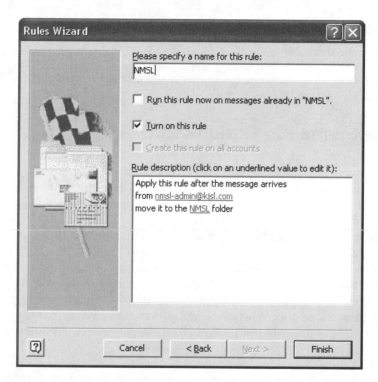

9. Click Finish when you are done.

After you create a rule, you can turn it off or edit it from the Rules Wizard dialog box. To create a new rule from scratch, display the Rules Wizard by choosing Tools | Rules Wizard and click the New button on the Rules Wizard dialog box. The Rules Wizard guides you through the process of defining the following aspects of a filter:

- **The type of rule that you want to create**   If you choose to create a rule based on a template (which we recommend), you see a list of types of filters. Most of these choices have to do with the type of message that the filter is examining and what the filter does with the message. Move New Messages From Someone is useful for sorting mailing-list mail or mail from a particular person. Move

Messages Based On Content is useful if you are looking at the content of the message rather than the message header. If you choose to start from a blank rule, you see only two choices: Check Messages When They Arrive and Check Messages After Sending.

- **The conditions that the message has to meet to be filtered** For instance, you may want to filter all messages that list you on the Bcc line or all messages sent to a particular distribution list.

- **What you want to do with the message** For example, move it to a specified folder or delete it.

- **Any exceptions to the filtering rule**

- **A name for the filter**

You can click any underlined text—names and folders, for instance—in the filter to edit it.

Deleting Junk E-mail in Outlook 2002

Outlook has a special "junk mail" feature that you can turn on. This feature looks for messages with words and phrases that are commonly used in junk mail, and messages from domains that are known for sending junk mail. A description of the filters included in the junk mail feature can be found in a file called Filters.txt, which is usually stored in the C:\Program Files\Microsoft Office\Office folder.

To turn on the Junk E-mail feature, click the Organize button that is on the toolbar when a mail folder is active or choose Tools | Organize. You see the Ways To Organize Inbox pane. Click the Junk E-mail tab to see the options shown in Figure 8-1.

The Junk E-Mail tab contains two options, one for junk messages and one for adult content messages. You can turn on or off these features by clicking the button next to the text describing the option. When these options are selected, messages identified as junk or adult content appear in your Inbox in a different color, enabling you to delete them quickly.

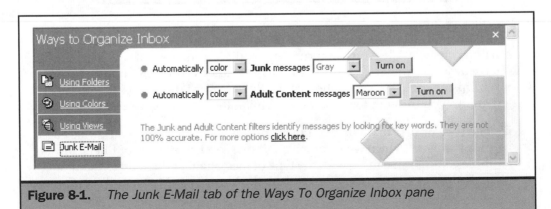

Figure 8-1. *The Junk E-Mail tab of the Ways To Organize Inbox pane*

Remember that filters like this are never foolproof, so you should at least scan the message information before deleting it, to make sure that it is indeed a message that you want to delete. If you choose to move junk mail to another folder, scan the contents of the folder once in a while to check for messages moved there mistakenly. You can access more options related to junk e-mail by clicking the Click Here link at the bottom of the panel.

You can add to the addresses identified as junk or adult content mail by following these steps:

1. When you receive a message that you wish Outlook had identified as junk or adult content, right-click the message information in the folder.

2. Choose Junk E-Mail from the menu that appears.

3. Choose either Add To Junk Senders List or Add To Adult Content Senders List.

Configuring Outlook 2002 Against Viruses

To change the Security settings in Outlook 2002, choose Tools | Options and click the Security tab, shown in Figure 8-2. In the Secure Content section, set the Zone to the Restricted Sites option, and click the Zone Settings button. By restricting what sites

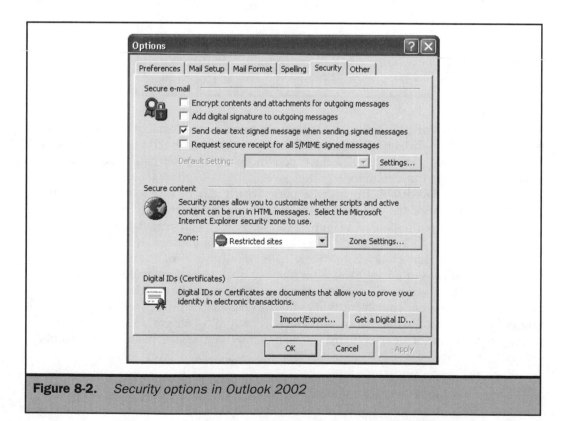

Figure 8-2.   *Security options in Outlook 2002*

can run scripts, you stop e-mail messages from unknown senders from running some viruses on your computer.

The second precaution you can take is to limit the ability of macros to run in Outlook. Choose Tools | Macros | Security to display the Security dialog box:

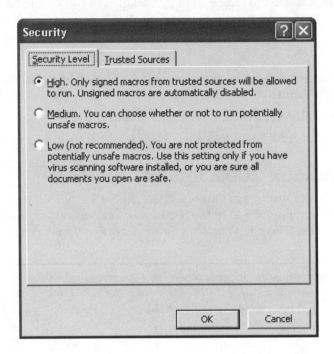

The default Security Level setting is High, but you may select any setting that feels safe to you. If you work on a local area network and have access to the Internet, using the Low setting should be fine, as long as you know where your mail comes from. Otherwise, use Medium or High.

The last step is to disable the preview pane, which may be able to execute certain scripts that are embedded in e-mail messages. (Microsoft has tried to disable scripts from running in the preview pane, but we can't predict whether malicious hackers will come up with a way.) You must disable the preview pane manually for each mailbox. To disable the preview pane, choose View | Preview Pane item. The pane disappears.

Based on Microsoft's less-than-stellar security track record, no matter how deeply you go to disable "features" in Microsoft software, someone, somewhere will find another way to bypass your security measures. A true and abiding sense of security comes from knowing what to look for, not taking anything for granted, and ongoing diligence. You cannot let your guard down, or something nasty can and will eventually slip in. Don't become a conspiracy-believing, tinfoil hat-wearing, alien ship–watching nutcase—just be savvy.

Filtering Mail, Deleting Spam, and Defending Against Viruses in Outlook Express

Like Outlook 2002, Outlook Express also has filtering, although it doesn't support the complex criteria that Outlook supports. You can delete spam by creating filters that identify spam messages and filter them into your Trash folder. Then choose File | Folder | New Folder.

Filtering Messages in Outlook Express

Before you create filters, make the folders into which you want to sort your messages. To create a folder, select the folder in which you want the new folder to be stored.

To set up a filter in Outlook Express, follow these steps:

1. Open a message with the criteria that you want to use for a filter, and make a note of the e-mail address or other information that identifies this type of message. You may want to copy an e-mail address to the Clipboard so that you can copy it into the filter definition.

2. Choose Message | Create Rule From Message from the message window menu to display the New Mail Rule window, shown in Figure 8-3.

3. Choose the conditions(s) for the rule by clicking the appropriate check box. The rule appears in the Rule Description box at the bottom of the dialog box. Click the underlined text and type or paste the appropriate text for the rule condition and click Add. You can add more than one block of text to the rule.

4. Choose the action(s) for the rule by clicking the appropriate check box. Click the underlined text in the Rule Description box and select or fill in the necessary information. (For example, choose the folder to move the message to or fill in the e-mail addresses of people to forward the message to.)

5. Type a name for the rule in the last box.

6. Click OK to create the rule.

You can choose Tools | Message Rules | Mail to display the Message Rules dialog box, which displays the filters that have already been defined. (If no rules have been defined yet, you see the New Mail Rule window first.) You can turn a filter on and off by clicking the check box next to the filter description.

  If you use Outlook Express to read Usenet newsgroups (which are described in Chapters 11 and 12), you can create rules for filtering newsgroup postings, too.

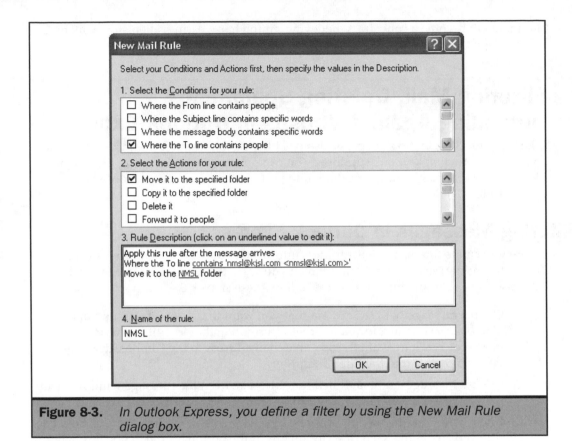

Figure 8-3. *In Outlook Express, you define a filter by using the New Mail Rule dialog box.*

Configuring Outlook Express Against Viruses

You can configure Outlook Express not to run programs embedded in HTML-formatted messages and to prevent other programs from accessing its address book. Outlook Express uses Internet Explorer's security settings, so you need to configure both programs (whether you use Internet Explorer or not). If you want to disable ActiveX and other scripting features for all incoming mail (which we recommend), you can set Outlook Express to use IE's Internet Zone security settings for mail messages and then disable the scripting features. If you are worried about receiving viruses from specific domains, you can add these domains to your IE Restricted Sites list.

First, follow these steps to specify which security settings Outlook Express uses for incoming messages:

1. In Outlook Express, choose Tools | Options to display the Options dialog box and click the Security tab, as shown in Figure 8-4.

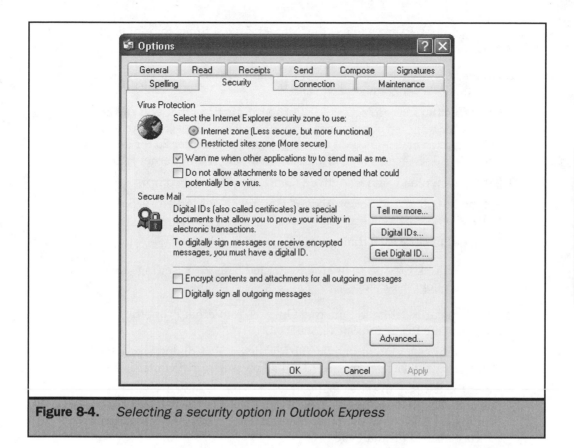

Figure 8-4.   *Selecting a security option in Outlook Express*

2. In the Virus Protection section, set the Internet security zone to either Restricted Sites Zone (More Secure) or Internet Zone (Less Secure, But More Functional). Unless you are worried about viruses only from specific sites, choose the Internet Zone.

3. Make sure that the Warn Me When Other Applications Try To Send Mail As Me check box is selected.

4. Click OK.

Next, you need to set the security settings for the zone you chose in step 2 (the Restricted Sites Zone or the Internet Zone). Either way, choose Start | Control Panel (Start | Settings | Control Panel in pre-XP Windows) and open the Internet Options item. Alternatively, in Internet Explorer, choose Tools | Internet Options to open the Internet Options or Internet Properties dialog box. Click the Security tab.

If you set Outlook Express to use the Internet Zone settings for e-mail, then follow these steps:

1. On the Security tab of the Internet Options or Internet Properties dialog box, click the Internet Zone icon.

2. Click Custom Level to access a list of specific actions that you can enable, disable, or be asked about for that zone. Most of the services are enabled, which makes malicious mail unsafe at best. See Chapter 20 for information about these settings, which also affect browsing with Internet Explorer.

3. Set the Download Signed ActiveX Controls option to Prompt.

4. Set the Initialize And Script ActiveX Controls Not Marked As Safe option to Disable.

5. Click OK to close each dialog box.

If you set Outlook Express to use the Restricted Sites Zone settings for e-mail messages, then follow these steps:

1. On the Security tab of the Internet Options or Internet Properties dialog box, click the Restricted Sites Zone icon.

2. Click the Sites button to display the Restricted Sites dialog box, where you specify which sites may send e-mail messages that contain viruses.

3. Enter the URLs of the sites that you want to block and click Add. Select a site and click Remove to take it off the list. Most of the services are disabled, limiting a malicious file's ability to wreak havoc, but also reducing the functionality of the mail client.

4. Click OK to close each dialog box.

*For more information about Outlook Express security, Microsoft's Knowledge Base contains an article called "OLEXP: Using Virus Protection Features in Outlook Express 6 (Q291387)." Start at **support.microsoft.com** and search the Knowledge Base (Database of Support Articles) for this title.*

To prevent additional attacks from certain viruses, turn off the preview pane. (Most viruses don't run in the preview pane, but why take a chance?) Here's how:

1. In Outlook Express, choose View | Layout to display the Window Layout Properties dialog box, as shown next.

2. In the Preview Pane section, uncheck the Show Preview Pane check box.

3. Click OK to save your changes.

Filtering Mail, Deleting Spam, and Defending Against Viruses in Eudora

Eudora has easy-to-use filter features and is not particularly susceptible to viruses—if you are careful. This section describes Eudora 5.1 in sponsored or paid mode.

Filtering Messages in Eudora

Before creating filters, create the folders into which you want to file your messages. Choose Mailbox | New from the menu. If a list of your mailboxes isn't already on the screen, choose Tools | Mailboxes to display it.

Eudora provides both the ease and complexity in its filter features—making a simple filter is easily done on the Make Filter dialog box. To make a more complex filter, select Tools | Filters to see the Filters dialog box.

Creating Filters in Eudora

The easiest way to create a filter is to select a message that meets your filtering criteria and then to follow these steps:

1. Select Special | Make Filter, or right-click the message and choose Make Filter, to see the Make Filter dialog box, shown in Figure 8-5. The Make Filter dialog box copies information from the selected message for your filter. You can take the settings that you need and delete the others to create your filter.

2. Change the Match Conditions settings as needed: choose the type of mail that you're filtering (that is, when Eudora should run the filter). Your choices are Incoming, Outgoing, and Manual. (You can run manual filters by pressing CTRL-J or choosing Special | Filter Messages.)

3. Select the header contents that you want to use to filter the message and use the accompanying text box to type the text you want the filter to find. *From* looks at the From field of the message, *Any Recipient* looks to match any single recipient in the To field, and *Subject* looks to match any part of the Subject field with the text you type.

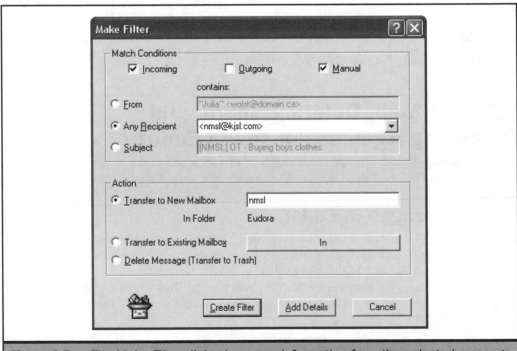

Figure 8-5.   *The Make Filter dialog box uses information from the selected message.*

4. Choose the Action settings—choose whether to transfer the message to a new or existing folder or to delete the message. If you're moving the message, be sure to name the folder or select the existing folder that you want to use.

5. Click Create Filter to make the filter.

If you want more control over the filter, click Add Details to see the filter in the Filters dialog box.

In Eudora you can also create filters by choosing Tools | Filters from the menu, which displays the Filters dialog box (shown in Figure 8-6). Click the New button to create a new filter. Define the criteria in the top half of the dialog box and, in the bottom half of the dialog box, define the action to take for the messages that match the defined criteria.

Making Filters That You Can Run Any Time

Eudora Pro has a neat feature that allows you to filter messages after they arrive on your computer—*manual filters*. If you get a bunch of messages that you want to filter, you can create a filter for them and set the filter type to Manual. To run the filter (and

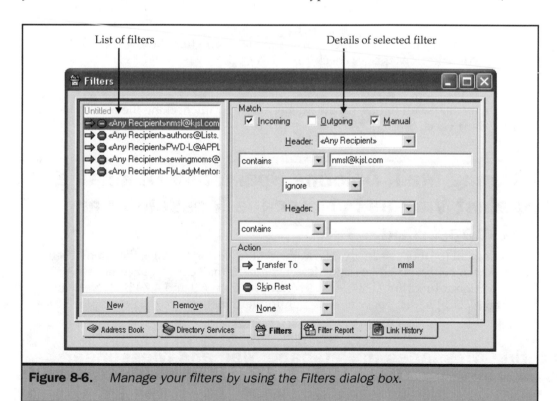

Figure 8-6.   *Manage your filters by using the Filters dialog box.*

EXCHANGING E-MAIL

all the other manual filters that you have set up), choose Special | Filter Messages from the menu.

Editing and Deleting Filters

You can use the Filters dialog box to edit existing filters, change the order in which Eudora executes the filters, or get rid of filters that you no longer want. Choose Tools | Filters from the menu to display the Filters dialog box. When you select a filter from the list on the left side of the window, the information about that filter appears in the boxes on the right side.

Avoiding Viruses with Eudora

To prevent Eudora from running programs that arrive by e-mail, follow these steps:

1. Choose Tools | Options to display the Options dialog box.
2. Click Viewing Mail from the Category list, and make sure that the Allow Executables In HTML Content check box is not selected.
3. Click Extra Warnings from the Category list, and make sure that the Launch A Program From A Message check box and Launch A Program Externally check box are selected.
4. Click MAPI from the Category list, and make sure that the Warn On MAPI Auto-Send Of Messages check box is selected.
5. Click OK to close the Options dialog box and save your changes.

You may also want to turn off the preview pane by unchecking the Show Message Preview Pane check box.

Filtering Mail, Deleting Spam, and Defending Against Viruses in Netscape Messenger and Netscape Mail

Netscape Mail (or more properly, Netscape Mail & Newsgroups) is the e-mail client that is part of Netscape 6. Netscape Messenger is the mail client that comes with Netscape Communicator. (This book describes versions 6.2 and 4.7.) Both Netscape Mail and Netscape Messenger offer straightforward methods to create simple or complex filters.

Filtering Messages in Netscape Mail and Messenger

Before creating filters, create the folders into which you plan to sort your mail. To create a folder, right-click in the folder list and choose New Folder from the menu that appears. In Netscape Messenger, choose File | New Folder.

To create a filter, choose Edit | Message Filters from the main menu, which displays the Message Filters dialog box. Existing filters are listed in this dialog box. Filters with a check mark to their right are turned on.

To create a new filter, click the New button to display the Filter Rules dialog box, shown in Figures 8-7 (Netscape Mail) and 8-8 (Netscape Messenger). To define a new filter, name the filter and use the drop-down lists and the text box to define the details of the rule. If you want to add additional rules, click the More button to display another row. If you use multiple rules, you need to choose how the rules work together—either they all must be met, or only one must be met—use the radio buttons to choose the appropriate setting. The description for the filter is optional (in Netscape Messenger only), but it gives you a place to describe how the filter works.

Avoiding Viruses with Netscape Mail and Netscape Messenger

Netscape Messenger doesn't include any configuration settings that control whether it runs programs that arrive by e-mail. Netscape Mail has only one: choose Edit | Preferences from the menu. Click the Advanced category and deselect the Enable JavaScript For Mail & Newsgroups check box.

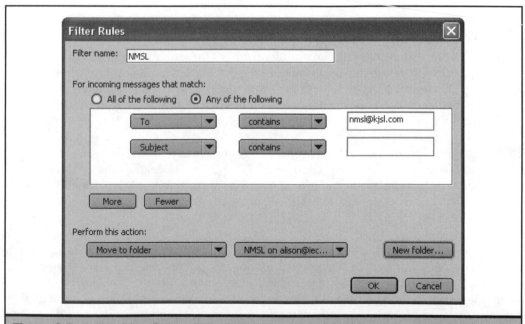

Figure 8-7.   *The Filter Rules dialog box in Netscape Mail gives you a straightforward way to create filtering rules.*

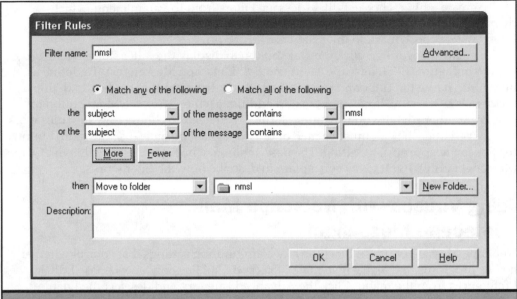

Figure 8-8. *Netscape Messenger provides a very similar Filter Rules dialog box to create filters.*

Blocking Junk Mail in AOL

AOL doesn't enable you to filter incoming messages into folders—a major drawback, in our opinion. However, it does allow you to block certain mail. Unlike a filter, which allows you to choose what to do with mail that meets your criteria (for example, file it in a particular folder or delete it), AOL's mail controls only allow you to block mail entirely.

 You never see the messages that you block, so you can never check that you're blocking only the mail that you don't want to read. Use AOL's mail controls conservatively, or you'll end up blocking incoming mail from friends and colleagues. We run into this a lot: we get a message from an AOL user, but when we reply, the message bounces because they've got their mail controls set too high!

To access AOL's mail controls, choose Mail | Mail Controls from the toolbar, which displays the Mail Controls dialog box. This dialog box guides you through setting e-mail controls. You can block e-mail to a particular screen name. Seven blocking levels are available, from allowing all mail to allowing only AOL mail to allowing no mail at all. Most options enable you to specify domains and/or AOL members whom you don't want to receive mail from.

AOL tries to block junk mail before it ever enters the AOL system. You can choose to report junk mail that does get through to AOL by forwarding the message to the screen name TOSReports. The only other option is to use Mail Controls to block mail from domains that you think send only junk mail. Be aware, though, that if someone sends you real mail from a blocked domain, you will never get it.

AOL has a Parental Controls feature that allows you to limit the content available to a particular screen name in your account. AOL has created the content screen so you can select the age of the child (who should have his/her own screen name) to block access to areas deemed inappropriate for that age group. You may prefer to use the set of Custom Controls, which gives you additional options. To access Parental Controls, choose Settings | Parental Controls from the toolbar.

If you want to be able to sort your AOL mail into folders, consider using Netscape Mail (part of Netscape 6) to read your messages. Netscape Mail is the only e-mail program that works with AOL. See Chapter 6 for how to configure it for your AOL mailbox.

Filtering Mail and Deleting Spam in Yahoo Mail

Yahoo Mail provides two features to help you control mail volume—you can create mail filters, and you can block mail from specified addresses. Yahoo has built-in virus-checking, so you can scan files you download for viruses before they arrive on your computer.

If you use an e-mail program like Outlook Express or Eudora to download and read your Yahoo Mail messages (as described in Chapter 6), you use your e-mail program's filtering features.

Filtering Messages in Yahoo Mail

Before creating filters, create the folders into which you want to sort your incoming messages. Click the Folders link, type a name for the folder in the Create A Personal Folder box, and click the Create Folder button.

To create filters to sort your mail into folders, click Options and click the Filters link. Click Create to create a filter. Choose one or more places in the message where you want to look for specific text (From header, To/Cc, Subject, or Body) and type in the text. Then choose the folder where you want the messages that meet the criteria to be stored. Click Save to create the filter.

Yahoo's Junk Mail Spamguard

Yahoo Mail can automatically create a Bulk Mail folder for you and filter all mail that it believes to be spam to that folder. To create the Bulk Mail folder, click Options and click the Filters link. Then click Create in the Spamguard box.

It's a good idea to scan the Bulk Mail folder periodically to check that no legitimate e-mail has ended up there. You can then delete the messages there so that they don't eat up your precious storage space.

Scanning Files for Viruses with Yahoo Mail

When you are reading messages in Yahoo Mail, your browser handles the messages. See Chapter 20 for how to configure your browser to avoid infection by viruses. If you receive a message with an attached file that you want to download to your computer, Yahoo offers to scan the file before downloading; always accept this option. Virus-scanning doesn't always catch the latest viruses, so if you don't know the person who sent the file, or you weren't expecting the file, don't download it.

Filtering Mail and Deleting Spam in Hotmail

Hotmail provides filters and an automatic junk mail filter for which you can choose a level of sensitivity. Hotmail contains a built-in virus checker.

Filtering Messages in Hotmail

Before creating filters, create the folders into which you plan to sort your incoming mail. Click the View All Folders link on the Home tab, and click the Create New button.

To create filters to sort your mail, click the Options tab at the top of the window. Then click Custom Filters in the Mail Handling column.

Hotmail allows you to define up to ten filters, which are processed in order. The filter definition allows you to choose to filter on the contents of the Subject, From Name, From Address, or To/Cc address. Select the field, the way the field and text should be used in the filter, and provide the text that the filter is looking for. Then choose the folder you want the message delivered to. Select the Enabled check box for the filter if you want the filter to be used. Click OK (at the bottom of the window) to create the filter and to run it on mail that arrives in your account. To run filters on mail already in your Inbox, click Apply Filters Now.

Deleting Junk Mail in Hotmail

Hotmail provides a junk mail filter, but doesn't provide details on how it decides when mail is junk. To turn on the junk mail filter, click Options and click Junk Mail Filter. Click a filter level to read a description of each level of protection. The Junk Mail Filter can be used with the Junk Mail Deletion option. You may also choose to block specific senders or specific domains using the Block Sender option.

If you use the junk mail filter, you should also use the Mailing Lists option (in Options, in the Mail Handling column) to ensure that your mailing list e-mail does not end up in your Junk Mail folder.

Scanning Files for Viruses with Hotmail

When you are reading messages in Hotmail, your browser displays the messages—check that your browser is set to avoid viruses (see Chapter 20). When you click to open an attachment, Hotmail scans the attached file for viruses and then offers to download the file to your computer.

EXCHANGING E-MAIL

The Complete Reference

Internet

Part III

Chatting and Conferencing on the Internet

Chapter 9

Online Chatting, Messaging, and Conferencing Concepts

The Internet enables groups of people to have discussions in which the participants may be anywhere in the world. This group communication can take the form of text on the screen, voice, or video, and messages and responses can be exchanged "live" or they may be read and responded to later. All these types of online communication can be referred to as *online chat* or *online conferencing*.

Forms of Chat, Messaging, and Conferencing

In some types of chatting, messaging, and conferencing, messages are sent immediately after they are complete (for example, as soon as you press ENTER after typing a message). This type of communication is called *real-time communication*. Other ways of chatting deliver messages more slowly; for example, via e-mail. These other types of communication are called *asynchronous,* because participants do not all read and respond to messages at the same time (synchronously). Each form of communication has advantages:

- **Real-time chat**   Each participant sees each message within seconds of when it is sent, so dialog can happen quickly. However, all the participants need to be online at the same time.

- **Asynchronous chat**   Messages are stored so that participants can read them when they have a chance, which allows participants to consider their responses, gather information, and formulate a response carefully. It also allows people from different time zones or with different schedules to participate. For example, there may not be a time when all the members of a group are available for a real-time meeting.

Table 9-1 lists the most commonly used forms of Internet-based chat and conferencing, along with the timing (real time or asynchronous), format of information (text, audio, video, or files), and type of software that you need to participate.

E-mail Mailing Lists

E-mail messages are sent to one or more people who are selected by the sender. An *e-mail mailing list* allows messages to be distributed to a list of preselected people, called *subscribers*. Depending on how the mailing list is set up, one, some, or all subscribers can post messages, so that mailing lists can be used to distribute newsletters or press releases, or to allow large group discussions. For more information on how to find, participate in, or create mailing lists, see Chapter 10.

Type	Timing	Format	Software Required
E-mail mailing list	Asynchronous	Text; HTML and attached files may be allowed	E-mail program
Usenet newsgroups	Asynchronous	Text with optional attached files	Newsreader (such as Free Agent, Outlook Express, or Netscape Newsgroups)
Internet Relay Chat (IRC)	Real time	Text with optional file transfer	Chat program (such as mIRC or Ircle)
Web-based chat	Real time	Text	Web browser
Web discussion boards	Asynchronous	Text; HTML and attached files may be allowed	Web browser
AOL and CompuServe chat rooms	Real time	Text	AOL or CompuServe software and paid subscription
Instant messaging	Real time	Text	ICQ, AOL Instant Messenger, or other program
Online conferencing	Real time	Text, voice, and video, depending on software used	Conferencing program (such as Yahoo Messenger, CUseeMe, or Microsoft NetMeeting)

Table 9-1.   *Types of Online Chat and Conferencing*

Usenet Newsgroups

Usenet is a system that allows messages to be distributed throughout the Internet. Because of the volume of messages, the messages are divided into *newsgroups,* or topics. You use a *newsreader* program to subscribe to a newsgroup, read the messages posted to that newsgroup, and post your own messages. Over 20,000 different public newsgroups exist, covering every conceivable topic. Private news servers host thousands of additional newsgroups. For general information about Usenet newsgroups, see Chapter 11. For help with the most widely used newsreaders, see Chapter 12.

Internet Relay Chat (IRC)

Internet Relay Chat (IRC) allows thousands of Internet users to participant in real-time text-based chat. When you use an IRC program to connect to a central IRC server and to join a conversation (called a *channel*), you see all the messages that are typed in that channel within seconds of when the messages are sent. The IRC program enables you to type and send your own messages, too. For guidance on how to choose an IRC program and use it to participate in Internet Relay Chat, see Chapter 13.

Web-Based Chat

Many people are daunted by the programs and commands required by IRC. Therefore, many web sites now provide a web-based way to participate in real-time text-based chat. For information about how to find and participate in live web-based chat, see Chapter 15.

Web Discussion Boards

Web discussion boards are sometimes referred to as *bulletin boards* because they are places where messages can be left and responded to. Like Usenet newsgroups, web discussion boards are dedicated to particular topics such as backgammon, pet health, or Basque culture. Generally, you need only your web browser to participate in a discussion, but some boards require that you register before reading or posting messages. Web discussion boards are covered further in Chapter 15.

AOL and CompuServe Chat Rooms

Many America Online users spend long hours in *chat rooms,* AOL services that allow real-time chat on a wide variety of subjects. A small number of AOL chat rooms are accessible by anyone with a web browser; but to participate in most AOL chat rooms, you must have an AOL account and use AOL's proprietary software to connect to your account. Other Internet users (those without AOL accounts) cannot participate in most AOL chat rooms.

CompuServe (an online service now owned by AOL) offers real-time chats on many different topics. As with AOL, you need a CompuServe account and CompuServe software to participate.

Both AOL and CompuServe also have discussion areas similar to the web discussion boards discussed in the preceding section.

Instant Messaging

ICQ (pronounced "I seek you"), AOL Instant Messenger, Yahoo Messenger, Windows Messenger, and other instant messaging programs enable you to send messages to other people when both you and they are connected to the Internet. These programs, which can usually be freely downloaded from the Internet, let you create a list of the people you want to chat with. When one of the people on your list connects to the Internet, your instant messaging program informs you that your friend is online, and you can then exchange messages. For more information on using instant messaging, see Chapter 14.

Online Conferencing

If text isn't enough, you can use one of several Internet-based online conferencing programs to confer with one or more people using voice and video. Some conferencing programs also allow all the participants to see or edit a document on their screens and to see or write on a digital *whiteboard* (a shared paint program that participants can use to share drawings). Your computer must have a microphone and speakers or a headphone/microphone combination if you plan to use voice conferencing features. If you want the other participants to see you, you must also have a *webcam* (a small, cheap, digital video camera designed for use with computers). Chapter 16 describes how to use some of the best-known voice and video conferencing programs.

MUDs, MOOs, and RPGs

In addition to unstructured chats and discussions, many multiuser games are in progress on the Internet at any hour of the day or night. *MUDs (multiuser dimensions)* are real-time text-based chats in which the participants play a game by following a set of rules enforced by the central server computer. A MUD is usually a fantasy or adventure game, but may be an online university or other group event. MOOs (MUDs Object Oriented) are user-programmable games that are similar to MUDs: by programming, participants can create objects in the shared world of the MOO.

Many game enthusiasts now play commercial *role-playing games (RPGs)*, so MUDs and MOOs are not as popular as they once were. If you would like to try one of these multiuser environments, **www.onlineroleplay.com** has many useful resources.

How Does Chat Work?

The following sections provide some general descriptions of how chat, message boards, and conferencing work.

Identifying Yourself

In mailing lists and newsgroups, you are identified by your name and e-mail address. When you join an IRC channel and some other real-time chats, you choose a name to go by—variously referred to as your *nickname, handle, ID,* or (on AOL) *screen name.* If someone is already using the name you planned to use, you must choose another one. On systems that allow you to choose a nickname each time you join, remember that the person who has a particular nickname today may not be the same person who had it yesterday.

Topics, Newsgroups, Channels, and Rooms

Tens of thousands of people can simultaneously participate in the various available forms of Internet chat and conferencing. Discussions are categorized by topic, enabling people who are interested in a particular topic to find and communicate with each other. Topics may include hobbies, personal problems, sports, research areas, religious beliefs, or other areas of interest; or participants may simply be grouped together by geographical area or age. Some discussions consist entirely of people looking for partners for romance, sex, or simple banter.

Depending on the system, topic groups may be called *newsgroups* (in Usenet), *channels* (in IRC), *forums, boards, groups,* or *rooms.* E-mail mailing lists are already divided by topic (one list per general topic), although some mailing lists ask you to include specific topic keywords in the subject lines of your messages, too.

Following the Discussion

In asynchronous chats and conferences, messages have subject lines. A *thread* is a message on a particular topic, along with all the responses to that message (and responses to the responses, and so forth)—it's more like a tree than a thread, as shown in Figure 9-1. The subject lines of responses usually begin with "Re:" (short for "regarding"). When you read a group of messages in a thread, you can often sort the messages by thread and choose which threads to read.

In real-time chat, the discussion consists of short messages from many participants, and each message is preceded by the name, nickname, or handle of the person who sent

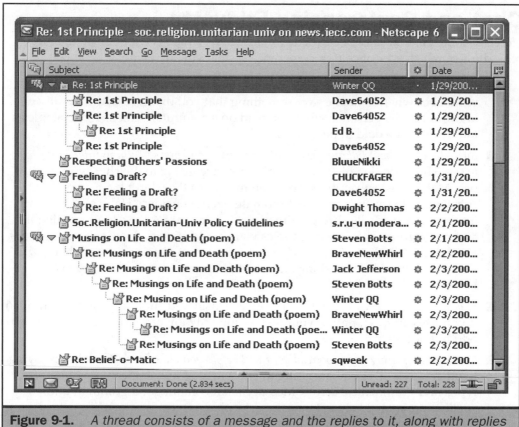

Figure 9-1. *A thread consists of a message and the replies to it, along with replies to replies.*

it. The messages are displayed on your screen in the order in which your computer received them, and several conversations may be happening at the same time.

Following a real-time chat can be tricky. When you join a channel or chat room, stay quiet for a few minutes until your screen fills up with messages. Start by reading one interesting-looking message, and then read down through the messages for responses to that message and for other messages from the same person who sent the original message. When you have something to say, jump in!

Chat and Conferencing Etiquette

Here are some general rules of etiquette (or *netiquette,* which is etiquette on the Net), regardless of which type of chat or conference system you are using:

- *Remember that you are talking to real people, not to computers.* This can be hard to remember when someone says something that you disagree with, and all you know about the person is what you read on a computer screen. Treat people as kindly as you would in person.

- *Lurk (listen without talking) first, and wait until you have something interesting to say.* The definition of "interesting" varies according to the chat system you use. Mailing list subscribers frown on messages that don't have something substantive to say, whereas chat room denizens consider "Hello all!" to be an intelligent remark. Be sure your message is relevant for the group: mailing lists and newsgroups have specific topics you should stick to. Lists and newsgroups also have *FAQs* (lists of *frequently asked questions* and their answers) that you should read before asking any questions; your question may already be answered in the FAQs.

- *Don't shout.* Typing in ALL CAPITALS is considered shouting. People complain if you use capitals for all of your text. Using only lowercase letters is considered odd but not offensive.

- *Check your spelling and proofread your text before you click Send.* It can be annoying to others (as well as embarrassing to you!) to read text that contains a lot of typos and grammatical errors. Messages that contain good grammar and spelling are more likely to be taken seriously.

- *Learn the rules.* Many groups, mailing lists, chat rooms, and channels have rules. You may receive a list of them when you join. By following the rules, you'll keep from looking foolish and avoid getting ejected from the discussion.

- *Precede your remark with the name (or nickname or handle) of the person to whom your remark is directed if several conversations are taking place simultaneously in a channel or chat room.* Otherwise, it is likely that the wrong person will answer your question, or that your question will be ignored altogether.

- *In mailing lists, message boards, and Usenet newsgroups, quote the relevant parts of the message to which you are responding.* Quoting messages is a good idea because it helps the people reading your message know what you are responding to. However, if subscribers already read the original message, they don't want to read the whole thing again. Delete all but the relevant parts of the quoted message. As a rule, the message that you write should always be longer than the quoted material in your message. Never quote an entire message and add only "I agree!"

- *Consider whether you really need to post a message to the entire list or newsgroup in which you are participating.* Messages of interest only to the original poster (such as "I agree!") should go privately by e-mail, because the rest of the subscribers aren't interested.

- *Don't try to manage the conversation unless you are the mailing list manager, channel operator, or other person in charge.* Don't send messages complaining about other messages; it's bad enough having to read an off-topic message without also having to wade through complaints about it. If you really have a problem with a message, use e-mail, a private chat room, or an instant message to talk privately to the person in charge or the person who posted the message.

- *Beware of* trolls, *messages that are intended to provoke a storm of responses.* If someone makes a provocative remark, silence is sometimes an appropriate response. If someone consistently acts obnoxious, the best response is to ignore him or her.

- *Don't post the same message to multiple lists or newsgroups.* Choose the list or newsgroup that is the most appropriate for your message.

- *Don't post chain letters, virus warnings, or calls to action unless you have checked their validity.* The Internet is remarkable for its ability to spread information rapidly. Unfortunately, incorrect and sometimes damaging information propagates just as quickly as correct information. If you're told to spread some information to as many people as possible—don't. To check out a virus warning or a call to action, look at **www.snopes.com**, **hoaxbusters.ciac.org**, or **urbanlegends .about.com**.

- *Don't send copyrighted material to mailing lists or newsgroups.* Doing so is probably an infringement of copyright. Most material on web sites is copyrighted, as are postings to mailing lists and newsgroups themselves. (Yes, you own the copyright on your messages.) When in doubt, contact the author of the material to request permission. Of course, quoting a message when you respond to that message is considered polite and proper, as long as the message to which you are replying was posted to the same mailing list or newsgroup to which you send the response.

Tip   *For all forms of online chat and conferencing, people frequently use abbreviations to save typing. These abbreviations may not be familiar. For a long list of frequently used abbreviations, see the Chatter's Jargon Dictionary at **www.SteveGrossman.com/ jargpge.htm**. This page also includes a listing of emoticons, diagrams of faces that are created by using punctuation, which are widely used to add emotion to chat messages.*

CHATTING AND
CONFERENCING ON
THE INTERNET

Safety While Chatting

Safety is a consideration when you participate in public chat systems. (Using a conferencing program for meetings with coworkers and clients doesn't carry the same risk because you already know the participants.) Here are some safety considerations:

■ *Remember that what you say may not be private.* Other people (or programs) may be capturing all the messages in the conversation. Usenet newsgroup messages are saved in a publicly searchable archive on the Web at **groups.google.com**. Similarly, many mailing lists and discussion areas maintain message archives.

■ *Be aware that your messages are not anonymous.* E-mail and newsgroup messages contain your e-mail address, as well as headers that contain other identifying information. Other chat and discussion messages may not contain obvious information that identifies you; but the system operators can, if necessary, trace your messages back to your Internet account, with help from your ISP.

■ *Don't believe everything you read.* A person's description of himself or herself may range anywhere from slightly optimistic to totally inaccurate. Many people use online chat and discussion as a way to experiment with their self-image. They may portray themselves as people of a gender, age, profession, or other characteristics that are different from real life. Others may present themselves inaccurately because they want to defraud you, gain your confidence, or otherwise trick you.

■ *Don't reveal more about yourself online than you want everyone in the universe to know.* Specifically, don't reveal your phone number, address, company, school, real name, or other identifying information. More than one person has received an unwanted phone call or visit from someone they met while chatting.

■ *Never type your password in a chat or conference.* Requests for your password are *always* bogus. Your Internet provider, AOL, or other password-protected system already knows your password, and employees of these systems *never* ask you to type your password in a chat or conference.

■ *Don't hang around in sexually oriented channels or chat rooms if you are not interested in sex.* If someone sends you a graphics file, delete it without looking at it unless you don't mind seeing a sexually explicit picture. If someone invites you into a private chat room or channel, consider what kind of chat you are looking for. If you don't like the conversation in one chat room or channel, find another.

■ *Don't allow your children to use chat or conferencing systems without supervision.* Be sure that your children know not to give out personal information and know never to agree to meet someone in person. Some malefactors offer prizes to kids in return for personal, identifying information; make sure your kids know not to go along with these scams.

- *Take advantage of AOL's guidelines if you use AOL.* Go to the Parental Controls keyword for more information.

- *Be sure to report inappropriate, abusive, or scary behavior when possible.* On AOL, go to the TOS keyword (Terms of Service) to report problems. On IRC, you can ask the channel operator in charge of the channel that you are in to have the person banned from the system.

Ways to Use Chat Effectively

Depending on the speed, formality, privacy, and availability you need when chatting online, consider which of the following types of chat to use:

- *For meeting people, socializing, and hanging around, consider the following programs.* If you don't mind a lot of banter that's frequently aimless (and ribald), you might like IRC or the chat rooms available with AOL and CompuServe. If you have specific people to converse with, instant messaging is probably your best bet.

- *For an informal discussion at a specific place and time, with a limited number of participants and immediate responses, consider a form of real-time chat.* Real-time chats can be hard to manage with more than about ten participants, but they offer many other advantages. Some types of real-time chat allow you to save a log of the proceedings, create a private room or channel, chat with voice and video, and share files. If you are planning to use a chat system that requires specific software, be sure all participants have installed the program and know how to use it before the scheduled chat time. Note that most free web-based chat systems display ads to support their service. Corporations that use instant messaging and real-time chat usually run their own servers or contract with private service companies to avoid the security risks of conducting business on public chat servers.

- *For an ongoing discussion that doesn't require everyone to be present at the same time, use a form of asynchronous chat.* Mailing lists and web discussion boards work well with almost any number of participants. They don't require any special software, so anyone with an e-mail address or web access can participate. Most mailing-list and discussion-board management programs can save all messages in an archive. If you want to control who can participate, configure the group to be private.

Note   *You might also consider a Usenet newsgroup: creating a newsgroup in one of the standard hierarchies (see Chapter 11) requires a long process of proposals, lobbying, and voting, but newsgroups can be easier for people to find than mailing lists. On the other hand, fewer people have used the newsreading programs that are built into most e-mail programs (including Outlook Express and Netscape). Also, newsgroups cannot be private unless you have access to a private news server.*

CHATTING AND
CONFERENCING ON
THE INTERNET

Corporations use chatting and messaging programs, too, although many larger organizations prefer to host their own instant messaging services, newsgroup servers, mailing lists, or discussion boards rather than relying on the security of public services.

The rest of the chapters in this part of the book give more detail about each of the ways to participate in Internet-based chats and conferences.

The
Complete
Reference

Internet

Chapter 10

E-mail Mailing Lists

235

E-mail mailing lists, which are generally referred to as *mailing lists, discussion lists,* or simply *lists,* enable groups of Internet users *(subscribers)* to communicate by e-mail on a subject of mutual interest. For example, a group of people working on a project might use a mailing list to plan and track the project, exchanging messages about their progress; a group of hobbyists could exchange tips and answer each other's questions; or a college professor and her class might conduct an ongoing discussion of the assigned readings for the class. Depending on how a mailing list is configured, it can be an online newsletter, a public forum for open discussion, a moderated discussion, or a private virtual meeting room with a complete transcript of the proceedings. This chapter describes how to find mailing lists of interest, how mailing lists work, how to join and participate in one, and how to set up and run a mailing list of your own.

Note   *Some people use the terms "listserv" or "listserve" instead of "e-mail mailing list." That's because the first mailing list management program was named LISTSERV. Using the word "listserv" to refer to any e-mail mailing list is like using the name of a popular brand of facial tissue to refer to all facial tissue, so in this book the more general "e-mail mailing list" is used.*

Finding Interesting Mailing Lists

Regardless of the subject you want to discuss or the kind of group you want to join, a special-interest mailing list probably already exists. No topic, from Estonian Buddhism to alien abduction of left-pawed cats, is too obscure.

To find a discussion list that interests you, start at the Google directory (**directory .google.com**), and choose Computers | Internet | Mailing Lists | Directories. This page gives a number of directories of mailing lists. You can also search for mailing lists from any search engine simply by typing **mailing list** (or **discussion list**) and one or two words about your topic into the Search box of Google, MSN Search, AOL Search, or some other search engine.

Once you find a list that seems to fit your needs, follow the instructions in the remainder of this chapter for subscribing to a list, participating, managing your subscription, and leaving the list.

    *The authors of this book maintain a web page with some of their favorite mailing lists at **net.gurus.com/lists**. More information is also available at **lists.gurus.com**.*

How Do Mailing Lists Work?

Most Internet mailing lists are automated, meaning that a *mailing list management program* or *list server* automatically handles the mailings. The mailing list management program stores a list of subscribers' addresses in a central location. When a subscriber sends a message to the list, the list server e-mails the message to each of the subscribers' addresses. If another subscriber *posts* (e-mails) a reply to the list, the reply is also e-mailed to each subscriber, and a discussion starts. The list server also handles tasks like letting people subscribe or change their subscriptions. Every list also has one human *list administrator* (sometimes confusingly called the *list manager*), who helps people who are having trouble with their subscriptions, enforces the rules for the list, and does other list management that requires human intervention.

Mailing List Types and Options

Mailing lists can be set up with controls on who can subscribe and who can post messages, and with several other options.

- **Open vs. closed subscriptions**   An *open subscription* list is configured to allow anyone to subscribe. A *closed subscription* list is configured to require that the list administrator approve each subscriber.

- **Open vs. closed posting**   An open posting list allows anyone to post messages, even nonsubscribers. A *closed posting* list allows only subscribers to post messages to the list.

- **Moderated**   *Moderated* lists have one or more human *moderators,* who sometimes also function as the list administrators. The moderator of a moderated list must approve each message before it is distributed to the subscribers. The moderator serves as an editor or gatekeeper who rejects off-topic postings, repetitive postings, or postings that break some other rule of the list. Some moderated lists allow only one person to post: in effect, this type of list serves as an online newsletter.

- **Digests**   On a *high volume* list—one with a large number of postings each day—some subscribers may prefer to receive each day's messages concatenated into one big e-mail (a *digest*) rather than separately. Digests are usually mailed daily, although they may be sent weekly or at some other interval. See "Receiving Messages in Digests," later in this chapter.

- **Reply-to-list vs. reply-to-sender**   Some mailing lists are configured so that any reply to a message will be automatically addressed and mailed to the list. Other mailing lists are configured so that replies are automatically addressed only to the original sender, and the rest of the subscribers don't see the response. *Reply-to-list* is often preferable for low-volume lists and those where discussion is desirable. *Reply-to-sender* is usually better for large lists and those on which minimal chatter is preferred.

- **Manually managed, e-mail managed, or web managed**   Some lists are managed manually, by human beings, but most are managed by a list server program. On occasion, as discussed later in this chapter, list subscribers need to communicate with the list server. Subscribers can communicate with some list servers over the Web, but other list servers can accept communications only by e-mail.

CHATTING AND CONFERENCING ON THE INTERNET

Note   *Your e-mail program doesn't have to be specially configured to work with mailing lists. Messages to and from mailing lists are sent and received the same way as other e-mail messages.*

Manually Managed Mailing Lists

Mailing lists have been part of the Internet for many years, but originally they were administered without the use of list server programs. This required lots of manual labor: each time someone wanted to subscribe, sign off, or change configuration settings, the list administrator had to make the appropriate changes to the list of subscribers' addresses. Some people who run mailing lists manually still do so completely by hand, keeping the subscriber list in their e-mail program's address book or in a text file.

If you want to subscribe to a manually managed list, just send a polite note to the administrative address that includes your name and the name of the list you want to join. Give the list administrator a few days to respond (don't nag!—some list administrators do things other than manage lists). To cancel your subscription, also send a polite note to the administrator. Be sure to include your thanks for his or her hard work.

List Server Programs

In 1986, someone had the idea of writing a program to do the work of running a list, and the first list server was born. Today, most lists are managed by one of these list server programs with help from a human list administrator.

Individuals who want to start a mailing list don't usually run list servers on their own computers; this would be beyond the ability of most computer users. Rather, people who want to create or join a mailing list generally turn to an organization that is already *hosting* a list server. List servers are hosted (run on host computers) at a variety of organizations that have an interest in fostering certain types of communications. Universities, for example, sometimes host a list server for mailing lists concerning the university's current areas of research; private companies may host a list server for mailing lists about their products and services; and Internet companies often host a list server for fee-based mailing lists or as a way to bring traffic to a portal and thereby boost advertising revenue.

Several commercial list servers are in wide use: ListProc, LISTSEV, Lyris ListManager, Mailman, and Majordomo are among the most popular. Proprietary list servers are operated by services such as Yahoo and Topica. Unfortunately, each list server works differently. This chapter describes how to interact with some of the more popular commercial and proprietary list servers.

- **ListProc**   This open source list server was designed to be very similar to LISTSERV and responds to most of the same commands. The ListProc web site at **www.listproc.net** contains additional information. This chapter describes ListProc version 8.2.09.

- **LISTSERV**   This was the first widely available list server. Now used to manage more than 200,000 mailing lists worldwide, LISTSERV is particularly popular among educational, nonprofit, and governmental institutions. For more information, see the LISTSERV web site at **www.lsoft.com/listserv.stm**. This chapter describes LISTSERV version 1.8d.

- **Lyris ListManager** This is often referred to simply as "Lyris," in spite of the existence of other Lyris Technologies products. Lyris ListManager was designed primarily for commercial use. It supports mail merging and integrates with several database standards. Additional information about it is available at **www.lyris.com/products/listmanager**. This chapter describes ListManager version 5.0.

- **Mailman** This open source list server can be entirely web managed and is very popular among Linux enthusiasts. Complete information about Mailman is at **www.list.org**. This chapter describes Mailman version 2.0.8.

- **Majordomo** The first widely used open source list server, Majordomo was the frequent choice of Internet pioneers on a budget and is still popular with many. For more information, see its web page at **www.greatcircle.com/majordomo**. This chapter describes Majordomo version 1.94.5.

- **Other commercial list servers** Many other list servers are available, including programs that run on Macintosh computers. To find out about commercial list server software, go to the Google directory (**directory.google.com**), and choose Computers | Software | Internet | Servers | Mail | List Management.

- **Proprietary list servers** Several services host mailing lists for people who want to start an e-mail mailing list, but who don't want to install a list server and don't belong to an organization that has one. Proprietary list server software, used by most of these services, can be found in the Google directory (**directory.google.com**) by choosing Computers | Internet | Mailing Lists | Hosting Companies.

Using the Web to Communicate with a List Server

Web interfaces to a list server are far easier and more intuitive to use than e-mail interfaces. Once you find the location of the web interface for your list, which should have been included in the list welcome message, the rest is easy. Just point and click! If you find a mailing list that uses a list server that doesn't have a web interface, see the section "Using E-mail to Communicate with a List Server," later in this chapter.

Most of the web software for list servers is modifiable, and the web pages are frequently customized by the individuals responsible for the computer where the list server resides. The web interfaces you find may differ from the ones shown in this book.

The ListProc Web Interface

Because ListProc is one of the older list servers that were written before the World Wide Web was in wide use, it was originally designed without a web interface. Its web interface is not as visually appealing as those of newer list servers, but it gets the job done. A typical ListProc web interface is shown in Figure 10-1.

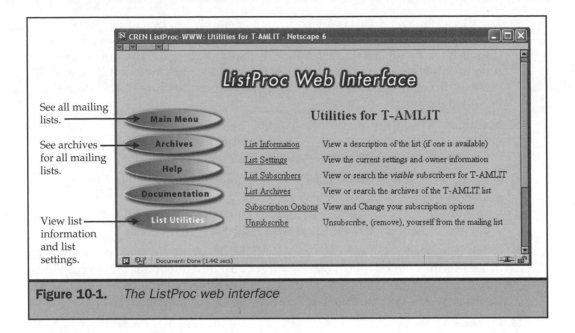

Figure 10-1. *The ListProc web interface*

The LISTSERV Web Interface

Like ListProc, LISTSERV was designed in the days before most Internet software was web enabled. Its web interface is unsophisticated, but it makes it possible to avoid using most e-mail commands. A typical LISTSERV web interface page is shown in Figure 10-2.

On a list settings page of the LISTSERV web interface, you can change your list settings to digest, no digest, postpone, and so on, as shown in Figure 10-3. Many of these settings are seldom used—for example, an "index" subscription is designed for people with very slow Internet connections. If you have an index subscription, you receive only summary information about each posting, such as the subject line, the name of the poster, and the number of lines in the posting.

The Lyris ListManager Web Interface

Lyris ListManager was originally designed to include a web interface, so its web tools have a modern appearance and are very comprehensive. A typical list entry page, like Figure 10-4, enables you to go to the user menu, join the list, or retrieve your password.

The Lyris user menu, shown in Figure 10-5, is the gateway to the functions a list subscriber needs. From this menu you can view old messages, write a new message, view or change your subscription options (your name, password, and mail delivery options), or sign off the list. All the Lyris ListManager web interface functions are easy for most subscribers to understand and use.

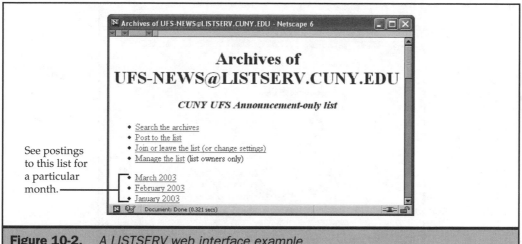

See postings to this list for a particular month.

Figure 10-2. *A LISTSERV web interface example*

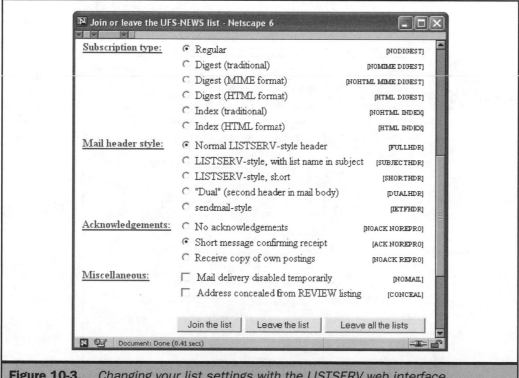

Figure 10-3. *Changing your list settings with the LISTSERV web interface*

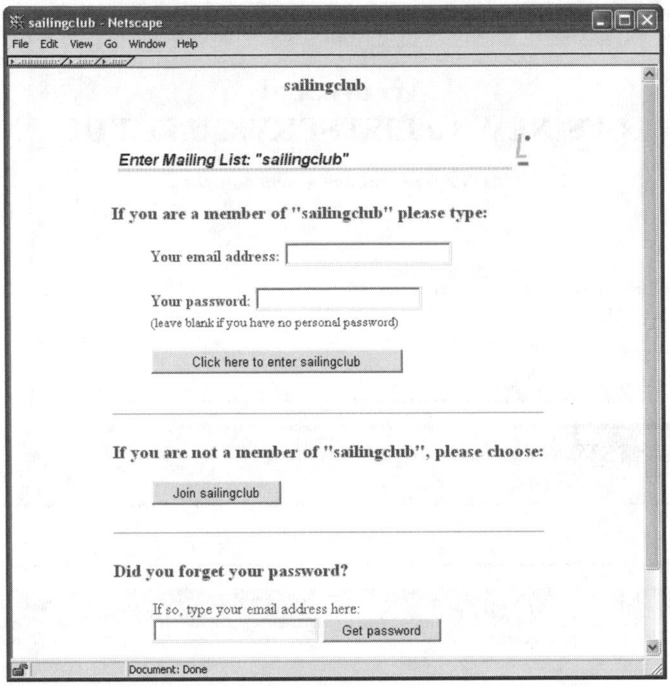

Figure 10-4. Lyris ListManager entry page

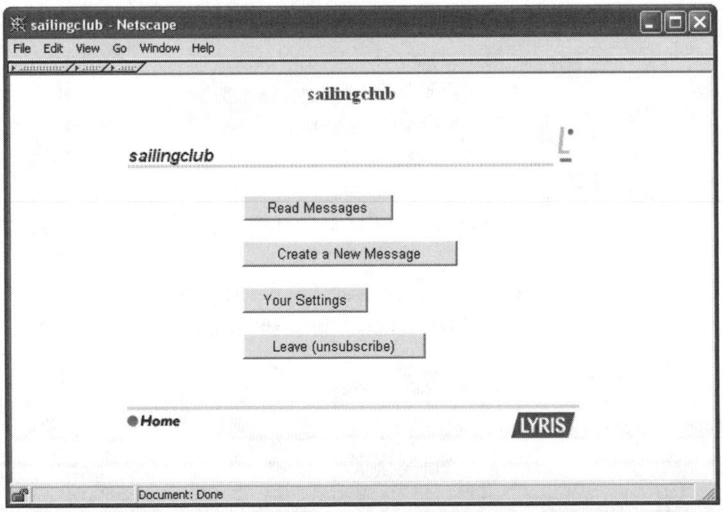

Figure 10-5. The Lyris ListManager user menu

The Mailman Web Interface

Like Lyris ListManager, Mailman was originally designed to include a professional-looking web interface. The Mailman web interface makes list information available and enables users to view or change any aspect of their subscription options.

You can subscribe to a Mailman list from a typical Mailman list information page, as in Figure 10-6. Note that the list information page allows you to choose to receive the list messages in a daily digest. If you're already subscribed to the list, type your subscription address at the bottom of the list information page to go to your configuration page.

Your Mailman configuration page (shown in Figure 10-7) enables you to remove yourself from the mailing list, change your password, request to have your current password e-mailed to you, and change any of your subscription options.

As you can see in Figure 10-7, the bottom portion of the configuration page provides all the usual subscription options. It enables you to disable mail delivery, set digest mode or change to the undigested version of the list, choose whether to receive your digests in MIME format or plain text format, select whether to receive copies of your own posts, choose to receive an acknowledgment e-mail of your posts, and indicate whether you want yourself to be visible among the list of subscribers.

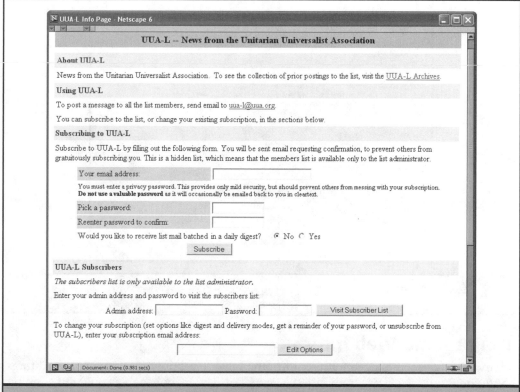

Figure 10-6. *Mailman list information page (a form for unsubscribing from the list appears lower on this web page)*

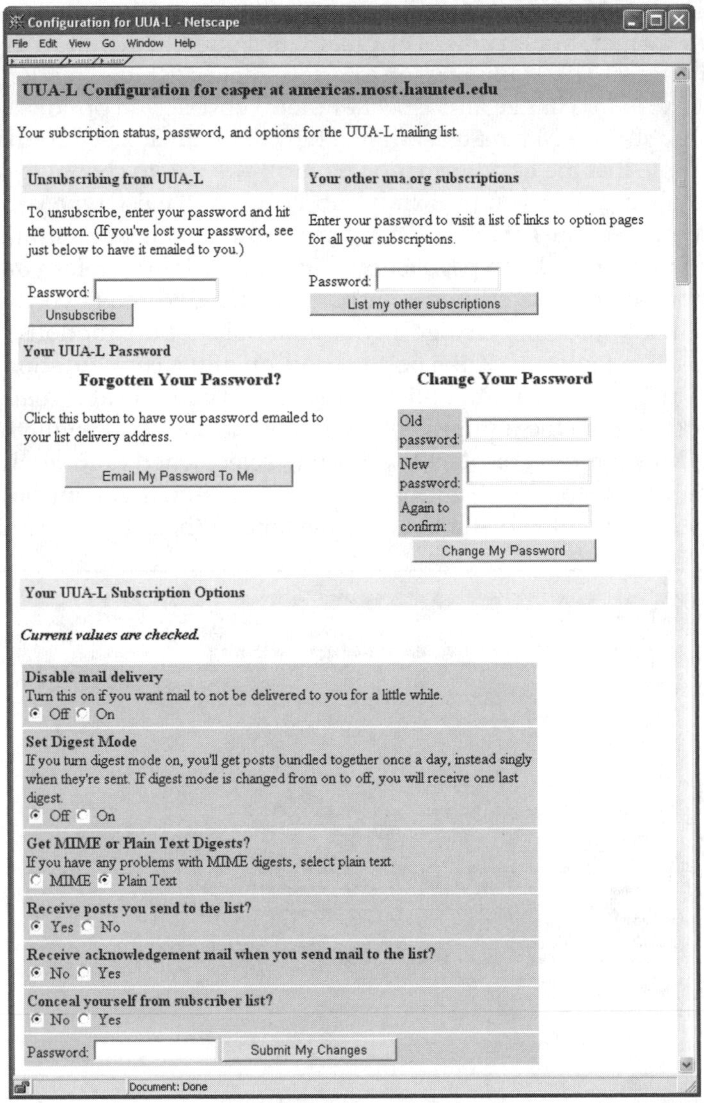

Figure 10-7. *Mailman list configuration page*

The Majordomo Web Interface

Relatively few lists managed with Majordomo have a web interface available, but those that do generally use a program called MajorCool. MajorCool enables only subscribing and signing off lists, and you must use the e-mail interface to make any other changes to your subscription. Majordomo 2 includes a web interface.

Proprietary Web Interfaces: Yahoo Groups and Topica

Several services host mailing lists for people who want to start an e-mail mailing list, but who don't want to install a list server and don't belong to an organization that has one. Two of the most popular free services are Topica and Yahoo Groups, both of which use web pages for communication between the list server and list subscribers.

The information in this book about Topica and Yahoo Groups was correct at the time of publication, but these services often update their proprietary software. You should have no difficulty adapting these directions for use with any version of Topica or Yahoo Groups.

To join a Yahoo Group or manage your subscription to a group you've already joined, go to the home page of the group. The home page for a Yahoo group is **groups .yahoo.com/group/***groupname*, where you substitute the actual name of the group for *groupname*. To join the group, click Join This Group. To view or change your subscription options, click Edit My Membership. From this page, which should be similar to the one in Figure 10-8, you can modify your e-mail delivery options, hide your e-mail address, or leave the list.

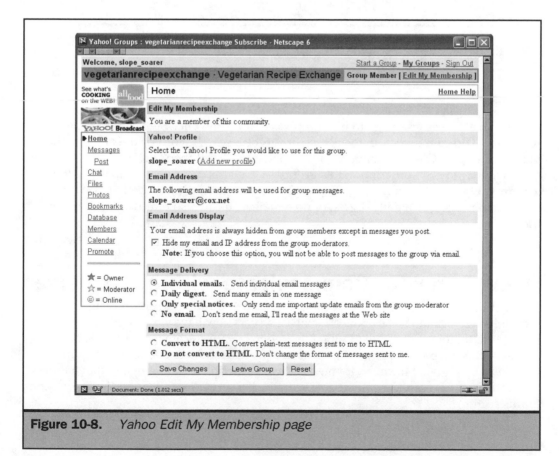

Figure 10-8. *Yahoo Edit My Membership page*

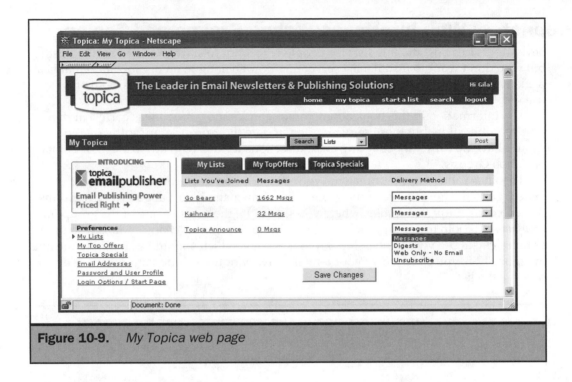

Figure 10-9.   *My Topica web page*

To join a Topica group, go to **www.topica.com/my** and click Sign Me Up to become a registered Topica member. In the Search box, type a search word or the name of the list you want to join. Click the name of any displayed list, and then click Join This List.

To manage your subscription to a group you've already joined, go to **www.topica .com/my**. On the My Topica page (Figure 10-9), you can indicate whether you want individual messages, a daily digest, or no e-mail. You can also remove yourself from the list.

Using E-mail to Communicate with a List Server

The first list servers were managed exclusively with commands sent to them in e-mail. Newer list servers and some of the original list servers now have web-based management tools (described in the section "Using the Web to Communicate with a List Server," earlier in this chapter), so you may never need to learn how to communicate with the list server by e-mail. However, if you decide to subscribe to a mailing list that has no web interface, you can learn to interact with the list server by following the instructions in this section.

Management, List, and Administrator Addresses

When interacting with any list server, it's important to understand that there are three types of addresses associated with every mailing list: the management address, the list address, and the administrator address:

- **Management address**   This is usually the name of the program, followed by @ and the domain name where the list server is running. For example, the management address for the Majordomo program installed at **gurus.com** is **majordomo@gurus.com**.

- **List address**   This is the list name followed by the same domain name. For example, the list address for the (fictional) RANT list managed by **majordomo@ gurus.com** is **rant@gurus.com**.

- **Administrator address**   Usually the same as the list address with the word "owner-" or "-owner" prepended or appended to the list name. For example, the administrator address for the RANT list is **owner-rant@gurus.com**.

Sound confusing? It's not too difficult once you get started, and Table 10-1 will help you understand the types of addresses and how to construct each one.

If you are interacting with a list server by e-mail, you can avoid personal embarrassment by being sure to send all commands to the management address. If you send a command to the list address, your command will just be e-mailed to the list subscribers, who can't execute your command for you and who may become annoyed.

List Server	Management Address	List Address	Administrator Address
	(For sending commands to the list server)	(For sending messages to the list subscribers)	(For sending e-mail to the human in charge of the list)
ListProc	listproc@*domain*	*listname@domain*	*listname*-request@*domain* or owner-*listname@domain*
LISTSERV	listserv@*domain*	*listname@domain*	owner-*listname@domain*

Table 10-1.   *Types of Mailing List Addresses*

List Server	Management Address	List Address	Administrator Address
Lyris ListManager	lyris@*domain* or *listname*-request@*domain*	*listname*@*domain*	owner-*listname*@*domain* or *listname*-owner@*domain*
Mailman	*listname*-request@*domain*	*listname*@*domain*	*listname*-owner@*domain* or *listname*-admin@*domain*
Majordomo	majordomo@*domain* or *listname*-request@ *domain*	*listname*@*domain*	owner-*listname*@*domain*

Table 10-1. *Types of Mailing List Addresses* (continued)

Common List Server Commands

You can communicate many different things to a list server, but only the most frequently needed commands are given in this chapter. When you type the commands given in the following sections, replace *listname* with the exact name of the list, *yourname* with your name (not your e-mail address), and *youraddress* with your e-mail address. If you received a password when you joined the list, replace *password* with that password. (If you've subsequently changed the password, use the current password.)

Remember that each command is to be sent to the list's management address. In the examples, a person named **Rosa Perez** is using the e-mail address of **rosaperez@ gurus.com** to subscribe to the fictional mailing list called **rant**. Her password (when required) is **lrkwdg**. When you send commands, be sure to substitute your real name and e-mail address, the name of the real list, and the actual password you've chosen or been assigned.

Tips for Sending Commands

When you send a command to the management address of a list server, follow these rules:

- ■ Put the command on the first line of the text of the message, not the subject line, which most list servers ignore.

- ■ Be sure to spell all parts of the command correctly.

- ■ Don't add any punctuation, spacing, or pleasantries. (Remember, a computer is reading this message.)

- ■ Put the whole command on one line.

■ Delete your signature if your e-mail program usually adds one. If you can't avoid a signature or other lines being added to the end of the message, type **end** on a line by itself after your command. The **end** command tells most list servers to skip the rest of the message.

If you fail to follow these rules exactly, the list server replies with a (probably confusing) error message. This isn't the time for creativity! Try to use the precise wording, spacing, and punctuation shown in this chapter.

LISTSERV has the annoying habit of responding to all commands with a message that tells you how much computer processing time your commands took. Just delete these messages.

Finding Out More About a Mailing List

Each mailing list should have an informational message about the list, which may include a FAQ (list of frequently asked questions and their answers). Most lists send you the informational message when you subscribe to the list, but you can get a copy at any time.

List Server	Put This Message in the Body of the E-mail
ListProc	info *listname* Example: **info rant**
LISTSERV	info *listname* Example: **info rant**
Lyris ListManager	review *listname* Example: **review rant**
Mailman	info
Majordomo	info *listname* Example: **info rant**

Subscribing to a List

To subscribe to a mailing list, send the appropriate command to the management address. These are the subscription command formats for the most popular list servers.

List Server	Put This Message in the Body of the E-mail
ListProc	subscribe *listname yourname* Example: **subscribe rant Rosa Perez**
LISTSERV	subscribe *listname yourname* Example: **subscribe rant Rosa Perez**
Lyris ListManager	subscribe *listname* "*yourname*" Example: **subscribe rant "Rosa Perez"**

List Server	Put This Message in the Body of the E-mail
Mailman	subscribe
Majordomo	subscribe *listname* Example: **subscribe rant**

Once you send your request, the list server reads your e-mail address from the headers of your message and processes your subscription command.

Confirming Your Subscription

Many lists send you a *confirmation message* to which you must reply before you are added to the subscription list. The use of confirmation messages prevents anyone from forging a subscription message and signing you up for lists without your permission. You may find the confirmation message to be poorly written and confusing; but if you follow these confirmation command formats for the most popular list servers, you should be able to confirm your subscription without difficulty.

Be sure to respond to the confirmation request from the same address from which you send the original subscription command.

List Server	Put This Message in the Body of the E-mail
ListProc	*Reply to the confirmation e-mail without making any changes to it.*
LISTSERV	Ok
Lyris ListManager	*Reply to the confirmation e-mail without making any changes to it.*
Mailman	*Reply to the confirmation e-mail without making any changes to it.*
Majordomo	auth *password* subscribe *listname youraddress* Example: **auth lrkwdg subscribe rant** **rosaperez@gurus.com**

If the mailing list has closed subscriptions, the list administrator may reject your request to subscribe, or she may write to you with a request for information about who you are and why you want to join. If the list allows open subscriptions, the list server adds you to the mailing list and sends you an automated response.

Be sure to save the welcome message you receive when you subscribe to a list. This message usually contains instructions for sending postings to the list, rules for postings, and instructions for signing off the list. The message may also contain a password that you can use to change the setting for your subscription, including changing your e-mail address. It's a good idea to create in your e-mail program a folder called Mailing Lists and to store all your welcome messages there.

Signing Off a Mailing List

To sign off (unsubscribe) from a list, send the appropriate command to the management address. Note that Lyris ListManager, Mailman, and Majordomo allow you to specify that you are signing off a specific e-mail address, which does not have to be the e-mail address you're using to send the command. Mailman requires you to include your list password, which was included in the welcome message you received from the list server when you subscribed.

List Server	Put This Message in the Body of the E-mail
ListProc	signoff *listname* Example: **signoff rant**
LISTSERV	signoff *listname* Example: **signoff rant**
Lyris ListManager	unsubscribe *listname* unsubscribe *listname youraddress* (depending on whether you want to remove your current address or another address) Example: **unsubscribe rant** or **unsubscribe rant rosaperez@gurus.com**
Mailman	unsubscribe *password* unsubscribe *password youraddress* (depending on whether you want to remove your current address or another address) Example: **unsubscribe lrkwdg** or **unsubscribe lrkwdg rosaperez@gurus.com**
Majordomo	unsubscribe *listname* unsubscribe *listname youraddress* (depending on whether you want to remove your current address or another address) Example: **unsubscribe rant** or **unsubscribe rant rosaperez@gurus.com**

The list server reads your e-mail address from the message headers, removes your name from the list, and sends you a confirmation message. Once the program has your new address, you can send a **signoff** command from your new e-mail account if you no longer want to subscribe to the list.

Changing Your Address

When your e-mail address changes, the easiest way to update your mailing list subscriptions is to sign off all the lists from your old address, and then resubscribe from your new account. Alternatively, if your list server is Lyris ListManager, Mailman, or Majordomo, you can sign off your old address by using the address-specific signoff command given in the previous section. However, what if your list isn't managed by one of these list servers, and your e-mail address has changed so you can't send a message from the account from which you subscribed? Simply write to the list administrator and politely ask him or her to change your address.

Finding Out What Lists You're Subscribed To

If you are subscribed to several lists run by the list server on a single computer, you can find out which lists you're subscribed to by using the **which** or **query** commands. Note that one of these commands includes an asterisk. That's a real asterisk that you need to type into the command, not a reference to an asterisked note elsewhere in the book!

List Server	Put This Message in the Body of the E-mail
ListProc	which
LISTSERV	query *
Lyris ListManager	which
Mailman	*This option is not available.*
Majordomo	which

Signing Off from All Lists Run by a Single List Server

You can sign off from all the lists run by the list server on a single computer with just one command. Note that some of these commands include asterisks. Those are real asterisks that you need to type into the command, not references to an asterisked note elsewhere in the book! ListProc requires you to provide your password for any list, which was included in the welcome message you received from the list server when you subscribed.

List Server	Put This Message in the Body of the E-mail
ListProc	purge *password* Example: **purge lrkwdg**
LISTSERV	signoff *
Lyris ListManager	purge
Mailman	*This option is not available.*
Majordomo	unsubscribe *

Receiving Messages in Digests

If you're too busy to read list postings all day, you might be happier if you choose to receive the list messages in a periodic digest rather than as separate e-mails. If you want to receive digests, you may also need to decide on the format you want to receive them in—many list servers give you a choice between MIME and plain text. *MIME* format means that each list message will be considered an *attachment* to the digest e-mail, as described in Chapter 7; *plain text* means that the various messages will be concatenated into one long e-mail. Note that Majordomo digests are actually separate lists: you subscribe either to the digested list or to the undigested list. Mailman requires you to include your list password, which was included in the welcome message you received from the list server when you subscribed.

List Server	Put This Message in the Body of the E-mail
ListProc	set *listname* mail digest set *listname* mail digest-nomime (depending on whether you want to receive the digest in MIME format or plain text) Example: **set rant mail digest** or **set rant mail digest-nomime**
LISTSERV	set *listname* digests set *listname* nomime (depending on whether you want to receive the digest in MIME format or plain text) Example: **set rant digests** or **set rant nomime**
Lyris ListManager	set *listname* digest set *listname* mimedigest (depending on whether you want to receive the digest in plain text or MIME format) Example: **set rant digest** or **set rant mimedigest**
Mailman	set digest on *password* Example: **set digest on lrkwdg**
Majordomo	Subscribe to the digest and unsubscribe from the undigested list, like this: subscribe *listname*-digest unsubscribe *listname* Example: **subscribe rant-digest unsubscribe rant**

Caution *When you reply to a message in a digest, be sure to quote only the message to which you are replying, not the whole digest. Also, change the subject line of your reply to include the subject of the message to which you are replying rather than the subject line of the digest.*

Stopping Receiving Messages in Digests

If you are receiving digests but want to begin to receive individual messages, you can change to that option. Note that Majordomo digests are actually separate lists: you either subscribe to the digested list or to the undigested list.

List Server	Put This Message in the Body of the E-mail
ListProc	set *listname* mail ack Example: **set rant mail ack**
LISTSERV	set *listname* nodigest Example: **set rant nodigest**
Lyris ListManager	set *listname* mail Example: **set rant mail**
Mailman	set digest off *password* Example: **set digest off lrkwdg**
Majordomo	Subscribe to the digest and unsubscribe from the undigested list, like this: unsubscribe *listname*-digest subscribe *listname* Example: **unsubscribe rant-digest** **subscribe rant**

Taking a Vacation from a List

There may be times when you temporarily want to stop receiving the messages from a list, but you don't want to sign off the list. Most list servers will let you do that, but they will not save the messages for you while you're away. If you want to be able to read the messages later, you should probably change your subscription to **digest** instead.

List Server	Put This Message in the Body of the E-mail
ListProc	set *listname* mail postpone Example: **set rant mail postpone**
LISTSERV	set *listname* nomail Example: **set rant nomail**
Lyris ListManager	set *listname* nomail Example: **set rant nomail**
Mailman	set nomail on *password* Example: **set nomail on lrkwdg**
Majordomo	*This option is not available.*

Returning from Vacation

When you're ready to start receiving messages from the list again, send one of the following commands.

List Server	Put This Message in the Body of the E-mail
ListProc	set *listname* mail ack set *listname* mail digest-nomime set *listname* mail digest (depending on whether you want to receive undigested mailings or to receive the digest in plain text or MIME format) Example: **set rant mail ack** or **set rant mail digest-nomime** or **set rant mail digest**
LISTSERV	set *listname* mail Example: **set rant mail**
Lyris ListManager	set *listname* mail Example: **set rant mail**
Mailman	set nomail off *password* Example: **set nomail off lrkwdg**
Majordomo	*This option is not available.*

Viewing the List Configuration and Subscribers

Most list servers will send you information about the configuration of the mailing list and/or a list of all the list's subscribers if you send the appropriate command.

List Server	Put This Message in the Body of the E-mail
ListProc	review *listname* Example: **review rant**
LISTSERV	review *listname* Example: **review rant**
Lyris ListManager	review *listname* Example: **review rant**
Mailman	who
Majordomo	who *listname* Example: **who rant**

List Server Communication Problems

If you run into trouble communicating with the list server, send the command **help** (or for LISTSERV lists, send the command **info refcard**) to the management address to get more information about how to use the various commands. If you still need help, write to the list administrator's address. The recipient of your e-mail will be an actual human, not a computer program, so politely ask for help with your problem.

Participating in Mailing Lists

To send a message to all the subscribers of a list, address the message to the list address (*not* the management address). The list address is the name of the list, followed by @, followed by the domain name where the list server is running. (For example, the fictional **rant** list hosted at **gurus.com** would have the list address **rant@gurus.com**.) When the list server receives your message, it distributes your message to the subscribers of the list. (If the list is moderated, your message first goes to the moderator, who must approve it before it's distributed.)

Before sending your first message to a list, remember to read the FAQ (list of frequently asked questions and their answers) for the list, if there is one, to be sure you understand the list rules.

Replying to List Messages

To respond to a posting with a message of your own to be sent to the entire list, first create a reply to a message from the list. Then look at the address in the *To* line of your reply. Some lists are configured so that replies are automatically addressed to the list address; others are automatically addressed to the person who sent the original message. You may need to change the address in the *To* line if you don't want to send your message to the address that the list configuration has supplied for you.

Consider whether the entire group of subscribers will be interested in your response. Perhaps a private e-mail message to the author of the message would be more appropriate. If the mailing list addresses replies to the list, you can copy the author's address from the original message to the *To* line of your reply.

If you want to refer to the original message in your response, quote the original message, deleting the parts of the original message that you don't plan to talk about. Don't bore subscribers by quoting the entire original message, which everyone else has already read once.

Posting a New Message

You don't have to respond to a message to participate in a mailing list discussion: you can also start a new topic. Address your message to the list address, choose a specific and informative subject line, and ask your question or make your comment.

Mailing List Dos and Don'ts

Here are some messages never to post to a mailing list:

- Commands intended for the list server (like **unsubscribe** or **signoff**) or questions intended for the list administrator. Send commands to the management address and questions to the administrator address.

- A message that quotes another message in its entirety, with the added comment "Me too!" or "I agree!"

- Chain letters, virus warnings, jokes about Microsoft buying God, get-rich-quick schemes, or other widely distributed e-mail messages.

- Advertisements about products or services. Rules about advertising vary from list to list, but advertisements are generally not welcome. If you sell something of interest to subscribers, you can discuss the technical merits of your product and include the URL of the product's web page in your signature, but don't try to solicit other subscribers to buy your product.

- Personal attacks on other subscribers. If you have a problem with something a subscriber said, write directly to that person rather than posting an attack to the list. Reply to the list only to discuss what the person said, not to discuss the person.

See the section on chat etiquette in Chapter 9 for general rules of behavior that are also applicable to mailing lists. Some other guidelines for participating in mailing lists include the following:

- *Make sure that the subject line reflects what the message is about.* Make your subject specific: "Trouble Importing Files into OmniData 6.2" is better than "Help!" If you are replying to a message, and the topic of your message has drifted from the topic shown in the subject line, change the subject line to reflect the actual current topic.

- *Don't send test messages.* If you're not sure whether you can post messages to a list, wait until you have something to say, and then try it.

- *Don't attach files to your messages, unless the mailing list specifically allows attachments.* Instead, send a message describing the file and asking anyone interested in receiving the file to e-mail you privately.

- *Don't send HTML-formatted messages.* Some e-mail programs can't read HTML, and others convert it into text that's full of annoying extra characters. Furthermore, when HTML-formatted messages go into the digest of the list, they fill it with duplicate copies of your message and other unwanted text.

Separating Mailing List Messages from Other Messages

Your personal messages and messages from various mailing lists arrive together in your e-mail mailbox. If you find it confusing to read all this mail jumbled together, you can arrange for all the messages from each mailing list to be displayed separately from your other mail.

Many e-mail programs can sort (or *filter*) your incoming messages into separate folders, so that you have one folder for each mailing list and one folder (usually your In or Inbox folder) for the rest of your incoming messages. Outlook, Outlook Express, Eudora, Netscape Mail, and Netscape Messenger can all sort your mail: see Chapter 8 for instructions.

Establishing Your Own Mailing List

If you haven't found a list to fit your needs or simply want to create your own mailing list, you have several choices:

- Use a service that hosts mailing lists at no cost or for a fee. (See the upcoming section "Free and Fee-Based Mailing List Servers.")

- Install a list server on your own computer. This approach is beyond the scope of this book. Refer to the web sites for LISTSERV, ListProc, Lyris, Mailman, and Majordomo for information about getting and installing each package. For information on other list servers, start at the Google directory (**directory.google .com**), and choose Computers | Software | Internet | Servers | Mail | List Management.

Note *Before you start a public mailing list, make sure that a similar list doesn't already exist. Search the directories discussed earlier in this chapter in "Finding Interesting Mailing Lists" for keywords that describe the subject or audience for your list. Hundreds of thousands of lists already exist—your new one may not be needed!*

Free and Fee-Based Mailing List Servers

A number of services host mailing lists at no cost to the list administrator. If you use a free list-hosting service, the service will either display advertisements on their web pages or append ads to the end of the e-mail messages that they distribute. If you don't want advertisements with your messages and don't want to host a list yourself, there are services that host ad-free lists at reasonable prices. Free and fee-based mailing list providers are listed in the Google directory at **directory.google.com** (Computers | Internet | Mailing Lists | Hosting Companies). The Mailing List Gurus page has links to other sites (**lists.gurus.com**).

Managing a Mailing List with a Mailing List Management Program

If you decide to establish your own mailing list, there are several steps to follow to set it up:

1. *Create the list.* The process of creating the list varies widely, depending on where your list is being hosted; but in all situations, you must decide on a name for your list. You must also specify whether the list will be open or closed, moderated, and other settings. Refer to "Mailing List Types and Options," early in this chapter.

2. *Write the informational and welcome messages.* Read the informational messages for some other mailing lists to get ideas of what yours should say. Be sure to include instructions for subscribing and signing off, for switching to and from digests (if digests are available), for postponing mailing list mail (if this option is available), and for contacting the mailing list administrator (you). Also provide guidelines for what subjects are welcome, what subjects are to be avoided, and other rules for subscribers. You'll need to install these messages and test that they look OK.

3. *Test the list.* Subscribe to your new list, and get a few friends or coworkers to subscribe, too. Then send a message to the list. Make sure that it is correctly distributed to the list and that replies to the message are addressed to the list or to the sender, depending on how you want the list configured. Check the list configuration, too. (See the next section, "Checking the List Configuration," for details on how to do this.)

4. *Advertise the list.* If the list is open only to a small group (for example, the list is for the board of trustees of an organization), let them know how to join. If the list is open to the public, you can ask to be added to each of the directories of Internet mailing lists (go to **directory.google.com** and choose Computers | Internet | Mailing Lists | Directories). Announce the new mailing list on some related existing mailing lists and Usenet newsgroups (but don't overdo it!), and add information about your mailing list to your organization's web site (if applicable).

5. *Consider making a web page for the list.* This web page can explain what the list is about, whom the list is for, and how to join. (In fact, you can use the informational message that you wrote in step 2.) After you upload the web page to the Web, submit your page to some search engines and directories as explained in Chapter 31.

6. *Start managing the list.* Think of a list of topics with which to seed the discussion once the list is running. Handle bounced mail and other problems as they arise.

CHATTING AND CONFERENCING ON THE INTERNET

Checking the List Configuration

List administrators can check the configuration of lists managed with Lyris List Manager by viewing List Info on the List Admin Menu, and configuration information for Mailman-based lists can be found on the List Administration page. Topica-based list configurations can be viewed and changed with the About Your List options at **www .topica.com/lists/***listname*/**prefs**, and the configurations for Yahoo Groups can be checked or modified at **groups.yahoo.com/group/***groupname*/**settings**. Changing the configuration of a list that has a web interface is quite straightforward and should need no further explanation.

For ListProc or Majordomo, send the command **config** *listname password*, or **get** *listname* (**header nolock** for LISTSERV—yes, that's an open parenthesis with no matching close parenthesis. In response, the list server sends you the configuration settings for the list (and possibly the informational message about the list and the subscribers list).

Note *The **nolock** part of the **get** command is important for LISTSERV lists. Otherwise, LISTSERV locks the settings for the mailing list, which prevents anyone from subscribing or unsubscribing.*

For example, here is part of the configuration for a ListProc mailing list:

```
VISIBLE-LIST
OPEN-SUBSCRIPTIONS
SUBSCRIPTION-MANAGERS [owners] (inactive)
SEND-BY-SUBSCRIBERS
ARCHIVES-TO-ALL
ARCHIVE /var/listmgr/archives/uua-l %h%y uua-l "" messages
MODERATED-NO-EDIT [owners]
DIGEST weekly Friday 0 0
MESSAGE-LIMIT 75
COMMENT "News from the Unitarian Universalist Association"
REPLY-TO-SENDER
OWNERS nettcr@gurus.com
```

The settings for a LISTSERV list might look like this (in part):

```
*   Review= Private
*   Subscription= Open,Confirm
*   Send= Private
*   Notify= No
*   Reply-to= Sender,Respect
```

```
*    Validate= No
*    Digest= Yes,/ssa/listserv/notebooks/uus-l,Daily,03:00,size(550)
*    Default-Options= REPRO, DIGESTS
*    Daily-Threshold= 150
*
*    Topics= Introduction, Announcements, Administration, GA, G,
*    Topics= UUA, E, D, C, B, A
*    Default-Topics= Introduction, Announcements, Other
*
*    Owner= nettcr@gurus.com
*    Owner= Quiet:
```

A Majordomo list's configuration might look like this:

```
subscribe_policy = open+confirm
restrict_post = kideo:kideo-digest
admin_passwd      =    kidzvidz
approve_passwd    =  kidzvidz
description       =    Videos for children
```

You can change some of these settings by sending **set** or **config** commands to the list server. For the details of each of these settings, as well as instructions for changing them, refer to the list administrator's manual for the list server you use. (See "Getting More Information," later in this chapter.)

Helping Others Subscribe

Some Internet users have difficulty subscribing to mailing lists, so you'll sometimes be asked to help a potential subscriber join your list. If your list has web administration, this task is very easy. List administrators who use Lyris can subscribe others (and cancel subscriptions) with the Members option of the List Admin Menu, and subscribers can be added to (or removed from) Mailman-based lists with the Membership Management section of the List Administration page. You can subscribe or unsubscribe others from Topica-based lists with the List Activity options at **www.topica.com/lists/***listname***/ prefs**. Add subscribers to Yahoo Groups at **groups .yahoo.com/group/***groupname***/ members_add**.

Subscribing someone else to ListProc, Majordomo, and LISTSERV lists generally requires that you send an e-mail message to the management address on that person's behalf. For ListProc lists, send this message:

add *listname password subscriberaddress subscribername*

Replace *listname* with the name of your list, *password* with the list administrator's password, *subscriberaddress* with the e-mail address of the person you want to add to the list, and *subscribername* with the person's full name. If you don't want the subscriber to receive a confirmation message, use **quiet add** instead of **add**.

For LISTSERV lists, send this command:

add *listname subscriberaddress subscribername*

For Majordomo lists, send this command:

approve *password* **subscribe** *listname subscriberaddress*

Helping Subscribers Sign Off

You can remove a subscriber from a Lyris, Mailman, or Topica list by going to the pages described in the previous section, "Helping Others Subscribe." To remove a subscriber from a Yahoo Group, go to **groups.yahoo.com/group/***groupname***/members**.

For ListProc lists, send this command:

delete *listname password subscriberaddress*

Add **quiet** to the beginning of the command if you don't want to send a confirmation message to that address (for example, if the address is no longer valid).

For LISTSERV lists, send this command:

delete *listname subscriberaddress*

For Majordomo lists, send this command:

approve *password* **unsubscribe** *listname subscriberaddress*

Handling Bounced Messages

From time to time (or many times a day, for lists with many subscribers and many messages), ListProc, LISTSERV, and Majordomo may inform you that mail to a subscriber has *bounced*—failed to be delivered. Your job as list administrator usually includes handling these *bounced messages*.

Take a look at the error message that the subscriber's mail host sent back. Many error messages include the phrase "non-fatal error," which usually means that the mail has been delayed but is expected to get through eventually. Other error messages include the phrase "fatal error": for these messages, continue reading to find out what the error was. Some fatal errors (errors that prevent the message from being delivered at all, ever) are temporary; for example, AOL's mail host produces a fatal error message when a subscriber's mailbox is full. Other fatal errors look permanent, like "Username unknown" or "Mailbox does not exist."

If the error looks non-fatal or temporary, ignore or delete the error message. If the error looks permanent and fatal, delete the subscriber from your list.

Some list servers (including Mailman, Yahoo Groups, and Topica) handle bounced mail themselves. Some delete any subscriber whose mail bounces at all, others delete subscribers with fatal mail errors, and others delete subscribers only after a specified number of messages have bounced within a short period. You may be able to configure your list to use one of these methods, depending on which list server you use.

Moderating a List

Often the administrator of a moderated list is also the list's moderator. If you are the moderator for a list, you approve all messages before they are distributed to subscribers. You act as the gatekeeper (or censor) for the list. When someone sends a message to the list address for the mailing list, the list server sends the message to you. You then tell the list server to tell it whether to distribute the message or to discard it.

ListProc gives each message a number. You tell ListProc what to do with the message by sending the command **approve *listname password number*** or **discard *listname password number***. For a LISTSERV list, if the message is okay to distribute to the list, reply to the message without editing the subject, and replace the text of the reply with the single command **ok**. For Majordomo, send the message (complete with the headers of the original message) to the list address for the list, adding the command **approve: *password*** as the first line of the message.

If a Yahoo Groups message is okay to post, go to **groups.yahoo.com/group/*groupname*/pending**. To approve a Mailman message, choose Tend To Pending Administrative Requests from the List Administration page. To allow a message to be posted to a Topica list, you must forward it to ***listname*-approve-*listpassword*@topica.com**.

If you choose to reject (discard) a message, be sure to inform the sender that you are doing so. The sender may want to rewrite the message to eliminate the issue that caused you to reject the message.

Editing the Informational and Welcome Messages

Every list should have an up-to-date informational message to tell subscribers how to sign off, how to change list settings, and what the rules of the list are. As list administrator, you are responsible for maintaining these messages, and you'll find that well-written and comprehensive informational messages will make your job easier! The informational messages for Mailman-based lists can be found on the List Administration page, and Lyris list administrators can modify the informational messages for their lists from the List Documents option on the List Admin Menu. Topica-based list informational messages can be viewed and changed with the About Your List options at **www.topica.com/lists/*listname*/prefs**, and messages for Yahoo Groups can be updated at **groups.yahoo.com/group/*groupname*/settings**.

For ListProc, LISTSERV, and Majordomo, the informational message is stored in the *info file* for the list. To receive a copy of the current message, send the command info *listname* to the management address. Once you receive the informational message, copy it into a text editor or word processor and edit the message. To send the updated message back to the list server for storage in your list's info file, compose a new message to the management address for the list. Turn off your signature or any other text added by your e-mail program.

For ListProc lists, type this command as the first line of the message:

put *listname password* **info**

For Majordomo lists, use this command:

newinfo *listname password*

For LISTSERV lists, type this command as the first line of the message:

put *listname* **welcome pw=***password*

Replace *password* with your personal LISTSERV password. (If you haven't created a personal LISTSERV password, before you use the **put** command, send the message **pw add** *newpassword* to LISTSERV to set your password to *newpassword*.)

On the second line of the message, copy the informational message. ListProc, LISTSERV, or Majordomo takes the text from the second line of the message to the end and uses it as the new informational message for the list.

 If you don't tell your e-mail program to suppress your signature when sending the informational file to the list server, your signature becomes part of the file!

Getting More Information

LISTSERV, ListProc, and Majordomo support many other configuration options. You can get more information about list administration commands on the World Wide Web.

- ■ **ListProc**   The ListProc manual is at **www.cren.net./listproc/docs**.
- ■ **LISTSERV**   LISTSERV manuals are at **www.lsoft.com/info/manuals.asp**.
- ■ **Lyris ListManager**   The Lyris manual is at **www.lyris.com/lm_help/5.0**.
- ■ **Mailman**   Mailman documentation is under the "Documentation" heading at **www.list.org**.
- ■ **Majordomo**   Ask your Majordomo site manager for the list-owner-info file in the Doc directory in the directory in which the Majordomo program is installed.
- ■ **Topica**   Topica documentation is at **www.topica.com/help**.
- ■ **Yahoo Groups**   Help for Yahoo Groups is at **help.yahoo.com/help/groups**.

Summary of List Administration Commands

Table 12-2 shows the most commonly used commands for administering mailing lists with LISTSERV, ListProc, and Majordomo.

Description	LISTSERV Command	ListProc Command	Majordomo Command
Get list configuration	get *listname* (header nolock	config *listname* *password*	config *listname* *password*
Add subscriber	add *listname* *subscriberaddress* *subscribername*	[quiet] add *listname* *subscriberaddress* *subscribername*	approve *password* subscribe *listname* *subscriberaddress*
Sign off subscriber	delete *listname* *subscriberaddress*	[quiet] delete *listname* *subscriberaddress*	approve *password* unsubscribe *listname* *subscriberaddress*
Approve message for moderated list	(Reply to message from LISTSERV)	approve *listname* *password number*	approve:*password* (Sent to the list address)
Reject message for moderated list	(Reply to message from LISTSERV)	discard *listname* *password number*	(Not applicable)
Install informational message	put *listname* welcome *password*	put *listname* *password* info	newinfo *listname* *password*

Table 10-2. *List Administration Commands for LISTSERV, ListProc, and Majordomo*

Chapter 11

Usenet Newsgroup Concepts

267

One of the oldest Internet services—a decade older than the World Wide Web—is Usenet, a system of thousands of newsgroups that enables people to exchange messages on a huge variety of subjects. Many novice Internet users consider Usenet dead (or have never heard of it), but Usenet still attracts tens of thousands of active participants. Many organizations run private newsgroups using Usenet technology. For example, Microsoft's beta testers receive support from Microsoft developers exclusively through a set of private newsgroups.

This chapter describes what newsgroups are, how they are named, what software you need to read newsgroups, problems that you may encounter, and how to create your own newsgroup. The next chapter gives step-by-step instructions for reading newsgroups, using the most popular programs. If you're looking for information on a specific subject— especially a technical one—searching and reading Usenet newsgroup postings is well worthwhile.

What Are Newsgroups?

Usenet is a distributed system of messages (also called *articles* or *postings*), like a worldwide bulletin-board system. Because so many messages are sent every day, they are divided into *newsgroups,* with each newsgroup concentrating on one topic. You can read the newsgroups' articles, post replies to articles, or post new articles. As with e-mail mailing lists, you can read articles on your own schedule rather than in real time (when people are writing them). Unlike with mailing lists, anyone can read articles without subscribing to the newsgroup.

Newsgroups are named by using a hierarchical system of words separated by dots. The first word of a newsgroup name indicates the category (or *newsgroup hierarchy*) into which the newsgroup falls. The additional words specify topics within the top-level category. The following are the original seven hierarchies and their respective topics:

- **comp**   Computer hardware, software, networking, and other computer-related topics
- **misc**   Miscellaneous topics
- **news**   Usenet itself
- **rec**   Recreational topics
- **sci**   Scientific topics
- **soc**   Social topics
- **talk**   General discussion

The **alt** newsgroup hierarchy was formed for "alternative" newsgroups (it may stand for Anarchists, Lunatics, and Terrorists, depending on whom you ask). Now there are hierarchies for countries (using two-letter abbreviations), other geographical areas (for example, **ny** for New York and **ba** for the San Francisco Bay area), colleges, ISPs, corporations, and other groups (for example, the **biz** hierarchy is for businesses).

Following the hierarchy name, the newsgroup name adds words that specify the topic of the newsgroup. For example, newsgroups about computers start with **comp**, newsgroups about computer systems start with **comp.systems**, and the newsgroup about laptop computers (one type of computer system) is called **comp.systems.laptops**. Newsgroups about social issues have names starting with **soc**, newsgroups about religion have names starting with **soc.religion**, and the newsgroup about Unitarian Universalism is called **soc.religion.unitarian-univ**.

Some newsgroups are *moderated*, which means that a moderator (usually a human being, but sometimes a program) reviews all messages for appropriateness and style. Moderation regulates the quality of the newsgroup's postings by eliminating garbage, repetitive posts, off-topic posts, and general whining. However, unless the moderator never sleeps, messages to moderated groups can be delayed, and if the moderator has opinions about the subject of the newsgroup, he or she may slant the discourse.

Some organizations run their own newsgroups that are not part of Usenet. For example, Microsoft uses private news servers to host public support forums about its products and uses private newsgroups for beta testers of unreleased products. These newsgroups are all in the **microsoft** hierarchy.

How Do You Read Newsgroups?

Articles posted on newsgroups are distributed over the Internet by *news servers*, Internet hosts running news server software. These servers store and forward Usenet articles, and provide articles to users running *news clients* or *newsreaders*. News servers and newsreaders communicate by using an Internet protocol called the *Network News Transfer Protocol (NNTP)*. To read Usenet newsgroups, you can use popular newsreaders, such as Netscape Mail & Newsgroups (which comes with Netscape 6), Netscape Messenger (which comes with Netscape Communicator), Outlook Express (which comes with Internet Explorer), Free Agent (a shareware newsreader), NewsWatch (a Mac newsreader), or one of many UNIX-based newsreaders (the easiest to use is called *tin*). Chapter 12 describes how to use some of the most popular newsreaders.

Some newsreaders allow you to download all the articles in newsgroups to which you are subscribed, to read the articles *offline* (when you are not connected to the Internet). If you compose new articles, the newsreader stores the articles and sends them the next time you connect to the Internet. For product support newsgroups, downloading and saving messages is a good way to have a library of questions and answers about the product.

An alternative way to read Usenet newsgroup articles is by using the Google Groups web site at **groups.google.com**. Google (which purchased the Deja News archive) stores all the articles in all the major newsgroups since about 1994 and enables you to search them by keyword. See the section on newsreading in Google Groups in Chapter 12 for details.

To start reading, you connect to a news server. Almost every ISP runs a news server, and it's usually named **news** followed by a dot and your ISP's domain name (for example, **news.sover.net**). These news servers distribute articles posted to most or all Usenet newsgroups. Many omit recreational newsgroups (like the **alt.sex** hierarchy), newsgroups that distribute large files (usually pictures), and illicit newsgroups (like those that distribute pirated software). You can also connect to a *private news server*, that is, a news server that carries only its own newsgroups, separate from Usenet. For example, Microsoft runs a news server named **news.microsoft.com** to which you can connect if you want to ask questions and read answers about Microsoft's products.

Once you are connected to a news server, you choose which newsgroups to read. When your newsreading program displays the list of available newsgroups, you see only the newsgroups carried by your news server. The list may not be complete: most ISPs and others who run news servers choose only the newsgroup hierarchies most likely to be of general interest, to save disk space. If your ISP is in Vermont, it may not carry newsgroups for the San Francisco Bay area. Some companies omit recreational newsgroups (like those in the **alt.sex** hierarchy, for example) from their news servers. Many news servers omit newsgroups with the word "binaries" in their titles because they carry either pictures (which may be prurient) or software (which may be stolen). Each news server has a *news administrator*, the system manager who makes these decisions. If you don't see a newsgroup that you are looking for and you are sure that it exists, search for it on Google Groups. You can ask your news administrator to add the newsgroup to your news server, if you have a good reason to read the newsgroup. You can also connect to more than one news server at the same time.

Looking at the list of newsgroups, you decide which to *subscribe* to. Unlike subscribing to a mailing list, subscribing to a newsgroup doesn't put you on a centralized list of people who read that newsgroup. Instead, subscribing only tells your newsreader that you want to read this group. (See Chapter 12 for specific instructions on how to subscribe to and read newsgroups in many popular newsreaders.)

Next, you instruct your newsreader to show you the headers of some or all of the articles in the newsgroup. The program usually shows you the subject, sender, and posting date for each article. You can select which articles to read. (See the section "Choosing What to Read," later in this chapter.) After you read articles, you can reply to the sender by e-mail or post a reply to the newsgroup.

How Are Newsgroups Different from Mailing Lists?

Technically, newsgroup articles are distributed differently than messages posted to e-mail mailing lists. When you post a message to a mailing list, it goes to the mailing list manager (usually a program), which sends copies of the message to each person subscribed to the list. The messages land in each subscriber's mailbox. When you post a message to a newsgroup, the message is forwarded from news server to news server until the message reaches all the news servers on the Internet. Each news server that carries the newsgroup stores one copy of the message. When people connect to a news server to get newsgroup messages, they see the messages that have arrived in the newsgroups they select. There's no such thing as a newsgroup mailbox: messages for all the newsgroups your news server carries are stored together on the news server. Your newsreader program has the job of keeping track of which newsgroups you subscribe to and which messages in each of those newsgroups you've already read.

Once you send a mailing list message to the list subscribers, you can't cancel it (or any other e-mail message). Because newsgroup articles are stored centrally on news servers, the sender of an article can cancel it. When you cancel an article that you've posted, a cancellation message is circulated to all news servers, and the servers delete the article from their list of current articles. If you cancel an article right after you post it ("Oops! What did I just say!?"), the article is deleted quickly and isn't on news servers long enough for many people to download it. However, the message remains on any PC that has already downloaded it from the news servers.

Another difference between mailing lists and newsgroups is the way in which past messages are stored. After mailing-list messages are distributed, they are saved only if the mailing list is archived. News servers usually store messages for a specific number of days, typically somewhere between 3 and 30 days, depending on the volume and size of newsgroup messages and the hard-disk limitations of the news server. You can browse the past messages that are stored on the news server. The Google Groups web site stores newsgroup articles for several years. Before posting an article, be aware that your words may be publicly available for years.

Finally, mailing lists can be closed (approved subscribers only), whereas newsgroups that are run on public news servers are all publicly readable. However, some organizations run private news servers, which require a user name and password to connect to. For example, some software companies maintain password-protected news servers, so that people who are testing unreleased products can exchange messages in private.

Finding Interesting Newsgroups

Here are some newsgroups to read while you are getting up to speed in Usenet:

- **News.announce.newusers** This is a must-read group. The newsgroup is moderated, so it contains only about 40 articles, with lots of introductory information.

- **News.announce.important** This useful group contains few articles, but the ones there are important.

- **News.answers** This is a collection of the FAQs (frequently asked questions and their answers) from thousands of Usenet newsgroups—a compendium of the collected knowledge of Usenet.

- **Rec.humor.funny** This moderated newsgroup consists entirely of jokes that the moderators (Brad Templeton and Jim Griffith) think are funny. (And they are usually right.)

After you are comfortable reading newsgroups, try searching for words in the list of newsgroup titles if your newsreader allows this. Alternatively, go to the Google Groups web site at **groups.google.com**, and search for words or phrases: when you see the list of articles that Google finds, you can also see to which newsgroups the articles are posted. Try subscribing to the newsgroups that have the most useful articles on your topic.

 For more general information about Usenet, see the Usenet Info Center at the **sunsite.unc.edu/usenet-i** *web site. Many of the regular postings from the* **news.announce.newuser** *newsgroup appear on the site as web pages, along with other Usenet advice.*

Choosing What to Read

When you read an article, your newsreader marks it as read, so that you can tell which articles you have and haven't read. If you decide after a quick scan of the subject lines that all the new articles in a newsgroup look boring, most newsreaders let you mark all the messages in a newsgroup as read. You may also be able to sort the messages by topic or sender and mark groups of messages as read.

 Many newsgroups include periodic postings, *which are articles that are automatically posted on a regular basis. Be sure to read these messages the first time that they go by: they usually contain the newsgroup's FAQ, newsgroup rules, or other useful information. If you are looking for the FAQ for a newsgroup and you don't see it in the list of articles, try the Usenet FAQ Archive web site, at* **www.faqs.org/faqs**. *(Click the Click To Pay button to donate $5 if you find the site useful.)*

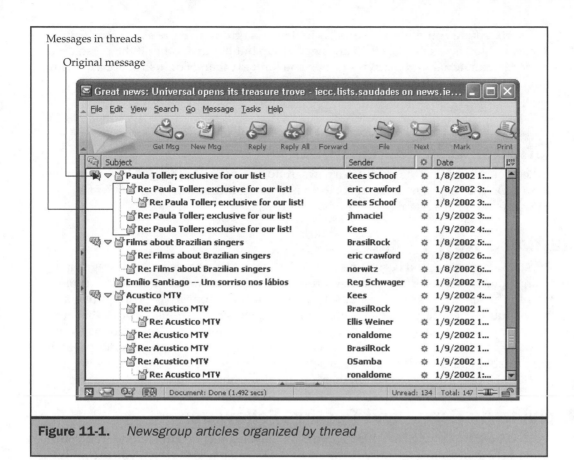

Figure 11-1. *Newsgroup articles organized by thread*

Most newsreaders present newsgroup articles in *threads*. A thread is an article, followed by all the replies to that article, replies to the replies, and so forth. These *threaded newsreaders* present the articles in each thread in an indented list, with the replies to each article shown indented below the message to which they reply. You can choose which threads you want to read, mark entire threads to skip, and perform other commands on threads, all of which make zeroing in on interesting topics easier.

Some newsreaders let you create *kill files,* which are files stored on your own system that specify which types of articles you never want to read and which types you always want to read. You can have one global kill file, which applies to all newsgroups, and other kill files that apply only to specific newsgroups. Using kill files, you can *kill* (automatically mark as read, so that you never see them) articles from a particular person, or you might want to kill specific topics in specific newsgroups. For example, you might want to blank all messages from **nettcr2@gurus.com** in all newsgroups (if this book annoys you). If you like to knit and you read the **rec.crafts.textiles.yarn** newsgroup, you could block all articles in that newsgroup that are about crocheting. You could kill a person's posts in one newsgroup but not in another if the person sends reasonable material to some newsgroups and junk to others. For instructions on using kill files, see the section on filtering messages for your newsreading program in Chapter 12.

Choosing What to Post

When you are reading the articles in a newsgroup, you may find that you have something to say. Or you may start a discussion on a new topic. Either way, you can post a message to one or several newsgroups.

Starting a New Thread

To start a new topic and begin a new thread, just post a message to the newsgroup by using your newsreader. If other newsgroups would be interested, too, you can *cross-post* the article to other newsgroups, but do so with caution: cross-posting to lots of newsgroups is considered spamming, and some newsgroups refuse articles that are cross-posted to many groups. Cross-post only if one or two other newsgroups would have a specific interest in your topic. When you cross-post, your newsreader program may enable you to designate one newsgroup to receive *follow-ups* (postings in reply), so that the ongoing discussion happens in only one newsgroup.

Replying by E-mail and Posting Follow-ups

When you compose a reply, think about who will be interested in reading it. If your remarks will be of interest only to the author of the message to which you are replying, send the reply by e-mail. Most newsreaders let you compose an e-mail reply easily. Don't waste everyone else's time, especially if your reply basically states "Me too!" or "I agree!"

On the other hand, if you are answering a question of general interest or have something good to contribute to the discussion, go ahead and post a *follow-up* article to the newsgroup. Quote the message to which you are replying, editing out all but the relevant material. After you send it, the article may take a few hours to appear on the newsgroup. Don't panic, and wait at least a day before reposting the message because your article is probably just slow to arrive. If the newsgroup to which you posted is moderated, the moderator may delay things. (Even newsgroup moderators take an occasional vacation!)

Usenet Netiquette

All the usual rules of "netiquette" (listed in the section on chat etiquette in Chapter 9) apply to newsgroups, too. Here are a few additional tips:

- Before you post a question, read the newsgroup's FAQ. (If you haven't seen it go by on the newsgroup, check in the **news.answers** newsgroup or the **www.faqs.org/faqs** web site.) Also, look through the existing newsgroup messages that appear in your newsreader—someone might have just asked the same question. People get peevish when you ask questions that have already been answered.

- If you are responding to a message, be sure to use the newsreader's command to reply or follow up, so that your message is marked as part of the same thread as the message to which you are responding. If you are starting a new subject, don't use the "reply" or "follow up" command: instead, use the "new article" command in your newsreader, so that your message starts a new thread.

- When you reply or follow up to an article, take a look at the headers of your message before you send it. If the original message was posted to several newsgroups, your reply may be, too. Most newsreaders let you edit the headers of your message so that you can post the reply to only the newsgroups that are appropriate.

- Just use plain text whenever possible, with no special characters, and with lines that are less than 80 characters wide.

- Don't post the same message to many newsgroups: this practice is called *cross-posting*. Choose the one or two most appropriate newsgroups for your message and post it there.

- If you realize that you made a mistake in an article that you posted, cancel it as soon as possible. Instructions for canceling articles for some popular newsreaders are in Chapter 12.

Sending and Receiving Attachments

Like e-mail messages, Usenet articles can contain files. And, like the e-mail system, Usenet was originally designed to accommodate only text, so the files have to be specially encoded to make it through the system. Usenet uses *uuencoding*, one of the encoding systems that e-mail uses, to convert binary (nontext) files to text for transmission. When your newsreader encounters a uuencoded message, it must decode the message to convert it to the original file. If the file is large, it may be split into several (or dozens of) messages, so that your newsreader has to reassemble the file before decoding it. Luckily, most newsreaders are up to the task.

Not all newsgroups allow you to post binary files: many specifically prohibit it. But over 800 newsgroups in the **alt.binaries** hierarchy are dedicated to the exchange of binary files. (And not all of them are for dirty pictures.) Binary files distributed on newsgroups are mainly graphics files (such as in **alt.binaries.clip-art** and the hundreds of newsgroups in the **alt.binaries.pictures** hierarchy), but some are audio files (such as in the newsgroups in the **alt.binaries.sounds** hierarchy) and executable program files (almost entirely bootlegged).

To decode and save a file distributed on a newsgroup, refer to Chapter 12, which contains instructions for some popular newsreaders. Some older newsreaders require you to save the messages that contain the file and to run a separate decoding program to turn the messages back into the file. Most newsreaders perform the decoding for you and display graphics files directly.

 Most of the binary files distributed via Usenet are bootlegged (that is, distributed without the permission of their copyright holders). Please don't use bootlegged material—buy the real thing!

Offensive Postings

Since the early days of Usenet newsgroups, people have posted off-color jokes. To avoid offending innocent readers, *rot13* was born (short for "rotate by 13"). Rot13 is the simplest encryption imaginable: any eight-year-old could easily crack the code. Each letter is replaced by the letter 13 places earlier or later in the alphabet; that is, letters in the first half and the second halves of the alphabet are swapped. The letter *a* is replaced by *n*, *b* by *o*, *c* by *p*, *m* by *z*, *n* by *a*, and so forth. The same swapping applies to capital letters. The code works well because its purpose is to avoid accidentally offending readers rather than truly concealing the text.

Rot13-encoded messages contain "rot13" in the subject line. When your newsreader displays a rot13-encoded message, it looks like Martian text, and you have to give a command to decode the message. (If your newsreader doesn't support rot13, you have to do the decoding by hand or by using a separate program.) If you'd rather not read something offensive, you can just skip decoding the message.

Avoiding Spam

Spam is a nickname for unsolicited commercial e-mail, but the term is used for Usenet postings, too. In fact, spam first became widespread on Usenet (when two lawyers blanketed most newsgroups with ads for a service that promised green cards to U.S. immigrants). Many Usenet newsgroups have virtually been taken over by spam, and many readers find advertising offensive, whether it's spam or not. If you want to post a commercial announcement on a newsgroup, make sure that it is directly related to the topic of the newsgroup, contains mainly technical information and no hype, is short, and contains your e-mail address for people who want more information. Also, make sure that you contribute regularly and constructively to the newsgroup, so that participants will feel you've "earned" the right to send an ad. Of course, it's always OK for the signature at the end of your messages to contain a one-line ad.

A pitfall of posting any article to any Usenet newsgroup is that the e-mail address on your article will be "harvested" by programs that scan all postings for e-mail addresses and add the addresses to databases that are sold to *spammers* (people who send spam). A common experience of people who post to Usenet for the first time is that within a few weeks, they start getting mountains of junk e-mail.

The most common method to avoid getting spammed is to use a garbled e-mail address when you post. Posting articles with fake e-mail addresses is discouraged, but you can easily garble your e-mail address so that a human can figure it out, but a harvesting program can't. For example, if your e-mail address were *nettcr2@gurus.com*, you could configure your newsreader to use *nettcr2-at-gurus-dot-com* as the return address in your postings. Anyone reading the address could figure out your correct address.

Many people add extra characters to their e-mail addresses (for example, turning *nettcr2@gurus.com* into *nettcr2ZZZ@gurusZZZ.comZZZ*), with instructions in the posted message (usually in the signature) for removing the letters that don't belong. Other people add *REMOVETHIS* or *DELETEME* right after the "@" in their addresses. Here are a few guidelines:

- Garble the domain part of your e-mail address (the part after @), not just the user name part (the part before @). If you garble only the user name, spam sent to your garbled address will reach a real domain, and the postmaster at that domain will have to deal with it for years. If you garble the domain, the e-mail will bounce back to the sender, without ever reaching a mail server.

- Don't use the same method of garbling forever. Spammers aren't stupid, and their harvesting programs get smarter every day. When they get wise to the idea of spelling out "at" and "dot," they will program their harvesting programs to convert *nettcr2-at-gurus-dot-com* back to *nettcr2@gurus.com*. The programs are already smart enough to remove *NOSPAM* from the middle of e-mail addresses.

- For more ideas, take a look at the headers and signatures of the messages in the newsgroups that you read. Other subscribers may come up with new, creative ways to foil the harvesting programs.

How to Create Newsgroups

To create a new Usenet newsgroup, someone must send a special command message that instructs news servers to create the newsgroup. However, most news servers ignore these commands unless the messages are the result of a process that has grown since the early days of Usenet. Specifically, few news servers will create newsgroups in the major hierarchies (**comp**, **misc**, **news**, **rec**, **sci**, **soc**, and **talk**) unless a procedure has been completed that involves proposals, discussion, and voting.

Many news servers will create newsgroups in the **alt** hierarchy at the drop of a hat (as you can tell, if you look at the huge and bizarre list of **alt** newsgroups). However, **alt** newsgroups are not as widely available as newsgroups in the major hierarchies, so your audience may be limited.

If you want to create a new newsgroup in one of the major hierarchies, see the article "How to Create a New Usenet Newsgroup," by Greg Woods, Gene Spafford, and David C. Lawrence, at **www.cis.ohio-state.edu/hypertext/faq/usenet/usenet/ creating-newsgroups/part1/faq.html**. The article is also posted on **news.groups** and **news.announce.newgroups**.

Creating a newsgroup in the **alt** hierarchy is a lot simpler: you propose the newsgroup in the **alt.config** newsgroup. If the consensus of the group is positive, then you either send the newgroup command message yourself or ask one of the Usenet experts in the newsgroup to send the command for you.

Many other hierarchies work similarly: look for a **config** newsgroup, subscribe to it, read the messages (and especially the FAQ), and ask questions. For example, if you live in New York City and want to create a newsgroup in the **nyc** hierarchy, subscribe to **nyc.config**. If there is no newsgroup called **config**, try **general** (for example, **nyc.general**).

For details, see the article "So You Want to Create an Alt Newsgroup," by Dave Barr, at **www.faqs.org/faqs/alt-creation-guide** on the Web.

Running Your Own News Server

You also have the option of running your own private news server and creating newsgroups on it. These newsgroups won't be distributed by the Usenet newsgroups around the globe, but you may not want them to be—private news servers are excellent ways to run narrowly targeted discussions. Many people find them easier to read than mailing lists because newsreader programs do a better job than mail clients of arranging messages into threads and include commands for ignoring topics or senders that you've decide not to read. Many organizations run private news servers that require a user name and password, to prevent the general public from reading, participating in, and spamming the newsgroups. For example, many software companies provide technical support to their advanced users and beta testers through private or public newsgroups.

If you want to set up your own newsgroup hierarchy, and optionally control who can read your newsgroups, you can run your own news server. You need a UNIX or

Linux system that is connected to the Internet and running a news server program. You also need an Internet connection with these characteristics to support a news server:

- **Broadband**   To effectively serve anything over the Internet, you need a fast connection, such as DSL or cable. Many ISPs, such as MSN, EarthLink, and CompuServe, do not allow any kind of server to be run on a regular Internet connection. Ask your ISP whether they forbid servers on your type of account. (Many networks formally forbid servers but, in practice, don't enforce the rule unless the server uses a great deal of bandwidth—which is rarely a problem with news servers.)

- **Static IP or Dynamic IP Service**   Although you are not required to have one, a static (unchanging) IP address makes hosting any kind of Internet server easier because your users can find your server at the same address each time they connect. If your ISP doesn't offer static IPs (or charges a mint for them), companies such as TZO and DynamIP offer dynamic IP services, which give you a static domain name that knows your dynamic IP at all times.

News Server Programs

If you decide to run your own news server, you'll need a news server program. Several free and shareware servers are available for Windows, Mac OS, and UNIX/Linux:

- **Tortoise (tortoise.maxwell.syr.edu)**   This is a simple but powerful news server for Windows NT Service Pack 3 (though it also runs on Windows 2000).

- **INN (www.isc.org/products/INN)**   This freely available, open source news server works on Linux, UNIX, and the various BSDs, and is included with most distributions. INN is not hard to set up if you know how to install and run UNIX/Linux software; I recommend reading *Managing Usenet* (by Henry Spencer and David Lawrence and published by O'Reilly & Associates).

- **Spaniel Server (www.spanielsoftware.com/newsserver.html)**   This free Java-based news server can be used on any server that supports Java 1.1.*x*.

- **DNews (netwinsite.com/dnews.htm)**   This commercial application is a well-respected high-performance news server. DNews is available in a 60-day demo version. Prices for the various versions are at **netwinsite.com/prices_dnews.htm**.

If you expect a lot of traffic, or have an organization with several offices, you can set up a private news network by installing INN on several servers that update each other with a shared set of newsgroups. For example, if you have three offices, you can set up three news servers that send updates to each other, and all the users get snappy response from their local server while seeing all the messages posted on all three servers.

CHATTING AND CONFERENCING ON THE INTERNET

Creating and Naming Newsgroups on Your Own Server

Once your news server is running, you are ready to create your local newsgroups (refer to your news server's documentation for specific instructions). Choose newsgroups names that are easy to remember, but unlikely to be the same as newsgroup names used elsewhere. A good approach is to use multipart names with the first part being the name of your organization and the second part being the specific topic area, something like *vtcooks.bread* and *vtcooks.cheeseballs* and *vtcooks.piecrust.lard* if you have a group of cooks in Vermont who want to swap recipes. Unique names are important because you may want to exchange messages with other news servers in the future, and mass confusion will ensue if two servers have identically named groups that are supposed to be different.

You also need to provide access to your newsgroup users. Don't just make the news server accessible to everyone; software pirates will promptly discover it and will fill your newsgroups with copies of stolen material they want to exchange among themselves. If your news server is on a LAN, you can configure it to permit access from addresses on your LAN. You can also set up user names and passwords that people elsewhere can use to connect to your news server. The user names need not be the same as a user's e-mail address; and it's quite possible for a group of people to use the same news password, even though they all have different e-mail addresses.

Finally, set an expiration policy for each of your newsgroups—that is, how long the news server stores messages before deleting them. If you have a lot of disk space and moderate traffic, you can keep all your news messages indefinitely, making the news server an archive for its messages.

The Complete Reference

Internet

Chapter 12

Reading Usenet Newsgroups

To read newsgroups (which are described in Chapter 11), you can use a newsreader program. No matter what system you use—PC or Mac or UNIX/Linux—there are several newsreader programs that enable you to access newsgroups. (An alternative to newsreaders is the Google Groups web site, described later in this chapter.) For those who use Linux or BSD UNIX, all the distributions come with at least three newsreaders, all of which are well documented.

If you use Netscape 6.*x* as your browser, you might want to use Netscape Mail (or more properly, Netscape Mail & Newsgroups, which is part of the Netscape 6 suite). Netscape 4.7 users might want to use Netscape Messenger, which is part of the Netscape Communicator 4.7 suite. If you use Microsoft Internet Explorer as your browser, you might prefer Outlook Express, which also comes from Microsoft. (Outlook, which comes with Microsoft Office, doesn't include a newsreader.)

> **Note**   *If you use a Mac, consider NewsWatcher, a stand-alone newsreader specifically designed to work on Macs. The latest version of NewsWatcher is 2.2.2. You can get a copy of NewsWatcher from TUCOWS (**www.tucows.com**) or from the Mac Orchard web site (**www.macorchard.com/usenet.html**). Alternatively, you can use Outlook Express's Mac version, which includes a newsreader.*

Common Newsreading Tasks

This section describes the general steps most newsreaders require you to follow for reading newsgroups: connecting to a news server, choosing newsgroups to subscribe to, choosing which articles to read, reading articles, and sending replies. The rest of this chapter gives specific instructions for performing these tasks with the most popular newsreaders: Outlook Express 6, Netscape Mail 6.2, and Netscape Messenger 4.7, as well as with the Google Groups web site.

Configuring Your Newsreader

When you install a newsreading program, you must tell it your news server (the server from which the newsreader gets Usenet newsgroup articles). If you don't know the name of a news server you can use, ask your ISP or system administrator. If you read newsgroups that are stored on different news servers, some newsreaders let you set up more than one news server. (For example, Microsoft, Netscape, and other software companies maintain publicly accessible news servers with newsgroups about their products.) You may also need to tell it your SMTP (Simple Mail Transfer Protocol) server for outgoing mail so that you can reply to newsgroup postings by private e-mail to the author.

Subscribing to Newsgroups

Once you are connected to your news server, you choose which newsgroups to subscribe to. News servers can carry 10,000 or more newsgroups, so downloading and displaying the list of available newsgroups can take several minutes. Sifting through the newsgroup names can take a while, too. Some newsreaders let you search for newsgroups that contain a word in the newsgroup name.

 Not all news servers carry all newsgroups. Many servers don't carry newsgroups that carry sexually explicit or bootleg material. Some news servers carry only private newsgroups.

Selecting and Reading Articles

Newsgroups can contain hundreds or thousands of messages, with dozens or hundreds of new messages every day. You can select which messages to read by thread (topic), date, or sender (using filters or kill files), or you can scan down through the message headers to spot messages that look interesting. If you read newsgroups with Outlook Express, Netscape Mail (in Netscape 6.*x*), or Netscape Messenger (in Netscape 4.*x*), see Chapter 8 for how to create filters that automatically skip or discard messages that you are unlikely to want to read.

If you pay for your Internet connection by the hour, reading newsgroups offline can save you money. Some newsreaders let you download some or all of the message headers in a newsgroup, or some or all of the message text, so that you can read them later, when you are offline. Once the newsreader has downloaded the messages for the newsgroups you want to read, you can read the messages in those newsgroups after disconnecting from the Internet.

Posting Messages

Sooner or later you may want to reply to a newsgroup message. You can either reply directly to the sender of the message by e-mail (if what you have to say is of interest only to the original author) or reply with a *follow-up* posting to the newsgroup so that everyone in the newsgroups can see your response. Most newsreaders let you reply either way.

If you want to bring up a new topic, you can post a new message, to one newsgroup or to many. (Don't send the same message to more than one or two newsgroups: choose only newsgroups that are directly related to your topic.)

A few newsreaders let you use HTML formatting when you compose e-mail or newsgroup messages. The messages look great (you can choose fonts, add lines, and insert pictures), but most people won't be able to see the formatting because most newsreaders can't display HTML formatting. Some people may even complain that they can't read your messages and request that you use text-only formatting. Use HTML formatting only in newsgroups that explicitly allow this type of message.

If you post a message and then have second thoughts about it, or one with an error, you might want to cancel the message after you've sent it. Usenet lets you cancel messages that you've posted, by sending out a cancellation message. Anyone who has already downloaded your message will see your message, but your cancellation message deletes the original message from some Usenet news servers. Once the message is deleted from a news server, anyone who downloads messages from that server won't get your canceled message.

Newsreading in Google Groups

Google Groups is a web site for searching and displaying newsgroups. It's a handy tool to use when you're looking for specific information in Usenet and don't want to spend hours hunting for it with a newsreader. Google Groups maintains a database of all the messages posted to all the Usenet newsgroups in the major news hierarchies for the last 20 years. You can search the newsgroup archives for messages that contain words or phrases, or messages posted by particular people.

Using Google Groups, you can locate the names of newsgroups within your interest areas and then use those names to subscribe to the newsgroups. Once you've found newsgroups of interest, you can read newsgroup articles using Google Groups, or you can subscribe to the newsgroups using your newsreader. This process saves you having to hunt through thousands of newsgroups from your news server.

 If you plan to read newsgroups regularly (for example, if you use a product whose manufacturer provides technical support through a newsgroup), Google Groups may not have all the features you want. However, it's great for occasional reading!

To use Google Groups, use your browser to go to the Google Groups site at **groups.google.com**. The exact layout of the web site changes, but you can

- Search for newsgroups that contain a specified word in the newsgroup name or description
- Search all newsgroup articles for individual messages that contain a word or phrase
- Browse newsgroups by newsgroup name

Once you find newsgroup names, you can click them to see listings of articles. Scroll through the message headers to find an article that interests you. Once you've found an article, click it, and Google Groups opens a new window displaying the message. Using the Back button in the browser's toolbar, you can go back to the message headers page to locate and read other articles. When you locate a message you want to print, click the Print icon in the toolbar. To save an article or message, click File | Save As, and select the directory and location you want to save the file to. Enter a name for the file and click the Save button. You can save any page you access in a browser, so you're not limited to only saving messages.

Tip *Search Google Groups' archive for your own name to see what articles you've posted to Usenet newsgroups or what other people have said about you (or to read postings from people anywhere in the world who have the same name as you).*

Newsreading in Outlook Express 6

Outlook Express is Microsoft's popular e-mail program (described in Chapter 6).
Outlook Express also acts as a newsreader, and Outlook runs Outlook Express when
you ask to read newsgroups by choosing Go | News from the menu bar.

When you run Outlook Express for the first time, the Internet Connection Wizard
helps you set up e-mail accounts and configure the newsreader to work with your ISP's
news server.

Finding and Subscribing to Newsgroups

If the Set Up A Newsgroup link appears in the middle of the Outlook Express window,
click it; the Internet Connection Wizard prompts you for information. Otherwise,
choose Tools | Accounts to display the Internet Accounts dialog box, click the News
tab to see whether any news servers are already configured, click the Add button,
and choose News from the menu that appears. Then follow the Internet Connection
Wizard's instructions. The wizard asks for your name and e-mail address (as you
want them to appear when posting to newsgroups), the name of the news server from
which you want to read newsgroups, and whether the news server requires you to
log in. When you are finished, the news server appears on the News tab of the Internet
Accounts dialog box. You can select it and click Properties if you need to change the
information about it.

After you've added your news server, you're ready to begin downloading newsgroups.
When you close the Internet Accounts dialog box, Outlook Express automatically
prompts you to subscribe to newsgroups. Downloading the list of available newsgroups
can take several minutes. When Outlook Express is done, you see the Newsgroup
Subscriptions dialog box shown in Figure 12-1. (You can also display this dialog box by
choosing Tools | Newsgroups or pressing CTRL-W. If your Outlook Express window is
wide enough, you can also click the Newsgroups button that appears near its right end.)

Once you see the list of newsgroups, you can choose which ones you want to subscribe
to by scrolling down the list to the newsgroup you want, clicking the newsgroup name,
and clicking the Subscribe button (or by double-clicking the newsgroup name). To see
only the newsgroups to which you have subscribed, click the Subscribed tab. When
you have finished choosing newsgroups, click OK. The newsgroups you chose appear
in the folder for your news server. (Click the plus button to the left of the news server
name or double-click the news server name if the newsgroups don't appear.)

Outlook Express also gives you a way to find specific newsgroups when you see
the Newsgroup Subscriptions dialog box. In the Display Newsgroups Which Contain
box, type the words you want to search for. (For example, if you are looking for a
newsgroup that discusses laptop computers, type **laptop**.) Outlook Express displays
all the newsgroups that contain that string of characters in the newsgroup name.

CHATTING AND
CONFERENCING ON
THE INTERNET

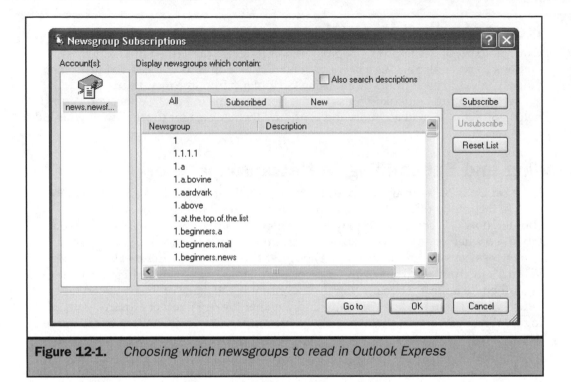

Figure 12-1.   *Choosing which newsgroups to read in Outlook Express*

    If you tire of a subscribed newsgroup, you can always unsubscribe by pressing CTRL-W *to see the Newsgroup Subscriptions window, clicking the Subscribed tab, clicking the newsgroup name, and clicking the Unsubscribe button.*

Selecting and Reading Messages

Once you have selected the newsgroups that interest you, there are several ways you can read the messages. You can read them while you're online, or you can read them offline without being connected to the Internet.

Reading Articles Offline

To set up newsgroups for offline reading, follow these steps:

1. Display the list of newsgroups you are subscribed to by clicking the plus box to the left of the news server name. Outlook Express lists the newsgroups indented below the news server name.

2. Click the newsgroup or newsgroups you want to read offline.

3. Choose File | Properties from the menu bar (or press ALT-ENTER) to display the Properties dialog box for the newsgroup.

4. Click the Synchronize tab and select the When Synchronizing This Newsgroup Download box. Choose the option you want: New Headers, New Messages, or All Messages.

5. Click OK to dismiss the Properties dialog box.

6. Repeat these steps for each newsgroup you want to read offline.

7. Choose Tools | Synchronize All from the menu bar. If you want to read only one newsgroup, you can select a newsgroup and then choose Tools | Synchronize This Newsgroup.

Outlook Express downloads all the message headers and (if you selected them) bodies (that is, the text of the messages) for the newsgroups you selected. You can disconnect from the Internet and read the articles as described in the next section.

Reading Articles Online

To read newsgroups online, click the plus box to the left of the news server and click the name of the newsgroup you want to read. Outlook Express downloads some or all of the message headers and displays them in the upper-right pane of the Outlook Express window. The selected message appears in the lower-right pane. You can double-click on specific messages to view them in a separate window.

If you don't like the layout or fonts used when displaying newsgroup messages, you can change them. Choose Tools | Options, click the Read tab, and click the Fonts button. Choose the font you want to read your messages in and click the OK button. When you see the Read tab, you can also set other options that control how e-mail and newsgroup messages appear.

Threading Messages

Outlook Express can sort messages by *threads* (an original message and all replies to that message), date posted, sender, subject, or several other ways. To keep threads together, choose View | Current View | Group Messages By Conversation. (A check mark appears by the Group Messages By Conversation command when it is selected; to turn this feature off, give the command again.) Outlook Express groups all the messages in each thread together and displays only the first message in each thread in the message list. To see the rest of the messages in a thread, click the plus box by the message.

To sort individual messages or threads by subject, sender, or other ways, choose View | Sort By and select the way you want the messages or threads sorted. You can also sort by subject, sender, or date by clicking on the column header in the message list (the upper-right pane in the Outlook Express window).

Selecting Articles and Threads

You can choose whether to see all the unread messages in the newsgroup or only replies to your newsgroup messages. To view unread messages, choose View | Current View | Hide Read Messages. To see only replies to your newsgroup messages, choose View | Current View | Show Replies To My Messages.

To search for messages from a particular person with a specific subject within a specific range of dates, choose Edit | Find Message or press CTRL-SHIFT-F to see the Find Message dialog box. To search again, press F3.

Sending Messages

You can reply to an existing message (that is, add your message to an existing thread), reply by e-mail to the author of a message, or post a message on a new topic.

Replying to Messages

When you want to reply to a message, either by e-mail or by posting a follow-up, first select or display the message.

To reply to the whole newsgroup, click the Reply Group button on the toolbar. The Newsgroups box in the new message header shows which newsgroups the article will be posted to. (You can also e-mail the message by typing addresses in the Cc box.) The original message appears quoted (with lines preceded by > characters) in the message box; delete everything but the part of the message you are specifically responding to. Type your message and click Send on the toolbar.

To reply only to the author of the message, click the Reply button in the toolbar of the Outlook Express window. If you haven't sent mail yet with Outlook, the Inbox Setup Wizard guides you through setting up your e-mail configuration. If your default e-mail program is a program other than Outlook Express, that program pops up to help you compose the message.

Posting a Message on a New Topic

To compose a new message, first click the newsgroup you wish to send your message to. Then click New Post on the toolbar. In the New Message window that appears, type your message and the subject and click the Send button on the toolbar.

When you want to post a message to more than one newsgroup, click Tools | Select Newsgroups from the New Message window menu bar. On the Pick Newsgroups dialog box that appears, choose a newsgroup from the list and click the Add button. You can send a message to any newsgroup whether you're subscribed to it or not.

Formatting Messages

When you post a message, you can determine how your message is formatted, as well as add your signature, a business card, attachments, or links to files or web addresses.

To ensure that everyone can read your messages, post them as plain text rather than formatted. Choose Tools | Options from the Outlook Express menu bar, click the Send tab, and click Plain Text in the News Sending Format part of the Options dialog box. Then click OK.

You can format your messages using HTML formatting, which lets you change font styles and sizes and indent or center your paragraphs. However, not everyone who participates in newsgroups is able to view HTML documents. To format a message with HTML, select Format | Rich Text (HTML) from the message composition window menu bar. Highlight the text you want to format. If you want to format all the text, select Edit | Select All from the menu bar (or press CTRL-A). Once you've selected the text you want formatted, choose the options you want from the formatting toolbar.

 Outlook Express lets you use stationery for newsgroup messages, too. You can include a background image, special fonts, signature files, or a business card. Chapter 6 describes how to set up stationery. Stationery uses HTML formatting, so most people won't be able to see the formatting. Don't use stationery when posting to newsgroups.

Canceling Messages

You can't cancel e-mail messages, but you can cancel messages to newsgroups. To cancel a message you've sent, select the newsgroup to which you sent the message, click the message you want to cancel, and choose Message | Cancel Message.

Printing Messages

To print a message, select the message header or display the message. Choose File | Print, click Print on the toolbar, or press CTRL-P.

Saving Messages

When a message catches your attention and you want to keep it indefinitely, you can save it. Outlook Express gives you two different ways to save messages you want to keep: moving them to an Outlook Express folder or saving them to a text file. To save the message in a folder, drag the message from the list of message headers to a folder in the folder list (in the left pane of the Outlook Express window). To save a message in a text file, choose File | Save As and select the folder and file into which you want to save the message. You can give the message a unique filename or use the subject line as the filename. (To create a new folder, click Local Folders in the folder list and choose File | Folder | New Folder.)

Unsubscribing from Newsgroups

As you get more proficient at using newsgroups, you'll find some of the groups you subscribed to either no longer interest you or that they never did. In that case, you can delete them from your folder list. Right-click the newsgroup in the folder list, and choose Unsubscribe from the menu that appears. Outlook Express may ask you to confirm that you want to unsubscribe.

Newsreading in Netscape Mail & Newsgroups 6

Netscape 6, which includes a completely new version of the popular Navigator browser, comes with its own e-mail and newsreader program. The program is called Mail & Newsgroups on Netscape's Task menu, but we'll just call it Netscape Mail. See Chapter 6 for how to get and configure Netscape 6.

To open Netscape Mail, choose Tasks | Mail & Newsgroups from the menu bar, or click the Mail icon in the lower-left corner of the Netscape window. When you run Netscape Mail for the first time, you need to tell the program which news server (or news servers) you plan to use:

1. In the Netscape Mail window, choose Edit | Mail & Newsgroup Account Settings from the menu bar.

2. In the dialog box that appears, click the New Account button. The New Account Setup Wizard appears. Click Next to move from screen to screen.

3. Choose the Newsgroup Account option.

4. On the Identity page, enter the name and e-mail address that you would like to identify yourself with in newsgroups. You do not have to use your regular e-mail address; to avoid spam, some people use a separate e-mail address for newsgroup postings (for example, a Hotmail or Yahoo Mail account).

5. On the Server Information page, enter the address of your NNTP (Network News Transfer Protocol) news server, which is usually something like news.*domain.com* or sometimes usenet.*domain.com*, where *domain.com* is the domain name part (not necessarily ending in "com") of your e-mail address. To read a public news server, ask your ISP for the name of their news server.

6. On the Account Name page, enter a nice name that's easy to remember. For our example, you could use "LarryNet's News Server" or something similar. Click Next and Finish.

When you are finished, you return to the Mail & Newsgroups Account Settings dialog box. There, the list of accounts on the left side of the dialog box now includes a new item—the news server. Categories appear below it (click the gray arrow to the left of the server name if the categories don't appear), as shown in Figure 12-2. Click these categories—Server Settings, Copies And Folders, Addressing, and Offline & Disk Space—to modify your news server settings as needed.

Note   *If the news server requires a user name and password to connect, Netscape Mail prompts you to enter this information when you first access it.*

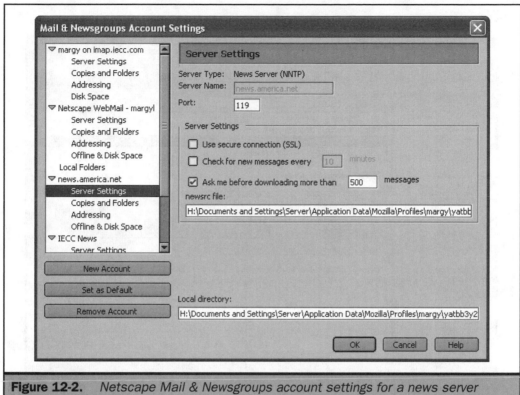

Figure 12-2.   *Netscape Mail & Newsgroups account settings for a news server*

Finding and Subscribing to Newsgroups

In the Netscape Mail window, your news server appears in the list of mail folders at the left side of the window, as shown in Figure 12-3.

To find newsgroups to subscribe to, click the news server you just created, and a new page appears in the right-hand pane. Under the Newsgroups heading, click the Subscribe To Newsgroups link. The Subscribe dialog box appears (as shown in Figure 12-4) and asks you if you would like to download the list of available newsgroups. After the list loads, which may take a long time, depending on your connection speed, you can select lists whose subjects interest you. Type a word into the Show Items That Contain field to narrow the list. Try using terms that are specific, like "surfing" or "Madonna" or "Access 2002." Vague terms like "computer," "software," and "music" can result in very large lists that are no help at all.

New newsgroups are added frequently. From time to time, take a look at the list of new newsgroups to see if any match your interest. Choose File | Subscribe and click the Refresh button.

News server   Message headers

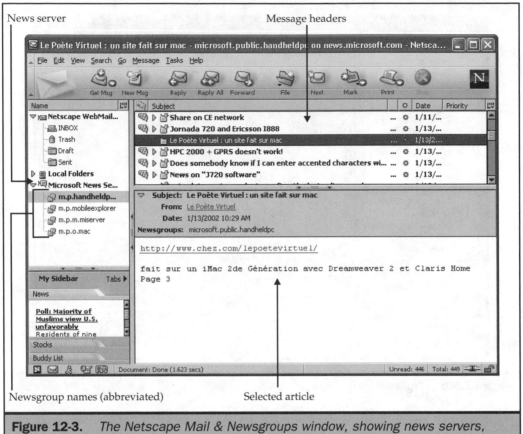

Newsgroup names (abbreviated)   Selected article

Figure 12-3.   *The Netscape Mail & Newsgroups window, showing news servers, newsgroups, message headers, and an article*

Downloading and Reading Messages

You can read the newsgroups you've subscribed to either online (while connected to the Internet) or offline (not connected). If your list of subscribed newsgroups doesn't appear under your news server name in the Netscape Messenger window, click the small triangle to the left of the news server name. Netscape Messenger automatically updates all the newsgroups you are subscribed to. This process can take several minutes.

Once you have subscribed to a newsgroup, you can begin reading its messages by clicking the newsgroup name in the left pane. If there are more than 500 messages that you haven't read, Netscape Mail asks how many *headers* (the part of the message that tells who it's for, who it's from, and what it's about) you want to download at one time.

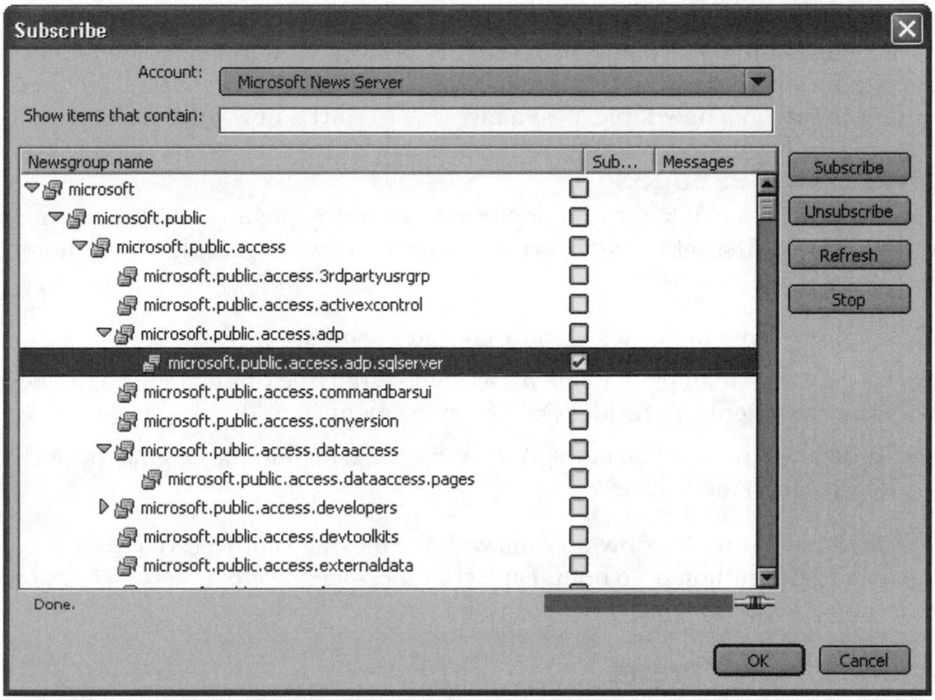

Figure 12-4.   *Subscribing to newsgroups with Netscape Mail & Newsgroups*

The default is 500. After Netscape Mail downloads the message headers, they appear in the upper-right part of the Netscape Mail window. To read a message, click the message header; the message appears in the lower-right part of the window.

To set Netscape Mail to retrieve messages so you can view them when you are not connected to the Internet, choose File | Offline | Offline Settings. You see the Mail & Newsgroups Account Settings dialog box, with the Offline & Disk Space settings for your news server. In the Offline section, click the Select button and choose which news servers you want to download for offline reading. Once you have saved your settings, choose File | Offline | Download/Sync Now. Netscape Mail asks whether you want to download mail messages or newsgroup messages, and whether to upload messages you've written.

Note   *Depending on the number of messages that are in the newsgroup and the filters you may have applied to the number of messages downloaded at any given time, downloading can take several minutes.*

CHATTING AND CONFERENCING ON THE INTERNET

Sending Messages

When responding to a message, you can either post a follow-up message to the newsgroup or reply by e-mail to the author of the message. When you may have something to say on a new topic, post a message to start a new thread.

Replying to Messages

To reply either via e-mail to the author of a message or by posting a follow-up message to the newsgroup, first select the message to which you want to reply. Then choose one of the following options:

- To post a reply to the newsgroup, click Reply on the toolbar.
- To send an e-mail reply to the person who wrote the original message, choose Message | Reply To Sender Only from the menu.
- To do both (post on the newsgroup and send e-mail to the original poster), click Reply All on the toolbar.

A message composition window appears with the message addressed to the newsgroup, to the author, or to both. Type your message, delete unnecessary quoted material, and click Send when you're finished.

Starting a New Thread

To compose a message on a new topic, click the newsgroup name and click New Msg on the toolbar (or press CTRL-M). When the message composition window opens, the newsgroup name appears in the Newsgroup box. Type the subject line, write the message you want to send to the newsgroup, and click Send on the toolbar. You can check your spelling by clicking the Spelling icon, or attach another document or file by clicking the Attach icon. (Remember that most newsgroups frown on attachments.)

Canceling Messages

If you realize after you sent a message to the newsgroup that you left something out or that you wish you hadn't been so hasty in clicking the Send button, you can cancel the message. Choose Edit | Cancel Message from the menu bar. Anyone who hasn't retrieved newsgroup messages before you canceled the message won't see it.

Printing Messages

When you see the text of a newsgroup message, you can print the message by choosing File | Print or clicking Print on the toolbar.

Saving Messages

To save a message, choose File | Save As | File from the menu bar. Select the directory and file where you want to save the message and type a filename (or let Netscape

Messenger use the subject of the messages as the filename). Click the Save button when you're finished.

Unsubscribing from Newsgroups

If you don't want to continue to read a newsgroup, unsubscribe from it so that Netscape Messenger doesn't waste time downloading its messages. In the list of subscribed newsgroups that appears below the news server name, right-click the newsgroup name and choose Unsubscribe from the menu that appears.

Newsreading in Netscape Messenger

Netscape Communicator 4.7, which includes the popular Netscape Navigator browser, comes with its own e-mail and newsreader program. The program is called Netscape Messenger when you are reading mail and Netscape Newsgroup when you are reading newsgroups, but it appears to be the same program. See Chapter 6 for how to get and configure Netscape Messenger 4.7.

   To open Netscape Messenger, choose Communicator | Newsgroups or Communicator | Messenger from Netscape, or click the Read Newsgroup icons (like two dialog balloons) in the Netscape component bar that appears in the lower-right corner of the Netscape window. When you run Netscape Messenger for the first time, you need to tell the program which news server(s) you plan to use:

1. In the Netscape Messenger window, choose Edit | Preferences from the menu bar.

2. In the Preferences dialog box that appears, click the plus box next to the Mail & Newsgroups category if its subitems aren't already displayed.

3. Click the Newsgroups Servers category to display the news server settings in the right part of this window, as shown in Figure 12-5.

4. Click Add and type the address for your Internet provider's news server in the Server box. Leave the Port box set to 119 (the default port number for news servers) unless your Internet provider or system administrator specifies another port. If the news server you use requires you to log in with a user name and password before retrieving newsgroup articles, click the Always Use Name And Password check box.

5. Click OK. The news server appears in the list of news servers in the Preferences dialog box.

6. Click OK again. Your news server appears in the folder list in the Netscape Messenger window, as shown in Figure 12-6.

Finding and Subscribing to Newsgroups

To subscribe to newsgroups, choose File | Subscribe. You see the Communicator Subscribe To Discussion Groups dialog box. From this dialog box, you can list all

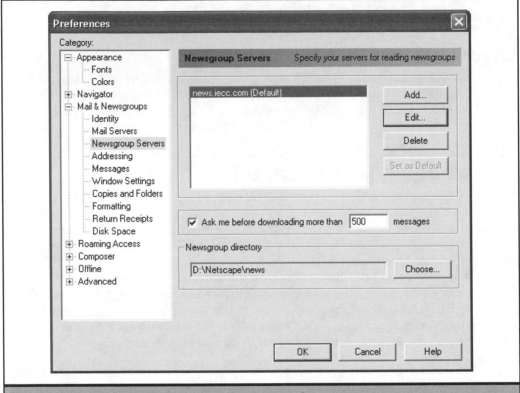

Figure 12-5. *Configuring Netscape Messenger for your news server*

newsgroups (by clicking the All tab), search for certain newsgroups you specify with a keyword (by clicking the Search tab), or list any new groups created since you last listed available newsgroups (by clicking the New tab).

When you click the All tab, you see the thousands of available newsgroups on the news server. Each newsgroup hierarchy (like **alt** and **comp**, described in Chapter 11) appears as a single heading, with a folder and plus box to its left. To see the newsgroups within a hierarchy, click the plus box. Hierarchies can contain subhierarchies: keep clicking plus boxes until you see newsgroup names, indicated by two-balloon icons. When you want to see only the top-level hierarchy names again, click the Collapse All button. If you know the beginning of the newsgroup name you want, type it in the Newsgroup box; Netscape Messenger scrolls the list of newsgroups down to the newsgroup you type, expanding hierarchies as needed.

When you see a newsgroup that looks interesting, subscribe to the newsgroup by clicking the newsgroup name and clicking Subscribe, clicking in the Subscribe

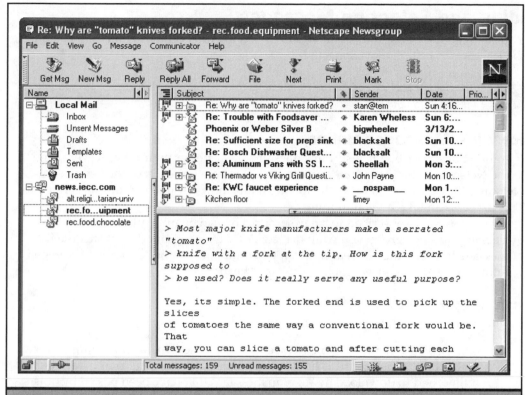

Figure 12-6. *The Netscape 4.7 Messenger window, showing news server, subscribed newsgroups, message headers, and an article*

column to the right of the newsgroup name, or double-clicking the newsgroup. A check mark appears in the Subscribe column next to the newsgroup name.

To bypass downloading what can be a very large list of newsgroups, you can search for specific newsgroups. Click the Search tab, make sure your news server appears in the Server box, type the keyword you want to search for in the Search For box, and click the Search Now button. Netscape Messenger displays a list of matching newsgroups. To subscribe to any of the newsgroups listed, click the dot in the Subscribe column to the right of the newsgroup name or double-click the newsgroup. Then click OK.

Tip   *New newsgroups are added daily. From time to time, take a look at the list of new newsgroups to see if any matches your interest. Choose File | Subscribe and click the New tab.*

Reading and Selecting Messages

You can read the newsgroups you've subscribed to either online (while connected to the Internet) or offline (not connected).

 If the lines of text extend off the right side of the window, choose View | Wrap Long Lines from the menu.

Reading Messages Online

If your list of subscribed newsgroups doesn't appear under your news server name in the Netscape Messenger window, click the plus box to the left of the news server. Netscape Messenger automatically updates all the newsgroups you are subscribed to. This process can take several minutes.

Once you have subscribed to a newsgroup, you can begin reading its messages by clicking the newsgroup you want to read. After the program downloads the list of message headers, they appear in the upper-right pane of the Netscape Messenger window. To read a message, click the message header.

Reading Messages Offline

If you prefer to read the newsgroup messages offline, follow these steps:

1. Choose File | Offline | Synchronize to display the Synchronize Offline Items dialog box, which controls how you send messages you've composed while offline, and to download newsgroup messages that have been posted by others while you were offline.

2. Click the Select Items button to choose the newsgroups you want to download before going offline and that you want updated when you go back online. In the Select Items For Download dialog box, click each newsgroup's dot icon so that it changes to a check mark and then click OK.

3. Back in the Synchronize Offline Items dialog box, click the Newsgroup Messages box so that it contains a check mark.

4. Click Synchronize to download the new messages in the newsgroups you selected. Netscape Messenger downloads new messages and uploads messages you have composed.

5. Once the download is finished, you can disconnect from the Internet and read the messages from the newsgroups at your leisure.

To tell Netscape Messenger that you want to work online again, choose File | Offline | Work Online.

Threading Messages

Reading newsgroups that have hundreds of postings a day can be overwhelming. You can sort the messages by thread, including either flagged messages only or all messages.

To organize a newsgroup's messages, follow these steps:

1. Click the newsgroup you want to read.

2. After all the messages load, click View | Sort By from the menu bar.

3. Choose how you want to sort messages.

You can sort by date, flags, order received, priority, sender, size, status, subject, thread, unread, ascending, or descending order. You can also combine ascending or descending order with one of the other sort criteria.

You can filter (sort) incoming messages to mark uninteresting (or offensive messages) as if you had already read them, so you don't have to see them again. Choose Edit | Message Filters to create and edit filters. See Chapter 8 for more information.

Sending Messages

If you have a response to a message, you can either post a follow-up message to the newsgroup or reply by e-mail to the author of the message. When you have something to say on a new topic, post a message to start a new thread.

Replying to Messages

To reply either via e-mail to the author of a message or by posting a follow-up message to the newsgroup, first select the message to which you want to reply. Then choose one of the following options:

- To post a reply to the newsgroup, click Reply on the toolbar.

- To send an e-mail reply to the person who wrote the original message, right-click Reply and choose To Sender Only from the menu that appears.

- To do both (post on the newsgroup and send e-mail to the original poster), click Reply All. A message composition window appears with the message addressed either to the author or the group.

Type your message, delete unnecessary quoted material, and click Send when you're finished.

Starting a New Thread

When you want to compose a message on a new topic (which may start a new thread), click the newsgroup name and click New Msg on the toolbar. When the message composition window opens, the newsgroup name appears in the Group box. Type the subject line, write the message you want to send to the newsgroup, and click Send on the toolbar.

You can check your spelling by clicking the Spelling icon, attach another document or file by clicking the Attach icon, or quote from another message sent to the newsgroup by clicking the Quote icon.

Canceling Messages

If you realize after you sent a message to the newsgroup that you left something out or that you wish you hadn't been so hasty in clicking the Send button, you can cancel the message. Choose Edit | Cancel Message from the menu bar. Anyone who hasn't retrieved newsgroup messages before you canceled the message won't see it.

Printing Messages

When you see the text of a newsgroup message, you can print the message by choosing File | Print or clicking Print on the toolbar.

Saving Messages

To save a message, choose File | Save As | File from the menu bar. Select the directory and file where you want to save the message and type a filename (or let Netscape Messenger use the subject of the messages as the filename). Click the Save button when you're finished.

Unsubscribing from Newsgroups

If you don't want to continue to read a newsgroup, unsubscribe from it so that Netscape Messenger doesn't waste time downloading its messages. In the list of subscribed newsgroups that appears below the news server name, right-click the newsgroup name, and choose Delete Selection from the menu that appears. Alternatively, choose File | Subscribe from the menu, click the All tab, scroll down to the newsgroup name (expanding newsgroup hierarchies as needed), click the newsgroup name, and click Unsubscribe.

Newsreading with Free Agent

Free Agent is a stand-alone Windows program that lets you access and read newsgroups. The latest version of Free Agent is 1.21. You can download a copy from its web site at **www.forteinc.com/agent** or from shareware sites like TUCOWS (**www.tucows.com**). Chapter 34 explains how to download and install programs from the Web. If you like Free Agent, you should also look at its inexpensive big brother, Agent, which adds more news and mail management features.

The first time you run Free Agent, it asks you for your news server, mail server, e-mail address, and name. Then it connects to the news server and offers to download the complete list of newsgroups. This can take a while, so you can choose to download them later. Then you see the Free Agent window, which is divided into three panes: the Groups pane, the Message List pane, and the Message pane (Figure 12-7).

Finding and Subscribing to Newsgroups

The Groups pane (in the upper-left part of the Free Agent window) lists newsgroup names. Click the pane header to switch from All Groups to Subscribed Groups (only those you are subscribed to) to New Groups (newsgroups that have been created recently).

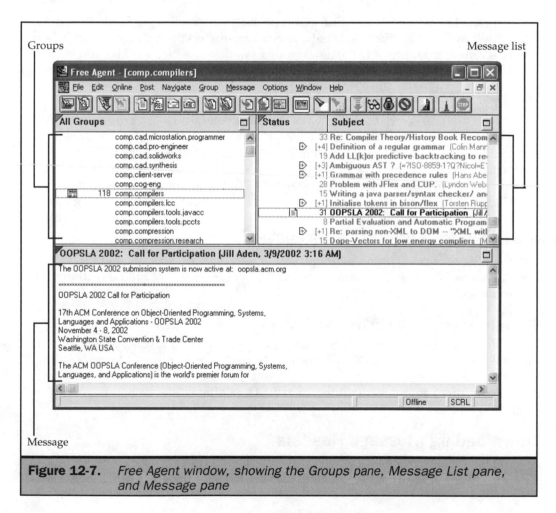

Groups

Message list

Message

Figure 12-7.   *Free Agent window, showing the Groups pane, Message List pane, and Message pane*

Subscribing to Newsgroups

To subscribe to a newsgroup, you can scroll down the list of all groups until you find
the newsgroup you want, and then double-click the newsgroup name. On the View
Empty Group dialog box that appears, you can click

- **Sample Message Headers** to see the headers of a few messages, to see if
  this newsgroup might interest you

- **Get All Message Headers** to see the message headers for all the current
  messages in the newsgroup

- **Subscribe To Group** to add the newsgroup to your list of subscribed
  newsgroups

You can also choose Group | Subscribe, press CTRL-S, or click the Subscribe To
Group button in the toolbar to subscribe to newsgroups as you run across them when
you're scrolling through the list of newsgroups. No matter which method you use to
subscribe, Free Agent inserts a newspaper icon next to the groups you've subscribed to.

Finding Newsgroups

Free Agent lets you search the huge list of available newsgroups for groups by name.
You can search individual messages by author or subject. To search for newsgroups
with a particular word in the newsgroup name, select the Groups pane. Click the Find
button on the toolbar or choose Edit | Find from the menu bar. In the Find dialog box
that appears, type a word you want to search for. To find other newsgroups that
contain the same word, click Edit | Find and click Find Next in the Find dialog box.

Selecting and Reading Messages

Once you have selected the newsgroups you're interested in, you can read the
messages several ways. You can read them while you're online or offline (without
being connected to the Internet).

Reading Articles Offline or Online

To set Free Agent to view newsgroup messages online or offline, choose Options |
General Preferences and click the Online tab. To configure Free Agent to work online,
click the Use Online Defaults button and set your preferences, as seen in Figure 12-8.
To set Free Agent as an offline reader, click the Use Offline Defaults button and set
your preferences.

Downloading Message Headers

To read the messages in a newsgroup, you can tell Free Agent to download the
message headers, mark those that interest you, and tell Free Agent to download the
text of the messages you choose. Click the Get New Headers In Subscribed Groups

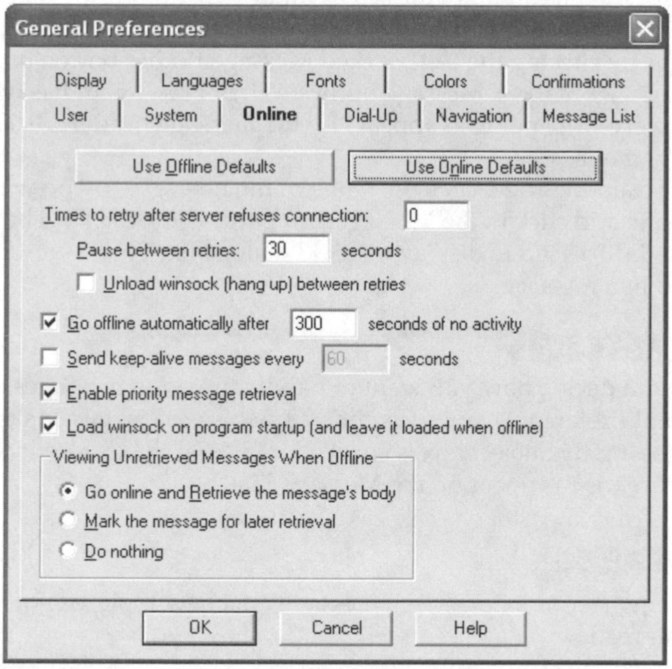

Figure 12-8. *Setting Free Agent for online or offline newsreading*

button (the leftmost button on the toolbar) or choose Online | Get New Headers In Subscribed Groups from the menu bar. Switch the Groups pane to list only the newsgroups you are subscribed to (by clicking the heading in the pane), to make it easier to switch among subscribed newsgroups. For the newsgroup that is selected in the Groups pane, you see the message headers in the Message List pane (the upper-right part of the Free Agent window).

Tip   *You can drag the divider lines between the panes to change the sizes of the panes. You can also click the Maximize button in the upper-right corner of a pane to maximize it, so that the pane occupies the entire Free Agent window. To return to seeing the three panes (Groups, Message List, and Message), click the Restore button in the upper-right corner of the maximized pane.*

Downloading and Reading Messages

New messages appear in red, and messages you've already read appear in black. Choose the message you want to read by double-clicking the message or by pressing

ENTER. Alternatively, you can mark messages for downloading by clicking the message and pressing M (an icon appears by the message header). Then download all your marked messages by clicking the Get Marked Message Bodies button on the toolbar or choosing Online | Get Marked Message Bodies. When Free Agent has downloaded the message text, a piece-of-paper icon appears by the message header: click the message header to display the message.

To locate a certain message, click the name of the newsgroup you want to search in the Groups pane and click in the Message List pane. Click the Find button on the toolbar or choose Edit | Find to display the Find dialog box. Type a word or name that you want to find in a message.

Threading Messages

Free Agent lets you decide how you want to handle threaded messages. Choose Options | General Preferences and then click the Message List tab. Make sure that the Enable Threading By Subject box is checked. This dialog box also lets you specify how you want threads to appear on the Message List.

Sending Messages

You can start a new thread by posting a message on a new topic, or you can reply to a message you read.

Replying to Messages

Free Agent lets you reply by e-mail to the author of the message or by posting a follow-up message to the newsgroup. Begin by selecting the message you want to reply to. To respond with a follow-up message to the newsgroup, click the Post Follow Up Message icon on the toolbar, choose Post | Follow-Up Usenet Message, or press F. To respond privately to the author of the message, click the Post Reply Via Email button on the toolbar, choose Post | Reply Via Email, or press R.

Either way, Free Agent displays a message composition window. If you are posting to a newsgroup, the name of the newsgroup appears in the Newsgroups box. If you are sending e-mail, the e-mail address of the author of the original message appears in the To box. The message you are responding to is quoted in the text of the message. Edit out the unimportant parts of the original message, add your response, and click Send Now (if you are working online) or Send Later (if you are working offline). If you decide not to send the message, click the Cancel button.

Starting a New Thread

To compose a new post to a newsgroup, select the newsgroup in the Groups pane. Click the Post New Usenet Message button on the toolbar, choose Post | New Usenet Message from the menu bar, or press P. The name of the current newsgroup appears in the Newsgroups box, but you can change it. Type the subject and your message and then click either Send Now or Send Later.

You can send e-mail to anyone, even if you don't feel like firing up your e-mail program. Click the Post New Email Message button on the toolbar, choose Post | New Email Message, or press CTRL-M.

Adding a Signature

When you post messages—replies to other messages or new threads you start—you can include a signature at the end of each message. Free Agent lets you set up as many different signatures as you want, so that you can use one (serious) signature on messages to business-oriented newsgroups and another (frivolous) signature on recreational newsgroups.

To set up signature files, click Options | Signatures. In the Signatures dialog box that appears, click the Add button and type a name for the signature (like **standard**) in the Names box. Then type the text you want to appear in the signature line to any messages you send. You can include any information you want, including your e-mail address, your web address, and your business name and address.

Canceling Messages

Free Agent also lets you cancel a message after it's sent. To cancel a message, select the message and choose Message | Cancel Usenet Message. When you see the Cancel Usenet Message window, click the Send Now button to send the cancellation message to the news server.

Printing Messages

When you want to print any of the messages you read in newsgroups, begin by selecting the message or messages you want to print. You can print an entire thread by selecting a collapsed thread header (where one header represents all the messages in the thread, and a plus box appears to the left of the header). Choose File | Print or press CTRL-P, and click OK to start the print job.

When printing a thread, Free Agent prints all the messages in the thread. If the thread contains many messages, printing can take a while.

Saving Messages

Occasionally you'll want to save messages permanently to your hard drive. To save messages, begin by selecting the message or thread and then choose File | Save Message As. In the dialog box that appears, choose the directory and file in which to save the message(s) and give the file a name. If you are saving more than one message, choose an option in the File Format box: Unix Message File (with a new-page character separating the messages), Precede Each Message With (and fill in what separator you'd like between messages), or No Separator Between Messages. Then click the Save button.

Deleting Messages and Groups

Free Agent automatically deletes old newsgroup messages for you. You can specify when you want these messages purged: when retrieving new headers, when closing the newsreader, or on demand. You can set these options for all newsgroups to which you are subscribed, or you can set different options for different newsgroups.

To specify when you want old messages deleted for a newsgroup, select the newsgroup in the Groups pane and choose Group | Properties (or press ALT-ENTER). In the Properties for Selected Newsgroups dialog box, click the What To Purge tab to control how Free Agent decides which messages are old enough to delete; click the When To Purge tab to control when Free Agent performs the deletions. If you don't like the What To Purge settings that Free Agent suggests, click the Override Default Settings button and check the options you want to use. To *purge* newsgroups (that is, to select old messages for deletion and delete them) immediately, choose Group | Purge Newsgroups and choose which newsgroups to purge.

To *delete* newsgroups from your subscribed list, select the group you want to delete. Then click Group | Delete or click the Subscribe button on the toolbar. Free Agent asks what to do with the messages for the newsgroup you are unsubscribing from.

Filtering Messages

You can tell Free Agent to ignore threads that you don't want to read or to automatically mark other threads for downloading. If you come across a particular thread that interests you and you want to keep track of all the responses to that thread, click the Watch Thread icon from the toolbar (the little pair of glasses), choose Message | Watch Thread, or press W. An eyeglasses icon appears next to each message in the thread along with a download icon, which means that Free Agent will automatically retrieve the bodies of these messages the next time you go online.

Ignoring threads works much the same way as watching threads. When you see a thread you're not interested in, click the Ignore Thread icon on the toolbar, choose Message | Ignore Thread, or press I. A circle-with-slash icon appears next to the threads you want to ignore. Free Agent then marks those threads as read, whether they've been downloaded or not, so the messages don't appear when you view only unread messages. Also, ignoring threads reduces the number of new unread messages you receive when retrieving messages from the news server.

The Complete Reference

Internet

Chapter 13

Internet Relay Chat (IRC)

nternet Relay Chat (IRC) is the original real-time group chat program. Predating AOL chat rooms, instant messaging, and the Web itself, IRC lets users type messages to each other. Although many new chat technologies have come along, IRC continues to be popular, with hundreds of thousands of simultaneous users. This chapter describes IRC, channels, nicknames, and other IRC-related concepts and then describes how to participate in IRC by using a popular chat program called mIRC, which runs under Windows. (Other IRC programs work similarly.)

> **Note**   *Some web-based chat sites actually use IRC in disguise: that is, the web pages provide a front end to IRC channels. Chapter 15 describes web-based chat rooms.*

What Is IRC?

IRC began in 1988 and is used in over 60 countries around the world. It gained international fame in 1991 during the Persian Gulf War, when people around the world gathered on IRC to hear reports from the war. Again, in 1993, IRC users from Moscow typed live reports about the situation during the coup against Boris Yeltsin.

As IRC gained in popularity, its main use changed. People still use IRC to discuss current events and news items, but also for general social banter and interaction. Little professional and business communication takes place on IRC.

IRC Networks

IRC networks (or *nets*) are the backbone of IRC. IRC networks are groups of IRC servers linked together to enable you to chat with people on any server. All the public IRC networks are accessible via the Internet and span the globe. IRC users connect to an IRC network to participate in chat channels hosted on that network. The networks do not connect to each other; each network hosts its own set of chat channels.

There are many different nets, mainly furnished or sponsored by local ISPs, university systems, other organizations, or individuals. The largest nets, each of which has over 20,000 participants active at the same time, 24 hours a day, are

- **EFnet** Short for "Eris Free net," this was the first net, but no longer is the largest. It was never designed; it just happened. If you find yourself on IRC and you are not sure what net you're on, chances are you're on EFnet. EFnet has few services, preferring to stick to its minimalist roots.

- **Undernet** This was formed in 1992, when a group grew discontented with what they perceived as privacy breaches and slowdowns and decided to form a new net. Since its inception, it has grown from 1,000 users in February 1995 to over 50,000 users in 2002, connected to 45 servers. Undernet, which has a home page at **www.undernet.org**, provides many more services than EFnet.

- **DALnet** This started as a role-playing-game alternative network in 1994. Originally, you could find an average of 130 users on this net. However, with the growth of the Internet and IRC usage, this net has grown to over 80,000 users during peak hours, and it frequently is the largest net. DALnet's home page is at **www.dal.net**.

- **QuakeNET**   With a home page at **www.quakenet.org**, this has as many as 70,000 active simultaneous users.

- **IRCnet**   This split off the EFnet in 1996 and works similarly, providing few services. It's larger than EFnet, with servers mainly in Europe.

Dozens of other nets are on the Internet. New nets are being added constantly. As more and more people get connected to the Internet, the older nets can't handle all the traffic.

*Nets come and go all the time on the Internet. Some disappear completely and some divide and evolve into other nets. For information about these and other IRC networks, start at Yahoo (**www.yahoo.com**) and choose Computers & Internet | Internet | Chats & Forums | Internet Relay Chat (IRC) | Networks.*

IRC Servers

IRC servers are computers that work like switchboards, connecting IRC users with each other. Most IRC servers are at universities or ISPs. IRC server computers run the programs that let you connect to an IRC net, keep track of users and channels, and make sure all the messages that all the users type get to the right place. To connect to an IRC net, you connect to a server that is part of that net. Each net has its own group of servers. For example, to access the Undernet, you connect to an IRC server that belongs to the Undernet. Each net has its own group of servers. Large nets may have over 50 servers positioned all over the world, whereas small regional nets may have only a few.

Each server has its own address, consisting of where the server is located and the net it accesses. For example, every Undernet server has an address ending with *undernet.org*. America Online (AOL) has its own Undernet server located in Washington, D.C., and the address for the server is **washington.dc.us.undernet.org**.

You may not always be allowed to connect to the server of your choice, usually because the server already has the maximum number of users connected. If this happens, keep trying, or try another server. Several European servers refuse connections from U.S. users, to avoid all their connections getting used up by U.S. users.

Widely Used Servers

Here are a few servers for some major IRC nets:

- **Undernet servers**   arlington.va.us.undernet.org (U.S.), austin.tx.us.undernet.org (U.S.), newyork.ny.us.undernet.org (U.S.), london.uk.eu.undernet.org (U.K.), and graz.at.eu.undernet.org (Austria)

CHATTING AND CONFERENCING ON THE INTERNET

■ **DALnet servers**   fork.ca.us.dal.net (U.S.), phoenix.nj.us.dal.net (U.S.), twisted.ma.us.dal.net (U.S.), typhoon.va.us.dal.net (U.S.), lineone.uk.eu.dal.net (U.K.), and powertech.no.eu.dal.net (Norway)

■ **QuakeNET**   us.quakenet.org (U.S.), uk.quakenet.org (U.K.), and se.quakenet.org (Sweden)

If these aren't already in the server lists of your IRC program, you can add them. These servers should give you a basis to start exploring IRC.

If one server fails to let you on, keep trying the other servers until you find one that will let you connect. If your IRC network has a web site, use it to find server addresses. As you use IRC, you'll learn which servers work best for you.

Ports on IRC Servers

When you try to connect to a server, you are often asked which port you wish to connect to. A *port* is like a line into the server, and each port has a number. The default port for IRC is 6667, and almost all IRC servers let you connect using port 6667. Most servers have additional ports you can use. If you are having a hard time getting connected to a server on port 6667, then try one of the alternative ports. IRC server ports usually range from 6660 to 6670. IRC network web sites frequently list the port numbers that are available on their servers.

For more information on ports, see Chapter 1.

Servers for Kids

Many parents are concerned about children being on IRC. You have heard the stories on the news about the pedophiles who stalk children, often luring them into their traps. Bad things can happen on IRC! We advise that young children not be allowed on IRC without supervision. All children who use IRC should know the basic rules listed in the safety section in Chapter 9.

Another option is to let your child connect only to a net that is for children only: Kidlink. Kidlink is a global network for youths up to age 15. Kidlink requires its users to register before using it, screens its users, and monitors users' activities to ensure that children are safe there. After you or your child registers for Kidlink, you get the server information to let you join. For more information, see their web site at **www.kidlink.org**. Many kids, especially teenagers, use instant messaging (IM) programs rather than IRC. (See Chapter 14.)

Channels

Users meet in *channels,* the IRC equivalent of a chat room. An unlimited number of users can be in a channel, and it only takes one user to open or create a channel. Each channel has a name, usually starting with a pound sign (#). For example, a channel for readers of this book might be called **#nettcr**.

Each time a person types a message and presses ENTER, the message appears on the screens of everyone else in the channel. Other people in the channel can then type their replies; this is how conversations are carried on in IRC.

Each net has its own set of channels. The number of channels varies according to when you log on. The three major nets usually have thousands of channels. Smaller nets may have from ten channels to hundreds during peak hours. The large nets usually have thousands of channels. The smaller nets average between 250 and 300 channels no matter what time of the day or night you join.

IRC channels frequently have their own topics, styles, and regular participants. Almost every topic imaginable has a channel somewhere on IRC. For example, here are some common types of channels:

- Channels for socializing, like **#teenchat** or **#teenland** for teenagers and **#letstalk** or **#friends** for adults.

- Channels for professionals, like **#writers** or **#realestate**.

- Channels for technical help, like **#techtalk** or **#WindowsXP**.

- Channels for help with IRC itself, like **#newbies**, **#mirc**, and **#wastelands**.

- Channels for collectors and crafters, like **#coins** or **#crafts**.

- Geographical channels for people from those areas, like **#michigan** or **#minnesota**. These include country channels, in which the discussions take place in the language of that country.

Finding a Channel

At any given moment, IRC users are chatting on over 10,000 different channels. With so many channels available, how can you find a channel you want to join? Once you are connected to an IRC server, your IRC program can display an alphabetized list of all the channels available on the net to which you are connected, showing the name of the channel, the number of people in the channel, and the topic that was set for the channel, if there is one.

The list of the channels on a major IRC net can be long and can take several minutes to download. Next to each channel name is a short description of the topic of the channel. Once the list appears, scroll through it to find a channel that interests you, based on the name of the channel, the channel description, and the number of people in it. (It's amazing how many channels consist of one person waiting for someone else to come along.)

Some Recommended Channels

The type of conversations you'll find on channels varies according to the type channel you choose. For instance, if you select one of the state or city channels, you are likely to find most of the people there are from that state or city. The conversation is generally centered around things to do, places to go, and current politics or events in that area.

Some channels you might want to try for fun are **#30plus**, **#40plus**, or **#webe30+**. In these channels you find people within that age group.

Several channels are available if you need technical help. For help with IRC itself, try **#irchelp**, **#ircnewbies**, **#wastelands**, **#beginners**, **#mirc** (if you use the mIRC program), or **#helpcastle**. When you need help with other parts of the Internet, try one of these: **#webmaster**, **#html**, or **#linpeople**.

These are just some examples of the channels you can expect to find on IRC. Each channel has its own regular participants whose personalities give the channel its unique character. Test the waters until you find the channel that feels right for you.

Creating Your Own Channel

You can create your own channel in a couple of ways. The easiest way is to pick a channel name that isn't already in use and join that channel. Then invite your friends to join you on your new channel. When you create a channel, you automatically become the *chanop* (channel operator, or manager) of that channel.

Normally, a channel disappears when the last person leaves the channel. However, a couple of nets (like Undernet and DALnet) allow you to register a channel, so that the channel exists permanently. In other words, the channel is there, even when you cannot be. When you register a channel, the administrators of that net put what is called a *bot* on your channel. A bot is a self-running program that participates in IRC channels. The bot belongs to the net organization, and its only purpose is to keep your channel open. (Bots may also have other purposes, like running games in game channels or kicking off people who post too much material.)

For details on creating and managing a channel, see the section "Starting and Managing a Channel" at the end of this chapter.

IRC Programs and IRC Commands

To participate in IRC, you need an IRC program (also called an *IRC client*). The original IRC programs were text-based UNIX programs named *irc* and *ircii*. These programs required you to type commands (all starting with /) to see listings of channels, join channels, leave channels, and other actions. For example, to see a list of available channels, you type the IRC command **/list**, and to join a channel, you type **/join** followed by the name of the channel.

Windows- and Mac-based IRC programs (including mIRC for Windows and Ircle for the Mac) provide buttons and menu choices instead of your having to remember and type IRC commands. Most of these programs also let you type the IRC commands, which is useful for commands that aren't included on the buttons and menus. This chapter describes how to use mIRC, the most popular Windows-based IRC program. Many other good IRC programs are available; browse the TUCOWS (at **www.tucows .com**), Mac Orchard (**www.macorchard.com**), and Consummate Winsock Applications List (at **cws.internet.com**) web sites for information.

Nicknames and Chanops

When you connect to an IRC server, you choose a *nickname* (or *nick*) by which you will be known during the session. Most nets restrict your nickname to nine characters. Only one person can use a nickname on a net at a time. However, when you sign off, you relinquish the use of your nickname, so nothing stops someone else from signing on and using it. When you use IRC, never assume that a person with a nickname you chatted with yesterday is the same person today.

> **Caution** *If you are female and chose a female sounding nickname for yourself, expect to get private, sexually oriented messages from strangers. To avoid these, choose an androgynous nickname. If you choose to stay with a feminine nickname, you must learn how to handle these kinds of messages.*

Some chatters have an at-sign (@) at the beginning of their nickname. An at-sign signifies that a person is a *channel operator* or *chanop*, the person who manages the channel. Chanops have the power to create a topic, give others operator's status, kick people off the channel, and prevent annoying people from coming back. (See the section "Starting and Managing a Channel" at the end of this chapter.)

Netsplits and Lags

Once you are connected to an IRC server and participating in a channel, you may experience two common problems: netsplits and lags.

A *netsplit* is when one or more servers split off from the rest of the net due to a communications problem. Usually a netsplit is caused by an overload of users. The servers that split from the rest of the net (and all their users) are still able to communicate with each other, but not with the rest of the net.

IRC nets are similar to a spider's web. The threads of the web are the connections between the IRC servers on the net. When a netsplit happens, it is as though someone swept away or disconnected a part of the web, severing connections between the servers. When the threads are brought back together, those servers rejoin the others, and users on them rejoin the channels they were on.

You can recognize a netsplit when a group of people appear to leave your channel at the same time, especially if they all have the same IRC server name. When communication is restored, the people all rejoin the channel. In reality, the people didn't leave; their IRC server lost contact with yours. Netsplits don't generally last very long. However, if you notice that your server seems to netsplit often, you may want to change servers.

Lags are sometimes associated with netsplits. The lag is the time it takes for your message to travel from your server to the net—the messages you type may not appear on the channel for many seconds, or even minutes. Before a netsplit, the lag is frequently long, which is an indication that the servers are overloaded and experiencing problems.

Sometimes a lag only affects one or two servers, and sometimes it affects many servers. Your best bet is to try to ride out the storm, but if your lag is so bad that you are unable to keep up or see anything anyone else might be saying in the channel, change servers. The only drawback to this solution is finding a server that isn't lagged.

If your IRC server is lagged, ask others in your channel which servers are not lagging, and then try one of those.

Direct Client to Client Protocol (DCC)

Direct Client to Client (DCC) protocol allows you to send files or to chat with other users by establishing a direct connection between your computer and theirs. This connection bypasses the IRC server and connects you directly from your ISP to the other person's ISP. You can use DCC when you want to hold a private conversation with one other person.

Don't accept DCC "sends" from someone you don't know. People have been known to send smutty pictures or computer viruses.

When sending files using DCC, it is advisable that the sender and receiver both be on the same IRC server. The lag is decreased, and in the event of a netsplit, you both remain together. When the net is experiencing significant lag, sending a file may take several tries, or you may have to try again at another time.

Chanserv and Nickserv

Originally, channels existed only when people were in them: when the last participant left a channel, the channel was deleted. Worse, when the last chanop left, the channel would be left with no operator. When a channel ended, anyone could come along and create a new channel with the same name, which other people would assume was run by the operators of the original channel. As channels developed their own followings and personalities, many IRC users wanted a way for channels to remain open and managed by a consistent set of chanops.

In response, some IRC networks added a service called *Chanserv*, which allows a user to register a channel and control who can be an operator. The specific features of Chanservs vary from net to net, and some nets (like EFnet) don't provide Chanserv. To find out whether a network has Chanserv, give this command:

```
/msg Chanserv help
```

Similarly, the original IRC networks let you choose a nickname when you connected to the net, but you lost your nickname when you disconnected. Someone

Clones May Be Banned

Many IRC channels don't let you log in more than once from the same machine. For example, you can run two mIRC windows on your computer at the same time and connect to IRC from both. This works as long as you don't connect to the same network and join the same channel. If you try, you may be kicked off the channel with a message like this: "You were kicked from #Beginner by Zeppy62 (Clone removal of redback-25.shoreham.net)." IRC can detect the Internet address of the computer from which you are connecting, and if two IRC users have the same address, both may be kicked off automatically by a bot.

This restriction also applies if you have several machines that share one Internet connection (for example, computers on a local area network). To the outside world, all the machines on the local area network have the same Internet address.

with the nickname CoolDude today might not be the same person who was CoolDude yesterday. Some networks have added *Nickserv* programs that enable you to reserve a nickname—for a specified time, no one but you can use it. The network identifies you both by a password and by the address from which you connect. If someone else logs in with your nickname, the Nickserv program gives the person a warning and kicks the person off if he or she doesn't change nicknames.

To find out whether a network provides Nickserv, give this command:

```
/msg Nickserv help
```

Note   *When you register a channel or nickname on a network, it's reserved only on that network. If you don't use the channel or nickname for a period (usually from 14 to 30 days, but it varies by network), your reservation is deleted.*

Chatting in mIRC

There are dozens of IRC programs to choose from, but mIRC is one of the best. mIRC not only automates most IRC commands, but also brings information to your fingertips quickly and conveniently. MIRC is available for all versions of Windows (not for the Macintosh). This section describes mIRC version 5.91, but new versions appear frequently.

Note   *If you use a Macintosh, consider running Ircle, another popular point-and-click IRC program. You can find it at **www.macorchard.com**.*

CHATTING AND CONFERENCING ON THE INTERNET

Getting mIRC

You can download mIRC from a number of web sites, including TUCOWS (at **www .tucows.com**), the Consummate Winsock Applications List (at **cws.internet.com**), or mIRC's web site at **www.mirc.com**. (See Chapter 34 for how to download and install software.) mIRC is shareware; if you decide to use the program, you should register it and then pay the small registration fee.

After you download and install mIRC, the program prompts you to configure it with your personal information and preferences, including your e-mail address and preferred nickname. Until you register the program, you see a dialog box about the program's author each time you start mIRC; click anywhere in the dialog box to proceed.

It's prudent to stay anonymous while chatting on IRC, so don't type your real name or e-mail address when mIRC asks for it. Instead, type a nickname or interesting quote in the Full Name box. Either leave the E-Mail Address box blank or type a web-based e-mail address (like a Yahoo Mail or HotMail address) that you use only for personal business.

Connecting to an IRC Server

After you have completed your setup information, you see the mIRC Options dialog box (shown in Figure 13-1). Click the IRC Servers drop-down arrow and choose the IRC network you want to use (for example, DALnet). The box below it lists servers on that network; choose a server near you. Then click the Connect To IRC Server button. mIRC tries to connect you to that server.

You can display the mIRC Options dialog box any time by choosing File | Setup, by clicking the Setup Info button on the toolbar, or by pressing CTRL-E.

Once a connection is established, a Status window opens, and information scrolls by about the server you connected to, the net, and general IRC information. The Status window in mIRC shows the activity for the server to which you are connected. In the input box at the bottom of that window, you can type commands to the server. Better yet, click buttons on the mIRC toolbar to give commands.

If you can't connect (servers are frequently full and not accepting any more connections), display the mIRC Options dialog box again, choose another server, and try again.

Listing Channels

When you connect to an IRC server, mIRC displays the mIRC Channels Folder dialog box. (See Figure 13-2.) You can see this window any time by clicking the Channels Folder button on the toolbar.

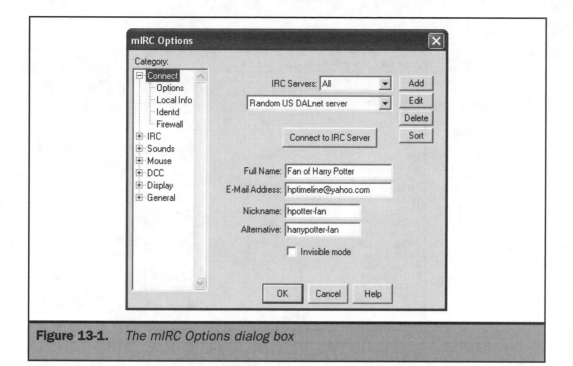

Figure 13-1. *The mIRC Options dialog box*

You can also find channels that have either specific text in the topic of the channel, or a range of numbers of participants. Click the List Channels button on the toolbar to display the List Channels dialog box, in which you can specify the types of channels you want to see. Then type the text that must appear in the channel topic, or specify the minimum or maximum number of people in the channel. When you click the Get List button, mIRC displays a window that contains a list of the channels that meet your criteria.

Joining Channels

The easiest way to join a channel is to click the Channels Folder button on the toolbar, choose the channel from the list, and click Join. If you have displayed a listing of channels that meet specific criteria, you can double-click a channel on the list to join that channel. A new window opens for the channel, as shown in Figure 13-3. At the right side of the window is a list of the people in the channel.

You can join several channels at the same time. Just display the mIRC Channels Folder again and select another channel. Each channel appears in its own window. Below the toolbar, a row of buttons appears, one for each open window in mIRC (including the Status window). You can click these buttons to select that channel's window.

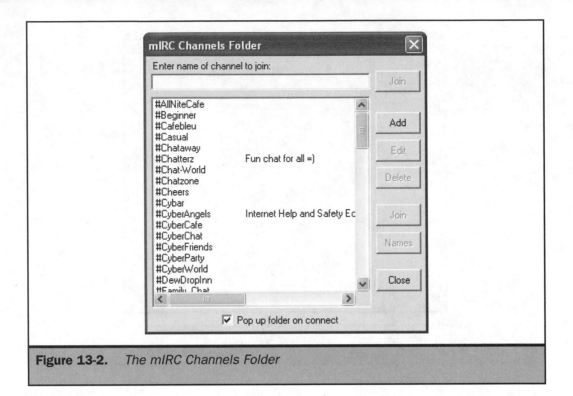

Figure 13-2.   *The mIRC Channels Folder*

Starting to Chat

Once you're in the channel of your choice, you can start chatting. Just type your message in the box at the bottom of the channel window and press ENTER. Within a few seconds, your message will appear for everyone on the channel to see, preceded by your nickname in angle brackets. For example, if your nickname is "katy" and you type **How do you all like mIRC?**, everyone in the channel sees

```
<katy> How do you all like mIRC?
```

You also see reports of people entering and leaving the channel and other events. These lines are preceded by asterisks.

Text messages can seem emotionless. To change the tone of the messages you send, you can send *actions*. Actions let you "perform" rather than talk. For instance, instead of sending the message "I'm chuckling," which would appear preceded by your nickname, you can send this as an action. Type the action command **/me** followed

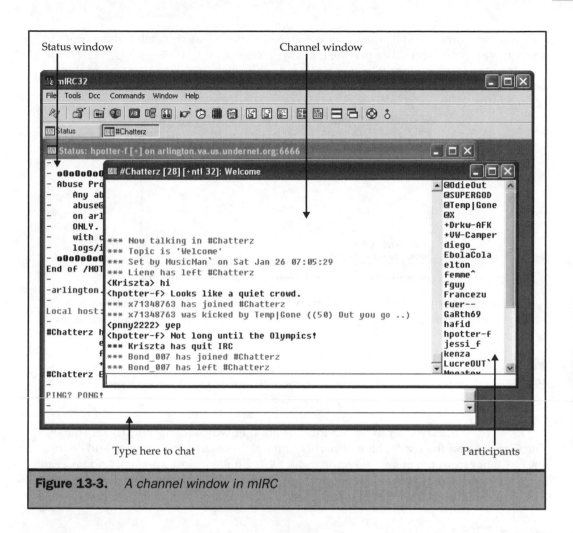

Figure 13-3. *A channel window in mIRC*

CHATTING AND
CONFERENCING ON
THE INTERNET

by the action you are taking. For example, if you type **/me is chuckling**, then everyone in the channel sees

```
katy is chuckling
```

In mIRC, actions appear in a different colored text than normal text.

Whispering

You can carry on a private conversation with someone you meet in a channel, so other channel participants don't see your exchange. Some call this *whispering,* some call it *querying,* and others call it *private messaging.* No matter what you call it, there are several ways you can initiate private chats with others.

One way to whisper with someone is to double-click the person's name in the list on the right-hand side of the channel window. A separate window appears:

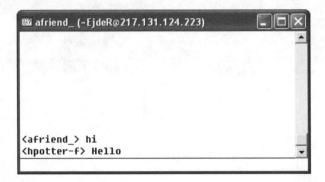

In the input box at the bottom of this new window, type the message you want to send privately to that user and press ENTER. The other person's replies appear in this window, too.

On many IRC networks, as soon as you connect, whisper windows start appearing as people decide to try to start private conversations with you. You can respond by typing in the window's input box, or you can close the window.

DCC (described earlier in this chapter) is another way to carry on private chats. Click a name on the list of channel participants, right-click to see a menu, and choose DCC | Chat from the menu that appears. A DCC Chat window appears, and you can type messages to each other. An advantage to using DCC is that if a netsplit happens, you two can still chat with each other, even if your servers can't communicate.

Sending Files

To send a file (perhaps a picture of yourself or your family) to another user, follow these steps:

1. In the list of channel participants, click the name of the person to whom you want to send the file. The name appears highlighted.

2. Right-click the name and choose DCC | Send from the menu that appears. You see the mIRC DCC Send dialog box, shown in Figure 13-4.

3. Select the file and click Send. mIRC sends the file to the other IRC user.

You can also start sending a file by clicking the DCC Send button in the toolbar. When you see the mIRC DCC Send dialog box, set the Nick box to the nickname of the person to whom you want to send the file.

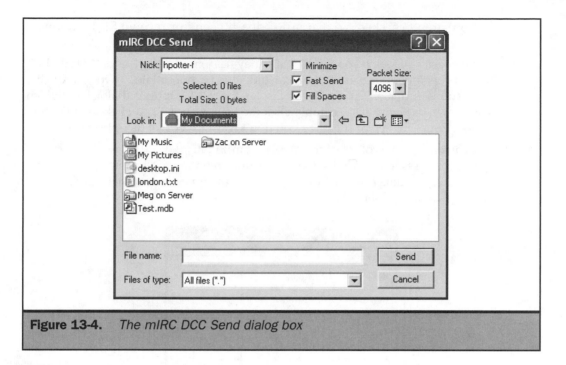

Figure 13-4.   *The mIRC DCC Send dialog box*

Caution   *Don't accept files, especially programs, from people you don't know.*

Leaving Channels and Disconnecting from Servers

To leave a channel, click the Close button (X) in the upper-right corner of the channel window. To disconnect from the server, click the Disconnect From IRC Server button on the toolbar.

mIRC Tips

Here are a few more tips for chatting using mIRC:

- Choose File | Options (or press ALT-O) to see the mIRC Options dialog box with many, many options you can set. The Category box down the left side of the dialog box lists the types of options: when you click a category, the dialog box shows those options. Click the Connect category to return to the IRC server settings that appear when you first open the dialog box.

- In the mIRC Options dialog box, click the IRC category and make sure that the Auto-Join On Invite check box is not checked. Otherwise you could find yourself joining channels that you would never go to on your own. Click the DCC category and make sure that the Auto-Get File check box (in the On-Send Request section) and the Auto-Accept check box (in the On-Chat Request section) aren't checked, so that mIRC doesn't send or receive files without your permission.

■ If you get sick of seeing so many "*** Bentley has joined #mirc" and "***PEL2PEL has left #beginners" messages, you can hide them. Choose Files | Options or click the Options button on the toolbar to display the mIRC Options dialog box, which was shown in Figure 13-1. Double-click the IRC category and click the Events button. For each type of message you don't want to see, set its option to Hide.

■ You can change the colors of the messages mIRC displays. Choose Tools | Colors (or press ALT-K or click the Colors button on the toolbar) to see the mIRC Colors dialog box. The dialog box lists the types of text that mIRC displays, as shown here:

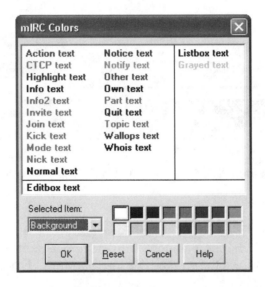

Click a type of message (Normal Text for most messages from other people, Action Text for actions, Own Text for the text of messages you send, and so on), and click the color in which you want that type of message to appear.

■ You can make your messages appear in color when other people receive them; press CTRL-K and click a color while you are typing a message. The colors don't appear until your message is sent; instead, you see codes to mIRC and other IRC programs as to what color to use for the text you've typed. You can also press CTRL-U to underline text and CTRL-B to make text bold.

For instructions for creating your own channel or helping to manage an existing channel, see "Starting and Managing a Channel" later in this chapter.

IRC Commands

The original IRC programs were command driven, predating the Windows and Mac programs like mIRC. If you have a UNIX shell account (described in Chapter 1), ircii is the best chat program available. If you see an error when you try to run ircii, try running irc instead (an older version). Even if you use a point-and-click program like mIRC, you can still type IRC commands. You may need to type commands on some IRC nets; for example, to communicate with some Chanserv and Nickserv systems, you need to type commands that aren't built into mIRC.

You can use IRC commands to list channels, join channels, perform actions—everything but sending messages once you are in a channel (for which no command is needed). All IRC commands being with a forward slash (/), and you press ENTER after typing the command.

Typing Commands

In mIRC, you can type commands in the same input box in which you type messages. You can type commands in the input box at the bottom of a channel window or in the Status window—either way, mIRC sends them to the IRC server to which you are connected. If you are using a UNIX or Linux command-line system, you run ircii by typing **ircii** or **irc** at the UNIX shell prompt, and then type IRC commands at its prompt, which is usually an angle bracket (>). Either way, press ENTER after you type each IRC command.

Connecting to a Server

To connect to an IRC server, type **/server** *servername* (replacing *servername* with the name of an IRC server). For example, to connect to an Undernet server in New Jersey, you can type

```
/server newbrunswick.nj.us.undernet.org
```

If someone is already connected to the server using your nickname, ircii prompts you for a different nickname. When you connect, you see the server's welcome message.

 IRC servers frequently refuse to allow you to connect because the maximum number of users are already connected. Try again in a few minutes, or try another server on the same network.

Listing Channels

Once you're connected to a server, type **/list** to see a list of channels. This list for can be so long that most of it flies off the top of the screen before you have a chance to read it. To make the list shorter and eliminate the channels with only one or two people, you can specify the minimum and maximum number of users on a channel. Type

```
/list -min #, -max #
```

Replace # with a number. For example, to limit your search to channels with a minimum of 5 and maximum of 10 users, type

```
/list -min 5, -max 10
```

Joining Channels and Chatting

To join a channel, type **/join #***channelname* (replacing *channelname* with the name of a channel). Your IRC program displays a list of the participants in the channel, followed by messages from that channel as they are sent. If the channel didn't exist, you just created it. (See "Starting and Managing a Channel" later in this chapter.)

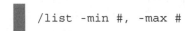

To see a list of the participants in the channel, type **/who channelname** *(replacing* channelname *with the name of a channel).*

Whispering

When you want to send a private message or whisper to another user, you type the command **/msg** *nickname* (replacing *nickname* with the person's nickname), followed by the message you want to whisper. In mIRC, the conversation appears in a separate window; in ircii, the messages appear preceded by stars.

Caution   *Be diligent in typing the /msg command before any message you want sent privately. Otherwise, your private message will appear in the channel you have joined.*

To initiate a DCC chat session with another user, type **/dcc chat** followed by the person's nickname. In mIRC, DCC sessions appear in a separate window. In ircii, DCC messages appear preceded by the sender's name enclosed in equal signs, like this:

```
=margyL= Can you believe how vacuous this conversation is?
```

Once you've established a DCC session with someone, send the message by typing **/msg =***nickname* (replacing *nickname* with the person's nickname), followed on the same line by the message you want to send to that person. The equal sign before the recipient's nickname indicates that this message should be sent via the existing DCC connection.

To close the DCC connection, type **/dcc close chat** followed by the nickname of the person you were chatting with.

Sending Files

When you want to send a file to another user, type this command:

```
/dcc send nickname pathname
```

Replace *nickname* with the person's nickname and *pathname* with the pathname of the file on your computer. For example, to send a picture to joebob, the command would look like this:

```
/dcc send joebob c:\gifs\katy.gif
```

To receive a file that someone is trying to send you, type this command:

```
/dcc get nickname filename
```

Replace *nickname* with the person sending you a file, and *filename* with the name you want to give the file when it arrives on your computer.

Leaving Channels

When you're ready to leave a channel, type **/leave #*channelname*** or **/part #*channelname*** (replacing *channelname* with the name of a channel). If you are running ircii, type **/bye** or **/exit** to leave the program.

Starting and Managing a Channel

No matter which IRC program you use, you can start your own channel rather than joining an existing channel. Simply join a channel with a new channel name. Before you join the channel, make sure there isn't already a channel with that name. One way to check for the existence of a channel is to type the command **/who #*channelname*** (replacing *channelname* with the name you want to create), which lists the participants in a channel. If you get an error message or no response, no channel by that name exists.

Once you've created the new channel, you are the first and only person in it. When you create your own channel, you are by default the channel operator (chanop). With this power you can perform chanop commands like changing the status of a user on your channel, changing or setting the topic and channel mode, and kicking off and/or banning users on your channel. Some of these commands are described in this section.

Many chanop commands are forms of the /mode command, which changes the characteristics of the channel or another person on the channel.

Setting the Topic

To set the topic for your new channel (the line that describes what the channel is about), type **/topic** followed by a phrase describing your intended subject or audience. Unless you've planned to meet specific people in your new channel at a specific time, you may have to wait awhile for people to join your channel. For example, type

```
/topic Microsoft Access database programming
```

Kicking and Banning Users

An inevitable fact of life on IRC is the presence of annoying and abusive personalities. However, you don't have to put up with this behavior. You can kick these people out of your channel and ban them from coming back if necessary.

In mIRC this is easy to do. Highlight the person's nickname in the list of channel participants, right-click the name, and choose Control | Kick or Control | Ban. In other programs, type **/kick #channelname nickname**. For example, to kick joebob out of the #webe30+ channel, you would type

```
/kick #webe30+ joebob
```

Kicking someone out of your channel doesn't prevent that person from rejoining. If someone is persistently bothersome, you can *ban* the person for good by typing this command:

```
/mode #channelname +b nickname
```

For example, to ban joebob from the #webe30+ channel, you would type

```
/mode #webe30+ +b joebob
```

If you want to ban someone from your channel, it is better to ban them before you kick them. Many users have their programs set up to automatically rejoin once they've been kicked from a channel. If you don't ban them first, they can often slip back into your channel before the ban has had a chance to take effect.

Designating Other Chanops

If you are a chanop, you can designate other people as chanops. Every channel should have at least one chanop, so don't leave a channel you created without creating a chanop to take your place. To make someone a chanop, type this command:

```
/mode #channelname +o nickname
```

(That's the letter *o*, not a zero.) To take away chanop status, replace the +o with -o in the /mode command.

    It is wise to give chanop status only to people you know. Some people like nothing better than causing trouble for others by coming to a channel, getting chanop status, and then kicking everyone off the channel.

Other Chanop Commands

Here are some other commands that channel operators can use to control how a channel works:

- **/mode #*channelname* +m**   This makes the channel moderated, so that only chanops can send messages. This feature is great if you have a guest speaker or if you use the channel as a classroom; the speakers can have their say without interruptions.

- **/mode #*channelname* +I**   This marks the channel as by-invitation only. When a channel is marked invitation only, no one can join that channel unless they are invited first. To invite someone into your channel, type **/invite *nickname channelname***.

- **/mode #*channelname* +p**   This marks the channel private. Marking a channel private prevents it from showing up on a channels list.

General IRC Tips

Here are some tips and warnings to make your time on IRC more productive, pleasant, and safe:

- When you join a large channel, it may be hard for you to keep up with what's going on there because the conversation on the channel scrolls by rather quickly. Try concentrating on the comments of just one or two people, ignoring the rest.

- IRC is not case sensitive; capitalization doesn't matter when typing IRC commands.

■ With the larger nets, requesting a list of channels can disconnect you from your server. These lists are so long some servers see them as *floods* (excessive lines of text being generated by one user).

■ If you log on with a nickname that is already in use or registered by someone else, the system notifies you. For example, from time to time, you may need to change servers due to lag. When the first server catches up to the second server and if you use the same nickname on both servers, you experience *nick collision*—the same nickname in use on two different servers. When this happens, you are disconnected from your server. Simply log back on with a different nickname until your old nickname disappears.

■ If you have a slow connection with your provider, you may experience lag or other problems when holding private chats via DCC.

■ To find out more about someone, you can type **/whois** *nickname* (replacing *nickname* with the person's nickname). It's a good idea to try this on your own nickname, to see what other people can find out about you!

■ Don't click on any URLs (web addresses) that appear in your IRC chats. A few malicious IRC users have created web pages that include Java or ActiveX programs that contain viruses.

■ Refer to Chapter 9 for more warnings about etiquette and safety when chatting.

Learning More

Although this isn't a comprehensive guide to IRC, it is a starting point. If you'd like to learn more, there are many web sites about IRC, and many channels have their own web sites. Start at the web site for the IRC net you use (see "IRC Networks" near the beginning of this chapter), or the Internet Gurus Guide to Internet Relay Chat web site at **net.gurus.com/irc**. Other useful sites are

■ IRChelp.org Internet Relay Chat help archive, at **www.irchelp.org**

■ International Federation of IRC, at **www.ifirc.com**

■ IRCTools, with more advanced information, at **www.irctools.com**

Chapter 14

Instant Messaging

A t times, using the Internet can be a very solitary experience. You're online, you're using the Web or checking your e-mail, but you have no idea whether anyone else is out there. Wouldn't it be nice if you knew when your friends were online and had an easy way to get in touch with them? Don't you sometimes want to send a quick message to the person working down the hall? That's probably what Mirabilis Ltd. was thinking about when they developed ICQ, the first *instant messaging (IM)* program to be widely used across the Internet.

This chapter describes ICQ as well as newer, more widely used instant messaging programs like Windows Messenger, AOL Instant Messenger, and Yahoo Messenger.

What Is Instant Messaging?

Instant messaging programs have a unique combination of useful chat features. With an instant messaging program, you can

- *Keep track of which of your contacts is currently available to chat.* Most programs enable you to keep a list of contacts, in the form of a "buddy" or friend list, which is used to notify you when your contacts log on.

- *Chat privately with a single person.* Unlike other forms of chat, instant messaging is private and one-on-one. Some IM programs now allow additional people to join a conversation, but the original idea of IM is one-on-one.

- *Send an immediate message that is likely to get quick attention.* When you send an instant message, you generally cause a chime to sound and a new window to open on the recipient's computer screen. Instant messages are hard to ignore.

- *Converse back and forth in a way that's similar to face-to-face communication.* Instant messaging is extremely interactive and is the most conversation-like of any text-based Internet chat capability. Some instant messaging programs even allow users to hand documents and pictures to each other and play online games together.

The most popular instant messaging programs include ICQ, AOL Instant Messenger (AIM), Windows (MSN) Messenger, and Yahoo Messenger. As of 2002, AIM is the market leader, but we expect Windows Messenger to gain users as Windows XP is more widely installed.

Unfortunately, these programs don't work together: if you're using ICQ, you can keep tabs only on your other friends who are using ICQ. If your friend uses AOL Instant Messenger only, then you can't communicate unless you use AOL Instant Messenger, too. However, each of these programs can be downloaded at no charge, so many instant messaging enthusiasts use more than one, sometimes simultaneously. (See the sidebar on Jabber and Trillian later in this chapter for programs that can connect with multiple IM services.)

ICQ

With over 100 million enrolled users, ICQ (pronounced "I Seek You") is a leader in direct messaging systems. ICQ (from ICQ Inc., formerly Mirabilis, now owned by AOL/Time Warner) was the first publicly available system to offer contact lists and instant messages. There are ICQ users all over the world, especially outside of the United States and Canada, making it an excellent instant messaging tool for those who want to communicate internationally. It's available in a number of languages, including Chinese and Arabic. ICQ enables you to talk with one other friend or join IRC-style group chats on a variety of subjects. The ICQ web site (**www.icq.com**) lists available topics.

ICQ is always being enhanced by ICQ, Inc., and on each operating system its use is slightly different. The instructions provided in this book are for use of ICQ version 2001b with Windows XP, but users of other versions and operating systems should have no difficulty adapting these directions for use with their configurations.

Installing and Getting Started with ICQ

You can use ICQ Lite at **lite.icq.com** without installing the ICQ software, but most people prefer to install and use the full-featured program. ICQ Lite plugs into your browser, rather than running as a separate program.

To download and install ICQ, go to its web site at **www.icq.com**, find the Download button amid the amazing clutter on the page, and follow the instructions. The ICQ program is available for all recent versions of Windows, Macintosh, several types of hand-held computers or personal data assistants (PDAs), and Java. (Refer to Chapter 34 for information about how to download software from the Web.)

Download the installation file and keep your computer connected to the Internet while you run the installation program. After the installation is complete, the ICQ registration program automatically starts. It asks you for a lot of personal information, and although only a password is absolutely necessary, personal information will help your friends and others who share your interests find you. You can add to or change your personal information after registering.

After the registration process is complete, the ICQ program starts. Type your password and click OK to log onto ICQ.

Tip *The ICQ program is designed to run whenever your computer is running. This enables the program to alert you when one of your friends comes online or when someone wants to contact you. Keep ICQ loaded if you want your friends to be able to contact you.*

ICQ is represented by a flower icon that appears in the notification area (system tray) of the Windows taskbar. The flower is green when you are connected to ICQ and red when you are not connected. Double-click the tray icon to open the ICQ window, shown in Figure 14-1. When you are not using the ICQ window, minimize it. When minimized, ICQ appears only as a flower on the taskbar.

ICQ knows when you are connected to the Internet and using ICQ, and you can configure it to automatically indicate to your contacts that you're "Away" if you don't use your computer for a while. Additionally, ICQ has dozens of configuration options you can explore by clicking the Main button on the ICQ window.

Finding People on ICQ

Before you can use ICQ, you need someone to talk to. No problem! Click the Add/ Invite Users button in the ICQ window to search the ICQ database for friends and acquaintances. Each ICQ user is issued a long number such as 20230642. This ICQ identification number is similar to a telephone number: if you want to contact another ICQ user, you need the person's number. ICQ users often include their ICQ numbers in e-mail messages or on their web pages, and the ICQ web site includes an online database that you can use to look up friends and associates who have agreed to be

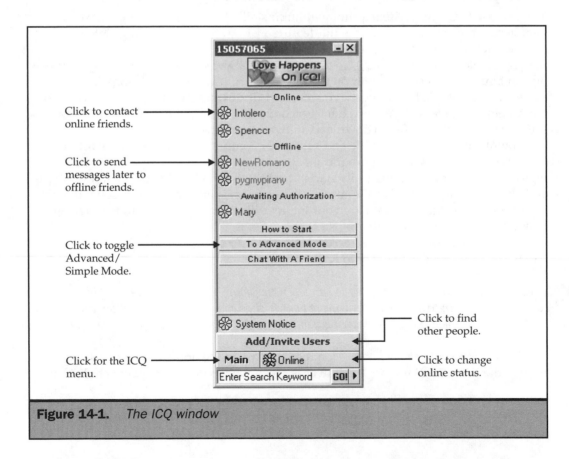

Figure 14-1.   *The ICQ window*

listed in the database. There are also lists of users grouped by interest, if you're seeking a new friend.

You can search for a friend's ICQ number if you don't know it. The most reliable way to find people is by e-mail address, although you can also search by name. Type some identifying information into the Find/Add Users To Your List window (as in Figure 14-2) and click Search. If ICQ finds a person who matches what you typed, it displays the person's ICQ number and other identifying information from the ICQ database. Highlight your friend's entry and click Add User to add the person to your contact list. Whenever this person starts ICQ while you are online, the person's nickname appears in the Online portion of your ICQ window.

Some people have configured ICQ to ask for their approval before you can add them to your contact list. When you try to add those people to your contact list, ICQ asks you to type a message to the person explaining why you'd like to be able to talk to them. (If it's a friend, you can type something like, "Hey, it's me!") Once the person approves, you receive a system message from ICQ: click the blinking ICQ taskbar button to read the message.

You can easily prevent people you don't know from adding you to their contact lists. Click Main in the ICQ window and then click Security & Privacy Permissions. In the Security & Privacy Permissions window, choose My Authorization Is Required Before Users Add Me To Their Contact List and click OK.

CHATTING AND
CONFERENCING ON
THE INTERNET

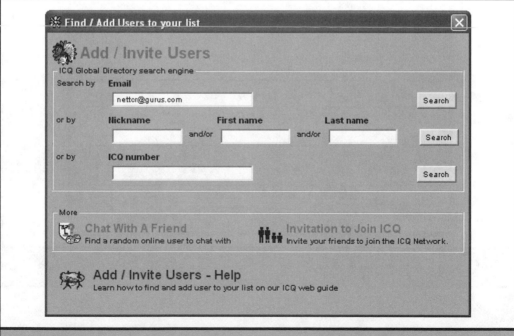

Figure 14-2.   *Finding other ICQ users*

Sending Messages with ICQ

Open the ICQ window, shown earlier in Figure 14-1, by double-clicking the ICQ flower icon in the system tray. The Online portion of the ICQ window lists the nicknames of people on your contact list who are online right now. The Offline portion lists your friends who aren't on the Internet right now or who don't have ICQ running. Double-click the nickname of the person from your contact list to whom you want to send a message or click the entry once and choose Message from the small window that appears. The Message Session window, shown in Figure 14-3, opens. Type your message in the lower portion of the window and click Send. If your contact is online, your message appears on his or her computer within seconds. If your contact is not online, ICQ can hold your message until the person connects.

When someone sends you a message, a blinking ICQ button opens in your taskbar or, if the ICQ window is already open, the icon to the left of the nickname begins to blink. Double-click the icon or click the blinking ICQ taskbar button to see the message.

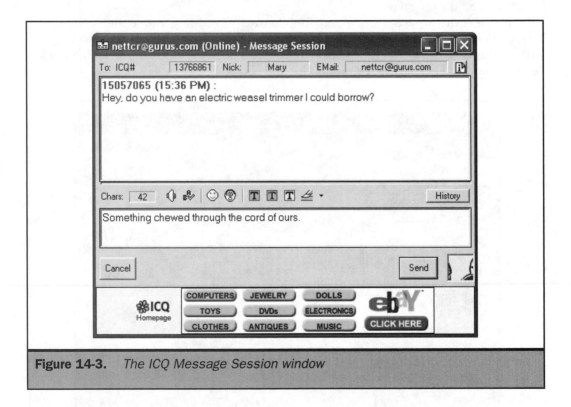

Figure 14-3.   *The ICQ Message Session window*

Another type of conversation is possible with the ICQ chat feature. ICQ chat is only available in Advanced Mode, so first you'll need to switch to that.

To enter Advanced Mode, click To Advanced Mode on the ICQ window and click Switch To Advanced Mode in the Simple/Advanced Mode Selection window. Your ICQ window will change slightly to include additional ICQ functions.

To use chat, click a nickname in the Online portion of your ICQ window and choose ICQ Chat from the small window that appears. When you see the Send Online ICQ Chat window, type a message to your prospective chat partner in the Enter Chat Subject box and click Send. If the other person accepts your chat request by clicking Accept, the ICQ programs on the two computers each open a chat window, like this:

What you
have typed

What your friend
has typed

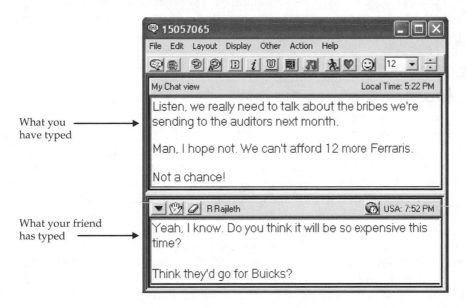

As you type messages, they appear character by character on the other person's screen.

Other ICQ Features

ICQ can do lots of other things, including voice telephony, file transfer, e-mail sending and receiving, and group chats. Much of the fun of using ICQ is in exploring its many features! For instructions, go to the ICQ web page at **www.icq.com**, and click one of the links that offers more information about the program. For voice features, see the ICQ section in Chapter 16.

AOL Instant Messenger (AIM)

Although there are AOL Instant Messenger users in many countries, the majority of users are located in the English-speaking world and particularly the United States. With over 100 million registered users, AIM has one distinct advantage over all other instant messaging tools: it connects to AOL's own messaging system, so that all AOL subscribers are part of its user base. In fact, AOL subscribers don't even have to sign up for or install AIM because it is part of their AOL software.

AOL continues to enhance AIM, and its use is slightly different depending on the configuration you use and whether you're an AOL subscriber. The instructions provided in this book are for use of stand-alone AIM version 4.8 and Windows XP, but users of other versions and operating systems should have no difficulty adapting these directions for use with their configurations.

Installing and Getting Started with AOL Instant Messenger

You may already have AIM because it's included at no cost with many other Internet programs, including Netscape. Search your computer for a file called aim.exe to determine if it's already installed. If you don't see AIM on your system, you can use AIM Express, a browser-based version of AIM, at **www.aim.com/get_aim/express/aim_expr.adp**, or you can download the AIM software from the AIM home page at **www.aim.com**. (See Chapter 34 for information about downloading and installing software.) AIM is available for all recent versions of Windows, Macintosh, Linux, and several versions of PDA.

After downloading and installing the software from the AIM home page, the AOL Instant Messenger Screen Name window appears. If you already have an AOL screen name, type it in the Screen Name box and click OK. Otherwise, click Get A Screen Name to be taken to an AOL web page where you can create one. You may have difficulty finding a screen name you're happy with because the millions of existing AOL and AIM users have already chosen many of the best ones. Make sure you enter your correct e-mail address because AIM will send you a confirmation e-mail message that you must reply to.

AIM is represented by an icon that looks like a person running in the notification area (system tray) of the Windows taskbar. When you are connected (logged on) to AIM, you see a blue circle around the running person, but when you're disconnected, no blue circle appears. Double-click the tray icon, and depending on whether you are already connected, either the Sign On window or the Buddy List window opens.

If you see the Sign On window, type your user name and password and click Sign On, like this:

The Buddy List window is shown in Figure 14-4.

AIM is designed to run whenever your computer is running. This enables the program to alert you when one of your friends comes online or when someone wants to contact you.

Finding People on AOL Instant Messenger

Now you need to find someone to talk to. You'll notice that the Buddy List window has two tabs, one to set up the Buddy List (the List Setup tab, shown in Figure 14-5) and one to see which of your contacts is online. To add someone to your list, click the List Setup tab, click the Add A Buddy button, and type a friend's AOL screen name or AIM user name. You can add as many friends as you like.

If you don't know your friend's AIM user name or AOL screen name, click the Find button (which looks like a magnifying glass) in the lower-right corner of the Buddy List

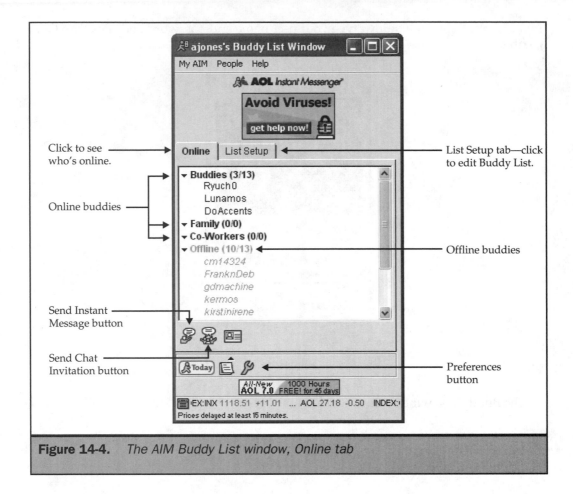

Figure 14-4. *The AIM Buddy List window, Online tab*

window and choose Find A Buddy. You can find a person by his or her e-mail address or name, or you can locate someone who shares an interest of yours.

Sending Instant Messages

Before sending an instant message to someone on your buddy list, be sure the Online tab of the Buddy List window is visible as in Figure 14-4.

The Online tab shows which of your contacts are currently connected to the Internet and signed onto either AOL or AIM. The numbers next to each group of friends

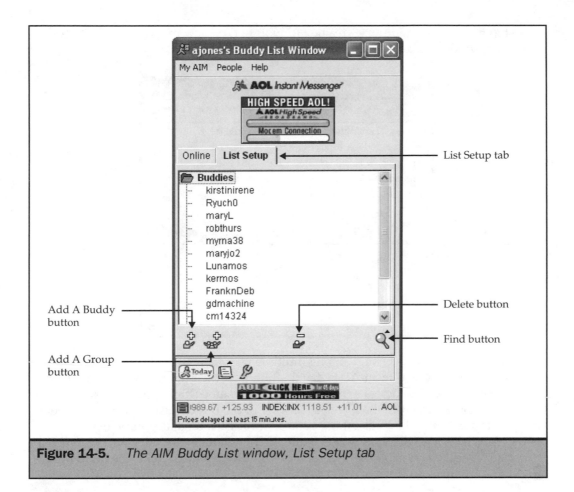

Figure 14-5. *The AIM Buddy List window, List Setup tab*

(Buddies, Family, or Co-Workers) show how many of your friends are online, followed by the total number of friends you have in that group. The last of the Buddy List groups, displayed in pale type, contains your AIM contacts who are Offline. Click the arrow next to any group to minimize or maximize it.

When you want to chat, double-click the name of an Online contact, or highlight it and click the Send Instant Message button near the lower-left corner of the Buddy List window. An Instant Message window will open. Type your message, click Send, and the Instant Message window changes to display the messages to and from your friend in the top part of the window, with a box for you to type new messages in the bottom part of the window, like this:

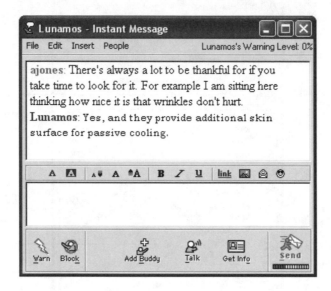

AIM also allows a discussion among multiple people, which AIM refers to as Chat. To invite several contacts to an AIM Chat, highlight all their names by holding down the CTRL key while you click each name. With all the names highlighted, click the Send Chat Invitation button near the lower-left corner of the Buddy List window. (The Send Chat Invitation button looks like three people with a cartoon dialog bubble over their heads.) Before clicking the Send button in the Chat Invitation window, you may type an Invitation Message and name the chat room. AOL subscribers can open the Buddy List window by going to the keyword BUDDYVIEW or by selecting People | Buddy List.

You can change your AIM user preferences by clicking the Setup button on the Sign On window or by clicking the Preferences button (which looks like a yellow wrench) in the Buddy List window. You may want to modify your Privacy settings to control who can send you messages; otherwise, you may be interrupted frequently when you're online.

AIM can do much more than instant messaging. If you enjoy using it, be sure to explore its ability to access e-mail, exchange files with your contacts, make telephone calls, and view news and stock market information. For voice features, see the AIM section of Chapter 16.

Yahoo Messenger

Yahoo, the web portal at **www.yahoo.com**, has its own instant messaging service, called Yahoo Messenger. (Yahoo! and Yahoo! Messenger actually include exclamation points in their names, but we omit these for readability.) Yahoo Messenger is very popular among people who use the many Yahoo functions such as e-mail, discussion boards, shopping services, maps, stock quotes, and more. Yahoo Messenger is available for Windows 95/98, NT, 2000, ME, and XP; PowerPC Mac 8.5 or higher; several versions of RedHat and FreeBSD Linux; Java; Palm handhelds; Windows CE; and web-enabled telephones. You can learn about and download Yahoo Messenger at the **messenger.yahoo.com** web site. (See Chapter 34 for information about how to download and install programs from the Web.)

Yahoo continually enhances Yahoo Messenger, and in each operating environment its use may be slightly different. The instructions provided in this book are for using Yahoo Messenger version 5.0 on Windows XP, but users of other versions should have no difficulty adapting these directions for use with their configurations.

Getting Started with Yahoo Messenger

After you've installed Yahoo Messenger, the Login window opens:

If you already have a Yahoo ID and password, type them in the fields provided; otherwise, click Get A Yahoo ID to register. In the Login window you can choose from three options. If you select Remember My ID & Password, your Yahoo ID and password are saved in a cookie file on your computer, and you won't have to type them each time you log onto Messenger. If you also choose to Automatically Login, you will completely bypass the Login window when you start Messenger and can thereby log into Messenger very quickly. The third option is to Login Under Invisible Mode. This privacy function prevents other Yahoo Messenger users from knowing you are logged in.

Yahoo Messenger is designed to run whenever your computer is running. This enables the program to alert you when one of your friends comes online or when someone wants to contact you. When Yahoo Messenger is running, you see a red *Y* behind a yellow smiley in the system tray. Double-click the tray icon to open the Yahoo Messenger window.

Finding People on Yahoo Messenger

The right-hand side of Figure 14-6 shows the Yahoo Messenger window, which is a list of the people you want to talk to. To find a contact to add to your Yahoo Messenger window, click the Add button and type your friend's e-mail address, Yahoo ID, or a keyword from his or her Yahoo profile.

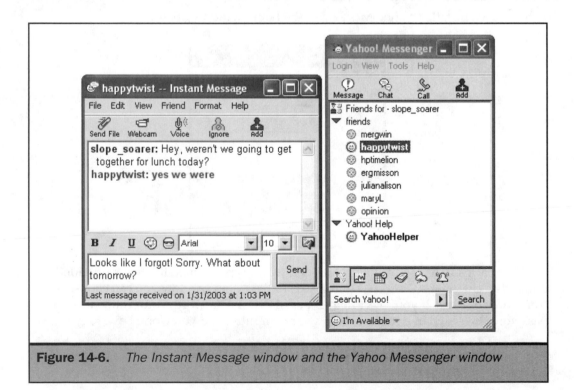

Figure 14-6.   *The Instant Message window and the Yahoo Messenger window*

Sending Messages with Yahoo Messenger

When you want to use Yahoo Messenger to send an instant message to one of your contacts, double-click a name in its window. The Instant Message window opens, as shown on the left side of Figure 14-6. Type your message in the bottom part of the window and click Send.

Part of the fun of Yahoo Messenger is in using its smileys or emoticons. Click the sunglass-clad smiley in the Instant Message window to see some of the available smileys. Surprise your friends by using one of the "hidden smileys" from **www.geocities.com/williampettrey**.

Yahoo Messenger also allows a discussion among multiple people, which is called a *chat* or *chat room*. Chat rooms can be publicly available or private, and they can include the use of live voice and video images. Yahoo Messenger is particularly strong when it comes to voice and video features: see Chapter 16 for details.

To create a chat room, click the Chat button in the Yahoo Messenger window. Select one of the listed Categories and click Create New Room. In the Create Chat Room window (Figure 14-7), choose your Access options and click Create Room. Once in the chat room, you can invite others with the Friend | Invite To Chat Room feature.

Figure 14-7.   *The Yahoo Messenger Create Chat Room window*

CHATTING AND
CONFERENCING ON
THE INTERNET

Jabber and Trillian Connect with Multiple IM Services

If you have friends or coworkers on several different IM services, it's annoying to have to load and run multiple IM programs (for example, AIM, Windows Messenger, and Yahoo Messenger). Trillian (**www.trillian.cc**) and Jabber (**www.jabber.com**) solve this problem, assuming that you run Windows. Trillian is an IM program that can connect to all the major services; download it from **www.trillian.cc/download.html**. In addition to large-scale IM server products for organizations that use IM for business purposes, Jabber offers Jabber IM (JIM) for Windows, which can connect to Windows Messenger, Yahoo Messenger, and ICQ. You can download JIM for free from **www.jabber.com/products/clients.shtml**.

Tip   *Yahoo Messenger can also let you know when e-mail messages arrive in your Yahoo Mail mailbox, when you get responses to your ad in Yahoo Personals, the current prices of the stocks in your portfolio, and more. See the Yahoo Messenger home page at **messenger.yahoo.com** for information.*

Windows Messenger (MSN Messenger)

Not to be outdone by AOL and others, in 1999 Microsoft released its own instant messaging option called MSN Messenger or Windows Messenger. Windows Messenger is integrated with Outlook Express, Hotmail, MSN TV, and some other MSN services, so it has a large following among users of those products. Windows Messenger is available for Windows 95/98, NT, 2000, ME, and XP; PowerPC Mac 8.6 or higher; Pocket PC; and MSN Companion.

You may already have Windows Messenger because it's included at no cost with some other Microsoft programs, including Windows XP. Search your computer for a file called Msmsgs.exe to determine if it's already installed. You can learn about or download Windows Messenger at **messenger.msn.com**. (See Chapter 34 for information about how to download and install programs from the Web.) To use Windows Messenger, you must have an e-mail address and a free Microsoft .NET Passport, but you can obtain a Passport (discussed in Chapter 18) when you begin using Windows Messenger.

Caution   *Some versions of Windows Messenger are extremely difficult to uninstall. If this bothers you, consider using another of the instant messaging systems described in this chapter.*

Microsoft continually enhances Windows Messenger, and in each operating environment its use may be slightly different. The instructions provided in this book are for using Windows Messenger version 4.6 on Windows XP, but users of other configurations should have no difficulty adapting these directions for use in their environments.

Getting Started with Windows Messenger

After you have installed Windows Messenger, its window opens. Click the Click Here To Sign In button, and the program takes you through its registration steps.

Finding People on Windows Messenger

Unlike many other instant messaging services, Windows Messenger does not tout itself as a "love connection," and it is not designed for making new acquaintances who share your interests. Instead, Windows Messenger is intended for communicating with people you already know. To send a Windows Messenger instant message to someone, you must first add the person to your list of contacts, which generally means you must know the person's e-mail address. If you have that information, click Add A Contact in the Windows Messenger window (Figure 14-8) and indicate whether you want to add a contact by e-mail address or search for a contact in the Hotmail directory.

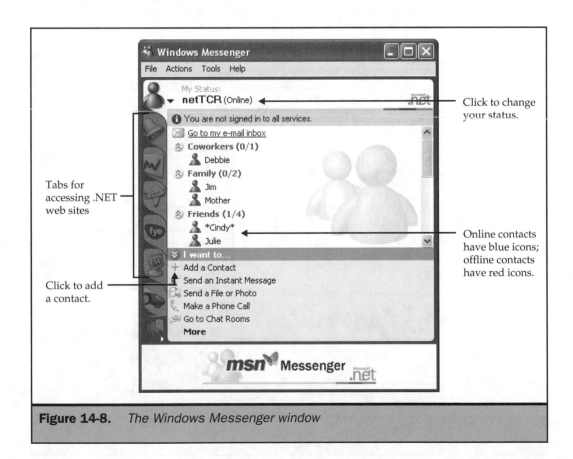

Figure 14-8.   *The Windows Messenger window*

Windows Messenger is designed to run whenever your computer is running. This enables the program to alert you when one of your friends comes online or when someone wants to contact you. Messenger knows when you are connected to the Internet and using Windows Messenger, and you can configure it to automatically indicate to your contacts that you're "Away" if you don't use your computer for a while.

Messenger appears as a stylized human torso icon in the notification area (system tray) of the Windows taskbar. The icon is green when your status is Online or red when your status is Offline. A red circle on the green icon indicates that youare online but not available. Double-click the tray icon to open the Windows Messenger window.

Sending Messages with Windows Messenger

When you want to use Windows Messenger to send an instant message to one of your contacts, double-click the name of an online contact in your Windows Messenger window. The Conversation window will open, as shown in Figure 14-9. Type your message in the bottom part of the window and click Send.

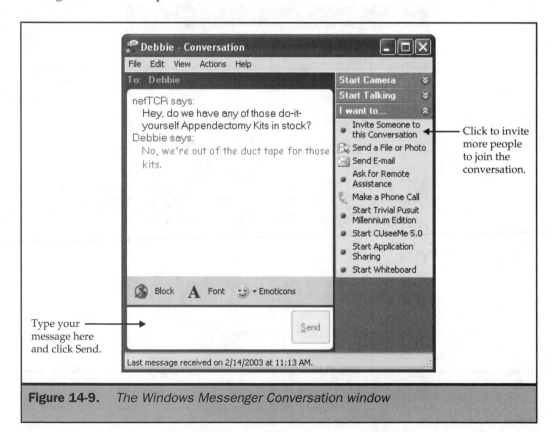

Figure 14-9.   *The Windows Messenger Conversation window*

Secure IM Services

Instant messaging can be used for business as well as individuals. However, businesses may not want to trust their internal corporate communications to a public IM service. Several private, secure IM services have sprung up to fill this need, including Bantu (**www.bantu.com**), iPlanet (from Sun Microsystems, at **www.iplanet.com**), Imici (**www.imici.com**), WiredRed (**www.wiredred.com**), and Jabber (**www.jabber.com**). These IM programs include other features for business users, such as logging of conversations.

Once a Conversation window is open, you can invite multiple contacts to join the discussion. Just click Invite Someone To This Conversation, click the name of the person you want to add, and click OK. All Windows Messenger Conversations are private, and no one can view or join a Conversation without being invited by one of the invited participants. Windows Messenger Conversations can also include the use of live voice and video images, as discussed in Chapter 16.

Windows Messenger has dozens of configuration options you can explore by clicking the File, Actions, and Tools menus of the Windows Messenger window. Furthermore, you can use Windows Messenger to make telephone calls, exchange files, play games, communicate on a whiteboard, directly access another person's computer, and more. Most of these features require the installation of a free add-in program. For information about add-ins for Windows Messenger, go to **messenger.microsoft.com/download/ addin.asp**.

Note *Although you have to jump through hoops to do it, it is possible to remove Windows Messenger from Windows XP if you don't plan to use it. To uninstall Windows Messenger, open up C:\Windows\Inf\Sysoc.inf in Notepad. (It's a hidden system file, but you can open it by choosing Start | Run and typing **notepad c:\windows\inf\sysoc.inf** in the Run dialog box.) Search for the line "msmsgs=" and remove the word "hide." Now you'll see Windows Messenger when you run Add/Remove Programs in the Control Panel, and you can uninstall the program.*

Chapter 15

Web-Based Chat Rooms and Discussion Boards

With the increasing popularity of the Web, both interactive and bulletin-board style chatting from web pages has become popular. Why use some new program—like an IRC client or newsreader—when you can use your familiar browser to participate in real-time chat or message boards?

A web site is often more than simply something to look at or a resource to use; many web site operators want to provide their users with a community that encourages them to be part of the experience. Web-based chat systems and message boards fill this goal, building an online network of people who interact not just with the web page, but with other users as well.

In many cases (especially for real-time chat), you may need to enable ActiveX, Java, or JavaScript in your browser (Chapter 20 explains why you may have disabled these features). You may also need to download a plug-in or ActiveX control, as described in Chapter 18.

Like other types of Internet communities, web-based communities provide real-time interactive chatting (like instant messaging or IRC), threaded discussion boards (like Usenet newsgroups or mailing lists), or both. Unlike IRC or Usenet, no standardized rules exist for how web chat should look or be used; each web site you visit could present another new system to learn. Fortunately, chatting on the Web is very simple—easier than using an IRC program or newsreader—so learning the basics will enable you to adapt to any system that a web site operator might provide.

Interactive Web Chat

Web sites that enable you to converse directly with other web users—in a manner similar to IRC or instant messaging—are providing *interactive web chat*. Usually, these sites are referred to as *chat rooms*, a concept popularized by America Online. However, only AOL users can use America Online chat rooms, whereas anyone on the Internet with the right software can access a web-based chatting system.

You can find two main categories of interactive chat systems. Some are basically textual in nature—you type something, and what you type appears on the screens of people around the world who are connected to the same site. Others use graphics and even 3-D animation to provide you with a visual *avatar*—your online representation in the chat room, which interacts with other users' avatars as you send and receive messages.

Most chat rooms are written in Java, a computer language that enables programs to be distributed and run over the Internet. To access a Java-based chat room, you need a web browser that can run Java applications, and you must configure it to do so. (Chapter 20's sections on managing Java tell you how.) When you click a link to enter a chat room, you may see an "Applet loading" message while your browser downloads the Java *applet* (small program) that displays the chat room. Other chat sites use autoloading HTML pages, so that your web browser doesn't need any extra software. Some chat sites offer both options.

Text Chat Rooms on the Web

Text-based chat rooms are very much like IRC (see Chapter 13) or instant messaging with lots of participants. You use your web browser to connect to the web site, choose a handle, and see the messages in the chat room. When you type messages, anyone using the same chat room can read what you type. For example, Figure 15-1 shows the Yahoo Chat site at **chat.yahoo.com**. When you click a chat topic, you may see a set of three icons: one for text chat, one for voice chat, and one for video chat. (See Chapter 16 for how voice and video chats work.)

Most web-based chat rooms display the ongoing conversation in most of the browser window, with a smaller box at the bottom of the window into which you

CHATTING AND
CONFERENCING ON
THE INTERNET

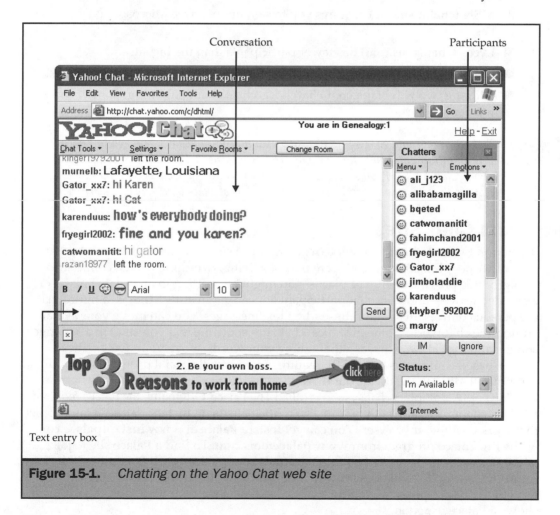

Figure 15-1.   *Chatting on the Yahoo Chat web site*

can type your comments. When you press ENTER or click Send, your message goes to the chat room and appears in the browser windows of the other chat participants. Nearly all chat rooms display a list of the other participants down the right side of the browser window.

Some chat systems include menus or buttons to enable you to send an emotion or action ("Margy laughs out loud") or to converse privately with people in the room. You may also be able to control the font, color, and size of the text of your messages.

Web sites that host real-time chats on a wide variety of topics include the following:

- **Excite SuperChat (communicate.excite.com)** requires downloading and installing the Excite SuperChat Private Messenger, which doesn't run on Macs.

- **MSN (chat.msn.com)** requires you to sign up for a free Microsoft .NET Passport.

- **Lycos (chat.lycos.com)** has fewer participants than the big sites.

- **ESPN (espn.go.com)** has celebrity sports chats; click the Chat Schedule link.

- **iVillage (www.ivillage.com/chat)** hosts chats about parenting, family, and women's issues.

Chat sites come and go. To find web sites that host lots of chat rooms, go to Yahoo (www.yahoo.com) and choose Computers & Internet | Internet | World Wide Web | Chat | Chat Rooms. Many other web sites host a few chats on topics that relate to the site. (For example, sports sites may host chats with sports celebrities.)

Graphical Chat Sites

If you don't want to limit yourself to text, graphical chat systems enable you to chat with other people as though you were part of a living, two-dimensional comic strip. Backgrounds provide a sense of place—you might be chatting in an ornate palace, or a wooded grove—and each chat participant appears as an *avatar,* that is, a figure that the person controls. In addition to sending text messages, you can move your avatar around the chat world. Some graphical chat sites show the text you send in a separate conversation window, whereas others show your words above your avatar's head. Avatar-based chat rooms frequently require you to install special programs on your computer to display the background, avatars, and text.

One popular graphics chat system is called The Palace. Originally, the Palace required a Palace client program, but you can also participate using Instant Palace, a Java applet that works with your browser. You can get Instant Palace at **www.instantpalace.com**, or the full Palace program from **www.palacetools.com**. To find a Palace site to join, go to the PalaceTools Directory (**www.palacetools.com/palace**); each Palace has links for connecting with "ip" (that is, with your browser using the Instant Palace Java applet) or with the Palace program. Many Palaces also have their own web sites. Figure 15-2 shows a Palace in action.

Figure 15-2.   *The Instant Palace Java applet enables you to participate in graphical chat rooms.*

In Palace, you can click to move around the graphical world, passing through doors to other chat rooms. You can also change your avatar (your character on the screen) or your name (which appears under your avatar).

Web Discussion Boards

An alternative to a real-time chat room is a *web discussion board, web message board,* or *web forum.* Web boards function like Usenet newsgroups or mailing lists—you can read messages, reply to them, and post your own thoughts whenever you like. Any number of people can participate, without having to be online at the same time; the drawback is that discussions are slower than live chatting.

Most web discussion boards don't require any special software to use them; a normal web browser is sufficient. Registration is sometimes required to participate on a web forum, which means that you may have to provide your name and e-mail address to the board operator before you can post messages.

The following sites host web discussion boards on a number of topics; many other sites have a few discussion boards related to the topic of the site:

- **About.com (www.about.com)**   This hosts thousands of sites about specific topics, each of which includes a message board.

- **Delphi Forums (www.delphiforums.com)**   This offers moderated discussions on a wide variety of topics.

- **EBay Community (pages.ebay.com/community)**   This hosts message boards about how to participate in online auctions, as well as on general topics, especially those related to things that are sold at auction.

- **iVillage (www.ivillage.com)**   This hosts discussion boards about family, parenting, and women's issues.

- **Lycos Communities (clubs.lycos.com)**   Click the Message Boards link for a list of discussion boards by topic.

- **MSN Communities (communities.msn.com/people)**   This hosts many communities that include discussion boards, but requires you to sign up for a Microsoft .NET Passport to participate. This board works only with Internet Explorer.

- **The WELL (www.thewell.com)**   One of the original message board sites, even before the Web, the WELL still hosts a wonderful collection of discussions. It costs $10 a month to participate.

- **Yahoo Groups (groups.yahoo.com)**   Groups include message boards, chat rooms, file sharing sites, calendars, and other features (as shown in Figure 15-3). You can choose to receive messages by e-mail, so the message board works more like a mailing list, although you still need to return to the web site to post messages.

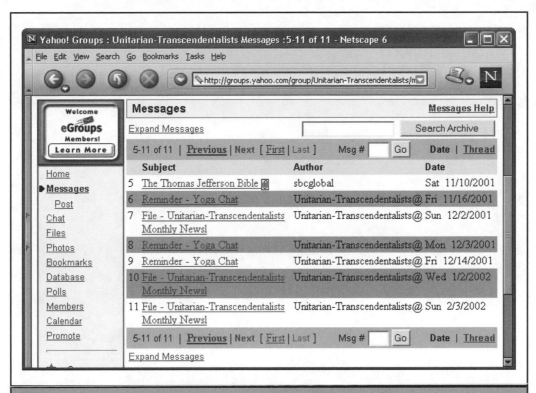

Figure 15-3.   *Yahoo Groups include discussion boards, and you can choose whether to receive messages by e-mail.*

The Complete Reference

Internet

Chapter 16

Voice and Video Conferencing

357

The Internet brings people together. As you saw in the preceding chapters on e-mail and various types of online chat, using the Internet is a great way to communicate with friends old and new. In this chapter, you will find out how to go a step beyond written messages by adding voice and video conferencing to your communication tools. This chapter describes Internet phone applications (like Net2Phone, PhoneFree, and iConnectHere PC-to-Phone), the voice and video conferencing features of instant messaging programs (Yahoo Messenger, AOL Instant Messenger, Windows Messenger, and ICQ), and a stand-alone conferencing program, Microsoft NetMeeting.

What Are Internet Phone, Voice Conferencing, and Video Conferencing?

Internet phone (or *Internet telephony* or *PC-to-PC phone*) programs are designed to simulate phone calls over the Internet, avoiding long-distance phone charges. Communicating on the Internet works the same way whether the two people are down the block, in different time zones, or on different continents. Each person on the Internet phone call needs a computer with a microphone and speakers. To participate, you download and install an Internet phone program and sign up for a user name on the system. You "dial" your Internet phone call by specifying your friend's user name. You chat using the microphone and speakers connected to your computer. Internet phone is one form of *voice-over-IP (VoIP)*—voice information transmitted over the Internet (using Internet Protocol, as explained in Chapter 1).

If you want to be able to call from your computer to someone's telephone (so the other person doesn't need a computer at all), VoIP programs are also available. However, these *PC-to-phone* programs and services aren't free; because they need to use local phone lines to connect to the other person's phone, the entire link isn't over the Internet.

Voice conferencing can be PC-to-PC or PC-to-phone, with two or more people in the conversation. It replaces conference calls, which get expensive when they include many people over long distances. PC-to-PC voice conferences can be free for up to 12 people if you use the right software.

Video conferencing enables you to send your image to one or more people through a camera attached to your computer and to receive pictures back. You can use voice or video conferencing (or both), depending on the peripheral equipment (microphone, speakers, and camera) connected to your computer and your conferencing software. Instead of typing messages to conduct a conversation, as you do in a chat room, with voice and video conferencing you can talk to other people, see their faces, and transmit your video so that they can see you, too.

Getting Your Telephone Service from Your ISP

Another form of VoIP (voice over IP) comes from cable Internet companies. Some cable Internet companies now offer telephone services using your existing cable lines. In addition to using your cable TV wire for television and the Internet, you can also use it for Plain Old Telephone Service (POTS). The cable company replaces your cable box with a box that has a phone jack into which you can plug a phone. This type of phone service is worth considering if the cable company's rates are competitive and if you hear good things from your neighbors about their service.

On the other hand, cable companies don't have the same long-term experience and reliability as most phone companies. They don't offer emergency-911 service and may not have three-way calling, caller ID, and other features. In addition, regular phones work even when the power is out, which is not true of your cable box.

Internet Telephony and Conferencing Sound Great—Why Don't We All Abandon Long-Distance Phone Calls?

If this question occurs to you as you read about Internet phone, voice, and video conferencing, you're not alone! Conferencing is very attractive—it saves you the cost of a long-distance phone call, you don't need to leave your desk to see the other person, and you can show your latest invention or interior decorating scheme to people who are far away.

Before you abandon your telephone and use the Internet for conversations, consider a few factors:

- Does the person you want to talk to have a computer and the hardware and software required for conferencing? Does everyone concerned have a high-speed line?

- A computer isn't as portable as, say, talking on a cellular phone. Will this lack of portability affect your conversations?

- Both parties have to be using their computers at the same time, so how will you schedule your conversation?

Note   *Using e-mail to exchange messages and set up a meeting time is a convenient way to schedule a conference.*

- How private does your conference have to be?

Some people are concerned that other people might eavesdrop on Internet conversations. As with any kind of public communication, you have to remember that absolute security does not exist. Your telephone can be tapped, and your cellular phone conversations can be recorded. However, when you use conferencing, the sheer number of other transmissions taking place at the same time makes it unlikely that your conversation will be overheard. The Internet is as secure as it can be without limiting how easy it is to use or how convenient it is to access.

Conferencing Is More Than Talking and Seeing

Most conferencing software lets you do more than just talk and exchange video. Software conferencing applications can simulate a business meeting where all participants are gathered in one conference room. In Table 16-1, many of the features seem like they are pulled right out of the business world (such as writing on a whiteboard, for example).

Conferencing features may be named after actions that take place in business, but you can use conferencing software in your personal life, too. To show how you can adapt conferencing software from a business conference venue to a different setting, suppose, for example, that you are planning a family reunion. Table 16-2 shows some ways to use the businesslike features of conferencing when you're not at work.

Feature	Function
Chat	This is used when you have many people in the conference. Most conferencing software allows you to talk to and see only one person at a time, so using the chat feature is a way to conduct an online discussion with a lot of people.
File transfer	This sends a copy of a file to one or all meeting participants.
Sharing an application	This opens an application and lets others see the application. For example, you can open your browser and jump from link to link in the browser window or open a word processing or spreadsheet program and make changes to a file, and everyone sees exactly what you are doing.
Whiteboard	This loads an existing graphics file for everyone to see, or you can create your own drawing. Everyone in the meeting sees and can draw on the whiteboard.
Collaboration	This lets other meeting participants edit one of your files.

Table 16-1. *Extra Features in Conferencing Software*

Feature	Business Use	Personal Use
Chat	Discuss a project by exchanging typed messages, which everyone in the meeting can see. Keep a record of the meeting minutes by saving the chat contents as a text file.	Connect all the cousins on your mother's side of the family and plan the reunion menu online.
File transfer	Send a hard copy of the meeting agenda to all participants.	Send the recipes that you've organized in text files on your computer to everyone haggling over the menu.
Sharing an application	Show the latest project status report in its original application.	Open your graphics editor and show everyone the invitations that you sent to be printed.
Whiteboard	Draw your department's organizational chart.	Diagram the best route to the reunion site.
Collaboration	Allow other meeting participants to add input to the project status report.	Allow other family members to edit your written directions to the reunion site.

Table 16-2. *Business and Personal Uses of Extra Features in Conferencing Software*

CHATTING AND
CONFERENCING ON
THE INTERNET

Getting Voice and Video Hardware

For Internet phone, voice, or video conferencing, you need a high-speed Internet connection. You can send and receive voice and video with a dial-up line, but expect *dropouts* (intermittent silence) and low general quality. If your computer is particularly slow, you may also run into quality problems.

You also need a microphone and speakers connected to your computer. Most computers come with sound cards and speakers, but you may have to get and plug in a mike. A computer-compatible microphone costs about $15 (available at any Radio Shack) and plugs into your computer's sound card.

Running Conferences with More than Ten People

What if you want to make a presentation over the Internet to 50 people? Neither Windows Messenger nor Yahoo Messenger supports large numbers of participants—in fact, no free product does (that we know of).

For presentations to large numbers of people, you can use web-based systems that charge by the participant or by the minute to "host" virtual meetings. Each participant registers at the web site, downloads browser plug-ins or other software, and connects to the meeting server. The organizer of the meeting pays the web site for the meeting. Participants can see and hear the presenter onscreen, as well as see whiteboards and software demonstrations from the presenter's computer. Some systems allow participants to collaborate on documents or test-drive software. Costs range from 35 cents per minute per participant (for systems that charge by the minute) to $10 per participant (for flat-fee sites). To find out more, go to WebEx (**www.webex.com**), Genesys (**www.genesys.com**), Raindance (**www.raindance.com**), or Communicast (**communicast.com**).

For video conferencing, you need a camera connected to your computer. (Note that a digital video camera that produces output for your computer is different from a video camcorder—and much cheaper.) Small, cheap video cameras designed for connection to computers are called *webcams* and can cost from $40 to $75, depending on the resolution. (Some webcams can also serve as digital still cameras.) Webcams connect to your computer via a USB or FireWire port and come with drivers that you install for Windows or Macs. Go to PC Connection (**www.pcconnection.com**) or Computer Discount Warehouse (**www.cdw.com**) and search for "webcam."

Note *Everyone in the conference needs a microphone and speakers, too, but not everyone needs a webcam. If one participant doesn't have a video camera, he can still see other people in the conference, but the other participants can't see him.*

Making Phone Calls over the Internet

If you're not interested in talking with groups, using video, or using other conferencing features, consider an Internet phone program. (On the other hand, if you already use an instant messaging program, as described in Chapter 14, check whether it has voice built in; you may be able to click a button to add voice to an instant messaging conversation.) PC-to-PC programs work only from one PC to another and are usually free, with no cost regardless of how many calls you make or how long they are. PC-to-phone programs usually charge for calls, with low rates (3.9 cents per minute or less within the United States as of mid-2002 and similarly cheap for international calls).

Be sure to check the rates and to check for monthly charges before signing up for a PC-to-phone service. Like long-distance plans, these services can have hidden costs or limitations. Some services limit the length or number of calls. (Net2Phone as of mid-2002 limits free calls within the United States to five minutes.) Others require you to deposit money in your account, even if you don't plan to make international calls.

Some Internet phone programs are separate programs, whereas others work through your web browser. Table 16-3 lists Internet phone programs with their web sites and features.

The next two sections describe instant messaging programs that support voice and stand-alone conferencing programs. Both can also work as PC-to-PC phone programs.

Tip

*For listings of other Internet phone programs, go to the Internet Phone Software web site at **www.internetphonesoftware.com**. Alternatively, search Download.com (**www.download.com**) or TUCOWS (**www.tucows.com**) for "phone."*

Program	Web Site	PC-to-PC	PC-to-Phone
BuddyPhone	www.buddyphone.com	✓	✓
Callserve (in Europe)	www.callserve.com		✓
DialPad	www.dialpad.com		✓
Go2Call	www.go2call.com		✓
iConnectHere.com PC-to-Phone	www.iconnecthere.com	✓	✓
Net2Phone	www.net2phone.com	✓	✓
NetTelephone.com	www.nettelephone.com		✓
PalTalk	www.paltalk.com/paltalk	✓	
PCCall	www.pccall.com		✓
PhoneFree	www.phonefree.com	✓	✓

Table 16-3. *Internet Phone Programs*

Voice and Video Conferencing Using Instant Messenger Programs

As the instant messenger wars heated up (pitting AOL, Microsoft, and Yahoo against each other), the software publishers started adding features. Now all the major IM programs have added voice, and some have added video. Not all have the same features, however: some IM programs enable only two people in a call to use voice and video, whereas others (notably Yahoo Messenger) enable up to 12 people to talk, see each other, and type in a conference.

Refer to Chapter 14 for how to install and use instant messaging programs. The next four sections contain instructions for using the voice and video conferencing features of ICQ, AOL Instant Messenger, Yahoo Messenger, and Windows Messenger (MSN Messenger).

Making Internet Phone Calls with ICQ

ICQ, the original instant messaging program, added a feature called ICQphone to handle voice connections. ICQ doesn't support video (yet).

To make a voice connection with another ICQ user, you need to be in Advanced mode. If you see the To Advanced Mode button in your ICQ window, click it. In Advanced mode, click someone's name on your contact list and choose ICQphone | Launch ICQphone Client from the menu that appears. The ICQphone window appears, like this:

You can also run ICQphone by choosing Services | ICQphone | Launch ICQphone Client from the ICQ window. Once ICQphone is running, you can connect to another

ICQ user by clicking the Call PC To PC button. To make PC-to-phone calls, click the phone number and click Call. PC-to-PC calls are free, whereas PC-to-phone calls require an account. To create an account, click the My Account button to display the Owner Preferences dialog box, click the ICQphone category if it's not already selected, and click the Create New Account Now button. You provide your name, address, and credit card information to pay for your calls.

For more information on voice over ICQ, see ICQ's www.icq.com/telephony/telephony.html web page.

Making Internet Phone Calls with AOL Instant Messenger (AIM)

AOL Instant Messenger 4.7 provides two ways to talk: BuddyTalk (or Talk) for PC-to-PC connections and AIM Phone for PC-to-phone. AIM doesn't include support for video conferencing.

BuddyTalk adds voice to your instant messaging conversations. To set your Talk privacy options, choose My AIM | Edit Options | Edit Preferences to display the AOL Instant Messenger Preferences dialog box. Click the Talk category and choose the way you want AIM to respond when others request to talk with you.

To talk to someone on your Buddy List, double-click the person to open an Instant Message window. Then click the Talk button on the toolbar at the bottom of the window. After a warning asking whether you want to enable voice, you see the Talk With window:

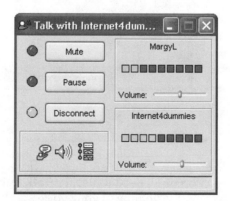

Another way to make a voice connection with someone on your buddy list is to select the person and choose People | Connect To Talk from the AIM menu (or press ALT-T).

If you want to make calls to people's phones, you can use AIM Phone, which is an AOL version of Net2Phone. Check the AIM Phone web site at **aimphone.aol.com/help.html** for U.S. and international rates.

Voice and Video Conferencing with Yahoo Messenger

Yahoo Messenger enables you to use both voice and video in one-on-one instant message conversations as well as in conferences of up to 12 people. No other free program we know can match it. Yahoo doesn't support PC-to-phone calls.

Voice Conferencing in Yahoo Messenger

Before you try Internet phone with the program, configure Yahoo Messenger to work with your microphone and speakers by choosing Help | Audio Setup Wizard from the Yahoo Messenger or Instant Message menu to adjust your settings. The wizard tests your microphone, speakers, volume settings, background noise level, and Internet connection.

When you are chatting with someone in Yahoo Messenger, click the Voice icon on the toolbar. The other person sees a dialog box asking whether to enable voice. If he or she agrees, both participants' Instant Message window gains buttons and indicators about voice, like this:

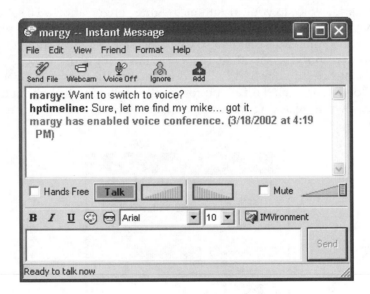

Click and hold the Talk button while you are talking. If you plan to talk a lot, click the Hands Free check box so you don't need to use the Talk button. The histograms to the right of the Talk button show the volume of your voice and the other person's voice. If you want to turn off the speakers so you can't hear the other person temporarily, click the Mute check box.

You can use voice in multiperson conferences, too. (This feature separates Yahoo Messenger from most other conferencing programs, which allow only two people to speak.) When you create a conference (by choosing Tools | Invite To Conference from the Yahoo Messenger menu), make sure that the Enable Voice For This Conference check box is selected. The Voice Conference window that appears has the same voice controls shown in the illustration earlier in this section. You can tell which conference participants have a mike; their icons on the participant list have headphones.

Video Conferencing in Yahoo Messenger

If you have a webcam connected to your computer, you can enable others in an IM conversation or conference to see you on camera. The first time you use your webcam, follow these steps:

1. Click the Webcam button on the Instant Message or Voice Conference window. You see the My Webcam window, shown in the picture that others will see. Adjust the camera to be the right distance and angle from your face.

2. Choose File | Preferences in the My Webcam window to display the Yahoo Messenger Preferences dialog box and click the Webcam category. Set the privacy settings to control who can see your image.

3. Click the Camera Settings button to display the Video Source dialog box. Move the sliders to make your image brighter or darker and to make other adjustments. Click OK when you are finished. Click OK to dismiss the Yahoo Messenger Preferences dialog box.

The next time you want to use your webcam, click the Webcam button on the Instant Message or Voice Conference window. The other people in your instant message conversation or conference see a dialog box saying that you have invited them to see your webcam. Those who click Yes see you in a window like this:

Close the My Webcam window to stop transmitting your picture.

 You can choose Login | Preferences (or press CTRL-P) from the Yahoo Messenger window to adjust your webcam or other settings, even when you aren't in a conference or conversation.

Conferencing with Windows Messenger and MSN Messenger

Windows Messenger comes with Windows XP (as explained in Chapter 14), whereas older versions of Windows and Internet Explorer come with MSN Messenger. You can download the latest version of either program from **messenger.microsoft.com**. This section describes Windows Messenger 4.6; MSN Messenger 4.6 works very similarly.

Windows Messenger supports PC-to-phone, PC-to-PC, and video conferencing, but only with one person at a time. If you have added more people to a conversation, the voice and video features are unavailable.

 If your computer connects to the Internet through a LAN or uses a firewall, Windows Messenger's voice, video, and other advanced features may not work. Check with your LAN administrator or check your Internet Connection Firewall settings, which are described in Chapter 3.

Making PC-to-Phone Calls with Windows Messenger

From the I Want To menu at the bottom of the Windows Messenger window, click Make A Phone Call. The program checks whether your Internet connection supports phone connections and displays the Phone window:

The first time you use the program, click the Get Started Here button to sign up for an Internet phone service. (Microsoft offered Callserve, Net2Phone, and iConnectHere last we checked, and other services for Canadian users.) Once you are signed up with a service, you can type the phone number (including the area code) or choose a number from the list of numbers you've called before. Click Dial to connect. When you are finished talking, click Hang Up.

Another way to make the call is to right-click an online contact and to choose Make A Phone Call from the menu that appears.

Making PC-to-PC Calls with Windows Messenger

To set up a voice conversation with another Windows Messenger user, right-click the person on your list of online contacts and select Start A Voice Conversation from the menu that appears. The first time you choose this command, the Audio And Video Tuning Wizard runs to set up your webcam. Follow its instructions.

The Start A Voice Conversation command opens a Conversation window, and Windows Messenger sends a message to ask the other person whether to start a voice conversation. The person can click Accept or press ALT-T to enable voice, or click Decline or press ALT-D to refuse. Slider controls appear to control the volume of your speakers and microphone, as shown in the lower-right section of Figure 16-1.

When you are done talking, click the Stop Talking button.

Video Conferencing in Windows Messenger

Video works similarly to voice in Windows Messenger conversations, and like voice, is limited to conversations with one other person. In a Conversation window, click the Start Camera to enable both voice and video. Windows Messenger sends a message to ask the other person whether they agree to use voice and video. If the other person agrees, the image appears in the upper-right corner of the Conversation window, as shown in Figure 16-1.

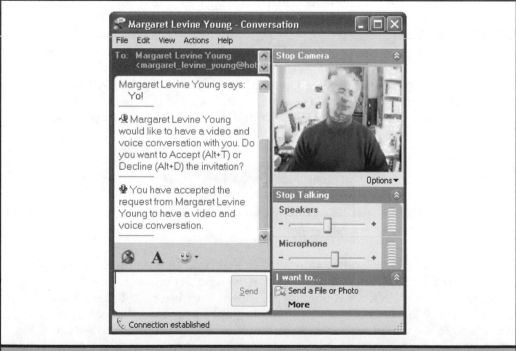

Figure 16-1. *Windows Messenger can add voice and video to a conversation with one other person, but not to conferences.*

If you want to be able to see your own picture, too, click the Options button below the video image and choose Show My Picture As Picture-In-Picture from the menu that appears. This command doesn't affect what the other person sees. When you are done with your video conference, click Stop Camera.

 To check your picture before letting anyone see you, choose View | Audio Tuning Wizard from the Conversation window's menu bar and click Next until you see the screen that includes your video image. Unlike Yahoo Messenger, Windows Messenger doesn't provide a way to adjust the picture quality, brightness, and contrast of your video image—that's why the picture in Figure 16-1 is too bright.

Sending Files to Others in a Conversation

To send a file to someone with whom you are having a conversation, click Send A File Or Photo in the Conversation window (or choose Actions | Send A File Or Photo from the menu). If you're not already chatting with the person, you can right-click the contact name in the Windows Messenger window and choose Send A File Or Photo from the menu that appears. Select the file and click Open. The contact has to click a button to accept the file.

When you receive a file, Windows usually stores it in the My Received Files subfolder of your My Documents folder. If you use Internet Connection Sharing, you may only be able to receive files—you may not be able to send them.

Sharing a Whiteboard

You can share a whiteboard—a drawing window on which everyone in the conversation can draw—as part of a Windows Messenger conversation. Click Start Whiteboard in the Conversation window (you may need to click More to see this option). Alternatively, choose Actions | Start Whiteboard from the menu. The other people in the conversation receive an invitation to start using Whiteboard. If they click Accept, you (and they) see a Sharing Session window, like this:

The Sharing Session window shows the shared items that Windows Messenger supports: App(lication) Sharing (described in the next section) and Whiteboard.

Then you see a Whiteboard window, as shown in Figure 16-2. The whiteboard works similarly to Microsoft Paint, the simple graphics program that comes with Windows. To see what a tool does, hover your mouse pointer over it to see a ToolTip. When you are finished with the drawing, close the Whiteboard window. (Choose File | Save As first if you want to save your joint work.)

Figure 16-2. *When you share a whiteboard with Windows Messenger, everyone in the conversation can draw on it.*

Sharing Control of a Program

If you would like to show the other people in a conversation how a program works or edit a document as a group, you can use Windows Messenger's Application Sharing feature. You can let the other people take control of the program and give commands, even if they don't have the program installed on their computers.

Showing a Program on Everyone's Screen In the Conversation window, click Start Application Sharing (you may need to click More to see this option). Alternatively, choose Actions | Start Application Sharing from the menu. Windows Messenger sends the other people in the conversation an invitation to share an application with you. If they click Accept, the small Sharing Session window appears (pictured in the previous section), and then you see the Sharing window shown in Figure 16-3. (If the other people want to share programs on their computers, they can display this window by clicking the App Sharing icon in the Sharing Session window.)

In the Sharing window, choose the program that you want to allow the other people in the conversation to share. For example, to edit a document as a group, choose to share a word processing program that is open with the document loaded. If you want to show the other people a presentation or some web pages, choose a presentation program or your web browser. Then click Share.

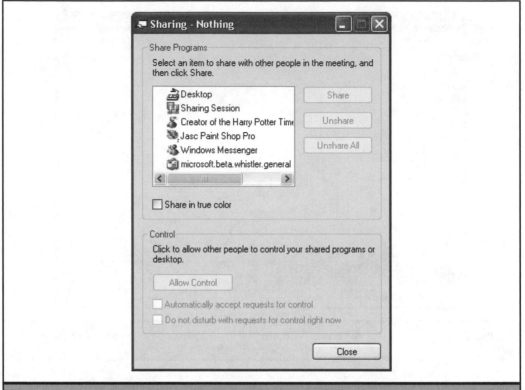

Figure 16-3. *Which application program do you want to share with the other people in your Windows Messenger conversation?*

Once you have selected a program to share, the program window appears on the screens of the other people in the Windows Messenger conversation. Bring the window to the front (that is, click in it to make it active) so that other windows don't obscure it on the other people's screens. The other people can see what you do but can't give commands themselves.

Here are a few pointers when sharing a program:

■ Before you start to share an application, agree on a screen resolution for everyone to use. Using the same resolution as the rest of the people in the conversation prevents the screen from jumping around as the cursor and mouse pointer move in the shared application.

■ Others in the conversation can see only as much of the program's window as you can see on your screen; when you click another window that overlaps the window that is editing the file, the obscured part of the window disappears on everyone else's screen, too.

- Unless you and everyone else in the conversation have fast Internet connections (faster than dial-up), displaying windows with a shared program can take a long time—a minute or two. Everyone in the conversation must wait for the shared window to appear, or everyone's screens will get hopelessly confusing. This feature works best for users connected by a high-speed LAN and is almost unusable on dial-up connections.

Enabling Others to Control the Program If you want other people to be able to control the application (giving commands and controlling the mouse), switch back to the Sharing window and click the Allow Control button. When someone else double-clicks in the window that displays your program, you see a Request Control window, indicating who wants to control the application. Click Accept or Reject to give or deny control to that person. The other person controls the mouse and keyboard for that application until you press a key. When you are finished sharing control of the application, switch back to the Sharing window and click the Prevent Control button. When you're done sharing the application, close the Sharing window (and the application, if you like).

While you are sharing control, you can select the Automatically Accept Request For Control check box in the Sharing window to skip having to accept requests for control. Alternatively, to temporarily disable control-sharing, select the Do Not Disturb With Requests For Control Right Now check box.

Note *Firewalls can prevent you from sharing applications with Windows Messenger.*

Here are some tips about sharing control of a program:

- If you share Windows Explorer, all Explorer windows are shared with the other callers, including windows that you open after clicking the Share button.

- If you are going to edit a file collaboratively, make a backup copy of the file first, just in case of disaster. When you have finished editing the file collaboratively, only the person who originally shared the file can save or print the file. If other callers want copies of the finished file, the owner of the file can send the file to the other callers, as described earlier in this chapter.

- Each person in the call does not need to have the program that the call is sharing; mouse clicks and keystrokes are transmitted to the program owner's computer.

Conferencing with Stand-Alone Programs: NetMeeting

Before instant messaging programs started adding voice and video conferencing features, people used stand-alone conferencing programs. The original conferencing program is CUseeMe, at **www.cuseeme.com/products/cuseeme5.htm**. The most widely distributed conferencing program is NetMeeting, which comes with Windows Me and Windows 2000. This section describes NetMeeting 3.

How NetMeeting Works

Windows Messenger has all of NetMeeting's features, but if you are working with someone who is not using Windows XP and Windows Messenger 4.*x*, you may want to use NetMeeting to chat, talk, video conference, or share applications or a whiteboard. As far as we know, Microsoft is no longer developing NetMeeting because Windows Messenger replaces it.

To connect to the other people with whom you want to meet, you have to provide a way for NetMeeting to find the person. NetMeeting uses several ways:

- **Windows Address Book**   If you are one of the few people who use the Windows Address Book to store e-mail addresses and other information, NetMeeting can search it for the person you want to talk to.

- **Directory server**   A *directory server* stores the addresses of people who use NetMeeting. When you are logged onto a directory server, your name appears on its lists, so that anyone else can "call" you. Once you have connected to a directory server, you can call another person or several other people. Large organizations may have their own directory servers for their employees, and Microsoft maintains a public directory server called the Microsoft Internet Directory, the same server that Windows Messenger uses. You must have a Microsoft .NET Passport to connect to the Microsoft Internet Directory.

- **IP address**   If you know the person's IP address (numeric Internet address, in the format *xxx.xxx.xxx.xxx*), you can type it directly. However, most Internet users have a different address each time they connect to the Internet or restart Windows, and if you are on a LAN that connects to the Internet, you can use IP addresses only for other people on the LAN. To find out your IP address, choose Help | About Windows NetMeeting from the menu bar in the NetMeeting window and look at the bottom of the About Windows NetMeeting dialog box that appears.

Note   *If there is a firewall (like the Internet Connection Firewall) between you and your directory server on the Internet, you will not be able to use many of NetMeeting's features. If you use your own corporation's directory server within the firewall, everything works fine.*

NetMeeting lets you connect only with other people who use NetMeeting. For example, you can't join a meeting with people who use Yahoo Messenger or AIM.

Running and Configuring NetMeeting

In Windows Me and 2000, NetMeeting is on the Start or Start | Programs menu. In Windows XP, choose Start | Run, type **conf** (for "conferencing"), and press ENTER. If you haven't already configured NetMeeting, you see a series of windows that tell you about the program and ask for the following information:

- **Your name, e-mail address, location, and comments**   You have to type your name and e-mail address, but you can leave the rest of the information blank.

- **Which directory server to use**   The default is Microsoft Internet Directory, which is the same directory you see when you use Windows Messenger. A number of other public directory servers are also available. If your organization uses NetMeeting, you may use a private directory server. You can choose the Log On To A Directory Server When NetMeeting Starts check box. (The alternative is to log on manually by choosing Call | Log On from the NetMeeting menu bar.) You can also choose whether you want to be listed in the directory on the server you choose—we recommend leaving the Do Not List My Name In The Directory check box unless you are using a private directory. If you choose a public server, you may prefer not to be listed so that strangers don't contact you.

- **Connection speed**   Choose the speed of your modem or specify that you are connected via a LAN. NetMeeting uses this information when sending audio or video data to you.

- **Shortcuts**   If you use NetMeeting often, you might want to add a shortcut to the desktop or to the Quick Launch toolbar on your taskbar.

NetMeeting runs the Audio And Video Tuning Wizard to make sure that your speakers are working, for use in audio chats. (Don't worry if you don't have a microphone—NetMeeting is still useful.) When it finishes, the configuration program displays the NetMeeting window, as shown in Figure 16-4.

You may want to make some other changes to your configuration by choosing Tools | Options. On the Options dialog box you can set these types of options:

- **General tab**   Make changes to the configuration information you typed when you first ran NetMeeting.

- **Security tab**   Specify whether to accept incoming calls automatically, whether to make secure outgoing calls, and other security options.

- **Audio tab**   Configure NetMeeting to work with your microphone and speakers.

- **Video tab**   Specify the size and quality of video images to display.

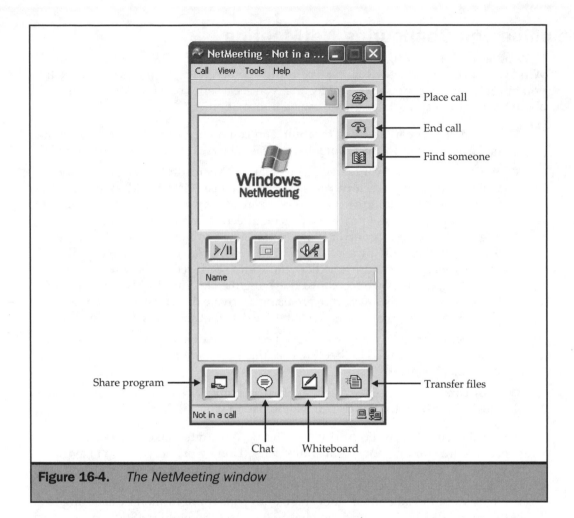

Figure 16-4.   *The NetMeeting window*

Connecting to a Directory Server

Once you see the NetMeeting window (as shown in Figure 16-4), you can start a meeting by clicking the Place Call button (the yellow telephone) if you know the e-mail address of the person you want to talk to. However, unless you know the person's IP address or have called this person before, you usually need to start the call by selecting the person from a directory.

When you click the Find Someone In A Directory button (the little open book) and you are connected to a directory server, you see the Find Someone window. (If your computer isn't connected to the Internet, you see a Connect dialog box first; click Connect.) Set the Select A Directory to the directory to which you want to connect. If you want to use the Microsoft Internet Directory, you may need to click a link to log in using your Microsoft .NET Passport name and password. Then you see a large window with a list of the people who are on your contact list. (This is the same list that appears in Windows Messenger.)

If you want to talk to someone who isn't on your Windows Messenger contact list, you and the other person need to connect to the same directory server. Choose Tools | Options from the NetMeeting window's menu bar, type the server name (usually ils.*domainname*) into the Directory box, and click OK. Now when you click the Find Someone In A Directory button, a list of people on the server appears, with a little PC icon to the left of each person's e-mail address (as shown in Figure 16-5). An icon with a blue screen and red twinkle means that the person is currently in a call, whereas a gray icon means that the person is not in a call. A little yellow speaker icon indicates that the person can communicate via audio. A little gray camera icon means that the person can communicate via video. On the listing of people, click the column headings to sort by that column; sorting by last name or e-mail address makes it easier to find the person you want.

Caution   *When you are connected to a public server and your name is listed, you are likely to get unwanted calls.*

CHATTING AND
CONFERENCING ON
THE INTERNET

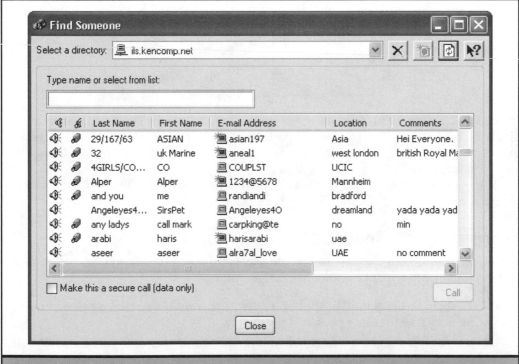

Figure 16-5.   *Clicking the Find Someone In A Directory icon displays a listing of people connected to your directory server.*

Making or Receiving a Call

To call someone, double-click the person's name on the contact or directory list, or type the name in the box and click the Call button. If you are using Microsoft Internet Directory, then the person is contacted through Windows Messenger. If the person accepts your invitation, Windows Messenger takes over on your computer, too. If you use another directory server, NetMeeting contacts the directory server to make the connection and displays a dialog box on that person's computer screen, asking whether they want to connect with you. If the person accepts your call, the lower white box in the NetMeeting window lists the people who are in your current call.

When someone calls you, you see a dialog box asking whether you want to take the call, or you see a message in Windows Messenger inviting you to join the meeting; click Accept in either case if you do. You see the NetMeeting window with the callers listed.

Another way to make a call is to click the Place Call button, choose Call | New Call, or press CTRL-N. You see the Place A Call dialog box:

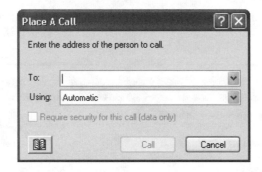

In the To box, type the name of the directory server to which the person is connected, followed by a slash (/) and the e-mail address of the person you want to call. If the person you are calling uses a computer with its own computer name or IP address, you can type that instead. Then click the Call button.

When you are done with the call, click the Hang Up button. NetMeeting maintains its connection with the directory server but disconnects from the call.

Once You Are Connected

Once you are connected to at least one other person, you can communicate using most of the same features that Windows Messenger offers:

- **Text chat**   Click the Chat button to display a window in which you can type messages to the other people in the chat.

- **Voice chat**   If both of you have microphones and speakers, you can just begin talking. Speak slowly, one at a time (as though you were using a walkie-talkie—"Over!"). Unless you have a very fast connection, you may experience "breaking up"—the sound may be interrupted and "staticky." Keep your microphone away from the speakers, or use headphones, to avoid feedback.

■ **Video conferencing**   If other people in your call have video cameras (even if you don't have one), you can see video from one of their cameras (one at a time) in your NetMeeting window. The video appears in the Remote Video window, a small box on the right side of the window when the Current Call icon is selected. If you don't see the video, click the button at the bottom of the Remote Video window. To set your video options, choose Tools | Options and click the Video tab. You can tell NetMeeting to enable your video camera automatically when you make a call; set the size of the video image; choose between faster, low-quality video and slower, high-quality video; and specify the properties of your camera. If you have a camera, be sure to light your face (or whatever the camera points at) from the front. You can't see more than one person at a time. To switch the person in the call you can see, choose Tools | Switch Audio And Video and choose the name of the person you want to see.

■ **Sharing a whiteboard**   If you and the other participants in your call want to draw diagrams or pictures that are visible to everyone in the call, use the Whiteboard feature. When you click the Whiteboard button near the bottom of the NetMeeting window, you see a window that works similarly to Microsoft Paint. (It's the same Whiteboard window that Windows Messenger displays, as shown in Figure 16-2 earlier in this chapter.) When anyone in the call makes a change to the Whiteboard window, everyone in the call sees the change.

■ **Sending and receiving files**   Choose Tools | File Transfer or click the File Transfer button at the bottom of the NetMeeting window to open the File Transfer window. Click the Add Files button and specify which file you want to send. Alternatively, drag the name of the file from Windows Explorer onto the File Transfer window. Click the Send All button to send the files. To send a file to one caller, rather than to everyone in the call, select the person from the drop-down list at the top right of the File Transfer window. If someone sends you a file, NetMeeting automatically receives the file, storing it in the C:\Program Files\NetMeeting\Received Files folder (assuming that Windows is installed on C:). You see a window telling you about the arrival of the file. To open the file with the default application for the type of file you received, click the Open button.

| **Caution** | *Beware of viruses in executable files and of generally offensive material when receiving files from people you don't know.* |

■ **Sharing programs**   You and the other people in your meeting can share the windows of a running program that one member has on his or her screen. For example, you could show a group around your web site by running a browser on your machine and sharing the browser window so that the other callers

CHATTING AND CONFERENCING ON THE INTERNET

could see the contents of the browser window on their screens, too. This feature works like Windows Messenger's application-sharing, described in the section "Sharing Control of a Program" earlier in this chapter.

 Firewalls, including the Internet Connection Firewall that comes with Windows XP, can prevent video and voice conferencing from working.

Hosting a Meeting or Joining an Existing Meeting

In addition to calls, you can communicate in *meetings,* calls that are scheduled in advance. Hosting a meeting allows you to define some properties for the meeting. To host a meeting, let everyone invited to the meeting know when the meeting will take place and how to call you using NetMeeting. At the time the meeting is scheduled to begin, choose Call | Host Meeting, and choose the options you want from the Host A Meeting dialog box:

When you click OK, you return to the NetMeeting window, with only you listed as a caller. When the other callers connect, you see a dialog box asking whether they can join; click Accept or Ignore.

Because you are the host of the meeting, the meeting ends when you hang up. Other participants can come and go without ending the meeting. As the host, you can also throw people out of your meeting: right-click the person's name on the list of callers, and choose Remove from the menu that appears.

To join an existing meeting, call someone who is in the meeting. You see a message that the person is currently in a meeting, asking whether you want to try to join the meeting; click Yes. When the person you called leaves the meeting, you leave too, so it's best to call the person who is hosting the meeting.

If you don't want anyone else to join the meeting (or to join any NetMeeting call), choose Call | Do Not Disturb. Remember to choose the same command again when you want to reenable receiving calls.

What's Next in Voice Conferencing and Video Conferencing?

As is the case with most things involving the Internet, conferencing software is in a constant state of change. Applications are upgraded, faster Internet connections become widely used, and new hardware is released. Programs sprout new features.

To keep up to date with what's going on in conferencing, use the Internet as your information resource. In addition to stopping by your hardware or software vendor's web sites periodically, do a quick search on "video conferencing" with your favorite search engine or visit some online computer magazines to see how conferencing is evolving. Also take a look at TUCOWS (**www.tucows.com**) for a listing of conferencing programs.

CHATTING AND CONFERENCING ON THE INTERNET

The Complete Reference

Internet

Part IV

Viewing the World Wide Web

The
Complete
Reference

Internet

Chapter 17

World Wide Web
Concepts

The *World Wide Web* (usually just referred to as "the Web") was invented in 1989, but it's hard to imagine the world without it. The Web includes over two billion files stored on tens of thousands of computers *(web servers)* all over the world. These files represent text documents, pictures, video, sounds, animations, programs, interactive environments, and just about any other kind of information that has ever been recorded in computer files. The Web is the largest and most diverse collection of information ever assembled in one place.

What unites these files is a system that allows computers to link one file to another and transmit them across the Internet. This concept was originally called *hypertext* by its inventor, Theodor Nelson, and was adapted for the Internet by Tim Berners-Lee, who created the Web.

The Web's Languages and Protocols

You probably have dozens of computers in your house—but very few of them speak the same language. The electronics in your microwave don't use the same sort of codes that, say, your television, digital watch, or PC use. Even getting a Mac and a PC, which are both home computers, to talk to each other takes effort. Getting computers to understand each other has always been an arduous process.

That's why the Internet is such an amazing technical achievement. The millions of computers that make up the Web represent every conceivable combination of computer hardware and software—but when a client computer requests a file from the Web, as long as it's using the proper Internet protocols, the two computers can talk to each other no matter what operating systems or chips they have. To make the Web work as smoothly as it does, computers that access the Internet must have a well-defined set of languages and protocols that are independent of the hardware or operating systems on which they run.

URLs and Transfer Protocols

When the pieces of a document are scattered all over the world, but you want to display them seamlessly to a viewer who could be anywhere, you need a *very* good addressing system. Each file on the Internet has an address, called a *Uniform Resource Locator (URL)*. For example, the URL of the BBC News Web site is **http://news.bbc.co.uk**.

The first part of a URL specifies the *transfer protocol*, which is the method a computer uses to access the file. Most web pages are accessed with the *Hypertext Transfer Protocol* (the language of web communication), which is why web addresses typically begin with *http* (or its secure version, *https* or *shttp*).

Because 99 percent of all web pages use Hypertext Transfer Protocol, most people assume that all pages are HTTP-transferred. In this book, for example, we don't write out the *http://* at the beginning of every web page; it's clunky to write "Go to **http://www.snopes2.com**" when we can simply say, "Go to **www.snopes2.com**." Leaving out the *http://* is so common that browsers assume the *http://* part if you don't type it—type **www.snopes2.com** into the address window of Internet Explorer or Netscape Navigator, and the browser fills in the *http://* by itself.

The next part of the address denotes the host name of the web server. (See the section about domain and host names in Chapter 1.) The URL doesn't tell you where the web server is actually located; you can't tell whether the BBC's server is in London or Bangkok from the URL alone. The domain name system (DNS, described in Chapter 2) routes your web page request to the web server no matter where it is physically— which is good. Otherwise, you'd have to memorize a new set of URLs every time the BBC got a new computer or changed buildings.

Some URLs contain information following the host name of the web server. This information specifies exactly which file you want to see, and what directory it is stored in. If the directory and filename aren't specified, you get the default web page for that web server. For example, the URL **http://net.gurus.com** takes you to the net.gurus.com web server (maintained by the Internet Gurus, including some of the authors of this book). The URL **http://net.gurus.com/nettcr2** displays the home page for this book.

 Not all URLs start with www *and end with* .com; *host names don't have to start with* www *(for example, net.gurus.com), and many domains don't end with* .com *(for example, news.bbc.co.uk).*

HTML

Hypertext Markup Language (HTML) is the universal language of the Web. It is a simple programming language that you use to lay out pages—*so* simple, in fact, that we teach you how to do it in Chapter 24. HTML pages are capable of displaying all the diverse kinds of information that the Web contains. The job of your web browser (Internet Explorer, Netscape Navigator, or another browser) is to display HTML pages and the other files that these pages refer to.

Although various software companies own and sell HTML-reading and HTML-writing programs, no one owns the HTML language itself. It is an international standard, maintained and updated by a complicated political process that has worked remarkably well so far. The World Wide Web Consortium (W3C), at **www.w3c.org**, manages the HTML standard. Tim Berners-Lee, who created HTML and invented the Web, is the W3C's director.

Java and JavaScript

Java is a language for sending small applications (called *applets*) over the Web, so that your computer can execute them. *JavaScript* is a language—which, contrary to popular misbelief, is *not* a smaller version of Java—that allows HTML to embed small programs called *scripts* in web pages. The main purpose of applets and scripts is to speed up web page interactivity; applets and scripts run directly on your computer, and they don't have to keep calling back to the web server to ask it what to do. Typically, this process is invisible—the interaction just happens, without calling your attention to how it happens. Chapter 28 includes a brief introduction to Java and JavaScript.

VIEWING THE
WORLD WIDE WEB

Beware of Pop-Up Downloads

A new and sleazy ad technique is *pop-up downloads*—small windows that certain web sites display that ask to install a program on your computer. A word of advice: *Never* install anything on your computer if you don't know what it is. Some web sites use pop-up downloads to update software that you already have on your PC, but some pop-ups install new software that you have no interest in running.

Some of these programs—"spy" programs—track your browsing and e-mail activity and send them back to a central database. More malicious programs can install viruses, reset your browser to automatically display adult-themed sites, or even rewrite your Internet dial-up program to call expensive 1-900 numbers.

Pop-up downloads rely on user confusion, betting that you are too ignorant to know the difference between a legitimate plug-in such as Adobe Acrobat or Macromedia Flash (plug-ins are described in Chapter 18) and a quasi-legal program that the advertising companies use to track your viewing habits. If you're not sure what a program does or is, click No in the pop-up window; you can always install the software later if it turns out you need it.

If you're afraid you have spyware on your system or clicked Yes accidentally, first scan your hard drive for viruses, as described in the section on protecting your computer from viruses in Chapter 1. Then install and run Ad-Aware, downloadable at **www.lavasoftusa.com**. Ad-Aware eliminates any intrusive spyware programs you may have unwittingly allowed onto your machine. For further information on installing (legitimate) programs such as Ad-Aware, see Chapter 34.

VBScript and ActiveX Controls

VBScript and ActiveX controls are Microsoft systems (not web standards) that work with Internet Explorer. *VBScript,* a language that resembles Microsoft's Visual Basic, can be used to add scripts to pages that are displayed by Internet Explorer. Anything that VBScript can do, JavaScript (which Microsoft calls *JScript*) can do, too, and vice versa.

ActiveX controls (AXCs), like Java, are used to embed executable programs into a web page. When Internet Explorer encounters a web page that uses ActiveX controls, it checks whether that particular control is already installed on your computer—and if it isn't, IE installs it. Netscape Navigator can't run plug-ins, ignoring the content that the plug-in provides. Except for the Microsoft web site, few sites use ActiveX controls for anything other than cute animations.

 VBScript and ActiveX controls can create security holes in your system; see Chapter 20 for details.

Plug-ins

A *plug-in* is a program that can "plug into" your browser to give the browser a new capability. Plug-ins were invented by Netscape for its Navigator browser, but most plug-ins work with Internet Explorer, too. Plug-ins work with your browser seamlessly, so that after you install them, you can forget that they are not part of your browser. See the section on finding and installing plug-ins and ActiveX controls in Chapter 18.

XML

HTML was designed for documents, with tags that control how the document looks on the screen. But with more and more types of information appearing on the Web, people have found a need to include other types of information, like price lists, product lists, and address lists, in a format that programs, rather than people, can read.

XML (Extensible Markup Language), HTML's younger but bigger and more capable brother, begins to solve this problem. Both languages are derived from SGML (Standard Generalized Markup Language), a language designed for describing pages that has extensive capabilities unrelated to the needs of the Web. XML is a standard created by the World Wide Web Consortium (**www.w3c.org**).

XML enables web pages to more easily and efficiently handle certain complex tasks, including passing data between unrelated programs, handling more of the processing load at the browser instead of the server, presenting different views of data to different users, and adjusting content according to the historical preferences of different users.

XML tends to be used for program-to-program communications, though it can also be used for documents intended for human consumption. Unlike HTML, it can do both quite easily. With the assistance of a style sheet, it's easy to present the same document (say, an invoice) to human readers in a browser and to computers that search the document for critical information (like how much is owed, to whom, and why). XML pages can be stored on web servers and viewed by web browsers, or they can be passed from program to program in other ways.

XML takes the markup technologies HTML made familiar and applies them to a much wider variety of information. XML makes two significant departures from HTML: it requires that markup syntax be applied much more consistently, while at the same time it permits developers to create their own vocabularies for marking up documents.

Documents may have only one *root element*, which contains all the other elements. In HTML, the root element of every web page is the <HTML> tag itself: the entire contents of the web page are enclosed in <HTML> and </HTML> tags. In XML documents, the root element may be <PERSON> (if the document consists of information about a member of an organization, for example), <PRODUCT> (if the document contains one product in a company's catalog), or whatever element the document is about.

XML also offers a new (to HTML) feature called a *processing instruction*. Processing instructions are much like comments, except that they begin with <? and end with ?>, and are considered suggestions to the application. Processing instructions might look like

```
<?do something here?>
```

or:

```
<?xml-stylesheet href="style.css" type="text/css"?>
```

(The latter is used to associate style sheets with XML documents for display in browsers.)

Using this stricter syntax as a foundation, XML permits developers to create their own *vocabularies*. Instead of display-oriented markup like HTML provides, developers can create tags that identify content more directly. For example, you could define a set of tags that store information about a person, like this:

```
<person>
 <name>
 <givenName>Joe</givenName>
 <familyName>Krinkles</familyName>
 </name>

 <address>
 <street>1093 Tinseltown Road</street>
 <city>Ithaca</city>
 <state>NY</state>
 <postalCode>14850</postalCode>
 <country>USA</country>
 </address>

 <phone>
 <home>607 555 1212</home>
 <work>607 555 2121</work>
 </phone>
</person>
```

Developers and organizations can create XML vocabularies describing nearly anything, and have. There are XML vocabularies for HTML (XHTML), Scalable Vector Graphics (SVG), Mathematical Markup Language (MathML), Synchronized Multimedia Integration Language (SMIL), and a wide variety of more industry-specific vocabularies covering subjects from auto parts to program models to DNA to weather.

Applications often need to check that documents follow the rules of particular vocabularies. XML 1.0 included Document Type Definitions (DTDs), a set of tools for describing document structures. DTDs permit the specification of document structures, like which element types may (or must) contain particular element types or attribute types. DTDs also provide a set of tools for providing default values for attributes (a value that is used if the author of a document doesn't include a particular attribute) and for defining entities (a tool for including content by reference). The World Wide

Web Consortium now suggests using XML Schema instead of DTDs because schemas can contain more detailed descriptions of the document elements.

A wide variety of tools is available for XML processing, largely built on standards like Extensible Stylesheet Language Transformations (XSLT), the Document Object Model (DOM), and the Simple API for XML (SAX). XML is also at the foundation of much current Web Services work, aimed at connecting programs with standards like XML-RPC (Remote Procedure Calls), SOAP (Simple Object Access Protocol), WSDL (Web Service Definition Language), and UDDI (Universal Description, Discovery, and Integration).

Browsers can view XML documents (at least, recent versions of IE, Netscape Navigator, and Opera can). To make sense of an XML document, the document must use the <?xml-stylesheet?> processing instruction to specify a style sheet that tells the browser how to display the information enclosed in the XML tags.

For more information about XML and its vocabularies and tools, see these web sites:

- **World Wide Web Consortium's XML site (www.w3.org/XML)** is the official XML site.

- **O'Reilly's xml.com (www.xml.com)** offers weekly stories in detail and great archives.

- **XMLhack (www.xmlhack.com)** posts XML developer news daily.

- **TopXML (www.topxml.com)** is a Microsoft-oriented community site for XML developers.

- **The XML Cover Pages (www.oasis-open.org/cover)** provides an incredible bibliography of XML-related material.

- **Web Developer's Virtual Library XML area (wdvl.Internet.com/Authoring/Languages/XML)** offers more developer information.

Excellent books on XML include *XML: A Primer, 3rd Edition* (by Simon St. Laurent, Hungry Minds, 1998), *The XML Bible* (by Elliotte Rusty Harold, Hungry Minds, 2001), *Just XML* (by John Simpson, Prentice Hall, 2000), and *Learning XML* (by Erik Ray, O'Reilly & Associates, 2001). (Thanks to Simon St. Laurent for this explanation of XML.)

Cascading Style Sheets (CSS)

Consistent with the vision of XML is the notion of a *style sheet*; a style sheet describes *how* information is presented, not *what* information is presented. An audio style sheet, for example, might describe the voice and accent of a speaker, and be associated with a text document. Changing the style sheet would change how the text is read, not the text itself. The W3C is working on two style sheet language specifications: the *Extensible Style Language (XSL)* and *Cascading Style Sheets (CSS)*. Learn about them at **www.w3.org/Style**.

HTML can also use Cascading Style Sheets; with CSS, the person who creates a web site creates a list of styles and their descriptions. When the web page creator links web pages to the style sheet, browsers use the style descriptions when they display the pages. Change the style definitions in the style sheet, and all of the other web pages immediately imitate that layout—which can save a lot of time. See Chapter 29 for how to use CSS when you create your own web pages.

Image Formats

Pictures, drawings, charts, and diagrams are available on the Web in a variety of formats. The most popular formats for displaying graphical information are JPEG and GIF. For more about graphic file formats, see Chapter 26.

Audio and Video Formats

Some files on the Web represent audio or video, and they can be played by browser plug-ins. (See "Plug-Ins" earlier in this chapter.) Web audio and video come in two flavors: your browser can download either the entire file and play it (which can take a long time even on fast connections because the files are huge) or only the part of the file that it needs to play next, discarding the parts that it has played already. The first flavor is called *static audio* or *static video*, and the second is called *streaming audio* or *streaming video*. See Chapter 22 for more information.

Animations

Until recently, you had three options for what visual information to put on web pages: picture files, text files (which had extremely limited animation but were quick to download), or video files (which were cool but took forever and a day to download). None of them offered interactivity. Now we have animation files that can be embedded in web pages—though they take longer than text and pictures to download, they're considerably smaller than video files and can also offer games, mutating menus, and *extremely* cool visual and audio effects.

Flash, by Macromedia, is the main program used to create (and view) web animations, and it requires a special plug-in to view it. For information on plug-ins, see the section "Plug-ins" earlier in this chapter. For how to get them, go to Chapter 18. Some animations are written in Java, which is described in Chapter 28.

Special Kinds of Web Sites and Pages

In one sense, web pages are all the same: they are files on web servers that are denoted by URLs. But in that sense, all planes are the same—even though some carry passengers, others carry cargo, and still others carry missiles and fly support missions. These are the different types of web sites, broken down by their content.

Portals

A *portal* is a web site that wants to be your start page—the page that your browser automatically loads every time you connect to the Internet. To attract you, a portal site tries to have everything, and all for free: web guides, search engines, chat rooms, e-mail accounts, customizable weather, and news services, just to name a few. Competition among the portal sites is intense, and any service provided by one is quickly copied by the others. All portal services are free (so far), but some (such as chat rooms, game rooms, e-mail, and anything personalized) require you to register and choose a password.

The most popular portal sites at this writing are My Yahoo (**my.yahoo.com**), MSN (**www.msn.com**), Netscape.com (**home.netscape.com**), My Excite (**www.excite.com**), and Lycos (**www.lycos.com**). They all make their money (such as it is) from advertising revenues, so expect to sit through a few ads while you browse. If you're feeling generous, click through to a few pages, and earn your favorite portal site some shekels.

 Yahoo began charging for the more advanced features of its free e-mail service, such as being able to read your Yahoo mail from your e-mail program. Expect other portals to follow suit.

To remember who you are and display information tailored to you, portals usually store a cookie on your computer. When you return to the portal, you see weather for your area, movie listings for local theaters, and news in categories you choose. You usually have to register to create a free account for the portal to remember information about you.

Web Directories and Search Engines

Web directories or *web guides* are a top-down approach to finding your way around the Web—they provide a system of categories and subcategories that organizes links to web pages—much like the Dewey decimal system organizes the books in a library.

Search engines are a bottom-up approach to finding your way around the Web. You give a search engine a list of keywords or phrases (called a *query*), and it returns to you a list of web pages that contain those words or phrases. Google, a newer search engine, has become so popular that it's become a verb. ("I Googled our new neighbor to find out what he did for a living.")

Searching efficiently is an art, and a more complete discussion of web directories, search engines, and techniques for using them can be found in Chapter 21.

 Because web directories were one of the first services provided by portals such as Yahoo and Excite, and because indexing all those pages on the Internet takes a considerable financial investment that needs to be recouped, the line between portal, search engine, and web directory is becoming increasingly blurred.

Home Pages

A *home page* is the front door of a web site, showing you what the site is for and providing links to the other useful stuff on the site. There are all sorts of sites, both personal and professional, but each site has a page you're supposed to start from. A *personal home page* is the front door of a web site that people put on the web to introduce themselves, to share interests with others, and to keep distant friends and acquaintances up to date on how they're doing. What you put on a personal web site—or whether you want one at all—depends on how attached you are to your privacy. Some people are afraid to put their address on their page, whereas others train webcams on themselves seven days a week so you can watch them sleeping.

Personal pages are easy to create, they're fun, they give you a sense of space on the Web—and it's cool to refer an online pal to your own little niche on the Web. You can get an idea of what sorts of things go in a personal site in Chapter 23.

A *business home page* is the front door to a business's web site. Like the front door of an office building, it should be attractive, easy to find, and provide enough information to get people quickly to the parts of the web site that they want to visit.

Similarly, any organization—a church, town, club, government office, school, or whatever—can have a web site, and the front door to that web site is its home page. Even inanimate objects can have home pages; this book's home page is **net.gurus.com/nettcr2**.

Creating web sites for organizations has become an industry; a great deal of professional help is available. The basic ideas and tools, however, are more common sense than rocket science.

The Mozilla Browser

If you want to try an open source web browser, consider Mozilla. In 1998, Netscape Communications Corporation released the source code (original programming) for the Netscape Navigator browser with open source license that allowed other programmers to work on it. They also created the Mozilla Organization (at **www.mozilla.org**) to oversee development of an open source browser created by volunteer programmers. Netscape Navigator 6.*x* uses the Mozilla source code, plus programming of their own.

The Mozilla browser is developed to run on a wide variety of computers, including Windows, Macs, UNIX, and Linux. It also adheres closely to the World Wide Web Consortium's web standards, including standards for HTML, JavaScript (ECMAscript), and cascading style sheets. Mozilla 1.0 includes a browser, e-mail program, and newsreader, but no web editor. Because it's open source, with hundreds of programmers working on it from around the world, Mozilla may evolve quickly, sprouting interesting new features.

You can download the Mozilla browser and try it out—go to the Mozilla web site (**www.mozilla.org**) or TUCOWS (**www.tucows.com**) to find the version of Mozilla 1.*x* for your computer. You can install Mozilla without disturbing your current version of Netscape Communicator 4.*x* or Internet Explorer, but it may overwrite files that are part of Netscape 6.*x*.

The
Complete
Reference

Chapter 18

Streamlining
Your Browsing

Aside from your e-mail program, you probably use your browser more than any other Internet program. You know how to browse, type URLs into the Address or Location box, and follow links. However, you can browse the Web more efficiently if you customize your browser for the things you like to do—eliminating buttons you never use to make more room for the web pages themselves. This chapter talks about how to customize Internet Explorer (IE) and Netscape Navigator, the two most popular browsers. We also include tips and tricks for efficient browsing in both programs.

You've also probably run into material that your browser can't handle, like Adobe Acrobat PDF files, video clips, and other files. To see or display this material, you need to download and install plug-ins or ActiveX controls. This chapter explains where to get them and how to install them. We also mention how to use Microsoft's .NET Passport to identify yourself when making purchases on the Web.

> **Tip** *You can install more than one browser on your computer; we like to install both Netscape Navigator and IE, so we can see how web pages look in both browsers. You can run both browsers at the same time, although there is rarely a reason to do so, unless you are testing web pages you are creating or editing.*

Opera: The Other Browser

Although Netscape Navigator and IE control about 97 percent of the browser market, a few renegade browsers are still out there. Opera is an excellent alternative. (Another less popular browser, Mozilla, is described at the end of Chapter 17).

Opera was created by Jon S. von Tetzchner and Geir Ivarsøy in 1994 as a small and efficient multiplatform browser that would work on every operating system. Along the way, Opera became widely viewed as the scrappy, independent alternative to the browsers presented by the twin monoliths of Netscape and (especially) Microsoft.

One of the Internet's dirty little secrets is that neither Netscape Navigator nor IE adheres 100 percent to the World Wide Web Consortium's HTML standard, creating some problems for web designers. Opera, however, complies with the HTML standard completely. In addition, it's much smaller and more efficient than either Navigator or IE, and many people believe it to be a much more secure browser.

This HTML compliance, however, is not a total benefit. Thanks to Netscape's and Microsoft's dominance, most web designers tailor their HTML code to accommodate the quirks of the Big Guns—and as a result, their technically improper code often looks funny when viewed through Opera. In addition, there are many Microsoft-powered sites that Opera just can't view—try going to Microsoft.com, for example, and you'll see that it doesn't work. (Microsoft's site looks odd in Navigator, too—we don't imagine that it's a coincidence.)

For most users, Opera is a fine program, but so are Navigator and Explorer. However, if you have a slower computer, want a secure and technically correct browser, or are just all for supporting the little guy, you can download a trial version of Opera at **www.opera.com**.

Customizing Internet Explorer

Internet Explorer (IE) comes with Windows, so it's rapidly become the most widely used browser. Though originally developed for Windows, Internet Explorer (IE) now is available for a wide variety of platforms, including the Macintosh and some versions of UNIX. (Currently, no Linux version exists.)

You can customize IE to reflect your tastes, your browsing habits, the other software that you use, and your security policies. This book describes IE 6, which comes with Windows XP. You can download the latest version of IE from **www.microsoft.com/windows/ie** or order a CD from Microsoft for a small shipping charge. Figure 18-1 shows an IE 6 window with its components labeled, so you'll know the names of features that we discuss in the following sections.

Choosing Which Toolbars to Display in IE

IE can display a variety of toolbars, but the more you display, the less space you have for the web page. To hide a toolbar, uncheck it from the View | Toolbars menu. You choose whether to display the Explorer Bar along the left-hand side by toggling the buttons on the Standard Buttons toolbar: Search, Favorites, Media, and History.

A new feature in IE6 is the ability to lock toolbars. Once the toolbars are arranged to your liking, you can right-click one of the toolbars and select Lock The Toolbars from the menu that appears. This command prevents them from being moved around accidentally.

Customizing the Standard Buttons Toolbar in IE

Most people like to keep the Standard Buttons toolbar on the screen because it contains the Back, Favorites, and Home buttons. You can customize the Standard Buttons toolbar in several ways. Start by choosing View | Toolbars | Customize to display the Customize Toolbar dialog box:

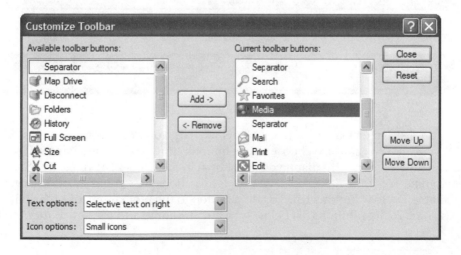

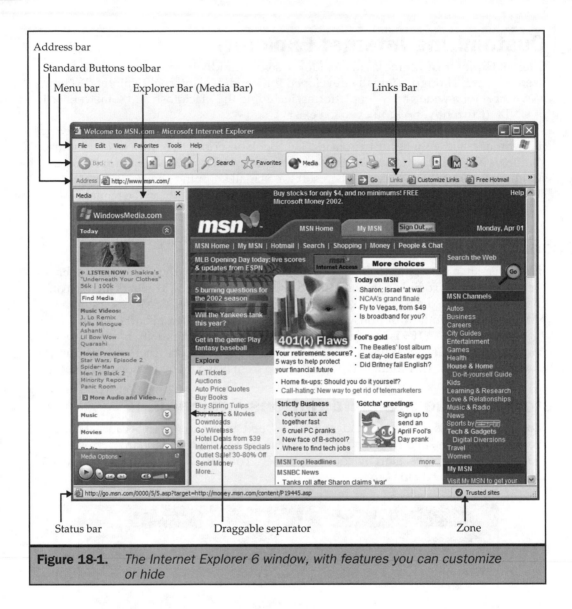

Figure 18-1.   *The Internet Explorer 6 window, with features you can customize or hide*

You can display text labels or not, and display large or small icons (or no icons, in the Mac version). You can also choose which buttons appear on the toolbar, and in what order. The buttons currently displayed are shown in the Current Toolbar Buttons list of the Customize Toolbars dialog box; the standard buttons that you may add appear in the Available Toolbar Buttons list. To add a button to the toolbar, choose which button in the Current Toolbar Buttons list below which you want to add the new button, choose the new button from the Available Toolbar Buttons list, and click the Add button. To remove a button, select it in the Current Toolbar Buttons list and click Remove.

Removing a button doesn't cause you to lose the button's corresponding function. All buttons have menu equivalents, and some have keyboard equivalents.

To reorder the buttons, select an entry on the Current Toolbar Buttons list and click the Move Up or Move Down button.

Customizing the Address Bar in IE

The Address bar displays the URL of the currently displayed web page or the file address of the currently displayed local file. You can open a web page by typing or pasting its URL into the Address bar and pressing ENTER. The AutoComplete feature tries to save you keystrokes by guessing what URL you are typing, based on URLs that you have visited before. The list that drops down from the Address bar remembers the last 25 URLs that you have typed in; you may select one from the list rather than typing it. In UNIX versions of Internet Explorer, AutoComplete doesn't always work for addresses with mixed upper- and lowercase characters.

If the text jumping ahead of your typing in the Address bar bothers you, turn off AutoComplete. In Windows, open the Internet Options dialog box (Tools | Internet Options) and go to the Advanced tab. Under Browsing, clear the check box Use Inline AutoComplete. On a Mac, open the Web Browser/Browser Display tab of the Internet Explorer Preferences dialog box (Edit | Preferences) and clear the Use AutoComplete check box.

Managing IE's Cache of Web Pages

Internet Explorer stores some of the pages that you view so that they can be redisplayed quickly if you return to them. In general, this speeds up the browsing experience, but if you are running short of disk space, you may decide to limit or eliminate these caches. IE stores these cached pages in a folder called Temporary Internet Files. On Windows 98/Me systems, this folder lives in the C:\Windows folder or (if you are using user profiles) in C:\Windows\Profiles*username.* In Windows XP, it's located at C:\Documents And Settings*username*\Local Settings\Temporary Internet Files. On UNIX systems, this folder is located in ~/.microsoft/TempInternetFiles, and on Macs, it is System Folder/Preferences/ Browser Cache.

If you use Windows, you control IE's cache of web pages from the General tab of the Internet Options dialog box, shown in Figure 18-2. Open this dialog box by selecting Tools | Internet Options. You can delete all the cached web pages by clicking the Delete Files button. To set limits on the amount of disk space that can be devoted to temporary Internet files, click the Settings button to open the Settings dialog box.

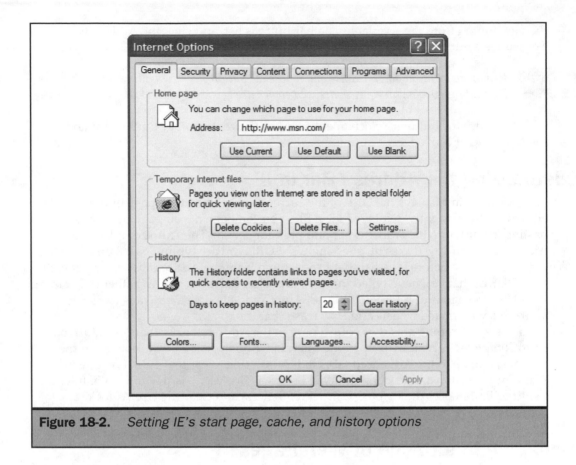

Figure 18-2.   *Setting IE's start page, cache, and history options*

Move the slider to raise or lower the percentage of your hard drive that the Temporary Internet Files folder is allowed to use. Click OK to apply your changes.

On a Mac, the cache is controlled from the Web Browser/Advanced tab of the Internet Explorer Preferences dialog box, which you open by selecting Edit | Preferences. To change the amount of disk space allotted to the cache, type a number of megabytes into the Size box. To delete all the cached web pages, click the Empty Now button. To move the Browser Cache folder, click the Change Location button and browse for a new location.

Sharing Internet Explorer with Other Users

The Windows version of IE inherits its user profiles from Windows. After you set up user profiles under Windows, each user has his or her own start page, Favorites menu, History folder, Links Bar, color schemes, and cookies folder.

You can create a new user profile either when you turn on your computer or by choosing Start | Log Off or Start | Log In As Different User. In either case, the Welcome To Windows box appears, asking for a user name and password. By typing an unclaimed user name, you establish a new user profile. Whatever password you type (including the possibility of a blank password) establishes the password for the new user profile.

Each user profile corresponds to a folder in C:\Windows\Profiles (when using Windows 98/Me) or C:\Documents And Settings (when using Windows XP). The name of the folder is the user name. Each user profile folder contains the information specific to that user, such as a Favorites folder.

The Macintosh version of IE doesn't include user profiles. The simplest way for two users to share a Mac and each have their own web browser settings is for one user to run Internet Explorer and the other to run Netscape Navigator, or to set up user profiles under Navigator.

Linking Internet Explorer to Other Programs

Some hyperlinks on a web page are intended to launch programs other than a web browser. For example, a linked e-mail address is better handled by an e-mail program, which can open a message window addressed to the linked address. Similarly, a newsgroup address can be bettered handled by a newsreading program. (Newsgroups are described in Chapter 11.)

For these handoffs to happen smoothly, IE needs to know which applications handle various jobs on your system. By default, IE launches the other Microsoft products that are part of the IE package: Outlook Express for e-mail and newsgroup links, Windows Messenger or NetMeeting for Internet telephone calls, and the Windows Address Book for contact information.

If you prefer to use other programs, you can change these defaults. Choose Tools | Internet Options to display the Internet Options dialog box and then click the Programs tab, as shown in Figure 18-3. Choose new programs from the drop-down lists.

On a Mac, open the Internet Explorer Preferences dialog box (Edit | Preferences) and go to the Network/Protocol Helpers tab, which lists the various Internet protocols. The protocol *mailto* invokes an e-mail program, and *news* invokes a Usenet newsreader. By default, Outlook Express is listed as the program to handle both e-mail and Usenet newsgroups. To change to another program, select from the list the protocol that you want to reassign and click the Change button. When the Edit Protocol Helper dialog box appears, click the Choose Helper button and browse for the location of the program that you want to handle this protocol. In newer Macs, there is an additional tab for mail where you can enter your details, including the SMTP server you use for sending mail. Newer Macs also have an Internet Control Panel, where you can specify which Internet applications to run.

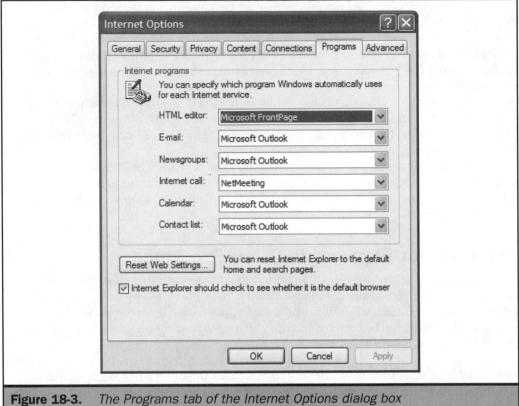

Figure 18-3.   *The Programs tab of the Internet Options dialog box*

Using IE on an Intranet

If your computer is on an intranet or LAN that uses a gateway or proxy server
(described in Chapter 4) to connect to the Internet, you may need to tell IE to contact
the proxy server to get web pages from the Internet. Contact your LAN administrator
to find out whether your proxy server uses manual or automatic configuration. For
automatic proxy configuration, find out the URL of the web page that contains the
proxy configuration information. For manual configuration, find out the numeric IP
address of the proxy server.

When you know your proxy configuration web page or IP address, follow these
steps in Internet Explorer:

1. Choose Tools | Internet Options and click the Connections tab, then the LAN
   Settings button. You see this dialog box:

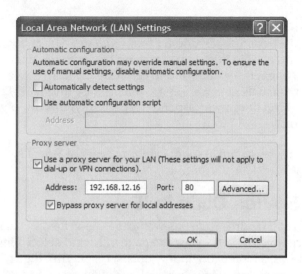

2. For automatic configuration, select either the Automatically Detect Settings or Use Automatic Configuration Script check box and type the URL in the Address box in the Automatic Configuration section of the dialog box. For manual configuration, type the numeric IP address of the proxy server in the Proxy Server Address box and **80** in the Port box.

3. Select the Bypass Proxy Server For Local Addresses check box if you are on a LAN with a local web server.

4. Click the Advanced button if you need to set up a proxy for other Internet protocols or if you have other addresses that bypass the proxy server.

5. Click OK.

 If your LAN connects to the Internet using Internet Connection Sharing, clear all the check boxes on the Local Area Network Settings dialog box.

Internet Explorer Browsing Tips

Here are commands and buttons you can use to find what you're looking for in a long web page, see the HTML code that makes up a web page, print pages that use frames, display more than one web page at the same time, and perform other useful tricks.

Searching Within a Page in IE

To find a word, phrase, or character string within a currently displayed web page, select Edit | Find (On This Page) from the menu or press CTRL-F (⌘-F on a Mac). A Find dialog box appears. Type what you want to find into the Find What box and select the appropriate check boxes within the Find dialog box. If you choose Match Whole Word Only, IE doesn't return words in which your search specification is only part of a larger word. For example, if you specify *book*, IE doesn't locate *bookend* or *bookstore*. If you check

Match Case, IE finds only those strings that match the capitalization that you type in the Find What box. For example, IE doesn't find *smith* or *SMITH* if you type *Smith*. Choose the Up or Down radio button to search up or down the document. Click the Find Next button to begin the search, and to continue the search after a match is found.

On a Macintosh, the only check boxes are Match Case and Start From Top. The Mac's Find box and Find button correspond, respectively, to Windows' Find What box and Find Next button.

Don't use the Search button to search within a page. The Search button is for finding pages on the Web, not for searching within pages.

Viewing HTML Source Code in IE

You can view the HTML source code of a web page (described in Chapter 24) and edit it with a word processor. To do so, view the page in IE and select View | Source from the menu. In Windows, a Notepad window opens, displaying the HTML source code. On Macs, the source opens in an Internet Explorer viewing window, which you can't edit. (If you want to edit the source code for your own use, save the file and open it with a word processor.)

Printing Pages with Frames in IE

Normally, you can print a page by choosing File | Print, pressing CTRL-P, or clicking the Print icon on the toolbar. However, if the page that you want to print is laid out in *frames* (individual panes that you can scroll through separately), you can print it several different ways, using settings on the Options tab of the Print dialog box, which you display by choosing File | Print:

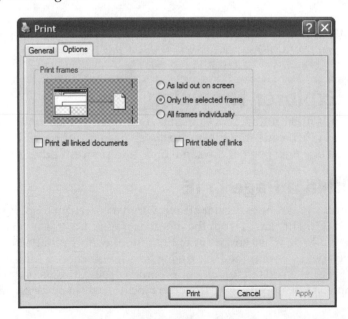

To print exactly what you see onscreen, select the As Laid Out On Screen setting. Only the currently displayed portions of a frame will print, regardless of the document's length. To print only the current frame (click in a frame to make it current, before you print it), select Only The Selected Frame. To print all the documents in all the frames, on separate pages, select All Frames Individually. This is equivalent to selecting the frames one by one and printing them with the Only The Selected Frame option.

Both the Only The Selected Frame and All Frames Individually options give you the ability to print information about the pages that are linked to the current one. The check boxes labeled "Print All Linked Documents" and "Print A Table Of Links" do exactly what they say. The table of links is a boxed table with two columns: the linked text on the printed page and the web address to which it is linked.

 Don't select Print All Linked Documents and then leave. The current page may be linked to more documents than you realize, and they may be longer than you think.

Opening Multiple Windows in IE

At times, you will find it convenient to open two or more browsing windows. You might, for example, want to compare two web pages. Perhaps you are bouncing back and forth among several browsing tasks and want each to have its own Back menu.

Select File | New | Window (or press CTRL-N) to open a new browsing window. The new window opens displaying the same page as the previous window. To open a new window displaying a particular page, select File | Open and then specify the file.

If the current page contains a link that you want to open without closing the current page, open a context menu over the link (right-click in Windows; hold down the mouse button on a Mac) and choose Open In New Window.

Customizing Netscape Navigator

Netscape Navigator was the most popular browser until Microsoft began bundling IE with Windows. Netscape recently released Netscape 6, a suite of Internet tools including Netscape Navigator browser and mail and newsgroup programs. The older Netscape Navigator version 4.79 browser is also available as part of the Communicator suite, which contains programs similar to those found in Netscape 6. New to Netscape 6 is the Sidebar, a customizable group of tabs providing quick access your favorite features, and of themes, which allow you to change the browser's appearance.

Netscape 6 is a complete Internet suite of programs, of which Navigator is only one component. The other components include the following:

- **Mail & Newsgroups** is a tool for participating in newsgroups or collaborative discussions in a newsgroup format. Using Netscape for e-mail is discussed in Chapter 6. Reading newsgroups with Netscape is covered in Chapter 12.
- **Composer** is a web page editing program, discussed in Chapter 25.

- **Net2Phone** is an Internet phone program that allows you to make calls (including international calls) over the Internet for free or at lower costs, discussed in Chapter 16.
- **AOL Instant Messenger (AIM)** is an instant messaging program, discussed in Chapter 14.

The Netscape Communicator suite 4.x includes most of the same programs, although with different names.

All versions of Netscape's browsers are free to download from Netscape's web site at **home.netscape.com/download**. You can also buy the program on CD. This book describes Netscape Navigator versions 4.7 and 6.2—when the instructions are different for the two versions, we'll let you know. Figure 18-4 shows the Netscape Navigator 6 window, with the component names that we'll use in this book.

Although Netscape 6 is newer, we prefer Netscape 4.7, which is more reliable.

Customizing the Toolbars in Navigator

Each visible toolbar has a vertical tab on its left edge. Click the tab to make the toolbar disappear. The tab turns horizontal and moves to a narrow bar just above the viewing window, as if the toolbar has been folded up. Click the horizontal tab to make the toolbar reappear. The tab disappears completely if you toggle the View | Show/Hide command for that toolbar. The toolbars can't be rearranged or placed next to each other on a single row.

The order of the items on the Navigation and Location toolbars is fixed, but the Personal Toolbar can be rearranged, and buttons can be added or deleted. (See the section on the Links Bar and Personal Toolbar in Chapter 19.)

You can remove buttons from the Navigation toolbar, but you can't change the size of the buttons. Open the Preferences dialog box by selecting Edit | Preferences, and select Navigator from the Category list. The right side of the dialog box displays Navigator settings, including the buttons to display on the toolbar, as shown in Figure 18-5.

Customizing the Navigator Sidebar

A new feature of Netscape 6 is the Sidebar. Like the Explorer Bar in Internet Explorer, it provides access to special features in a small window on the left edge of the browser. You can resize or hide the Sidebar window when you aren't using it. You can also choose what to display in the Sidebar.

The Sidebar is visible by default; click the handle on its right side to close it, and click the handle on the browser's left edge to open it. The handle has two parallel lines between two triangles; the triangles point toward the window edge when the sidebar is open and toward the web page when it's closed.

Personal Toolbar   Navigation Toolbar

Toolbar tab

Menu bar

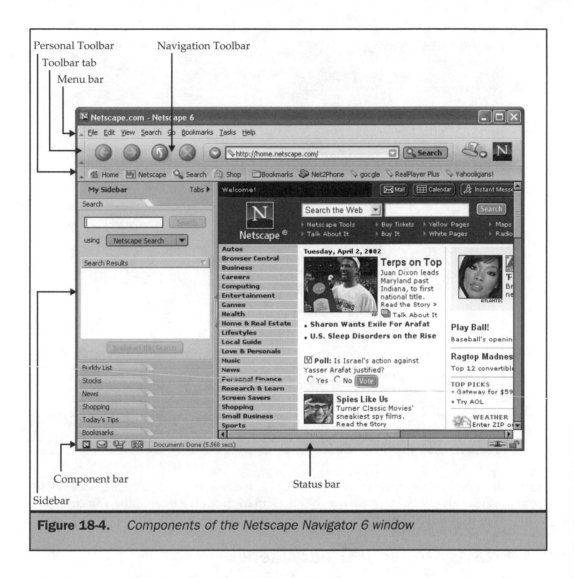

Component bar

Status bar

Sidebar

Figure 18-4.   *Components of the Netscape Navigator 6 window*

The Sidebar normally displays a vertical stack of tabs you can click to see many types of information. If there are tabs you never use, you can easily remove them and add more useful tabs. Click the Tabs button in the upper-right corner of the Sidebar and uncheck the items you don't want displayed. Select the items you want displayed and, if nothing on the initial list suits your fancy, click Customize My Sidebar. You see the Customize My Sidebar dialog box (as shown in Figure 18-6) containing additional Sidebar options, including offerings from Google, MapQuest, and FedEx. If you can't find what you want, click the Find More Tabs button at the bottom of the dialog box. This takes you to Netscape's Sidebar Directory, where you'll find more tabs and

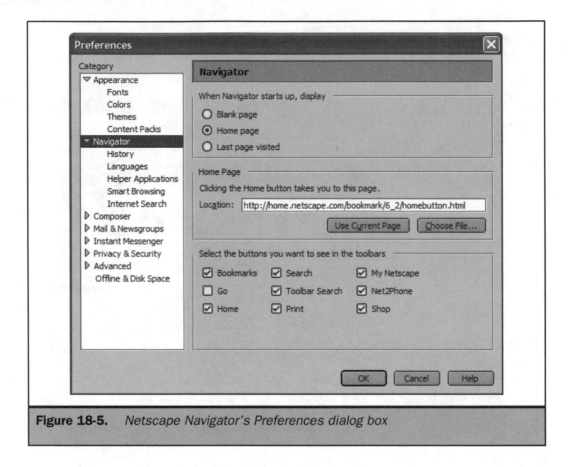

Figure 18-5. *Netscape Navigator's Preferences dialog box*

instructions on how to create your own tabs. If you don't use a tab often, remove it from the Sidebar, either by removing the check mark from the item in the Tabs menu or by deleting it from the Tabs In Sidebar pane in the Customize My Sidebar dialog box.

Sharing Navigator with Other Users

On Windows and Macintosh systems, use Netscape's User Profile Manager to create a profile for each user on your machine. This allows each user to have an independent Bookmarks file, History list, Address book, stored messages, and preferences. On UNIX systems, user profiles are not available within Netscape; instead, use UNIX system tools to create different UNIX accounts for each user.

Unlike in Internet Explorer, Netscape user profiles are different than Windows user profiles. You may have a different user name or password for your Netscape profile than you have for your Windows profile.

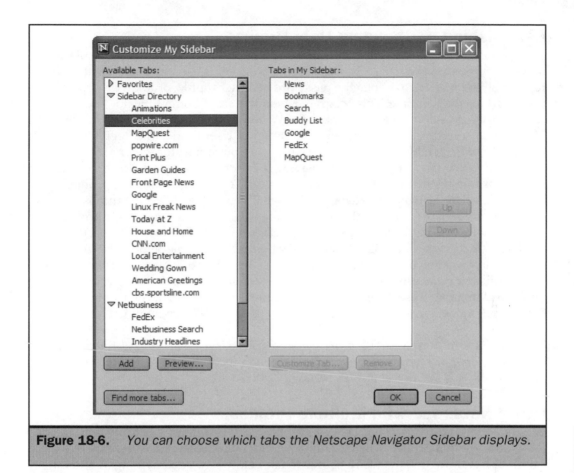

Figure 18-6.   *You can choose which tabs the Netscape Navigator Sidebar displays.*

Netscape user profiles on Windows systems can have passwords that make them unavailable to other users. User profiles on the Mac are not password protected.

You may even find it handy to have several user profiles just for yourself, if you use Netscape differently for different purposes. For example, you might set up home and work profiles. In this way, family members could use your Messenger program without seeing your work messages, and coworkers could use your Messenger program without seeing your personal messages.

In Windows, each user profile has a folder inside the folder C:\Documents And Settings*username*\Application Data\Mozilla\Profiles if using Netscape 6 or C:\Program Files\Netscape\Users when using Navigator version 4.7. This folder contains all the information connected with the user profile, such as its bookmarks file. On Macs, the user profile folders are in System Folder/Preferences/Netscape Users.

Establishing or Changing User Profiles

The User Profile Manager is installed automatically when you install Communicator on Windows or Mac systems. The User Profile Manager is used to create, remove, or rename a user profile, to change the password of a user profile, or to give a profile a password for the first time. This program is separate from Communicator and can be run only when Communicator is closed. On Windows systems, open User Profile Manager by selecting Start | Programs | Netscape | User Profile Manager. On Macs, find the User Profile Manager inside the Netscape Communicator folder.

User Profile Manager opens by displaying the Profile Manager dialog box, which lists the profiles Communicator has set up already. To change an existing profile, select it on the list. This activates the Rename, Change Password, and Delete buttons, which enable you to rename or delete the profile or to change its password. (User profiles on a Macintosh are not password protected, so it has no Change Password button.)

To create a new user profile, click the New button. The Profile Setup Wizard starts. Enter the information that the wizard requests. You need to know the names of the new user's mail and news servers, and the new user's e-mail address. (In the Mac version, you don't need to know these things; the e-mail address can be skipped, and Communicator doesn't ask for server information until you try to access Messenger or Collabra.

Profiles are easy to delete. Anyone with access to your computer can delete any profile, including password-protected profiles. Deleting a profile destroys access to the e-mail messages stored in that profile's Message Center.

Using Netscape with Multiple Profiles

When Communicator has only a single user profile, it opens automatically with the preferences in that profile. When multiple profiles have been established, however, Communicator must know which profile to use before it can do anything. (Different users, for example, might set up Communicator to open with different components.) Consequently, when multiple profiles are enabled, Communicator starts with the User Profile Manager. Choose the appropriate profile name from the list provided, and give that profile's password, if any.

You can also open the Profile Manager dialog box (discussed in the preceding section) by clicking the Manage Profiles button.

Using Navigator on an Intranet

If your computer is on an intranet or LAN that uses a proxy server (described in Chapter 4), you may need to tell Navigator to contact the proxy server to get web pages from the Internet. Contact your LAN administrator to find out whether your proxy server uses manual or automatic configuration. For automatic proxy configuration, find out the URL of the web page that contains the proxy configuration information.

For manual configuration, find out the numeric IP address of the proxy server. Then follow these steps:

1. Choose Edit | Preferences in Navigator to display the Preferences dialog box.

2. Click the plus box by the Advanced category and then click the Proxies category. The right side of the Preferences dialog box displays proxy settings.

3. For automatic configuration, click Automatic Proxy Configuration and type the URL in the box. For manual configuration, click Manual Proxy Configuration, click the View button (in Netscape 4.*x* only), type the proxy server's numeric address into the HTTP Proxy box, type **80** into the HTTP Port box, and click OK.

 If your LAN connects to the Internet through Internet Connection Sharing, leave the proxy setting as Direct Connection To The Internet.

Netscape Navigator Browsing Tips

Web browsing is more than a passive experience of viewing web pages. Once a page is open in the viewing window, you may want to search the page for a word or phrase, view the page's HTML source code, check the security of the connection with the web server, or display more than one page at the same time.

Searching Within a Page in Navigator

To find a word, phrase, or character string within a currently displayed web page, select Edit | Find In Page from the menu or press CTRL-F (⌘-F on a Mac). A Find dialog box appears. Type what you want to find into the Find What (or Find) box. If you check Match Case (Case Sensitive in the Mac version), the process finds only those strings that agree in capitalization. For example, the word *smith* will not be found in the name *Smith* or *SMITH*. In Windows, choose the Up or Down radio button to search up or down the document. In Mac, the search goes down the page, unless you check the Find Backwards check box; the Wrap Search check box causes the search to continue at the beginning of the document when it reaches the end. After you make your choices, start the search by clicking the Find Next button (the Find button on a Macintosh).

 Don't use the Search button to search within a page. The Search button is used to find pages on the Web, not to search within pages.

Viewing Information About a Page in Navigator

In addition to the information *on* a web page, Navigator also allows you to access information *about* the web page.

Viewing Page Information

To display a web page, Navigator has to know quite a bit about it, such as how many pieces it has, what servers all the buttons are connected to, where on the Web the page's images are stored, and what method of encoding is used for all the action-generating items in the page.

Navigator hides all this information from you because you usually don't want to know, and you might not know how to interpret all this information even if you had it. Nonetheless, if you want all this information, Navigator gives it to you if you select View | Page Info. A separate window appears with two panes. The top pane gives the structure of the web page, with all of its attendant pieces, and the bottom lists facts about the core HTML document addressed by the URL.

If the page was encrypted, the security information is listed at the bottom of the lower pane of the Page Info window. This section contains all the information on the Security Info page, plus information on the method of encryption.

Viewing a Page's HTML Source Code

You can view the HTML source code of the currently displayed page by selecting View | Page Source. Windows displays the HTML code in a viewing window that has no menu and allows no editing. If you want to edit this text in a word processor and save it for your own use, either select what you want to save with the mouse or press CTRL-A to select all. Then press CTRL-C to copy it onto the Clipboard. You may then paste the text from the Clipboard into any text editor or word processor.

On a Mac, you can still use the mouse and the menu bar to work with the window displaying the HTML source code. In particular, the Edit | Select All and the Edit | Copy commands work.

Printing Frames in Navigator

If you want to print a web page that contains more than one frame, you are out of luck with Navigator. When you choose File | Print, click the Print button on the toolbar, or press CTRL-P, Netscape prints only the current frame (the one you last clicked in). You can't print the page as it appears onscreen, as you can with Internet Explorer. At least you can't do this from within Navigator. (In Windows, you can press the PRINT SCREEN key to capture a picture of what's on the screen, paste this picture into the Paint program that comes with Windows, and print the results, but this process is cumbersome and prints only one screenful of information.)

Opening Multiple Windows in Navigator

Sometimes, you will want to open two or more Navigator windows. For example, you may want to compare two web pages, or bounce back and forth among several browsing tasks, and want each to have its own Back menu.

Select File | New | Navigator Window to open a new window displaying whatever page is specified on the Navigator panel of the Preferences dialog box. (The choices there are Home page, blank page, or last page visited.)

When the current page contains a link that you want to open without closing the current page, open a context menu over the link (right-click in Windows or hold down the mouse button on a Mac) and choose Open In New Window (on a Mac, New Window With This Link).

Finding and Installing Plug-Ins and ActiveX Controls

Browsers were designed to display text and graphics, but many web pages contain other types of nontext information, such as audio files, video files, animated graphics, and moving stock tickers. Chapter 17 describes the technology behind some of these web components: plug-ins (which work with both IE and Netscape), ActiveX controls (which work only in IE), and various types of scripts that are embedded right in the web page.

Typically, a plug-in or ActiveX control is born when a software company develops a new type of information to play or display on the Web—for example, sound or video. Rather than trying to convince Microsoft and Netscape to make their browsers capable of playing or displaying this new type of information, the software company creates a plug-in or ActiveX control (or both) that can handle the task of playing or displaying the new information within the browser. People who want to extend the capabilities of their browsers can download and install the plug-in or ActiveX control. Many plug-ins include a stand-alone player, in case you want to display files when you are not browsing the Web.

Caution

As with any downloaded program, plug-ins and ActiveX controls pose a security risk to your system. Theoretically, a plug-in or ActiveX control could introduce a virus, delete files, or relay information from your hard disk to the Internet. Downloading and installing plug-ins and digitally signed ActiveX controls from reputable sources— such as BrowserWatch, Netscape, and Microsoft—is perfectly safe, but think twice before you use a plug-in or ActiveX control from a site you know nothing about.

Many plug-ins and ActiveX controls are available for download from the Web. Frequently, if a page contains information that requires a plug-in or ActiveX control, the page usually also contains a link that leads to a page from which you can download what you need. A variety of plug-ins and ActiveX controls are available for Windows, Macs, and UNIX at the following web sites:

- Netscape, at **home.netscape.com/plugins** (plug-ins only).
- BrowserWatch, at **browserwatch.internet.com/plug-in.html** (for plug-ins) or **browserwatch.internet.com/activex.html** (for ActiveX controls).
- TUCOWS, at **www.tucows.com**. (Choose a site that is geographically close to you, choose your operating system, and choose Browser Add-Ons.)

- CWSApps, at **cws.internet.com**. (Click the button for your operating system and then click the Browser Plug-Ins or ActiveX Controls links.)

- Download.com: for plug-ins, start at **www.download.com** and search for "plug-in." For ActiveX controls, start at **www.download.com/PC/Activex** and click Browser Enhancements.

For instructions on how to download and install programs (including plug-ins and ActiveX controls) from the Web, see Chapter 34.

Plug-Ins in Navigator

When you are browsing the Web, you may click a link that requires Navigator to have a plug-in. If Navigator knows about the plug-in that you need, you see the Plug-in Not Loaded dialog box. Click the Get The Plug-in button to download the plug-in that the web page requires. If Netscape isn't familiar with the plug-in that you need, you see the Unknown File Type dialog box, with an indication of the type of data file that requires the plug-in. Click the More Info button to see a page that lists a lot of plug-ins. Pick a plug-in whose description seems to match what you need and then follow the instructions on the page to download and install it.

You can ask Navigator to display a list of the plug-ins that you already have installed. To see a list, choose Help | About Plug-ins from the menu or type **about:plugins** in the Location box.

 *ActiveX controls don't work in Netscape Navigator. If you load a web page with ActiveX controls in Navigator, the browser omits the material that the ActiveX would have displayed, and pages may look odd. Try browsing the **www.microsoft.com** site with Navigator, and you'll see what we mean.*

Plug-Ins and ActiveX Controls in IE

Internet Explorer stores all ActiveX controls and plug-ins in a single folder. In Windows, this folder is called C:\Windows\Downloaded Program Files or C:\Winnt\Downloaded Program Files (assuming that Windows is installed on your C: drive). On a Mac, it is System Folder/Extensions/ActiveX Controls. You can check this folder to see what applications IE has downloaded by choosing Tools | Internet Options, clicking the General tab, clicking the Settings button to display the Settings dialog box, and clicking the View Objects button.

See Chapter 20 for how to disable ActiveX controls in IE, to minimize your security risk.

Recommended Plug-Ins and ActiveX Controls

Here are a few plug-ins and ActiveX controls that you should consider downloading and installing:

- **Adobe Acrobat Reader**   Displays *Portable Document Format (PDF)* files, documents that are saved with all of their formatting for uploading to the

Web. (Acrobat Reader is available as a plug-in, an ActiveX control, and a stand-alone player.) Unlike with regular web pages, the author of a PDF file can control the exact formatting of each page of the document. PDF is used for documents that are to be printed (like IRS forms) and documents with formatting too elaborate for HTML. For more information on Adobe Acrobat, see its web site at **www.adobe.com/prodindex/acrobat**.

■ **Apple QuickTime**   QuickTime is a standard audio and video format. (See Chapter 22 for more information.) You can download a QuickTime plug-in at **apple.com/quicktime/download**.

■ **RealOne Player**   This plug-in plays RealNetworks streaming audio and video files, as described in Chapter 22. You can download it from **www.real.com/download**.

■ **Shockwave and Flash**   These two animation systems from Macromedia are both widely used on the Web. They display animated graphics, play sound, and let you interact with the web page. Shockwave is the older plug-in, and has largely been superceded by Flash. You can download these plug-ins from their web pages at **www.macromedia.com/shockwave** and **www.macromedia.com/flash**.

 If you have Adobe Acrobat or Microsoft Office programs installed, you may already have the necessary plug-ins or ActiveX controls installed and configured for use.

Uninstalling Plug-Ins and ActiveX Controls

Uninstalling plug-ins and ActiveX controls is not always easy—in fact, sometimes it's impossible. Some plug-ins come with uninstall programs, but most do not. If you use Windows, you can also choose Start | Control Panel or Start | Settings | Control Panel, open the Add/Remove Programs icon, and see whether the plug-in or ActiveX control appears on the list of installed software that you can remove.

Identifying Yourself Online with Microsoft .NET Passport

Shopping is one of the most popular features of the Internet, for a variety of good reasons: web sites are open all night, you can move from one store to another in seconds, it's usually easy to find reliable product information, and you don't have to worry about overaggressive salespeople.

However, credit card numbers, billing addresses, and shipping addresses are things you would like to think about once, get right, and never have to consider again. That's the idea behind Microsoft's *.NET Passport program*; sign up for a Passport account and, simply by entering a Passport logon ID and confirming it with a password, the site can automatically access all your credit card and address information.

Pop-Up Windows

It used to be that Internet advertisers relied on *banner ads* on their web pages—those small, flashing graphics that invite you to click the monkey or that tell you about a new online casino. The sites that used banner ads were paid by *clickthroughs*—the more people who clicked the ad, the more they got paid.

However, few people clicked. "How else can we attract their attention?" the advertisers asked in despair. "*I got it!*" one brave marketroid said. "We can *have separate windows automatically start* when people go to a site, forcing them to close the window! They'll be annoyed, but at least they won't be able to avoid it!"

These are called *pop-up ads* and are the bane of many casual surfers. Not only do they interrupt your work, but they also tend to include large graphics files. If you have a slow connection, your precious bandwidth may be wasted on loading advertisements, rather than on the site you want to see. Worse yet, some pop-up ads have pop-up ads embedded in them that start up when you close them, leading to an endless array of clicking and closing, clicking and closing. Pop-up ads also take up memory on your computer, which may lead to crashes if you encounter enough of them and don't close them.

Several programs are available that claim to block pop-up ads, and some are free, though none are perfect because advertisers are always working on new ways to create pop-up ads that get past the blockers. In addition, many sites create legitimate pop-up windows; for example, when you click on a link that takes you to another site, many web sites open another window for that link rather than risk you actually leaving their site.

We suggest Pop-Up Stopper, downloadable at **www.panicware.com**, as the easiest and most efficient stopper. For instructions on downloading and installing software, see Chapter 34.

Signing Up for .NET Passport

You sign up for a .NET Passport account by going to **www.passport.com** and signing up for an account. Your logon ID can be any valid e-mail address; all Hotmail and MSN email accounts are automatically Passport accounts, although you'll still have to enter your credit card and billing information if you want to use them to purchase anything. Microsoft asks you to create a password (with a minimum of six characters) and agree to Microsoft's terms. You see a secure page where you can enter your credit card number, your address, and other demographic information that can be used at all Passport-enabled sites.

Windows XP users can link your user accounts to a .NET Passport by choosing Start | Control Panel, selecting User Accounts, clicking your user name, and selecting Set Up My Account To Use A .NET Passport. You have the option of either linking the User Name you're logged in under to a .NET Passport account or creating an entirely new .NET Passport account and then linking it to the User Name you're logged in under.

If you link your User Account to a .NET passport, every time you click a link on a web site to identify yourself via Passport, Windows XP automatically uses the Passport account that you've linked to the User Account you're logged in under. In other words, if you're logged into Windows XP under a User Account named Ferrett and you've linked that account to the .NET Passport account named **notarealemailaddress@hotmail.com**, when you click a .NET Passport Sign In button, Windows automatically tries to log you in under the **notarealemailaddress@hotmail.com** account.

Other users logged on that same machine who click on a .NET Passport Sign In button need to enter their own .NET Passport accounts manually, unless they link their own accounts.

Once you've actually linked your .NET Passport account to your Windows XP User Account, you can change the linking by selecting User Accounts under Control Panel, then clicking Change My .NET Passport. You can then change your Passport information or link your User Account to an entirely different .NET Passport account.

Using .NET Passport

Using .NET Passport is reasonably simple: you shop at a .NET-enabled web site, adding items to the shopping cart just like you normally would. When it comes time to check out, you click the .NET Passport Sign In button or the Passport Express Purchase button. Enter your Passport account and your password, and—assuming you've entered your credit card information and shipping address into your Passport account—all of the billing is filled in for you. Presto!

Problems with .NET Passport

The biggest problem with .NET Passport is that few merchants actually use it—some of the largest players in the e-business industry, like Amazon.com and Dell, don't accept .NET Passport at all. You can find a list of the businesses that *do* accept it at **www.passport.com/Directory**.

Another problem is privacy and security. Several privacy groups, including the Electronic Privacy Information Center (**www.epic.org**), allege that Microsoft will use Passport to collect an unprecedented amount of information on consumers, tracking all of their purchases. (Microsoft denies these claims.) Furthermore, Passport accounts have suffered some notable security breaches, where programmers testing Microsoft's security were able to access secret Passport data by breaching Hotmail security. As of mid-2002, no hacker has stolen data from .NET Passport (that we know of). However, considering that Microsoft is the highest-profile computer company in the world, it's safe to assume that hackers everywhere are trying to breach Microsoft's security in ways that lesser-known companies wouldn't have to worry about. If security and privacy are concerns of yours, you may want to read more about EPIC's concerns about .NET Passport at **www.epic.org/privacy/consumer/microsoft/default.html#complaint**.

Many other organizations have expressed concern, too. If Microsoft succeeds at making the .NET Passport the way that most users identify themselves on the Internet, they will essentially own and operate the database of all of our online identities. (One wag quipped that Microsoft plans to collect our online identities and then rent them back to us at reasonable rates.)

Alternatives to .NET Passport

Sun Microsystems, one of Microsoft's biggest competitors, has created The Liberty Alliance (**www.projectliberty.org**), which hopes to create a set of standards for a secure, private, central repository of personal information that isn't owned by any single company. As of this writing, the alliance had not actually created anything that would help you buy anything, but they were expected to take their first steps toward it in late 2002. The alliance has some heavy hitters on its council, including Visa, Cisco Systems, Novell, and Sabre (a major player in the airline reservation industry)—so if they produce a viable product, it should meet with some success.

The
Complete
Reference

Chapter 19

Keeping Track of Your Favorite Web Sites

Internet Explorer (IE) and Netscape Navigator each provide five tools that you can use to return to previously visited web sites. Microsoft and Netscape are competitors, so they give their tools different names, but both programs catalog web sites in pretty much the same way. The five critical tools are

Internet Explorer Tool	Netscape Tool
Address bar	Location bar
History folder	History folder
Links bar	Personal Toolbar
Favorites menu	Bookmark menu
Home button	Home button

The Address bar (in Internet Explorer), Location bar (in Netscape Navigator 4.7 and 6), and the History folder record web sites *automatically*. The Address/Location bar tracks web sites you've typed in manually, while the History folder records all of the most recent URLs you visited. However, favorites, links, and Internet shortcuts, to be discussed shortly, are voluntary—they keep track only of the web sites that you (or Microsoft or Apple or Netscape) have decided to record.

The most valuable pieces of URL-recording real estate are IE's Links bar (called the Favorites bar or Toolbar Favorites in IE's Mac version) and Netscape Navigator's Personal Toolbar. Both usually appear just below the main toolbar and comfortably display only about six links. So choose them wisely. Instructions on adding and deleting entries from the Links bar and Personal Toolbar are given shortly.

Your main tool for remembering the URLs of favorite web sites, however, is IE's Favorites menu or Navigator's Bookmarks. They provide a combination of easy access, memorable organization, and high capacity.

You'd better like the look of your home page (known as the start page in Netscape) because your browser automatically displays it every time you start it up. We'll discuss how to choose your Home page in "Choosing Your Start and Home Pages" later in this chapter.

Another handy thing to do with a few frequently accessed URLs (or URLs that you plan to visit soon and then dispose of) is to make Internet shortcuts for them and put them on your desktop. See "Using Internet Shortcuts" later in this chapter.

The Address/Location Bar

Internet Explorer's Address bar remembers the last 25 URLs that you typed in and successfully reached, whereas Netscape's Location bar remembers only the last 15.

To access previously typed URLs, click the drop-down arrow to the right of the bar, and select a URL from the list. If the URL you entered wasn't reached (either because you mistyped it or the browser couldn't find the page), it doesn't show up on the list.

 If you remember only part of a URL you've been to, both IE and Navigator 6 have the AutoComplete feature. When you type in the first few letters of a web site, the program searches its History file for URLs that start with those letters and offers a drop-down menu for you to choose from. You can clear your menu by clearing the History; see "Using the History Folder" for details.

Choosing Your Start and Home Pages

When you open your browser without specifying a particular web page, the browser opens a page by default. Navigator calls this URL the *start page,* whereas IE calls it the *home page.*

Whether it's called "start" or "home," choosing the page that you connect to every time you start up your browser is important—and both Microsoft and Netscape want you to go to their sites daily, which is why their default home pages are usually on their news sites. (Microsoft has MSN.com; Netscape uses Netscape.com.)

Both sites are *portal sites* that act as a customizable gateway to the rest of the Web, and both allow you to search the Web, get local news, display your local weather, and so forth.

Setting the Internet Explorer Home Page

You can choose a new home page for IE from the Internet Options dialog box, which you open by choosing View | Internet Options in IE 5.5 or lower or by choosing Tools | Internet Options in IE 6. (See Figure 19-1.) The Internet Options dialog box opens with the General tab on top. You can type the URL of the new home page into the Home Page box on this tab, or you can click one of the following buttons:

- **Use Current** The page currently displayed by IE becomes the home page. (If IE isn't open, this button is grayed out.) This can be any page on the Web, on your local area network (LAN), or even on your own hard drive.
- **Use Default** The home page becomes the default (usually **www.msn.com**).
- **Use Blank** The home page is blank. This is handy if you want IE to start up as quickly as possible and don't necessarily want to open your Internet connection.

To return to your home page, click the Home button on the IE toolbar.

Figure 19-1.   *Setting the page that IE displays when you start the program*

Setting the Netscape Navigator Home and Start Pages

In Navigator, however, it's slightly more complicated. Navigator draws a distinction between the URL you see when you start your browser (the start page) and the URL you go to when you click the Home button (the home page). You can change both pages or simply make them the same page.

In Navigator, choose Edit | Preferences. (See Figure 19-2.) The When Navigator Starts Up, Display box gives you three choices for your Start page: it can be the same as the home page, a blank page, or the last page that you visited in your previous session. To change the home page, enter a URL into the Location box, click the Use Current Page button (to make the home page the page that Navigator is currently displaying), or click the Choose File button (to make the home page a page on your system).

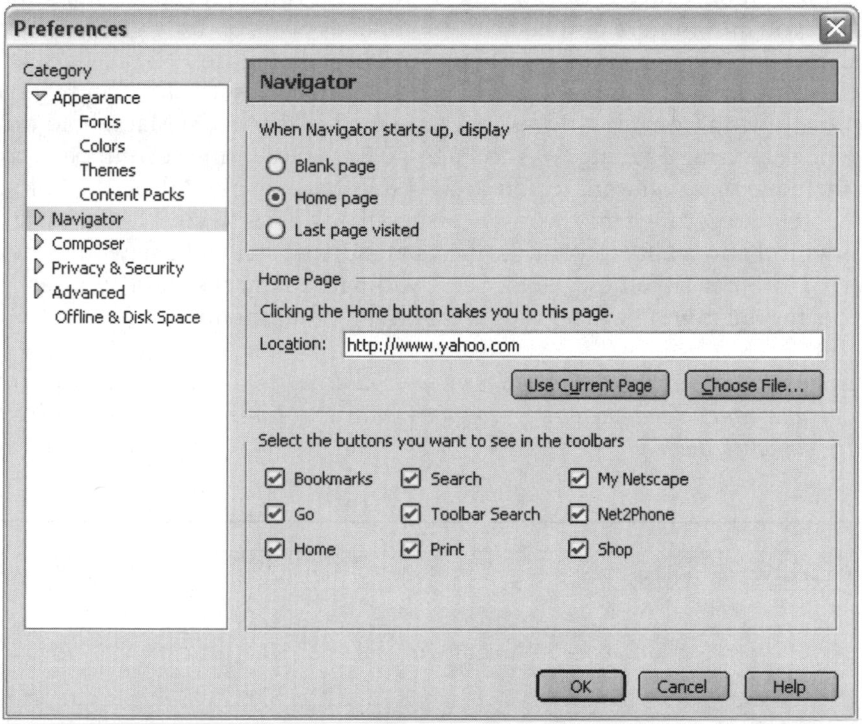

Figure 19-2.   *Setting Netscape Navigator's start page*

The Links Bar and Personal Toolbar

You'll find a couple of sites that you check every time you fire up your browser. When you go to sites daily, the Personal Toolbar and the Links bar put them right up front, where you can find them. One click accesses any URL on the bar.

Tip   *To save space in your Links bar, rename your favorites so they're as short as possible. The default name is the page's title, which is often quite long—one link can take up your entire Links bar! You can learn how to rename favorites in "Managing the Favorites and Bookmarks Menu" later in this chapter.*

Internet Explorer's Links Bar

To add a button to the Links bar, drag the bookmark or favorites icon from the Address toolbar onto it. The new button is created in the place where you set down the icon.

The Links bar can only hold about six links before you run out of space along the top. However, if you add more, a double-arrow symbol appears on the right-hand side that you can click to access the rest of your links, as shown in Figure 19-3.

To add a link to the Links bar, open the page that you want to link, and then drag and drop the IE icon from the Address bar onto the Links bar. On Macs, hold down ⌘-SHIFT while selecting Favorites | Add Page To Favorites. If the current page contains a link to the page that you want to add to the Links bar, drag and drop the link to the bar. If you feel like getting fancy, you can also add any URL to your Links bar in the same way you'd add a URL to your Favorites menu; just create the new favorite inside the Links (or Toolbar Favorites) folder. See "Adding Bookmarks and Favorites" later in this chapter for the myriad ways to add a favorite to your menu.

Tip	*You're not restricted to just favorites on your Links bar. You can drag any shortcut from your Start menu, including programs, onto your Links bar, and they'll start up once you click them.*

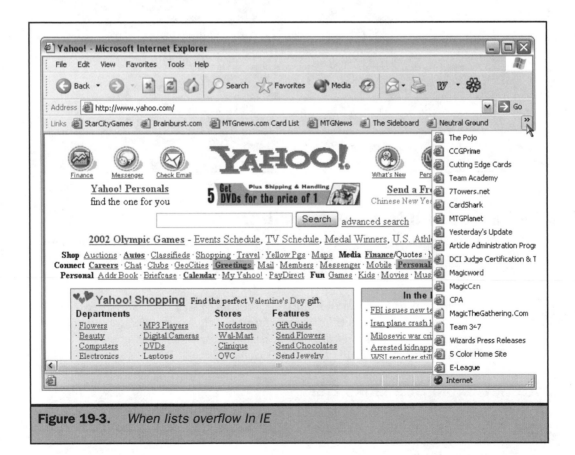

Figure 19-3. *When lists overflow In IE*

To rearrange the Links bar, drag and drop individual links to their new locations. In Windows, you can do this on the Links bar itself. On Macs, drag and drop within the Toolbar Favorites folder of the Favorites Explorer bar. You can drop a link between other links; when a link is in the location to be dropped, the cursor changes to a separator bar. Your final option is to arrange your favorites in the Links folder via the Organize Favorites command—which we'll show you how to do in "Managing the Favorites and Bookmarks Menu" later on.

To delete a link from the Links bar in Windows, right-click the link and choose Delete from the context menu. On Macs, click the Favorites tab (left side of the screen) to display the Favorites Explorer bar, find the link in the Toolbar Favorites folder, and drag the link into trash.

Netscape Navigator's Personal Toolbar

Much as you can with Internet Explorer's Links toolbar, you can drag and drop icons from other components of Netscape Communicator—a mailbox or newsgroup icon from Netscape Messenger, for example. After you drop such an icon onto the Personal Toolbar, it turns into a button that opens the corresponding object. There are also preset buttons you can put on the Personal Toolbar (see "Adding Links Bar Buttons in Netscape Navigator" later on). Unfortunately, unlike in IE, you're limited only to Netscape programs—you can't drag programs off the Start menu and onto the Personal Toolbar.

You can add bookmarks to your Personal Toolbar in two ways: you can click and drag the icon from your Address bar onto your Personal Toolbar, or you can drag and drop a bookmark into the Personal Toolbar folder. (See "Organizing Bookmarks in Netscape Navigator.") You can rearrange the bookmarks on your toolbar simply by dragging and dropping them into a different place on the toolbar, or you can arrange them within the Personal Toolbar folder in the same way you would organize any other Bookmarks.

The Personal Toolbar is linked to the Personal Toolbar folder on the Bookmarks menu. When the Personal Toolbar is hidden, you can still access its contents by clicking the Bookmarks button on the Location toolbar and looking in the Personal Toolbar folder.

   Space on the Personal Toolbar is limited. If you add too many items to the Personal Toolbar, those on the far right are pushed off the screen and become unavailable. However, you can increase the number of web sites available from the Personal Toolbar by placing folders of bookmarks on the toolbar, rather than individual bookmarks.

Managing the Favorites and Bookmarks Menu

Microsoft calls them "favorites," Netscape calls them "bookmarks"; whatever you call them, they're the primary place to store URLs that you want to revisit. With a single click, you can return to any web site. Favorites and bookmarks are only slightly less convenient than the Links bar and Personal Toolbar, and they can contain a vast number of URLs.

In Windows 95 and later, you can use the Favorites menu from the Start menu, even if IE isn't open. If you choose an entry from the Start | Favorites menu, both the default web browser and your Internet connection (if you're not already connected) open. This feature eliminates one of the main hassles of changing browsers: losing your bookmarks. Favorites stay with the operating system, not with the browser.

If you don't see a list of Favorites on the Start menu in Windows XP, it may have been disabled. You can enable Favorites from the Start menu in Windows XP by choosing Start | Control Panel, double-clicking Taskbar And Start Menu, clicking the Advanced tab, and selecting Favorites Menu from the Start menu items list.

Adding Bookmarks and Favorites

To add the current page to Bookmarks or Favorites, use any of the following methods:

- **Click and drag**   Drag the Bookmark (or Favorites) icon on the Location toolbar, which is just to the left of the URL, onto the Bookmarks (or Favorites) menu. When the menu appears, continue to drag the icon into whichever menu or submenu that you want this page's bookmark to be in.

- **Menu selection**   In IE, select Favorites | Add To Favorites. In Navigator, select Bookmarks | Add Bookmarks.

- **Context menus**   Open a context menu in the viewing window, and select Add Bookmark or Add To Favorites.

- **Dragging links**   You can save a page that is linked to the current page (without opening the linked page) by dragging the link from the current page onto the Bookmarks (or Favorites) menu.

Additionally, Netscape Navigator has a special button for Bookmarks: click the Bookmarks button and choose Add Bookmark or File Bookmark from the menu that appears. Add Bookmark puts the new bookmark at the bottom of the main Bookmarks list; File Bookmark lets you put the new bookmark into a subfolder of the Bookmarks folder.

IE's link-organizing capabilities aren't as comprehensive as Navigator's, so adding a favorite via a menu always gives you a dialog box. You can either enter a name for the link or accept the suggested one. To put the new favorite into a subfolder, click the Create In button and choose the subfolder into which you want to put the new favorite. If you want to define a new folder for the favorite, select a folder in which to put the new folder and then click New Folder.

Navigator, on the other hand, only displays a dialog box if you add a bookmark through a context menu and always puts the bookmark in the main bookmark menu, counting on you to organize your bookmarks into subfolders and rename them later.

Any of these methods results in a new item on your Bookmarks or Favorites menu. This icon is associated with the web page that was current when the bookmark was created and is labeled with the name that the author of the web page chose as the page title. Many web pages have ridiculously long titles to increase their chances of being picked up by a search engine (see Chapter 30 for more details), so you may wish to rename your bookmark.

Editing a Favorite or Favorite Folder in IE

To change the name of a folder or favorite, choose Favorites | Organize Favorites, select the link or folder, and click the Rename button. Then type in the name you want. Alternatively, you can change the name by opening a context menu on the favorite, selecting Properties, clicking the General tab, and typing the new name at the top.

You may want to change the URL of a favorite, either because the web site it refers to has moved or because you now want a different web site assigned to a bookmark named, for example, "My Girlfriend's Home Page." To change the URL of a favorite, open a context menu on the favorite, select Properties, and type the new URL into the URL field.

Editing a Bookmark or Bookmark Folder in Navigator

You can change the name or URL of a bookmark or assign a description to it. All these changes are done from the Properties dialog box.

To open the Properties dialog box in Navigator, open the Bookmarks window and select the bookmark. Then choose Bookmark Properties from the context menu. On a Macintosh, choose Edit | Get Info. If you want to choose a different name for the bookmark, type the new name into the Name line of the bookmark's Bookmark Properties dialog box.

To change the URL of a bookmark, type the new URL into the Location (URL) line of the bookmark's Bookmark Properties dialog box.

You may decide to add a description to a bookmark, either to remind yourself why you bookmarked this site or to provide keywords that you can use in a search. (See "Finding Bookmarks in Netscape Navigator" later in this chapter.) Type the description into the Description box of the bookmark's Bookmark Properties dialog box.

A bookmark folder also has a Bookmark Properties dialog box. Though the folder has no URL, its name and description can be edited from this dialog box, just as you would do with a bookmark.

Organizing Favorites and Favorites Folders in IE for Windows

You can organize the Favorites folder from within Internet Explorer by selecting Favorites | Organize Favorites. This opens the Organize Favorites window, shown in Figure 19-4.

Many PC manufacturers preload their computers with lots of favorites they want you to go to—so before you even start, you have 50 URLs that you may never visit clogging up your screen. Pruning your Favorites periodically and organizing them into folders makes it easier for you to find what you need.

When you first open the Organize Favorites window, it displays the contents of the Favorites folder, including its subfolders. To look at the contents of one of the subfolders, double-click its icon. If you are viewing the contents of a subfolder and want to examine the folder that contains it, double-click the folder icon.

To move or delete a favorite (or a folder within the Favorites folder), you must first find it in the Organize Favorites window. If the favorite is inside a subfolder of the Favorites folder, open that subfolder by clicking (or double-clicking) its icon. When you find the favorite's icon, select it.

To delete the favorite, click the Delete button, select Delete from a context menu, or press DELETE on the keyboard.

To move the favorite to another folder within the Favorites folder, click the Move To Folder button. A Browse For Folder window appears. Select the folder to which

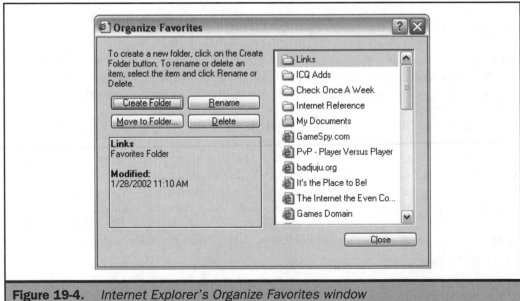

Figure 19-4.   *Internet Explorer's Organize Favorites window*

you want to move the favorite and then click OK. Alternatively, you may drag and drop the favorite to the desired location without using the Move To Folder button.

To create a subfolder of the Favorites folder, click the Create Folder button in the Organize Favorites window. The folder is created within the currently displayed folder. The new folder has the default name New Folder, which appears with a text-editing box around it. Type into the box the name that you want the folder to have. After you create the folder, you can rename, move, or delete it, as previously described.

Favorites is a folder in Windows, so you can organize it as you would any other folder in your file system, without learning how to use the Organize Favorites window. You can also search for favorites through Window's Find command.

In Windows 95/98/NT/ME, the Favorites folder is inside the C:\Windows folder; it's inside C:\Windows\Profiles*username* if user profiles are set up on your machine. In Windows 2000 and XP, your favorites are in C:\Documents And Settings\ *username*\Favorites. The entries on the Favorites menu are Internet shortcuts inside the Favorites folder.

After you find the Favorites folder, you can organize it (and search through it) in the same way that you organize any other folder: create and delete subfolders, move objects from one subfolder to another, or delete objects by using your usual file commands.

Organizing Favorites on IE for UNIX

In non-Windows systems, Favorites is an HTML file, not a folder of Internet shortcuts. In UNIX, the location of the Favorites file is (relative to where IE is installed) ~/.microsoft/Favorites. When Favorites is an HTML file, any browser that opens it has access to its links.

Organizing Favorites on IE for Macintosh

On Macs, favorites are stored in an HTML file called System Folder/Preferences/ Explorer/Favorites.html. You can open this file and view it in your browser.

Click the Favorites tab to expand the Favorites Explorer bar. Drag and drop favorites or folders to wherever you want them. To create a new folder, select Favorites | New Folder. To rename a favorite or folder of favorites, select Favorites | Open Favorites. When the Favorites window appears, click the item's name and type in a new name. You can remove a favorite, favorite folder, or divider by dragging it to the Trash icon in the dock.

Organizing Bookmarks in Netscape Navigator

When you are ready to organize your bookmarks (or maybe just thin them out a little), open the Bookmarks window, as shown in Figure 19-5. (The title bar also includes the name from your Netscape profile, or *for default* if you don't use Netscape profiles.) Navigator 6 has moved Bookmarks into their own menu, and you can organize your Bookmarks by selecting Bookmarks | Manage Bookmarks in Navigator 6. In older

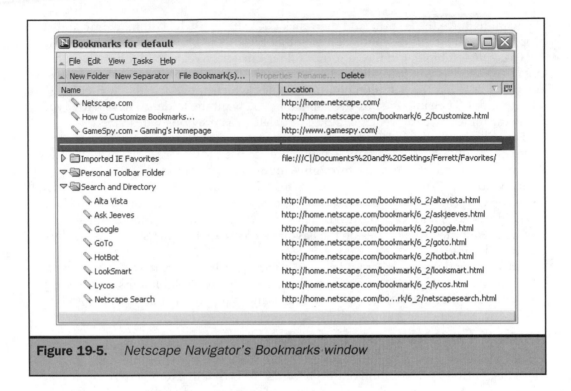

Figure 19-5.   *Netscape Navigator's Bookmarks window*

versions of Navigator, you'll have to settle for selecting Bookmarks | Edit Bookmarks, Communicator | Bookmarks, or Communicator | Bookmarks | Edit Bookmarks.

 Of course, if you just want to shuffle a couple of Bookmarks around, you can click and drag bookmarks into new places on the Bookmarks menu.

Folders in the Bookmarks window have arrowheads next to them (see Figure 19-5); a right-arrow denotes a contracted folder, and a down-arrow signifies an expanded folder. Click an arrow to expand or contract the folder contents. (In Navigator 4.7 and earlier, the folder's contents are expanded when a minus sign [–] shows and contracted when a plus sign [+] shows.) Continue expanding folders until you can see all the bookmarks and folders that you want to organize.

To move bookmarks or folders in the Bookmarks window, drag and drop them, or select bookmarks or folders, and then select Cut, Copy, or Paste from the Edit menu. To delete bookmarks or folders, select them and press DELETE or select Edit | Delete. If you delete something by mistake, select Edit | Undo to get it back.

To create new bookmark folders, choose File | New Folder. A Bookmark Properties box appears for the new folder. Use this box to give the folder a name, or even a short description. The new folder appears at the bottom of the Bookmarks menu; move it wherever you want it. You can even put it inside other folders.

To organize your Bookmarks menu into sections, add separators. Select the entry that you want to appear immediately above the separator and then select File | New Separator. To delete separators, select the separator in the Bookmarks window and press DELETE. To move separators, drag and drop them in the Bookmarks window.

In the Windows version, the View menu of the Bookmarks window provides several automatic ways to rearrange your bookmarks: by name of the bookmark, by location (alphabetical arrangement by URL), by date last viewed, or by the date the bookmark was created.

Finding Bookmarks in Netscape Navigator

Bookmarks have a tendency to accumulate with time, just as index cards and yellow sticky notes do. When you have only a couple dozen bookmarks, you can just scan them—but when you have hundreds, it becomes convenient to let the computer help you find the one that you're looking for.

To find a bookmark automatically, open the Bookmarks window and choose Edit | Find Bookmarks from its menu bar. In Netscape 6, you see the Find Bookmarks window, like this:

Type into the text box a word or character string that you want to search for.

In Netscape 4.7 and earlier, use the check boxes in the Look In line to specify whether the word or string should be in the name, location, URL, or description of the bookmark. (Adding keywords to a bookmark's description is one way to make it easier to find. (See "Editing a Bookmark or Bookmark Folder in Navigator" earlier in this chapter.)

For Netscape 6 and later, type your word or phrase in the right-hand box, and then choose in which part of the bookmark you'll be searching for your word (or phrase). You can choose to look in the bookmark name, location (the URL), description, or keyword from the drop-down menu on the left. Navigator then allows you to refine your search by selecting from a list of qualifiers: for most searches, a simple "contains" will do, finding the bookmark if your word or phrase is anywhere in the place you've selected—but you can also specify that Netscape search in the following ways:

- **Starts with** returns a match if the field starts with the word (or phrase) you're searching for.

- **Ends with** returns a match if the field ends with the word (or phrase) you're searching for.

- **Is** returns a match only if the entire field equals the word exactly. Thus, searching for "Netscape" when the bookmark name is "Netscape.com" will not return a match.

- **Is not** returns a match only if the entire field *doesn't* equal the keyword exactly. So using "Is Not Netscape" will still return "Netscape.com."

- **Doesn't contain** returns a match if the field does not contain the keyword.

In Navigator 4.7's Find Bookmarks window, check the Match Case check box if the search should pay attention to the capitalization that you use in the Find box, or check the Whole Word check box to instruct the search to ignore bookmarks in which the word in the Find line appears only as part of some longer word or string.

After you specify everything that you want, click OK ("Find" on a Macintosh) to begin the search. Older versions of Navigator find bookmarks one at a time; press CTRL-G (⌘-G on a Mac), or choose Edit | Find Again to find the next bookmark. (Navigator 6, thankfully, finds them all at once.) To examine the found bookmark in more detail, open its Bookmark Properties dialog box by selecting Edit | Bookmark Properties in Navigator 4.*x* for Windows, choosing File | Properties in Netscape 6, or selecting Edit | Get Info on a Macintosh.

Adding Links Bar Buttons in Netscape Navigator

In addition to the bookmarks you can place on the Links bar, Netscape 6 allows you to add several pre-generated buttons there, simply by going to Edit | Preferences and selecting the buttons you'd like to see in the section at the bottom. Unfortunately, you can't add, delete, or change any of the button URLs, most of which point to a section on Netscape's site.

Importing and Converting Bookmarks to Favorites, and Vice Versa

In addition to building up your bookmarks and favorites files one entry at a time, you may get whole lists of links simultaneously—or give lists of links to others. For example, you may download a file of bookmarks from the Web, you may get a file of favorites on a disk from a friend, or you may wish to transfer your Navigator bookmarks over to IE on your laptop. The process of saving favorites and bookmarks is known as *exporting*; bringing lists of links into your browser is known as *importing*.

 Tip *If you install Netscape Navigator when IE is already on your machine (and vice versa), it automatically imports all of your old favorites/bookmarks into its new bookmarks/favorites.*

Exporting Favorites from Internet Explorer

To export a list of IE favorites, choose File | Import And Export, which runs the Import/Export Wizard. Click the Next button, select Export Favorites from the menu on the left and click Next again. IE gives you a choice of exporting a single folder of favorites (and all of its subfolders) or of exporting all the favorites you have. To export a single favorites folder, click that folder. If you want to export all favorites, select Favorites from the top. (See Figure 19-6.) Unfortunately, there's no way to export more than one top-level folder at a time—so if you wanted to export Links and ICQ Adds from the example shown in Figure 19-6, but *not* any of the others, you'd have to export twice. However, exporting Favorites exports all the links in the Favorites folder and everything contained in Favorites.) When you've selected the folder you want, click Next.

Internet Explorer gives you a choice: export your favorites to an application or export to a file. (See Figure 19-7.) If you have another browser installed on your system and Windows recognizes it, that browser appears in a drop-down menu under Export To An Application. To export directly into the other program, select the radio button, choose the browser from the drop-down menu, and click Next. IE displays an Export Favorites warning box, asking you if you want to replace the file. If you click Yes, you overwrite any links in that other browser and replace them with the exported favorites.

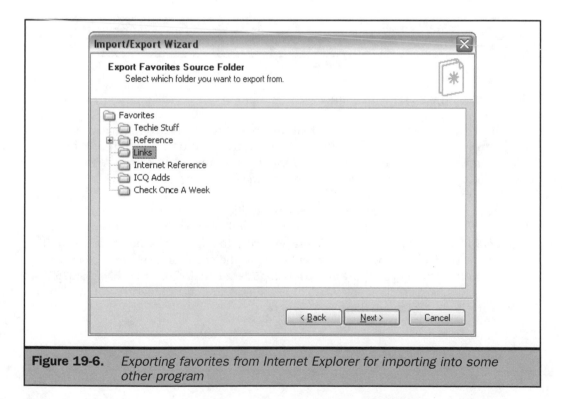

Figure 19-6.   *Exporting favorites from Internet Explorer for importing into some other program*

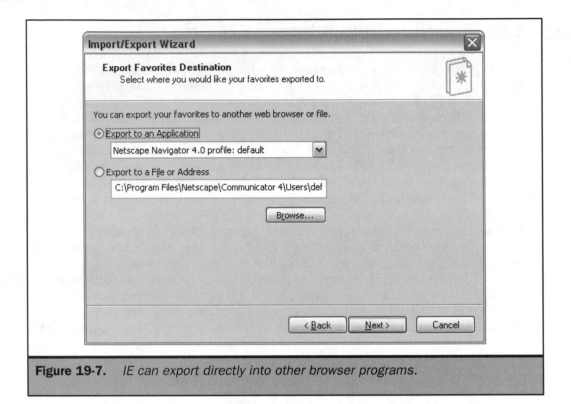

Figure 19-7. *IE can export directly into other browser programs.*

If that's fine with you, click Yes; otherwise, click No to cancel. Once you've said Yes, click Finish and you're done.

To export your favorites into a file that can be sent or imported manually into another program, click the Export To A File Or Address radio button. Either type the location where you want the file saved into the text box or click Browse to point-and-click to a new location. You can save the file by any name, though it defaults to bookmark.htm.

In previous versions of Internet Explorer (5 and lower), Favorites is not an HTML document, so the process is more complicated. Microsoft had a free utility for Windows 95/98 called *favtool* that converts favorites to bookmarks, and vice versa. It's become quite difficult to find this in recent years as the need for it dropped. Last we knew, you could find it at **support.microsoft.com/default.aspx?scid=kb;EN-US;q152681**, but occasionally Microsoft moves it. All else failing, search for the word "favtool" on the Web; it's bound to be out there somewhere.

Exporting favorites is a lot simpler in non-Windows systems because favorites are automatically saved as an HTML document, as are bookmarks in Navigator no matter what the platform. You can import the URLs from the favorites file into IE, Navigator, or another browser.

Importing Favorites into Internet Explorer

Internet Explorer gives you a choice of importing new favorites from another application on your PC or importing from an HTML file. You start by choosing File | Import And Export, which runs the Import/Export Wizard, and clicking Next. Choose Import Favorites and click Next. If another browser is installed on your system and Windows recognizes it, that browser appears in a drop-down menu under Import To An Application. To import favorites in from another browser (generally Navigator), select Import From An Application, choose the browser from the drop-down menu, and click Next. IE asks you what folder you'd like to bring the new links into; click the folder and click Next. (Unfortunately, there's no way of adding a new folder from here—so if you want your new favorites in a new folder, be sure to add it before you start to import them!) Then click Finish.

To import your favorites from a file (or from a browser that IE doesn't recognize), click the Import From A File Or Address radio button. Either type the file's location in the text box, or click Browse to point-and-click your way to the HTML file. Select the file and click Save. IE asks you what folder you'd like the new favorites saved in; select that folder, click Next, and then click Finish.

Importing and Exporting Bookmarks in Netscape Navigator

Unlike IE, Navigator doesn't give you the choice of exporting a single folder—it's all or nothing. To export bookmarks from Netscape Navigator, choose Bookmarks | Manage Bookmarks in Netscape Navigator 6 and later, or Bookmarks | Edit Bookmarks in Netscape Navigator 4.7 and earlier. In the Bookmarks window, choose File | Export Bookmarks from the menu, and choose the name and location of where you'd like to save it to. Click OK.

To import a set of bookmarks in Netscape Navigator, go to Bookmarks | Manage Bookmarks in Navigator 6 and later, or Bookmarks | Edit Bookmarks in Netscape Navigator 4.7 and earlier. Select File | Import Bookmarks and choose the HTML document you want to import files from. The links in that HTML file are added to your current set of bookmarks in a folder called IE Favorites and are alphabetized by name, whether or not they were that way in the original HTML file.

Using the History Folder

Clicking the History button on the IE toolbar opens the History Explorer Bar in the IE window. To display it in Netscape Navigator 6 as a separate window, choose Tasks | Tools | History, or in older versions, press CTRL-H. Each of these commands displays the contents of that browser's History folder, as shown in Figure 19-8. Selecting a closed folder expands the tree to show its contents; selecting an open folder compresses the tree to hide its contents. You can search for a specific page by pressing CTRL-F.

Clicking the History button again (or the X in the corner of the History pane) causes the History pane to disappear in IE; all you have to do in Netscape is close the window.

Returning to a Web Page in the History Folder

In Netscape Navigator 4.7 and 6.2, the History folder (shown in Figure 19-8) is organized into subfolders—one for each day of the current week, and one for each previous week, going back a default of 20 days in IE, and 9 days in Navigator. (You can change the number of days that History remembers, as explained later in this section.) Each day's folder contains one subfolder for each web site visited. Inside the web site folders are Internet shortcuts to each of the pages viewed on that web site; you can return to a web

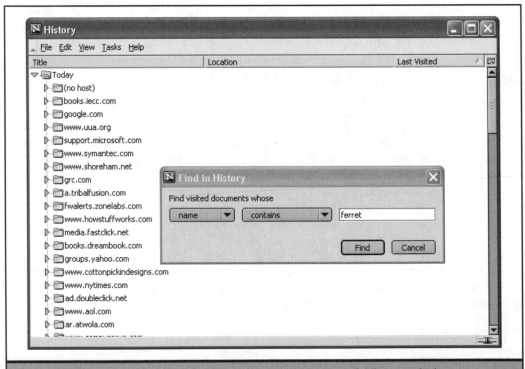

Figure 19-8.   *Searching for a web page in the Netscape 6 History window*

page by opening its shortcut, or add it as a favorite or a bookmark by right-clicking the shortcut. Delete a shortcut or subfolder from the History folder by selecting Delete from the right-click menu.

In IE, selecting a shortcut displays its title and address in a ToolTip window. You can look up the exact time the page was accessed and the number of times it has been visited by choosing Properties from the right-click menu.

Configuring and Clearing the History Folder

To change the number of days that IE remembers your History, open the Internet Options dialog box by selecting View | Internet Options (in IE 4 and 5), or Tools | Internet Options (in IE 6), where you find the settings on the General tab. Enter a new number into the Days To Keep Pages In History box and click OK. To do the same in Netscape Navigator, go to Edit | Preferences and select Navigator | History from the drop-down menu on the left side. (See Figure 19-9.) Type a number in the Remember Visited Pages For The Last *xx* Days box.

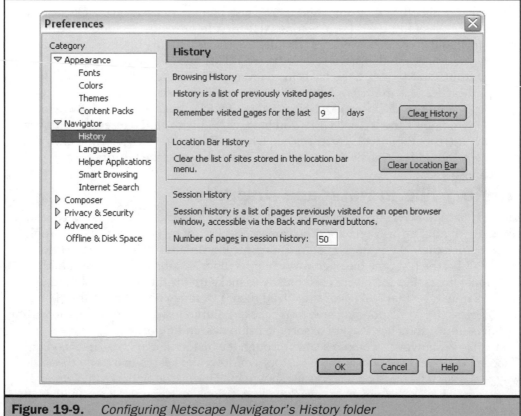

Figure 19-9.   *Configuring Netscape Navigator's History folder*

To delete all the entries in the History folder, click the Clear History button in the History box of the General tab in either program.

The History File in Internet Explorer

You can access and change your History files in IE the same way you can access and change your favorites. In Windows 95/98/NT/ME, the IE History folder has the address C:\Windows\History if you haven't activated user profiles and has the address C:\Windows\Profiles*username*\History if you have. For Windows 2000 and XP, the folder is C:\Documents And Settings*username*\Local Settings\ History. You can edit it (and search through it) as you would any other folder.

In Mac versions of IE, you display History by clicking a tab on the right side of the viewing window. The tab expands into an Explorer bar that displays a list of previously visited URLs in the order in which they were visited, organized into daily folders.

An entry in the History file can be clicked to open its corresponding web site, dragged to the Links bar, or dragged onto the desktop to create an Internet shortcut. In Windows XP, every user has a history folder at C:\Documents And Settings\ *username*\Local Settings\History, and there's also one for all users, at C:\Documents And Settings\Default User\Local Settings\History. In previous versions of Windows, the history folder is at C:\Windows\Profiles*username*\History or at C:\Windows\ History. On Macs, the IE history is stored as an HTML file (web page) named History.html. On Mac OS X, the file is in ~/Library/Preferences/Explorer. On Mac OS 9 and earlier, it is in System Folder/Preferences/Explorer.

The History file keeps track of a set number of URLs, not a set period. By default, History remembers the last 300 URLs you have visited with IE. To reset this number, open the Internet Explorer Preferences box (choose Edit | Preferences), and click the Advanced tab under Web Browser. Type a new number into the History box.

The History File in Netscape Navigator

Sadly, Netscape Navigator does not store its history as Internet shortcuts, so you can't access them outside of Navigator. You can access History by choosing Tasks | Tools | History. Netscape Navigator 6 History is organized into three columns: page title, location, and the last time the page was visited. (Older versions of Navigator had additional fields, but they were used mostly to make up for the way—or should we say lack of way?—that Navigator organized them.) Double-click a line in the History list to access the corresponding web page, click a column head to sort the list according to that column, and click it again to sort the list in descending order.

Unlike IE, however, you can search through the history list in Netscape Navigator. Choose Edit | Search History in the History window, and search in exactly the same way you search through bookmarks (as shown in "Finding Bookmarks in Netscape Navigator"), except that you only have two places to look in: name and location (the URL).

Figure 19-8 (which appears earlier in this chapter) shows the Find In History dialog box.

Older versions of Netscape Navigator did not organize their History list into folders and subfolders, as IE does, but had a fairly complex searching function to make up for it. Search the History list in old versions of Navigator by selecting Edit | Search History List from the menu of the History window (not the Navigator window). A Search History List dialog box opens.

A History search in older versions of Netscape Navigator consists of a set of conditions. In the preceding example, two conditions are defined. Define a condition by filling out three boxes on a horizontal line. In the first box, choose (from a drop-down list) the column of the History list to which the condition applies. In the second box, choose from a drop-down list of verbs that go with that column. In the third box, type something to compare the column entries against. When you are done, the condition should be a sentence that describes what you are looking for. In the example, the first condition reads "Visit Count Is Greater Than 5."

If you want to enter another condition, click the More button. A second condition-definition line appears. In this way, you can define as many conditions as you want. If you change your mind about the number of conditions that you want to use, click the Fewer button to make the bottommost condition-definition line go away.

When you are done defining conditions, click the Search button. A list of the entries on the History list that satisfy all the conditions appears at the bottom of the Search History List dialog box. If the list is still too long, refine your search by defining more conditions or by narrowing the ones that you have. Then click Search again. If what you want is not on the list, refine your search by eliminating conditions (using the Fewer button) or by broadening conditions. Click Search again.

History works differently on Windows systems than on Mac or UNIX systems. In Windows, History is a folder of shortcuts. On Mac and UNIX systems, History is an HTML file of links. On UNIX systems, the location of the History folder is relative to where IE is installed and has the relative pathname ~/.microsoft/History.

Using Internet Shortcuts

To create an Internet shortcut to the current page, drag the bookmark icon off the Location or Address bar and onto the desktop. In Windows, the shortcut bears the icon of the default browser. On a Macintosh, the shortcut is automatically associated with Navigator.

You may also create Internet shortcuts by dragging a link off the current page or dragging a bookmark out of the Bookmarks or Organize Favorites window and onto the desktop or the Start menu. In IE, choosing Create Shortcut from the context menu of the viewing window puts an Internet shortcut on the desktop.

To return to the web page, double-click the shortcut. If your browser isn't already running, it runs, and you see the shortcut's page. To delete a shortcut, right-click the shortcut and select Delete from the context menu.

The Complete Reference

Chapter 20

Web Security, Privacy, and Site-Blocking

Web browsers are intended to be simple enough for novice users. For this reason, most of what the browser does is invisible. Some choices that your browser makes for you, however, have implications for your system's vulnerability to viruses or other security lapses—implications that more-advanced users may want to consider.

This chapter discusses several topics that relate to what web sites you can see with your browser, what programs your browser will run on your computer, and how much web site operators can find out about you from your web browsing habits. Internet Explorer and Netscape Navigator use different approaches to security, privacy, and site-blocking, so this chapter begins with an overview of the concepts involved, followed by instructions for each browser.

 *To keep up-to-date on what's going on with Internet security, bookmark the Electronic Privacy Information Center at **www.epic.org** and the Center for Democracy and Privacy at **www.cdt.org**.*

Web Security and Privacy Concepts

Web security defines what your browser will allow web pages to run or store on your computer—what programs the browser will run, both within the browser and as separate programs, and what files the browser will create or modify. Browsers have *security policies,* or systems that enable you to specify which web sites can take what types of actions on your computer. For example, you can specify that certain web sites can run Java applets (programs embedded in web pages, as described in Chapter 17) on your computer, while others cannot.

Another aspect of web security specifies what information web sites can store on your computer, to track your use of the web site. Many sites use *cookies* (tiny files) to store information about you, as explained in the section "What Are Cookies?" later in this chapter.

How Security Policies Work

Internet Explorer's security policy is based on *trust,* and the decisions that you are asked to make involve who to trust and who not to trust. For example, when a web page wants to run an ActiveX control on your machine, IE verifies who wrote the control (Microsoft, for example), and that it hasn't been tampered with by anyone. You aren't told what the control intends to do or what privileges it requests on your system (rewriting files, for example). Instead, you are asked to decide whether you trust its author. (See Chapter 18 for information about plug-ins, ActiveX controls, and applets that your browser may ask you about.)

By contrast, Netscape Navigator's security policy is based on *action,* and you are asked to decide which actions to allow or disallow. This approach has its pluses and minuses. Trust is an intuitive concept that makes sense to the novice user. Deciding to trust Microsoft or your company's information technology department (or not to trust a web site offering free pornography) is simpler than deciding a large number of technical issues about your computer's security. On the other hand, more experienced users may want more direct control over their computer systems than a simple trust/don't trust decision allows. Navigator allows you to "get under the hood" and make choices about caching web pages, accepting cookies, and running applets in Java. Fortunately, IE also allows some ability to make security policy for these choices and for ActiveX controls.

This chapter includes instructions for setting your browser's security policies: see the sections "Configuring IE's Security Zones" and "Security in Netscape Navigator" later in this chapter.

What Are Cookies?

At last you broke down and ordered that pink flamingo from www.trashytrinkets.com to spruce up your lawn. The next time you went there, Trashy Trinkets' site not only greeted you by name, but suggested you buy a birdbath to go with it. How did the site know? Is it reading your mind? Not exactly. Welcome to the world of cookies.

A *cookie* is a tiny file that a web server stores on your machine. Its purpose is to allow a web server to personalize a web page, serving as a small record of your personal preferences that the server can access. When you ordered that garish oaken statue, the server set a cookie on your machine that recorded your name and previous purchases; when you returned to Trashy Trinkets, it simply read the cookie and reconfigured its page to say, "Howdy, PHIL SMITHERS!" and to suggest items that you were likely to buy based on what it read in the cookie.

Much has been written about whether cookies create a security or privacy hazard for you. If your browser is working properly, the security hazard is minimal. It is, at first glance, unsettling to think that web servers are storing information on your hard drive without your knowledge—but cookies aren't executable programs. They can't search for and accumulate information from elsewhere on your system. They simply record information that you have already given to (or gotten from) a web server.

Cookies *do* make it easier for advertising companies to gather information about your browsing habits. For example, a company that advertises on web sites can use cookies to keep track of where you have seen its ads before and which ads (if any) you clicked. Advertising agencies are coming up with slimier and more efficient ways of tracking your movements all the time.

For example, in 2000, the ad company DoubleClick used cookies to invisibly track all sites users were surfing to—along with their names, street addresses, and e-mail addresses, which would be stored in a large database used for targeted advertising. The only way to avoid being tracked by this program was either to disable cookies from DoubleClick or to go to DoubleClick's web site and specifically opt out. They never signed up for DoubleClick's tracking program, so most people were unaware that their web surfing habits were being cataloged and thus never knew to opt out.

> ## Does Your Browser Do Strong Encryption?
> The latest versions of both Netscape Navigator (4.*x* and 6.*x*) and Internet Explorer (6.*x*) support full-strength (128-bit) encryption when used to visit sites that support encryption. Some older browser versions only support a weak, 40-bit encryption scheme. If you are using an older browser, choose Help | About to find out what kind of encryption it supports. If it mentions "40-bit" or "International Strength" encryption, upgrade to a later version.

Thankfully, the Electronic Privacy Information Center (**www.epic.org**) sued DoubleClick and caused them to stop this rather sleazy practice. If the possibility of future weaseling like this bothers you—because advertising agencies continue to try and find new ways to watch what you're doing—both Netscape Navigator and IE let you control their use of cookies, including the option to disable the storage of all cookies.

However, disabling all cookies makes browsing more difficult because many sites need cookies to function properly. Instead, you may want to accept *first-party cookies* (which are stored for the web site's own use) and refuse *third-party cookies* (which are accessible by other web sites and can be used to track your movement from site to site and serve you appropriate advertisements). You can also accept only *session cookies*, which are stored only until you close your browser.

For instructions for controlling cookies in IE and Netscape Navigator, see the sections "Managing Cookies in Internet Explorer" and "Managing Cookies in Netscape Navigator" later in this chapter.

Blocking Offensive or Inappropriate Web Sites

Almost anything that people want to see, hear, or read is on the Web somewhere—and one of the less thrilling aspects of the Internet is that some people are mighty sick. You may decide that you want to block your browser's access to certain kinds of content because you find it offensive, don't want your children to see it, or don't want your workers to waste their time on it. Recent versions of popular browsers allow you to participate in a voluntary system for blocking offensive or inappropriate content.

How PICS Site-Blocking Systems Work

The World Wide Web Consortium (W3C, the same folks who maintain the HTML standards) has created a system called *Platform for Internet Content Selection (PICS)* for making web site ratings systems possible. Ratings organizations (such as the Recreational Software Advisory Council [RSAC] and SafeSurf) have created ratings systems based on questionnaires. When web site owners fill out the questionnaires, the ratings organizations issue ratings labels for their sites. The site owners display these labels on their web sites. Browsers such as Navigator and IE contain software that reads these labels and compares them to your stated standards of acceptability. Web pages whose ratings exceed your acceptable standards aren't displayed unless someone gives the appropriate password. As long as your children don't know the password, they have to ask you before they can see web sites that might be objectionable. The rest of this section fills in some of the details.

PICS, the Enabling Technology

It's a great idea with some flaws.

The Platform for Internet Content Selection (PICS) is an Internet protocol that enables ratings to be transferred and understood across the Internet. Basically, PICS associates a web page with a label containing information about its content. A browser reads the label first, compares it to criteria set by the user, and then decides whether to display the page.

PICS itself is not a ratings system; in theory, anyone could use PICS to rate web sites according to their values and standards, whatever those might happen to be. (Paul Resnick, who has written many articles on Internet filtering, has given the hypothetical example of rating pages for literary merit. But despite that, usually PICS is used to block kid-unfriendly sites.) Ratings systems based on PICS are called *PICS-compliant*. You can find out more about PICS at **www.w3.org/PICS**.

So what's the catch? There are two ways of attaching PICS rating labels to web pages, but only one of them works. In addition, the system requires that the people who own the web page *submit their own site* for rating and then embed the rating as an HTML tag within their page. That means exactly what you think it means: the conscientious sites that are concerned about children's welfare rate their pages scrupulously, thus sometimes barring legitimate content unnecessarily, and the fly-by-night sex sites and underground pages may not even bother to submit their pages at all.

(Incidentally, the other method involves someone creating a large database of approved web sites that your browser would check each page against, but nobody has done this, to the best of our knowledge.)

That leaves you with two options: you can set your browser to only accept pages that have PICS ratings, thus blocking those who haven't submitted their site to a PICS rater. Sounds good, but many legitimate sites (including the Children's Television Workshop, creators of *Sesame Street*, at **www.ctw.org**) haven't bothered to submit their sites, ensuring that your child may not be able to see a significant (yet inoffensive) portion of the Internet.

The other option, blocking only sites that have bothered to submit themselves as unsafe for family viewing—presents obvious problems. Still, either method may be better than nothing if you have children, and it can help restrict the sites you want your family to see.

E-mail Encryption

Electronic mail can pass through many computers on its way from sender to receiver. If your message is not encrypted, someone might be able to read it along the way. One popular program for protecting your mail is Pretty Good Privacy (PGP), originally developed by Philip Zimmermann. Unfortunately, PGP is in limbo at the time of this writing. Network Associates, the company that now owns the rights to PGP, stopped development before new versions for Windows XP and Macintosh OS X were released. Older versions are still available through the International PGP Home Page (**www.pgpi.com**) and MIT's PGP Distribution Site (**web.mit.edu/network/pgp.html**). There are also efforts to develop a free encryption program based on the Internet Engineering Task Force's OpenPGP specification (RFC2440). One such program is GNU Privacy Guard (GnuPG), which is available from **www.gnupg.org**, as well as from **www.pgpi.com**. Check these pages for the latest news on e-mail encryption.

If you have some elementary knowledge of programming, you might want to try writing you own encryption program. It's easier than it sounds. Visit **ciphersaber.gurus.com** to learn how.

Content-Rating Services: SafeSurf and RSAC

Although any organization *could* set up a PICS-compliant ratings system, rate the millions of pages on the Internet, and persuade the authors of those pages to display its rating labels, only a handful of organizations are making a major effort to do so. The two whose ratings systems are built into Netscape NetWatch are SafeSurf (**www.safesurf.com**) and the Recreational Software Advisory Council (RSAC, at **www.rsac .org**). Microsoft's Content Advisor includes only RSAC's system. (Microsoft is a founding sponsor of RSAC.)

Other ratings services exist and can be added to NetWatch or Content Advisor by downloading a RAT file from the service's web page. W3C maintains a list of the PICS-compliant ratings systems that it knows about at **www.w3.org/PICS/raters**.

SafeSurf and RSAC arose in very different ways. SafeSurf is a parents' group trying to make the Internet a safe and useful tool for children. (Its web site is a good reference for finding links to other kid-friendly and educational web sites.) RSAC is a nonprofit corporation created by the Software Publishers Association together with computer and entertainment powerhouses, such as Microsoft, Disney, and IBM. RSAC's original mission was to issue a ratings system for computer games, and it later extended its game-rating system to the Internet. What the two organizations have in common is a belief that a voluntary rating-and-blocking system for web sites is better than government censorship.

How SafeSurf and RSACi Rate Their Content

At the heart of SafeSurf and *RSACi (Recreational Software Advisory Council for the Internet)* is a set of categories of possibly offensive content, with defined levels for each category.

The RSACi system (an adaptation of RSAC's computer-game rating system) has four categories (language, nudity, sex, and violence) and five levels for each category (from "0–none" to 4). The SafeSurf system has nine categories (profanity, heterosexual themes, homosexual themes, nudity, violence, intolerance, glorifying drug use, other adult themes, and gambling) and nine levels for each category (ranging from "1–subtle innuendo" to "9–explicit and crude or explicitly inviting participation"). The Netscape NetWatch web site gives the explicit definition of each level in each category for both RSACi (**home.netscape.com/comprod/products/communicator/netwatch/b_rsaci.html**) and SafeSurf (**home.netscape.com/comprod/products/communicator/netwatch/c_safesurf.html**).

Web site owners rate their sites voluntarily by going to the rating organization's web site and filling out a form. To rate a web site with SafeSurf, go to **www.safesurf.com/classify**. To rate with RSACi, go to **www.rsac.org**. Once a site is rated, the rating organization e-mails the web site owner a piece of HTML code to attach to the rated web pages. This piece of code is the rating tag that is read by browsers.

Other PICS-compliant ratings services include Safe for Kids (**www.weburbia.com/safe**), and the Vancouver Webpages Ratings Service (**vancouver-webpages.com/VWP1.0**). These systems resemble RSACi and SafeSurf in that the web site owners have to rate their own sites (though Vancouver's system is unique in having some positive categories, such as educational content and environmental awareness). None of these systems is preinstalled in IE's Content Advisor or Netscape's NetWatch, but any can be added by downloading the ratings file (.rat) from the rating service's web site—which we show you how to do in the next section.

PICS-Reading Browsers: Navigator's NetWatch and Internet Explorer's Content Advisor

PICS-compliant ratings systems would be useless if browsers couldn't read the PICS labels. The most recent versions of the two programs that dominate the browser market, Microsoft's Internet Explorer and Netscape's Navigator, do so. Internet Explorer contains a component called *Content Advisor*, and Navigator has a similar component called *NetWatch*. Each lets you set your own acceptable rating levels. After you enable Content Advisor or NetWatch (and choose a password), it blocks web sites whose ratings exceed your selected level of acceptability, unless the password is given.

Both browsers support RSACi and SafeSurf. Content Advisor comes with RSACi already enabled—but you can download a file to enable SafeSurf as well. NetWatch comes with both RSACi and SafeSurf. You can use more than one ratings system simultaneously.

At present, both Content Advisor and NetWatch suffer from the same deficiency: neither has a memory. If you decide that a particular web site is sufficiently worthwhile to allow your child to access it, even though it is unrated or has a high rating for some objectionable material, you can only give once-and-for-all permission in IE 6 and above.

Unrated Web Sites

The most difficult task in establishing a ratings system is to get the cooperation of the web site owners. Sites that are trying to be kid-friendly, such as Yahoo's Yahooligans (**www.yahooligans.com**), have a motivation to cooperate with the system. And adult sites, such as Playboy's (**www.playboy.com**), are motivated to support voluntary ratings in order to avoid government censorship or possible lawsuits. However, for the broad range of sites in between Yahooligans and Playboy, the motivation to rate is less clear, and cooperation has so far been variable. The Weather Channel site (**www.weather .com**) has an RSACi rating, whereas CNN (**cnn.com**) does not.

RSAC claims that tens of thousands of sites have been rated and that 5,000 more are rated every month, but given the size of the Web and the rate at which the number of web sites is increasing, it's not clear whether RSAC is gaining or losing ground in the battle to get the Web rated. SafeSurf gave us no estimate, but our own browsing experience convinced us that SafeSurf has rated even fewer sites.

Recommendations for PICS Web Site Blocking

The two biggest decisions that you need to make regarding PICS-compliant web site–blocking programs (such as Content Advisor and NetWatch) are whether to use them at all—and if you do use them, whether to block unrated web sites.

Currently, so many sites are unrated that if you *don't* block them, you really aren't protecting anyone. Playboy's web site may be rated with both RSACi and SafeSurf, but Penthouse's (**www.penthouse.com**) wasn't rated by either service when we looked, and neither was Bianca's Smut Shack (**www.bianca.com/shack**). No actively predatory web site is going to bother getting itself rated. On the other hand, if you do block unrated sites, you make the Web a much smaller place: no CNN, no Library of Congress (**lcweb.loc.gov**), no Children's Television Workshop—just to name a few of the many web sites that were unrated by either RSACi or SafeSurf when we last checked.

Our conclusion is that Content Advisor and NetWatch are useful mainly for very small children, who are going to want to visit a small list of web sites over and over. Teenagers would find the blocking of unrated sites very restrictive, and most of the worthwhile content of the Web would be lost to them (unless a sudden upturn in the number of rated sites occurs). Moreover, children who are computer-smart enough to download a second copy of Navigator and install it in an obscure directory, or to simply delete all RAT files, are not going to be constrained by the rating systems unless they want to be.

For children of an in-between age, make a list of the things that you want them to be able to do on the Web, and look for rated web sites that allow them to do it. (The simplest way to check whether a site is rated is to turn on Content Advisor or NetWatch and try to look at the site.) After you determine exactly what you are giving up by using a rating system, you will be in a better position to decide whether to use one.

Other Site-Blocking Options

Although NetWatch and Content Advisor are free components of Navigator and Internet Explorer, respectively, there are other commercial products that filter the web sites that your browser can receive. A list of the products available, with links to the web sites of the companies marketing the products, can be found at The Internet Filter Assessment Project (TIFAP), at **www.bluehighways.com/tifap**. TIFAP is a project created and run by librarians, who have a special interest in Internet filtering, now that many libraries contain public-access Internet terminals.

Commercial blocking packages may include access to proprietary databases of "good" and "bad" URLs, and may block pages based on the presence of specific words. (The TIFAP report contains an amusing story about a program that included "XXX" among its objectionable character strings, and so refused to display anything about Super Bowl XXX.)

Security in Internet Explorer

IE provides two systems for controlling security on your computer: zones and content blocking.

Configuring IE's Security Zones

The central concept of IE's security policy is the *security zone*. There are four zones: Local Intranet, Trusted Sites, Internet, and Restricted Sites. To establish your security policy, you assign web sites to security zones and then choose a security level (High, Medium, Low, or Custom) for each zone. Default settings make this process invisible, unless you choose to tinker with it. As you browse the Web, the status bar displays the security zone of the current page.

What Security Zones Mean

Internet Explorer has the following four security zones:

- **Local Intranet zone** This consists of web pages that you can access without going through a proxy server. In general, these are resources on your home LAN or within your company or place of business. You may not have any web sites in this zone if you are not on a network and connect to the Internet through a modem. The default security setting is Medium.

- **Trusted Sites zone** This consists of sites that you trust as much as you trust the files on your hard drive. The default security setting is Low.

- **Internet zone**   This consists of web sites that you have not assigned to any other zone. The default security setting is Medium.

- **Restricted Sites zone**   This consists of web sites that you have explicitly decided not to trust. The default security setting is High.

What IE Security Levels Mean

When you set a zone's security level, you actually are making numerous decisions simultaneously. You can set the security level of a zone to High, Medium, Medium-Low, or Low, to use a pre-defined set of settings for that zone. Alternatively, you can set the security level to Custom, which allows you to make the technical decisions one by one. If you choose Custom, you can disable or enable a range of features, including ActiveX controls, file downloads, and Java applets.

Changing a Zone's Security Level in IE

To see a list of the current settings for each security zone:

1. In Internet Explorer, choose Tools | Internet Options. Click the Security tab, shown in Figure 20-1. (On Macs, select Edit | Preferences to open the

Figure 20-1.   *Internet Explorer divides the Web into zones to which you can assign security levels.*

Preferences dialog box and choose the Web Browser/Security panel from the category list.)

2. Select the zone.

3. Choose the Custom Level button to display the Security Settings dialog box:

After you examine the settings, you can (if you want) reset to one of the default security levels by setting the Reset To box at the bottom of the Settings dialog box to High, Medium, Medium-Low, or Low and clicking the Reset button. If you don't want to change any of the settings, click Cancel.

Security settings are divided into six categories: ActiveX Controls And Plug-Ins, Downloads, User Authentication, Java, Scripting, and Miscellaneous. For each security setting, you choose one of the following:

- **Disable**   Internet Explorer will not do the activity.
- **Enable**   The activity is allowed to happen without warning.
- **Prompt**   Internet Explorer asks you whether to do the activity.

A few settings don't allow the Prompt option, and a few use other options.

Assigning Web Sites to IE Security Zones

Any web site that you haven't explicitly assigned to some other security zone is, by default, assigned to the Internet zone. Therefore, you can't add web sites to the Internet zone explicitly. Removing a web site from some other zone automatically adds it to the Internet zone.

To assign a web site to (or remove it from) one of the other security zones:

1. Choose Tools | Internet Options from the Internet Explorer menu. In the Internet Options dialog box, click the Security tab (shown back in Figure 20-1). Macintosh users select Edit | Preferences to open the Preferences dialog box and choose the Web Browser/Security panel from the category list. (The Macintosh version is functionally identical.)

2. Click the zone and click the Sites button. If you are adding sites to (or removing them from) the Trusted or Restricted zones, go to step 4.

3. If you are adding sites to (or removing sites from) the Local Intranet zone, you see a dialog box with three check boxes: Include All Local (Intranet) Sites Not Listed In Other Zones, Include All Sites That Bypass The Proxy Server, and Include All Network Paths (UNCs). (The third choice doesn't exist in the Mac version.) Include or exclude sites fitting these descriptions by checking or clearing the boxes. To add or remove specific sites, click the Advanced button.

4. A dialog box appears listing the web sites assigned to this zone. To remove a site from the zone, select it on the Web Sites list and click the Remove button.

5. To add a web site to the zone in Windows, type its URL (complete with the protocol—**http://** for regular web sites and **https://** for secure web sites) into the Add This Web Site To The Zone box and then click the Add button. On a Macintosh, click the Add button and type the URL into the Add This Web Site To The Zone box when it appears.

Note   *IE normally refuses to add a site to the Trusted zone unless the site uses a secure server and its URL starts with* **https://**. *If you'd like to relax this restriction and add other sites to the Trusted zone, uncheck the Require Server Verification (https:) For All Sites In This Zone check box, at the bottom of the Trusted Zone dialog box.*

Setting Other IE Security Policies

Not all security policies are set by choosing security levels for the various security zones. Several decisions about Java and ActiveX can be changed without changing security levels, particularly in the Macintosh version.

Controlling IE's Security Warning Messages

Internet Explorer can be set up to warn you before it does anything potentially dangerous. Most of these warnings are set up by choosing Prompt when you customize the settings of security zones. (Refer to "Changing a Zone's Security Level in IE" earlier in this chapter.) But a few warnings are controlled from the Security section of the Advanced tab of the Internet Options dialog box—choose Tools | Internet Options, click the Advanced tab, and scroll down until you come to the Security heading, followed by a list of check boxes. (On a Mac, these warnings are controlled from the Web Browser/Security panel of the Internet Explorer Preferences dialog box.)

In Windows, you can choose to be warned about the following:

- A submitted form is being redirected to a server other than the one it came from.
- Internet Explorer is changing between secure and insecure modes.
- The certificate that a site is using to establish a secure connection is invalid.

On a Macintosh, you can choose to be warned

- When entering a page that is secure
- When entering a page that isn't secure
- Before submitting a form that isn't secure
- Before submitting a form through e-mail
- Before downloading an ActiveX control

Managing Cookies in Internet Explorer

Cookies are small files that your browser stores on your hard disk so that a web site can store a small amount of information about you. (See the section "What Are Cookies?" earlier in this chapter.) Internet Explorer gives you the choice of three policies for handling cookies: accept all cookies (default option), refuse all cookies, and accept or refuse cookies on a cookie-by-cookie basis. The Mac version gives you a fourth choice (which we prefer to the other three): accept or reject cookies on a web-site-by-web-site basis.

In IE 5 and 6, cookie management is part of the privacy settings for the Internet security zone. The defaults are always to accept cookies in Low and Medium security levels, and to disable them in High levels. If this isn't what you want, choose Tools | Internet Options from IE's menu bar, click the Privacy tab, and slide the Settings slider up (for higher security) or down (for lower security). Alternatively, click the Advanced button to display the Advanced Privacy Settings dialog box:

Click the Override Automatic Cookie Handling check box and choose whether to accept, block, or prompt you when a web site wants to store a first-party or third-party cookie. Click the Always Allow Session Cookies check box if you are willing to accept all cookies that last only for the current browser session.

In Windows, IE cookies are stored as text files in a folder called *Cookies*, located in C:\Windows (if user profiles aren't being used on your system) or in C:\Windows\ Profiles*username*. Some cookies may also be in C:\Documents And Settings*username*\ Cookies, C:\Documents And Settings\Default User\Cookies, C:\Windows\Temporary Internet Files (or one of its subfolders), or C:\Windows\Profiles*username*\Temporary Internet Files (or one of its subfolders). Reading a cookie as a text file probably will not tell you much, though it may set your mind at ease to realize just how little information is there. Delete cookies from your system by deleting the corresponding text files.

Managing Java and JavaScript in IE

Java and JavaScript are programming languages that are used to give some web pages advanced features. (See Chapter 17.) Java policy is controlled by the security level settings in the Java and Scripting sections. Refer to "What IE Security Levels Mean," earlier in this chapter, in which we describe Java settings that can be changed independently of the security levels.

Managing Java in Windows IE   You can deactivate Java and JavaScript in the Windows version of IE from the Advanced tab of the Internet Options dialog box. (Choose Tools | Internet Options and then click the Advanced tab.) The check boxes Java Console Enabled, Java JIT Compiler Enabled, and Java Logging Enabled control Internet Explorer's use of Java.

Managing Java in Macintosh IE   In the Mac version of IE, Java is managed from the Web Browser/Java panel of the Internet Explorer Preferences dialog box. Enable or disable Java with the Enable Java check box. The Java Options section of the Java tab has check boxes to select whether to log Java output and Java exceptions. It's a good policy to select these boxes.

The Apple Java Virtual Machine (JVM) has policies that are also controlled from the Web Browser/Java tab. The Byte-code Verification drop-down list gives you three options for verifying Java applets: Check All Code, Check Remote Code, and Don't Check Code. The default, Check All Code, is safest.

The Network Access drop-down list controls whether a Java applet running on your machine can exchange information over the Internet. The default, Applet Host Access, allows the applet to exchange data with the server that it came from. No Network

Access is safer, of course, but disables some potentially useful applets. Unrestricted Access lets an applet exchange data with any server on the Internet, which for most people is an unnecessary risk.

The Restrict Access to Non-Java Class Files box is checked by default. It prevents Java applets from reading or changing non-Java files on your computer. This is a good safety precaution; unless you know that you want to run a particular applet that needs file access, leave the box checked.

Managing ActiveX Controls in IE

Internet Explorer stores all ActiveX controls in a single folder. In Windows, this folder is C:\Windows\ Downloaded Program Files. On a Mac, it is System Folder/Extensions/ ActiveX Controls. Check this folder periodically to see what applications IE has downloaded. Deleting files from this folder uninstalls the associated applications. (ActiveX is described in Chapter 17.)

Disabling ActiveX controls entirely isn't a bad idea. You seldom run into them, except on web sites that are somehow connected with Microsoft (like MSNBC); because ActiveX controls have fewer restrictions than Java applets, they open a large can of worms. On the Mac, you can disable ActiveX controls with a single click: on the Web Browser/Web Content panel (under Web Browser) of the Internet Explorer Preferences dialog box, uncheck Enable ActiveX.

Disabling ActiveX on Windows versions of IE is possible, but more difficult, because ActiveX controls are controlled by the security level settings. To disable ActiveX controls for a security zone without affecting anything else, you have to customize the security level of that zone. (Refer to "Changing a Zone's Security Level in IE" earlier in this chapter.)

Blocking Web Sites with IE's Content Advisor

Internet Explorer includes the web site–blocking application Content Advisor. Content Advisor works with any PICS-compatible ratings system and comes with the Recreational Software Advisory Council for the Internet (RSACi) ratings system already installed. For a general discussion of PICS and PICS-compatible ratings systems, see the section "Blocking Offensive or Inappropriate Web Sites" earlier in this chapter.

Enabling and Disabling Content Advisor in IE

To set up Content Advisor for the first time, display the Content Advisor dialog box. (Choose Tools | Internet Options in IE, click the Content tab, and then click the Enable button.) On Macs, select Edit | Preferences to open the Preferences dialog box and choose the Web Browser/Ratings panel from the category list. In either case, click the Settings button to display this dialog box:

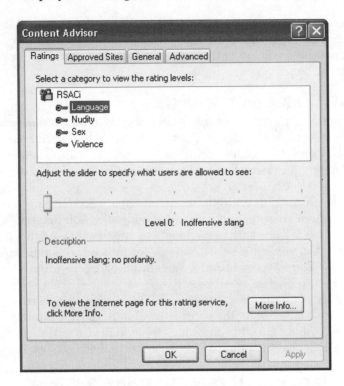

In Windows Me and earlier, Content Advisor makes you choose a password. In Windows XP and on Macs, the default password is blank, and you can set a password by clicking the Create Password button. (In Windows, it's on the General tab of the Content Advisor dialog box.)

IE initially includes only the RSACi ratings system, and the default settings are the most restrictive. If this is what you want, you can click OK and be done. Otherwise, you can use the Content Advisor dialog box to change the settings, as described in the section "Changing IE Content Advisor Preferences" later in this chapter.

To disable Content Advisor, open the Content tab of the Internet Options dialog box as you did when you enabled Content Advisor. Click the Disable button and enter your Content Advisor password when requested.

Enabling Content Advisor again (after disabling it) is simpler than setting it up the first time: click the Enable button on the Content tab of the Internet Options dialog box and then give the supervisor password when asked. Content Advisor remembers your previous settings.

Adding or Removing Ratings Systems in IE

Before you add a ratings system other than RSACi to Content Advisor, you should enable Content Advisor, as described in the preceding section.

Ratings systems are described by RAT files. Thus, to add a ratings system to Content Advisor, you first need to get a copy of the rating system's corresponding RAT file. (SafeSurf's ratings file, for example, is SafeSurf.rat. Based on SafeSurf's web page at **www.safesurf.com**, you might guess that this file works only for Windows versions of IE, but this isn't true.) Typically, the RAT file can be downloaded from the web site of the ratings organization. After you download the RAT file, save it. In Windows, the installation process is simplest if you save the RAT file in C:\Windows\System folder.

After you obtain the RAT file of the ratings system that you want to install, you need to tell Content Advisor about it. To do this in Windows,

1. Go to the Content tab of the Internet Options dialog box. (Choose Tools | Internet Options in IE and click the Content tab.)

2. Click the Settings button and then enter your Content Advisor password to display the Content Advisor dialog box.

3. Click the Ratings Systems button on the General tab of the Content Advisor dialog box. You see the Ratings Systems dialog box. In this box, you find a list of the RAT files that correspond to the ratings systems that Content Advisor knows about.

4. Click the Add button.

5. When the Open Ratings System File dialog box appears, browse until you find the RAT file of the ratings system that you want to add. When you select this file, the Open Ratings System File dialog box disappears, and the new RAT file appears in the Ratings Systems dialog box.

6. Click OK to return to the Content Advisor dialog box. Click the Ratings tab to set the blocking levels for your new ratings system.

To remove a ratings system from Content Advisor under Windows, display the Ratings Systems dialog box by repeating steps 1 through 3. Select the corresponding RAT file on the list in the Ratings Systems dialog box and then click the Remove button.

On Macs, you add or remove ratings systems from Content Advisor from the Web Browser/Ratings panel of the Internet Explorer Preferences dialog box (select Edit | Preferences). To remove a ratings system, select it from the Ratings Settings section of the Web Browser/Ratings tab of the dialog box and click the Remove Service button. If you have set a password, Content Advisor asks for it before removing the ratings system. To add a ratings system on Macs, click the Add Service button and find the service's RAT file in the window that appears. Click Open to install the ratings service.

Any smart teenager will figure out that the backdoor way to uninstall a Content Advisor ratings system is to delete its RAT file. No password is required. Internet Explorer then treats sites rated by that ratings service as unrated sites.

Changing IE Content Advisor Preferences

Content Advisor's default settings are its most restrictive. You can change these settings, change your Content Advisor password, and choose whether to let users see unrated sites.

Changing Content Advisor Preferences in Windows IE   To makes changes to the ratings levels, open the Content tab of the Internet Options dialog box as you did when you set up Content Advisor. Click the Settings button and enter your supervisor password, when requested. When the Content Advisor dialog box appears, click the category (Language, Nudity, Sex, or Violence) whose rating you want to change and then move the slider that appears to the desired level.

To allow (or not allow) users to see unrated web sites, open the Content Advisor dialog box and click the General tab. One check box on this tab enables users to view unrated web sites without the supervisor password; the other check box allows viewing of unrated sites with a supervisor password. Make your changes and type your supervisor password when prompted.

To change the supervisor password, click the Change Password button on the General tab of the Content Advisor dialog box. Enter the old password into the first line of the Change Supervisor Password box and enter the new password into the second and third lines of the Change Supervisor Password box.

Changing IE Content Advisor Preferences on a Macintosh   To change the Content Advisor rating levels on a Mac, open the Web Browser/Ratings panel of the Internet Explorer Preferences dialog box. Find the category whose rating you want to change and make a new choice in the corresponding drop-down list.

To make decisions about unrated sites, click the Options button. One check box on this tab enables users to view unrated web sites without the supervisor password; the other allows viewing of unrated sites with a supervisor password. Make your changes and enter your supervisor password when prompted.

To change the supervisor password, click the Change Password button. Enter the old password into the first line of the Change Supervisor Password box and enter the new password into the second and third lines of the Change Supervisor Password box.

Browsing with Content Advisor Enabled in IE

As long as you view only rated web pages whose rating is within your acceptability criteria, Content Advisor is invisible. When a user attempts to see a web site that violates your criteria, Content Advisor displays a dialog box listing the areas in which the site's ratings exceed the criteria and requests the Content Advisor password before continuing:

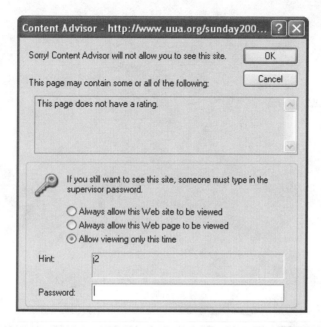

To allow IE to display the requested page, type the Content Advisor password into the Password box and click OK. Otherwise, click Cancel to return to the previously displayed page.

Security in Netscape Navigator

Some choices that Netscape Navigator makes for you have implications for your system's use of disk space or its security—implications that more-advanced users may want to consider. Navigator allows you some opportunities to "get under the hood" and make choices about caching web pages, accepting cookies, and running applets in Java.

The Security Info window enables you to review security information related to the current page (whether it was encrypted, for example). Open this page by clicking the lock icon on the left or right end of the status bar. Netscape Navigator 4.7's Security Info window is shown in Figure 20-2, and the Netscape 6.2 version is shown in Figure 20-3. (Click the Security tab when the Page Info window appears.)

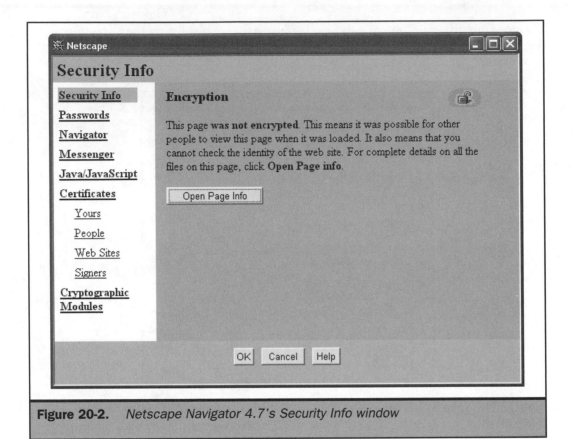

Figure 20-2.   Netscape Navigator 4.7's Security Info window

Managing Cookies in Netscape Navigator

Navigator lets you control how it uses cookies. The default option is to accept all cookies. You also have the option to refuse all cookies, be asked whether to accept or refuse cookies on a case-by-case basis or accept only those cookies that get sent back to the originating server. For an explanation of what cookies are, see "What Are Cookies?" earlier in this chapter.

Select Edit | Preferences to open the Preferences dialog box. In Netscape 6.2, double-click Privacy & Security from the Category list and then click Cookies from the list that appears. In Netscape 4.7, click Advanced from the Category list. The right panel lists the three cookie-policy options as radio buttons: Accept All Cookies, Accept Only Cookies That Get Send Back To The Originating Server (that is, first-party cookies), and Disable Cookies. In addition, a check box controls whether Navigator should warn you before accepting a cookie. The warning includes the option to refuse the cookie. In Netscape 6.2, you can also choose to view a list of stored cookies.

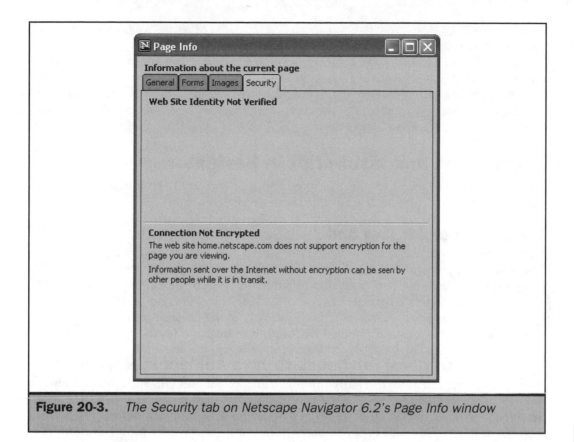

Figure 20-3.   *The Security tab on Netscape Navigator 6.2's Page Info window*

Navigator stores your cookies in a text file named Cookies.txt. In the default Windows installation, this file is in the folder C:\Program Files\Netscape\Users\ *username*. On a Mac the file is stored in your profile folder, and it's easiest to search for the Cookies.txt file. Delete cookies from your system by deleting the corresponding text files.

Managing Navigator's Caches of Web Pages

Navigator stores some of the pages that you view, so that they can be redisplayed quickly if you return to them. In general, this speeds up the browsing experience, but if you are running short of disk space, you may decide to limit or eliminate these caches. You should also empty them if you don't want anyone to find these web pages on your computer.

Navigator has two caches for web pages: a small but extremely fast cache in your computer's memory (RAM), and a larger but slower one in the Windows folder

C:\Program Files\Netscape\Users*username*\Cache. On Macs the cache is stored in your Profile folder.

To empty or change the size of either cache, select Edit | Preferences to open the Preferences dialog box and then choose the Advanced/Cache panel from the Category list. The panel contains windows displaying the size of each cache. You can resize a cache by typing a new number into the corresponding window, or empty the cache by clicking the corresponding Clear button.

Managing Java and JavaScript in Navigator

Java and JavaScript are programming languages that are used to give some web pages advanced features. They are discussed in more detail in Chapter 17.

Turning On or Off Java and JavaScript in Navigator

The simplest way to avoid any security issue connected with Java is to deactivate it. The downside: you lose some of the more advanced functionality of web pages, and you won't be able to use NetWatch (described in the section "Blocking Web Sites with NetWatch" later in this chapter). If you want to deactivate Java and JavaScript, select Edit | Preferences and click the Advanced category in the Preferences dialog box. Two check boxes, Enable Java and Enable JavaScript, turn Java and JavaScript on or off.

Granting Additional Privileges to Java Applets in Navigator

Java applets run in a *sandbox,* a software construction that prevents the applets from having direct access to the resources on your computer or network. If your Java virtual machine (JVM) is working properly, even a malicious applet should not be able to do significant harm. That said, security holes in Java are occasionally found. Netscape patches them as fast as it can. This is a good reason to make sure that you are running the most recent available version of Navigator (whether in the 4.*x* or 6.*x* series).

Some applets may require access to more of your system's resources than the JVM provides. So far this is fairly rare, though it may become more frequent as increasingly complex applets are written. Navigator allows you to grant these privileges, should you decide to do so. In general, we recommend extreme caution in granting these privileges, which are comparable to those enjoyed by ActiveX Controls under IE.

A privilege-requesting applet must be digitally signed and carry a digital certificate (which are described in Chapter 32). Navigator keeps track of all applets, their certificates, and the privileges they have been granted. To examine these certificates in Netscape 4.7 and review or revoke the privileges granted, open the Security Info window by clicking the lock icon on the status bar. Click Java/JavaScript in the left pane of the Security Info. The right pane displays a list of vendors, distributors, and web sites whose Java applets or JavaScript scripts have been granted privileges. (Our own list is blank. Don't be surprised if yours is also.)

To remove an entry from this list (and thereby revoke the privileges granted), select the entry and click the Remove button. To examine the certificate, click View

Certificate. To examine precisely which privileges the vendor, distributor, or web site's applets and scripts have been given or to change those privileges, select an entry from the list and click Edit Privileges.

In Netscape 6.2, choose Edit | Preferences to display the Preferences dialog box, click the Privacy & Security category, and click the Certificates subcategory. Click the Manage Certificates button to display the Certificate Manager window, listing the certificates you've installed.

Blocking Web Sites with NetWatch

Netscape Navigator 4.7 includes the web site–blocking application NetWatch, which works with the PICS-compatible ratings systems SafeSurf and Recreational Software Advisory Council for the Internet (RSACi). For a general discussion of PICS and PICS-compatible ratings systems, see "Blocking Offensive or Inappropriate Web Sites" earlier in this chapter.

Note   *Netscape 6.2 doesn't include NetWatch.*

Enabling NetWatch in Navigator

To begin the setup of NetWatch, choose Help | NetWatch from the menu bar. Navigator then opens the Netscape web page that explains NetWatch, **home.netscape.com/communicator/netwatch**. (You can also go to this URL directly.) This web page explains PICS and the two ratings services that NetWatch uses—SafeSurf and RSACi. Near the top of this page is a button labeled "Click To Set Up NetWatch."

Note   *Java and JavaScript must be enabled for Navigator to work with NetWatch enabled. To check or change these settings, select Edit | Preferences and choose Advanced in the Category list.*

Clicking the button takes you to a simple form that sets up NetWatch. The form asks you to set up one or both of the preinstalled ratings systems, and to make choices of ratings levels. These systems and levels are explained in "Blocking Offensive or Inappropriate Web Sites" earlier in this chapter and from links on the page that you view by selecting Help | NetWatch. At the bottom of the form is an Allow Users To See Unrated Sites check box, an option discussed in "Unrated Web Sites" earlier in this chapter. After you make your choices, you need to choose a NetWatch password, which is the password that users need to disable NetWatch for a single session or to change the NetWatch settings. To turn on NetWatch, select the NetWatch On radio button at the bottom of the form and click the Save Changes button.

Disabling NetWatch or Changing Its Settings

You can disable NetWatch or change its settings by selecting Help | NetWatch again. This returns you to the page from which you set up Navigator. Click the Set Up NetWatch button, enter your NetWatch password, and click the Log In button. If your password is correct, you see the Setup form to fill out again.

To change passwords, proceed as in the previous paragraph, but click the Change Password button instead of the Log In button. You are asked to type your new password twice. Click the Change Password button at the bottom of the form to complete the process.

If NetWatch prevents you from viewing a page that you ask for, you can disable NetWatch for a single session from the NetWatch Protection Alert screen that it displays. Click the Disable NetWatch For This Session link and give the NetWatch password when requested.

 If you forget your NetWatch password, don't call Netscape. They don't know your password and can't help you. See the section "Circumventing NetWatch in Navigator," coming right up.

Browsing with NetWatch Enabled

NetWatch is invisible as long as the web sites that you visit either satisfy your acceptability ratings or are unrated (and you allow the viewing of unrated sites). When anyone using your NetWatch-enabled user profile tries to open a page that violates your acceptability ratings or is unrated (and you have not allowed the viewing of unrated sites), Navigator doesn't display the page. Instead, Navigator displays the NetWatch Protection Alert message, explaining that the page violates your standards.

From this screen, you may view the page's ratings, disable NetWatch for this session (if you have the NetWatch password), or change the NetWatch settings. (See the preceding two sections.)

Circumventing NetWatch in Navigator

NetWatch settings are maintained separately for each Netscape Communicator user profile. This is both a convenience and a hole in the system. You can use this hole to work around NetWatch if you forget the password, but if you have clever children, they also can work around NetWatch.

The user profile dependence of NetWatch is convenient if you are sharing a computer with small children because you can establish a password-protected user profile for yourself (except in Netscape Communicator's Macintosh version) and a password-free user profile for your children. You can then set up NetWatch on your children's user profile without interfering with your own browsing. To gain access to forbidden web sites, a child would have to know either your user profile password or the NetWatch password.

A hole in the system is that any user can create a new user profile, and the new profile is free from NetWatch restrictions. (See the section on sharing Navigator with other users in Chapter 18.)

Inspecting Saved Form Data in Navigator

Netscape 6 can remember information that you type when filling out forms at web sites. The information Netscape can save includes your name, address, telephone number, e-mail address, credit card number, and social security number. You can see just what data Netscape has already saved by selecting Edit | Preferences to open the Preferences dialog box, choosing the Privacy & Security/Forms category, and clicking the Forms subcategory. Then click the View Stored Form Data button in the right panel to display the Form Manager window. Click on each category of information displayed to see what Netscape is saving and to correct errors or delete data you don't want saved.

If you don't want Netscape to collect the information that you type, providing it the next time you need to fill out a similar form, you can turn this feature off. On the Preferences dialog box, in the Privacy & Security category, Forms subcategory, clear the Save Form Data From Web Pages When Completing Forms check box.

Changing Navigator's Security Warnings and Encryption Options

Navigator is set up to warn you whenever you are about to do something that has security implications, such as send unencrypted information over the Internet. Depending on how risky your browsing habits are and your general attitudes about security, these warnings may either be important reminders or annoying nuisances. To choose which actions you want to be warned about in Netscape 6.2, select Edit | Preferences to open the Preferences dialog box, choose the Privacy & Security category, choose the SSL (Secure Sockets Layer) subcategory, and then make your choices from the SSL Warnings check boxes. In Netscape 4.7, select Communicator | Tools | Security Info (or click the lock icon on the status bar), click Navigator on the list of the categories, and choose from the Show A Warning Before check boxes.

In Netscape 6.2, the SSL subcategory of Privacy & Security also allows you to select what encryption technology you will accept when visiting a secure site. (In Netscape 4.7, choose Communicator | Tools | Security Info and click Navigator.) Those who are particularly security conscious may wish to uncheck Enable SSL Version 2 because this version has security issues that have been fixed in version 3. The security conscious may also wish to click the Edit Ciphers button and uncheck the buttons that offer 40-bit, 56-bit, and single DES encryption. Triple DES is safe and should be left checked. Clearing these options may limit your access to some web sites, however.

The
Complete
Reference

Chapter 21

Searching the Web

L ooking for information on the Internet without a guide is like searching for a book in a library without a card catalog. This chapter describes how to find what you're looking for on the Internet, whether you're searching for web pages on a specific topic, the e-mail address of a friend, or information on a particular company.

What Are Search Engines?

Back in the old days (the 1980s), the Internet was primarily a research medium. Files were stored separately, with no way to go from one file to another easily. A few systems appeared (Gopher and WAIS) to make it easier to find things on the Internet. In 1989, Tim Berners-Lee developed a network of files connected by hypertext links and dubbed it the World Wide Web. The popularity of the Web exploded after the creation of user-friendly browser applications that enabled people to view text and graphics and to jump quickly from page to page. The next thing that was needed was a way for users to find what they wanted, and that's why search engines were created.

A *search engine* is a database application that retrieves information, based on words or a phrase you enter. How do web-based search engines work? A web search engine employs a program called a *search agent* (or a *spider*) that goes out and looks for information on web pages. This information is indexed and stored in a huge database. When you conduct a search, the search engine looks through its database to find entries that match the information you entered. Then the search engine displays a list of the web pages it determines are most relevant to your search criteria.

How Do Search Engines Work?

Dozens of search engines are available on the Web. Each search engine gathers information a little differently. Some engines scan the entire web page; others focus on the page title; some analyze the references from one web page to another; still others read keywords and information included in *meta tags* (tags that include keywords about the page) on the web page. These different methods are the reason you can get different results from different search engines. Popular search engines include Google (**www.google.com**), MSN Search (**search.msn.com**), AltaVista (**www.altavista.com**), and Yahoo (**www.yahoo.com**).

Most search engines go beyond just searching for web pages. Some search engines allow you to search for information from Usenet newsgroups (described in Chapter 11) or for specific types of information, such as pictures or sound files.

Tip *If you are the author of a web page and want to know how to get your page noticed by a search engine, review the Help file of each search engine. Most search engines provide information that tells you how to code your web pages so they will be included in the search engine's database. See Chapter 31 for more information about building traffic to your web site.*

Although the way each search engine gathers information is unique, all search engines share a common purpose—to help you find the information you're looking for.

 If you're interested in keeping up with the latest news about search engines or in reading reviews and comparisons of search engines, visit the Search Engine Watch page at **www.searchenginewatch.com**. *Search engines rise and fall in popularity as innovators develop new methods of indexing and retrieving web site information. Google, the most popular search engine, is a relative latecomer.*

Search Result Rankings

How does a search engine determine which query results to list first? Search engines have formulas they use to rank each page they index, and their ranking methods consider the number of times a word appears on the page, the word's position on the page (words near the top of a page give it a higher ranking), and whether the word is included in the page's title or meta tags. They may also consider *backlinks*—the pages that link back to a site—and how popular a page has been with previous searchers.

Top rankings, though, are frequently available to the highest bidder. Other than Google, most search engine results show *sponsored sites*—web pages of organizations that paid for a high ranking—ahead of other pages. Some search engines do disclose that these sponsored pages bought their way to the top of the rank by referring to them as "sponsor matches" or "partner link results," but others neglect to acknowledge the profit motive behind their rankings.

What Are Web Directories?

A *web directory* (or *web guide*) is a web site that categorizes web pages so you can browse links to web pages by topic. For example, the Yahoo web directory (**www.yahoo.com**) includes categories for Arts and Humanities, Business and Economy, Computers and Internet, Education, and a dozen others. Each of these major categories contains many subcategories: for example, if you click the Recreation and Sports category, you see Sports, Games, Travel, Fitness, Outdoors, and many other subcategories. Keep clicking categories to see their subcategories until you find the specific types of web pages you are looking for.

The advantage of a web directory over a search engine is that human beings have categorized the web pages, so all the links in a category usually belong there. Web directories are great for browsing when you don't know the exact name of what you are looking for. For example, if you want to know which gourmet shops sell merchandise online, you can browse to the page listing online gourmet stores without knowing the exact name of a store and without stumbling over other food-related sites.

On the other hand, search engines are quicker than web directories if you are looking for information about a specific, unusual term. For example, if you need pages

---

The Open Directory Project

During the late 1990s, many web directory sites created and maintained their own proprietary directories. Eventually the labor costs of keeping these directories up-to-date became prohibitive for some, and a number of web directory sites began to use a large, nonproprietary directory called the Open Directory Project (at **dmoz.org**) for all or part of their directory services. Among the general-purpose directories that use the Open Directory Project are AOL Search, Ask Jeeves, Google, HotBot, InfoSpace, Lycos, and Netscape Search.

The contents of any web directory based on the Open Directory Project are generally very similar to any other web directory that uses it.

---

about fibromyalgia and aspirin, using a search engine to search for the terms gives you pages on your specific topic.

> **Note**   *Some web directories also include search engines. For example, Yahoo includes both a web directory and a search engine.*

What Are Databases?

A *database* is a collection of pieces of related information that is organized so its various informational items can be located and retrieved when needed. Billions of electronic databases exist, but only some of them can be accessed on the Web. Your health insurer, for example, probably has a searchable database that contains information about your recent health history, but that database is not available on the Web.

On the other hand, many databases are indeed available on the Web. Some databases on the Web can be used by anyone at no charge, and others require that users belong to a particular organization or pay a fee. Web-accessible databases are part of what is sometimes referred to as the *hidden Web,* the *deep Web,* or the *invisible Web*: information that cannot be directly located with today's general-purpose search engines because it is "hidden" behind query forms. To locate information in most web-accessible databases, you need to be able to find the database itself and make your query. Databases on the Web include library catalogs, telephone books, public records, and news and magazine archives. For example, if you use a web search engine to look for a specific book, you probably won't find Amazon.com's page about the book because Amazon's book information is stored in a database that isn't indexed by search engines.

Some databases are fully indexed, meaning that you can search the entire database for the occurrence of any word. Other databases are indexed only by fields. For example, to find someone in a white pages database, you need to search for information for a particular field. If you type "McKinley" into the last name field of a white pages search, you see only people with the last name of McKinley rather than people who live on McKinley Avenue.

Using Search Engines for General-Purpose Web Searching

Most searches can be successfully completed with the use of a good search engine and the correct search words. At the time this book was being written, the most popular search engines were Google (**www.google.com**), Yahoo (**www.yahoo.com**), and MSN Search (**search.msn.com**). Google is the clear choice of people who are experienced and successful web searchers; it's fast, it's big, and it finds the pages you're looking for. In fact, Google is so good that some other search engine providers gave up trying to compete with it and simply began using Google as the engine behind their own searches. Yahoo, AOL, and Netscape Search, among others, are really Google searches.

One reason Google is able to find most things better than other search engines is that it strongly weights backlinks when it ranks web pages. This process is a little like asking for recommendations. If you asked ten people to recommend a plumber, wouldn't you choose the plumber most frequently named? That's more or less how Google decides which web pages are the best.

Choosing Your Search Words

Whether you use Google or another comprehensive search engine such as FAST (**www.alltheweb.com**), AltaVista (**www.altavista.com**), or Teoma (**www.teoma.com**), it's important to use the right search words in the right way. You must narrow your focus so the search engine can find a small number of relevant pages out of the billions of possible pages on the Web. For example, if you're a bird-watcher, it's better to search for a specific type of bird (for example, "blue heron") than to search only for "birds."

Table 21-1 shows some quick ways, which work in most search engines, to narrow your search. (For detailed information about the search methods used by a specific search engine, consult the search engine's Help page.)

To start your search, go to the main page of the search engine and think of some words that are likely to appear on the kinds of pages you want to see. Type these words into the search field. If you receive too many results, narrow your focus. If you searched for "Hawaii vacation" in Google, for example, you probably found hundreds of thousands of sites. Look over these results and determine what you might add or subtract. Do you see a lot of rental offers? If you do, and you're looking for rentals, change your search to "Hawaii vacation rental." If you are specifically looking for something other than rentals, rerun the search using "Hawaii vacation -rental." Continue with this process until the results reflect exactly what you're seeking.

Sometimes a search yields too few results. If you search for "espresso" but can't find the particular espresso bar you're seeking, try typing "espresso OR expresso." The Web is full of inaccurate spelling! Try several different forms of the same root word. A search for "wash" yields different results than a search for "washing." You may want to search for "wash OR washes OR washing OR washer."

Method	Example	Results
Multiple words	Hawaii vacation	Pages containing all entered words, with the most likely matches listed first on the list of results. The words you enter don't have to appear together, or in the order you specified. Some search engines return pages containing any of the words, not necessarily all of them.
Phrase in quotation marks	"Baltimore Orioles"	Pages containing an exact phrase.
Plus sign (+) to include words, and minus sign (-) to exclude words	+penguins -hockey	Pages about penguins, excluding hockey teams named "penguins."
Boolean search	Cats AND obedience NOT zoo	Pages about cats and obedience that do not mention zoos. You can also use "OR" to search for pages containing one word or another; for example, "cats OR obedience."

Table 21-1.   *Common Search Methods*

Each search engine employs specific rules to conduct a focused search. Nearly every search engine has easy-to-use Help pages that show you the rules and expectations peculiar to the search engine. If the common search methods don't give you the results you want, look at the Help page and try rewording your search according to the syntax of the search engine you're using.

Google Tricks

One of the biggest annoyances of using the Web is the disappearing page. Your search yields a URL which, from its brief description, appears to be about to yield the precise information you were looking for. Alas, when you click the link, you find that the page "no longer exists," or its content has been changed to eliminate the information you wanted. Google's solution to this particular frustration is to enable you to view a copy of the page it stored when it indexed the site. This copy is *cached* (stored) on the Google servers and can be viewed by clicking the gray Cached link at the end of each individual search result.

Take advantage of the Advanced Search function of Google, shown in Figure 21-1, at **www.google.com/advanced_search**. This page lets you expand or limit your search in a number of useful ways.

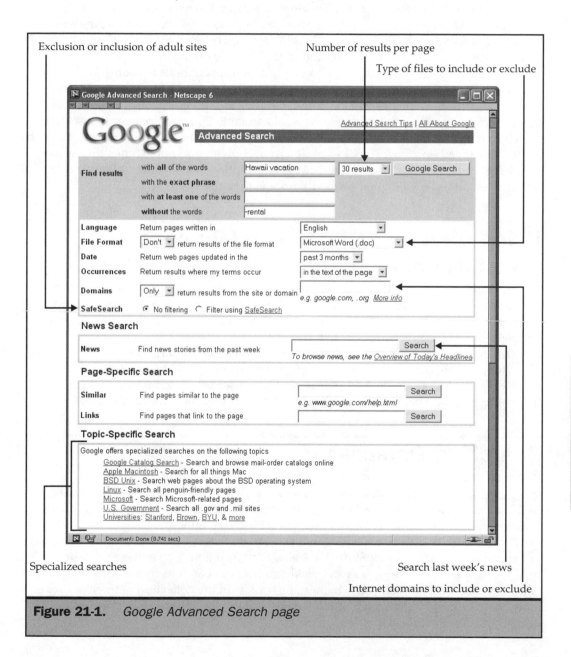

Figure 21-1.   *Google Advanced Search page*

VIEWING THE
WORLD WIDE WEB

Many web sites have search engines that search the pages of their site, but some do not. No problem! To use Google to find all mentions of "financial aid" on the Princeton Review web site, type **"financial aid" site:www.review.com** in the Google search box. This function is also available from Google's Advanced Search page.

In addition to general searching, specialized searches, and the Google Directory, the Groups and Images tabs on the main Google page can be used to search the archives of Usenet newsgroups (see Chapter 11) and to find images on the Web.

Be sure to explore the Preferences and Language Tools options available on the main Google page. With these options you can change the language of the Google interface (available languages include Pig Latin and Klingon, as well as Spanish, Russian, and others), translate web pages between several available language pairs, narrow your search to pages that originate in specific countries, change the default number of search results displayed on a page, block explicit sexual content, and make other choices.

There's much more to Google, including maps, phonebooks, and toolbars, and features are added on a regular basis. Take some time to explore it!

Using Directories for General-Purpose Web Searching

Search engines are fine when you know what words to look for, but when words fail you, a web directory can help. Perhaps someone suggested a name for that rash on your arm, but you can't remember what you were told. Typing "rash" into a search engine yields far too many results to be helpful.

Instead, go to a directory such as Yahoo (**www.yahoo.com**), Google (**directory.google.com**), or its source, the Open Directory Project (**dmoz.org**), and choose Health | Conditions And Diseases | Skin Disorders. The information presented in the subdirectory should help you find the name of the condition you're looking for.

Searching Databases

A large amount of information on the Web simply can't be found even with the biggest and best general-purpose search engine, and even if you know exactly what you're looking for. In most cases, this "hidden" information can't be found because it's located in databases whose contents are not indexed by search engines.

For example, there's no general search you can do to learn whether Manuela Negrete is a member of the California State Bar Association, but if you go to the association's web site at **www.calsb.org**, you can quickly and easily search its member database. A general search won't tell you whether this book is in the collection of the Harvard University Library, but a search of the library's catalog at **hollisweb.harvard.edu** quickly yields this information.

> ## Time-Traveling the Internet with the Wayback Machine
> Many societies attempt to record their culture, and the Internet is no exception. Much of the Internet is preserved as it was at particular moments since 1996 by the Internet Archive, a public nonprofit organization. It is searchable with the archive's Wayback Machine at **www.archive.org**. Although many sites are not included in Internet Archive, and some sites are incomplete, the Wayback Machine provides an interesting glimpse of "the Web as it was." At the time this book was published, the Internet Archive contained over 100 terabytes of information and was growing at a rate of 10 terabytes per month. It is the largest known database in existence.

Finding Searchable Databases

So, how do you find the databases you want to search? It's a little trickier than a general-purpose search, but it can be done. The key is to re-orient your query toward finding a database that might contain the information you want, rather than finding the information itself. For example, if you want to find the social security number of Denzel Bailey, you need to find a database of social security numbers. Type **"social security database"** into the search field of a general-purpose web directory or search engine. Once the search engine locates the web page for a social security number query form, such as **ssdi.genealogy.rootsweb.com**, you can enter Denzel Bailey's name, and try to find his Social Security Number within the database. (Online Social Security information is available only for people who are no longer living.)

Some specialized search engines search only for databases. Among these are Complete Planet at **www.completeplanet.com** and the Librarian's Index to the Internet at **www.lii.org**. Although these specialized search engines probably can't find anything more than a large general-purpose search engine can, a database-focused search engine can be useful because its search results include only pages that are entry points to databases—all other types of web pages are excluded. When using a database-focused search engine, remember that you are searching *for* a database, rather than *within* the database. The specialized search engine only helps you find the database; once you've found the proper database, you must then search *within* it.

Fee-Based Databases

Many owners of searchable databases allow access to their information for a fee. The fee may take the form of a membership or subscription, or there may be a charge for each search or each retrieval.

Some popular fee-based databases include LexisNexis (**www.lexisnexis.com**), an accumulation of business and legal information; eLibrary (**ask.elibrary.com**), an archive of periodicals, books, photographs, transcripts, and maps; Ancestry.com (**www.ancestry.com**), a collection of genealogical information for the United States and other countries; and Dialog (**www.dialog.com**), a compilation of information sources for market research and other business purposes.

One interesting hybrid, Northern Light, is both a general-purpose search engine and an aggregator of fee-based content. When you go to **www.northernlight.com** and perform a search, the results include both free content and pay-per-view content from the Northern Light Special Collection. The Special Collection includes documents from books, periodicals, news wires, and other sources, most of which can be viewed for between one and four dollars per article.

A number of organizations provide fee-based access to their own databases. These differ from the previously mentioned database aggregators that act as gateways to collections of databases rather than a single database. Examples of searchable stand-alone databases that can be viewed for a fee include Consumer Reports at **www.consumerreports.org**, the Wall Street Journal at **www.wsj.com**, and research reports from Gartner Group at **www.gartner.com**.

Searching Usenet Newsgroups

Archived Usenet newsgroups, described earlier in this book, are a potential information resource that is often overlooked. Though often compared to the output of a billion monkeys in front of a billion keyboards, Usenet is a wealth of opinions and experiences of millions of Internet users with too much time on their hands. If you remember that most of these opinions are worth precisely what you pay for them, you may also uncover some extremely useful pieces of arcane information unavailable elsewhere. Usenet can be an excellent source for real-world product information, help with software difficulties, do-it-yourself inspiration, and the like.

As described in Chapter 12, Google's Usenet archive is searchable at **groups.google.com**.

Finding People

Looking for people on the Web is a popular pastime, whether you want to find a phone number, locate a family member or old high school friend, or learn the name of your neighbor. The information you find in web-based personal directories is either from public sources, such as yellow pages and white pages, or is added to the directories' databases by the individuals themselves.

A variety of people finders are available on the Web. Many allow reverse lookups—lookup by telephone number or address or other demographic—as well as name lookups. Here is a small sample of some you may want to try.

Directory and URL	Specialty	Interesting Features
Alumni.Net **www.alumni.net**	Alumni directory	Faculty and staff directories, message boards
AnyWho **www.anywho.com**	Electronic white and yellow pages	World directories
Classmates **www.classmates.com**	Fee-based alumni directory with some free content	Elementary schools, military directories, message boards
Infospace **www.infospace.com**	General-purpose search engine	World directories, city guides, maps, e-mail search
Roots Web **www.rootsweb.com**	Family research	Mailing lists, message boards, database searches
Switchboard **www.switchboard.com**	Electronic white and yellow pages	City guides, maps, e-mail search
WhitePages.com **www.whitepages.com**	Electronic white pages	Area code search, ZIP code search, maps, world directories

The
Complete
Reference

Chapter 22

Audio and Video
on the Web

479

The Web has gone beyond text and pictures: many web pages now include sound and video. With the increased popularity of broadband connections, many sites feature music, movie, and television clips you can view or download. However, even with a broadband connection, audio or video files that are more than a few seconds long can be large and take a long time to download to your computer.

Audio and video files are stored in several standard formats. Windows and Macs come with players for many of these formats, or you can download an audio/video player from the Internet. You can use plug-ins and ActiveX controls to play the files within your browser or play the files in a separate program. Internet Explorer 6 has a Media Bar, adding a media player to the browser window.

This chapter describes how to find, download, and play audio and video from web sites, including streaming, MP3, and video files. The last sections of the chapter contain directions for how to use the Windows Media Player, RealOne Player, and Internet Explorer's Media Bar.

Playing Streaming Audio and Video

Because audio and video files can be large, and to avoid a long wait before you can start playing them, *streaming* was invented. Streaming enables your computer to play the beginning of an audio or video file while the rest of the file is still downloading. If the file arrives more slowly than your computer plays it, the playback has gaps while your computer waits for more data to play. (Players usually display a "Buffering…" message when this happens.) Several streaming formats are widely used on the Web, and you can install plug-ins and ActiveX controls to enable your browser to play them.

When you click an audio link on a web page, your audio plug-in or ActiveX control plays the file. Some plug-ins and ActiveX controls display a little window with VCR-like controls that let you stop, rewind, or fast-forward the file, as well as adjust the volume of the sound played by the file. When you click a video link, the video appears in your browser. Because these video files are highly edited and compressed, the video is usually very small and jerky, especially with the smallest files, which may have been optimized for modem users. Many sites now provide a broadband version for users with faster connection speeds, and the quality of these clips is much better.

Popular Audio and Video Players

Here are the popular audio and video plug-ins and ActiveX controls that can play the most common file formats:

- **RealOne Player** (formerly known as RealPlayer) plays most popular audio formats and video files, including streaming audio and video. RealOne Player supports burning audio files on CDs, so you can create your own music CDs, provided you have a CD-R/RW drive. You can download RealOne Player from **www.real.com**. For more information, see "Using RealOne Player," later in this chapter.

■ **QuickTime** plays audio and video files stored in the QuickTime format. You can download Windows or Mac versions of the Apple QuickTime player from **www.apple.com/quicktime**. QuickTime is available in a Pro version if you want to create your own QuickTime files.

■ **Windows Media Player** (shown in Figure 22-1) plays both regular and streaming audio and video files, including most audio files and CDs. It supports burning to CDs or copying files to portable media players that support WMA format. It's included with Windows, and you can download the latest version from **www.microsoft.com/windows/mediaplayer**. In addition to versions for Windows and Mac, there are also versions for the Palm and Pocket PC operating systems. For more information, see "Using Windows Media Player," later in this chapter.

Figure 22-1.   *Windows Media Player's featured radio stations*

■ **WinAmp** plays MP3 and Windows Media files, as well as many other popular music formats, CDs, and streaming audio. WinAmp is free, available for both Windows and Mac, and can be found at **www.winamp.com/download**.

■ **MusicMatch** comes in a free version that plays MP3s and CDs, copies and creates CDs, transfers MP3s to portable media players, and supports Internet radio broadcasts. The paid version, MusicMatch Plus, has advanced options for copying music and creating CDs. It's available for both Windows and Mac from **www.musicmatch.com**.

| Note | *Internet Explorer 6 includes the Media Bar, which uses Windows Media Player ActiveX controls to play streaming audio and video in a small bar on the left side of the browser window. The bar is turned on and off using the Media button on the standard toolbar. You can stop it from playing web audio and video files by clicking the Media Options button, selecting Settings, and unchecking Play Web Media.* |

Internet Radio

With the growing popularity of high-speed Internet access and improvements in broadcasting technology, it's now possible to listen to high-quality radio broadcasts via streaming audio. Because of the current licensing policies enforced by ASCAP, the American Society of Composers, Authors and Publishers (**www.ascap.com**), few American radio music stations provide Internet feeds, but you will find many news-only, Internet-only, and non-U.S. stations broadcasting on the Internet. Although the sound quality is not very good using dial-up modem speeds, cable and DSL users will find the quality very good—how else could you hear broadcasts originating halfway around the world?

RealOne, WinAmp, MusicMatch, and Windows Media players provide links to featured Internet radio stations and search tools to locate others. RealOne and MusicMatch also have paid services that include additional radio stations and other specialized media content. Figure 22-1 shows Windows Media Player's built-in Internet radio tuner.

Most players include links to all categories of web content, from music and music videos to news and sports videos, but if you want to browse the Web for additional audio and video sources, here are some web sites to try:

■ National Public Radio (NPR), at **www.npr.org**, has today's news and some of your favorite public radio shows.

■ Broadcast.com, at **www.broadcast.com**, lists live radio and TV stations, music, audio books, and other audio and video sources.

- For listings of live and recorded audio and video that is "broadcast" over the Internet, start at Yahoo (**www.yahoo.com**), click News And Media, and then click Internet Broadcasts.

- CDNOW, at **www.cdnow.com**, is an online CD and audio cassette store that lets you listen to RealAudio clips of many of its recordings before you decide whether to buy.

- SHOUTcast.com, at **www.shoutcast.com**, lists streaming MP3 audio sites.

- IFILM.com, at **www.ifilm.com**, has many movie trailers and short films listed on its site.

 Most major news sites, including CNN.com, ABCNews.com, CBSNews.com, and MSNBC.com, broadcast audio and video clips from some of their televised newscasts online.

To look for stations that are broadcast over the Internet, you can go to Yahoo Broadcast (**broadcast.yahoo.com**) or Nullsoft's SHOUTcast (**www.shoutcast.com**) and search for stations. To listen to stations listed on either site, you need to have a player installed that supports Windows Media or RealAudio.

Playing MP3 Music

MPEG3 or *MP3* is a highly compressed audio format that is used for storing audio data, mainly music. Many music files are available on the Internet in MP3 format, which has the file extension .mp3. The problem with many MP3 files is that they are *bootlegged,* recorded illegally without the permission of the copyright holder. Some files are put on the Web by small bands that are just getting their start, and they use MP3 and the Web as a great way to get wide exposure legally and inexpensively.

To play an MP3 format file, you need an MP3 player. Windows Media Player, WinAmp, RealOne Player, and MusicMatch, which were mentioned earlier in this chapter, can play MP3s, or you can look for other MP3 players to download from the Internet. These players and many others are also available from TUCOWS (**www .tucows.com**), MP3.com (**www.mp3.com**), or CMJ New Music First (**www.mp3now .com**), which have lots of other MP3-related information.

 *Many people think that because music is available on the Internet and so many people download and play it, this must be legal. It's not, unless the copyright holder of the music (usually the publisher) has given permission. If you live in the United States, see **www.loc.gov/copyright** for information about copyright.*

Ripping MP3 Files from CDs

If your computer has a CD-ROM drive, you can also convert songs from CDs that you own into MP3 files. Converting your music CD songs into MP3 files is legal as long as only you use the MP3 files that you create, and you don't give or sell them to anyone else. All newer CD-ROM drives can be used to create MP3 files, but older drives may not able to read raw data from music CDs, which is a must to create MP3s. Most MP3 players can copy, or *rip,* the songs from your music CDs and save the songs as individual files on your hard drive, often complete with the song title, and saved in folders named for the artist and album title. Figure 22-2 shows the RealOne Player playing music that was copied from a CD to the computer's hard disk.

Figure 22-2.   *RealOne Player playing music ripped from a CD*

Customizing Your Player with Skins

WinAmp pioneered the concept of customizing the look of the player interfaces with *skins*, making the program look even cooler than it usually looks. For example, here's WinAmp with a wild (and almost unusably confusing) skin applied:

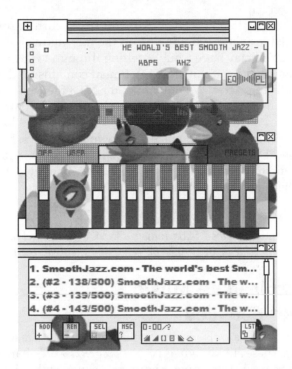

RealOne, MusicMatch, and Windows Media Player all support skins, and you can find many free skins for each program on the Internet. You can even create your own skins—all it takes is a graphics editor (such as Microsoft Paint or Paint Shop Pro) and a text editor like Notepad to create a basic skin. Specific instructions for creating skins for each player can be found at each player's web site or in the Windows Media Player SDK at MSDN (**msdn.microsoft.com**).

Finding MP3 Music on the Web

Many players include a start or search page to help you find music, or you can use one of the many MP3 search sites, including the following:

- MP3 Master List, at **www.mp3masterlist.com**
- MP3Board, at **www.mp3board.com**

- MediaFind, at **search.mp3.de**
- Scour.net Media Search, at **www.scour.com** (requires IE)

You can find additional MP3 sites using your favorite search engine. Some of these sites include audio and video files in other formats, but you can identify MP3 files by the filename extension .mp3.

Once you find the song that you are looking for (most current songs and many older songs are available online), you download the file, many of which are three megabytes or larger. You may have trouble getting through to sites that have MP3 files because they can be very busy: if you get "Document contains no data" or "Site busy" messages, just keep trying. After you download the MP3 file, you can play it as many times as you want by using an MP3 player. If you have a slow computer, the music may sound terrible; but on faster computers, MP3 files can sound like CDs.

If you have a CD burner, you can make your own music CDs. Not all CD boom boxes can play these CDs, but many newer ones will play them. You can also copy the songs to a portable media player, which is a small Walkman-style device that holds music on Compact Flash or Smart Media cards.

 Other popular formats for music include WAV, which is the original sound format for Windows, and Windows Media Player's WMA. RealOne Player saves music using RMJ format, which can only be played using the RealOne Player at this time.

Finding and Downloading Music with Peer-to-Peer Services

A new breed of MP3 players are also search engines and file servers to find and download the music you want. These are known as *peer-to-peer (P2P)* file-sharing services. Using a P2P program, you can easily find songs, share your songs with others, and play songs from your collection. Downloading music using a P2P program is easy: type in a song title or artist in the search field, select the song from the search results (which list the servers on which the song is stored), and click Download. Once the file is downloaded, you can listen to the music using the same program.

P2P systems can be used for any type of files, as described in Chapter 33. But the most popular use of P2P (to date) has been for sharing songs. Not all P2P programs include MP3 players; some require you to use another program to play the music you download.

P2P Services

The first and most famous program to use the P2P concept was Napster (**www.napster .com**). The music industry closed Napster down in 2001 because it was providing a way for people to share pirated music. Napster used a central database to keep track of who had what file. When Napster was forced to turn off its central servers, the whole network ground to a halt. Scour (**www.scour.com**), a similar service, was closed down at about the same time. (Napster may reopen as a commercial site where you pay a subscription fee to download music.)

The shutdown of Napster was immediately followed by the release of many similar programs. Some are based on an open source system called Gnutella (**www.gnutella .com**), which takes P2P networking a step further—it's a protocol for searching for and exchanging files that avoids centralized servers completely. Many Gnutella client programs are available, including BearShare (**www.bearshare.com**) and LimeWire (**www.limewire.com**). However, the Gnutella network slowed down as more users joined because every search was handled by many computers on the network.

FastTrack, an improved P2P system developed in the Netherlands, was designed to solve Gnutella's speed problems. Several sites use FastTrack's technology, including Grokster (**www.grokster.com**) and KaZaA (**www.kazaa.com**). Music City's Morpheus (**www.musiccity.com**, shown in Figure 22-3) started life as a FastTrack program and then switched to Gnutella in mid-2002. KaZaA changed hands and may have switched to a pay-per-download system by the time you read this.

Other clients have been written to work with OpenNap, an open source version of Napster (**opennap.sourceforge.net**). WinMX (**www.winmx.com**) is an OpenNap client and can connect to OpenNap servers listed at **www.napigator.com**. (WinMX has also developed its own decentralized network.) OpenNap is designed for sharing files other than music files. Servers are run by independent organizations, may be public or

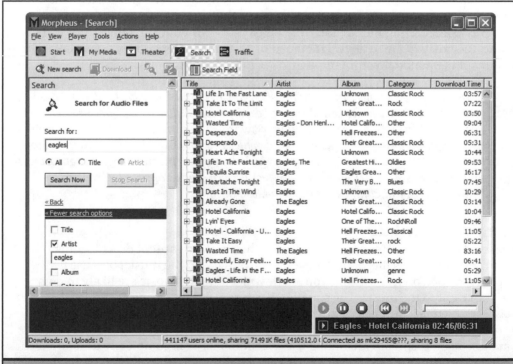

Figure 22-3. *Morpheus helps you find music files that are stored on other people's hard disks.*

private, and may distribute different types of files. However, OpenNap servers that enable people to share copyrighted music are liable to be shut down by law enforcement authorities.

A few other P2P file-sharing services emerged after the shutdown of Napster. AudioGalaxy (**www.audiogalaxy.com**) maintains its own database of songs. (We're not sure why it hasn't been shut down for piracy.) eDonkey2000 (**www.edonkey2000 .com**), Blubster (**www.blubster.com**), and URLBlaze (**www.urlblaze.com**) are decentralized, like Gnutella.

Using P2P Services

When you install a P2P program on your computer, you connect to a network of file-sharing systems. The music you can find on the system depends entirely on the other users; the index of available songs consists of the music that other people have uploaded to their computers. If you are looking for an aria from a Verdi opera, you may be out of luck, although Britney Spears songs appear in great profusion. The information about songs consists of whatever title the other users typed when they digitized the song; so if you can't find what you are looking for, try misspellings of the title.

If you run a P2P program on a DSL or cable modem, that makes you a server on most systems (because DSL and cable connections usually give you a fixed IP address, which servers require). If you happen to have a desirable file, your computer will be very busy transferring files to and from other people. If your ISP notices this increase in traffic, they may get mad at you for violating their no-servers policy, regardless of the legality of the material you're serving.

Caution   *Peer-to-peer programs can be used to share any or all files on your hard disk. Make sure you are not sharing confidential or copy-protected files using these programs. In addition, some P2P programs include* spyware, *which transmits information about you, your browsing history, and your downloading habits back to the software maker. We can't tell you which P2P programs include spyware because the situation changes monthly. Research P2P programs at Slyck (**www.slyck.com**) and Zeropaid.com (**www.zeropaid.com**) before you download them!*

The Future of P2P

The legal status of P2P services is still up in the air. It's clear that downloading copyrighted music is illegal (unless you have purchased the music) because neither you nor the person from whom you are downloading the music are likely to own the copyright to the music. The situation has turned into a technical and legal race between the music recording industry and file-sharing enthusiasts.

Most newer P2P systems don't have a central database server—instead, the database itself is spread out among users' computers. This completely decentralized architecture makes P2P systems almost impossible to shut down. If one company providing Gnutella, FastTrack, or other decentralized client programs is shut down, users can switch to another client program and keep working.

P2P cases are still (as of 2002) working their way through the courts. Services with central servers or databases, like Napster, are clearly liable for piracy by their users because they can track or block downloads by their users based on the title or artist of the song. However, companies that only provide software, without maintaining music databases or servers, don't know what files are passing through the system and may not be liable for their P2P system's use. The courts will have to decide.

The music industry proposes to replace the current free system with paid subscription-based P2P services; Napster is working with Bertelsmann AG (a large publishing company) and MusicNet to reopen as a legal, fee-based music downloading site. The music industry is also trying to build copy-protection into new digital music devices and CDs (including all new computers). MusicNet and Real.com premiered a legal service called RealOne MusicPass (**www.real.com/realone/services/music.html**) that costs $10 per month for up to 100 downloads from their catalog. The question is: How can sites that charge for downloads compete with free P2P sites?

Because of the ongoing controversy and legal maneuvering, P2P web sites come and go, programs change names, and tracking currently available (and legal) systems can be hard. For the latest news about P2P software, try Slyck (**www.slyck.com**) and Zeropaid.com (**www.zeropaid.com**).

| Tip | *Support artists! If you like an artist's work, buy his or her music—don't rip it off.* |

Playing Video on the Internet

Video is supposed to be exciting and entertaining; but in the early days of the Internet, it was slow and boring. The files are large and most people had slow Internet connections, meaning a video clip just a few seconds long could take ten minutes or more to download. Even using streaming media, where the content is played as it is downloaded, the images were often blocky, jumpy, and tiny. Technology has improved since then. With improved video compression and faster Internet connections, now almost everyone can enjoy rich multimedia content delivered over the Internet.

Prerecorded Video

Several video formats are in use on the Internet. Many videos play in Windows Media Player, whereas other videos require that you have RealOne Player or a QuickTime player installed. If you don't have the right player installed, many sites offer to install it for you on the spot.

Popular web sites for videos include movie studio sites (like Warner Bros. at **www.warnerbros.com**) and sites dedicated to specific movies. Music publishers and recording artist's sites have music videos online. Many popular commercials and movie trailers are also available online. IFILM (at **www.ifilm.com**) features many short films and trailers, and The FeedRoom (**www.feedroom.com**) has many news, sports, and entertainment clips.

Web sites use Windows Media Player, RealOne Player, or QuickTime to play videos. Some open a separate window to display the video, whereas others display the video image within the browser window.

Live Video with Webcams

Another source for video broadcasts is the ever-popular *webcam*. These are digital video cameras broadcast from a specific location, usually stationary, and often broadcasting 24 hours a day, even after dark when there is nothing to see. You'll find webcams at many popular tourist attractions and natural areas, such as Mount Washington (**www.mountwashington.org/cam**, shown in Figure 22-4) and Disney parks (**home.disney.com/DisneyWorld/cgi-bin/allCameras.cgi**), with more webcams listed at EarthCam (**www.earthcam.com**). Search Google (or the search engine of your choice) for webcams—dozens of sites show webcams of zoos and animals in general. Additionally, you'll find many webcams used by businesses and individuals, often showing views of parking lots, coffee makers, and backyards. These are referred to as

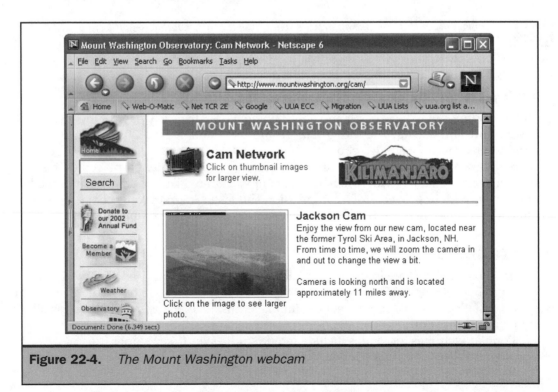

Figure 22-4. *The Mount Washington webcam*

"vanity cams" because they feature subjects few people (besides the cam operator) are interested in.

Webcam images are usually updated between every few seconds and five minutes, or longer, although some sites use streaming video for their webcams.

Caution *Many webcam sites are pornographic; these usually charge for viewing.*

If you'd like to have a webcam of your own, all you need is a video camera hooked to your computer, webcam software to snap the pictures and upload them to your web site, and a web site to publish the pictures to. You can find webcam software at many shareware sites, including TUCOWS (**www.tucows.com**). Webcams are not expensive, starting at under $100. You can also use webcams with video conferencing software like Yahoo Messenger.

Using Windows Media Player

Windows Media Player is included with Windows XP, and users of older operating systems can download the newest version from the Windows Media web site (**www .microsoft.com/windows/mediaplayer**). Windows Media Player does more than play audio and video clips and help you organize your media library; you can use it to copy music CDs to your hard drive. One drawback is that, although Windows Media Player can play several formats, it can only rip music in WMA format. If you have a CD-R/RW drive or portable media player, you can use Windows Media Player to copy songs to a CD or device. As with many players, you can change the look of the player by changing the "skin" and be entertained by its visualizations.

To start Windows Media Player, choose Start | All Programs | Windows Media Player (in Windows XP). Once the program is running, click the buttons on the toolbar (down the left side of the window). Click the Now Playing button to play files on your own computer.

Note *The Windows Media Player has many features, but only those used for web content are described here.*

Finding Files with the Media Guide

To find audio and video files on the Web, click the Media Guide button on the toolbar on the left side of the player. The Media Guide (shown in Figure 22-5) includes a list of categories you can browse for media content. Media Guide is actually the **www.windowsmedia.com** web site—if you prefer browsing the site in a browser window, you can.

The Media Guide includes a search field that you can use to find audio or video content on the **windowsmedia.com** web site. You can clear the search and return to the main media guide page by clicking the WindowsMedia.com logo. Some of the content plays in the media player; other content opens new browser windows.

Figure 22-5. *Windows Media Player displaying the Media Guide*

Creating a Media Library

The Media Library displays a list of all audio and video files that the program has cataloged on your hard drives. The first time you click the Media Library button on the toolbar on the left side of the player, the program asks if you want to scan your drives for files. You can limit the locations it looks in and skip smaller file sizes (click the Advanced button to display these settings) to keep small Windows sound and video clips out of your media library (like the sounds that Windows makes during normal operation). To add more files later, choose Tools | Search or press F3. If the clip is encoded with *tags* (information about the album, artist, and genre), the program properly categorizes the clip. Video clips are grouped by author.

After you've searched your hard drive and added your audio and video files to the library, you can create *playlists* for your favorite media. Playlists make it easy to play your favorite songs or videos when your collection is large. You can move songs on and off playlists, and include one song on multiple playlists. Click the Media Library button to display and manage your playlists.

Finding Internet Radio Stations with the Radio Tuner

Select the Radio Tuner button on the toolbar on the left side of the player to load a list of currently featured stations (shown in Figure 22-1, earlier in this chapter). You can listen to one of the featured stations or browse stations by type. Recently played stations are cached on this page, so you can return to them easily, or you can add favorites to your My Stations list.

Using RealOne Player

The RealOne Player is available for download from Real.com (at **www.real.com**). There are two versions: a free version and a Pro version that is available as part of a subscription service. The free RealOne Player provides basic features, such as an MP3 player, streaming audio, and streaming video. If you have a CD burner, you can use it to make your own music CDs. The Pro version offers higher-quality video and premium content. When you install RealOne Player, a button appears on the Quick Launch toolbar on the Windows taskbar (if your taskbar includes this toolbar).

 Many of the options on the menus are available only to Pro subscribers, including Channels and advanced CD burning features.

RealOne Player has many features to enhance your multimedia enjoyment, but only those features that deliver web content are described in this chapter.

The RealOne Player Windows

When you run the RealOne Player, you see two connected windows, one above the other, as shown in Figure 22-6. The RealOne Player window (on the top) displays videos, while the RealOne Media Browser (on the bottom) helps you find audio and video files to play. If you haven't yet played a video, the top window may not contain anything.

Along the bottom of the RealOne Player window is a toolbar with tab-like buttons. These buttons switch among the different features of RealOne. These buttons are also found on the Player's View menu.

Note *The Now Playing button displays a list of the files you are playing now and what you've played recently.*

Browsing RealOne's Web Site

Click the Web button on the toolbar to see the Media Browser, which displays a home page containing links to current events and other content in the Media Browser

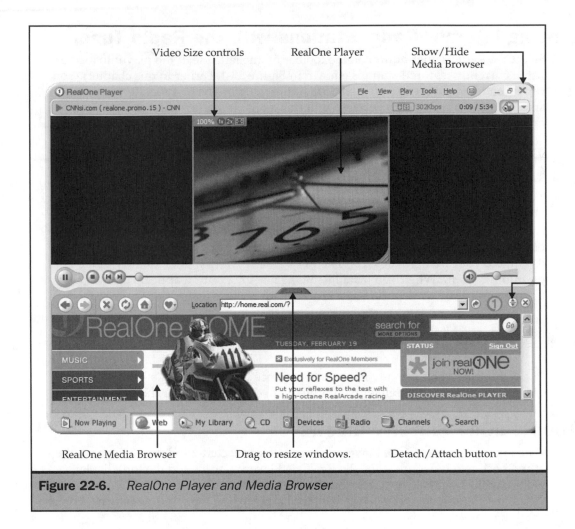

Figure 22-6. *RealOne Player and Media Browser*

window and a video (usually an advertisement) in the player window. Video content is marked with a small filmstrip icon, and premium content is indicated with a gold star icon. To listen to a selection, click it in the Media Browser window, and it loads in the player window.

You can detach the Media Browser window from the player by clicking the double-arrow icon in the upper-right corner of the Media Browser window. You can hide the Media Browser window by clicking the small globe icon near the top right of the player window. Click the globe icon to show the Media Browser again.

Creating Playlists

Like the Windows Media Player, RealOne Player organizes your audio and video files into *playlists.* The Now Playing button shows the playlist you are currently playing, with each song listed by name. You can rearrange the order by selecting one item in the list and right-clicking it, or use the Edit menu at the bottom of the window. If you are playing an audio or video stream from the Internet, the filename and source is listed in this window. You can right-click the name and choose Copy To | My Library to add it to your library. It doesn't copy the actual file to your hard drive, but it adds a shortcut to the file stored on the Internet.

To create or maintain your library of audio and video files, click the My Library button on the toolbar at the bottom of the RealOne Player window. To search your hard disk for files you already have and to add them to your RealOne library, click the Options button along the top of the My Library pane and choose Scan Disk For Media from the menu that appears. The program lists them in the All Media list, shown in Figure 22-7.

You can also add any MP3s or videos downloaded from the Internet by scanning your drive for new media again or by clicking Options | Add Files To My Library if you know where the files are.

Figure 22-7. *The RealOne Player can scan your disk for audio and video files and arrange them in playlists.*

You can use My Library as a favorites list of Internet radio sites or favorite videos. To make a new playlist, click the New Playlist button and name the playlist. When you display a playlist, RealOne displays the Add Clips button (to add files to the playlist), the Burn CD button (to copy the songs on the playlist to a CD), and the Copy To button (to copy the songs to another playlist).

Playing Internet Radio

Click the Radio button on the toolbar to see a searchable list of Internet radio stations, grouped by genre, recently played, and any local stations broadcasting over the Internet. (To get local stations, scroll the radio web page to the right, and click Local Radio Settings to enter your ZIP code or country.)

Using Internet Explorer's Media Bar

In Internet Explorer (IE) 6, you can click the Media Bar button on the toolbar to display the Media Bar, shown here:

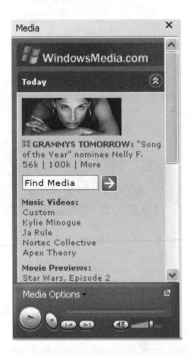

The Media Bar gives you the choice to play Windows Media-compatible videos in the Media Bar or in a separate browser window. You can play multimedia clips in the browser every time, or choose between your default media player and the Media Bar each time you select a video to watch. Playing the video in the browser means a small, postage-stamp picture, but you can undock the player and resize the window for a larger video screen. Click Media Options at the bottom of the Media Bar, choose Settings, and set your preferences on the menu that appears. The Settings menu lets you turn on and off the Ask For Preferred Types option, which always asks if you want to play a video link in the browser or your default player. If Play Web Media In The Bar is unchecked, the video (or audio clips) always play in the default player.

Regardless of your settings, not all audio and video files use the Media Bar. Many sites open a small browser window instead, with the playback controls embedded in the page.

The
Complete
Reference

Internet

Part V

Creating and Maintaining Web Sites

The Complete Reference

Internet

Chapter 23

Web Site Creation Concepts

E very day, more and more people are putting up their own web sites. If you own a business, having your own site is almost a requirement; if you're just an everyday Joe, you might have noticed that your friends are starting to post pictures and essays on the Internet. It's not as hard as it looks.

Silly as it sounds, there's still a certain cachet in having your own place on the Web to speak your mind—and to help people from all over the world get in touch with you. Whatever you're a fan of, someone else somewhere shares your love, and they'll be happy to find your page about it.

So how do you share all that knowledge? Create your own web page! Having your own web page can be a lot of fun (a lot of work is involved, too, but don't let *that* scare you), and it's a great way to express yourself.

This chapter is split into two parts: the first section, the planning process, helps you figure out what kind of content you want to present on your site and highlights things to keep in mind as you flesh out what your site will be. The second part deals with the technology and concepts you'll use as you take on the title of webmaster. Chapters 24 and 25 explain how to create web pages using a text editor or web page editor, and Chapters 26 through 29 explain how to add graphics, sound, video, forms, and other more advanced features. Once your web pages are ready to go, Chapter 30 explains how to upload them to your web server and Chapter 31 describes how to announce them to the world. If you want sell something on the Web, Chapter 32 tells you how.

Planning Your Web Site

Before you start creating web pages, you need to plan what you want to say, who your audience is, and how people will find their way around your site.

What Do You Need to Create an Interesting Site?

The most important ingredient for a successful web site is your enthusiasm for the subject matter and your willingness to put up solid content. Well, let's be honest—the most important thing is the content; that's the stuff that keeps people coming back, but if you're truly interested in a subject, coming up with something new and interesting to say shouldn't be a problem. Visitors to your site should come away with the feeling that you know your stuff and are eager to share it with the world.

In your journeys around the Web, you've probably found sites that impressed you, even if you weren't particularly interested in the subject matter. It's like going to a well-kept garden, when you're strictly a city dweller—even though you're not interested in gardening, you can enjoy the garden and appreciate the time that the gardener spent creating and maintaining the place. By the time visitors leave your web site, they might not share your fascination with whatever it is that you're raving about, but they *will* appreciate the time and care that you put into the production of the site.

To keep people coming back to your site, keep the site fresh by adding new information, deleting out-of-date topics, and updating pages regularly. Occasionally, you'll see sites that haven't been updated in months, or even years. It's disappointing to find a site that you look forward to revisiting, then scroll to the bottom of the page and find the site hasn't been updated in two years. Some sites, like news sites, need daily content for people to keep coming back; others with slightly less timely topics, like a Gilbert and Sullivan fan page, probably can get away with updates about once a month. Still, some dedicated fans do update their pages daily on the darnedest topics, finding new things in the most obscure places, and the longest you should probably go without adding something to your page is about a month. Professional sites for businesses should try to update once a week.

 No shortcuts—it's not fair to your visitors to change the revised date on a page unless you actually update something.

Basic Steps in Creating a Site

Here are the general steps you follow to create and maintain a web site:

1. Plan the structure of the site, so that you have an idea what information will be on at least the home page and other key pages. Be sure that you've thought about the audience for the site, what your main purpose is, how often you plan to update the site, and whether you'll want a database-driven site. A three-page site about your hobby needs a different structure than a 100-page database-driven site that provides an online catalog. (For example, larger sites need to provide multiple ways for people to find the pages they need.)

2. Using a text editor or web page editor, create the pages for your site (or some of them, anyway) and save them as HTML files. Use a graphics editor to create or view graphics for the pages. The next few chapters describe how to create web pages.

3. Using your own browser, view the HTML files that you created. (In Netscape Navigator and Internet Explorer, press CTRL-O to open a page that is stored on your own computer.) Check that the text is spelled correctly, that the graphics look good, and that links among your pages work. There are subtle differences in the way that different versions of Netscape Navigator and Internet Explorer read HTML, so look at your pages with both programs to make sure your site is compatible with both browsers. Repeat steps 2 and 3 until your site looks good enough to publish.

4. Publish your web site by putting all of its files (HTML files and graphics files) on a web server (as described in the section "Publishing Your Site," later in this chapter).

5. Using your browser, view the web pages as stored on the web server. Also, view the pages from a computer other than the one on which you created the pages, so that you can spot accidental references to files on your own hard disk.

6. Publicize your site, get feedback, get new ideas, and repeat the steps!

Planning Your Site

Planning is crucial to the success of your web site, so you'll know how many pages you need and how the pages will be linked. A *web page* is each separate file you format for viewing on the Web, a *web site* refers to all of the pages you are making available, and your *home page* is the first page visitors see when they visit your site.

The pages of your web site are connected together by *hyperlinks* (or *links*), which are the spots on the web page that users can click to move to another location on the page or to another page. You need to plan your site so that visitors can navigate from page to page quickly and can easily find the information you're providing.

You've probably seen sites that look like the author just added pages randomly, without thought to the organization of the site. The last thing that you want is for visitors to your site to get lost, be confused, or have trouble finding information.

The planning process involves answering these questions:

- Who is the audience for your site?

- What can you put on your site that will interest people?

- How can you make it easy for people to navigate your site?

- How will you store the pages on your site?

- What tools will you need to develop your site?

Who Is the Audience for Your Site?

Defining your target audience helps you to develop the content for your site. To determine your audience, you can start with global audience characteristics (Is the intended audience primarily adults or children?) and work your way down to specific characteristics (Do you expect visitors to be avid gardeners, home-schoolers, or fans of *They Might Be Giants*?). Here is a list of types of sites and their audiences:

Type of Web Site	Audience
Personal	Family members (adults and children), friends, colleagues
Small business	Other businesses, customers, employees

Type of Web Site	Audience
Large business	Other businesses, customers, employees, vendors
School	Parents, current students, prospective students, alumni
Church	Church members, other churches
Community groups or clubs	Current members, potential members, anyone with an interest in the group or club's activity
Special interest	Anyone who shares your special interest

You don't have to include a lot of fancy graphics or designs on your web pages to convey your information. For instance, Figure 23-1 is a personal web site, Figure 23-2 shows a small business site that makes it easy to order products via the Internet, and Figure 23-3 is a site for a church.

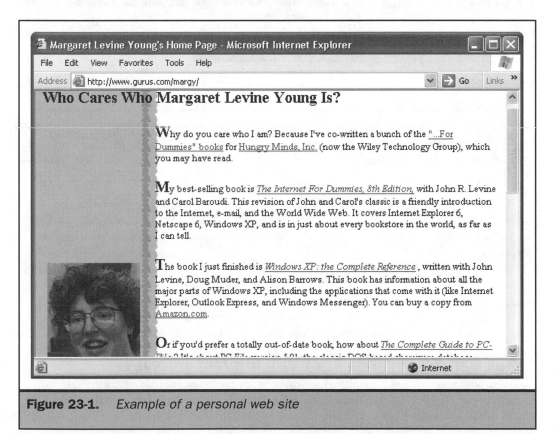

Figure 23-1.   *Example of a personal web site*

Figure 23-2.   *Example of a small business web site*

When you figure out who the audience is for your web site, you can tailor the site to fit the audience. Figure 23-4 shows the home page of a *Star Wars* fan site. The audience for this site is *Star Wars* fans, and the home page shows something familiar to most fans—an AT-AT Walker.

Your graphics don't have to be elaborate, but you get the idea. Keep your audience in mind when you create your site, and use symbols and graphics that they'll relate to and understand.

With the purpose and audience of your site in mind, the next thing you need to resolve is what tools you need to produce the kind of site you want.

What Can You Include That Will Interest People?

A good web site is there for one reason only: to provide useful information. The definition of "useful" gets spread thin on the Net. For every news site packed with the latest details on educational reform, there's a site with dancing hamsters. Even so, you have to admit that before the Internet came along, your chances of seeing dancing hamsters were pretty slim. Useful information can be anything from a detailed analysis

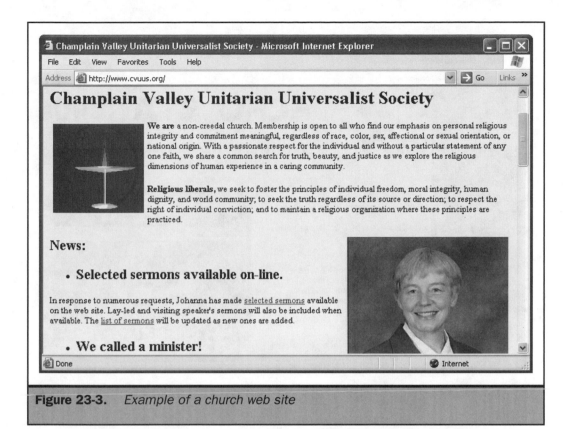

Figure 23-3.   *Example of a church web site*

of a company you're interviewing with to a simple, "Wow—people spent a lot of time to create something this silly!" Your site has to provide something unique and interesting if you want people to go see it.

There are probably as many different reasons for wanting to publish a site on the Web as there are web sites. Table 23-1 lists some types of web sites and common things people put on them, to help you figure out the purpose of your site. Which category fits your web site?

How Can You Make Navigation Easy?

The first question you should always ask yourself when designing a web site is this: "What's the most important thing about my site?"

The answer is usually simple. If you're a business, the most important thing is what you're selling—you want your visitors to buy your product, or at least to take a look at it. If you're running a personal site, you might decide the most important part is your pictures of your friends. If you're designing a fan site, your treasure-trove of *X-Files* fan fiction might be the largest on the Net.

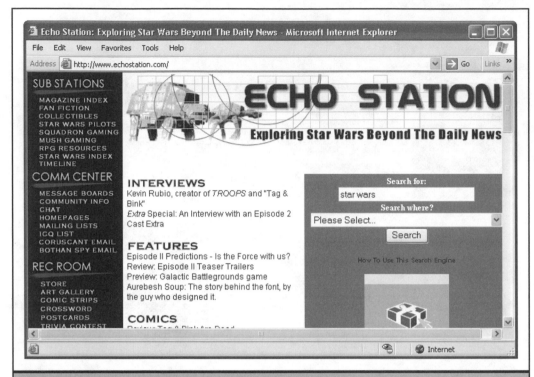

Figure 23-4.   Star Wars Fan site with Star Wars graphics

Type of Web Site	Things You Can Put on It
Personal	Personal interests, hobbies, and activities; pictures of friends and family; personal writings, like online journals and poetry; extremely silly things like dancing hamsters
Business	Product information and advertising; event schedules; testimonials; product sales; customer service and feedback; how-to guides using your products; community-building features such as customer recommendations and mailing lists; address, phone, and e-mail information

Table 23-1.   Common Web Site Content

Type of Web Site	Things You Can Put on It
School	Hands-on training for students to create their own web pages; online newspapers; school events and class schedules; access to mailing lists
Church	Days and times of services and meetings; a map to the church; dates of special events; publicity to attract new members and young converts; signing people up for mailing lists
Community groups, clubs, or organizations	Meeting announcements; sharing information and news; asking for new members; opinion articles; pictures of celebrities or noteworthy participants
Special-interest pages, like baseball or chess	History; statistics; how-to pieces; analyses of past games; reviews of new products; weekly summaries of shows; gossip and upcoming news; links to other related pages

Table 23-1.   *Common Web Site Content* (continued)

Once you've decided what's critical, design the site so users can get there quickly. Always. Internet visitors are fickle—they can leave at the click of a button, and if you bore or confuse them, they will. Too many business sites make you click through three or four pages to find whatever it is they're selling. Too many personal sites cheerfully lead you off to look at cool pictures, then leave no way for you to get back to where the rest of the fun stuff is. Too many fan sites are stuffed with great content, but you'll never see any of it because the interesting links are buried under a bunch of boring dreck.

If it's something important, put a link to it on the home page—and put it near the top, so people don't have to scroll down to see it. Then put a link to it on every page. Whatever you're selling or showing, make sure your visitor can get to the best parts no matter where they are on the site—you don't want them to feel lost.

Make sure the viewers always know where they are and how to get somewhere else. Always put a link to your home page on every page. (Thanks to search engines, as discussed in Chapter 21, people might be entering your site from all sorts of interesting places. Not all of them will be your home page.)

You can make navigating your site easier by applying a consistent design to all of your web pages. Place the navigation buttons or links (such as Next, Previous, and Home) in the same place on each page, so that they are easy to find. Use the same colors, lines, buttons, and icons from page to page so that your pages are easily distinguished as belonging to the same site. For example, the web site shown in Figure 23-5 uses the same title and row of buttons on all the pages of the site.

Figure 23-5.   *Use the same navigation buttons on each page of your site.*

If you're not inclined to create your own design or to hire a design firm, select a design from the choices included with your web editor. Many web authoring software packages contain an excellent selection of themes from which to choose. The themes provide page layouts with matching colors, borders, horizontal lines, and navigation buttons—in short, everything you need to create your web site. We'll go over some web design programs later in this chapter in "HTML Editors," and Chapter 25 describes in more detail what popular web authoring programs can do.

If you're having trouble choosing a design or figuring out what to do, the Web is a great source of inspiration. By looking at existing pages, you can get an idea of what you do and don't like when it comes to web page design. Reviewing existing sites on the Web gives you ideas about how you want your web page to look. Before you construct your site, go to your favorite search engine and search for sites on your proposed topic. Take a look at the existing sites and write down things that you'd like to emulate and things to avoid. Make special notes about what they do to make their site interesting— and what they do to keep people coming back.

Caution	*Looking at existing sites to gather ideas is acceptable, but don't copy things from the site without securing the author's permission! There are web sites that provide buttons, icons, and graphics free for everyone to use, and the authors always state these intentions clearly on the site. See Chapter 26 for more information on clip art.*

If you're interested in getting more involved in web design, articles on that subject are available on the Web, and numerous excellent books are devoted to the subject. To see what others think of your design, use the Web as an information-gathering medium—consider adding a survey to your site and asking visitors what they think.

Other General Tips for Web Site Design

Here are some other dos and don'ts:

- *What does each page do?* Each page on a site should fulfill some function, whether that's showcasing a product, sharing pictures of your kids with the world, or helping someone to find an old college buddy. Make sure that function is clear to the viewer.

- *Remember the five-second rule.* Studies have shown that most web visitors stay at a page for five seconds, and if they haven't seen anything interesting by then, they move on. Put anything you want people to see at the upper-left corner, where it catches their attention quickly.

- *Remember the other five-second rule.* That five seconds just mentioned includes the amount of time it takes your page to load.

- *The simpler, the better.* You'll be tempted to put every menu, button, and search engine on your site, but the fewer choices your visitors have to make, the less likely they'll get confused, and the cleaner and more professional your site will look.

- *Name and address.* Particularly if you're a business, have a link on every page that leads to a "Contact Us!" page—and have that page contain your e-mail address, your physical address, and your phone number.

Things You Might Not Have Thought Of

Just when you thought your plan was complete, here are some issues to be aware of when planning your web site:

- **Text size** Try not to use specific fonts or text sizes on your pages, unless it is necessary to the design of the page. Some people like to control fonts and text size via the browser settings to make the page more comfortable to read.

- **Colors** Don't use color-coded text to relay important parts of your message. Many people can't distinguish between colors and might miss the meaning that you intend.

■ **Writing for an international audience**   Remember that the Web is a worldwide resource, open to people from many different cultures and countries. What is acceptable in your culture might be vulgar in another culture. One general rule: Don't use pictures of hand symbols (like a "thumbs up" or the "OK" sign) on your site. Every hand symbol is considered obscene in at least one country in the world. Make sure that addresses, phone numbers, prices, and shipping costs include information for those outside of your country.

■ **Privacy**   Never include personal information about people on web pages without their consent. For example, suppose you create a web site for a church and you include the church's weekly newsletter. Omit people's addresses, e-mail addresses, and phone numbers, unless you have their permission to include them. Get the person's permission before mentioning sensitive information; for example, reporting that someone is out of town for a month might be an invitation to burglars, and reporting a wedding date and location invites pickpockets to the event. The Web is much more public than a small printed newsletter!

■ **Maintenance**   Don't commit to updating the web site more than you can actually follow through on. To continue with the church web site example, it's easy to make a site with information about your church, and the only maintenance the site requires is when staff or contact information changes. However, if you decide to include information about upcoming events, you are committing to updating the web site often enough to remove events as they pass and to add future events. If you decide to publish the weekly church newsletter, you are committing to updating the web site weekly. The Web is full of sites advertising events that happened in 1997—don't embarrass your organization by doing the same!

■ **Accessibility**   Make your web site usable by vision-impaired people, as well as people with all types of software and hardware. For information about designing web sites for people with disabilities, see **www.cast.org/bobby**. To make sure that your web pages look good on all types of browsers, try viewing your pages on the two most-recent versions of Internet Explorer and Netscape Navigator. You might also want to see how your pages look on MSN-TV (WebTV) or on handhelds.

How Will You Store the Pages on Your Site?

For a small site, all the HTML files and graphics files are usually stored in one directory (folder). If you plan a large site, you might want commonly used graphics files to be stored in a separate subdirectory, so that all pages can use the same copies. You might also want a subdirectory for each major section of the web site.

Larger sites may not even have HTML files at all; some of them have databases that create web pages on the fly as you request data. That is a database-driven site, as described in Chapter 28.

Creating Your Site

To create a web site, you create lots of files, containing the text, pictures, audio, video, and programming for the site.

Elements of a Web Page

Web page files are text files, including the text that appears on the page and the text commands to format the page, show links, and display pictures. These web page formatting commands are called *HTML tags*, the commands that are included in the formatting language that web browsers understand when displaying web pages. Web page files usually have the filename extension .htm or .html.

Each web page that you create is stored in a separate file—an *HTML file*. You use a text editor or web page editor to create HTML files. The main (home) page for a web site usually has the name index.html or index.htm because this is the default filename that most web servers provide. For example, if a user types **www.greattapes.com** into a browser, the web page that appears is the page named index.html at that web site. (Database-generated sites may have the default filename default.asp or index.php.)

In addition to HTML files, your web site will probably include graphics files—lots of them. Each picture that appears on a web page is stored in a separate file, usually with the extension .gif (for GIF files) or .jpg or .jpeg (for JPEG files). An HTML tag controls where each picture appears on your web pages. For example, if you use a tiny picture as a bullet for lists on your web pages, you need only one graphics file, with an HTML tag containing the filename in each place on the web pages where you want the bullet to appear. You may also have graphics files for page backgrounds. But remember: the greater the total size of all the files required to display a web page, the longer it takes to view the web page, especially for users with slow Internet connections. Keep your graphics files small, and don't use too many. For tips on using and creating graphics for your web pages, see Chapter 26.

If your web site requires forms, databases, or other programmable features, you'll also need scripts and other files. See Chapter 28 for more information.

What Else Can You Put on a Web Page?

You can put almost anything you want on a web page nowadays, from streaming video to custom-made cartoons, but it all comes at a price: bandwidth.

Bandwidth (data transfer capacity) is a fancy way of reminding you that no matter how cool your page is, it still has to be sent out across the Internet before people can see it. You can come up with the neatest page in the world—but if it's a 10-megabyte page that takes three hours to download, then nobody will wait for it to finish. As such, sticking to the old standbys—words and pictures—may seem a little boring at times, but has the advantage of being quick.

Still, if you want something a little snazzier, there are all sorts of things you can add to your web page:

- **Animated GIFs** This type of picture contains frames that loop back and forth, like the frames in a movie. They're easy to make and quick to download, but they only show one animated image and don't do much else. You can learn how to create animated graphics in Chapter 26.

- **Audio files** These come in two varieties: static and streaming. We go into more depth on audio files in Chapter 27.

- **Video files** These consume unbelievable amounts of bandwidth and server space, and as such are generally used only by sites that absolutely need them—like news sites. (And even then, they're used sparingly.) See the section in Chapter 27 on adding video to web pages for more information.

- **Flash** If you want complex animation, fancy web-based games, or buttons that morph and twist into menus when you click on them, Flash (a program from Macromedia, Inc.) is definitely the way to go. Flash allows you to do almost anything you can imagine in a web page, but creating your own Flash files is a complicated process and takes a while to learn. In addition, Flash files—though smaller than any other animation files—still take a while to load, and not everyone has the Flash plug-in. (See Chapter 18.) If you'd like to see some examples of how exotic Flash can get, grab the Flash plug-in and check out Macromedia's Flash Showcase at **dynamic.macromedia.com**. (Click Products | Flash | Showcase, or search the site.)

- **Shockwave** Made by the same company that makes Flash, Shockwave is an early web animation tool, but its files are bigger than Flash's, and it's not as widely used.

- **JavaScript** This scripting language is for programs that are stored as part of web pages and are run by your browser when it loads the page. JavaScript is generally used for small tasks—like creating a picture that changes when you roll the mouse over it (called, creatively, a *rollover*), drop-down menus in the web page itself, putting and tracking cookies (small text files) on the viewer's computer, or popping up a separate advertising window. JavaScript is easy to learn as languages go, but all JavaScripts run in the browser—so the more creative you get, the more likely you'll encounter a browser-specific bug that won't work on, say, Netscape 4.7 or Internet Explorer 6.0. Still, JavaScript is very popular and flexible, and many people have created scripts that you can cut and paste into your own web page. See Chapter 20 for an explanation of how cookies work, and see Chapter 28 for more about JavaScript.

- **Java** JavaScript is not a smaller version of (or a bigger version of) Java. They're two separate programs. Java was originally intended to be the "run anywhere, on any system" way of providing web page interactivity, but has since settled down into a more nitty-gritty language that's used to connect different systems and run on small appliances. You can, however, still write small applications that will run on people's browsers using Java—it just requires a lot of programming expertise and requires your viewer to download the program. For all your Java needs, go to **java.sun.com**.

- **Databases** When you look up all the films that Harrison Ford was in on the Internet Movie Database (**www.imdb.com**), you're asking the server to search through a large file that contains the names of a bunch of movies, actors, and directors and return all the ones that contain the words "Harrison Ford." This large file is called a *database*. If you sell products, you can create a database of information about whatever it is you sell and then allow your customers to search for specific answers. Also, many sites enter their articles and news items in a database so that people can find news the way they want it. We get into an overview of how database technology can help streamline large sites later in this chapter—or you can just cut to the chase and skip to Chapter 28.

- **Forms** A form on your web page is just like a form on paper. Visitors fill out the form to order products, give you answers to a survey, or any other uses you can think of for a form. You can see how to create forms in Chapter 24.

What Tools Do You Need to Develop the Site?

Determining the tools that you need depends on the type of content that you have planned for your web pages. The components that make up web pages are the following:

- Text
- Pictures
- Animated graphics
- Audio files
- Video files
- Animation files
- Forms and database information

You don't need to put every one of these on your pages—in fact, because audio files and graphics can take a long time to load, in many cases it's best to get by with as bare-bones a site look as you feel comfortable with. The first priority is to make sure that your pages are easy to read and well organized. You don't need to include animated icons or half-megabyte Flash animations to make a page visually interesting; the bulk of successful sites on the Internet are just plain text and pictures.

To create web pages, you need these tools:

- A text editor (if you know HTML), or a web page editor that adds the HTML codes for you. (Chapters 24 and 25 describe both.) We'll help you choose the web page editor that's right for you in "HTML Editors," later in this chapter.

- A drawing program, if you want to create your own graphics. (Chapter 26 describes creating graphics for web pages.)

- A supply of clip art if you do *not* want to create your own graphics. (Lots of clip art is available on the Web.)

- Sound or video equipment if you plan to make audio or video files to include on your site. (Chapter 27 describes how to record and format audio files for the Web.)

Your site may require more advanced features, such as forms that users can fill in, or a connection to a database of information from which web pages can be created based on user requests. Based on the information your users provide by using forms, your web site can run *scripts,* which are programs that process the information visitors fill in on forms. For web sites with forms, you'll need additional tools: see Chapter 28.

HTML Editors

In the old days of web design, back when pictures and words were all you needed, every page could be constructed easily using just good old-fashioned HTML know-how and a text editor. Today, web sites are more complicated in terms of both content and pictures; people expect more than five pages of text with your mug shot at the top. Take a look at the web site in Figure 23-2 earlier in this chapter, for example. On the surface, it looks simple, but when you look at the site in a WYSIWYG (What You See Is What You Get) web editor like Dreamweaver (see Figure 23-6), you see that the HTML is boiling with complexity underneath. The simple graphic stashed in the upper-left side? That's actually two graphics lined up vertically with one another—a common trick in HTML pages, thanks to the limitations of simple HTML. That list of links on the left? Each link is in a separate box in a table. And let's not forget that this is a database-driven web site, so the Search box needs to be coded so it can accept names and hand them off to the server properly.

Now, you *could* create all of this HTML by hand if you really wanted to—we show you the basics of manual coding in Chapter 24. However, creating it manually would be

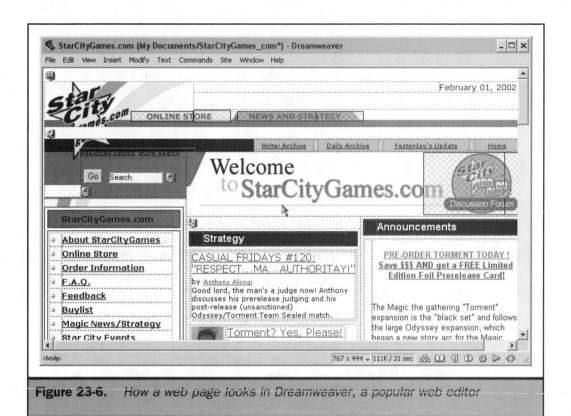

Figure 23-6.   *How a web page looks in Dreamweaver, a popular web editor*

complicated, it would take you a long time, and you'd probably get a lot of it wrong at first, requiring you to go through line-by-line and check for errors. Wouldn't it be easier to just put the graphics and text where you want them and let a web-editing program create the HTML for you automatically?

Of course, web editors aren't for everyone. For one thing, most of them cost money, so if thriftiness is your main goal, then coding by hand is still your best bet. For another thing, the HTML code that web editors create isn't always perfect. Microsoft FrontPage, for example, creates HTML that works perfectly when viewed under Internet Explorer (go figure), but doesn't always look good when seen through Netscape Navigator. Also, the HTML that web editors create is not as efficient as it would be if you hand-coded it yourself, but in the end, most professional web designers use web editors for the bulk of their designing and tweak it by hand afterward. If you're a casual web designer, just creating something for fun, it's doubtful you'll even need to look at your code.

Table 23-2 shows a list of the major web editors, sorted by price.

Web Editor	Price	Pros	Cons
Netscape Composer	Free	Free and simple to use, as web editors go; comes with Netscape Communicator suite	Not suited for large, complicated sites; doesn't handle multimedia files or scripting well; no picture editing features
Microsoft FrontPage	Under $175	One of the cheapest professional web editors; widely supported; highly visual and easy to use; has special features that work on servers that support it; comes with themes for pre-made web sites; comes with simple picture editing tools; integrated with Office	Tends to create HTML code that can cause viewing problems under non-Explorer browsers; can handle medium-sized sites, but large enterprise sites cause problems; doesn't always accept manual changes made to HTML code
Macromedia Dreamweaver	Under $300	High-powered tool with immensely customizable interface; handles large-scale web sites well; able to handle almost any kind of scripting, multimedia, and anything else you can throw at it; integrated with Flash and Fireworks	Steep learning curve; more windows and buttons than you may ever need; requires separate picture-editing program; expensive
Adobe GoLive	Under $350	High-powered tool with customizable interface; handles large-scale web sites well; handles scripting and multimedia with ease; integrated with Photoshop, Illustrator, and LiveMotion	Moderate learning curve; most expensive software package

Table 23-2. *Popular Web Editors*

Database-Driven Sites

For small sites, individual HTML files work fine. Say you're publishing your poetry to the Web to share with your friends. If you have five poems, that's no problem; just create five pages.

But suppose you get really prolific and write a hundred poems. Now, you *could* create a hundred HTML files and put them on your server, but keeping track of all those files would be cumbersome. Furthermore, every time you add a new poem, you'll have to update the page that has your list of poems—which, incidentally, would take up about four screens. Eventually, keeping track of all those folders and files and subdirectories gets to be completely overwhelming, and updating the site becomes a nightmare.

Wouldn't it be easier to store all of your poems in a database on the server and have the server create an HTML page for each poem whenever someone asked for it?

That's called *server-side scripting,* and it's a way to create what's called *dynamic content.* You can create a template of a web page, and the server will then drop information—like your poem—into it wherever you want. You can also use scripting to customize your pages for each visitor, showing different items, depending on what day of the week it is, what sorts of news items they like to see, and so on.

Tip   *If you want to be able to change all the pages on your site at once and don't want to use a database, you can use an HTML enhancement called* Cascading Style Sheets (CSS). *We talk about CSS in Chapter 29.*

Most e-commerce catalogs use server-side scripting to store their products, but it's becoming more and more common for large sites to store *all* of their information dynamically. ZENtertainment, for example, is a news site that has hourly updates and keeps them all in a database. You can identify a database-driven page by the question mark in the URL in Figure 23-7: see the way it ends with "article.php?sid=1519"? That's how it accesses its database.

There are three basic server-side scripting languages:

- **Perl and CGI**   Perl, the oldest of the scripting languages, is by far the most established. It's the most difficult to learn, but has unparalleled text-handling abilities. CGI is the method that web pages use to call Perl scripts.

- **Active Server Pages**   This is Microsoft's system. It is highly integrated with Visual Basic and is fairly easy to learn.

- **PHP**   This is a free program that is relatively easy to learn and was written specifically to create web pages dynamically.

ColdFusion is another program that isn't quite a server-side scripting language, but is very easy to use. Chapter 28 describes how designers can use databases and programs to create dynamic web sites.

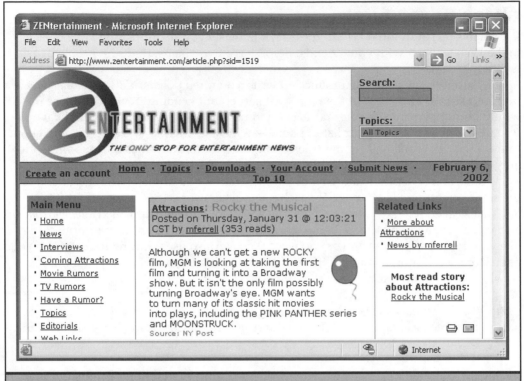

Figure 23-7. Some web pages are created on the fly using information from databases.

Publishing Your Site

Deciding where to store your pages is one of the final steps in creating your web site plan. To make your site available to everyone on the Web, you need to publish the site on a web server. You can either set up your own server or post your files to someone else's server.

File transfer procedures are different for each web server. Your web hosting company or ISP can give you the instructions that you need to transfer files to its web server. As soon as the files are transferred, your site is available for viewing on the Web. For more information about transferring web pages, see Chapter 30.

Maintaining Your Own Server

You probably don't want to set up your own web server, and here's why: it's expensive and it eats up all your time. Setting up and maintaining your own web server requires that you have the following items:

- A computer capable of handling web traffic that is up and running 24 hours a day
- Web server software
- A dedicated, high-speed Internet connection (such as an ISDN, DSL, or fractional T1 line) that supports a web server (most ISPs charge extra if you want to runs servers over a DSL or ISDN line) and that has a static IP address

The setup fees and monthly charges required when you use your own server are substantial. Factor in the additional job of being the server administrator, and other alternatives start to look good.

Using a Web Hosting Service

A *web hosting service* is a company that rents space on its web servers, and it's what most mid-level businesses and serious techies use. For $10 to $50 per month, you can store your web pages on the service's web server. Web hosting companies usually offer multiple web servers (so that one server is always running, even during system maintenance), a fast connection to the Internet, domain hosting (so that you can use your domain name for your web pages, like **www.greattapes.com**), frequent backups, unlimited access by the webmaster (you) to update your pages, and use of whatever scripts they support, like ASP, Perl, and PHP. In addition, if you're running any kind of database services, a serious web hosting service is generally the only way to go if you want to guarantee it's available at all times. Charges may be fixed, or they may depend on how much space your web pages occupy and how many visitors you have.

To find a web hosting service, start at Yahoo (**www.yahoo.com**) and choose Business & Economy | B2B | Communications And Networking | Internet And World Wide Web | Network Service Providers | Hosting | Web Site Hosting. Check around to get references on their reliability and customer service—what is their guaranteed uptime, and will they guarantee that in their contract? (You want uptime percentages in the very high 90s.) How quickly do they respond when their servers crash? Call their customer service line with a problem, and see how long you're put on hold. The CNET web site includes useful reviews of web hosting services. (Start at **www.cnet.com** and search for "web hosting reviews.") If the web hosting service hosts a domain for you, make sure you get e-mail addresses included with the service, and ask how many e-mail addresses you can host at your own site. (You may be able to set up e-mail addresses at your domain for your family and friends if your hosting service is generous enough.) Also, if you're starting a business site, check to see whether there's a bandwidth limit, and make sure your estimated traffic won't go over that limit. Nothing's more embarrassing than having a popular site that isn't available because your web host won't send out an extra 10 megabytes that day!

Using Your ISP's Server

If you're planning a more casual site, most ISPs include a few megabytes of web server space free of charge with a dial-up or DSL account, and nearly all offer additional space for a few dollars a month. For most people, storing web files on their ISP's server is the most convenient and economical way to publish a site on the Web.

The downside to all of this free space is that ISP-hosted web sites tend to be limited in terms of what you can do. If you need databases and forms on your site, many ISPs won't support them. In addition, some ISPs won't host domains, meaning your web site address will be something clunky like **webpages.yourisp.com/~yourname**, as opposed to the more memorable **www.yourname.com**.

Using a Free Hosting Service

Many sites, like Geocities.com and Netscape, offer free web site hosting. The advantage is pretty clear: it's *free*. Like ISP-hosted sites, the URLs of free web hosts tend to be long and hard to remember. But if you're using your ISP for web hosting and you change ISPs, your old address will disappear unless you've registered your own domain. (See Chapter 2 for details on what's involved in getting your own domain name.) If you host your site at Geocities, the address will always be the same, no matter *what* ISP you use to connect to the Web.

In addition, many free hosting services offer cute little add-ons you can add to your pages at absolutely no cost to you—things like hit counters, slot machine games, and web-based e-mail accounts. And because these sites are for the novice webmaster, you generally upload everything onto the site through your browser in a very easy process. If you want ease of use and no cost, free hosting is the way to go.

What are the drawbacks? For one thing, most free hosting services insert an advertisement somewhere on every one of your pages—they have to make their money *somewhere*, right? Also, many use the personal information you give them to bury you in spam. (See Chapter 8 for a definition of what spam is and how to reduce it.) For another thing, you're not guaranteed any set amount of uptime, the way you are with a paid web hosting service. (Though to be fair, most free services want you to eventually upgrade your hosting service to a paid account, so long periods of downtime generally aren't an issue.) Finally, the bandwidth is severely limited. If *People* magazine suddenly talks about your dancing hamsters page and 10,000 people go to see it, the free web hosting service will shut down your site for the day until traffic stabilizes. (Again, though, to be fair, those who *do* overload their free hosting sites are very lucky—and popular—people.)

A final issue is one that affects fan sites: free web hosting services tend to be very nervous about what they have on their servers, and they're the first to close up shop when the lawyers come knocking. The entertainment industry is very concerned about copyright these days, so their legal departments frequently make noises about unlicensed content. Rather than trying to figure out which Harrison Ford sites are legal and which have copyrighted photos, free web services are more likely to shut *all* Harrison Ford sites down and work it out later. If you're a fan of an actor, a show, or a movie, be warned.

For a list of free web sites and what services they offer, go to **www.freewebsiteproviders.com**.

Publicizing Your Site

After your site is published on the Web and you've joined the global online community, how are you going to publicize the site? The first step is to register your site with search engines, so that people doing online searches can find the site. For more information on registering your site with search engines (and on putting the right keywords in your HTML code to attract traffic there), see Chapter 31.

Chapter 24

Creating Web Pages by Hand

525

ypertext Markup Language (HTML) is the language of web pages. The formats
that you see applied to text, headings, and graphics on web pages are controlled
by HTML. Entering the world of web page authoring is like being a traveler in
a foreign land—the best way to feel at home and get around easily is to know the language.
Even if you plan to use a web editor that adds HTML codes for you, you'll find it
useful to know what HTML is, how it works, and what effect HTML codes have on the
appearance of your web pages. This chapter describes how to enter HTML codes on
pages manually in order to build web pages by hand.

Where Did HTML Come From?

HTML was developed (by Tim Berners-Lee, the architect of the World Wide Web) to
provide a way to format text and graphics to be read by web browsers. HTML is a
markup language rather than a programming language: it is a way of coding information
so that all types of browsers can read and display the page. HTML is evolving constantly;
new codes are added and outdated codes are retired. The evolution of HTML is
governed by the World Wide Web Consortium (W3C). The consortium membership
is made up of organizations and companies with an interest in the future of HTML.

| Tip | *For information about W3C, see its web site at **www.w3.org**. To see a list of W3C members, visit **www.w3.org** and click the link to access the member list.* |

Within the W3C are working groups that propose changes to HTML. Consortium
members vote on changes, and the W3C develops the approved changes into a
specification, which is posted in a variety of different formats at the W3C web site.

| Tip | *If you want to stay up to date on proposed changes to HTML, visit the W3C web site's HTML pages at **www.w3.org/MarkUp** periodically. Creating a new specification is a big undertaking, and proposed changes go through months of review and feedback.* |

At the time this book was written, HTML 4 was the current specification, and this
chapter describes HTML codes from HTML 4. HTML may eventually be supplanted by
XML (Extensible Markup Language) or XHTML, as described in Chapter 17. For more
information about HTML, see *HTML: The Complete Reference, Third Edition*, by Thomas A.
Powell (Osborne/McGraw-Hill, 2000).

Creating a New Web Page

To start creating a web page manually, open a text editor. Any text editor will work;
the examples in this chapter were created using Windows Notepad. Don't use a word
processor, which stores formatting characters that browsers won't understand. For
example, many word processors use special characters for line endings. Stick with a
text editor that stores only what you type.

HTML Isn't as Standard as It Should Be

The original idea of the Web was that any browser could display any web page because pages would use standard HTML that all browsers would support. Unfortunately, the Web hasn't completely worked out that way. Netscape has added extensions that their browsers support, and Microsoft has added extensions that they support. The World Wide Web Consortium has created new standards (like Cascading Style Sheets) that are supported differently in different versions of the two browsers.

Even if you don't try anything fancy, your pages may look different in various versions of Netscape Navigator and Internet Explorer. Ideally, you should make sure that they look acceptable in the last two or three versions of each, as well as in Opera, another popular browser. If your web site absolutely needs to use a feature that looks right only in a specific browser, be sure to mention this fact on your home page—many web sites include a note that "This web site looks best in Internet Explorer" or another browser. Another option is to use JavaScript to provide different page coding depending on which browser the person uses (see Chapter 29 for an example).

 Web pages look different when they are displayed in different browsers. The figures you see in this chapter may not match exactly the screen contents you see when you view your pages in your browser. When you make web pages, test the way they look in various browsers.

Seeing How You Are Doing

As you create your web page, you can periodically save what you have accomplished to that point and view it in your web browser. To display your web page in a browser, follow these steps:

1. Save the file by using the Save command in your web page editor or text editor.

2. In your browser, choose File | Open Page or press CTRL-O, and then choose the name of the file that contains your web page. Alternatively, you can type **file://pathname/filename** in the Location or URL box, replacing *pathname* and *filename* with the exact location and filename of your web page, and then press ENTER. (You are viewing a file stored on your computer or local drive, so you do not have to be connected to the Internet.)

HTML Tags

Web pages contain *HTML tags*, the codes that add formatting, pictures, and links to web pages. Some HTML tags appear by themselves, whereas others have a beginning tag and an ending tag. Tags are enclosed by < and > symbols.

If you've used word processing programs, you may already be familiar with the way that tags work. For example, HTML tags are similar to the formatting commands that precede and follow text in WordPerfect. The heading tags in HTML (Heading 1 through Heading 6) mark levels of importance in the same way that the built-in Heading styles do in Word.

For example, to enter a typical heading on a web page, type this line of HTML:

```
<H1>The Book Lovers Book Club</H1>
```

The <H1> tag indicates the beginning of the heading, and the </H1> tag marks the end of the heading. For tags that appear in pairs (such as <H1> and </H1>), the closing tab is the same as the opening tag, with the addition of a /.

In this chapter, tags appear in uppercase so that they stand out from the text, but you can use any combination of upper- and lowercase in your web pages. (In other words, HTML is not case sensitive.) Because tags always appear enclosed in < and > in HTML, they appear that way in this book, too.

Standard Tags on a Web Page

All HTML pages contain some common tags. The basic structure of a (very short!) page looks like this:

```
<HTML>
<HEAD>
<TITLE>A Sample Web Page</TITLE>
</HEAD>
<BODY>
<P>...The substance (text and graphics) of your page goes
here...</P>
</BODY>
</HTML>
```

This sample HTML would look like this in a browser. (We've turned off the toolbars and status bar in the browser to unclutter the picture.)

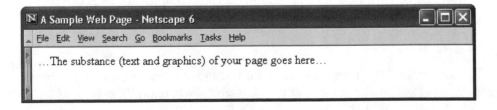

Here is an explanation of each HTML tag in this example:

- **<HTML>** Every HTML page starts with an <HTML> tag and ends with an </HTML> tag. This tag simply denotes that the page is coded in HTML, the language of web pages.

- **<HEAD>** The HEAD section is reserved for tags that apply to the entire document, including the <TITLE> tag. The HEAD section can also include *<META> tags* (discussed in Chapter 31), which provide keywords and other information about the page, and *style sheets* (described in Chapter 29), which control the formatting of text on your web page.

- **<TITLE>** The <TITLE> tag is required in the HEAD section. The text between the <TITLE> and </TITLE> tags is displayed on the title bar of the browser window when you view the page.

- **<BODY>** The BODY section, starting with a <BODY> tag and ending with a </BODY> tag, contains the content of your web page. Most of the tags described in the rest of this chapter—including tags to format text, links, and graphics on your page—are included in the BODY section.

- **<P>** Each normal paragraph in the web page is enclosed in <P> and </P> tags. Headings and other specially formatted text use other tags, as described in the section "Formatting Headings" later in this chapter.

Adding Hidden Comments

You can type comments that don't appear on the web page when it is displayed in a browser. For example, you might want to add notes to yourself, the names of people who worked on the page, or other information to the web page file, but you might not want this information to appear on the page.

Looking at the Codes in Other Web Pages

Have you ever wondered how other web authors make their pages look so good? You can see the HTML codes that format a page by choosing View | Source in your browser. The browser displays the HTML code for the current page (you may see JavaScript mixed in, too). You can get some good formatting ideas by looking at other people's pages.

However, the design of most web sites is copyrighted, so simply using the HTML and switching a few pictures around is generally illegal. Don't steal someone's design! If you want non-copyrighted web page designs that you can use, check out **www.netscape.com/browsers/templates**; otherwise, feel free to look at the HTML of popular web sites to see how they work, but don't call the design your own.

To add a hidden comment, precede the comment text with **<!--** and follow it with **-->**. For example, the following line would not appear in the page when displayed by a user with a browser:

```
<!-- Written for use with The Internet: The Complete Reference
book -->
```

Controlling the Overall Appearance of the Page

You can include some information inside the <BODY> tag to govern the overall appearance of the page. Some tags, like the <BODY> tag, can contain extra information, called *attributes*, before the closing angle bracket of the tag (for example, <BODY BGCOLOR="blue">). These attributes set the background that is displayed on the page, the color of text on the page, and the color of the links on the page. Each attribute consists of the name of the attribute (such as BGCOLOR), an equal sign, and the value that you want to use for that attribute (such as blue). The value should appear enclosed in quotes, although for many types of attributes, the quotes are optional.

Tip   *Setting colors for the background, text, and links is optional. If you omit color choices, the page is displayed in the colors used by each reader's browser. In fact, many browsers give readers the choice of overriding the colors set on the page with the colors used by the browser. Vision-impaired people, for example, might want to set their font sizes very large and their colors very bold.*

Displaying Wallpaper in the Background

The background of your page can be either an image or a specific color. To set an image as the background of your page, use the BACKGROUND attribute in the <BODY> tag and place the name of your image file within quotes:

```
<BODY BACKGROUND="image.gif">
```

Like tags, attribute names can appear in uppercase or lowercase letters. For the filename, be sure to use the same capitalization that is used in the actual filename. (Most web servers run the UNIX operating system, in which capitalization matters.) See "Absolute vs. Relative Pathnames" later in this chapter for more information about where the background image file can be stored and how to refer to it.

When a browser displays the page, the image in the file that you specify is *tiled* to fill the background of the web page: that is, it is repeated across and down the page.

*You can find some backgrounds to use for your web pages at Netscape's web site (**www.netscape.com/assist/net_sites/bg/backgrounds.html**), HowAmazing.com Web Page Backgrounds site (**www.webpagebackground.com**), or the Enders Design site (**www.ender-design.com/rg/backidx.html**).*

Choosing a Background Color

Instead of using wallpaper, you can specify a solid background color for your web page. Use the BGCOLOR attribute in the <BODY> tag. For the color, you can enter either a hexadecimal (hex, or base 16) value that represents the color or one of 140 standard color names, which are shown on the color charts at **www.projectcool.com/developer/reference/color-chart.html** or **www.gotomy.com/color.html**.

To indicate a standard color, use this tag:

```
<BODY BGCOLOR="blue">
```

Using a hexadecimal value is safer if you want your colors to be read by a wide variety of browsers. Also, only 16 colors have names, whereas you've got millions of colors to choose from if you specify in hex. The hexadecimal value is six characters that represent the amount of red, green, and blue in the color. The first two characters indicate the amount of red; the next two characters, the amount of green; and the final two characters, the amount of blue. Hexadecimal values range from white (FFFFFF) to black (000000). For example, this code specifies light aqua:

```
<BODY BGCOLOR="#99FFFF">
```

How do you obtain the six digits of hexadecimal value for a color? Here are two methods to use:

- Consult a conversion chart, such as the charts at **html-color-codes.com** or **www.gotomy.com/color.html**. To find other color conversion charts on the Web, go to your favorite search engine and search for "hexadecimal colors."

- Calculate the six digits of the color, as follows:
  1. Open any graphics program and display the color palette. (For example, in Windows, open the Paint program, select Options | Edit Colors, and click the Define Custom Colors button.)
  2. Move the color indicator until you see the color that you want. Note the Red, Green, and Blue numeric values.

3. Open a calculator and convert the numeric codes to hexadecimal values. (In Windows, open the Calculator and select View | Scientific. Click Dec, enter the numbers that you wrote down for Red, and click Hex. The result is the first two entries for your hexadecimal value: the result can be numbers or letters. Repeat these steps for the Green and Blue numbers. When you have the Red, Green, and Blue hexadecimal values, combine them into one six-character value, and that is your color code.)

Choosing Colors for Text and Links

If you're using an unusual background color, you may need to set the text color so that the text is readable. For example, black text tends to disappear on dark-colored backgrounds; if you're using a dark background, you need to reset the text to a light color that is easy to read against the background.

After you set your colors, test the text and link colors to make sure the text and links are visible. Four attributes in the <BODY> tag set the text and link colors on a page:

- **TEXT** controls the color of text on the page.
- **LINK** controls the color of an unvisited link.
- **ALINK** controls the color the link turns when a reader clicks it.
- **VLINK** controls the color of a visited link.

The following tag specifies colors for the background, text, and all links. This tag results in a page with a light-blue background, dark-blue text, green unvisited links, red active links, and hot-pink visited links. When you experiment, the color combinations are not always pretty.

```
<BODY BGCOLOR="#99FFFF" TEXT="#2C148F" LINK="#218F14"
ALINK="#CC0000" VLINK="#FF00CC">
```

Unless the use of multiple bright colors matches the feeling that you're trying to convey on your page, use colors sparingly, especially on the first pages that you create. You can always go back and add color attributes after the site is developed. If you have a lot of text on your pages, leave the text black and use a white or neutral background. The content on your page is important, and people should be able to read the text without interference from the page design.

Formatting Text

Most of the text on your web pages is formatted in paragraphs that begin with a <P> tag and end with a </P> tag. (The closing </P> tag is optional, and many web authors leave it out, but using it is a good habit to get into.) The <P> tag starts a new paragraph by leaving a blank line and starting at the left margin, without indenting the first line of the paragraph.

Here are some other tags that are used to format text:

- **
** inserts a line break, so that the following text starts on a new line. A single <BR> tag does not leave any vertical space between the preceding and following text. For example, you can use <BR> tags to start each line of a mailing address on a new line:

```
<P>Osborne McGraw-Hill
<BR>2600 Tenth Street
<BR>Berkeley, CA 94710 USA
```

  You can use multiple <BR> tags, or <P> and <BR> tags together to leave various amounts of vertical blank space.

- **<DIV align="center">** tells the browser to center text across the line (or lines), up to the matching </DIV> tag. (Older web pages use the tags <CENTER> and </CENTER>, which are left over from earlier versions of HTML and still work.)

Formatting Headings

An easy way to organize text is to divide it by headings. Six heading tags are available in HTML; it is rare to use all six on one page. The heading tags are <H1> through <H6> and come in pairs. (<H1> appears at the beginning of the first-level heading, and </H1> appears at the end.) The heading numbers indicate the size of the headings in relation to each other. H1 is the largest heading, and H6 is the smallest heading. The exact sizes and fonts that appear depend on the user's browser settings or on style sheets. You can control the format of the H1 through H6 headings by creating a style sheet for your web page. (See Chapter 29 for instructions.)

Heading text is enclosed between the heading tags. Text paragraphs are marked with the paragraph tags <P> and </P>:

```
<H1>The Book Lovers Book Club</H1>
<P>The Book Lovers Book Club meets online once each month. Books
are selected by a consensus vote of the book club members. We
discuss fiction and non-fiction books.</P>
<H2>Book Suggestions</H2>
<P>We're always open to new book suggestions!</P>
```

To emphasize specific words within a paragraph, you can enclose the words in a <B> tag to mark bold text, or an <I> tag to mark italic text, such as the following:

```
<P>We're <B>always</B> open to <I>new</I> book suggestions!</P>
```

Figure 24-1 shows how the Book Lovers Book Club web page would look.

Figure 24-1. Use the H1 tag for the major headings on your web page and H2 for minor headings.

> **Caution** *Stay away from underlining text. People expect underlined text to be a link, so don't use underlining for anything else.*

Controlling Fonts

Browsers display text and headings in standard typefaces and sizes, and users can control the default fonts that are used. Web authors can also specify the typefaces and sizes for the text on web pages, although you never know exactly which fonts are available on users' computers. In most cases, if you specify a font, and that font is not available on the user's computer, the browser will display the web page in the browser's default font.

To specify the font, you enclose the text in <FONT> and </FONT> codes. In the <FONT> tag, you specify the attributes that you want to use:

- **COLOR** This specifies the color of the text, using the same color codes described in "Choosing a Background Color," earlier in this chapter.

- **SIZE** This specifies the size of the text, usually relative to the size it would otherwise be. For example, this code displays one word a little bigger than the surrounding text:

```
Really <FONT SIZE=+1>Big</FONT> Show!
```

Another way to display text a little larger or smaller than normal text is to use the <BIG> and </BIG> tags or the <SMALL> and </SMALL> tags.

- **FACE** This specifies exactly which typeface you want to use. Using FACE isn't a good idea, however, because you don't know which fonts are installed on users' computers. If you want to control the fonts used in your web pages, use style sheets instead, as described in the section on formatting web pages using Cascading Style Sheets in Chapter 29.

Adding Special Characters

HTML is not limited to standard ASCII characters—this is a lucky thing because ASCII does not include special characters such as trademark symbols. You can use *character entities* to create many other characters. Each of these extra characters has both a name and a number. To include a character entity in the text of your web page, type an ampersand (&), the name or number of the character, and a semicolon (;). If you use the character number, precede it by #. For example, to include a copyright symbol, you can type **©** or **©** in your text. Not all character entities have names; some only have numbers.

Table 24-1 lists some useful character entities; you can use the version in either the second or third column of the table (unless only one version is available). For a complete listing of all the standard character entities, see one of the following sites:

- **hotwired.lycos.com/webmonkey/reference/special_characters**
- **www.natural-innovations.com/boo/doc-charset.html**
- **www.htmlhelp.com/reference/html40/entities**

Character	Character Entity (Name)	Character Entity (Number)
Less than (<)	&lt;	&#060;
Greater than (>)	&gt;	&#062;
Bullet (•)		&#149;
Em dash (—)		&#150;
En dash (–)		&#151;
Trademark (™)		&#153;
Nonbreaking space		
Inverted exclamation point (¡)	&iexcl;	&#161;
Copyright (©)	&copy;	&#169;
Registered trademark (®)	&reg;	&#174;
Paragraph sign (¶)	&para;	&#182;
One-half (½)	&frac12;	&#189;
Inverted question mark (¿)	&iquest;	&#191;

Table 24-1.   *Some HTML Character Entities*

When displaying text, browsers throw away repeated characters. For example, if you include a series of <P> codes (<P><P><P><P>), browsers display the same amount of vertical space that one <P> code leaves. Similarly, if you type ten spaces, browsers display only one. To leave extra vertical space, mix <P> and <BR> tags; to leave extra horizontal space, mix regular spaces with nonbreaking spaces ( ).

 If you don't want the paragraphs on your web pages to be separated by blank space and want them to start with an indented first line, use styles to control the way that paragraphs are formatted: see the section on formatting web pages using Cascading Style Sheets in Chapter 29.

Presenting Information in Lists

A good way to break up text on a page is to use lists:

- **Numbered lists** show a progression of steps in sequence. Numbered lists use the <OL> (Ordered List) tag at the beginning of the list, the <LI> tag at the beginning of each list item, and the </OL> tag at the end of the list.

- **Bulleted lists** highlight short sentences or present a series of items that can be read quickly (like this list). Bulleted lists use the <UL> (Unordered List) tag at the beginning of the list, <LI> for each list item, and </UL> at the end of the list.

- **Definition lists** present information in a glossary-type format (one short line, followed by an indented paragraph). These lists use the <DL> (Definition List) tag at the beginning of the list, a <DT> for each term, a <DD> tag for each definition, and a </DL> tag at the end of the list.

For example, the following is code for a numbered list. (Figure 24-2 shows how it looks in Netscape Navigator.)

```
<OL>
<LI>Select the books and authors you want to recommend.
<LI>Write a brief summary of each book.
<LI>Send your recommendations to the host.
</OL>
```

A bulleted list (with an introductory paragraph) looks like this:

```
<P>The most recent books we've read are:</P>
<UL>
<LI><I>John Adams</I>, by David McCullough
<LI><I>The Battle for God</i>, by Karen Armstrong
<LI><I>The Fellowship of the Ring</i>, by J.R.R. Tolkien
</UL>
```

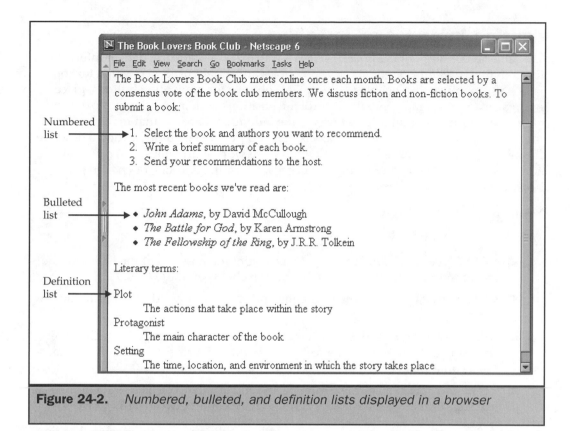

Numbered list

Bulleted list

Definition list

Figure 24-2. *Numbered, bulleted, and definition lists displayed in a browser*

The entries in a definition list (with an opening paragraph) look like this:

```
<P>Literary terms:</P>
<DL>
<DT>Plot
<DD>The actions that take place within the story
<DT>Protagonist
<DD>The main character of the book
<DT>Setting
<DD>The time, location, and environment in which the story takes
place
</DL>
```

CREATING AND
MAINTAINING WEB SITES

Presenting Information in Tables

The table layout was originally designed as a way to show statistical data or information that can fit easily into columns. However, tables are widely used to position text on web pages because they enable you to create columns for navigation buttons, place figures next to text, and generally control the positions of items on the web page.

Table data is stored in cells, which are the individual "boxes" that make up the rows and columns of the table. The labels that you put on a column or row to describe the table's content are called *table headings*. As you work with tables, you can apply additional formatting to align data within cells, adjust the borders, or change the background color of the table.

Laying Out the Table

Tables use the following tags:

- **<TABLE> and </TABLE>** indicate the beginning and end of the table. All the rest of the tags and text in the table must be between these tags.

- **<TR> and </TR>** mark the beginning and end of a row. All the cells in the row come between these tags.

- **<TH> and </TH>** mark the beginning and end of a header cell, which usually appears in boldface. A header cell must be part of a row, so <TH></TH> tags must come between <TR></TR> tags.

- **<TD> and </TD>** mark the beginning and end of a data cell on a row. One row can have one or many cells. <TD></TD> tags must come between <TR></TR> tags.

The following example shows a table with three columns and three rows. The first row is a header row. The BORDER attribute in the <TABLE> tag indicates that the table cells have lines around them. To omit the lines, delete the BORDER attribute.

```
<TABLE BORDER>
<TR>
<TH>Member's Name</TH>
<TH>Hosted the Book Club?</TH>
<TH>Host Dates</TH>
</TR>
<TR>
<TD>Ellen</TD>
<TD>No</TD>
<TD>Not Applicable</TD>
</TR>
<TR>
<TD>Samuel</TD>
<TD>Yes</TD>
<TD>May 10, August 23</TD>
```

```
</TR>
</TABLE>
```

In a browser, the table looks like this:

Member's Name	Hosted the Book Club?	Host Dates
Ellen	No	Not Applicable
Samuel	Yes	May 10, August 23

Formatting the Table

To control the appearance of the table, you can use the following attributes in the <TABLE>, <TR>, <TH>, and <TD> tags:

- **ALIGN** controls the horizontal alignment of the row (if you add it to a <TR> tag) or the data in a cell (if you add it to a <TD> or <TH> tag). The most common values are LEFT, CENTER, and RIGHT. For example, this tag starts a table with rows aligned to the right:

  ```
  <TR ALIGN=RIGHT>
  ```

- **VALIGN** controls the vertical alignment of the row (if you add it to the <TR> tag) or the data in a cell (if you add it to the <TD> or <TH> tag). The most common values are TOP, CENTER, and BOTTOM. The following tag starts a table with entries at the top of each cell:

  ```
  <TR VALIGN=TOP>
  ```

- **CELLPADDING** controls the amount of space between the information within cells and the border. The space is measured in pixels. This attribute is set in the <TABLE> tag. This tag starts a table with five pixels of space between the contents of each cell and its border:

  ```
  <TABLE CELLPADDING=5>
  ```

- **BGCOLOR** controls the background color of the entire table (if you add it to the <TABLE> tag), a row (if you add it to the <TR> tag), or a cell (if you add it to the <TD> or <TH> tag). The color can be the name of a standard color or the hexadecimal value for a color. This tag starts a row with the background color of bright aqua:

  ```
  <TR BGCOLOR="#66FFFF">
  ```

- **BACKGROUND** displays a graphics file in the background of the table, row, or cell (like the BACKGROUND attribute of the <BODY> tag).

- **WIDTH** sets the width of the table, either in pixels or as a percentage of the width of the browser window.

Using Tables for Page Layout

Even if a web page doesn't appear to contain a table, it may use tables to position the objects on the page. For example, take a look at the web page shown in Figure 24-3. The body of the web page is contained in a table with one row and two columns. The left column contains the navigation links, and the right column contains the text of the page.

You can also use a table to make a sidebar or boxed text. Create a table with one row and one column, like this:

```
<TABLE BORDER ALIGN=left WIDTH="30%">
<TR>
<TD>
Warning! The following text has not yet bin proofread!
</TD>
</TR>
</TABLE>
```

Set the table apart from the rest of the web page text by giving it a border (as in this example) or by setting its background color in the <TABLE> tag. Set its width with the WIDTH attribute. (We usually set the width to a percentage of the available space; in

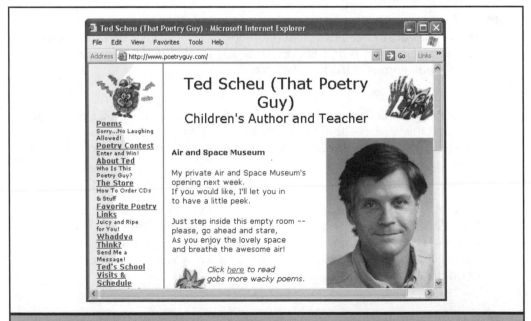

Figure 24-3.   *Many web pages use tables to position text in columns.*

this example it's 30 percent.) The little table appears on the web side to the left or right, depending on the ALIGN attribute, like this:

> Warning! The following text has not
> yet bin proofread!

Adding Horizontal Lines

You can separate one section of the web page from the next section with a horizontal line by using the <HR> (horizontal rule) tag, which moves down a line, inserts a horizontal line, and starts the following material on the next line. You can control the length of the horizontal line relative to the width of the browser window in which the web page is displayed by using the WIDTH attribute. You can also specify the thickness of the line in pixels by using the SIZE attribute. You can align the line to the left, right, or center by using the ALIGN attribute. For example, the following tag displays a centered, two-pixel-thick line that is 80 percent of the width of the browser window:

```
<HR SIZE=2 WIDTH=80% ALIGN="CENTER">
```

Adding Pictures

A page of all text and no graphics is usually boring. To spice up your web page, consider adding some pictures.

Where do you get pictures to add to your web page? You can use clip art, create your own pictures with a drawing program or graphics program, load pictures from a digital camera, or use a scanner to import a drawing or photograph. There are also many web sites that offer images free for downloading. Chapter 26 describes how to create graphics for web pages.

To add a picture, use the <IMG> (image) tag, entering the tag at the place in the BODY section of the web page where you want the graphic to appear. You use the SRC (source) attribute to specify the name of the file that contains the picture that you want displayed on the web page, like this:

```
<IMG SRC="picture.gif">
```

Tip   *On most web servers, capitalization counts in filenames. Use lowercase for all filenames (including images), and refer to them in lowercase in your <IMG> tags.*

CREATING AND
MAINTAINING WEB SITES

Before you add a picture to your page, determine where the picture will be stored. The filename is either an absolute pathname or a relative pathname.

Absolute vs. Relative Pathnames

An *absolute pathname* includes the full pathname of the file. This means that if you move your files or if you change your directory (folder) names, you have to edit every <IMG> tag in every HTML file that contains the absolute pathname. For that reason, this naming convention is not recommended.

A *relative pathname* indicates the pathname of the image file relative to the pathname of the HTML file. This is the recommended naming convention for graphics files. For example, if your image file is stored in the same directory as your HTML file, you can use just the image filename in your <IMG> tag, with no pathname, as in the example in the previous section. If the image file is in the same directory as your HTML file, but in a subdirectory, include the subdirectory name in the <IMG> tag, like this:

```
<IMG SRC="images/picture.gif">
```

If the image file is stored one directory level up from your HTML file, use two dots (..) in the pathname to move up a directory level, as follows:

```
<IMG SRC="../picture.gif">
```

Some web authors like to store their frequently used graphics in a directory called *images* or *pix,* so that all the <IMG> tags in all the pages in the rest of the directories of the web site can refer to one set of graphics files.

Image Attributes

You can add the following attributes to the <IMG> tag to adjust the picture and to control how text flows around the picture:

■ **HEIGHT and WIDTH** control the size (in pixels) at which the graphic appears on the web page. These attributes are optional; use them only if you do not like the default size and need to resize the picture. The web browser that displays the web page adjusts the height and width of the graph to the sizes that you specify. When you use the HEIGHT and WIDTH attributes, make sure that you keep the same proportions as the original graphic; if you don't, the picture looks like you s-t-r-e-t-c-h-e-d it either horizontally or vertically. Resizing a graphic to be larger than the original is rare. The larger the number of pixels, the bigger the picture. For example, the following <IMG> tag displays the picture in the file picture.gif as 30 by 50 pixels, regardless of the size of the stored picture:

```
<IMG SRC="picture.gif" HEIGHT=30 WIDTH=50>
```

> **Tip**
>
> *Using small (but legible) graphics on web pages is best because they load faster than large graphics. To make a graphic small, be sure to use a graphics program to reduce the size of the file. Don't just change HEIGHT and WIDTH attributes, which don't change the file size (or speed up downloading time), only the way it is displayed by the browser. For information on resizing web graphics, see Chapter 26.*

- **ALIGN** controls how text flows around the graphic. ALIGN has five possible values:

  - **TOP** places one line of text even with the top of the image.

  - **MIDDLE** places one line of text at the middle of the image.

  - **BOTTOM** places one line of text even with the bottom of the image. TOP, MIDDLE, and BOTTOM are useful when you have a *single* line of text that you want placed next to a graphic.

  - **LEFT** places the graphic on the left side of the page, with your text paragraph wrapped around the right side of the graphic.

  - **RIGHT** places the graphic on the right side of the page, with your text paragraph wrapped around the left side of the graphic. LEFT and RIGHT are useful when you have paragraphs of text that you want to wrap around a graphic. For example, the following tag displays a picture on the left side of the web page, with the surrounding text wrapped around its right side:

    ```
    <IMG SRC="picture.gif" ALIGN=LEFT>
    ```

- **HSPACE and VSPACE** control the amount of white space around the image. Both values are indicated in pixels. HSPACE sets the amount of space at the left and right of the image; you use this attribute to control the distance between the text that is wrapped around your graphic and the graphic itself. VSPACE sets the amount of space above and below the graphic. The following tag inserts a picture with 25 blank pixels to either side, and 10 blank pixels above and below the picture:

  ```
  <IMG SRC="picture.gif" HSPACE=25 VSPACE=10>
  ```

- **BORDER** indicates that a border should be placed around the image and also controls the width of the border. The width is measured in pixels. The next tag inserts a picture with a border that is three pixels wide (a heavy line):

  ```
  <IMG SRC="picture.gif" BORDER=3>
  ```

- **ALT** contains the text that appears while the picture is loading, if a user has a browser that does not display graphics, or if the user has opted not to load graphics when viewing web pages. Always include ALT attributes in all image tags to make your web site accessible to vision-impaired users, who use special software to read the text on the screen. For example:

  ```
  <IMG SRC="picture.gif" ALT="Book cover of this week's selection">
  ```

> **Note** *You can use as many or as few of the attributes as you need. Only the SRC attribute, which specifies the filename, is necessary. All attributes are placed in the same <IMG>, separated by spaces. For example, if you decided to use all the attributes listed here, your image tag might look like this:*
> ```
> <IMG SRC="picture.gif" HEIGHT=30 WIDTH=50 ALIGN=LEFT HSPACE=25
> VSPACE=10 BORDER=3 ALT="Book cover of this week's selection">
> ```

You can do other things with graphics besides wrapping text around them. A graphic can be displayed in a table by including the <IMG> tag between the <TD> and </TD> tags , like this:

```
<TD><IMG SRC="picture.gif" ALT="Book cover of this week's
selection"></TD>
```

You can center an image by enclosing the <IMG> tag between the <CENTER> and </CENTER> tags, like this:

```
<CENTER><IMG SRC="picture.gif" ALT="Book cover of this week's
selection"></CENTER>
```

An image can also be a link that takes readers to a new destination, as described in the next section.

Adding Links

The ability to jump from one location or web page to another is what makes the Web so powerful. No matter what you call them (*hyperlinks, hypertext links,* or just *links*), the purpose of links is to help you navigate though a web site or jump to other, related web sites.

Links use an <A> tag with an HREF (hypertext reference) attribute to specify the URL to which the link connects. Between the starting <A> tag and the ending </A> tag is the text or graphic that appears on the web page as the link. A basic link looks like this:

```
Visit the <A HREF="suggest.htm">Book Club Suggestions Page</A>.
```

The value of the HREF attribute ("suggest.htm") indicates what the browser displays when the user clicks the link. The text between the beginning and ending tags is the text that appears on the screen, marked as a link (usually blue and underlined).

Translated by a browser, this link looks as follows to readers who visit your page:

Visit the Book Club Suggestions Page.

The link's destination (the HREF value) can be a filename or the URL of another web page. If the destination is a filename, the link leads to a web page stored on your web site, and you need to decide whether you're going to use absolute or relative pathnames. Relative pathnames are recommended. (For a discussion of the difference between absolute and relative pathnames, refer to "Absolute vs. Relative Pathnames" earlier in this chapter.)

To link to any web page on the Internet, type the full URL of the destination page in the HREF attribute, like this:

```
<A HREF="http://www.mcgraw-hill.com">McGraw-Hill Books</A>
```

Links that readers click are not confined to text only. You can also use graphics as links. Many web pages use navigation buttons, such as Next, Previous, Home, or Index, to guide readers through the site. To display an image as a link, include the <IMG> tag between the <A> tag and the </A> tag. The following HTML code displays a link that leads to the schedule.html page on the same site. The link is a picture called next.gif (a small picture that looks like a Next button):

```
<A HREF="schedule.htm"><IMG SRC="next.gif" ALT="Next button"></A>
```

Tip   *Whenever you use graphical navigation buttons, also include text-only navigation options somewhere on your page for readers who are not viewing graphics.*

Adding a Link That Jumps Within the Page

A link doesn't have to take a reader off the current page. If you have a long page made up of text divided by headings, add links at the top and bottom of the page so that readers can jump to the topics they want to read—you can make a little table of contents with links to each heading. To implement a link to a spot on the current page, you add two tags: one tag to mark the destination on the page (called an *anchor*) and one tag to add the link that the reader uses to get to the destination.

To mark the destination on the page, move your cursor to the header or text of the destination, and enter an <A> tag that uses the NAME attribute. (You can place the tags around existing text, or add new text between the tags.) The following tag assigns the anchor name "members" to the text "Book Club Members":

```
<A NAME="members">Book Club Members</A>
```

To create a link that leads to the anchor, move your cursor to the location where you want to place the link, and enter an <A> tag with an HREF attribute. The value of the HREF attribute uses a # to indicate that it links to an anchor name. For example, the next tag creates a link that jumps to the anchor named "members":

```
Take a look at the <A HREF="#members">list of our members</A>.
```

When readers click the "list of our members" link, they jump to the Book Club Members anchor. You can add an anchor name to jump to an existing anchor in any web page (not only in the current page), like this:

```
<A HREF="http://www.sample.com/index.html#members">list of book
club members</A>
```

 If you are creating a long web page, consider adding links that allow the reader to jump back to an anchor at the top of the page.

Adding a Link to Your E-mail Address

Most web pages contain a contact link at the bottom of the page. The link often goes to the webmaster or to the person responsible for the page.

You can set up the link so that when a reader clicks the link, an e-mail window opens with your address filled in, so that the reader can simply enter a message and send it to you. When a reader clicks the link, the browser sends a message to the reader's e-mail program, which pops up the window.

To add a link to your e-mail address, use *MAILTO:* and your e-mail address in place of the URL in an <A> tag. For example:

```
<A HREF="MAILTO:nettcr2@gurus.com">Internet Complete Reference
Authors</A>
```

 Some people advocate including the e-mail address in the text of the link, so that the address is visible on the web page. This is probably a good idea, especially if you want to make sure that all readers, including those whose browsers don't support the MAILTO feature, can contact you via e-mail.

Gathering Information in Forms

Up to this point, you have been giving readers information on your page. Now, it is time to receive a little feedback, by using *forms*. A form is useful to your readers because it enables them to send information to you. You benefit because you get answers to the questions that you ask. Forms are used on web pages for a variety of tasks, including

- Gathering information from readers (similar to an electronic suggestion box)
- Performing a survey to find out what readers think
- Taking orders for products

Creating a form involves two tasks:

- Creating the form page in HTML
- Creating a Common Gateway Interface (CGI) script that processes the responses

This section describes how to create a form page in HTML. For information on CGI scripts, see Chapter 28. Many ISPs provide CGI scripting services as part of their web page–hosting capabilities, providing standard, tested scripts that you can use.

Creating a Form

The <FORM> tag defines the beginning and end of the form. The information that the reader fills in falls between these tags. The following are two attributes that you need to set within the <FORM> tag:

- **METHOD**   This indicates how the information from the reader will be sent to the CGI script. Use the POST option on your METHOD attribute, unless the CGI script documentation indicates otherwise.
- **ACTION**   This specifies the location of the CGI script to run when the user fills in and submits the form.

For example, the following tag begins a form that will be processed by the bookform script stored in the web server's cgi-bin directory:

```
<FORM METHOD="post" ACTION="cgi-bin/bookform">
```

Fill In the Blanks

The body of a form contains objects that the user can use to input information. In addition to text boxes in which readers can type information, you can display these other types of controls:

- **Radio buttons**   Readers are limited to one selection from the list.
- **Check boxes**   Readers can mark as many selections as they want.
- **Drop-down boxes**   Readers make a selection from a drop-down list.

You create each of these items by entering an <INPUT> tag. The TYPE attribute of the <INPUT> tag determines what type of box or button you are creating, and the NAME attribute gives the input a name. Depending on the type of input that you are creating, you can also specify other attributes.

Text Boxes

Text boxes are blank boxes into which readers type free-form responses. You create a text box by using an <INPUT> tag with the TYPE attribute set to "TEXT." You can also specify the size of the box (measured in number of characters). The following tag creates an input box named *source* that is 40 characters wide. (The top of Figure 24-4 shows how this text box looks in a browser.)

```
<INPUT TYPE="TEXT" NAME="howlearned" SIZE=40>
```

To give readers more than one line into which they can type responses, use the <TEXTAREA> tag. You control the size of the text box by using the attributes COLUMNS and ROWS. The NAME attribute names the box. This following tag creates a large text box that is 5 rows high and 40 characters wide:

```
<TEXTAREA NAME="resource" COLS=40 ROWS=5>
</TEXTAREA>
```

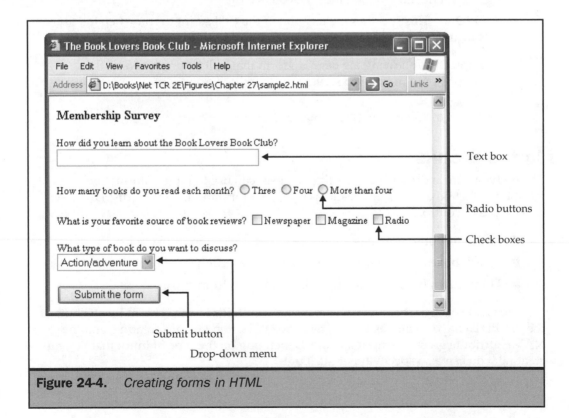

Figure 24-4. *Creating forms in HTML*

Radio Buttons

Use radio buttons when you want to present a set of choices to readers, from which the user can choose only one. You create each radio button with an <INPUT> tag that sets the TYPE attribute to "RADIO." Each radio button in the group must have the same name (specified with the NAME attribute). If you have more than one set of radio buttons on your form, make up a unique name for each set. The VALUE attribute indicates the value of the button's input if the user chooses that button. When the user submits a form, the browser uses the value of the chosen radio button as the value for the set of buttons.

For example, these three <INPUT> tags create a set of three radio buttons, from which the user can choose only one. (Figure 24-4 shows the resulting radio buttons.)

```
<INPUT TYPE="RADIO" NAME="bknumber" VALUE="three">Three
<INPUT TYPE="RADIO" NAME="bknumber" VALUE="four">Four
<INPUT TYPE="RADIO" NAME="bknumber" VALUE="more">More than four
```

Check Boxes

Use check boxes when the reader can choose more than one of the options in a set of inputs. Sets of check boxes are similar to sets of radio buttons, and the tags contain the same attributes as radio button tags. However, with check boxes, readers can select as many options as they want. For example, this set of check boxes lets the user choose as many media types as he or she wants. (Figure 24-4 shows the resulting check boxes.)

```
<INPUT TYPE="CHECKBOX" NAME="media" VALUE="newspaper">Newspaper<BR>
<INPUT TYPE="CHECKBOX" NAME="media" VALUE="magazine">Magazine<BR>
<INPUT TYPE="CHECKBOX" NAME="media" VALUE="radio">Radio<BR>
```

To force each selection on a radio button list or check box list to be displayed on a separate line, add a <BR> tag at the end of each <INPUT> tag.

Drop-Down Menus

Drop-down menus are useful if you need to conserve space on your form. The selections do not appear onscreen; they are displayed only when the reader clicks the drop-down arrow.

Most drop-down menus allow only one item to be selected. However, you can set a Multiple option to allow readers to select more than one item. (To select more than one item, the reader's browser must support this feature, and the reader must know which keys to use to select more than one item on a list. In Windows, you can select more than one item from a list by pressing SHIFT-DOWN ARROW.)

Every drop-down menu that you create on your form must be assigned a unique name.

Type a <SELECT> tag to start a drop-down menu, and type a matching </SELECT> tag at the end of the tags for the menu. The <SELECT> tag must include the NAME attribute, to assign the menu a name. After the <SELECT> tag, enter an <OPTION> tag for each option that you want to appear in the drop-down menu. For example, these lines create one drop-down menu with four options. (Figure 24-4 shows the drop-down menu.)

```
<SELECT NAME="booktypes">
<OPTION>Action/adventure
<OPTION>Historical
<OPTION>Mystery
<OPTION>Political thriller
</SELECT>
```

Submit Button

Somewhere on your form (usually at the bottom), you need a *submit button* that the user clicks to send the information on the form to the web server. (The button doesn't have to say "Submit" on it, but many buttons to submit information do, and readers are comfortable with it.)

Readers click the submit button (or whatever you call it) when they complete the form and want to send their entries to your web server for processing. The CGI script specified in the <FORM> tag goes into action when the submit button is clicked to process the answers on the form.

To add a submit button to your form, use an <INPUT> tag with the TYPE attribute set to "SUBMIT." If you don't want the button to read "Submit," enter something else for the VALUE attribute of the tag. For example, the following tag defines a submit button labeled "Submit the form" (as shown in Figure 24-4):

```
<INPUT TYPE="SUBMIT" VALUE="Submit the form">
```

Putting the Form Together

The form shown in Figure 24-4 is made up of the following HTML:

```
<H3>Membership Survey</H3>

<P>How did you learn about the Book Lovers Book Club?<BR>
<INPUT TYPE="TEXT" NAME="howlearned" SIZE=40></P>

<P>How many books do you read each month?
<INPUT TYPE="RADIO" NAME="bknumber" VALUE="three">Three
<INPUT TYPE="RADIO" NAME="bknumber" VALUE="four">Four
<INPUT TYPE="RADIO" NAME="bknumber" VALUE="more">More than four</P>

<P>What is your favorite source of book reviews?
<INPUT TYPE="CHECKBOX" NAME="media" VALUE="newspaper">Newspaper
```

```
<INPUT TYPE="CHECKBOX" NAME="media" VALUE="magazine">Magazine
<INPUT TYPE="CHECKBOX" NAME="media" VALUE="radio">Radio

<P>What type of book do you want to discuss?<BR>
<SELECT NAME="booktypes">
<OPTION>Action/adventure
<OPTION>Historical
<OPTION>Mystery
<OPTION>Political thriller
</SELECT>

<P><INPUT TYPE="SUBMIT" VALUE="Submit the form"></P>
```

Tip *If you want the controls in the form to line up evenly, you can put the text, check boxes, radio buttons, and other form components into a table.*

Formatting Your Page in Frames

Frames let you divide your web pages into rectangular sections of the browser window. They are useful if you want part of the web page to stay the same while other parts of the page change as the reader clicks links. The most common use for frames is to add a list of links in a narrow space on the left side of the window and to present information on the larger, right portion of the window. The links in the left frame remain onscreen as the reader goes through each page of information. The links serve as a table of contents of the site, although the frame is rarely labeled "Table of Contents."

To use frames, the web page contains tags that define the layouts of the frames on the page. The contents of each frame are stored in a separate file. For example, a web page that displays two frames is stored in three files: the main file with the frame layout tags, and a file for each frame. The files that appear in each frame are ordinary web pages, with no special frame-related formatting.

Drawbacks of Frames

When frames were introduced in the late 1990s, web designers were excited about the possibilities. However, most designers have determined that frames have more drawbacks than advantages, including these:

- Frames are slower to load because each page is stored in multiple files.

- Frames interfere with the user's ability to "bookmark" a page because the URL in the browser's Address or Location box frequently displays only the address of the original web page with the frames, even after the user has moved from page to page within the frames.

- Frames interfere with some screen readers, so people with vision impairments can't use the web site.

- Frames interfere with some search engines' ability to index your web site, so people who are searching for your web pages may not be find them.

Setting Up Frames

The main file for the web page contains a <FRAMESET> tag, which specifies the layout of the page, and <FRAME> tags, which indicate the name of the file that appears in each frame. You omit the BODY section from this web page file because the body of the page is contained in the separate files for the frames.

Not all browsers are capable of displaying frames, but the last few versions of both Netscape Navigator and Internet Explorer are frames-capable. Whenever you use frames, be sure to include a paragraph of information for readers whose browsers do not display frames. This information is included under the <NOFRAME> tag, so that readers whose browsers can display frames don't see it.

Controlling the Frame Layout

The <FRAMESET> tag indicates whether the page is divided horizontally (by using the ROWS attribute) or vertically (by using the COLS attribute). You can specify the size of each frame either in pixels or as a percentage of the whole browser window in which the web page is displayed. For example, the following tags divide the page into two vertical frames; the first frame consumes 20 percent of the page, and the second frame uses the rest of the page (noted by the asterisk):

```
<FRAMESET COLS="20%,*">
</FRAMESET>
```

Displaying Web Pages in Frames

Between the <FRAMESET> and </FRAMESET> tags, you add a <FRAME> tag for each frame. The SRC attribute of the <FRAME> tag specifies the name of the file that contains the web page to appear in that frame. The files that you specify appear in order across and down the browser window. If you define two columnar frames, the first file that you add with the <FRAME> tag is displayed in the left column; the second file that you add is displayed in the right column. (If the <FRAMESET> code used the ROWS attribute to divide the browser window horizontally, the first file would appear above the second.)

For example, these tags specify the names of files to appear in the two frames:

```
<FRAME SRC="firstdoc.htm">
<FRAME SRC="secondfile.htm">
```

> **Tip** *You can set the SCROLLING attribute of the <FRAME> tag to control whether the contents of the frame can scroll—if it's too big to fit in the frame. SCROLLING defaults to Yes unless you set it to No.*

Displaying Text for Non–Frame-Enabled Browsers

Finally, enclose text in between the <NOFRAMES> and </NOFRAMES> tags to appear in browsers that don't support frames, as follows:

```
<NOFRAMES>
```

This page uses frames, which are not supported by your browser:

```
</NOFRAMES>
```

Putting It All Together

The following is an example of an entire web page. (The finished page is shown in Figure 24-5.)

```
<HTML>
<HEAD>
<TITLE>The Internet Complete Reference Home Page</TITLE>
</HEAD>
<FRAMESET COLS="25%,*">
<FRAME SRC="toc.html">
<FRAME SRC="pagetext.html">
<NOFRAMES>
This page uses frames, which are not supported by your browser.
Click <A HREF="noframes.html">here</A> to see a non-framed version.
</NOFRAMES>
</FRAMESET>
</HTML>
```

Changing What Appears in a Frame

If you use the web page in one frame as a table of contents for the web site, you want links in the one frame to control what appears in another frame. For example, clicking a link in the left frame displays a specific web page in the right frame. To create this kind of link, you name the right frame and then refer to that name in your link.

To name a frame, add the NAME attribute to the <FRAME> tag. For example, the following <FRAME> tag for the right frame names the frame "Data":

```
<FRAME SRC="pagetext.html" NAME="Data">
```

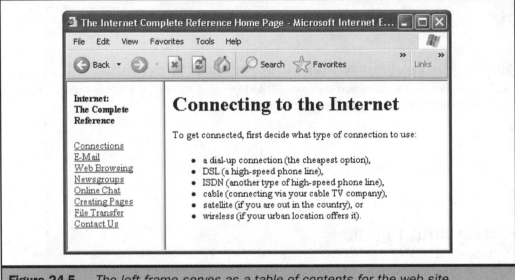

Figure 24-5.   *The left frame serves as a table of contents for the web site.*

Then, include the frame name in an <A> tag in the left frame, using the TARGET attribute to specify the frame in which the linked file should appear. For example, the table of contents web page displayed in the left frame might contain the following <A> tag, which displays the connections.html file in the Data frame:

```
<A HREF="connections.html" TARGET="Data">Connecting to the Internet</A>
```

When readers click the link in the left frame, the file is displayed in the right frame.

Note *If you leave out the TARGET attribute, the file is displayed in the same frame as the link (in other words, the left frame) when readers click the link.*

The left frame in Figure 24-5 displays the toc.html file, which contains this HTML code:

```
<HTML>
<BODY>
<P>
<B>Internet:
<BR>The Complete
<BR>Reference</B></P>
```

```
<P><A HREF="connections.html" TARGET="Data">Connections</A>
<BR><A HREF="email.html" TARGET="Data">E-Mail</A>
<BR><A HREF="browsing" TARGET="Data">Web Browsing</A>
<BR><A HREF="usenet.html" TARGET="Data">Newsgroups</A>
<BR><A HREF="chat.html" TARGET="Data">Online Chat</A>
<BR><A HREF="creating.html" TARGET="Data">Creating Pages</A>
<BR><A HREF="ftp.html" TARGET="Data">File Transfer</A>
<BR><A HREF="authors.html" TARGET="Data">Contact Us</A></P>
</BODY>
</HTML>
```

Summary of HTML Tags

Table 24-2 lists the HTML tags and attributes defined in this chapter. The next chapter describes how to create web pages without having to type all of these tags.

Tag	Definition and Attributes	
<HTML>	Indicates that the page is an HTML page.	
<HEAD>	Provides information about the page.	
<TITLE>	Specifies text to appear on the title bar of the browser.	
<!-- -->	Defines a hidden comment that doesn't appear on the web page.	
<BODY>	Defines the main segment of the page, which contains the content of the page. Attributes:	
	BACKGROUND	Image displayed behind the text
	BGCOLOR	Color displayed behind the text
	TEXT	Color of the text
	LINK	Color of unvisited links
	ALINK	Color of active links
	VLINK	Color of visited links
<P>	Marks a paragraph.	
 	Starts a new line.	

Table 24-2.   *Summary of HTML Tags*

Tag	Definition and Attributes
\<DIV ALIGN=center\>	Centers text or other information.
\<H1\> through \<H6\>	Denotes headings on the page.
\<FONT\>	Controls the typeface, size, and color. Attributes:

	COLOR	Color of the text
	SIZE	Type size in points
	FACE	Typeface (not recommended)

Tag	Definition and Attributes
\<OL\>	Indicates a numbered list.
\<LI\>	Specifies an element in a numbered or bulleted list.
\<UL\>	Indicates a bulleted (or unordered) list.
\<DL\>	Shows a definition list.
\<DT\>	Marks the term being defined in a definition list.
\<DD\>	Indicates the definition paragraph in a definition list.
\<TABLE\>	Defines information presented in rows and columns. Attributes:

	ALIGN	How table is aligned with surrounding text
	BACKGROUND	Image displayed behind the text in the table
	BGCOLOR	Background color of the table
	BORDER	Width of the table border
	CELLPADDING	Amount of space between data and table border
	WIDTH	Width of the table in pixels or as a percentage of the browser window

Tag	Definition and Attributes
\<TR\>	Indicates a row in a table. Attributes:

	ALIGN	Horizontal alignment of the row
	VALIGN	Vertical alignment of the row
	BGCOLOR	Background color of the table
	BACKGROUND	Image displayed behind the text in the table

Table 24-2.   *Summary of HTML Tags* (continued)

Tag	Definition and Attributes	
<TH>	Marks the heading of a table. Attributes:	
	ALIGN	Horizontal alignment of the row
	VALIGN	Vertical alignment of the row
	BGCOLOR	Background color of the table
	BACKGROUND	Image displayed behind the text in the table
<TD>	Defines a data cell in a table. Attributes:	
	ALIGN	Horizontal alignment of the data
	VALIGN	Vertical alignment of the data
	BGCOLOR	Background color of the table
	BACKGROUND	Image displayed behind the text in the table
<HR>	Adds a horizontal line. Attributes:	
	ALIGN	Controls the horizontal alignment
	WIDTH	Specifies the width in pixels or as a percentage of the browser window width
<IMG>	Adds an image to the page. Attributes:	
	SRC	Filename or URL of the graphic
	HEIGHT	Number of pixels in height
	WIDTH	Number of pixels in width
	ALIGN	Controls text flow around graphic
	HSPACE	Space at left and right of graphic
	VSPACE	Space at top and bottom of graphic
	BORDER	Line around graphic
	ALT	Text displayed while graphic is loading, or instead of graphic

Table 24-2.   *Summary of HTML Tags* (continued)

Tag	Definition and Attributes	
<A>	Specifies a link. Attributes:	
	HREF (Hypertext reference)	File, anchor, or URL that is the destination of the link
	NAME	Name of anchor to create at this position on the web page
	TARGET	Frame in which to display the linked page
<FORM>	Marks a section where readers can enter information and make selections from lists. Attributes:	
	METHOD	How information is sent to the CGI script (usually POST)
	ACTION	CGI script name to run when form contents are submitted
<INPUT>	Defines areas where readers enter information on a form. Attributes:	
	TYPE	Format of input
	NAME	Name of input
	SIZE	Size in characters (for text boxes)
	VALUE	Unique identifier of input (for radio buttons, check boxes, and submit buttons)
<TEXTAREA>	Defines a multiline text box in a form. Attributes:	
	NAME	Name of text box
	COLS	Number of columns (characters) across the text box
	ROWS	Number of rows (lines) in the text box
<SELECT>	Creates a drop-down list on a form.	
<OPTION>	Specifies the selections in a drop-down list on a form.	
<FRAMESET>	Defines the overall format of a page constructed in frames. Attributes:	
	ROWS	Number and size of frames across the web page
	COLS	Number and size of frames down the web page

Table 24-2. *Summary of HTML Tags* (continued)

Tag	Definition and Attributes	
<FRAME>	Contains the name of the file that fills the frame. Attributes:	
	SRC	The filename or URL of the web page to appear in the frame
	NAME	Unique identifier assigned to frame
	SCROLLING	Controls whether the contents of the frame can scroll if the web page is too big to fit in the frame
<NOFRAMES>	Information displayed by browsers that cannot display frames.	

Table 24-2.   *Summary of HTML Tags* (continued)

The
Complete
Reference

Internet

Chapter 25

Using Web Page Editors

Web pages are coded using Hypertext Markup Language (HTML) tags to specify the way text and graphics are displayed (as described in Chapter 24). HTML controls the layout and format that you see on web pages. When you create your own web pages, you *can* type all of those tags into a text editor—but most web designers use a *web page editor* to lay out their site and let the editor generate the HTML tags for them. (If necessary, they go back and tweak the code manually later.) This chapter describes how to use web page editors to create pages and to build your web site using several popular packages: Dreamweaver, FrontPage, Netscape Composer, and GoLive. If you use another web editor, the ideas are the same, although the commands and dialog boxes are different.

When all of your pages are finished, you upload the pages to a web server. For more information on uploading files to a web server, see Chapter 30.

What Is a Web Page Editor and Why Would I Use One?

Although the phrase "web page editor" sounds like it refers to a person who edits the web section of a newspaper, in Internet jargon this phrase describes the applications that web authors use to code pages in HTML. Rather than coding everything blindly and then looking at it through a browser to see whether it looks right—as you would do if you coded it with a text editor—web page editors allow you to lay out the page as it will appear in a browser and then write HTML code that will create that page for you.

Another advantage to using a web page editor is the amount of time that you save by not having to type all the HTML tags. Because the web page editor adds the tags for you, you can focus on the layout and content of your page. Most editors also check the tags to be sure that you haven't forgotten the beginning or ending tag, which is a laborious task to do manually. Some help you with the syntax of more complex tags, displaying dialog boxes with the options for the tag.

The WYSIWYG (What You See Is What You Get) capability and the amount of time saved by not typing all the HTML tags leads practically all serious web authors to use a web page editor. Advanced web pages editors like GoLive and Dreamweaver include other useful features like these:

- **HTML help**   The program reminds you what options are available for each HTML tag and what attributes are available for any object.

- **Graphics editing**   The web editor includes or links to a graphics editor that you can use to create or update the graphics in your web page.

- **Site management**   These editors keep track of which files are included in the site (HTML files, graphics files, CSS style sheet files, and others). The program can also check that links within your site are right. If you decide to rename a file, the web editor can update all the references to that file within your site. Some web editors can draw a map of the files in your site.

- **Built-in file transfer**   You don't have use a separate FTP program to upload a finished web site to your web server.

- **Link-checking**   The program can check the external links (links to pages outside your web site) to make sure that the links aren't dead.

- **Script cookbooks**   Simple JavaScript programs are built-in, so that you can create rollovers and other commonly used scripts by choosing from menus.

Web Page Editing Tasks

Within a web page editor, HTML tags are included as options on menus and as buttons on toolbars. Even if you aren't coding pages manually, a basic knowledge of HTML is important for two reasons: one, it helps you to know which button to click in the editor. Two, the HTML that web page editors create isn't always perfect, and sometimes it's necessary to go back and change the code manually. (The simpler the page, the less likely that you'll need to change anything.) You can also experiment in a web page editor and see how different menu options, palettes, and toolbar buttons would look on your page.

All web page editors deal with the same set of HTML codes and create HTML pages that can be viewed in any web browser and reedited with any web page editor. HTML codes are fairly standard, so the differences that exist among web page editors are primarily in the way that they arrange their windows and in the extra features that they offer. The extra features offered are often ways to manage your web site, usually by verifying links or showing all the files that make up your site. The higher-end programs also make it easier to put advanced features in your web pages—things like server-side scripting, XML coding, multimedia, and CSS. This chapter shows what some web page editors look like and explains their extra features.

Microsoft's programs are exceptions to the standard use of HTML. FrontPage may use WebBot components, which require FrontPage Server Extensions to be installed on the web server. Don't use these WebBot components unless your ISP's or web hosting company's web server supports them. Instead, use only standard HTML codes, which work with all browsers, web editors, and web servers.

All web page editors work in pretty much the same way. They all enable you to create a new page, starting with a blank page, a template, or help from a Wizard; edit an existing page; see what your page looks like in a browser; alter the HTML after the editor has created it; and save the page on disk. When you are done creating or editing a page, you can customize your web page in many ways:

- **Text**   Type the text to appear on the web page, and use formatting buttons on the toolbar to change it afterward. Web page editors have formatting buttons that are similar to those of a word processor. However, if you want to do much text formatting, consider using style sheets instead of formatting codes. (See the section on formatting web pages using Cascading Style Sheets in Chapter 29.)

- **Pictures** Insert a picture in the web page by clicking an Insert Image button on the toolbar and specifying the filename and what size the picture should appear.

- **Lists** Format instructions as a numbered list, or format a list of items as a bulleted list, by clicking a button on the toolbar.

- **Tables** To format text as a table, most web page editors have an Insert Table toolbar button to create and format the table. Then you can type or copy text and insert pictures into the rows and columns of the table.

- **Links** Add links to other web pages related to your subject by clicking an Insert Link toolbar button.

- **Lines** Click a toolbar button to place a horizontal line on the page to mark the end of a section.

Most web page editors can show you what your web page will look like in a browser: some have built-in browser previewers, and others pass your web page to a browser that you already have installed. You can also look at the underlying HTML and make changes directly to the code.

Where to Find Web Page Editors

Web page editors are available as stand-alone applications or bundled into Internet software packages. This chapter describes how to use some popular editors, including Netscape Composer (which is part of Netscape Communicator 4.x and Netscape 6.x), FrontPage (from Microsoft), Dreamweaver (from Macromedia), and GoLive (from Adobe). All run under Windows 95 and later. With the exception of FrontPage, each of these main editors is also available for the Mac. GoLive 6 runs on Mac OS X as well.

Dozens of excellent web page editors are available. For information about all editors reviewed and/or available on the web, go to your favorite search engine and search for "HTML editors"; you'll find a lot of them. You can also go to **www.download.com** and choose Web Developer | HTML Editors or go to **www.versiontracker.com**, click your operating system, and click HTML Tools. For how to download and install software, see Chapter 34.

  *1st Page 2000 (**www.evrsoft.com**) is a completely free web authoring tool. Although the learning curve is steep, is comes with over 400 VBScript and JavaScript scripts to get you started.*

This chapter describes Netscape Composer in some detail as an example of how a web page editor works because it's simpler than the others, and Netscape users already have it installed. The other editors listed in this chapter work similarly, but have more features, as we note.

Tip *If you create occasional web pages and already have Netscape installed, start with Netscape Composer. If you have to create web pages that use Microsoft's web objects, use FrontPage. If you are a serious web designer—or want to become one—get Dreamweaver or GoLive.*

Editing Pages with Netscape Composer

Composer is part of Netscape Communicator 4.*x* and 6.*x* and can be downloaded from the Netscape web site at **home.netscape.com**. This section describes Netscape Composer version 6, which is quite different from previous versions. (The program is free, so go ahead and upgrade if you have an earlier version.)

Note *Netscape Composer is easy to use, but it doesn't support frames or style sheets. If you need either of these features, consider GoLive or Dreamweaver instead. Netscape Composer doesn't help you create forms, either, although you can type in the tags yourself (as described in the previous chapter).*

To start Composer from within Netscape 6 and above, choose Tasks | Composer. You can also start Composer from within Netscape Navigator 6 by clicking the Composer button next to the Netscape icon at the bottom of the Navigator window.

Tip *When you are running Netscape Navigator and choose File | Open Web Location to see a web page, you can specify whether to open the page in a Navigator window or a Composer window. Also while browsing in Netscape Navigator, you can choose File | Edit Page to switch to Composer to edit the page that you are looking at.*

You can get more information about Netscape Composer at **help.netscape.com/ netscape6**.

Creating a New Page

To make a new web page, you can start from scratch, from a web page on the Internet, or from a web page that you've already saved on your hard drive. To make a new page from scratch, you just fire up Netscape Composer and start typing.

Editing a Page

To edit an existing web page—whether it's stored on the Internet or on your own hard disk—select File | Open Web Location to display the Open Web Location dialog box:

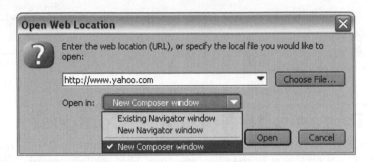

(If the file is on your computer, you can also choose File | Open File or press CTRL-O.) If you want to edit a web page on the Internet, type the URL or select it from the drop-down address box menu by clicking the down arrow. (This address box displays the same addresses as Netscape's Address bar; for information about how the Address bar works and what URLs it displays, see the section on the Address/Location bar in Chapter 19.) If you want to edit a web page stored on your computer, click Choose File and select the file.

The Open Web Location dialog box's Open In box offers three options to open the web page, but only one of them lets you edit it:

- **Existing Navigator Window** This opens the page for browsing in your current Netscape Navigator window.

- **New Navigator Window** This opens the page for browsing in another Netscape Navigator window.

- **New Composer Window** This downloads the HTML of the page and allows you to edit it in Netscape Composer.

Choose New Composer Window and click Open to begin editing.

If the page you've selected uses frames, *Composer will not open it; other web page editors, like Dreamweaver, help you edit pages with frames. For more information on frames, see Chapter 24.*

Once you are in Netscape Composer, you can select from a list of recently edited files by selecting File | Recent Pages. The Netscape Composer window includes the

Composition toolbar (choose View | Show/Hide | Composition Toolbar if it doesn't appear) and the Format toolbar (choose View | Show/Hide | Format Toolbar).

Choosing a View

Once you have opened (or created) a web page in Netscape Composer, you see a window that looks like Figure 25-1. Netscape Composer can work as a WYSIWYG (What You See Is What You Get) editor, but you may want to see the HTML tags on occasion. Along the bottom of the Netscape Composer page is a row of tabs—the Edit Mode toolbar that controls what view you see.

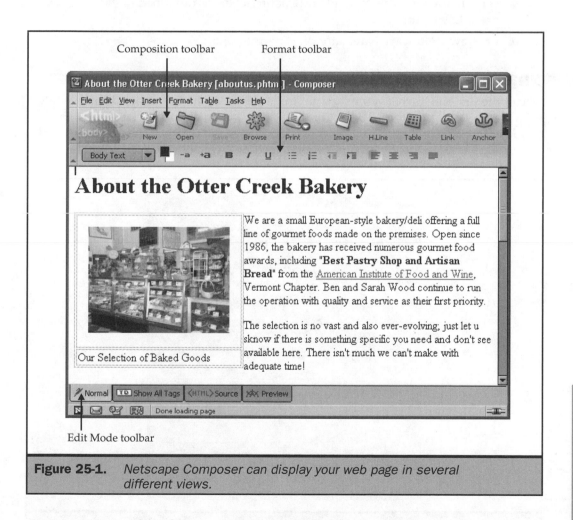

Figure 25-1. *Netscape Composer can display your web page in several different views.*

If this toolbar doesn't appear, select View | Show/Hide | Edit Mode Toolbar. You can click these tabs (or choose from the View menu on the menu bar) to choose among these views:

- **Normal**   This is Netscape Composer's WYSIWYG view, which looks approximately the way that the page will look in Netscape Navigator, with additional formatting markings.

- **Show All Tags**   Tags appear as little boxes that you can right-click to see the tag's properties.

- **HTML Source**   This shows HTML source code, as described in the preceding chapter.

- **Preview**   Netscape Navigator displays the page.

Setting the Background, Text, and Links Colors

One of the first things that you may want to do is change the background color; white is so bland, don't you think? Select Format | Page Colors And Background. The dialog box shown in Figure 25-2 allows you to change the colors of the text, links, and background of the page. If you don't want to choose any specific colors, select Reader's

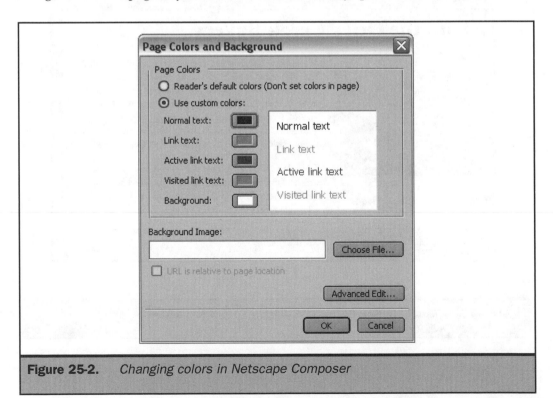

Figure 25-2.   *Changing colors in Netscape Composer*

Default Colors and click OK; that setting lets the viewer's browser set the colors on the page.

Changing the color of Normal Text allows you to set the default color for all nonlinked text. (Of course, you can still override the color for a specific section of text by changing it in the page.)

The next three options allow you to set colors for the hyperlinks in your page. Although there's theoretically a difference between Active Links, Visited Links, and Link Text—Active Links are hyperlinks you're clicking on, Visited Links are links you've already been to, Link Text is for default hyperlinks—browsers don't always pick up on that difference. Even though you may visit a particular URL several times, sometimes it just won't show up as the "Visited" color. Be aware of that when coloring links.

To change a color, click the swatch of color immediately to the right of the setting. You'll see the dialog box shown in Figure 25-3 with an array of web-safe colors. If you are changing several settings to the same color, you can click the Last-Picked Color box to choose the same color you chose the last time you used this dialog box. Pick a color and click OK—or, if you happen to know the hexadecimal code for the color you want (*riiiight*), you can enter it in the box just above and to the left of the OK button.

Tip   *Numerous studies have shown that white text on a black background is the least readable color combination. Dark on dark or light on light are bad, too.*

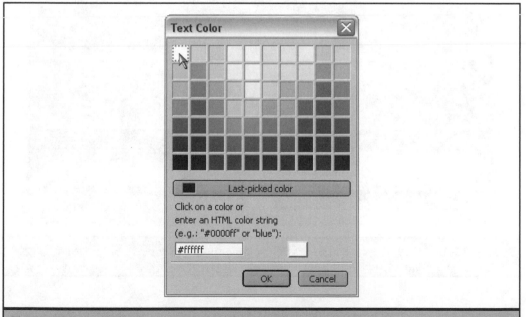

Figure 25-3.   *The color selector window, in black and white*

If you'd like to display a picture or graphic as the background of your web page, click the Choose File button to browse your way to the photo you want behind your text and click OK. The background picture will be tiled (repeated horizontally and vertically to fill the page), as in Figure 25-4.

  If you use a background picture, make it simple and keep the colors pale. You don't want to make it hard to read your text!

Setting the Page Title and Properties

The page title is the first place web search engines look to rank your site, and it's also the name used in people's browsers when they bookmark you. So make sure to set it to something short, accurate, and complete.

Figure 25-4.   *Even the clean design of Yahoo can be made ugly with a bad background!*

Select Format | Page Title And Properties to display this dialog box:

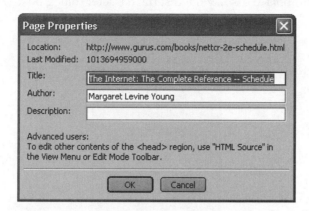

Type the name of your page into the Title box. If you want to keep track of who created what page (it's not used for anything else), type your name in the Author box. Typing a bunch of keywords in the Description field includes those words in the keywords <META> tag; for why *that's* so important, check out Chapter 31.

Entering and Formatting Text

In Normal Edit view, you can type text into your web page or edit the existing text. Netscape Composer adds the <P> and </P> codes around your paragraphs. You can use the Formatting toolbar and commands to format your text:

- **Headings (H1 through H6)**   Click the Paragraph button and choose Heading 1 through Heading 6 from the menu that appears, or choose Format | Paragraph and choose the built-in HTML style from the menu.

- **Boldface, italics, and underlining**   Select the text and click the appropriate toolbar button, or (with the text selected) choose Format | Text Style and choose from the menu, which also includes other text formatting.

- **Alignment and centering**   Select the paragraph to align and click the Align Left, Align Right, Align Center, or Align Justified button.

You can also control the font, size, and color of your text by selecting it and choosing Format | Font, Format | Size, and Format | Text Color from the menu. These commands add <FONT> codes to your web page.

To insert a special character (HTML calls these *character entities*), choose Insert |
Characters And Symbols to display the Insert Character dialog box:

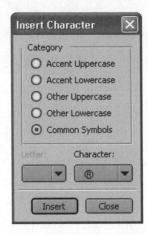

Choose the category of character you want, choose the character from the Letter
or Character drop-down menu, and click Insert. Chapter 24 describes the special
characters that HTML pages can contain.

Adding Horizontal Lines

Horizontal lines (<HR> codes) divide your page into readable sections. To insert
a horizontal line, click the H. Line button on the Composition toolbar or select Insert |
Horizontal Line.

The line appears at the cursor position. The default size of the line is 100 percent
of the window. To resize the line, right-click the line and select Horizontal Line
Properties. On the dialog box that appears, you can also change the color and thickness
of the line.

Formatting Lists

Formatting text as a list is a good way to make instructions, short paragraphs, or
a series of items easier to read. Numbered lists work well for sequential items or
instructions. Bulleted lists work well for short, related paragraphs or to highlight
items that you would normally separate by commas in a paragraph.

To add a numbered list (the <NL> and <LI> tags), click the Numbered List button
or select Format | List | Numbered. To add a bulleted list (the <UL> and <LI> tags),
click the Bullet List button or select Format | List | Bulleted.

Adding Pictures

Before you add a picture to your web page, store it in the same folder as your web
page or in a nearby folder for images. For example, some web authors like to store

all their pictures in an Images subfolder. When you add the picture to the page, the <IMG> tag will contain the current path and filename of the picture, which is usually written relative to the current location of the web page.

To add a picture to your page, follow these steps:

1. Position the cursor where you want the image to appear and either click the Image button on the Composition toolbar or select Insert | Image. You see the Image Properties dialog box, shown in Figure 25-5. Click the More Properties button if you don't see everything that appears in Figure 25-5.

2. Click the Choose File button, select the image file, and click Open. Make sure that the URL Is Relative To Page Location check box is selected. (Otherwise, Netscape Composer may store the complete URL of the exact location of the

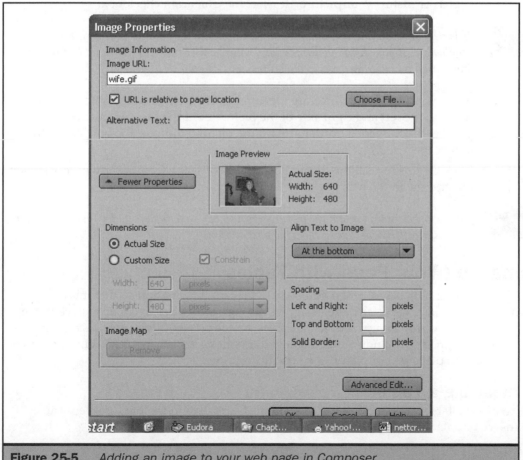

Figure 25-5. *Adding an image to your web page in Composer*

file on your computer, which won't work at all once the web page is uploaded to a web server.)

3. In the Alternative Text section, type the text you want to appear while the image is loading. (It's also helpful for vision-impaired people and for people who turn their graphics off to enhance their downloading speed.) If you don't put Alternative Text in, Composer suggests that you do.

4. In the Align Text To Image section, select one of the options to indicate how text wraps around the picture.

5. In the Dimensions section, choose the size of the image. To display the picture using its actual pixel size, select Actual Size. To shrink it or enlarge it, select Custom Size and type in the dimensions you'd like it to appear as. (You can set the size of the graphic in pixels or as a percentage of the screen.) By default, Composer shrinks the picture horizontally and vertically at the same time; to stretch or distort your picture, deselect the Constrain check box.

 Shrinking your picture in Composer doesn't decrease the amount of time it takes to download it! If you shrink pictures a lot, create smaller pictures instead. For further information on creating good web pictures, see Chapter 26.

6. In the Spacing section, indicate the number of pixels of white space that you want on the left and right side of the picture or at the top and bottom of the picture. If you want a border around the picture, indicate the border width in pixels.

7. Click OK to close all the dialog boxes. The Netscape Composer window shows the graphic in the web page.

 If you want a caption below the picture, create a two-row table, one for the picture and one for the caption, as described in the next section.

Formatting Your Page with Tables

The table format is useful when you need to present information so that it is aligned in columns and rows. Web page designers also use tables to leave blank space to the left of their text, to line up complex graphics, and for many other uses. Because HTML wasn't designed to include many page-layout options, tables are used almost any time you want to place text or pictures in specific locations.

Inserting a Table

To insert a table, click the Table button on the Composition toolbar, or select Table | Insert | Table to display the Insert Table dialog box:

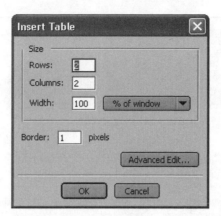

Specify the number of rows and columns that you want. Fill out any of the following optional fields that you want to use:

- **Width** By default, Composer sets a table to 100 percent of the entire page, but you can adjust that to a lesser percentage—or set an exact width in pixels.
- **Border** This creates a gray border around the table.

Creating a Table from Existing Text

You can also create a table from text that you've already typed in. To do so, select the text and then select Table | Create Table From Selection, or click the Table button on the Composition toolbar. You see the Convert To Table dialog box, shown here:

When you click OK, Netscape Composer creates a new row for each paragraph in the selection, but you have to show it where to create columns. By default, Composer creates a new column whenever it sees a comma, as shown in Figure 25-6.

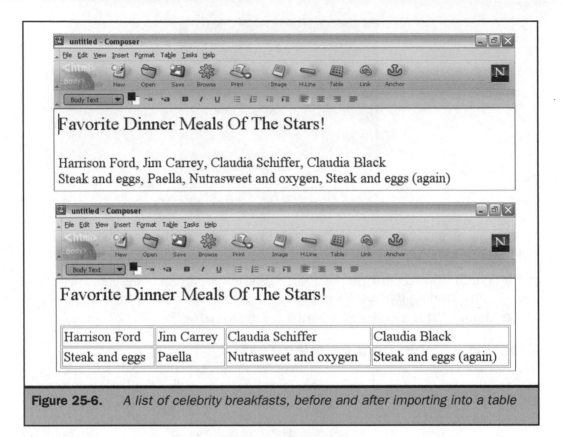

Figure 25-6. *A list of celebrity breakfasts, before and after importing into a table*

You can also tell Netscape Composer to create a new column whenever it sees a character of your choice, like a % or a #. In the Convert To Table dialog box, choose Other Character and type whatever character appears in your text between columns—make sure it's something that won't appear by mistake. If you're simply using that character to tell Composer when to create a new column and want it deleted from the table, click the Delete Separator Character check box.

Editing a Table

Once you have created a table, you can type text or insert pictures into the cells of the table. When you press TAB in the lower-right cell of a table, Netscape Composer adds a new row and moves you to the first column in it. You can also insert or delete rows and columns by positioning the cursor in an adjacent row or column and choosing Table | Insert or Table | Delete.

Formatting a Table

You can control the borders, background colors, positioning, and other properties of a table. Click in any cell and select Table | Table Properties, or just click the Table button and select the Table tab. On the Table Properties dialog box (shown in Figure 25-7), you can change the number of rows and columns in the table from here, as well as what kind of border the table has, the spacing between cells, the spacing between cell border and content, the table alignment, the color of the table, and whether the table has a caption. Make your changes and click OK.

If you want to change the properties of a row, column, or cell in a table, you use the same Table Properties dialog box. Click the Cells tab (shown in Figure 25-8). You can change specific cells in your table, or change them all at once.

First, decide whether you want to alter a single cell, a row, a column, or all cells. The first three are easy: Choose Cell, Row, or Column from the drop-down menu under Selection. Clicking the Previous and Next buttons cycles you through cells, columns, and rows; keep clicking until you see the selection you want highlighted on the window underneath.

Changing all cells in a table is a bit different; select Cell from the drop-down menu, but in this case you have to click the check box next to the aspect that you want altered in all cells. For example, if you want to change every cell's height in a table to 100 pixels, click the Height check box, type **100** in the text box next to it, and click OK. If you are changing the format of individual cells, don't select those check boxes!

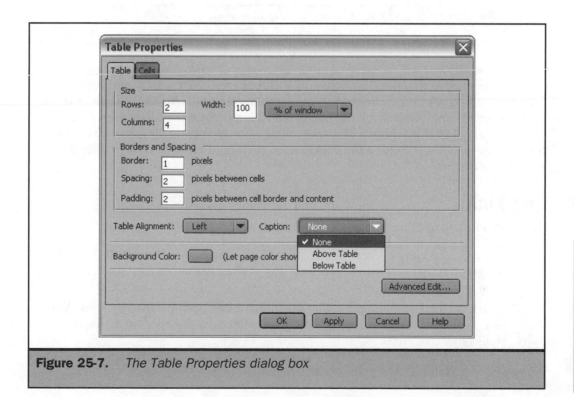

Figure 25-7.   *The Table Properties dialog box*

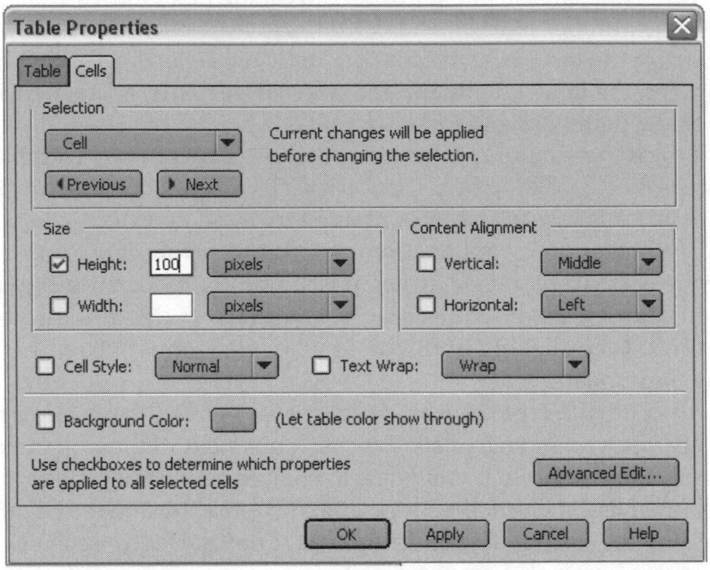

Figure 25-8. The Cells tab of the Table Properties dialog box

You can choose the specific height and width of each cell, column, and row (although you can't make a single cell smaller than other cells in that column or row), how the words and pictures are aligned in the cells, whether the text wraps, and the background color. (You choose the background color for a table the same way you do for the page itself; see "Setting the Background, Text, and Links Colors" earlier in this chapter for details.)

Adding Links

To insert a link to another web page:

1. Position the cursor where you want the link to appear in the text. If the text or graphic that you want to use as a link is already in your web page, select the text or graphic.

2. Click the Link button on the Composition toolbar or select Insert | Link. You see the Link Properties dialog box. If you selected an image, the dialog box looks like this:

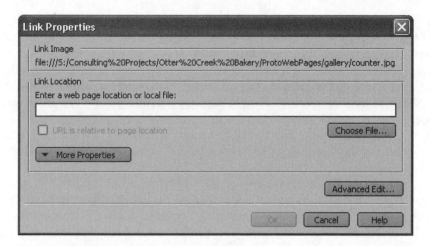

3. If you selected text or a graph as the link, Composer already knows what information on the web page will turn into a link. Otherwise, enter the text of the link as it you want it to appear on your page in the Link Text box.

4. In the Link Location box, type the URL or filename of the page to which you want to link. Click OK.

Changing the Underlying HTML Code

If you decide that Composer isn't cutting it, and you need to tinker with your page's HTML directly, click the HTML Source tab on the Edit Mode toolbar (below the main window). Doing so lets you change the code that Composer has generated in the same way you'd use a word processor; all you need to do is type in whatever new HTML tags or text you want in your page and to delete the HTML code you don't need. To see how these changes will affect your page, click the Preview tab to see how it will look in Netscape Navigator.

Be careful when changing HTML! You can sometimes accidentally delete a tag, which changes the layout of the entire page. For more information on what's important and what's not, see Chapter 24.

Saving the Web Page

After you complete your page, save the file on your local drive. Select File | Save As and enter a filename. If you want to put the page on a web server, see Chapter 30.

Editing Pages with FrontPage

FrontPage is a web page editor from Microsoft that is ideal for the casual user who wants a simple business site or a solid-looking personal page. (FrontPage used to come as part of the Microsoft Office suite, but no longer.) This section describes FrontPage 2000 and 2002. More information about FrontPage is available at **www.microsoft.com/frontpage**.

To start FrontPage, choose Start | All Programs | Microsoft FrontPage. Accept the default selection in the Getting Started dialog box. You see the FrontPage window in Figure 25-9.

Caution   *FrontPage supports nonstandard web extensions that work only on web servers that have FrontPage Server Extensions installed. Be careful not to use these extensions, also called WebBots, which won't work if your web server doesn't have this Microsoft program installed.*

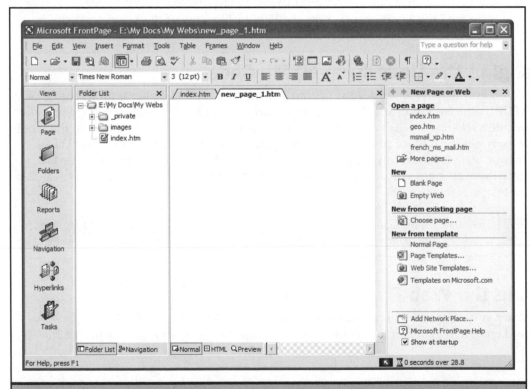

Figure 25-9.   *Microsoft FrontPage*

Creating Web Sites in FrontPage

To create a blank web site that you can fill in on your own, select Web Site Templates from the Task pane at the right of the FrontPage window. Otherwise choose File | New | Page Or Web. You have ten options:

- **One Page Web** is a web site with a single blank page for you to work on. If you're starting from scratch, this is what you'll use most of the time.

- **Personal Web** is a web site designed for personal sites, with pages for photo collections and favorite links.

- **Corporate Presence Wizard** is a web site wizard that creates a site featuring corporate news, products and services.

- **Customer Support Web** is a web site that features product help and information.

- **Database Interface Wizard** is a wizard that connects to an Access database, creating a web site where visitors can submit new information or search the database. This option creates pages using the .asp extension and requires a host that supports Active Server Pages (ASP) and FrontPage extensions.

- **Discussion Web Wizard** is a wizard that helps you create a message board (like those described in Chapter 15). It requires a web host that supports FrontPage extensions.

- **Import Web Wizard** is a wizard that helps you import an existing web site or files into a new web site.

- **Project Web** is a web site that enables you to track the status of projects, collect reports, and archive information.

- **SharePoint-Based Team Web Site** is a project collaboration web site that gives out specific pages for each login ID. The web server must be running SharePoint Team Services. This feature is new in FrontPage 2002.

- **Empty Web** is a web site with no pages whatsoever. You see a blank folder.

By default, FrontPage creates each of your web sites as a separate subfolder called *My Webs* in your My Documents folder.

If you are using Windows XP Professional, you can install IIS Server (which is included in Windows Components), and "publish" your web site using the IIS web server on your computer. If you plan to use non-HTML FrontPage extensions, installing the IIS Server allows you to work on your site without maintaining a connection to your web server and to publish it online when you're ready. If your web server does not support FrontPage extensions, use the My Webs folder for your local copies (but your pages won't work when you upload them to the web server). You don't need the extra load of running a web server locally, and you might accidentally use features only available with FrontPage extensions.

After creating a new web site, choose Tools | Web Settings, click the Advanced tab, and check the option to Show Hidden Files And Folders. FrontPage creates several hidden folders that it uses to keep track of updates and files. These folders are needed only by servers that use FrontPage extensions; you don't need to upload these when uploading your web site to your web server.

Although FrontPage is a WYSIWYG web editor, you still have the option of hand-coding or editing the raw HTML, instead of using wizards and dialog boxes to set the properties of web elements. Click the HTML tab at the bottom of the editor interface.

FrontPage Page Options

Using the Page Options dialog box, you can set the default options used for all new web pages. Open this dialog box by choosing Tools | Page Options. Always check these settings when creating a new web site because the options apply to all new pages you create. By setting the compatibility options before you begin to design your site, you won't accidentally use features that are not compatible with your web server or older browsers.

FrontPage has a bad reputation for mangling HTML code. FrontPage 2002 isn't quite as bad as previous versions, and you even have some control how FrontPage writes HTML code. The HTML Source tab has options to preserve existing HTML code and to format new code.

The most important tab on this dialog box may be Compatibility. This tab is where you tell FrontPage which browsers, versions, and servers you want your web site to work with. The features not supported by your choices are disabled, preventing you from accidentally using them in your site. You should use this dialog box if your site does not support FrontPage extensions and for Internet sites that will be viewed by the public using older browsers.

Using Templates

Most of the time, you'll probably just want to use the normal template so you can start with a blank canvas for new web pages. However, if you're in a hurry to set up your site or just not feeling very creative, you can use a template to help you get started. Some templates, like the Photo Gallery template, are useful for specific tasks, like setting up a slide show of your favorite digital photos. FrontPage includes 27 page templates, covering layouts from one-, two-, and three-column layouts to specialty templates, including templates for bibliography, feedback forms, and guest books. Templates have the advantage of giving your web pages a uniform look across your web site.

To open the Page Template dialog box, select File | New | Page Or Web to show the Task pane and then choose Page Templates.

You can save your own page layouts as templates, so it's easier to keep the pages on your site looking uniform. Once you're happy with a layout, including colors and background images, use the File | Save As menu.

Setting the Background, Text, and Links Colors

Once you've selected the web or page template you want to use, you're ready to work on the look of your web site.

Most of the global page settings are on the Page Properties dialog box. You can open it from the Format | Background menu or by right-clicking the page and choosing Page Properties from the menu that appears. From the Background tab, you can choose a background picture for the page and enable hyperlink rollover effects, as well as set the colors used for the background, text, and links.

If you're adding a page to an existing web site, you can use the same formatting selections used on other pages on your site by adding a check to Get Background Information From Another Page and choosing the page you want to copy formatting from. Using this option helps you maintain consistency across your site.

One of the background picture options is Watermark. A watermark is a background image, often one that is larger and wouldn't look good tiled, that remains stationary on the page. When the page scrolls, the text scrolls over the background. However, not all browsers can display watermarks. Pages don't scroll smoothly, so don't use watermarks on large pages.

Setting the Page Title and Properties

The Page Properties dialog has other important options you need to check:

- **Title** Found on the General tab, this adds a descriptive title (which appears in the title bar when a browser displays the page).

- **Margins** Use the Margins tab to set the top and left margins, based on pixels. The default (unchecked) is about 10 pixels; with it set on 0 (zero), text and images will be against the edge of the browser. If you have a border background, you can set the left margin to clear the border's edge, instead of using tables to control your margins.

- **<META> Tags** On the Custom tab, click the Add button and enter the name of the <META> tag (keywords or description, as explained in Chapter 31) in the Name field. Type the text, such as several keywords or a description of the page, in the Value field.

Adding and Formatting Text

Once you've created a blank page and a folder ready for your HTML files, type your text onto your page, and format it with the Formatting toolbar along the top. Microsoft has tried to make FrontPage work very much the same as Microsoft Word, so if you've ever used Word, you know how to format text in FrontPage.

The Format menu has another formatting option you can use, Dynamic HTML Effects. This applies dynamic features to text when events, such as clicks or mouseovers (that is, when a mouse moves across an item without clicking), occur.

If your site will have more than a few pages, consider formatting your text using Cascading Style Sheets, as described in Chapter 29.

Adding Links and Pictures

To create a hyperlink, select the text or image and click the Hyperlink button to display the Edit Hyperlink dialog box:

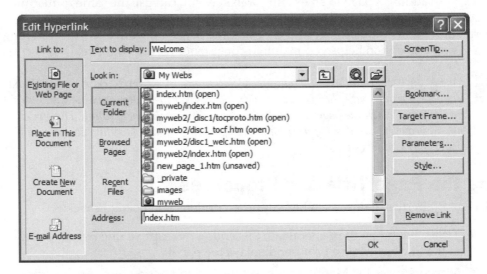

Click Existing File Or Web Page on the left. You can type in the URL or web page you'd like it to link to, or you can click the globe button to browse for it on the Web. Click OK when you're done.

To add a picture, click the Insert Picture From File button, browse to the picture you'd like to use, and click OK. Double-click the picture to choose the various options for it.

Formatting Your Page Using Tables

To create a table, select Table | Insert | Table and then specify the size, layout, and width of the table. Click OK when you're done. To change the way the table looks or the size of the cells, right-click the table and select Table Properties. You can click in table cells and type text or insert pictures.

Using Themes in FrontPage

FrontPage comes with color and graphic themes that can be overlaid on your web pages to gussy up otherwise dull sites. You can browse through the themes by selecting Format | Theme to display the Themes dialog box shown in Figure 25-10. Two radio buttons in the upper-left corner control which pages the theme applies to: the All Pages button applies the theme to all pages on your site—and despite the confusing wording, the Selected Page(s) button formats a single page at a time.

Select the themes by scrolling down and selecting them from on the right side, which will give you a preview of what it will look like in the pane. FrontPage gives you four different options for how the theme can be applied, including bright colors and whether it has a background picture. Fool around with the various options until you find the page you like and then click OK to apply it.

To preview the themes supplied with FrontPage, click the Themes icon on the Views bar. When you see a theme that you like, click the theme name. The background, images, and buttons that you see in the preview will be available on all of your pages.

You can easily modify any theme by clicking the Modify button to expand the window to show the Colors, Graphics, and Text buttons, as shown in Figure 25-10.

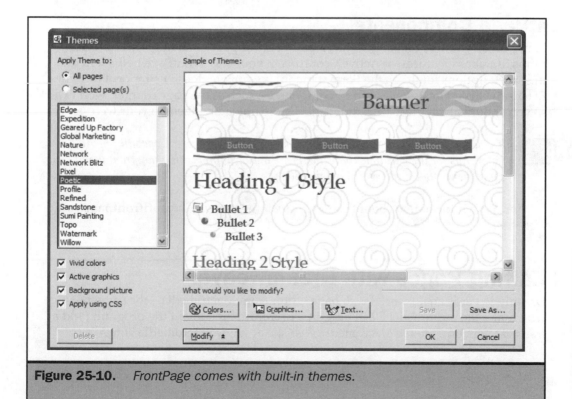

Figure 25-10. *FrontPage comes with built-in themes.*

When you are satisfied with your changes, save the new theme. Click Save As and save the changes as a new theme because you may want to use the original theme later.

Breaking Your Page into Frames

If you want to use frames in your web site, FrontPage includes predefined templates for them. To select the frameset layout, choose File | New Page Or Web to open the Task pane, and select Frames Pages. You can see previews of the frame layout. When you've found one you like, click OK.

Once you've picked the frameset layout to use, click the buttons in each frame to set the pages to use. Changing the frame sizes is as easy as dragging the edge or right-clicking on the frame page and choosing Frame Properties. If you'd like a customized No Frames page (a page displayed by browsers that don't support frames), select the No Frames tab and edit the page. The No Frames page should contain links to the pages that contain the main content of your site.

 Frames have some disadvantages; see the section on the drawbacks of frames in Chapter 24.

FrontPage Components

Many times you want more than just a plain HTML page. You might want to add forms, database features, or ActiveX controls to your site. FrontPage helps you do this, with options found on the Format menu. If your site doesn't support FrontPage Extensions (WebBots), some of these components, such as the page counter, won't work, so you should always test the components before uploading them to your web server.

 If you set the site compatibility on the Tools | Page Options | Capability menu, the menus for incompatible components are disabled, preventing you from using components that won't work on your site.

For more information about FrontPage, visit the **www.microsoftfrontpage.com** web site.

Editing Pages with Dreamweaver

Dreamweaver is an advanced web page editor from Macromedia—the same people who make the multimedia Flash plug-in. For information about the program (and a free trial version), see the Macromedia web site at **www.macromedia.com**.

Creating and Editing Pages

When you run Dreamweaver, you see the edit window, as shown in Figure 25-11. You may also see additional windows, which you can close by clicking the X box in their upper-right corners. To display these various information windows again, choose Window and the name of the window.

To create a new page, type the title of your page in the Title box on the toolbar and then click in the blank space in the central work area. Type the text that you want to include on your page; to put in images, choose Insert | Image.

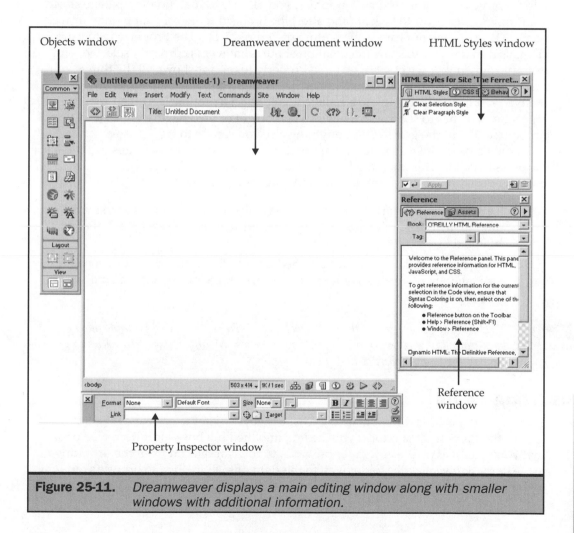

Figure 25-11. *Dreamweaver displays a main editing window along with smaller windows with additional information.*

Be sure to display the Objects window, a floating vertical window that contains buttons for many common tasks, as shown on the left side of Figure 25-11. If it doesn't appear, choose Window | Objects (or press CTRL-F2).

When you are ready to upload your pages to a web server, see Chapter 30 for how to use Dreamweaver's built-in FTP program.

Formatting Text, Images, and Other Page Components

After you've put in your text and graphics, you can use a small floating palette called the Property Inspector to look at (and alter) the properties of everything on your web page. (This window appears at the bottom of Figure 25-11.) The Property Inspector changes dynamically to show information about whatever is currently selected—for example, when you select some text, the Property Inspector shows all the things you can do to text (like turning it into a hyperlink, bolding and italicizing it, changing the type size, and turning it into a bulleted list). Select a graphic, and the Property Inspector switches to show you the width and height of the image, the alternate text, the source file for the graphic, and anything else you can do to it.

If the Property Inspector doesn't appear, choose Window | Properties to get it back (or press CTRL-F3). This mutating box is a little strange at first, but you get used to it quickly. You can use it to format many web page components:

- **Text**   Select the text and use the Property Inspector to set the font, size, style, alignment, color, indent, or outdent, or to format the text as a numbered or bulleted list.

- **Image**   Select the image and use the Property Inspector to set the filename, size, alignment, alternative text, or border, or the vertical or horizontal space around the image.

   To change the properties of the entire web page—like the title, background color, background image, text color, and link color, choose Modify | Page Properties to display the Page Properties dialog box.

Inserting Links

To create a hyperlink, select the text or image that you want to appear as the link and look at the Property Inspector. Type the link into the Link box—or if it's a web page that you've edited in Dreamweaver previously, you can select it from the drop-down list. Alternatively, click the folder icon to the right of the Link box to browse your way to the file you want linked.

Formatting Text and Images in Tables

Clicking the Insert Table button in the Objects window (or choosing Insert | Table from the menu) pops up the Insert Table dialog box. You use it to specify how many rows and columns you want in your table. To change the properties of the table, click and drag your mouse to select the entire table and change the values in the Property Inspector. To format a specific cell, click and drag to select the cell (or cells) and use the Property Inspector again.

Using Frames in Dreamweaver

To insert a frame into a Dreamweaver page, select Insert | Frames. You'll be given a list of several places to put your frame, ranging from the simple "top" all the way to the slightly more complex "left top," which will actually give you two frames—one along the left and one along the top. To switch between frames, just click within the frame you want to edit. Insert text and images the way you would in any other web page, but when you save, you'll have to save each frame separately by clicking in the frame and choosing File | Save Frame As. Alternatively, you can save all of them at once by choosing File | Save All Frames, though you'll still have to give a separate name to each frame.

 Frames have some disadvantages; see the section on drawbacks of frames in Chapter 24.

Advanced (But Helpful!) Features of Dreamweaver

Dreamweaver also makes some advanced tasks easier, including creating rollovers, adding Flash to your page, laying out pages with layers, and editing complex graphics.

Creating Rollovers

For example, creating a rollover image (one where the image "flips" from one picture to another when you mouse over it) usually involves knowing JavaScript, or you can select Insert | Interactive Images | Rollover Image, and Dreamweaver displays a dialog box that asks you for the location of the two pictures and the URL it takes you to when clicked. Dreamweaver writes all of the JavaScript code *for* you to make the rollover work.

Inserting Flash Buttons and Text

Likewise—which isn't surprising, considering Macromedia also makes Flash— Dreamweaver makes it easy to insert Flash buttons and SWF files for the cutting edge in multimedia web presentations. To select from a list of built-in Flash buttons that morph and change in cool ways when you click or mouse over them, click the Insert

Flash Button in the Objects window (or choose Insert | Interactive Images | Flash Button from the menu). Dreamweaver presents you with a list of button styles:

You can change the text, the color, the size, the URL the button links to, and the background color. When you click OK, Dreamweaver generates a Flash button for you, automatically inserted into your web page and saved on your hard drive as an SWF Flash file, all without you ever having to open Flash (or even having Flash installed on your computer, for that matter).

Dreamweaver also allows you to do limited tricks with Flash text in the same way. This feature is useful if you want the text of a button to use a nonstandard font that may not be installed on other computers.

Working with Layers

Dreamweaver allows you to work directly with layers, which is both good and bad. Layers are an advanced feature, usable in some newer browsers, that allows for *absolute positioning* of text and graphics. In basic HTML, you can't say, "I want this picture half an inch away from the left edge and three inches down from the top," the way you would in a brochure or a catalogue, mainly because HTML changes the way a web page looks dynamically, depending on the size of the browser window and the available fonts. You can use tables to position text and graphics—and most designers do—but it's a large pain to get right.

Layers *do* allow absolute positioning—you can put a picture or text box anywhere on the screen with precision, and even have portions of your page overlap! The downside is that many earlier browsers still in use can't interpret layers correctly; to them, it's just strange HTML code that doesn't look right.

So how can you use layers? Many designers use layers to lay out the web page the way they want it, shifting everything into a precise position—and then they use Dreamweaver to convert their layers into very large and complex tables that are the next best thing to absolute positioning. Dreamweaver layers are outside the scope of this book, but the help files are (for once) helpful on the topic, and you can simply use Modify | Convert | Layers To Table once you've got everything where you want it.

The only thing that Dreamweaver cannot do is convert overlapping layers into a table. HTML tables don't let you overlap—so before you convert, make sure your layers don't step on each other's toes!

Editing Pictures with Fireworks

By far, Dreamweaver's coolest feature is its integration with its companion graphics program, Fireworks. Fireworks has a steep learning curve and isn't recommended for beginning graphics jockeys, but once you learn it, you can save tons of time designing your pages. Thanks to Dreamweaver and Fireworks integration, you can use Fireworks to draw a picture of the way you want your web page to look—creating the design of your page. Tweak your layout in Fireworks, redrawing it until you get all the elements just the way you like them. Then you can give Fireworks some guidelines as to how to section it up, and Fireworks creates a Dreamweaver-ready HTML page, using the graphics from the picture of your page, *for* you. This feature can save hours for the serious designer, both in preparing "sample" web pages for clients and in allowing you to lay out your page without worrying about all of the HTML code you'll need to make it work.

*You can also download a trial copy of Fireworks at **www.macromedia.com**—but it's considerably different from a graphics editor like Paint Shop Pro!*

Dreamweaver Extensions

Macromedia encourages people to write Dreamweaver Extensions, programs that add features to Dreamweaver and the pages it can create. You can find out about the available extensions by visiting the Dreamweaver web site at **www.macromedia.com/ software/Dreamweaver** and clicking the Dreamweaver Exchange link. You can download extensions for free that enable your web pages to display slide shows or to include e-commerce features.

Managing the Files That Make Up Your Web Site

Dreamweaver helps you to keep track of all the files that make up your site. As you expand your site, you might find yourself managing HTML files, graphics files, audio files, and video files. Before you use the site management features of Dreamweaver, you need to create a directory to store all of your web files in. You can create subdirectories for images, videos, and audio files from within the Site Management window.

To tell Dreamweaver about your web site, so that it can help you manage its files, select Site | New Site. Give the site a name, and select as the location the main directory that you just created. Click the New Folder button, and create folders for each type of file that you have at your site. You can check here for dead hyperlinks, see whether your site is compatible with designated web browsers, replace certain chunks of text or HTML globally within your site, and keep track of who's been changing what web pages and when.

Editing Pages with Adobe GoLive

Adobe GoLive is a full-featured web site authoring tool; you can download a trial version at **www.adobe.com/golive**—and while you're there, you can read about GoLive's numerous features, which also include support for XHTML, XML, wireless browser authoring, dynamic (database driven) web site creation, and collaborative (workgroup) authoring. GoLive is fully cross-platform; it runs on Windows XP, 2000, Me, and 98, as well as on Mac OS-X 10.1 (Native and Classic) and Mac OS 9.1 and 9.2. It runs exactly the same on Mac and Windows (with the exception of keyboard shortcuts). In fact, the files can be seamlessly transferred between Mac and Windows.

Creating and Editing Pages

To run GoLive from Windows, choose Start | Programs | Adobe GoLive 6. On the Mac, locate and double-click its application icon. As GoLive launches, you're greeted by a startup window (shown in Figure 25-12) that asks you to choose to create a new page, a new site, or to open a site you've already begun. You can turn this wizard off and make the same choices from the File menu if you prefer. If you are starting a new web site, choose New Site and follow the directions.

After the wizard is finished, your new site window opens, as shown in Figure 25-13. It contains one page, called index.html (the default web home page filename). You can change the default name or extension to match your web server's guidelines.

The GoLive Site Window

The site window, shown in Figure 25-13, is the key to GoLive's power—it's where you add and organize your pages, images, style sheets, external JavaScript files, and other

Figure 25-12.   *Adobe GoLive's introductory window*

files that will reside on the web server when you're ready to go public (go live!). Whenever you work on your site, you work in the site window.

To open the site window, double-click the file with the .site filename extension. A toolbar appears at the top of your screen with a collection of menus grouped by task. The Files tab (shown in Figure 25-13) lists the files that make up your web site. You can see folders for web pages, graphics, stationery, scripts, templates, and other types of files. The External tab lists links to external addresses, so you can point to them when using them in your web pages. If you change a link on the External tab, GoLive changes it throughout your site. The Diagrams tab can display a diagram of the files in your site. If you want to save a table, text, or other piece of a web page for use in other pages, you can save it by using the Library tab.

Most of your page building is done by using GoLive's floating palettes. The Objects palette looks like this:

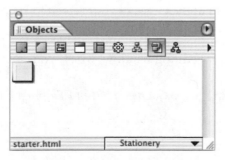

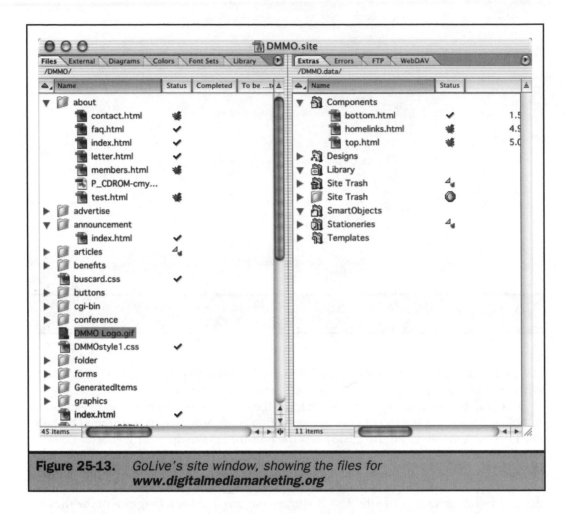

Figure 25-13. GoLive's site window, showing the files for
www.digitalmediamarketing.org

If you're used to working in any other Adobe application, such as Photoshop, floating palettes (windows) will be familiar. As a rule, keep the most commonly needed floating palettes open. When you are adding objects to your pages, keep the Objects palette open. When you are formatting objects, keep the Inspector palette open. You can dock these palettes at the edges of your screen to keep them out of the way until needed.

To start working on your first page, double-click the page (index.html) in the site window. You see the GoLive editing window, where you can type text into the page.

 See Chapter 30 for how to use GoLive's built-in FTP program to upload web site files to your web server.

Creating a New Page

To create a new page, add it to the site window. The fastest way is to right-click (or CONTROL-click on Mac) in any white space in the site window's Files tab (where your index.html page already appears) and choose New | New Page. The new page appears in the Files tab of the site window, with the name selected so you can name it right away.

 Rather than starting from scratch with a new blank file for each page in your web site, set up one page with all the common design elements, such as backgrounds, colors, page title, properties, graphics, text, and links, and save it as Stationery. This technique enables you to create a new page with these design elements already in place by dragging the Stationery name from the Objects palette.

Setting the Background, Text, and Links Color

One of the first things you'll probably want to do is give your page a background color other than white. Open the page and click the page icon at the upper left of the page. As you do, the Inspector palette displays the Page tab, where you can set basic page properties:

To set or change a color, click the colored button to open the Color palette. Colors are divided by color space to make selection easier. Figure 25-14 shows the Color palette and the editing window.

If you prefer to use an image as the background of your page, find a graphic that works well as a background and drag it from Windows Explorer or your hard drive folder into the Files tab of the site window, where the pages are. Then check Image under the Background section of the Page Inspector and select the graphic.

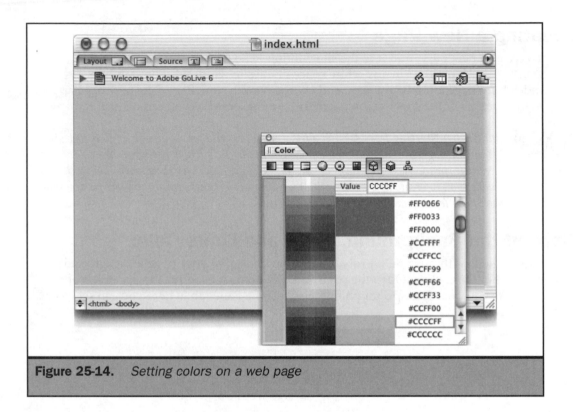

Figure 25-14. *Setting colors on a web page*

> **Note**   *Setting background, text, and link colors is a good idea so that people with older browsers will see the colors, but use style sheets to set these colors and background, too, for newer browsers. (See Chapter 29 for how to use style sheets.)*

Setting the Page Title

Every web page has a few proprieties that can be used to make your page more valuable. For example, giving the page a title not only provides a description when visitors bookmark your page, but also helps people find your site via search engines. In the Page tab of the Inspector palette, you can select and change the title. However, there's another common way to do this. At the top of each open GoLive page, beside the page icon, you'll see the words, "Welcome to Adobe GoLive 6." Select this name and enter your own page name.

To add description and keywords <META> tags (as described in Chapter 31), select any desired word or phrase on your page, and choose Special | Add To Keywords. GoLive creates the <META> tag for you and adds the selected words within the tag. You can rearrange them later to fine-tune their priority. To do so, open the Head section by clicking the arrow at the upper left of the page and double-click the Keywords icon there. The Inspector palette morphs into the Keywords Inspector to enable you to view and edit them, as in Figure 25-15, or if you're so inclined, you can edit the keywords in any of the HTML views.

To add a <META> tag for a site or page description, drag a Meta icon from the Head tab of the Objects palette onto any area of your page. GoLive opens the Head section; drop the icon there, preselected. In the Meta Inspector palette, choose Description from the list of <META> tags.

Adding and Formatting Text

As you work in the Layout tab of the editing window, you can add text by tying it or by pasting it in or by dragging it from another window. (The big exception is that on a Mac, you cannot drag Microsoft Word clippings because Word doesn't write its Text Clippings properly.) When you want to start a new paragraph, press ENTER. GoLive ends the existing paragraph with a </P> end-paragraph tag and starts a paragraph with a <P> tag.

Text formatting controls are located in the toolbar and in the Type menu. GoLive provides several types of formatting to give designers the greatest freedom, but you

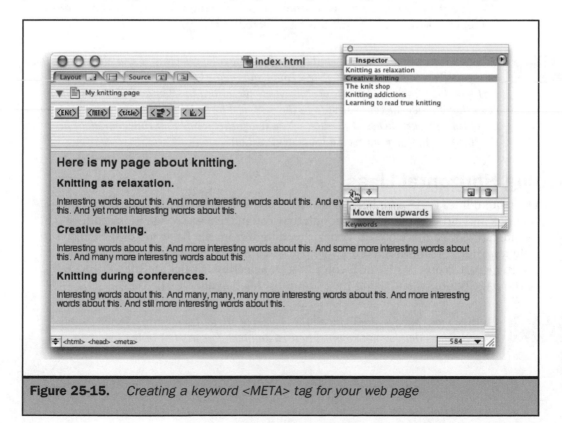

Figure 25-15. *Creating a keyword <META> tag for your web page*

should avoid some if you want the maximum flexibility and accessibility. Your formatting options are

■ **Headings (H1 through H6)**   Use <H1>, <H2>, and other heading tags to supply the basic organization needed to make your page most accessible. Click anywhere within the heading and choose Heading 1 through Heading 6 from the pop-up menu at the left of the toolbar, or choose a heading from under the Type | Paragraph Style menu. The entire paragraph is formatted as a heading.

■ **Boldface, italics, and underlining**   Avoid these, and use formatting from under the Type | Structure menu instead. The results are the same, but these structural tags carry a meaning that web accessibility tools can understand and interpret.

■ **Alignment and centering**   As with headings, alignment applies to an entire paragraph. Click anywhere within the paragraph and use the toolbar, clicking the button that represents your desired alignment: Left, Center, Right, or Justified.

■ **Lists**   To create a list, start your first list item and click the Numbered List or Unnumbered List button in the toolbar. Next, use the Increase or Decrease List Level buttons to organize as desired. To remove the list formatting and return to regular text, decrease the indent back to the margin.

Caution *You can control the font, size, and color of your text by selecting it and clicking buttons in the toolbar, but please don't. These commands add <FONT> tags around your text—and conflict with the use of style sheets (described in Chapter 29). Resist them, even though they appear at first to be the easy, fast formatting solution. Invest the bit of time to learn to use style sheets. You'll definitely save that time manyfold in the future—and save yourself a lot of aggravation.*

Adding Horizontal Lines

Horizontal lines (<HR> for horizontal rule) can be used to divide your page into sections and aid organization, although they can make a web page look crude and old-fashioned. To place one on your page, drag it from the Basic tab of the Objects palette. After you add it to your page, you can adjust its size and a bit of its look in the Inspector. You can also add color to it by selecting it, clicking the Outline tab of the page window, and using the pop-up list of all available attributes.

Tip *Outline mode always gives you all the choices of attributes for any selected object, even the ones that are not commonly used and therefore are not in the Inspector.*

Adding Pictures

What would a web site be without images? Also, what do you or your client look like when visitors to your site get a missing image icon instead of the graphic you intended them to see?

The first step to adding a picture to your page is to drag the file (from Windows Explorer or your hard disk folder) to the Files tab of your site window. GoLive copies the file, leaving your original in place. Once the image is in the site window, you can place it on your page.

To place the image on your page, open the page and drag the graphic from the Files tab into place on your page. The image will fall into line anywhere your cursor has passed by. You can also drag an image to a table cell. Alternatively, you can place an image icon on the page and link from the Image Inspector to the graphic.

If you want to add other objects, like videos, Flash (SWF) files, Scalable Vector Graphics (SVG) files, or other special graphics files, the process is the same. These files have their own icons in the Objects palette. GoLive knows what codes to insert when you drag them to a web page. Files created by Adobe graphic applications have special features that enable you to alter the graphic and to regenerate the graphic actually used on the page.

Adding Links

You can create a link from either text or a graphic. To turn text into a link, select the text and click the New Link icon in the Text Inspector palette. To turn a graphic into a link, select the graphic, display to the Link tab of the Image Inspector palette, and click the New Link icon. Either way you create the link, you next have to tell GoLive what web page to link to: a file on your Files tab or an external web page.

Creating and Using Tables

Until the next generation of style sheets becomes standard, tables remain the best way to define the page width and columnar structure of your page.

Inserting a Table

You can create a default three-by-three table by dragging it from the Basic tab of the Objects palette to your page. GoLive adds the <TABLE>, <TR>, and <TD> codes to create the tables, or you can click where you want the table, right-click (or CONTROL-click on Mac) there, and choose Insert Object | Basic | Table from the menu that appears.

In GoLive 6, you can also create the table with the exact number of rows and columns that you need. Press CTRL (in Windows) or COMMAND (on Macs), click the

Table icon in the Objects palette, and drag it to the desired numbers of rows and columns. Then release the CTRL or COMMAND key and drag the table from the Objects palette into place on the page.

Regardless of how you add it, a new table is 180 pixels wide by default. You can select the table and change its size, units of measure, number of rows and columns, and background color or image by using the Table Inspector palette.

Adding and Formatting Rows, Columns, or Cells

You can add rows or columns to a table on either side of any selected cell: above, below, left, or right. Select a cell or row, and click the Add and Delete buttons in the Table Inspector palette, as shown in Figure 25-16. Alternatively, you can make the same additions or deletions by right-clicking (in Windows) or CONTROL-clicking (on Macs) in any table cell's border or in the Table palette (opened via Window | Table).

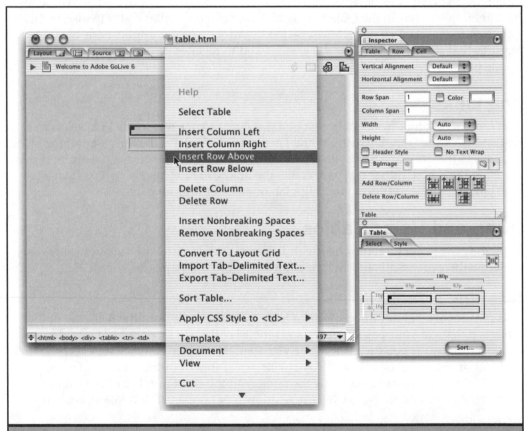

Figure 25-16.   *Adding a row to a table in GoLive*

You may want to merge cells to create longer columns or rows so they span across others. Before you do, know that anything in the to-be-merged-over cells will be lost. Move that stuff out before you do the merge. To merge cells, select the rightmost or topmost cell, and enter a row or column span in the Table Inspector palette. However, it's more fun to select the rightmost or topmost cell and press SHIFT and the DOWN ARROW or RIGHT ARROW. Pressing the LEFT ARROW separates the cells.

Adding Content to a Table

Adding text and images to a table is similar to adding it directly onto your page. You can drag an image or text to any cell, or you can click in any cell and type or paste.

Importing Text into a Table

You can export text from programs such as Excel or FileMaker Pro and import it into GoLive, creating a table containing the information from the other program. First export the text or table data, preferably as tab-delimited. (You can also use the comma, space, or semicolon as your separator.) Back in GoLive, place a table on the page. Right-click (or CONTROL-click on Macs) in the table and choose Import Tab Delimited Text from the menu. In the Open File dialog box that appears, choose the filename and delimiter, and import the file. GoLive automatically adds rows and columns to your table to accommodate your text.

To add a caption that moves along with the table, check Caption in the Table Inspector palette, choose where the caption should be placed, and enter the text within the page layout.

Breaking Your Page into Frames

If you want to use frames in your web pages, GoLive provides a tab full of starter framesets in the Frames tab of the Objects palette. Create the new blank page that will contain the frameset and click the Frame Layout tab. Then drag a frameset from the Frames tab of the Objects palette onto that page. Use the Frameset Inspector palette to set the exact frames you want, their sizes, borders, scrolling, and so on. Then click within each frame section to display the Frame Inspector so you can name that section, specify the first page that will fill it, and set the target frame.

 Frames have some disadvantages; see the section on drawbacks of frames in Chapter 24.

Viewing Your HTML as You Work

The power to see your pages take their shape as you build them is a great time saver, but there are times you want to work in the actual code. For example, you might want to check the HTML in your page, or you might want to do something the Inspector and other WYSIWYG tools don't provide. (GoLive's menus and Inspector provide all standard/common code, but there may be something nonstandard that you want to do, such as color a horizontal rule.) GoLive contains a full-featured HTML editor for you.

The best way to view your HTML is the Split Source view. Click the double-headed arrow (the Show/Hide Split Source button) at the lower left of the page layout window. GoLive splits the window, revealing the HTML in the lower part. As you select an element in the layout, the lower section scrolls to that code. If you'd like to focus on that code only, right-click (CONTROL-click on Macs) anywhere in the code section and choose View | Local Mode. The same contextual menu enables you to choose various other viewing options such as syntax coloring.

*Thanks to Deborah Shadovitz for writing the introduction to GoLive in this chapter. You can find more of her coverage of GoLive at **www.shadovitz.com/writing.***

The Complete Reference

Internet

Chapter 26

Creating and Optimizing Web Graphics

Graphical images have become ubiquitous on the Web. You can brighten up your web pages with nearly any image, simply by storing the image in one of the graphics file types *(formats)* that browsers can display. For the fastest downloading, highest quality images, however, you may need to do some fine-tuning. This chapter tells you how to use popular graphics programs to create, fine-tune, compress, and then add popular special effects to your web graphics.

Perhaps the most important fine-tuning that web images need is for their files to be made as small as possible (in kilobytes) so that the images download quickly. You can keep file size small by saving an image in the file format that is best suited for its content. The quality of web images doesn't need to be as high as the quality for printed images, so you also can keep down file size by compromising quality where you don't need it. Where image quality is important, you can adapt images to the special needs of web browsers and computer displays.

You may also want to add popular, special graphics features common on the Web. You can animate an image (similar to a tiny movie), make selected areas transparent so that the image appears to be pasted on the page, or make the image fade in gradually (display it *progressively*) as it arrives from the web server.

You control some graphics features by how you design the web page, not by doing anything to the image. You use tags on the web page to position or align images on the page, turn images into clickable hyperlinks, or assemble them into an array. You control such features either by writing HTML code or by using a web design tool (discussed in Chapters 24 and 25). Some graphics programs, discussed in this chapter, also help you to control those images on the web page.

Graphics File Formats for the Web

Computer graphics are stored in many different file formats, but come in only two main types:

- **Vector images** consist of lines and various shapes, outlined and filled with colors or shadings. Web browsers can't display vector images (yet).

- **Bitmap images** consist of colored dots, or *pixels*. Web documents commonly use only bitmap images, and in two principal formats: *Graphics Interchange Format (GIF)* and *Joint Photographic Experts Group (JPEG)*. A third bitmap format, Portable Network Graphics (PNG) is less common but is slowly increasing in popularity.

This chapter concentrates on creating GIF and JPEG files for web pages. Choosing the best format can give you better looking or faster downloading graphics. Because smaller files download faster, all web graphics formats rely on *compression*, a way to pack more information into a smaller file. Each format compresses data in its own way, and some ways trade off image quality for a smaller file size.

Using GIF

For drawings and artwork created on a computer (including clip art, icons, screen captures, and text), use GIF. Specifically, when an image consists of uniformly colored pieces with sharp contrasts between them—colored lines and shapes, for instance—GIF is the best format for getting smaller, faster-downloading files, without losing image quality.

GIF can also be used for scanned-in photographs and artwork, but because the GIF format is limited to 256 colors, the image quality is often poorer than the main alternative, JPEG. GIF files of photos may also be much larger than JPEG files. JPEG, however, may distort certain parts or qualities of the image in the process of making the file smaller, particularly parts with high-contrast boundaries between colors.

GIF is also the only choice if you want to do special effects, such as animations and images with transparent areas. (See the discussions of those features later in this chapter.)

Using JPEG for Color Photographs

For color photographs, JPEG files are usually much smaller than GIF files and offer better handling of color gradients. The JPEG format can accommodate 16.7 million colors, whereas the GIF format is limited to 256 colors. (For black-and-white photographs, JPEG doesn't offer any big advantage over GIF.) Even if an image is not actually a photograph, try using JPEG when you can see (under magnification) that most regions of the image are made up of dots of many colors. (Some drawings that have undergone *dithering*—a process of simulating a color by mixing dots of other colors—are also more efficiently stored in JPEG than in GIF.)

JPEG is not perfect for all photographs. JPEG is a *lossy* format, meaning that it discards some data to create a small file. Most graphics programs allow you to trade off JPEG quality for image size, but even the highest quality JPEG image loses some image quality. JPEG images have small distortions, especially around sharp edges, such as the edges of text characters.

Other File Formats

Most of today's browsers display (*support*) only a few file formats other than GIF and JPEG. Most (but not all) newer browsers can display PNG format, which offers good compression and better color fidelity than GIF and also supports transparency and progressive delivery (discussed later in this chapter). A few browsers also support the X Window BitMap (XBM, which is widely used on UNIX systems) and portable bitmap (PBM) formats—but don't use these formats in your web pages unless you are sure that your target audience will have browsers that can display them.

Other image formats can be used on the Web for specific applications. Browsers display other formats (such as multimedia formats) if the file format is supported by special browser options. By installing a *plug-in* (Netscape) or *ActiveX control* (Internet Explorer), which typically displays images directly in the browser window or embedded in the web document, or a *player*, which displays an image by itself in a separate player window, you can "teach" your browser to display other graphic formats. (See Chapter 18 for information about plug-ins and ActiveX controls.)

In the future, browsers may support other file formats *intrinsically* (without plug-ins, ActiveX controls, or players). In particular, Netscape and Microsoft browsers may soon support vector images, such as those created by drawing programs or that come with clip art collections. Currently, you can use vector images on conventional web documents only if you first convert them to bitmap formats such as GIF or JPEG. If vector files could be used directly, they would download much faster because of their smaller size. Two major vendors of web graphics software, Adobe and Macromedia, support web vector formats, and Microsoft's Internet Explorer 5 and 6 support a vector format called VML once you install the VML option. Macromedia promotes its Flash (SWF) format, and Adobe promotes its Scalable Vector Graphics (SVG) format, but both apparently are seeking a common standard.

Getting GIFs and JPEGs

How do you create images in GIF or JPEG format? The latest versions of nearly all graphics programs can output graphics to GIF or JPEG formats. If you don't already have a graphics program on your computer that can save pictures as GIF or JPEG, you can easily download one from the Internet. This section offers a few suggestions for graphics editing programs.

Creating GIFs and JPEGs with Word Processors

The latest versions of many word processors can create web pages with graphics. If you are using a word processor to create your web pages, the program may generate GIF or JPEG images from inserted pictures, drawings, charts, or other nontext objects on your page.

If, for instance, you use Microsoft Word or WordPerfect to create a web page and that page contains images, the images are saved as GIF files. Equations and other inserted objects, such as spreadsheets and charts, may also be translated into GIF files. (Note that the HTML file that results, the newly generated GIF files, and any folders that contain them must be copied to your web server without changes—otherwise, the documents may not display the images.)

Some word processors provide additional support for web graphics. In WordPerfect's web view, for instance, you can right-click a graphic, choose HTML Properties, and on the Publish tab of the dialog box that appears, choose JPEG or GIF. You can choose Interlaced GIF to make the image gradually fade in, or you can choose Transparent color and then select a color in the image to be displayed transparently. WordPerfect also translates symbols, text boxes, and TextArt into bitmapped graphics.

Common Programs for Creating GIF and JPEG Files

Graphics programs come in three main varieties:

- **Paint and photo programs** enable you to read different image files and customize them for web use or create a web image of your own by using a paintbrush and other tools. Two popular examples are Adobe Photoshop and Macromedia Fireworks.

- **Illustration programs** focus on creating images, principally vector graphics, and thus typically have fewer features for optimizing the bitmap files (such as GIF and JPEG) used on the Web. Examples include Adobe Illustrator, Macromedia Freehand, and CorelDRAW.

- **Graphics utilities** are small programs with simple features that focus on converting images from one format to another and fine-tuning those images.

The following are just a few graphics programs that are widely available:

- **Microsoft Paint (Windows XP version)** The most recent version of Microsoft Paint, this enables PC users to paint a simple image or read in an image in Windows bitmap (BMP), PNG, JPEG, or GIF format and then edit it. You can then save the image in GIF or JPEG rather than Paint's native PCX format.

- **Adobe Photoshop** This professional-level, general-purpose graphics program enables you to scan, edit, paint, and enhance images on PCs and Macs. Photoshop also reads a variety of graphics file formats. It helps you to fine-tune your images and then to output them to GIF and JPEG, as well as many other formats. Photoshop Limited Edition (LE) does the same basic tasks and often comes bundled with scanners. Adobe's web editing program GoLive, described in Chapter 25, is designed to integrate seamlessly with Photoshop and ImageReady (described next). In GoLive, when you edit a Smart Photoshop Object containing a GIF or JPEG, GoLive launches Photoshop so you can edit the original Photoshop file. You can download an evaluation copy of Photoshop from the Adobe web site (**www.adobe.com**).

- **Adobe ImageReady** This Adobe tool for Macintosh and PC computers is a companion program to Photoshop and offers many features geared toward web graphics.

- **Macromedia Fireworks** This professional-level graphics program offers many advanced features and is specifically designed for web development work. It also reads a variety of graphics formats and outputs as GIF or JPEG, as well as many other formats. It uses PNG as its native format, rather than a proprietary format. Macromedia's web editing program Dreamweaver, described in Chapter 25, is designed to integrate seamlessly with Fireworks. Editing a GIF or JPEG image from Dreamweaver launches Fireworks, allows you to edit the original PNG file, and automatically saves a new GIF or JPEG file. You can download an evaluation copy of Fireworks from the Macromedia web site (**www.macromedia.com**).

- **Paint Shop Pro**   This popular and inexpensive PC program is similar in many respects to Photoshop and Fireworks. As in Photoshop or Fireworks, you can read various image files, scan images with a scanner, and edit, paint, add text, and enhance images. Paint Shop Pro offers a free evaluation period. You can download an evaluation copy from the JASC web site (**www.jasc.com**).

- **Lview Pro**   This is another popular and inexpensive PC paint and photo tool (similar to Paint Shop Pro) that also offers a free evaluation period. Its help files are a little less helpful than Paint Shop Pro's, but it offers some special features for web images. You can download a free evaluation copy from the Lview web site (**www.lview.com**).

Dozens of other excellent graphics programs are available on the Web. In general, two good places to look for downloadable graphics software are **www.download.com** and **www.shareware.com**. TUCOWS (**www.tucows.com**) also lists graphics programs used for the Web. For more information on downloading and installing programs from the Web, see Chapter 34.

Creating a GIF or JPEG Image File

How do you actually create a GIF or JPEG image file with a graphics program? You can either paint or draw an image from scratch, scan an image, or convert an existing file to GIF or JPEG with a paint program or graphics utility.

- *Paint or draw an image from scratch.* Use a paint program, such as Photoshop or Paint Shop Pro, to create your own GIF or JPEG image. Start with the File | New command. In some paint programs, you then proceed through a dialog box in which you can choose image size, number of colors, and other attributes that are described in this chapter. In other paint programs, these choices are made for you by default.

- *Scan a paper image.* If you have a scanner installed on your computer, you can use a paint program to acquire the image. Choose File | Acquire (or a similar command) to begin the scanning process.

- *Convert an existing file to GIF or JPEG with a paint program or graphics utility.* Open an image in the drawing program's native (vector) format and save it as a GIF or JPEG image:

    1. Select File | Open or a similar command. In the dialog box that appears in most programs, you generally must either specify which type of file you want

to open (such as an Adobe Illustrator AI file or a Windows BMP file) or choose "all types," to see a list of file types from which you can choose.

2. Choose File | Save As or a similar command to save a copy of your image. In the dialog box that appears, choose a file type of GIF or JPEG.

3. Look for an options button in that dialog box to control some of the attributes that are discussed in this chapter. (See the next section, "Issues in Converting Images to GIF and JPEG," for a discussion of conversion issues.)

Even if you are using a text-based UNIX system, you may be able to do graphics file conversions. To use text-based UNIX graphics utilities, you type a command line to convert a file to GIF or JPEG. Display the program's help files for details, but the command line usually consists of the program's name, the name of the file to be read, the name of the file that you want to create, and various "switches" (options), consisting of dashes, slashes, and letters. The switches tell the program which file type to create and any special attributes that the file should include.

Issues in Converting Images to GIF and JPEG

Converting an image from its original format into GIF or JPEG can require you to make certain choices that involve trade-offs. Some programs make those choices for you, unless you find the controls for those variables. Look for a Tools | Options, View | Options, or Edit | Preferences command in your program and then look for settings that relate to file types. Here are a few of the choices that you or the program may make:

■ **Colors**   Using fewer colors means creating smaller files, but may mean poorer quality or poor fidelity to the original image. If you change the number of colors, you may have the option of telling the program how to choose new colors: use dithering or the nearest color. See "Optimizing Images for the Web" later in this chapter for more details about color depth and palettes.

■ **JPEG quality**   Many programs offer an image quality control for JPEG output. Lower quality creates a significantly smaller file, but can introduce unwanted color blurs, especially near the abrupt color changes that occur at sharp edges and text.

■ **GIF version and interlacing**   Choose GIF89a if you want to use interlacing (progressive display) and then also choose interlacing. See "Special Effects: Progressive Display and Transparency" later in this chapter for details.

If you have an image in a program that can't store the image in GIF or JPEG format, copy the image from that program's window to your computer's Clipboard (in Microsoft Windows, select the file and press CTRL-C). Then, open a new, blank image in a program that can output to GIF or JPEG (such as Microsoft Paint in Windows XP) and paste the image (CTRL-V in Windows). Now you can save the file as a GIF or JPEG file.

Getting Images and Clip Art from the Internet

An amazing amount of artwork is available free of charge on the Internet. You must be careful to ensure that you obtain any such art from its legal owner (the person or entity who has the authority to give rights) and that you have the owner's permission to use it on the Web. Ask non-exclusive worldwide rights to use the artwork on your web site, along with rights for any derivation from the web site (such as pictures of or articles about the web site). Some amateur collections that are offered free are collections of other people's work, obtained without permission. Do not use art from such collections without first obtaining the true owner's permission.

Free sources come and go quickly on the Internet, so the best way to explore the world of web clip art is through a search engine or web directory. At Google (**google.com**), for instance, choose the Image tab and then enter keywords to search.

Tip	*Art Today (**www.arttoday.com**) requires you to register to access its collection of clip art, but the fee is small ($3–8 per week, depending on the length of the subscription), and the collection is huge (more than 1.5 million images). Art Today is especially useful if you are looking for classical or antique-style pictures.*

Special Effects: Progressive Display and Transparency

The Web uses many special effects involving graphics. Some special effects require that you do something in the web page, such as write HTML code or use an advanced web page development program. Two of those special effects, however, are special options of the graphics file itself: progressive display and transparency.

What Is Progressive Display?

Progressive display is one way of coping with a long download time. On many web pages, the images don't appear until after they have been completely downloaded, or they appear gradually from top to bottom. With progressive display, the image starts blurry and gradually becomes more detailed over the entire image area as it is downloaded. Some people simply like that effect better.

A GIF file that the browser displays progressively is called an *interlaced* GIF image. Interlacing is an option only in files in the latest GIF format, called GIF89a. (The other common GIF format is GIF87a.) Most tools that create GIF files give you the option of creating an interlaced GIF89a file.

A JPEG file that displays progressively is simply called *progressive JPEG*. Progressive JPEG is a fairly new effect, so only more recent browsers and graphics programs support the effect. (If a program does not support progressive JPEG, it doesn't just fail to display the file progressively; it won't be able to display the file at all.)

The PNG file format also supports progressive display.

What Is Transparency?

Transparency is a way of making graphics look like they are drawn directly on a web page, rather than drawn on a rectangular piece of paper and then pasted on. How does the transparency effect work? Web pages often have a background color, image, or pattern. When an image on a web page has transparent portions, that page background shows through the image's transparent portions. Without transparency, the image appears in a rectangular area with its own background color. Transparency is only available for GIF and PNG images, not JPEG images.

The alternative to transparency is to match background colors exactly between the image and the web page, but that can be tricky. Where there is a background pattern or image on the web page, matching is next to impossible because you can't align the graphic precisely enough with the page background.

Setting a GIF Color to Be Transparent

The way to make a GIF image file transparent is to designate one of the colors in that image as the *transparent color.* Any part of the image that is in the color you choose then disappears entirely when the image is viewed in a web browser. Although you usually use transparency for image backgrounds, the chosen color can be any color in the image, not just the background color. Many graphics programs that output GIF89a file formats give you some way to choose one color as transparent.

Note that many graphics programs don't automatically show the transparent color *as* transparent! You may need to look for a special viewing option (usually in the program's View menu) to actually see the transparency. You can also open the image in your web browser to check its transparency, with the File | Open or a similar command. See the section "Avoiding or Fixing Transparency Problems" later in this chapter if you have troubles with transparency.

The following three sections provide detailed instructions of typical ways to create transparency using Photoshop, Fireworks, and Paint Shop Pro.

Transparent Images in Adobe Photoshop

You can set transparency in Photoshop by first setting a transparent background and then specifying transparency again during the process of exporting the file in GIF format. The steps are

1. Select the background layer of the image.

2. Set the opacity of the background layer to **0%.**

3. Save the file in GIF format by selecting File | Save For Web.

4. Select GIF as the format to save.

5. Check the Transparency box.

6. For Matte, select None from the pull-down menu.

7. Click OK and give the file a name.

Transparent Images in Macromedia Fireworks

You set transparency in Fireworks when you export the Fireworks document as a GIF file. Follow these steps:

1. Choose File | Export Preview to begin exporting the file as a GIF image.

2. In the dialog box that pops up, select GIF as the format.

3. Change the pull-down menu from its default of No Transparency to Index Transparency.

4. By default, Fireworks selects the predominant background color to be transparent. If you want to designate a different color to be transparent, click the eyedropper tool, and then click the color in the image that you want to make transparent.

5. Click the Export button, and give the file a name.

Transparent Images in Paint Shop Pro

The simplest way to create a transparent GIF in Paint Shop Pro is to designate one color as the *background* color and then specify that the background color should be transparent. The following are the steps to take:

1. Click the eyedropper icon on the Tool palette, on the left side of the window.

2. In the image, *right*-click the color that you want to become transparent.

3. Choose Colors | Set Palette Transparency (or press CTRL-SHIFT-V). If a dialog box informs you that Paint Shop Pro must decrease the palette, click Yes. Read the upcoming section "Optimizing Images for the Web" to make the best choices in the Set Palette Transparency dialog box that appears after you click Yes (or, simply click OK in that dialog box to accept the default settings).

4. In the Set Palette Transparency dialog box, choose Set The Transparency Value To The Current Background Color and then click OK. To view the result of your transparent color selection, choose Colors | View Palette Transparency (or press SHIFT-V).

5. Choose File | Save As and in the Save As dialog box, select CompuServe Graphics Interchange (GIF) as the file type.

6. Click the Options button in the Save As dialog box and in the Save Options dialog box that appears, make sure that Version 89a is chosen. Click OK.

7. Click Save in the Save As dialog box.

Avoiding or Fixing Transparency Problems

Several problems can afflict your transparent image, including pinholes, ragged edges, and incomplete (spotty) transparency. You can avoid or fix many such problems.

The root of the problem is that GIF uses a *palette* (limited selection of colors) of no more than 256 colors, and each color may be used in many pixels throughout the image. If a color in the palette (distinguished not actually by its color, but by an index number in the palette, 0 to 255) is designated transparent, any pixel anywhere in the image that uses that index number will be transparent—even those outside of the area that you want to be transparent. The opposite side of the problem is that pixels in the area that you want to appear transparent may remain opaque. They may only be *similar* to your designated transparent color, not actually *of* the color whose index number you chose in the palette.

The first step in avoiding such problems is to choose a color for transparency that appears only in the area that you want transparent. You can then use that color to *fill* (replace) or paint the color in the area that you want to become transparent. One way to ensure that a palette color is not used in the image is to add a unique color to the palette. See the next section, "Optimizing Images for the Web," for more information on palette control.

Transparency sometimes leaves rough edges or unwanted, fuzzy borders around objects. The problem is caused by a gradual color transition along the edge, instead of a sharp one, or by a non-uniform background color. Several causes, to be avoided if possible, exist for this problem:

- *Objects in the image (typically text) have been anti-aliased. Aliasing* is the staircase-like edge that appears around slanted or rounded edges on computer screens. *Anti-aliasing* is the removal of that staircase-like edge by making the edge less distinct: blending the object and the background colors in the pixels along the edge. Avoid anti-aliased images where transparency is needed.

- *The image originated as a JPEG image.* JPEG images invariably have subtle color variations around edges. Try to obtain an original image in another format, or plan to spend a lot of time editing the colors in the image.

- *The image was scanned from a drawing or photograph or is the result of a realistic computer rendering of a 3-D scene.* Realistic or hand-drawn images invariably have blurred edges, which means less color uniformity. Try rescanning (or rerendering) the image with fewer colors selected in the scanning or rendering software and with anti-aliasing turned off.

- *The image was dithered.* In *dithered* images, dots of different colors in the palette are sprinkled near each other, to give the illusion of a color that isn't in the palette. You get holes in your image in places where dots appear on the otherwise-opaque object and happen to be in the transparent color, and you get spots where dots appear on the background and are not transparent.

Dithering has a positive side, however. If you want an image either to fade gradually to a transparent background or to be partially transparent, you need dithering. No matter how close in color value a pixel is to the chosen transparent background color, that pixel will not be partially transparent. Dithering allows you to sprinkle transparent pixels in various proportions among the opaque pixels to achieve partial transparency. The image palette, however, must not have any colors available between the foreground and background color for this effect to work, or else an intermediate, nontransparent color will be introduced.

Dithering is a double-edged sword for transparency. If given a dithered image, try to obtain the undithered original so that the option to dither is yours. You can avoid dithering an image by careful palette control, as described in "Optimizing Images for the Web," or by changing settings in your graphics program.

If you have problems with an image because it has non-uniform colors, dithering, or any of the other reasons just listed, you may be able to clean up the image. See "Optimizing for Quality" in the next section for suggestions.

Optimizing Images for the Web

Creating good web graphics is mainly a matter of balancing download speed and image quality. If you aim for speed, you reduce the number of colors and the amount of detail an image can contain. If you aim for color fidelity, use a highly detailed image, or add certain special effects, you may actually diminish image quality slightly for certain viewers of your web graphics and will almost certainly worsen downloading speed. Certain optimizations help minimize the trade-off, and some graphics programs can do much of the optimization process for you. Adobe Photoshop and Macromedia Fireworks both have tools that allow you to compare JPEG and GIF versions of an image and select the best quality or color palette for balancing this trade-off between download speed and image quality. In Photoshop, optimize an image by choosing File | Save For Web. In Fireworks, display the Export Preview dialog box by choosing File | Export Preview. These dialog boxes are illustrated in Figures 26-1 (Photoshop) and 26-2 (Fireworks).

The quality problems that you get in the normal course of creating web graphics are subtle. (Too subtle, even, to be visible in illustrations in this book.) For casual web sites, sizing your image properly and choosing GIF or JPEG appropriately is enough. Only for professional or business web sites do you usually need to consider doing more.

Optimizing for Speed

Images need to download fast, or people won't wait for them before moving to another page. Download speed is essentially a matter of small file size and reusing images where possible. Four principal factors affect file size, as follows:

- Choice of format (GIF, JPEG, or PNG), and JPEG "quality." (Refer to "Graphics File Formats for the Web" earlier in this chapter for a discussion of format issues.)
- Image dimensions.
- Image content.
- Number of colors.

This section focuses on the last three factors in file size: dimensions, content, and colors.

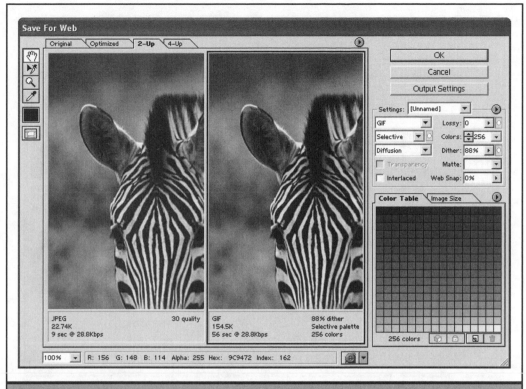

Figure 26-1. *The Save For Web dialog box in Adobe Photoshop helps you balance download speed and image quality.*

Tip *Reuse images where possible to save download time. Browsers don't download the same image file more than once in any given browsing session, even if the image (such as a button, bullet, or icon) is repeated within or among your web pages. Some web page development tools (especially word processors), however, create a separate file for each instance of an identical bullet or icon. You may need to edit the HTML file to ensure that all the IMG tags for the bullet or icon refer to the same image file.*

Minimizing Image Dimensions

One important way to keep files small is to use the smallest practical image height and width (in pixels). If you reduce both height and width by half, for example, most image files diminish in size to about one-quarter of the original file size and download from the Web in one-quarter of the time. For drawings, where images are stored in vector format, image dimensions don't matter until you convert the image to bitmap format (GIF or JPEG).

You obtain best results by making the image the right size from the start, although you can also reduce a larger image. (Going the other direction, enlarging a smaller

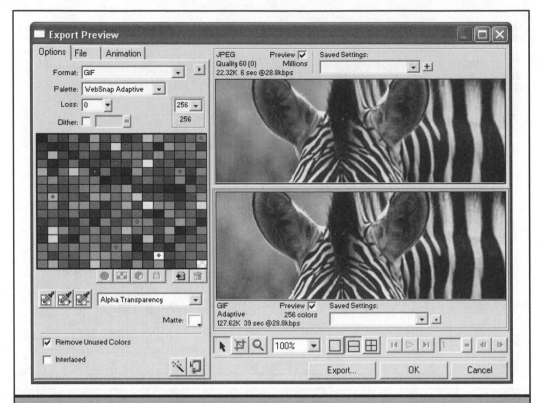

Figure 26-2.   *The Export Preview dialog box in Macromedia Fireworks also helps you balance speed and quality.*

image, usually results in unacceptably poor quality.) Most graphics programs provide a resize, stretch, shrink, or size attribute control that you can use to reduce image size. (You usually find the sizing commands in the Image menu, if you use Photoshop, Paint Shop Pro, or one of the many other popular PC and Macintosh graphics programs.)

Note   *To avoid distorting an image any more than necessary, don't crop, shrink, or otherwise edit an image that is in JPEG format. In some programs, doing any of these things may make the image dimmer, as well as distort it. Save the image to another format before you edit it.*

Only one kind of dimension is relevant in web images: *pixels.* Some graphics programs show image dimensions in inches or centimeters (cm) by default. (Look on the status bar, in many programs, to see which scale it uses for image dimensions.) If you can set dimensions in pixels in your program, don't be concerned with dimensions displayed in other units or with resolution. If your graphics program does not show dimensions in pixels, you can calculate pixel dimensions. Multiply the dimensions in inches (or cm) by the resolution in pixels per inch (or cm) that the program displays. Adjust image size in such a program by adjusting either the dimension in inches (or cm) or the resolution; the result is the same. Some drawing programs may not even discuss pixels until you try to save your file in a GIF format.

If you are using a program to create your web pages and shrinking the graphics in that program doesn't seem to make them download faster, try reducing the image size in a graphics program. When you're creating a web page, you may be able to force an image into a space smaller than its pixel dimensions, but forcing won't reduce the file size, and it hurts the image quality. For instance, the following HTML code forces Image.gif to be displayed in a space 126 by 126 pixels, regardless of its actual dimensions:

```
<img src="Image.gif" width=126 height=126>
```

The file is still transmitted in its entirety, so it takes just as long to download as if it were not forced into smaller dimensions. The browser receiving this document performs the job of reducing the image size to 126 by 126 pixels on the screen. Browsers are not as good as most graphics programs at this kind of task, so you achieve better quality and a smaller file by reducing the image size in a graphics program rather than in a browser.

Reducing a GIF image's size affects its quality because the program must eliminate pixels, a process that can distort or eliminate small features and introduce rough edges. Some programs can smooth the result by anti-aliasing. Anti-aliasing can become objectionable, however, if the background color is transparent or if the image is displayed on computer hardware or browser software that has only limited color range. See "Optimizing for Quality" later in this chapter for information on controlling anti-aliasing.

Minimizing or Avoiding Certain Types of Image Content

Images with less detail (or, more precisely, more uniformity among their pixels) create smaller files. All graphics formats for the Web rely on data compression, and uniformity aids compression. In data compression, if a group of pixels is identical in color, each pixel doesn't require its own color value in the file—the group can be represented by a single value. The fewer color changes that occur in a row of pixels, the fewer groups that are needed, and thus the smaller the file. For that reason, certain image attributes are costly in file size, such as the following: horizontally graduated fills (where a color changes gradually from left to right), patterned backgrounds, dithering, speckling, high-resolution photographs, images with printing screens applied, images scanned from coarsely screened media such as newspapers, and scanned image files for which the color palette is larger than the original number of colors in the artwork.

The best solution is to seek better original artwork. Failing that, you need to make the image's colors more uniform, blur or despeckle the image, or choose a different way to minimize file size, such as reducing the number of colors, described in the following section. To make colors more uniform, see "Optimizing for Quality" later in this chapter. To blur or despeckle the image, look for a blur or despeckle filter in your graphics program. Photoshop, Paint Shop Pro, Lview Pro, and other common graphics programs offer a variety of filters for removing excessive detail and color variation. Some scanner software also offers descreening settings.

Minimizing and Flattening Colors

Usually, the fewer colors your image uses, the smaller the file. If you are drawing a picture, use as few colors as possible right from the start. In addition, many graphics programs let you reduce the color palette of an existing image, which is called *flattening* the colors. Reducing the palette reduces the size of the image file, but not because the file has less palette data. (Palette data is a small part of the image file.) When the program removes colors, it gives the affected pixels new colors. It has fewer colors to choose from, so a pixel is more likely to match a neighboring pixel's color. The pixels are then part of a same-color pixel group and no longer require their own data in the file.

If you use a graphics program to reduce colors, be aware that how it reduces the colors is important. If a program removes a color from the palette, the image file gets smaller only if the program simply reassigns the next closest color to the pixels that had the removed color. If the program compensates by dithering, the file may not get significantly smaller because dithering makes pixels different from their neighbors, thus requiring each pixel to have its own data in the file.

Most graphics programs that offer color reduction let you choose a reduction process. Look for options in the dialog box that appears when you reduce colors. The process that helps to minimize file size is often called *nearest color substitution.* The other process, dithering, goes under various names, but a common one is *error diffusion.*

Optimizing for Quality

Rapid downloading is important, but you also need to maintain a level of quality. Given a certain size and content, the way to ensure quality is to choose the file format well and to control the depth and uniformity of color in the image.

Choosing Color Depth and Palettes in GIF and JPEG

The number of different colors an image file can contain is called its *color depth.* GIF files have a maximum color depth of 256 colors, which is called *8-bit color,* but can also have depths of 7 bits (128 colors), 6 bits (64 colors), 5, 4, 3, 2, or 1 bit. JPEG files have a fixed color depth of 16.7 million colors, called *24-bit color,* a depth that makes JPEG images generally better for color photographs. Within a given depth, the actual number of colors used in the image (the *palette*) can be fewer than the color depth allows. An 8-bit GIF image (256 colors possible), for instance, might use only 200 colors.

Today, most computers can display 16.7 million different colors. Many older computers can still display only 256 or fewer colors, but those can be *any* 256 colors out of 16.7 million, 64,000, or some other very large number.

GIF images are equally flexible. You (or your graphics program) can *choose* the 256 colors out of 16.7 million colors that best match the colors in your original image. You can also choose a smaller palette or color depth to reduce file size, or choose a specific palette to better match the palette of a broad range of computer displays (as described in the following section).

So-called *true color* formats, such as JPEG or 24-bit PCX, do not use a palette: each pixel can be any color out of 16.7 million. However, if a computer cannot display a particular color in a JPEG image, it either chooses the closest color it can display or approximates the missing color by dithering other colors, depending on the browser. To minimize quality problems caused by such compromises on older computers, you can create your image in (or convert your image to) a palette format such as GIF and then convert the file to JPEG.

If your web page has several images on it, make sure that all images use the same palette. Computers that use screen palettes can display the colors of only one palette at a time. If you have images with different palettes, you may force the computer to substitute or dither colors.

Choosing Between Quality and Control

Web images sometimes look worse when they are viewed in a browser or on someone else's computer than they looked originally. This problem arises because the browser, the computer's display adapter, or its operating system doesn't have as many different display colors as the original hardware and software. To compensate for the colors that it doesn't have, the displaying system must either dither the image by mixing dots of colors that it does have, or substitute colors for the original ones. The result can be speckled images or peculiar colors.

To avoid having some other computer dither or substitute colors in your image, you need to use the smallest commonly used color palette. That minimal palette, sometimes called a *web-safe* or *Netscape palette,* consists of 216 specific color values that were chosen by Netscape years ago. (An even more minimal palette is the set of 16 fixed, so-called *Windows colors.*)

If you choose to create images in the limited web-safe palette, you sacrifice the maximum quality that your image could provide in order to gain control. You, not the system on which your image is viewed, now control how the dithering is done and what colors appear where. In gaining that control, you reduce your image to the lowest common denominator. You lose the quality that a larger palette offers: a crisper, richer, higher-fidelity image.

Should you make the trade-off? The decision depends on how much you care about delivering top image quality to the viewers in your audience, but with lower graphics capability. The web-safe, 216-color standard assumes people are running the lowest color quality commonly available in Microsoft Windows: 256 colors (8-bit color). Some systems, however (certain UNIX systems, for instance), actually use even lower color depth than that. The majority of computers and browsers today use much higher color depth. Many run at least 16-bit color (32,000 or 64,000 colors). By adopting web-safe colors, you deprive those viewers of higher quality. Many web sites now optimize their graphics for this higher color depth.

Using a Web-Safe Palette

If you decide to use the web-safe colors for maximum control, how do you do so? All but the most basic graphics programs let you construct a palette, load a palette from a file, or customize a palette of an existing image by removing, adding, or adjusting colors. Some programs, such as Photoshop and Fireworks, offer web-safe palettes built into the program.

If your graphics program does not have a web-safe palette included, one practical way to get one is to obtain an image in web-safe colors, save the palette as a separate file (if your graphics program allows it), and then apply that palette file to your own images. An example of such an image file is on the Web at **the-light.com/netcolpc.gif**, a graphic created by Victor S. Engle. You can find other examples on the Web by searching for the phrase "web-safe palette." Open a web-safe image in your graphics program, and look for a command that saves the image's palette as a file. In Paint Shop Pro, for instance, choose Colors | Save Palette. In Photoshop, use File | Save For Web, and click the Color Palette Menu button next to the color table. Once you have this palette as a file, you can load it either before you create a new image or after you open an existing image, to convert that image to web-safe colors.

Eliminating Problems with Photographs in GIF

The GIF format sometimes displays photographs poorly. If a photograph in GIF format is blotchy or speckled, uses unrealistic colors, or has bands of color instead of gradation, it may have been scanned using too few colors, or its palette may have been reduced too far. Repeat the scan or palette reduction from the original image, using a larger palette. You can also reduce a speckled or banded area to a uniform color. (See the following section.) A more attractive way to replace blotches, pools, or bands of colors may be to "smudge" certain areas of the image or to apply a "blur" filter if your graphics program provides those tools. If possible, a more satisfactory alternative in many cases is to rescan the image and save it as a JPEG.

Reducing Mixed Colors to a Single Color

Reducing an area of mixed colors to a uniform color can improve image quality, minimize file size, and help you get uniform transparency for that color with no unwanted holes or spots. The simplest approach is to paint over a non-uniform area with a single color, using the painting or drawing tools common in many graphics programs. Click a distinctive (and for transparency, unused) color in the palette that your program displays, click a paintbrush or other drawing tool, and then drag across the area of the image that you want to paint.

If the area that you want to repaint has irregular edges, however, such as the background behind a flower, manually repainting the area is difficult. If the mixed colors in that area are similar to each other (say, a variety of lighter and darker greens), you can sometimes improve uniformity by reducing the number of colors in the image palette.

More advanced programs, such as Photoshop, Fireworks, and Paint Shop Pro, offer tools that allow you to replace a range of colors with a single color. The next three sections tell you how to do it.

Photoshop   Photoshop provides a "magic wand" that lets you select an area of similar colors and then fill that area with a single color. Click the Magic Wand button on the toolbar and then click the area of the image that you want to reduce to a uniform color. To adjust the range of colors selected, choose Window | Show Options to display the Options palette. In the Tolerance box, enter a larger value to expand the range of colors or a smaller value to reduce the range and then click the image again. You will need several tries to select the pixels that you want. To expand or contract an area, choose Select | Modify | Expand (or Contract). To add individual areas to the selection, press SHIFT while clicking areas of the image; to remove areas, press ALT while clicking. To fill the selection with a single color, choose a foreground color on the toolbar, click the Paint Bucket tool (the spilling paint can), and then click the selected area.

Fireworks   The Magic Wand tool in Fireworks is practically identical to the one in Photoshop. To adjust the range of colors selected by the tool, choose Window | Tool Options to display the Tool Options dialog box. Adjust the Tolerance box the same as described for Photoshop earlier. To expand or contract an area, choose Modify | Marquee | Expand (or Contract). To fill the selection with a single color, choose a fill color on the toolbar, click the Paint Bucket tool (the spilling paint can), and then click the selected area.

Paint Shop Pro   Paint Shop Pro has magic wand and fill functions very similar to Photoshop's. To select a range of colors, click the Magic Wand tool and then click the image. To adjust the range of colors that the wand selects when you click, use the Tool Options window. If that window is not on your screen, either click the Toggle Tool Options button on the toolbar or choose View | Toolbars and click to place a check mark in the Tool Options check box.

In the Tool Options window, as in Photoshop's Options palette, is a Tolerance box for adjusting the range of colors selected. You will need several tries with different tolerance values to select the pixels that you want. Between tries, remove your previous selection by pressing CTRL-D; then adjust the tolerance value and click the image again to try your new tolerance. Paint Shop Pro's Magic Wand allows you to select pixels by *hue* (color, such as blue, regardless of brightness or darkness), brightness, or *RGB value* (color and brightness combined). Choose one of these methods in the Match Mode selection box of the Tool Options window.

Animating GIF Graphics

Animated graphics for the Web take various forms; a simple, common form is an *animated GIF* file, a single file containing multiple images that your browser can play in succession. You can place animated GIF images on a web page just as you would regular GIF images. Each image is a frame of the animation, like a frame of a movie. You can set the time between frames and make the animation loop either indefinitely or a fixed number of times. Netscape Navigator and Microsoft Internet Explorer display animated GIFs without additional software. Some graphics utilities and paint programs designed for single images, however, display only the first or last frame of the animation.

Other forms of animated graphics may use the vector-based Flash format. These are created using Macromedia's Flash authoring program. Viewing Flash animations requires a special browser plug-in, but the Flash viewer has become so common that it is now a *de facto* standard format, and the viewer comes bundled with both Internet Explorer and Netscape Navigator. Adobe's SVG (discussed in the first section of this chapter), can also provide animation, but as of this writing is much less common on the Web.

You can also create animation using Java, which you can code by hand, or you can use a development tool that outputs Java. Such tools can often help you to convert standard presentations, done in Microsoft or Corel presentation formats, into web slide shows or animations. The person viewing the file needs a Java-compatible browser to see the animation. Java does not, as a rule, transmit multiple images the way animated GIF does, but instead transmits code that draws a sequence of images on the browser screen. The code can be extensive and can require long download times.

GIF animations are very easy to create—with the right graphics tools. Among the commonly used tools for animations are the following:

- **Adobe ImageReady** is a professional web development tool (distributed with Adobe Photoshop) that runs on a variety of computers and includes animated GIF output, palette optimization, and special effects. ImageReady integrates tightly with both Adobe Photoshop and Illustrator, which you can use to create the original artwork to be animated.

- **Macromedia Fireworks** allows you to create animated GIF files by defining frames within the image file.

- **Animation Shop** is an inexpensive, capable, and easy-to-use program (distributed with Paint Shop Pro) available from **www.jasc.com** on the Web. Animation Shop helps you assemble multiple GIF images into an animation, generate animated special effects from single images, and optimize your palette.

- **CorelDRAW** is a high-end graphics suite that is available for a variety of computers. The drawing module enables you to create images for animation, and the paint module can assemble and output the images as an animated GIF file with optimized palettes.

- **GifBuilder** is a popular and simple freeware GIF animator for the Macintosh, developed by Yves Piguet and available at **www.download.com**.

- **GIF Construction Set** is an inexpensive program that is available as shareware from Alchemy Mindworks at **www.mindworkshop.com**. It includes clever GIF animation wizards, performs palette optimization, and can create animations by generating transition effects (such as wipes or fades) between individual GIF images.

- **Ulead GIF Animator** is a program that offers a variety of inexpensive and nicely featured web graphics tools at its site, **www.webutilities.com**. One such tool, GIF Animator, provides animation and optimization wizards, plus a variety of transition effects for creating animations based on one or two original images.

For a list of GIF, Java, or JavaScript animation tools, go to TUCOWS (**www.tucows.com**) or CNET Download.com (**www.download.com**) and search for "animation."

Creating and Animating Image Sequences

The best way to create the series of images that you need for an animation usually is with a drawing program, not a paint program. With a drawing program, you can move and adjust shapes very flexibly. (A paint program with multiple-layer capability, such as Photoshop, also works.)

Drawing programs, however, normally store their images as vector-format (drawing) files, not as GIF files. Some professional drawing programs intended for web development may directly create animated GIF files from a sequence of vector images, but most drawing tools will not. In most drawing tools, the process involves creating a series of drawing files (one for each frame), converting each one to a GIF file, and then using a GIF animation tool to assemble those GIF images into a single animated GIF file. In more detail, the process usually looks like this:

1. Using your drawing program, draw the image that you want to animate. Group together any shapes that make up an object that you want to animate. Save your starting image (the first frame) as a drawing file.

2. Create a single frame of your animation by slightly moving, rotating, resizing, or changing the coloring or shape of the object(s) that you want to animate. Do not change the dimensions or palette of your drawing, however. If your drawing program offers a motion-blur feature, apply that feature to your moving object to enhance the illusion of motion between frames.

3. Save your modified image as a separate drawing file.

4. Repeat steps 2 and 3 until you have finished all the frames of your animation and saved them as separate files.

5. If your GIF animation program can't directly read the format in which you have stored your frame drawings, convert each frame drawing file to a separate GIF file by using a graphics utility or paint program. (Photoshop, for example, can read Adobe Illustrator, EPS, or PICT drawing files and output GIF files.)

6. Run your GIF animation software to assemble the frame images into a single GIF file. The details of this process vary from program to program, but most make the process simple. Some programs, such as the PC-based Animation Shop, provide a wizard that steps you through the process. In other programs, such as the Mac-based GifBuilder, you can simply drag the frame files into the Frame window of the program.

Your GIF animation software may offer a variety of options for your animation. It can let you set the time interval between frames and how many times the animation repeats before it stops. The better programs provide automatic features that can optimize the palette for speed or image quality. In addition, a good program can often apply to your animated images the same features of transparency and interlacing that you use in still GIF images.

Some GIF animation software, including Ulead GIF Animator and Animation Shop, can also convert movies (such as Microsoft's AVI files) and other animations (such as AutoDesk's FLC or FLI files) to animated GIFs. Animated GIFs offer the advantages of not requiring special software and downloading faster than many movie formats. The usual trade-off is lower image quality.

Here are some tips for creating a GIF animation:

- Some drawing programs can output directly to GIF, possibly saving you a conversion step (step 5, earlier in this section). You may, however, get better conversion results by converting the file to GIF in a paint program or graphics utility.

- A word processor that has drawing features and writes text and graphics to HTML, such as Microsoft Word or Corel WordPerfect, can be a simple animation tool. In a blank document, draw an image or insert clip art and then copy the image repeatedly, moving or changing some object each time that you copy, to animate the object. When you output to HTML, you get a series of GIF images that you can animate with a GIF animation tool (and a blank HTML document that you can discard).

- Use images that are the same size and from the same palette. Changing palettes in mid-animation can cause peculiar coloring effects.

- If your drawing program does not output a format that your graphics utility or paint program can read and convert to GIF, try using your computer's copy-and-paste techniques to copy each image between your drawing software and your graphics utility or paint program.

- Continuous looping is an option, but is distracting and usually annoying to watch.

- Time intervals between frames do not apply while the image is being downloaded to someone's browser. As a result, the first playing of the animation will be uneven.

- Keep it short! People generally don't wait for long graphics downloads, and the longer the animation, the bigger the GIF file.

Animating with JavaScript: Rollovers

JavaScript is slightly off the topic of creating web graphics because it is part of the HTML document, not part of an image. Nonetheless, you can use JavaScript to animate graphics interactively (in response to user activity). The user must have a JavaScript-enabled browser, which includes most current browsers.

JavaScript can load and unload images in response to a variety of events. A common use of JavaScript is the *rollover*, which calls attention to an HTML link by replacing the linked image with another image when the cursor passes over the link. (See Chapter 28 for more details on JavaScript rollover code.) A simple (but slow-responding) example is the following:

```
<A HREF="nextpage.html"
onmouseover = "document.mysymbol.src = 'image2.gif' "
onmouseout = "document.mysymbol.scr = 'image1.gif'"
<IMG SRC = "image1.gif" width = "100" height = "100" border = "0"
name = "mysymbol"></A>
```

As the user passes a cursor over the link to Nextpage.html, the Image1.gif image is replaced by Image2.gif. The downloading time for Image2.gif makes the effect slow when it is first used.

Creating Clickable Graphics by Using Image Maps

A popular feature of web pages allows the user to click various parts of an image to go to various pages. These web pages rely on *image maps* in the HTML document or on the web server. The image is associated with the map by the HTML code that inserts the image in the document. The image file itself has no map information in it.

Another popular way to create an image with different clickable regions is to slice the image into rectangles, put the pieces into a table so that they appear as one seamless image on the web page, and link each piece of the image to a different address.

Overview of Image Maps

An image map is code that either is part of a web page's HTML (a *client-side* image map) or is in a separate file on the web server (a *server-side* image map). Most developers today use the client-side image map because it's easier to implement, gives users faster response, and reduces demand on the server.

Image maps do two things: they identify areas of the image (often called *hot spots*) and link these areas to different URLs. Each hot spot consists of a shape (circle, rectangle, polygon, or point) and a location on the image.

For example, an automobile manufacturer could place hot spots on the image of an automobile, so that users clicking on a portion of the car would be shown a document about that portion. The manufacturer might use circular hot spots for the wheels, a rectangular hot spot for the rear passenger compartment, and a polygon for the front compartment (to extend under the dashboard).

Client-Side Image Maps

Following is image map code for an image of an automobile as the map might appear in client-side form (in the HTML of a web document):

```
<MAP NAME="car">
<AREA SHAPE=CIRCLE COORDS="86,144,36" HREF="AWD.html">
```

```
<AREA SHAPE=CIRCLE COORDS="481,144,36" HREF="AWD.html">
<AREA SHAPE=RECT COORDS="168,31,261,138" HREF="passenger.html">
<AREA SHAPE=POLY
COORDS="266,33,266,82,296,137,386,139,383,71,331,33,266,33"
HREF="frontseat.html">
</MAP>
```

The image map code is bounded by <MAP> tags, which also name the image map ("car" in this example). Hot spots are defined by <AREA> tags with SHAPE and COORD (coordinate) attributes, as follows:

- A circle shape (CIRCLE) uses the following coordinates, in order: column (or X position) of circle's center, row (or Y position) of circle's center, and radius.

- Rectangle shapes (RECT) use two column-row coordinate pairs to define diagonally opposite corners (X_1, Y_1, X_2, Y_2).

- Polygon shapes (POLY) list any number of X, Y coordinate pairs in a connect-the-dots scheme.

- The default shape (DEFAULT) is not really a shape; it gives a URL for the rest of the image, outside of the hot spots. Clicking outside of a hot spot takes the visitor to that default URL.

You associate the image map with the image in the <IMG> tag that displays the image. You use the USEMAP attribute, like this:

```
<IMG SRC="newcar.gif" USEMAP="#car" BORDER=0 WIDTH=600 HEIGHT=200>
```

This example uses the image map code just listed, which is part of the same document (that's what the # means) and has the name "car."

You can include alternate text with each <AREA> tag: text that appears in the hot spot if the web site visitor's browser is not displaying images. Write the attribute in this form:

```
ALT="Drivers seat"
```

Creating Image Map Code

You can write image map code using any text or HTML editor, but using image mapping software is easier. Dreamweaver and GoLive include features to help make image maps, as do their partner graphics programs, Fireworks and Photoshop. (We find Dreamweaver's image mapping feature confusing and recommend Fireworks' instead.) In these programs, you outline the parts of the image that will have links. The program then outputs the map code—either by writing the code into a separate file or by inserting the code directly into your existing HTML file.

Two stand-alone image mapping tools are the following:

■ LiveImage (for Windows), at **www.liveimage.com**
■ Web Hotspots Imagemapper (for Windows), at
www.1automata.com/hotspots/mapper.html

Advanced Features of Graphics Programs

Many graphics and drawing programs today have various advanced features that are useful for web graphics. Many of the graphics programs already mentioned, such as Photoshop, Fireworks, and Paint Shop Pro, offer some or all of these advanced features. The following sections describe some of the advanced features that you will find useful for web graphics in the preceding programs and other programs.

Anti-Aliasing

Anti-aliasing is a method of reducing the "jaggies," a staircase-like effect more properly called *aliasing*, that appears along slanted lines on computer images. Anti-aliasing works by creating color values that are intermediate between the object color and the background color and then using those values to fill in the steps of the staircase. Anti-aliasing also helps display fine detail, such as the *serifs* (small protrusions) that many fonts have. Where a serif or other detail is smaller than a single pixel, anti-aliasing uses a faded version of the object color to give the illusion of less than one pixel.

The disadvantages of anti-aliasing are that file size increases, and you get unintended intermediate colors along the edges of your objects. If you create a transparent background, you get an opaque fringe around the edges of objects.

Some programs do anti-aliasing automatically. The process is used in two common circumstances: to reduce the dimensions of an image and to apply text or other sharp-edged objects. Some tools refrain from automatically anti-aliasing GIF and other palette-based images, but only anti-alias 24-bit, "true color" images. If you are converting a 24-bit image to a palette (GIF) image, convert it before you shrink it or apply text to it, if you want to avoid anti-aliasing. On the other hand, if you want maximum image quality, do the conversion last and make sure anti-aliasing is turned on.

Image Slicing

Many web page designs let the visitor click graphics, instead of text, to navigate to various documents of the site. (The images may still contain text, but in some font or graphical treatment that regular HTML document text would not allow.) You can accomplish the incorporation of graphics as links in two ways:

■ Use a single image linked to an *image map*, a special feature of the HTML document, in which clicking different parts of an image links the viewer to different URLs.

■ Slice the image into several pieces, arrange them seamlessly in a table, and then link them separately.

In the second method, you can give each piece of the image *alternate text* that appears if the image hasn't yet downloaded or if the visitor has disabled browser graphics. The visitor can then explore your site without a long wait or a special effort. The second method also enables you to substitute a new piece of the image (in a different color, perhaps, to indicate a previously explored link) without requiring the visitor's browser to download an entire image. This method requires a graphics program that can *slice* an image into several parts and save each part as an image.

Background (Seamless) Tiling

Web pages can have an image for a background (a feature coded into the HTML page, not the image itself, as described in Chapters 24 and 25). That image automatically *tiles*—repeats itself in rows and columns—across the width and height of the browser window. Only one copy of the image file is downloaded; the browser does the repetition. To make the background image into a continuous surface, especially a textured surface, such as pebbles, flocked paper, or granite, the image must not appear to repeat; or if it does appear to repeat, like wallpaper, it should not show seams. Some advanced programs offer special features for *seamless tiling*, matching the left side of an image to its right side, and its top to its bottom, so that no obvious border appears. Such background images can be quite small, requiring little download time, yet still fill the page.

Advanced Compression and Optimization

Optimizing an image for speed and quality is no easy task. You must consider the different computers and browsers viewing the image, the image content, the palette, and more. Some web graphics optimizing tools can help you trim file size in half, even after your best manual efforts. Many of the tools already mentioned include optimizations of various sorts. More advanced tools are available, either in the form of programs or filters. Filters often conform to the Photoshop plug-in filter standard, which means that a wide variety of programs can use them. Some advanced tools may require that you have a good comprehension of computer graphics issues to use the tool properly. The following are two examples of filters especially designed for compression and optimization:

■ **Boxtop Software** offers a variety of Photoshop-standard filters for the Mac and PC. Image Vice is one such filter that performs advanced palette optimization as well as *clipping, smoothing,* and *convergence* operations that reduce areas of mixed colors into sets of uniform colors for better compression. A small preview is offered.

■ **Ulead SmartSaver** is a PC Photoshop-standard filter that lets you create GIF, JPEG, and PNG images with optimized palettes and provides a useful preview of the image and its file size as you make adjustments.

Using Special Effects to Create Animations or Enhance Graphics

Animation programs often can create a GIF animation from individual images either by *tweening* (creating transition frames between images) or by expanding upon a single image, using such special effects as wipes, fades, dissolves, and explodes. Some programs contain all that you need to do text-only animations using those effects. Figure 26-3 shows a waving "flag" animation of text in Animation Shop.

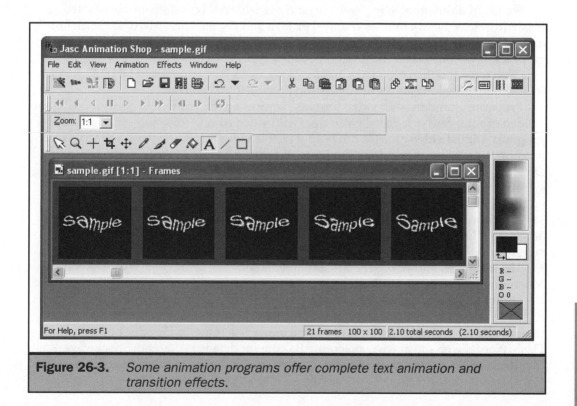

Figure 26-3.   *Some animation programs offer complete text animation and transition effects.*

Multimedia Graphics

Multimedia generally refers to movies, animations, audio, and *interactivity* (response to user input). You can think of multimedia on the Web as coming in two forms: *standard* video, audio, and animation files in formats supported by more than one vendor, and *proprietary* multimedia that requires acquiring a particular vendor's proprietary software to either create or play. (This book discusses audio files in Chapter 27.)

Standard multimedia graphics include animation in GIF and Java, and video in several forms: MPEG (Motion Picture Experts Group), AVI (Microsoft's audio/video format, Audio Video Interleave), WMF (Windows Media Format), and QuickTime (Apple's audio/video format). Exactly *how* standard these formats are is open to debate. In earlier web browsers, you needed additional plug-ins to view all of these formats. Gradually, browser vendors are including in web browsers the capability to view these formats (or to use the operating system's ability to view them). Still, not all users can view all of these formats or their variants without adding plug-ins or players.

Standard animation on the Web currently is achieved by using animated GIFs or Flash, (discussed earlier in this chapter) or Java and Dynamic HTML (DHTML). Java is a programming language that runs within Java-capable browsers and that can animate graphics in various ways. The programs, called *applets,* are downloaded to your browser by a web page and then executed. Chapter 28 discusses Java applets and DHTML further. In addition, new formats are always being proposed for the Web.

Preparing standard web video formats requires a video source (a camera, VCR, and a video capture card or a digital video disc) with video editing software—or an animation program. Digital video cameras can output usable video for use on the Web. Most video or animation programs (Adobe Premiere, Windows Movie Maker, or Macromedia Director, for instance) can output movie files in standard video formats. Video requires significant data compression to be useful on the Web and uses various compression engines (software). One problem with video is that the browser or player requires the same compression engine that the creator program used, and not all computers have access to all the different engines. Even with compression, most video files require significant download time.

The most well-known proprietary multimedia software on the Web is by Macromedia. Macromedia distributes its Flash players (plug-ins) aggressively, so many people have the ability to view Macromedia's multimedia formats. Macromedia's principal formats are its movie and Flash (vector graphics) formats. You can create Macromedia video movies and animations with audio by using either Macromedia Director or Macromedia Flash. (See its web site at **www.macromedia.com** for details.) Although Shockwave was the dominant Web multimedia format, it has fallen by the wayside to Macromedia Flash.

The Complete Reference

Internet

Chapter 27

Creating Web Audio Files

The Web includes every sort of interesting combination of sound, video, synchronized photo slide shows, and animated graphics. Audio is perhaps the most useful medium beyond ordinary text and graphics, the most practical for ordinary modems, and essential to mixed media productions. A good knowledge of web audio also carries over directly to other multimedia that you may tackle in the future. This chapter concentrates on how to create audio files for inclusion on web pages.

Although digitized sounds can be of very high quality, they may not be. The truth is that *digital* audio simply refers to any sounds stored as a series of numbers, and the quality varies tremendously. Essentially, the better the quality, the more numbers that are required: a three-minute popular song, for example, consumes about 30 million bytes on an ordinary CD. This is too much data to place on the Web for transfer to modem users. The data size becomes manageable only by starting with recording format options that give less than CD quality. Often, you can then further reduce the size with *encoding* software.

Types of Web Audio Files

Audio comes in a variety of file formats, just as graphics do. Different formats use different *encoding* methods (methods of translating sound information into digital data). A program that stores audio (or video) data is called a *codec* (coder-decoder). Your choice of format depends on what degree of sound quality you want, the audio software tools that you have available on your computer, and the degree to which various formats are supported on the Web.

Static vs. Streaming Audio Files

Web audio formats generally fall into two categories: static and streaming. Ordinary audio files are also called *static* files and can be of various formats and quality. You upload these files to your web server much as you would your own web pages and then link to them. The user links to your audio file and waits for the *entire file* to download. Then an associated sound program begins to play the file. Commonly used formats include WAV, AIFF, AU, and MP3 files.

Streaming audio files allow the user to start hearing the sound within a few seconds of the beginning of the download. After several seconds, during which the user's streaming player program *buffers* (stores temporarily) the first part of the data (the *preroll time*), the audio begins playing and continues as the program downloads further portions of the file. If the downloading data is not interrupted, the audio can continue to play indefinitely as the audio data *streams* into your PC, keeping just ahead of what you're hearing.

To implement streaming, your web pages link to a *metafile,* a small text file that contains the name and location of the actual audio file. Why this complication? If you link directly to the audio file, the browser program dutifully downloads the entire file before turning it over to the player program, defeating the purpose of streaming. By first linking to a tiny metafile, your browser hands the metafile over to the player, which can then stream the actual sound file appropriately. However, if the average throughput of the user's Internet link is less than required for your stream, either the player refuses to play it, or inevitable tiresome pauses occur during playback while the player rebuffers.

This chapter describes the most prevalent audio and video streaming standards: RealNetworks' *RealSystem* (formerly called RealAudio), Microsoft's *Windows Media*, and Apple's *QuickTime*. For more information about RealSystem, see **www.real.com** on the Web; the RealNetworks Resources page is at **www.realnetworks.com/resources**. For information about Microsoft Windows Media, see **www.microsoft.com/windows/ windowsmedia**. Information about Apple's QuickTime is at **www.apple.com/quicktime**. The following are the advantages of using ordinary static audio:

- **Quality**   You can send small amounts of high-quality sound if the user tolerates the wait. Musicians' web sites sometimes include 20-second clips of some of their songs in static audio so their visitors can sample the full richness of their work.

- **No midstream pauses**   A static file may take a long time to download, but once it does, the static file should always play perfectly, and you can save it and play it again and again.

- **No plug-ins to download**   The programs to play many formats may already be part of the user's operating system. (Windows and Macs come with audio software to play many static audio file formats.)

- **No need for a special server**   Streaming audio often works without a special streaming server program running on the web server, but it usually works better through such a server.

The following are the advantages of streaming audio:

- **Long programs are practical**   People can listen to a three-hour presentation with only a few seconds of initial delay—truly a remarkable advantage. With static audio, even the delay for a three-minute clip may be more than most of your users will tolerate. Streaming audio also allows live feeds, in which the web site creates the audio stream on-the-fly and serves the audio just a few seconds after it happens.

- **More features**   The same encoder and player that you use for your streaming system may allow many additional features, such as merging video, graphics, and slide shows. Because streaming audio formats are of adjustable size and quality, just like static audio, you can choose to serve a high-quality audio file without streaming to modem users—it being no worse than and often faster than other static audio formats.

Types of Static Audio Files

Audio files can contain sound with varying degrees of quality, with higher quality coming at the cost of slower downloading. Some of the media file formats in popular use are shown in Table 27-1.

Name	File Extension	MIME Type/Subtype	Features
Windows Media	WMA, WM, WAX	audio/x-ms-wma, audio/x-ms-wm, audio/x-ms-wax	Wide range of sampling quality, multichannel; designed for static audio
Windows Media (Streaming)	ASF, ASX	video/x-ms-asf	Wide range of sampling quality, multichannel; designed for audio streaming
RealSystem	RA, RM, RAM, RPM, RMX	audio/ x-pn-realaudio	Wide range of sampling quality, multichannel; quite compact; designed for audio and video streaming, not static files
QuickTime	MOV, QT	video/quicktime	Wide range of sampling quality, multichannel; designed for static and streamed audio and video
MPEG Audio Layer 3	MP3	audio/x-mpeg	Wide range of quality, multichannel; quite compact
Resource Interchange File Format, Waveform Audio Format	WAV	audio/x-wav	Wide range of sampling quality; regular and multichannel audio, similar to AIFF

Table 27-1.   *Popular Web Audio Formats*

Name	File Extension	MIME Type/Subtype	Features
Apple's Audio Interchange File Format	AIF, AIFF	audio/x-aiff	Regular and stereo (multichannel), varying sample rates; not compact
Mu-law (u-law)	AU, SND	audio/basic	Telephone quality audio, sampled at 8 Kbps; fairly compact; commonly used
Modules	MOD	audio/x-mod mod	8-bit sampled audio at various rates, plus data for special playing effects; fairly compact
MIDI (Musical Instrument Digital Interface)	MID, MIDI	audio/x-midi	Not for sampled audio, but a music description language; far more compact than sampled music

Table 27-1.   *Popular Web Audio Formats* (continued)

One consideration in your choice of format is quality. The basic factors that affect audio quality are the following:

■ **Sampling rate, given in samples per second (or hertz [Hz], which means the same thing)**   Most common audio files deliver "sampled" audio (with the notable exception of MIDI), which means that they represent sound waves by a series of numbers, called *samples*. The more samples recorded per second, the higher the quality and fidelity of the sound file. A sample rate of 44,100 Hz is considered CD quality.

■ **Sample depth (in bits per sample, such as 8, 16, or 32)**   The more bits per sample, the more closely the sample represents the original (or intended) sound wave, and the higher the audio quality.

- **Number of channels** One channel gives monaural sound, two channels allow stereo, and more channels can be used for a variety of purposes.

- **Compression** The more efficient the compression, the greater the sample rate and depth that is possible for a given download time. MPEG audio is generally considered to offer the best compression/quality trade-off.

Most tools for developing static audio files offer a variety of file types. In general, however, you will find that audio tools on the PC tend to favor the WAV format, tools on Macintoshes favor the AIFF format, and tools on UNIX workstations favor the Mu-law format. The RealSystem streaming file format is supported on a wide variety of computers. (For more on RealSystem, see the following section.)

How to Create Audio Files for the Web

The typical steps in putting sound recordings on the Web—whether they are in static or streaming format—are the following:

1. Capture the audio with a recording device, such as a cassette, minidisc, or digital audio tape (DAT).

2. Generate an uncompressed audio file on your computer by using its sound card.

3. (*Optional*) Edit and process the uncompressed audio.

4. Encode the file into a different audio format, which usually compresses the file size in the process.

5. Load the resulting audio onto your web server and add links to the audio files from your web pages.

Step 1. Capturing the Audio

The secret to creating successful web audio is to start with a good, clean recording. The following pointers can help you to get your digital audio project off to a good start.

- *Always obtain rights to post your recording.* Don't just ask "May I record your speech?" Instead, be specific: ask "May I have your permission to place a recording of your speech on my organization's web site? You would retain copyright, and I'll note that on the web page." Written releases are even better. Obtaining permission to use a recording for one purpose doesn't necessarily give you rights to use it for other purposes. Even though you may be making nonprofit use of a recording, you are still subject to copyright laws. Be especially careful when posting music on the Web because performers, composers, and publishers may all have rights to grant.

- *Don't rely on post-processing to clean up recording deficiencies.* If the original recording is muddled, distorted, or noisy, a good final product may be impossible to obtain.

■ *Suit the tools to the task.* A recording of a PTA meeting for the Web doesn't require the same degree of attention to detail as does a music recording intended for both the Web and a demonstration CD. You don't need to spend lavishly to get very acceptable web audio.

■ *For speech or singing, place the microphone within a foot of the performer's mouth.* In general, your ears can perceive sound cleanly at a much greater distance than can your microphone. (A microphone *too* close, though, can result in pops, distortion, or excessive breath sounds.) Remind the speaker to repeat comments made by anyone who is not at one of your microphones.

■ *Get a feed.* When an existing public address system or professional music-mixing board is already set up at the recording venue, in most cases, get a direct feed (that is, a cable connection) from the board to your recording device. Be certain that you have a compatible adapter and line levels.

■ *Monitor your recordings.* As you record, listen with headphones and trust your ears. With a setup that you've used before and where volume levels don't change greatly, you may not need to monitor the entire recording, but listening is your best insurance against Murphy's Law foul-ups. Headphones that cover the ears completely are best, so that you can distinguish the recorded sounds from the live sounds: even an inexpensive pair can save you from audio disaster.

Recording Devices

Although it's possible to record directly from a microphone or sound system to your computer's hard disk, for most situations, a separate audio recorder is more practical. Portable minidisc recorders are ideal for capturing web audio, combining a very low noise level with quick, random access. A DAT recorder is another choice that eliminates tape noise. Without venturing into expensive commercial recording equipment, consider not only a home cassette deck (use Type II cassettes) as a recording device, but also perhaps your 8mm video camera—just ignore the video portion and use an external microphone. (The soundtracks of non-HiFi VHS or non-HiFi VHS-C recorders are not as capable.) For many types of web audio, ordinary portable cassette recorders, or, in a pinch, even microcassette units, may be sufficient. Depending on how much you compress the audio files later, much of the frequency response and subtleties that high-grade recorders preserve may be sacrificed anyway.

Set, and preferably monitor, your recording volume levels carefully. With ordinary analog recording devices, don't be so conservative with a low recording level that you increase noise needlessly. With digital devices, don't be so liberal with high recording levels that you cross over into their unforgiving distortion overload range.

Microphones

The trick to capturing a clear recording for the Web is to position your microphone correctly. Using a recorder's built-in microphone is often a bad idea because you risk three things: pickup of tape motor noise, muddled sound resulting from improper positioning, and overzealous analog compressor circuits that may raise the volume far too much during quiet passages.

Unless you're using a sophisticated shotgun or parabolic microphone, be sure that your microphone is 6 to 12 inches from the speaker's lips. Even a $20 to $50 microphone can often give you clear speech recordings, but if you run long extensions of 25 feet or more of unbalanced cables, which are used on most such consumer microphones, you may pick up hum. You can avoid long cables and free up your presenter by using a wireless microphone. If you do so, however, plan to spend at least a few hundred dollars for decent quality, remember to check with your venue to be sure that your microphone's radio frequencies won't conflict with existing equipment, and bring a wired microphone, just in case the wireless mike doesn't work. Whenever possible, though, take the easy way out: obtain a direct-feed cable from an existing professional sound system, and save your microphone as an emergency backup.

Sound Card

You need a sound card to get audio in and out of your computer. You may not require an expensive sound card—give any existing card a tryout with your intended application. Older sound cards sometimes advertised "CD quality recording," referring to the rate of sampling, but their background noise levels were not good for critical music recordings. Many newer cards offer about 70 decibels (dB) of *quieting* (a high ratio of signal to noise) and are quite good. Some sound cards, when recording in mono, discard the right channel. If your card does this and you have stereo input, be sure to mix the left and right channels into a mono signal when you specify mono output.

Step 2. Generating a Digital File

When you have a good audio recording, you can store it on your PC in digital form by using either of the following methods:

- Encode it directly into the ultimate format that you want to use on the Web, which is usually a compressed format.

- Convert it first to an uncompressed format, usually a WAV file on PCs or an AIFF file on Macs, and then encode it into a compressed format.

By encoding your recording directly into the final format, you need a lot less disk space, you save a bit of time, and you don't need an audio processing program (apart from your streaming encoder, if you plan to use streaming audio). However, after your audio file is in a compressed format, editing the file is hard. On the other hand, by first converting your recording to a WAV or AIFF file, you can edit and process the audio before you commit it to its final format. To encode directly, connect your sound source to your sound card, and then skip to "Step 4. Encoding the File into a Compressed Audio Format."

To capture an uncompressed audio file on your hard disk, you can use a sound utility program included in your operating system (for example, Windows comes with the Sound Recorder program) or bundled with your sound card. The built-in sound programs on laptops usually work fine as well. If you recorded the sound in an analog format, you digitize the sound in this step. Typically, you connect the LINE OUT connector on your recording device to the LINE IN jack on your computer's sound card. If you consistently get low recording volumes, try the MICROPHONE input on your sound card and check for distortion. Monitor the audio transfer with headphones, at least until you're confident of the sound levels.

If you're transferring sound from a digital device (DAT or minidisc) into a high-end sound card, the sound has already been digitized, and you simply need to move it to your PC and store it in standard format. You may be able to connect the recording device to your PC with a digital wire or fiber optic cable: consult your manuals. A digital connection eliminates the need to convert the signal to analog and then back to digital (*redigitizing*), with a resulting loss in quality. If your sound card is at all worthy, though, you won't lose noticeable quality on the Web by redigitizing.

Most sound formats—not only compressed formats—give you many choices that enable you to balance quality and file size. Choose a quality that is considerably higher than your target users' modem rates can handle, so that you have more options later when you process the data. Digitizing at around 22,000 Hz at 16-bit resolution is sufficient for a modem-using audience.

 More precise recommendations are contained in the RealSystem Production Guide *(available free from **www.realnetworks.com/resources/producer**). This document also contains a table of* RealSystem *codecs (coder/decoders) that denotes which codecs are backward compatible, suggests ideal sampling frequencies, and provides a host of other helpful information.*

Step 3. Editing and Processing the Uncompressed Audio

Many audio processing programs are available, and you don't have to use one from the maker of your streaming software. PC and Mac users can find downloadable audio programs at repositories such as **www.download.com** or TUCOWS, at **www.tucows.com**. UNIX users have a fine resource at **sound.condorow.net**. Look for programs for your operating system, and then for multimedia programs. (See Chapter 34 for more information about downloading and installing programs.)

The most useful processing functions for web preparation are the following:

- **Editing**   Most often, you just edit out a few seconds of leading and trailing time. Attempting to edit out coughs or profanity is much more time consuming—avoid such editing if possible. Most streaming formats also provide tools that enable you to perform simple editing later if needed.

- **Removing direct current offset**   Also called *removing DC bias*, this process centers the waveform around the zero line.

- **Automatic normalization of volume**   The audio processing program can seek out the loudest portion and adjust the volume of the entire recording, so that the loudest portion is just below the distortion level. RealNetworks recommends normalizing to 95 percent or –0.5 dB.

■ **Volume (dynamic) compression**   If you haven't used an analog compression device in front of the recorder, compression can help bring all parts of the recording to within a narrow range of volume. This process is terrible for a fine CD music recording, but is often wonderful for web audio that is to be delivered via modem. The *RealNetworks Production Guide* suggests adjusting the volume to a threshold of –10 dB, a ratio of 4:1, and attack and release times of 100 milliseconds (ms). Then adjust the input volume level until you get about 3 dB of compression, and set the output level to around 0 dB.

Step 4. Encoding the File into a Compressed Audio Format

Now that you have a digitized and processed, but uncompressed, audio file, it's time to get small. Which format you choose depends on whether you want a static or streaming file, and which static or streaming format best suits your sound. If your target is a hi-fidelity, nonstreaming MP3 file, several downloadable encoders are available at the shareware sites listed in the preceding section. If streaming Real audio is your goal, use the RealSystem Producer (available at **www.realnetworks.com/products/producer**) or the free RealSystem Authoring Kit (available at **www.realnetworks.com/resources/smil/downloads/authkit**). For streaming Windows Media, use Microsoft's Windows Media (available at **www.microsoft.com/windows/windowsmedia/wm7/encoder.asp**). For QuickTime audio, both streaming and static, use Apple's QuickTime Pro (available at **www.apple.com/quicktime/upgrade**).

In general, remember that audio compressed with a newer encoder version may not be playable by an older player. Usually, the user can simply upgrade the player for free, but sometimes the new technology player may actually require a hardware upgrade. Check the specs: you may need to restrict your encoding options so that compatibility is maintained, or perhaps simply download an earlier encoder version.

The simple secret to encoding good audio for modem users is to be conservative with your *target bit rate*, the connection speed at which you expect users to be able to download the file. RealSystem, Windows Media, and QuickTime, the predominant audio streaming methods, are in fierce competition, and each company wants to showcase its higher bit-rate modes. You may also want every bit of increased fidelity that you can produce. However, if you can rein in your optimism about how high a throughput your users can obtain, you'll have much smoother sailing. You may think that you're through with picking formats, but each encoder supports several *codecs* (coder/decoders), low-level software engines that do the real encoding work and determine the final bit rate.

If you are creating a streaming file, consider that both Microsoft and RealNetworks enable you to encode a single file at more than one bit rate, so that during playback, the server can choose a different encoding if the user connection is slower than expected. RealNetworks calls this feature *SureStream*. Before you choose this option, though, make sure that the following is true:

■ Your web site includes a true RealSystem or Windows Media server because ordinary web server streaming (HTTP streaming) can't handle the combined streams.

■ You don't need to support users with Real Players and Windows Media Players that are older than the ones that support this option.

If you're encoding from a file to a streaming format, you may find that you encode much faster than real time. This makes sense when you consider what the encoder must accomplish if you encode directly from a sound source! (Compare this to MP3 encoders, which are sometimes *much* slower than real time.) Encoding at higher bit rates may take *less* time because less compression work needs to be done. The multiple–bit-rate mode understandably takes much longer, so recording to a WAV or AIFF file first often is better.

When you run your encoding program, configure the program (by choosing Options or Preferences from the menu bar) to specify the speed at which most users will connect to the Internet ("network bandwidth"), whether the user can save the file for later replay, and where the audio input will come from (a sound card or a previously recorded file). Try choosing Options or Preferences from the menu bar, depending on the program. When you begin encoding an audio file, you specify the file that contains the audio data, the name to give the encoded file, network bandwidth, copyright information, and whether the audio contains voice, music, or both.

Here are some tips for successfully encoding an audio file:

■ If you're encoding directly from an external sound source, experiment a few times until you get the recording volume level just right. Be sure the appropriate inputs are selected, and then adjust the volume to the level at which the loudest passages light the red bars on the encoder's level meter, but they don't activate the overload indicator.

■ Avoid frequent overloads, which cause lots of ugly distortion.

■ When using a Microsoft encoder, unless you're encoding for an intranet application, stay with the MetaSound, MetaVoice, or MP3 codecs for your audio. These are the *core codecs* included with your users' Media Player program. Otherwise, you may produce some great audio that many in your intended audience can't decode.

■ Likewise, when using a RealSystem encoder, unless you're encoding for an intranet application, do not use the secure option. Otherwise, you will produce a file with an .rmx extension that many listeners will not be able to decode.

■ If you're in a hurry to encode a lot of material, turn off automatic indexing. Although this feature allows users to use rewind and fast-forward, by turning it off during encoding, you save time, and you can use other utilities to set index points later.

Adding Audio Files to Web Pages

The simplest way to include audio in your web page is to add a hyperlink to your audio file just as you would link to another web page. When you click the hyperlink, the browser either plays the audio file directly or passes the job to separate plug-in or player software.

Alternatively, web page developers often prefer to include the audio automatically as part of a page, called *embedding* the media. With embedding, you can allow people to experience embedded media immediately, without clicking anything; and if the medium is visual, like video or an animation, it appears right on the web page itself.

When you offer audio files on the Web, it's polite to include a link on your web page to a site from which the user can download the player that your audio file requires. For example, if you include a RealSystem streaming audio file, include a link to **www.real.com/realone,** *where the user can get the RealPlayer program.*

Adding a Link to an Audio File

Web pages may contain links to both static and streaming audio files.

Linking to Static Files

If you have created a static audio file, just upload it to your directory on the web server. When uploading, be sure to specify that it is a binary (not ASCII) file; otherwise, the file transfer process garbles the file in transit.

On the web page from which you want the static audio file to be accessible, add a link with the name of the audio file. For example, you could add a sentence like this:

```
Fred Smith's <A HREF="http://www.myisp.com/mydir/conf/speech.wav">
State of the Club Report</A> has details about next year's plans.
```

Linking to Streaming Files

If you have created a streaming audio file, you need to perform an extra step before you upload the file. Instead of linking directly to the file that contains your audio (usually an RM file for RealNetworks, or an ASF file for Microsoft Windows Media), you link to a *metafile,* a small text file—located on the web server—that contains the name and location of your audio file. However, if you link directly, your listener's browser downloads the entire sound file before the player program gets a chance to play it, defeating the purpose of the streaming aspect.

Consult the documentation for your encoding program, the RealEncoder, or Microsoft NetShow Encoder, for situations in which metafiles may not be necessary.

Whether you have a RealSystem or Windows Media streaming audio file, here are the general steps for creating a metafile, linking to it from your web page, and uploading the files:

1. Using Windows Notepad or any text editor, create a tiny, text-only metafile containing the name of the actual audio file that you want to play. The line contains the URL of the streaming audio file. For the streaming to work, the URL must start with the protocol used by your streaming file (RealSystem or Windows Media). The exact format for the line contained in the file depends on your streaming format; see the next two sections for the exact format. Most people use the same name for the metafile that they use for the audio file (except for the extension) to avoid confusion.

2. Using your web page editor or any text editor, add a link to the web page from which you want the streaming audio file to be accessible. This link is a normal HTTP (web) link to the metafile that you just created. For example, you might add this line to your web page:

```
Click <A HREF="showersong.ram">here</A>to hear my singing!
```

This link uses relative addressing because the metafile (a RealSystem RAM file in this example) is stored in the same directory as the web page, but you can also use a complete URL identifier, like this:

```
Click <A HREF="http://www.myisp.com/xyz/showersong.ram">here</A>
to hear my singing!
```

3. Upload the large audio file to your ISP's RealSystem or Windows Media server directory, and upload your tiny metafile to the directory that contains your web pages. When using FTP to transfer your small metafile, be sure to use ASCII transfer.

4. Test your new audio file to be sure that it plays the audio file that you intended. If it's the correct file, then you're ready to wow the world.

Tip   *If your ISP doesn't provide you with a RealSystem or Windows Media server to transmit the streaming files to your users, you can still stream your audio (with lower performance quality) simply by specifying the ordinary web transfer protocol, HTTP, in the metafile. Your ISP need only define the proper MIME types (that is, types of multimedia files) on its web server; contact your ISP to ask. Then upload both the metafile and the audio file to your directory on the web server.*

Linking to RealSystem Media Files   For a RealSystem audio file, you create a metafile with the extension .ram. The metafile contains a single line indicating the URL of the audio file. If you are using a regular web server, the URL starts with the usual

http://. If your web server runs the RealServer program to provide streaming audio, the URL starts with *rtsp* (RealTime Streaming Protocol) instead of **http**. The **rtsp://** at the beginning indicates that this is a RealSystem file. If your ISP runs an older, version 5, Real server, use **pnm://** instead of **rtsp://**. You can have multiple lines (with one URL per line) if you want to play several audio files in succession.

For example, if your ISP's domain is **MyIsp.com**, your audio file is named mysongs.rm, and your ISP's RealSystem directory is named myaudio, you would create a RAM file named mysongs.ram containing this line:

```
rtsp://www.myisp.com:554/myaudio/mysongs.rm
```

The **554** port identifier can vary with your ISP. When the port number is 544, which is the default port for RealSystem, you can omit the **:554**. Note that your webmaster must configure your server for the RealSystem MIME type before your web page will work properly. Ordinary web servers cannot deliver many RealSystem files at once, so your webmaster may impose constraints on your use of RealSystem unless the server is a streaming server.

Linking to Microsoft Windows Media Files   For a Windows Media streaming file with the file extension .asf, the metafile has the extension .asx. The latest ASX format uses an *XML (Extensible Markup Language)* structure. For example, if your ISP's domain is **myisp.com**, your audio file is named mysong.asf, and your ISP's Windows Media directory is named aud, the ASX file would look like this:

```
<ASX version="3.0">
<ENTRY>
   <REF HREF="mms://www.myisp.com/audio/mysong.asf" />
</ENTRY>
</ASX>
```

ASX files have tags that look similar to HTML. The protocol to specify at the beginning of the second line (in place of the usual **http://**) is **mms://** (Microsoft Media Server protocol).

Note   *If you ever work with RealSystem SMIL files, you'll find them similar in structure to ASX files.*

Embedding a Multimedia File in a Web Page

Many types of objects can be embedded in a web page, including, but not limited to, multimedia files. The following sections describe the process of embedding objects in general, followed by a description of embedding audio files in particular.

Embedding Objects That the Browser Can Handle Without Downloading Additional Viewing Software

Many browsers can handle objects in a variety of multimedia formats intrinsically (without special additional software). Here are some of the types of multimedia files that popular browsers commonly support without help:

- Microsoft video (AVI files)
- Apple QuickTime (QT, movie, MOV, or MOOV files)
- MPEG (Motion Picture Experts Group) video (MPG or MPEG files)
- Audio (AU, WAV, AIFF, MID, or MIDI files)

In addition, browsers are often already equipped with the plug-ins, viewers, ActiveX components, or other technology needed for viewing various types of multimedia. If you expect the browser to be able to display the multimedia object without downloading additional software (either because the browser can handle the multimedia intrinsically, or because you expect the user has previously downloaded whatever plug-in or viewer is needed), you can write the OBJECT element as simply as in the following example:

```
<OBJECT WIDTH="500" HEIGHT="500" DATA="glennlaunch.mpg"
TYPE="application/mpeg">
</OBJECT>
```

The attributes of the <OBJECT> tag in this example provide the following information:

- **DATA**   The location and name of the multimedia file. If a relative address (which, like the one in the example, does not begin with **http://**) is used, the location is assumed to be the same as for this web page, unless the optional CODEBASE attribute is used.

- **WIDTH and HEIGHT**   The size of the area in which the multimedia appears (optional).

- **TYPE**   The file's MIME type (optional). (See "Understanding and Using Multimedia MIME Types" later in this chapter.)

An additional and useful optional attribute to add to the <OBJECT> tag if your multimedia file is large is the STANDBY attribute, like this: STANDBY="Please wait". The text in quotes is displayed while your object downloads.

Embedding Objects with the <EMBED> Tag for Older Browsers

For older browsers that do not process the OBJECT element properly, you can use the <EMBED> tag. This tag was originally extended HTML developed by Netscape. An example of the <EMBED> tag is as follows:

```
<EMBED width="500" height="500" src="glennlaunch.mpg">
```

To ensure that your page is usable by older browsers and yet is HTML 4–compliant, you can include the <EMBED> tag within an OBJECT element as described in the upcoming section, "Embedding a RealSystem File in a Web Page." The <EMBED> tag can also use the ALIGN, BORDER, VSPACE, and HSPACE attributes that are used in the <IMG> tag. See Chapter 24 for more about the <IMG> tag. Depending upon the plug-in or viewer handling the multimedia, other attributes may include AUTOSTART= "true" or "false" to determine whether the multimedia begins to play immediately or not, CONTROLS=*value*, and CONSOLE=*value*, where *value* is determined by the plug-in or viewer.

Embedding Objects That Need Additional Browser Software

Multimedia that the browser can't play on its own requires the user to download a viewer, plug-in, or ActiveX control. In that case, you need to add the CLASSID attribute to the <OBJECT> tag, as in the following example, which gives the URL where the viewer (in this case, 3d_games, a hypothetical viewer) can be found:

```
<OBJECT WIDTH="500" HEIGHT="500"
CLASSID="http://www.radviewers.com/3d_games"
DATA="wheykewl.gam">
</OBJECT>
```

If the browser has not already downloaded the viewer or other software identified in CLASSID, it begins to download (with the user's approval) that software. In this example, the viewer is presumably designed to read the developer's own GAM file format, and it is located at the URL given by CLASSID.

If you are using Java applets, ActiveX controls, or other popular add-on software, you do not give the URL (which begins with *http:*) for the software as the preceding example describes, but instead use special URI (Uniform Resource Identifier) code within the CLASSID attribute, as follows:

- For Java applets, the CLASSID URI begins with *java:*, as in classid="java:myjavathing.class"

- For ActiveX controls, the CLASSID URI begins with *clsid:* and continues with the ActiveX component's very long, unique code, as in the following code for a Macromedia Director ActiveX control:

```
classid="clsid:166B1BCA-3F9C-11CF-8075-444553540000"
```

If the Java or ActiveX component is not in the same directory as the web page file, you need to include a CODEBASE attribute inside the <OBJECT> tag to give its URL, as in the following example:

```
<OBJECT CLASSID=="java:myjavathing.class"
CODEBASE="http://www.radviewers.com/java">
```

The CODEBASE might not even be on your own web site. For instance, if you were embedding a Shockwave Director ActiveX control, your CODEBASE attribute might look like the following line, which points to the URI at Macromedia for a Shockwave player:

```
CODEBASE="http://active.macromedia.com/director/cabs/sw.cab#version=
6,0,0,0"
```

Embedding Audio Files in Web Pages

You can embed a RealAudio file in your web page so that the RealPlayer program runs in the browser window. The main advantage of embedding is that it allows the player controls to appear on the web page instead of in a separate window. It also allows the audio to start automatically, rather than waiting for the web page visitor to click a link. (Linked files can, however, also start automatically if you use JavaScript or other advanced tricks to execute the link.) Embedding can be done using the OBJECT element or <EMBED> tag, as described in the earlier section of this chapter, "Embedding a Multimedia File in a Web Page."

The current HTML specification, 4, includes a standard way of embedding multimedia, called *object embedding*. Object embedding uses the tags <OBJECT> and </OBJECT>. The *OBJECT element* includes <OBJECT>, </OBJECT>, and everything in between. Of course, an HTML 4 browser is necessary for it to work. Prior to HTML 4, the usual way to include multimedia was Netscape's invention, the <EMBED> tag, which is still in common use today.

Exactly how you write the object embedding statement in HTML depends on whether you need the browser to download a plug-in, viewer, or other resource such as an ActiveX control in order to display your multimedia.

Embedding a RealSystem File in a Web Page

To embed the RealPlayer control on your web page so that the RealPlayer runs in the browser window, use the OBJECT element or <EMBED> tag described in the section "Embedding a Multimedia File in a Web Page" earlier in this chapter. As that section indicates, until all browsers fully support the HTML 4 OBJECT element, an approach that covers all contingencies is to include an <EMBED> tag within the OBJECT element.

If the browser cannot process the OBJECT element, it proceeds to the <EMBED> tag. Here is an example of the RealPlayer control in an HTML page:

```
<OBJECT CLASSID="clsid:CFCDAA03-8BE4-11cf-B84B-0020AFBBCCFA"
HEIGHT=140 WIDTH=312>
<PARAM NAME="src" VALUE="sample.ram">
<PARAM NAME="controls" VALUE="Default">
<PARAM NAME="autostart" VALUE="true">
<EMBED SRC="sample.rm" CONTROLS="Default" AUTOSTART="true">
</OBJECT>
```

Notice that the example does not quite follow the usual form for an OBJECT element in HTML 4. Instead of using the DATA attribute of the OBJECT element to identify the audio file, as would be conventional in HTML 4, it uses the <PARAM> tag with an SRC attribute. The example reflects the current state of affairs for RealAudio at this writing: the DATA attribute (and the CODEBASE attribute) of the OBJECT element are not used.

Understanding and Using Multimedia MIME Types

Each kind of media file commonly used on the Internet has a MIME (Multipurpose Internet Mail Extension) type. You can find a good, readable list of MIME types at **www.ltsw.se/knbase/internet/mime.htp**.

Browsers differ in their intrinsic capabilities for handling various MIME types. If a browser cannot display a certain MIME type, it tries to turn the job over to an additional chunk of software like a viewer, plug-in, or ActiveX control. If it has no such software to display the embedded media, it then either displays any alternative text that you have included in the <OBJECT> tag using the ALT attribute or proceeds to display an alternative object using the <NOEMBED> tag.

In the <OBJECT> tag, you can identify the MIME type of your multimedia file by using the TYPE attribute. The TYPE attribute is optional, but by including it, you allow the browser to avoid wasting time downloading the file if it has no way of displaying the file. If you don't include the TYPE attribute, the browser uses the file extension to figure out what kind of file it is.

MIME type names have two parts, the type and subtype, separated by a slash in the MIME name as in application/x-msvideo. Common multimedia types are application, audio, and video; application is a catch-all type that simply implies that the file's format is generally native to a particular application.

MIME subtypes are of two varieties: registered and unregistered. Registered subtypes are registered by the Internet Assigned Numbers Authority (IANA), after a formal process. Unregistered subtypes can be anything at all—in fact, you can create your own—but the subtype must begin with x-. Audio files in WAV format, for instance, are of the MIME type audio/x-wav.

You can choose a variety of RealPlayer controls with the CONTROLS attribute of the <PARAM> tag. By setting CONTROLS to ControlPanel, PlayButton, StopButton, InfoVolumePanel, and other values, you can place various controls for the audio on your web page. See the technical support web pages at **www.realnetworks.com** for details.

The AUTOSTART parameter allows you to start the audio flow immediately. Otherwise, the user must click the Play button on the control panel to begin the sound.

Adding Video to Web Pages

Video is popular for multimedia presentations on CD, but is not yet as popular as audio on the Web. The main reason is that only the fastest networks can handle the rate of data transmission that quality video requires. In addition, the Web does not transmit data at a steady rate, leading to gaps, pauses, and quality lapses in the video. (This variable rate is also a problem for audio, but less so.) Finally, getting video from the video source and into the computer requires a video capture card, which requires an additional expenditure in hardware on many computers.

As with web audio, two approaches are used to get around the bandwidth and variable data-rate problems. One approach is to use static video, which requires the user to download a file (which typically makes use of advanced data compression to shorten download time) before playing it. The alternative is to use *streaming video*. Streaming video not only uses advanced compression in the data stream to overcome the bandwidth problem, but must also solve the problem of variable transmission rate. Solving the latter problem usually involves a special streaming web server.

To date, broadcast- or CD-quality streaming video cannot be delivered over typical dial-up connections to the Internet. The quality of streaming video possible today over a typical dial-up connection is limited to color images a few centimeters square, with audio. Broadband connections such as DSL, T1, and T3 are much better suited for streaming video.

Static Video

Adding static video to a web page is identical to adding static audio. Simply embed or link to a file that is in one of the standard video formats. The video file formats most commonly supported by browsers are

- Apple QuickTime
- Motion Picture Experts Group (MPEG)
- Microsoft AVI

The big technical achievement of video file formats is compression. All these formats offer varying degrees and types of compression, which they implement by using different compression and decompression *engines*—software that encodes or decodes the format.

One practical challenge for web developers is ensuring that the type of compression engine used for creating the video clip is also available in browsers or viewers. AVI files, for instance, can use compression types of Microsoft Video or any of several variants of Intel Indeo, Cinepak, and others. QuickTime movies can use Video, Compact Video, Animation, or Raw (uncompressed) compressors. QuickTime files also come in two forms: the native Macintosh file and a "flattened" file used by other computers. MPEG videos come in a variety of flavors as well, and the standards are progressing rapidly, with MPEG-4 being the latest in the progression.

Streaming Video

Adding streaming video to a web page is identical to adding streaming audio. The most common streaming video formats are RealSystem, Windows Media, and QuickTime. To date, most applications for streaming video have been on corporate intranets, not the Internet, because of the generally higher bandwidth available on an intranet. New streaming technologies and faster modems are gradually making Internet video more attractive to a broader base of users and developers.

Chapter 28

Forms, Interactivity,
and Database-Driven
Web Sites

651

Ordinary web pages are simply documents. They have clickable links to other documents, and they might contain singing, dancing multimedia, but they never get beyond simply displaying fixed information to you. Computer programs, however, can be more flexible. Program screens change immediately in response to your actions, without downloading an entire new page: a menu drops down, text appears, a window opens, or an image changes. Perhaps you type information into the program, and the computer stores that information, computes an answer from it, or uses it to retrieve other information for you from a central database. These capabilities require a program—ordinary web pages can't do these things.

Some methods of adding programs to your web pages involve the web server. In the simplest and most common case, a web page is stored in a file on the computer on which the web server program is located, and the server merely retrieves the page and sends it to the browser when needed. To make the contents of a web page change, you add some form of program—by writing it yourself, using a program writing tool, or using an existing program.

You can add programming in three main ways:

- **Browser scripting, or embedding client-side scripts**   Place program code in the web page that runs in the user's browser, using JavaScript, Java, VBScript, ActiveX, or other technologies. The web server is not involved in running the program code. For example, many pages use browser scripting to display animated graphics, text, or images that appear as you move the mouse around the page, or to show different formatting for differing browsers.

- **Calling external scripts**   Place programs (called *CGI scripts*) on the web server, and include tags in the web page that direct the web server to run those programs. CGI scripts can be written in any programming language the server supports, most commonly Perl, C, or C++. Many web pages call CGI scripts to handle what users type into web page forms.

- **Embedding server-side scripts**   Place program code in the web page that runs on the web server as the page is processed to create the individualized web page sent to the user. The web server needs to be able to run the scripts, which usually means installing extra server software. Popular server-side script systems include PHP (an open source server scripting language), Microsoft's FrontPage WebBots, Microsoft's *Active Server Pages (ASP),* and Macromedia's ColdFusion. You can also use *Server Side Includes (SSI)* to include text files, which may contain scripts. For example, shopping cart systems and web-based message boards use embedded server scripts.

Server-based programs can do things that browser-based programs cannot; in particular, only server programs can enter data into, or distribute data from, a central source such as a database. You cannot create an online store or visitor registration (guest) book, for instance, without employing server software of some kind. Programs run in the browser are limited to using whatever data is stored within a page or entered into the page by the user. They can, however, communicate with server programs to transmit or receive data.

Programs run in the browser can also perform useful interactive effects. Rather than a web page being a fixed combination of text and graphics, every element of the page can be generated or modified by the program. This way of creating the content of a web page from its programming is called *Dynamic HTML (DHTML)*. Common DHTML applications include cascading menus (multilevel menus that appear dynamically) and checking the user input values in forms before sending them off to the server.

Adding program code to the web page is generally easier than writing CGI programs. On the other hand, if your web server already has standard programs or server extensions installed, running server programs from commands in your web page can be quite easy.

Browser Scripting with JavaScript

The easiest kind of program code to create and debug is JavaScript in the web page. The script code runs in your browser, so you can create the pages on your own PC and test and debug them in the browser on the PC before you upload them to your web server.

What Is JavaScript?

JavaScript is a scripting language developed by Netscape and used in its web browser. *ECMAScript*, named after the European standards body, ECMA, is a standardized version of JavaScript. Microsoft's version of ECMAScript is *JScript*. JavaScript is the name still in common use for all these variants, and with moderate care it is possible to write your JavaScript, ECMAScript, or JScript script so that it runs in Netscape, Internet Explorer, and other browsers. This chapter refers to all three scripting languages as JavaScript.

With JavaScript you can do a variety of actions on a web page, such as

- Read what kind of browser and display the user has and adjust the page accordingly

- Open additional browser windows and write content, title, and status bar text to them

- Control frames and the documents within them

- Provide mouseover feedback with images and sounds (that is, events that happen when the user moves the mouse over an object)

- Create forms, set form defaults, read and check form input, and change the page in response

- Create and read cookies and respond according to the cookie data

- Read and write the date and time

- Execute Java applets with varying parameters depending on user input or on which browser is displaying the page

- Animate objects by sliding document layers over each other

The JavaScript language offers features common to other programming languages. Features include variables, loops, conditional statements, numeric and string operators, user-defined functions (similar to subroutines), and comments.

What Is VBScript?

Microsoft has its own technologies for making web pages more interactive. In addition to its JScript version JavaScript, Microsoft has a fully proprietary scripting language for Internet Explorer called *VBScript*, an extension of Microsoft's Visual Basic language. You can use VBScript in web pages for many of the same functions you might perform in JavaScript, but the language is very different and works only in Internet Explorer.

 We suggest using JScript or JavaScript rather than VBScript so your scripts run in Netscape, Opera, and other browsers, as well as in IE.

How JavaScript Works

Browsers use the *object and event model* to describe the structure of a displayed web page and to handle user input. Each item a browser displays (or holds hidden within the HTML code of a page) is an *object*. When scripts run, they can create, change, and read objects. Scripts can create objects of their own as well.

In a browser scripting language like JavaScript, each object has a *name*, either inherently or assigned by the programmer. The entire web page is named *document*, for instance. The main browser window is named (unremarkably) *window*. You might create additional objects of the window type (new browser windows) with names assigned by you.

Objects have *properties*. For example, one property of a window object is the text that appears in its title bar. That property would be referred to as *window.title*. Properties can have subproperties of their own.

Scripts can apply actions, called *methods*, to the objects in a web page. A script executes a method like this:

```
document.write("<I>Hi, Mom!</I>")
```

This line of JavaScript makes the browser add *Hi, Mom!* to the current document.

You can assign pieces of script code to particular objects to be run when something happens to the object—for example, when someone moves the mouse over an image or clicks on a button. Such a happening is called an *event*. Moving the mouse cursor over an object, for instance, is a *mouseover* event. By associating code with an object and an event, the code can change the properties of the object when the event happens. Code can change the filename of an image object when a mouseover happens, for instance, so the image content can change when the cursor passes over the image.

Using JavaScript in Web Pages

JavaScript code can be embedded in the HTML document or contained in a separate, associated file. If JavaScript code is written within a document, it can appear within conventional HTML tags or within a separate script area. A separate script area may appear in either the head or body of the HTML document and is usually written as follows:

```
<SCRIPT LANGUAGE="JavaScript">
<!-- A line that causes non-JavaScript browsers to interpret
the following lines as comments, not display them.

Your JavaScript code goes here.

// A single comment line to a JavaScript browser; an end-of-comment
to non-JavaScript browsers -->
</SCRIPT>
```

For non-JavaScript browsers, which cannot interpret the <SCRIPT> tag, two special lines are added to make the JavaScript code appear to be a comment, which is ignored by browsers. (Otherwise, your JavaScript code may appear on the web page when displayed by older browsers.)

In addition to the script definitions, which usually appear in a separate script area of your page, you also include calls to the scripts in the page itself, usually in <IMG> or <A HREF> tags.

The following "mouse rollover" code is an example of JavaScript objects, events, and properties in action. The JavaScript in the example signals the user that the mouse cursor is over a hyperlinked image by changing the image.

```
<HTML>
<BODY>
<SCRIPT LANGUAGE="JavaScript">
<!-- This line begins protection for non-JavaScript browsers
image1 = new Image
image2 = new Image
image1.src = 'firstpicture.gif'
image2.src = 'secondpicture.gif'
// This line ends protection for non-JavaScript browsers -->
</SCRIPT>
<A HREF = "somedoc.html">
    <IMG SRC = "firstpicture.gif" WIDTH="100' HEIGHT="100"
```

```
        BORDER="0" NAME="picture"
        onmouseover = "document.picture.src = image2.src"
        onmouseout = "document.picture.src = image1.src">
</A>
</BODY>
</HTML>
```

The JavaScript within the <SCRIPT> tags creates two objects (image1 and image2), assigning each to a different image file. The browser downloads the two image files to its cache (storage), but does not yet display them. The JavaScript within the <IMG> tag makes the tag sensitive to the mouseover event. The NAME attribute (picture) for the <IMG> tag enables the mouseover code to control the image by its object and property name (document.picture.src). When the event occurs (onmouseover), the image changes and returns to the original image afterward (onmouseout).

Getting Predesigned Scripts

Many people make their scripts available for your use or education on the Web. A good starting place to find these scripts is Yahoo. From **www.yahoo.com**, choose Computers & Internet | Programming And Development | Languages | JavaScript (or choose Visual Basic | VBScript for that language). Following are some specific web sites to visit for JavaScript examples or usable samples:

- A good starting place for documentation and examples is EarthWeb.com's JavaScripts.com site at **www.javascripts.com**.

- Netscape offers sample JavaScript code on its developer web site at **developer.netscape.com/docs/examples/javascript.html**.

Extending Browsers with Java and ActiveX

Although JavaScript lets you extend your browser in many useful ways, many kinds of browser extensions are not practical to write in JavaScript, either because JavaScript is relatively slow or because of the limits to what parts of the browser JavaScript can control. The Java programming language has become the most popular way to write more sophisticated browser extensions. We also look briefly at Microsoft's competing ActiveX technology.

What Is Java?

Java is an advanced, standardized, object-oriented programming language that can be used for many applications, not just web pages. Java has a unique quality, however, that has made it particularly useful for web pages: programs written in Java can run without modification on a broad variety of computers (*platforms*)—that is, Java is *multiplatform* or *platform-neutral*. For Java to run on a computer, the computer must have software that can understand Java, called a *Java engine*. Today, most computers don't have Java engines built into their operating systems, but all popular web browsers include them. (These browsers are said to be *Java-enabled*.)

As a result, you can equip your web pages with Java *applets* (downloadable application programs), and when users with Java-enabled browsers view your pages, your programs run. Java programs on web pages are run in a *sandbox*, a limited programming environment that provides access to the screen, keyboard, mouse, and network, but not the rest of the computer, to thwart buggy or malicious code.

Java programs on the Web can do everything a scripting language like JavaScript can do—and more. They generally run faster, too, because Java applets are provided in a binary form designed to run quickly. Java programs can use Internet services such as e-mail, file transfer, telnet, and web services to interact with server programs around the world.

Chapter 29 contains examples of ways you can use Java in your web pages, without programming. The section on adding advanced features to your web site explains how to link to existing Java applets that provide free message boards, calendars, and other interactive web page goodies.

What Are Java Applets?

A Java program for a web page usually comes in a form called an *applet* (because it is a small *application*). Applets are contained in separate binary files called *class files* that must be downloaded to your browser in addition to the HTML web page. (Sometimes, the applet relies in turn on other binary files, called *library class files*, that must also be downloaded.) <OBJECT> or <APPLET> tags in the HTML code of the web page associate applet files with the web page and transmit data to the applet that tells it how to operate.

Getting Java Applets

To write a Java applet, you must have good programming skills and understand how to use a compiled object-oriented language. You also need the same sorts of special tools that developers in other sophisticated languages like C or C++ require: compilers, linkers, libraries, debuggers, documentation, and the like. The original collection of tools for this purpose is called the Java Development Kit (by Sun Microsystems, who pioneered the Java language) and is available at **java.sun.com**. Many other vendors offer development software, containing similar tools.

Rather than write Java applets, most web designers obtain them free or buy them. Java applets are available at various sites on the Web. A starting place is Yahoo: choose Computers & Internet | Programming And Development | Languages | Java | Applets to see a list of links to sites offering applets. Another good starting point for sites offering applets and instructions on using them is **java.sun.com/applets**.

CREATING AND
MAINTAINING WEB SITES

Applets themselves are files generally ending in the extension *.class*. Often they are contained in compressed files, such as ZIP or TAR files, that also contain documentation. (See Chapter 34 for information on dealing with ZIP and TAR files.)

Running Java Applets

To use an applet with your web page, you add tags to the web page and place the class file (the applet file) on your web site, usually in the same directory as your web pages. Originally, Java applets were enclosed in <APPLET> and </APPLET> tags, but more recent versions of HTML require applets to appear within <OBJECT> and </OBJECT> tags.

Here is an example of one way the code is often written, using a hypothetical applet called sitemap.class that creates a graphical image displaying a table of contents (site map) for your web site:

```
<OBJECT CODETYPE="application/java" CLASSID="java:sitemap.class"
WIDTH="400" HEIGHT="400">
<PARAM NAME="bgcolor" VALUE="white">
<PARAM NAME="font" VALUE="medium | bold">
<PARAM NAME="url" VALUE="http://yoursite.com/">
</OBJECT>
```

Within the <OBJECT> tag, the CODETYPE attribute is optional, but helps browsers that are not Java-enabled to avoid downloading the applet. The CLASSID attribute is required because it specifies the applet filename (sitemap.class in this example). The WIDTH and HEIGHT attributes are optional, but are usually included to give the dimensions (in pixels) of the area of the page where the applet is allowed to write. The <OBJECT> tag can also include the following optional attributes:

CODEBASE	The URL where the applet file resides, if it is not in the same directory as the web page
ALIGN	Horizontal alignment; for example, center
VSPACE and HSPACE	The vertical and horizontal white space, respectively, around the applet's writing area
ALT	Alternate text that appears if the browser can't process the applet

Most applets allow the page developer to choose details about how the applet operates. You give those details by using <PARAM> tags that contain NAME and VALUE attributes. Depending on the applet, you may need no <PARAM> tags or you may need many. In the preceding example, the web page developer has set three parameters named bgcolor (background color), font, and url to various values. You must read the applet's documentation to know how to set its parameters.

What Is Microsoft's ActiveX?

ActiveX is a technology called an *application programming interface (API)* that enables web developers to write small (or not so small) Windows programs that are invoked from web pages in a browser. As a web page creator, you can use ActiveX features by using special terms within JavaScript or VBScript, similar to the terms used to invoke a Java applet. Microsoft's ActiveX Control Pad is an authoring tool that lets developers add ActiveX controls and features (as well as JavaScript and VBScript code). In principle, you could write ActiveX programs for Macintosh, UNIX, or other systems, but in practice ActiveX is only available on Windows.

 ActiveX has security problems not present in Java because ActiveX programs have full access to Windows, so a buggy or malicious program can delete files, install viruses, or otherwise damage a user's computer.

For more information about ActiveX controls, see Microsoft's developers' web site at **msdn.microsoft.com**.

Running Server Programs from Your Web Pages

An alternative to putting a program (a script or Java applet) in a web page is to store the program on the web server and run the program from a command in the web page. Server-side programs are essential, for instance, if you want your visitors to be able to enter data in a central database or to read data from that database. Pages that use forms for registering, signing in, or placing orders run a server program to do those tasks. In fact, the original intent of forms, and still one of the most common uses for forms, is to gather information and pass that information to a server program. (Today, forms may also be used in conjunction with browser-side programs.)

For some web applications, you need one program running in the browser and another on the server. If the browser program is a Java applet, you can even make your web page communicate with an e-mail or chat server instead of the web server.

The most popular methods of running programs on the web server are the following:

■ **CGI scripts**   Programs written in C, Perl, or other programming languages. Codes in the web page call these programs. Figure 28-1 shows what happens when a web site visitor clicks a link that calls CGI script: the web server runs the script and sends the output of the CGI script back to the browser for display.

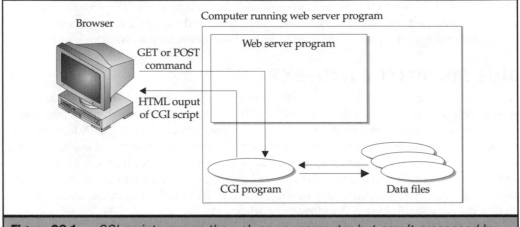

Figure 28-1. *CGI scripts run on the web server computer but aren't processed by the web server program itself.*

■ **Embedded code**   Another increasingly popular technique is to *embed* the program code to be run on the server in the web page itself, in much the same way that you embed JavaScript in web pages. The most popular embedded languages are the open source PHP, Microsoft's ASP, and Macromedia's ColdFusion. Microsoft's FrontPage Extensions (or WebBots) also work this way. Figure 28-2 shows what happens when a web site visitor clicks a link

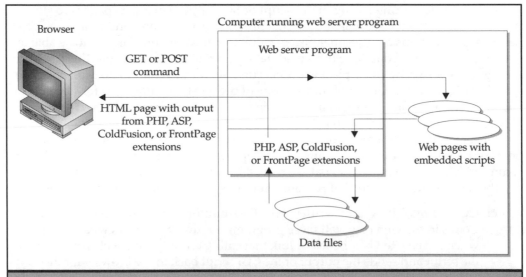

Figure 28-2. *Embedded scripts require the web server to have extra programs installed to execute the embedded code.*

to a web page that contains PHP, ASP, ColdFusion CFML code, or WebBots: the web server retrieves the web page; calls on PHP, ASP, ColdFusion, or FrontPage Extensions to execute the embedded code; includes the output in the web page in place of the code; and sends the resulting web page to the browser.

The rest of this chapter describes how to use both of these approaches: CGI scripts and embedded scripts, including PHP, ASP, WebBots, and ColdFusion.

Creating Web Pages That Run CGI Scripts

The traditional way for web pages to run your server programs is through a server feature called the *Common Gateway Interface (CGI)*.

What Are CGI Scripts?

The programs that your web page can run on the web server are called *CGI scripts*. (The word "script" doesn't imply that these programs are written in web scripting languages such as JavaScript or VBScript—it's just another word for "program.") CGI is neither a programming language nor a program; CGI scripts are generally written in either the C or Perl programming language, although other languages can also be used to create the executable script file. CGI is built into the Web's HTTP protocol for communications between browsers and web servers.

Creating a CGI script for a web server is harder than browser-side programming. Most ISPs and web hosting companies require you to submit each CGI script to them and pay for them to review it before you (or they) install it on the server. This precaution protects the web servers from running malicious scripts (or scripts with serious bugs). For most web page developers, attractive alternatives include using predesigned or preinstalled scripts that the ISP or web hosting company have already approved and installed. Another alternative is to buy special tools that create the scripts for you.

Advantages of CGI scripts are that they can be written in C or C++ and compiled, and that they run faster than other interpreted types of scripts. Another advantage is that on UNIX/Linux systems, CGI scripts can run under another user name, so that they can read and update files that aren't directly accessible to the web server.

Creating Links That Run CGI Scripts

To write a web page command that runs a CGI script, you must know a few things about that script. Pages that run server scripts refer to the scripts by the script's URL. To run a server script, therefore, you must know the script's URL: its name and the subdirectory where it is located on your web server. (Note that it must usually be *your* web server—the server the web page comes from. You are not usually permitted to run a script on a different server.) You must also know what kind of data the script wants passed to it and what method must be used for passing the data.

There are two basic ways of running a CGI script located at a particular URL, depending on how that script requires data to be passed to it. (The way you pass data is officially called the *method*.) The two methods of passing data that a script may use are as follows:

- GET transmits small amounts of data.
- POST transmits data from forms.

Some scripts require one particular method to be used. Others can use either method. The GET method in its simplest form uses a conventional <A HREF> (hyperlink reference) tag in HTML with the script's URL. Here is an example of a link using the GET method to run a program that takes a Canadian province name and language as inputs:

```
<A HREF = "/cgi-bin/myscript.bin?province=quebec&language=french">
Click here to run the script.</A>
```

The script file's name is myscript.bin, and it is in the cgi-bin directory of the web server. (The directory name cgi-bin is commonly used for CGI scripts.) The URL includes the pathname of the script file (cgi-bin/myscript.bin) followed by a question mark (?) and the values to pass to the CGI script as inputs. The parameters in the example are named province and language, and they have the values quebec and french, respectively. The ampersand (&) separates the two values. This script might produce a listing of radio stations that are available in the Canadian province specified and that broadcast in the specified language.

The CGI script and the HTML code that runs the script must work together, as they must both use the same method and variables. To read the data in the example, for instance, the CGI script must be designed to accept data that was transmitted using the GET method. The CGI script looks in a special variable (an *environment variable*) that usually has the name QUERYSTRING (or QUERY_STRING) to find the data that was passed (that is, that appears after the question mark in the URL). The data is passed as a single string of characters, so the script must separate (*parse*) the data. It does so by looking for the variables by their names (in this example, province and language) or by their position in the string, and reading whatever data follows each variable's equal sign (=).

Passing Data from Web Forms to CGI Scripts

If you want to create a form on your web site and process the information from the form, you might want to run a server script. To pass data from forms to server scripts, you use special attributes within the <FORM> tags. Chapter 24 describes how forms and <FORM> tags work.

Here is an example of the HTML for a web page in which a form is used. The example acquires and transmits the same data as the example in the preceding section. The user fills out a form (this one happens to use radio buttons) and clicks the Display Radio Stations button to run the CGI script and transmit form data to it:

```
<FORM ACTION="/cgi-bin/myscript.bin" METHOD="post">
    <P> Choose your province and language:</P>
<INPUT TYPE="radio" NAME="province" VALUE="New Brunswick" CHECKED>
    <P> New Brunswick</P>
<INPUT TYPE="radio" NAME="province" VALUE="Quebec">
    <P> Quebec</P>
<INPUT TYPE="radio" NAME="language" VALUE="english" CHECKED>
    <P> English</P>
<INPUT TYPE="radio" NAME="language" VALUE="french">
    <P> Francais</P>
<INPUT type="submit" value="Display Radio Stations">
</FORM>
```

In the <FORM> tag, the ACTION attribute gives the URL of the script file. As in the earlier example, the script file is myscript.bin located in the server's cgi-bin directory. The METHOD attribute in this instance is POST, not GET. The script, as in the script described in the previous section for the GET method, receives the data from the QUERYSTRING variable and must parse the contents to extract the values submitted for province and language. Each value has the same name as the form input field that acquired the value. For instance, clicking the top radio button assigns the value New Brunswick to the variable province.

Writing CGI Scripts

Writing CGI scripts requires a good deal of technical knowledge, for example:

- Knowledge of some compiled language such as C or C++, or a script language the server can interpret, such as Perl

- Understanding of how data is passed between the web page and the server script, as the preceding sections describe

- Understanding of how to perform processing in the UNIX or other environment in which the server runs

- Understanding of how to write HTML to a web browser from a CGI script, so that the CGI script can display pages that result from its processing

This section provides an overview of this information, describing in general terms the actions of a simple CGI script that reads data from a form and writes the data back as a confirmation page. To actually write the CGI script, you must translate this overview into the language of your choice.

A CGI script that processes data from a form and displays a web page must perform the following steps:

1. Perform any initial tasks that enable the server to execute your program, such as telling it what directory the language interpreter is in.

2. Parse the environment variable QUERYSTRING (or its equivalent) into its separate data values, breaking the string at ampersand (&) characters.

3. Perform any processing necessary on the web server, such as writing to a file or handing database transactions.

4. Begin outputting the web document to the standard output (*stdout*). First output a header giving the web document MIME type: "content-type text/html" followed by a blank line.

5. Output "<HTML>" to begin the web page that the user will see.

6. Output whatever material the script has generated based on the inputs.

7. Output "</HTML>" to end the web page.

Getting, Installing, and Using Prewritten CGI Scripts

To avoid writing your own CGI scripts, you can obtain prewritten CGI scripts, written in various languages. However, you usually must customize the scripts before they will run on your web server, so you need to understand the program's language and your web server. You may also need a compiler and programming skills to recompile that modified script if it is in C, C++, or another compiled language. Finally, once you obtain a script, someone still needs to install it on the server.

The most common scripts that are easily customized are those in the Perl language, although server-side VBScript and other languages are also available on some servers. For an introduction to Perl, read *Perl: A Beginner's Guide,* by R. Allen Wyke and Donald B. Thomas (Osborne/McGraw-Hill) or *Perl For Dummies,* by Paul Hoffman (John Wiley Technology Group).

To find prewritten CGI scripts, start at Yahoo and choose Computers & Internet | WWW | CGI-Common Gateway Interface.

CGI script files are usually placed in a directory on the web server to which only the webmaster has access for security reasons. The webmaster must configure the server to recognize this directory as the place where scripts live and must set the files in the directory to be executable. Moreover, either you or your webmaster must set ownership of your script files (usually a UNIX file attribute) so that anyone can read and execute them. (In UNIXese, these attributes are called *world-readable* and *world-executable*.)

E-mailing Form Information

One of the most popular kinds of CGI script takes information that web site visitors enter into a form and transmits the information to you by e-mail. Some of these forms-to-e-mail scripts limit you to asking for only certain information. Many commercial scripts exist, but one of the most flexible free versions is called cgiemail, created by Bruce Lewis at MIT. You or your webmaster can download cgiemail and its documentation at **web.mit.edu/wwwdev/cgiemail**. Your ISP or web hosting company may already have installed the script.

Once cgiemail is installed on your web server, create your web page with a form whose ACTION attribute is the URL of the cgiemail script on your server. Follow the instructions on the cgiemail web site to create a text template file listing the form fields used on your web page and install both your web page file and the template file in your regular web site directory on the server. The cgiemail script takes it from there.

 Some sites use an older e-mail script called formmail.pl, which you should avoid due to severe security problems.

Embedding PHP Scripts in Your Pages

An alternative to CGI scripts, which are stored in separate files on the web server, are embedded scripts, which are stored in your web pages. One of the most popular languages for embedded server scripts is PHP.

What Is PHP?

PHP (which stands for *PHP Hypertext Preprocessor*) is an open source programming language similar to Perl. It is most often used with the open source Apache web server on Linux and other UNIX-like systems, but PHP can also be used with nearly every UNIX, Mac, and Windows web server including Netscape iPlanet, Microsoft IIS, and dozens of others. PHP is estimated to be installed on over 20 percent of all web servers.

Embedded PHP scripts provide nearly all of the power of CGI scripts but are much easier to write and use. You can upload web pages with embedded PHP the same way that you upload regular web pages, except that the names of the pages end with *.php* or *.phtml* rather than *.html*. (The exact naming convention is up to the manager of the web server.)

Writing PHP Code

Embedded PHP resembles HTML tags, but is handled on the server, before the page is sent to the user's browser. Here's a sample PHP script that sends different text on Sundays than other days:

```
<?php
  $day = date("w"); /* Store numeric weekday in $day /
  if($day == 0): /* 0 is Sunday */
```

```
?>
... HTML code for Sunday ...
<?php else: ?>
... HTML code for other days ...
<?php endif; ?>
```

PHP code is enclosed between *<?php* and *?>*. You can and usually do intermix PHP code and HTML in a web page. Before the web server sends the page out to the user's browser, the server interprets the PHP code, replacing the PHP scripts with the results of the scripts. The version of the web page that arrives at the browser no longer contains any PHP code and contains only the HTML code for the appropriate day.

PHP includes an extensive library of built-in routines that do everything from string processing to database management to building GIF and PDF documents on-the-fly. The database libraries are used extensively to create database-backed web sites, with the contents of web pages created dynamically from databases. PHP has built-in support to connect to most popular databases including Informix, Interbase, Microsoft's SQL Server, MySQL, Oracle, and many other databases that support ODBC.

PHP also handles parameters from both GET and POST, just like CGI scripts. PHP automatically interprets named parameters and puts the parameter values into PHP variables. Assume this line appeared in a PHP web page called mypage.php:

```
The square root of <?php print $N; ?> is <?php print sqrt($N); ?>
```

If you request the page by clicking a link with a URL like this:

```
http://myserver/mypage.php?N=3
```

the value 3 is assigned to the variable $N, and the line of the web page becomes

```
The square root of 3 is 1.7320508075689
```

(The print operator "prints" to the web page being sent to the browser.)

PHP can also read the text in a URL after the name of the web page. This feature enables it to do tricks like the ones in our web page at **net.gurus.com/scale.phtml/ 500/bishbash.jpg**

The PHP code in the file scale.phtml takes a number of pixels (500, in this URL) and the name of an image file (bishbash.jpg) from the URL and generates a web page on-the-fly, showing that image scaled to the given width. If you change the *500* to any other number, you see a page displaying the image at that size. The PHP code gives the effect of a folder with an unlimited number of pages showing images at various sizes. This URL shows a different image (maidmist.jpg) at a different size (400 pixels wide): **net.gurus.com/ scale.phtml/400/maidmist.jpg**

Getting Prewritten PHP Scripts

Many people have written entire applications in PHP with databases, such as calendars and online stores with shopping carts. Many of these applications are freely available on the Web. You can also find libraries of PHP code that you can include in applications you write. Here are places to look for PHP scripts and general information about PHP:

- **The PHP Home Page (www.php.net)**   This site contains a huge amount of information, but a good place to start is the tutorial at **www.php.net/tut.php**.

- **The PHP Resource Index (php.resourceindex.com)**   This site lists hundreds of scripts, libraries, documentation, and other material.

Standardizing Web Page Formatting by Using Server Side Includes or PHP

One of the most tedious aspects of maintaining a web site is to make the formatting of all the pages consistent. This job is particularly time consuming if many elements appear on all your pages, like page headers and footers, menu bars, and comment boxes. If you (the web designer) want to change one of the elements, you would have to change every web page on the site. In modern browsers, you can use frames to define areas of the browser window with fixed headers or footers, but web designers still end up putting repetitive chunks of HTML code into pages to get consistent appearance from page to page.

What Are Server Side Includes (SSI)?

An early web server feature that helped solve this problem was *Server Side Includes (SSI)*, which let web pages logically include other files on the server and set and use simple parameters. For example, this line tells the server to include the contents of the file /ssi/header.shtml in its place:

```
<!--#include virtual="/ssi/header.shtml" -->
```

Before the web server sends the web page out to the user's browser, it includes the header.shtml file, replacing the #include command. By using a Server Side Include for the standard elements in your web pages, you can update one file (the included file) to update all the pages in your site.

SSI also provides clumsy ways to define and refer to parameters that you can use to set background colors and other web design elements.

Caution   *Not all web servers support SSI. If your web server supports PHP, use PHP instead.*

CREATING AND MAINTAINING WEB SITES

Standardizing Page Formats Using PHP

Although many web servers still support SSI for existing users, PHP can do everything that SSI can do, but better. PHP can include files and define and use parameter variables like SSI, but can also use the full power and flexibility of the PHP language. You can include code that displays the page differently, depending on whether the page appears in a frame, for example.

Creating Web Pages with FrontPage WebBots

FrontPage (Microsoft's web page editor, described in Chapter 25) allows you to use *WebBots*, Microsoft's term for their proprietary web server features. For WebBots to work, the web server must be equipped with Microsoft Front Page Extensions—many ISPs and web hosting companies run web servers that are so equipped. WebBots can do tasks like searching the Web, providing a simple web message board, automatically displaying the last date and time, or adding forms and navigation bars. If your server provides FrontPage Extensions, you need only put HTML-like codes in your pages to tell the server to activate the extension you want. Not surprisingly, the FrontPage editor can insert the codes automatically, but with any other editor you can add them by hand.

 Before using WebBots in pages you create in FrontPage, be sure to ask your ISP or web hosting company whether they support WebBots and which ones you can use.

Creating Active Server Pages (ASPs)

Microsoft has a proprietary technology called *Active Server Pages (ASP)* that is functionally similar to PHP. ASP can add interactivity to your web pages, including such server-side tasks as running databases, without CGI scripting. Originally, using ASP required your web server to run Microsoft's Internet Information Services (IIS), which only runs on Windows NT, 2000, and XP, but a handful of other ASP server components are now available that allow ASP code to work on web servers that run UNIX and Linux. Sun's Chili!Soft ASP (**www.chilisoft.com**) extends the popular Apache web server to support ASP, and iASP from Halcyon Software (**www.halcyonsoft.com**) is an ASP support program written in Java, which works with any server that supports server-side Java applets. Both of these packages are commercial software, not freeware.

Including ASP Code in Web Pages

Like PHP, ASP is interpreted on your web server. If a web page has the filename extension *.asp*, a program on the web server looks in the web page for ASP commands, which are enclosed in <% and %> tags. ASP scripts are usually written in Microsoft's VBScript, but can also be JavaScript, ECMAScript, or Perl. The web server program reads the ASP commands and scripts and executes them before sending the web page out to the user's browser for display.

The following is an example of a web page that includes ASP commands written using VBScript:

```
<%@ Language=VBScript %>
<HTML>
<HEAD>
<TITLE>This is an ASP page, </TITLE>
</HEAD>
<BODY>
<%Response.Write("and I'm executed ASP code!!")%>
</BODY>
</HTML>
```

At the top of the page is an ASP command that specifies that the ASP code is written in VBScript. In the body of the page is a VBScript command, also enclosed in <% and %>. This VBScript command reads the object (Response) and its associated method (Write) and displays the result on the web page. The Response.Write command is so commonly used (because it displays the results of a script on the page) that you can also write it this way:

```
<%="and I'm executed ASP code!!"%>
```

What You Can Do with ASP

Because ASP code runs on the web server, it can refer to information stored on the server, including text files and databases. If your server has a database that conforms to Microsoft's Open Database Connectivity (ODBC) standard, you can even use commands to write to or read from the database. Those commands are in yet another language, Structured Query Language (SQL). Shopping cart systems, product catalogs, and many other types of web sites can be written using ASP.

Activating your pages with some server-side ASP code is simple, and the process is similar to include PHP in a web page. However, to get more than the most basic functionality out of your web applications, you can use additional tools that work with ASP code. Here are two powerful ASP tools:

- **Microsoft Visual InterDev (msdn.microsoft.com/vinterdev)**   This application was designed specifically for developing ASP and related technologies. It's also good for XML code management. The last stand-alone version was InterDev 6.0; later versions come integrated into Visual .NET Studio.

- **Macromedia Dreamweaver UltraDev (www.macromedia.com/software/ ultradev)**   Designed like Macromedia's own Dreamweaver web authoring tool, UltraDev makes coding ASP, Java Server Pages (JSP), and ColdFusion pages easier. (ColdFusion is described in the next section.)

Although the basics of ASP scripting are simple, ASP scripts can be long and complicated, to create entire applications implemented in a web server. These resources can be useful in finding and writing ASP scripts:

- **ASP Resource Index (www.aspin.com)** This site is a very large, well-organized portal to the growing ASP industry. You can also find a large selection of free software and information.

- **Visual InterDev Tutorial (www.aspdeveloper.net/VInterDev/page1.asp)** Though a bit dated from the Windows XP perspective, this very helpful tutorial on accessing databases through ASP is a big help. After experimenting with Access, we suggest you move to a more robust database system like Microsoft's SQL Server or FileMaker's FileMaker Pro 6.0 Unlimited. Access simply cannot handle the high demand of a web site.

- **15 Seconds (www.15seconds.com)** If you're seeking to learn how to code for ASP and not just reuse components, 15 Seconds is the right place to start. If you have little to no programming experience, be sure to check out the Beginning section.

- **eDEVCafé (www.edevcafe.com)** This site's articles are clearly written and come from people apparently in the know. They cover all of the bases, not just ASP.

- **ASP.net (www.asp.net)** Microsoft's own site covers ASP.NET—ASP programs that work with Microsoft's .NET platform.

- **MSDN (msdn.microsoft.com/asp)** The core of Microsoft development lies at this site, which is part of the Microsoft Developer's Network site.

Creating ColdFusion Pages with CFML

ColdFusion is a server-side scripting system from Macromedia. ColdFusion uses tags in ColdFusion Markup Language (CFML), which are similar enough to HTML to be easy and quick to learn. On the other hand, it doesn't include support for JavaScript or VBScript.

CFML tags look like HTML tags. For example, here's the CFML to display a line of text that includes a calculated number:

```
<cfoutput>
Your total cost will be #ProductTotal.
</cfoutput>
```

You can't use ColdFusion in your web pages unless your web server runs ColdFusion Server. Check with your ISP or web hosting company to find out whether they do.

Alternatively, find a ColdFusion-enabled web hosting company to host your site; start at the ISP list at Forta.com (**www.forta.com/cf/isp**).

 To try ColdFusion, download the free trial version, ColdFusion Express, from ***www.macromedia.com/software/coldfusion/trial/cf_server_express.html****.*

For more information about ColdFusion, look at these web sites:

- **CFHub.com (www.cfhub.com)**   This site includes tutorials, articles, and links.
- **CFM-Resources (www.cfm-resources.com)**   This is both an informational site and a ColdFusion web host.
- **ColdFusion Developer's Journal (www.sys-con.com/coldfusion)**   This site includes information about ColdFusion web hosts, product reviews, and the archives of articles from the magazine.
- **Macromedia (www.macromedia.com/coldfusion)**   Macromedia provides technical support for ColdFusion at this site. (ColdFusion was created by Allaire, which was later acquired by Macromedia.)

Content Management Systems

A *Content Management System (CMS)* is a program that manages the content (text, graphics, programs, and other information) on your web site and that makes the site easier to update. CMSes are becoming popular with large web sites to keep track of who is supposed to update what page and what pages need to be updated when. A CMS can provide web-based editing of pages, so that people who provide information for the web site can update pages without using a web page editor.

A CMS stores the content of your web site in a database and creates either static or dynamic web pages that make up your web site, based on the information in the database. By using a CMS, you can ensure that all the pages on your site use the same style and format and present the same information. For example, if product information is stored in one place in the CMS database, changing a product price in the database should update the price everywhere it appears on your web site.

CMS software is expensive, and implementing it is a big project, so only large web sites use CMS. For smaller sites, stick with Perl and PHP scripts, which can read information from a MySQL or other SQL database.

For more information about CMS software, see the CMSWatch site at **www.cmswatch.com**.

The
Complete
Reference

Internet

Chapter 29

Advanced
Web Page Options

Whether you use a text editor or web editor to create your pages, you may want to use *Cascading Style Sheets (CSS)* to control the overall look of the site. This chapter describes how style sheets work and why you might want to use them.

You may also want to add a web-based chat room, message board, or other fancy feature to a page on your web site. You don't need to learn to program to include these interactive features—many web sites offer services that allow you to include them on your own pages. The section "Adding Advanced Features to Your Web Site Without Programming" tells you how.

Formatting Web Pages Using Cascading Style Sheets

HTML has always had the concept of *styles*—preformatted types of text that you can use in your web pages. HTML's built-in styles include the body text style used for unformatted text and the headers <H1> through <H6>. However, HTML originally had no way to change how these built-in styles looked until the invention of *Cascading Style Sheets (CSS)*. CSS revolutionized the way web pages are conceived and structured and opened up worlds of flexibility for the web page designer. CSS has many attractive features, but two of the most attractive benefits of CSS are

■ Changing the appearance of text and other objects throughout all the pages in a web site without editing all the pages

■ Positioning and even animating text and other objects on web pages

The following sections explain how to create and use styles and how to use them in positioning objects on web pages.

Note   *This chapter describes only the most widely used features of CSS. To get the full story, go to the World Wide Web Consortium site at **www.w3.org** and follow the link to Cascading Style Sheets.*

Style Sheet Concepts

With styles, you can change the appearance of text and other objects throughout a web site by making changes in the style sheet. You begin by creating the style sheet and then use those styles in your web pages.

    You don't have to hand-code HTML to use CSS. The most recent versions of many popular web page design tools employ CSS, or at least the most important features of styles. For example, FrontPage, Macromedia Dreamweaver, and Adobe GoLive help you create and use styles.

Types of Style Sheets

Styles can apply to a single item, a single document, or any set of documents, depending on where you store the style declarations:

- **Single items**   You can define the style of a single tag in a web page, so that it applies only to one piece of text. This type of style is called an *inline style.* Inline styles are useful for styles that you use in only one or two places in your web site.

- **Single web page**   Defining a style in the header of the same document where you use it is called *embedding* a style sheet. The styles you define apply to the entire web page. If your web site consists of only a few pages, embedded styles provide an easy way to standardize the styles on each page.

- **Multiple web pages**   You can store your style sheet in a separate file and refer to it from as many web pages as you like. The file that contains the style sheet is called an *external style sheet,* and it has the filename extension *.css.* External style sheets enable you to control the look of all your web pages in one place—if you have a web site with more than a few pages, consider using an external style sheet.

No matter of where you store your style declarations—in an individual tag, in the header of the web page, or in an external file—the declarations work the same way.

Style Declarations

An embedded or external style sheet contains a list of *style declarations,* each consisting of a name and properties (including the font or color of text, for instance), like this:

```
element { properties }
```

You can use any of the standard HTML elements (like <P>, <H1>, and <H2>). The properties of the style can control its size, font, color, spacing, and other formatting. Properties usually look like this:

```
propertyname: value
```

You can add spaces before the colon; browsers don't care. Table 29-1 lists many commonly used formatting properties and their values. Some properties require you to specify colors, sizes, and filenames, like this:

- **Colors**   You can use one of the 16 Windows VGA colors names (**aqua**, **black**, **blue**, **fuchsia**, **gray**, **green**, **lime**, **maroon**, **navy**, **olive**, **purple**, **red**, **silver**, **teal**, **white**, or **yellow**). Alternatively, use the numeric values described in the section on choosing a background color in Chapter 24.

■ **Measurements** The values are in *ems*, where 1em is the height of a capital letter in the element's font. Alternatively, you can specify pixels (by using the abbreviation *px*), inches (*in*), or centimeters (*cm*); however, these methods may look odd depending on the size and resolution of the screen. Another way to specify measurements is as a percentage of the standard size for the element. For example, if you want text to appear 150 percent of its usual size, you can use "150%" as the value of the font-size property.

■ **Filenames** Type **url(*name*)**. The name can be the name of a file on the same web server, for example, **url(fill.gif)** or **url(images/fill.gif)**; or the URL of a web page, for example, **url(http://www.uua.org/chalice.gif)**.

The Web Design Group has a list of style properties at
www.htmlhelp.com/reference/css/properties.html.

You can assign more than one property to an element, defining its font, color, and background, for example. Separate the properties with semicolons. For example, this style declaration sets the H2 element as a sans-serif font (Arial, if it is available), in blue italics:

```
H2 { font-family: Arial, sans-serif;
  font-style: italic; color: blue }
```

Style Property	Description	Example
background-color	Solid color for the element's background.	background-color: red
background-image	Graphics file to use as the element's background.	background-image: url(fill.gif)
border-color	Color of a line around the element. If you provide one number, it controls all four sides. If you provide four numbers, they control the top, right, bottom, and left sides, respectively.	border-color: black

Table 29-1. *Some CSS Properties*

Style Property	Description	Example
border-width	Width of a line around the element: **thin**, **medium**, or **thick**. If you provide one number, it controls all four sides. If you provide four numbers, they control the top, right, bottom, and left sides, respectively.	border-width: medium
color	Solid color for the element's foreground (e.g., the text color).	color: white
font	Characteristics of the font, using any of the font-family, font-size, font-style, font-variant, or font-weight values.	font: bold large
font-family	Specific font or a general description (e.g., **serif**, **sans-serif**, **cursive**, or **monospace**). You can list several, separated by commas; the browser uses the first font that is available.	font-family: Verdana, Arial, sans-serif
font-size	Size (**small, medium, large**, etc.) or size compared to the normal size (**smaller, larger**, etc.).	font-size: large
font-style	Slant, usually **normal** or **italic**.	font-style: normal
font-variant	Either **normal** or **small-caps**.	font-variant: small-caps
font-weight	Boldness of the text, usually **normal**, **bold**, **bolder**, or **lighter**.	font-weight: bold
margin-bottom	Space at the bottom of the element, in ems.	margin-bottom: 2em
margin-left	Space at the left of the element, in ems.	margin-left: 1em

Table 29-1.   *Some CSS Properties* (continued)

Style Property	Description	Example
margin-right	Space at the right of the element, in ems.	margin-right: 0em
margin-top	Space at the top of the element, in ems.	margin-top: 3em
text-alignment	Horizontal positioning, like **left**, **right**, **center**, or **justify**.	text-alignment: center
text-decoration	Miscellaneous formatting, including **underline**, **overline**, **line-through**, **blink**, or **none**.	text-decoration: underline
text-indent	First-line indentation.	text-indent: 2em

Table 29-1. *Some CSS Properties* (continued)

Redefining HTML Styles Using Classes

You can control the style of any of HTML's elements: P, H1 through H6, and other items that change the way text looks. However, what if you want to create your own style? For example, what if you are creating a site of children's poetry, and you want one style for poem titles and another for poem text?

CSS doesn't allow you to create new HTML elements, but you can do something close: create a class. A *class* is a subset of an existing HTML element; for example, you can create a POEMTITLE class as a subset of the P (paragraph) HTML element. Your style sheet can contain the formatting declarations for that class, like this:

```
p.poemtitle { font-size: large; color: blue }
```

In your web pages, you can format text using the element and class, like this:

```
<P CLASS=poemtitle>Stopping by Woods on a Snowy Evening</P>
```

You can also create classes that can be used with any element by omitting the element in the style declaration for the class, like this:

```
.poemtitle { font-size: large; color: blue }
```

You can use this type of class with any element. Either of these would work:

```
<P CLASS=poemtitle>Stopping by Woods on a Snowy Evening</P>
<H1 CLASS=poemtitle>Stopping by Woods on a Snowy Evening</H1>
```

Defining Single-Use Styles Using IDs

Another type of style that you can create is an *ID*, a style that you plan to use only once on each web page. IDs begin with a pound sign (#), like this:

```
#logo { font-size: xx-large; color: green; text-alignment: right }
```

You can use the ID name with any element in your web page. For example, you can use the #logo ID like this:

```
<P ID=logo>ABC Industries</P>
```

Creating and Applying Text Styles by Hand

This section describes creating a style sheet and using it to reformat the text in your web pages. To format a few web pages, use embedded style sheets; to format lots of web pages with the same formats, use external style sheets.

Creating an Embedded Style Sheet

If you hand-code your web pages (rather than using a web editor), you include an embedded style sheet in a web page by adding a *STYLE element* to the page. A STYLE element consists of the <STYLE> and </STYLE> tags and everything between them, and you add them to the header of a web page (between the <HEAD> and </HEAD> tags). The following example illustrates how to assign a style to a standard HTML element, H3, and how to define a class called SIDEBAR:

```
<HEAD>
<STYLE TYPE="text/css">
<!--
H3 { font-family: Desdemona, cursive;
 font-style: normal;
 color: green }
.sidebar { font-family: Arial, sans-serif;
 font-style: italic; color: blue }
-->
</STYLE>
</HEAD>
```

The STYLE element contains these parts:

- <STYLE TYPE="text/css"> begins the style sheet element, and </STYLE> ends it. The TYPE value tells the browser that this is a CSS style sheet (the only type that currently exists).

- Comment lines begin with <!-- and end with -->. They keep earlier browsers that don't recognize style sheets from being confused by the definition lines in the style sheet. Browsers that can handle CSS ignore the comment lines. Older browsers (IE 3, Navigator 3, and others) see the comment lines and ignore the style definitions. Without the comment lines, older browsers display the style definitions on the web page!

- Style declarations follow, as many as you need.

- The </STYLE> tag ends the STYLE element.

Applying Styles in Your Web Page

The styles you define (in the example in the preceding section, a class called SIDEBAR and standard style H3) will apply automatically to all instances of like-named tags throughout this document. For instance, any headings formatted with the <H3> tag appear in green, Desdemona font, or a cursive font if the computer doesn't have Desdemona. To apply a class to any tag, you use the CLASS attribute like this:

```
<P CLASS=sidebar>Technical Note</P>
```

In this example, the class is applied to an ordinary <P> tag. You can apply a class to any tag of the appropriate type (as in this case, where text styles are being applied to text tags). To apply a class to just a portion of text, use the <SPAN> tag, like this:

```
This text is normal, but <SPAN CLASS=sidebar>this text is in
Sidebar style.</SPAN>
```

Creating an External Style Sheet

An external style sheet is a text file containing only the style definition lines. The file must have the extension .css (for example, mystyles.css). External style sheets are usually stored in the same directory as your web pages or (if you use several style sheets) in a separate style sheet directory. For each web page that uses the styles in the external style sheet, include a <LINK> tag in the <HEAD> section of the web page like this:

```
<LINK REL="StyleSheet" HREF="mystyles.css" TYPE="text/css">
```

Replace "mystyles.css" with the name of your style sheet file. The REL and TYPE attributes must appear just as shown in this example, to indicate that you are using a Cascading Style Sheet. (Other types of style sheets may come along in the future.)

Once you add this <LINK> tag, when you view the web page, the styles from the external style sheet apply to the text on your page. If you change the formatting of the styles in the style sheet file, the formatting changes automatically for all the pages that link to the style sheet—that's the feature that designers love because you can change the look of your entire site by changing the style declarations in one file.

Using Different Style Sheets for Different Browsers

Internet Explorer and Netscape Navigator don't use the same size fonts for the same values of the font-size style sheet property. Other differences also exist between the ways that the two browser families display web pages. To make sure that your pages look approximately the same in Internet Explorer or Netscape Navigator, you can create two external style sheets, one for IE and one for Netscape. A small JavaScript program can select which style sheet is connected to the web page based on which browser is running.

In the HEAD section (between the <HEAD> and </HEAD> tags) of each of your web pages, include this script:

```
<script language="JavaScript" type="text/javascript">
var isN = /Netscape/.test(navigator.appName);
if (isN) { document.write ("<link href=\"mystyle-ns.css\"
rel=\"stylesheet\" type=\"text/css\">"); }
else {
document.write("<link href=\"mystyle-ie.css\" rel=\"stylesheet\"
type=\"text/css\">");}
</script>
```

This text defines a script written in JavaScript. The script checks whether IE or Netscape is displaying the page and links either the Mystyle-ie.css (for IE) or the Mystyle-ns.css (for Netscape) external style sheet. You can replace these style sheet filenames with the names of style sheets you create.

Any style that you apply locally to text (or any other object) takes precedence over the applied style. For instance, even if the style is not in boldface, you can apply bold style locally with the <B> tag.

Using Inline Styles

Another use of styles is to format specific pieces of text. You can use the style properties listed in Table 29-1 earlier to format a paragraph or even a few words. This use of style properties doesn't give you the key advantage of style sheets—that you can update the styles of text throughout a web page or site by changing codes in one place. However, *inline styles* (that is, using style properties within a page) can be useful where one item needs to be formatted a particular way.

To use an inline style, add **style="*properties*"** to the tag that formats the text. For example, if you want one paragraph to be in large, Arial, blue type, you can format it like this:

```
<P STYLE="font-family: Arial; font-size: 18pt; color: blue">
Important Notice</p>
```

You can use the <SPAN> tag to format text within a paragraph, like this:

```
<P>Many people find poetry to be both
<SPAN STYLE="color: red">mysterious and inspiring</SPAN>.</P>
```

Creating and Applying Text Styles in Web Editors

Most web page editors can handle style sheets, although some basic editors cannot. Here's how to work with style sheets in each of the web editors described in Chapter 25.

 Netscape Composer doesn't support style sheets.

FrontPage

FrontPage includes predefined style sheets in the Page Templates dialog box, or you can create your own. Editing style sheets is easy: open the style sheet in the FrontPage editor and select the Style button, or use the Format | Style menu. You see the Style dialog box:

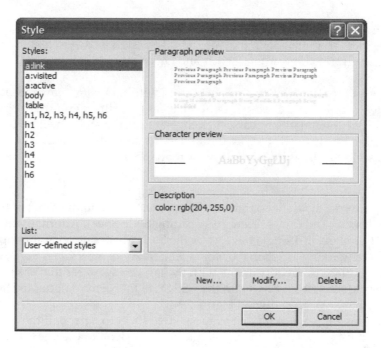

You can use CSS styles to format your text, using either inline styles, where the style is applied to individual text, or style sheets, where the style is applied to an entire page or web site. Use the Format | Styles menu to apply styles to selected text. If you're not happy with the look of your web pages, edit the styles in the style sheet, or apply a new style sheet to your site. All the pages on your site use the new or modified style instantly.

Dreamweaver

Choose Window | CSS Styles (or press SHIFT-F11) to display the CSS Styles window. Click the CSS Styles tab to see the styles that are defined in the current web page, like this:

To attach an external style sheet, right-click in the CSS Styles window and choose Attach Style Sheet from the menu that appears. To assign a style to text in the page, click in the paragraph you want to format and choose the style from the CSS Styles window.

You can edit the styles in the style sheet from within Dreamweaver. Right-click in the CSS Styles window and choose Edit Style Sheet from the menu that appears. When the Edit Style Sheet window appears, click the name of the style sheet and click Edit. You see a dialog box listing the styles defined in the style sheet. Click a style, click Edit, and edit the style's settings in the dialog box that appears.

GoLive

To create an external style sheet, right-click (CONTROL-click on the Mac) in the Site Window's Files tab, and choose New | Cascading Style Sheet. Alternatively, to create an internal style sheet in a single page, click the Style Sheet button at the top right of the page you're working in. Click the New Element Style, New Class Style, or New ID Style button. Replace the generic name with the tag you want for that style. Then use the Inspector palette (which turns into the CSS Style Inspector palette) to choose your attributes for that style, as shown in Figure 29-1.

There are several ways to link an external style sheet to a page. If the page is open, you can drag the external style sheet file onto the page icon in the page. If your page is closed or you want to link many pages at once, select the pages in the Files tab, open the CSS palette (by choosing Window | CSS), specify the style sheet name in the CSS palette, and click Add.

To edit the style sheet at any time, open the style sheet file and make your changes, which will affect all the web pages linked to the style sheet.

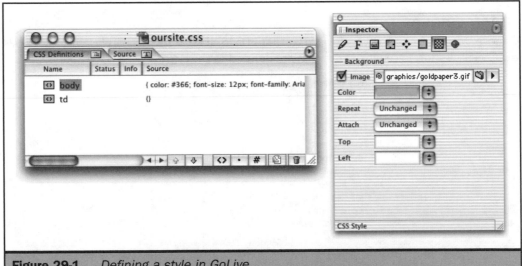

Figure 29-1. *Defining a style in GoLive*

Positioning Objects on Web Pages

One valuable aspect of styles is that not only can you, from one central location, set such properties as font, color, and size for any set of objects on the page, but you can set any individual object's position, too. You use the **position** property, which wasn't in the original CSS standard (CSS1), but was added in the next version (CSS2). With the aid of JavaScript or some other scripting language, you can also make that position vary in time, which animates the object. (See Chapter 28 for how JavaScript works.)

> **Note** *Not all browsers support CSS2, so be sure to test your web pages in various browsers if you use the **position** property.*

To position something on a web page, you set the **position** property to **absolute** in a style declaration and specify the position for the object in inches (*in*) or centimeters (*cm*) from the edges of the web page. For example, this style declaration positions an object absolutely:

```
#textA { position: absolute; left: 4in; top: 2in; width: 3in;
height: 3in }
```

This style declaration can go either within the <STYLE> element in a web page, or in an external style sheet. You usually use ID styles for absolute positioning because only one item will be at that position on each web page. When you use the **position:absolute** property, the **left**, **top**, **width**, and **height** properties define the position and size of a rectangular area in which the text (or other object) appears.

Once you define an ID style using absolute positioning, you can use it in your web pages. For instance, here is the HTML code for a paragraph that is formatted with the textA ID:

```
<SPAN ID="textA">This text is 4 inches from the left, and 2 inches
down.</SPAN>
```

You can even animate objects on your web page by using JavaScript, ECMAScript, or another page scripting language (as described in Chapter 28). In the **position:absolute** style declaration, you use a variable than the script can set to change the position of the object.

> **Note** *Different browsers handle web page objects differently. Most notably, Microsoft's Internet Explorer differs from Netscape Navigator. These distinctions should disappear now that a standard Document Object Model has been recommended by the World Wide Web Consortium (W3C) and ECMAScript has emerged as a standard JavaScript-like language. Until those standards are commonly supported, however, your script must be able to cope with distinctions by checking which type of browser is displaying the text and defining the positions accordingly.*

Adding Advanced Features to Your Web Site Without Programming

Originally, you needed to be a programmer to add advanced features like calendars, chat rooms, news tickers, and message boards to your web pages. However, many services can now provide these features—all you have to do is copy a few lines of code into your web pages. Some services are free and others cost money. These services include

- **Calendars** Not only can you add a calendar to your site for the current and future months, but you and your web site visitors can also add events to the calendar. Some calendar services even allow you to download the events and synchronize them with your Outlook or Palm calendar.

- **Chat rooms** If you'd like your web site visitors to be able to talk to other visitors who are currently at the site, you can include a chat room on one of your web pages. Chapter 15 describes what web-based chat rooms are like.

- **Guestbooks** If you'd like visitors to your web site to be able to leave notes for you—like a guestbook in a hotel—these services can add this feature.

- **Hit counters** To track how many people have visited your site, you can add a free hit counter to your home page.

- **Message boards** Web-based discussion boards are described in Chapter 15 and allow visitors to the web site to leave messages that others can read. You can include message boards on your site for free, if you don't mind ads appearing as part of the web page. Some message boards are simple—the coding projects of a few hackers—whereas others are provided by full-fledged businesses that serve message board technology to larger sites.

- **News tickers** News headline services are readily available on a variety of topics and in an array of protocols (HTML, RDF, XML, and so on). However, some require programming to add to your site.

These services all use programming languages (see Chapter 28 for what languages and how they work)—most of these services provide you with pre-programmed Java applets. Fortunately, you don't need to know how to program to add the services described in this section. Instead, you copy the Java applets (or other code) into your web pages that call on programs provided by other web sites. Some of these features are integrated directly into your site, which, in turn, will require you to add at least some code. Others provide customizable services that are hosted on the provider's site but offer links back to your own. In this section we look at a handful of providers that give you some very cool features for your site with little work required.

Adding a Calendar

The granddaddy of all web calendar services is Calendars Net (**www.calendars.net**) and you'll soon see why. Though the colors on the home page may be eye catching (we're being kind), the service is extraordinary. For the cost of your time, you can add a highly configurable calendar to your web site that you can synchronize with Outlook and soon, with your Palm organizer. Figure 29-2 shows a sample calendar.

Creating a new calendar takes just a few clicks. (These steps may change if the Calendars Net site is redesigned.) Go to **www.calendars.net** and click the Create Free Calendar link. Agree to the license agreement, terms, and conditions (or you can't make a calendar), type a filename for your calendar filename (up to 16 characters, including letters, numbers, and underscores), and type a title and description for your calendar. The description of your calendar is helpful if you plan to allow other people to share the calendar. When you click the Create button, Calendars Net creates your calendar. The system tells you if the name you chose is already in use so you can try another name.

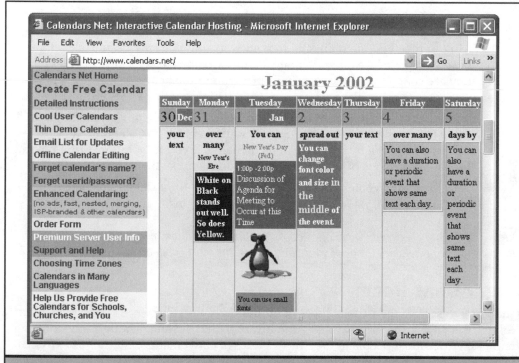

Figure 29-2. *You can set up a sharable web-based calendar for free and add calendar pages to your web site.*

Calendars Net offers a wide assortment of options for your calendars. After you modify your options, don't forget to click Save at the bottom of each page to keep your changes. Your options include

- **Display Options** control the way your calendar displays data and links.

- **Colors and Fonts** change the colors that appear on your calendar. Keep in mind that few fonts are installed on most people's computers. You may be able to see the Impact font on your computer, but not everyone can.

- **Event Categories** allow you to assign different colors to different types of events (business meetings in red, family events in blue, trips in green).

- **Add-ins** are predefined groups of events and dates that you can add to your calendar.

- **Security Access Codes** can protect various components of your calendar. Normally, anyone can change the settings, edit or delete entries, add new entries, and view the calendar. You can restrict who can view the calendar and who can add items.

- **Publish Calendar** copies events from the calendar to static web pages. These files are stored on Calendars Net's web servers for download to your computer. You can then add them directly to your web site. The only drawback is that these web pages are not automatically updated by changes in your calendar— they are snapshots of the calendar when you published it.

- **Data Importing** imports events from another source, such as Microsoft Outlook. You can import events in Tab Delimited (*.tab) or Comma Separated Value (*.csv) file formats. First upload your event file to Calendar Net's server, and then import it by referring to its filename. If you use Outlook, first rename the file to the name of your calendar by adding a .csv filename extension.

- **Data Exporting** copies your calendar data back out of Calendars Net so that you can import it into Outlook or other applications.

 Be sure to check out Calendars Net's extensive help section, which has instructions for showing calendars inside of your site's pages, the most common form being in a frame.

Adding a Chat Room

Chapter 9 describes the various types of online chats, and Chapter 13 describes Internet Relay Chat (IRC), the original real-time Internet chat system. Though live chatting tends to reduce most people to the simple basics of conversation, chatting is extremely popular, which is why some services give your site live chat for free.

One such service is called QuickChat (**www.quickchat.org**), which offers free access to code that places their Java-based IRC chat client into your site and free access to their IRC-compliant chat servers. We're amazed that they can provide this service for free without advertising because chat and IM take up a great deal of bandwidth.

QuickChat reserves an IRC channel for your chat room and provides a web interface to the IRC channel. Alternatively, your web page can provide access to a public channel on which people from other web sites may be chatting. (The default channel name is #webchat.)

Other web sites that offer free chat services you can add to your web pages include ChatPod (**www.chatpod.com**), Bravenet (**www.bravenet.com**), and Beseen (**www.beseen.com**).

Adding QuickChat's Code to Your Web Page

To request your own chat room, you must register at the QuickChat site (it's free) by clicking the Register link. QuickChat displays a form in which you can customize your chat room, specifying the size and colors of the chat box (in which the conversation will appear), the fonts, and the name of the IRC channel that will be used. When you click the Generate Code button, QuickChat shows a page with the HTML code that you need to add to your own web page. Cut and paste the HTML into your web page editor where you want the chat room box to appear. QuickChat's HTML code calls a Java program that runs on their web server.

 The QuickChat chat application requires that your browser run Java applets. If you use a browser that doesn't support Java, click the icon in the Chat box to download a Java plug-in.

Chatting on Your Custom Chat Web Page

Once you have added QuickChat's HTML code to your page, display the page in your browser. It looks something like Figure 29-3. (The formatting and text on the rest of the web page depend on what's on your page.)

Like most IRC programs, the chat box has three parts:

- The *main box* in the upper-left part displays the messages that have appeared in the channel.

- The *user list* on the right side displays the list of people in the channel.

- The *input box* is where you can type messages and commands.

 *You can display the chat box in its own window by typing **/float** in the input box. If you close the window, the chat program exits.*

When you first join the channel, your nickname may already be in use or registered to another user. If you see a message that tells you to change your nickname within 40 seconds, type this command in the input box:

```
/nick nickname
```

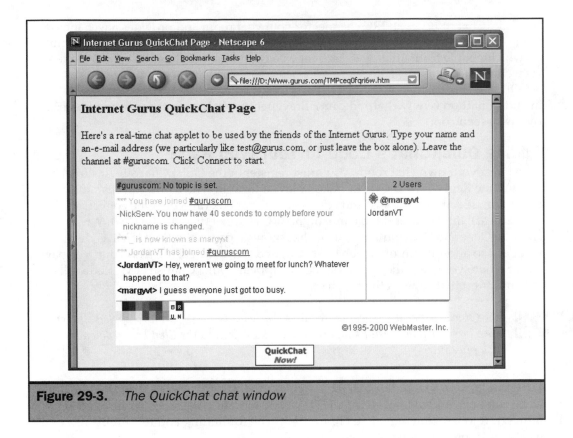

Figure 29-3.   *The QuickChat chat window*

Replace *nickname* with the nickname you want to use.

If you plan to use your chat web page often (and why create it if you don't?), register your nickname, also called a *nick,* to NICKSERV so that you can retain it permanently (as long as you use it at least once every 21 days). Also register your chat room's channel name so that it is always there, even if you are not. Registering your channel name also prevents anyone else from taking it and using it for something else. To register your nickname and channel name, go to **www.quickchat.org/reg.shtml**.

Adding a Guestbook

Before there were news tickers and message boards, there were web-based guestbooks. These pages urged visitors to sign a virtual guestbook. A large guestbook was a sign of prestige, indicating that a lot of people visited the site. These days, however, hit counters are better indicators of how many people visit a page, and message boards (covered later in this chapter) provide more interest than guestbooks do for visitors to come back.

If you do want a guestbook on your web site, the most popular service is Bravenet (**www.bravenet.com**), which is described next. Other sites that provide free guestbooks include Escati (**www.escati.com**), Beseen (**www.beseen.com**), and Sparklit (**www.sparklit.com**).

Bravenet offers a free and a fee-based guestbook. With the free version, which you can use if you sign up for a free Bravenet membership, advertisements appear on the guestbook page. You can sign up for a premium account that removes the ads from your guestbook, but there's a fee.

To add a guestbook to your site, click Join Bravenet to sign up for a free membership, click the Members Area link to log in, and click the Guestbook link on the Bravenet home page. Bravenet displays a page with the HTML code that you need to copy to your web page.

Bravenet also offers an array of tools to customize your guestbook. You can control the color, type size, images, and messages that appear on the guestbook page. You can also archive old guestbook entries to a file and clear the guestbook entries so that they no longer appear on the web page.

Adding a Hit Counter

If you want to know how many people visit your web site, you can add a hit counter to one or more pages. These web sites offer free hit counters that you can use on your site: Beseen (**www.beseen.com**), Bravenet (**www.bravenet.com**), Digits.com WebCounter (**www.digits.com**), Sparklit (**www.sparklit.com**), and Escati (**www.escati.com**). Follow the directions on the site to copy the HTML code to your web page. Most sites give you a choice of type styles.

Adding a Message Board

As described in Chapter 15, message boards allow web site visitors to post messages and reply to other people's messages. Message boards are popular because they allow people to ask questions and answer other people's questions and are a great tool for getting visitors to come back to your web site regularly.

The most common form of message board display is a hierarchical list. The first page shows general topics. Each topic page shows existing discussions. Each discussion contains individual messages and their associated replies. The most used message board system comes from EZBoard (**www.ezboard.com**), which offers both free and subscription services for people needing a message board for their site. Other sites that offer free message boards are Bravenet (**www.bravenet.com**), Beseen (**www.beseen.com**), Boardhost (**www.boardhost.com**), Boards2Go (**www.boards2go.com**), and HomepageTools (**www.homepagetools.com**).

To start a message board using EZBoard, go to **www.ezboard.com** and sign up for a free membership by clicking the Join link. EZBoard will send you a confirmation message by e-mail; use the information in the e-mail message to confirm your membership.

Be sure to uncheck the check boxes that allow EZBoard to add your address to a million spammers' mailing lists.

To manage the community that you created when you established your account, click the My EZBoard tab at the top of the page. EZBoard sets up a *community,* within which are *forums* (message boards). Each forum contains the messages posted in that forum. You can customize your community and the forums in it by setting colors, fonts, and images. You can also control how messages and their replies are arranged on the web page.

If you plan to have many forums, you can use the *categories* feature to group the forums. If you turn Categories on, you can apply category names to groups of forums. EZBoard groups the forums by category on your main community page.

Adding a News Ticker

News services provide headlines that link to web pages that contain the stories. Headlines are commonly grouped by category so you can customize them for your audience. Some web-based news feeds are provided by large corporations and charge seemingly insane fees for customized delivery (and the obligatory "News Powered by WalletVac Enterprises" advertisements), while others happily provide headlines for free, provided that you make a small mention of them.

Moreover.com (**www.moreover.com**) works both ways. Moreover.com is a fully featured, wide reaching news feed service that is customizable and free (up to a point). It provides free services to noncommercial webmasters who do not receive significant amounts of revenue for their services (which, in this case, include Moreover's news headlines). If you start at **www.moreover.com**, you can follow links to examples of large corporate sites that use Moveover to provide news headlines.

To add free news headlines to your site, go to the following URL:

```
w.moreover.com/webmaster
```

Note   *The URL starts with only one* w. *This is not a typographical error.*

Follow the links to run the Moreover Webfeed Wizard (shown in Figure 29-4) to generate the code for a free news feed for your web site. Choose the content (types of news to include) and layout (how the headlines look on your page). Click the Advanced Options link at the bottom of the Layout section to adjust your fonts, font size, and formatting. When you like the look of the preview in the right-hand part of the page, click Get The Code.

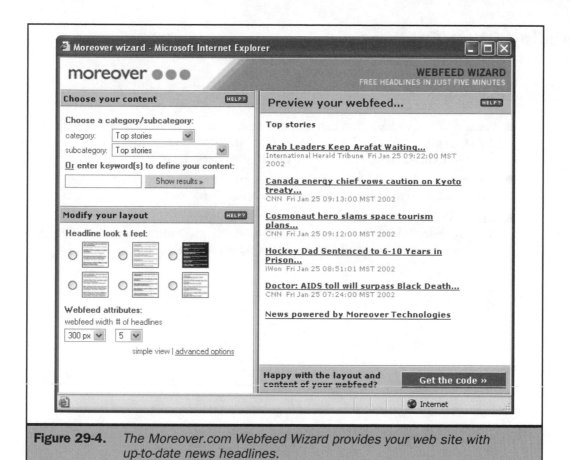

Figure 29-4. *The Moreover.com Webfeed Wizard provides your web site with up-to-date news headlines.*

> **Note** *If you use Pop-up Stopper or a similar utility, disable it while you use this wizard because the utility may cause the main window or the color picker windows to close before you get a chance to use them.*

Before the Moreover Webfeed Wizard shows you the HTML code that you need to copy to your web page, it asks for the URL of your page and your e-mail address. You can paste the Moreover code into your HTML editor or text editor. The web page with code will have consistently updated news headlines that you won't have to write yourself!

> **Note** *Bravenet (**www.bravenet.com**) also provides a free news feed service.*

Adding Other Features

Other features you can add to your web pages include

■ **Polls**   Find out what your web visitors think about a specific question. Available from Bravenet (**www.bravenet.com**) and Sparklit (**www.sparklit.com**).

■ **Forms**   Your web visitors can fill out a form to send you an e-mail message. (See Chapters 24 and 25.) Available from Bravenet (**www.bravenet.com**), Sparklit (**www.sparklit.com**), and Escati (**www.escati.com**).

■ **Greeting cards**   Enable your visitors to e-mail greeting cards from your site. Available from Bravenet (**www.bravenet.com**).

■ **Clock or countdown clock**   A regular clock shows the current time and date. A countdown clock shows the days, hours, and minutes until a time you specify. Both are available from Escati (**www.escati.com**).

The Complete Reference

Chapter 30

Uploading Web Pages

You've finished the first draft of your web site and it's looking good. The files are all on your computer, and you've tested the pages to make sure that all the links work. You've even checked all your pages with the latest versions of both Internet Explorer and Netscape to see how the pages lay out in each browser. You're ready to upload your files to the web server, so that the rest of the world can see them.

This chapter describes how to upload your web pages, graphics files, external style sheets, and the other files that make up your web site. You can use file transfer programs—web-based systems, stand-alone FTP programs, or the file transfer features of many web editors. You'll also learn some pitfalls that can create broken links and "404 - Not Found" errors.

The Uploading Process

You first need to find a web server on which to publish your pages. Where do you find a web server? Contact your ISP, shop for a web hosting service, or (if you are on an intranet) ask your system administrator. Most ISPs offer web hosting services either free with your Internet account or for a low monthly fee. (See the section on publishing your site in Chapter 23 for more information.)

You have a choice of methods of uploading your web site files, depending on your web server. Some web hosting companies or ISPs provide a web-based uploading system, which is very convenient, although it may not provide a way for renaming, deleting, or moving the files on the web server. Other web servers provide FTP (file transfer protocol) access so that you can use an FTP program to move your files. (Chapter 33 covers how to use FTP programs for file transfer, including Windows XP's built-in Web Folders.) If your web editor has a built-in FTP program, uploading may be as simple as clicking the Publish button on your web editor's toolbar.

The third thing that you need to do is prepare your files to be uploaded so that they have the right filenames and folder structure. You may need to create or rename folders on the web server. With luck, your FTP program provides these commands. If you need to make changes that your FTP program can't handle (like changing the permissions on files), and your web server provides telnet or ssh access, you can log into the web server and give commands to list, rename, delete, and move your files, as well as creating, renaming, and deleting folders (directories) on the web server. Most ISPs use UNIX-based systems, so it helps to know at least some basic UNIX commands so that you can manage the files in your directories. See Chapter 33 for how to use telnet, ssh, and some of the most useful UNIX commands.

Web Server Login and Site Location

Before you can upload your files, you need to be able to log into the web server using your FTP program or web editor Publish feature. The web server administrator can give you the information you need:

■ **Host name of the web server computer**   The host name is the name of the FTP
server that accepts files for the web server. This is not necessarily the same as
the domain name of the web site you are creating or updating. One web hosting
company or ISP may host hundreds or thousands of domain names, but may
have one or a few FTP servers. For example, your domain name may be **www
.greattapes.com**, but the computer to which you log in for uploading might be
named **ftp3.burlee.com**.

■ **User name and password**   This information enables you to log into the FTP
server and usually also tells the server which web site you are updating. For
example, if you log in with the user name *greattapes,* the FTP server allows you
to access the directories owned by that user.

■ **Base directory name**   When you log into the FTP server, you may see several
folders (directories). You need to know which to store your web site files in.
For example, when you log in, you may see folders named *web, logs,* and
mail—your web site files probably go in the *web* folder.

If you are going to use the uploading feature of a web page editor, ask for the
information in the form of a URL (Internet address), which will look like one of the
following:

ftp://ftp.hostname.com/directory
http://ftp.hostname.com/directory

 *To avoid confusion when you store your web page files in directories on the web server,
use the same structure as the set of folders on your hard drive. Most uploading programs
do this for you. For example, many web designers put all their graphics in a folder called*
images, *both on their own computer and on the web server.*

File Preparation

Before you upload your pages, verify that everything is in place and looks the way that
you want it to on all pages:

■ Make sure that your directory structure makes sense. You should have a
main directory, with subdirectories for images, video files, and audio files.
Your home page, usually named index.html, should be in the main directory.
Unless you have a large number of HTML pages, the rest of your HTML files
can also stay in the main directory.

Note   *If you have a large site with many HTML files, you might want to set up subdirectories
to organize the HTML files. Just make sure that the index.html file (the starting page)
remains in the main directory. If your pages fall into categories, you can create a folder
for each category. (For example, your poetry fan site might have a bunch of pages about
poets and another bunch of pages with poems.)*

CREATING AND
MAINTAINING WEB SITES

- Check the spelling on every page.
- Verify that graphics are displayed properly.
- Test all the links to be sure that you arrive at the proper destination when you click the link. If you coded your pages manually or if your web page editor does not verify links, open the HTML file in your browser and make sure that all the links work.

When you have the administrative information from your ISP or server administrator, and your files have been checked, you're ready to upload your pages to the Web.

Uploading Through a Web Interface

A few web servers provide a web interface for uploading files. For example, if you sign up for a web site with GeoCities (**geocities.yahoo.com**), you can use the Yahoo File Manager to copy, rename, and delete files on your web site, as shown in Figure 30-1. You can also create directories (folders). If you click the Upload Files button, you can type the filenames to upload to the web server.

The exact buttons and links to use depend on your web server's design; most are self-explanatory. Check your web host's or ISP's support pages to find out whether they provide a web interface for maintaining web sites.

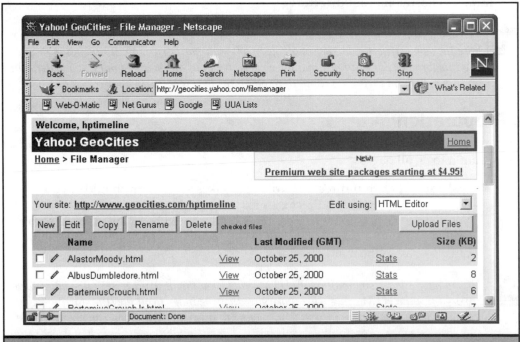

Figure 30-1. *Yahoo's GeoCities web server provides a web interface for uploading and managing the files on your web site.*

Uploading Through Your Web Editor

Many web editors include uploading (FTP) programs. As you work on your web pages, you can upload them and see how they work on the server. Here are instructions for uploading pages from the web editors described in Chapter 25: Netscape Composer, FrontPage, Dreamweaver, and GoLive.

 Note   *The FTP programs built into web editors automatically upload text files (HTML, HTML, CSS, and other text-only files) in FTP's ASCII mode and the graphics and other binary files in FTP's IMAGE or BINARY mode.*

Netscape Composer 4.*x*

Netscape Composer is part of Netscape Communicator 4.*x* and Netscape 6.*x*. See Chapter 18 for where to get Netscape Communicator and Netscape 6 (which both include Composer) and Chapter 25 for how to create web pages. Strangely, Netscape Composer 6 doesn't include an FTP program—there's no Publish or Upload button to click.

In Netscape Composer 4.*x*, follow these steps to upload your web page files:

1. Open the main file for your site (usually named index.html).

2. Choose File | Publish to display the Publish dialog box, shown next.

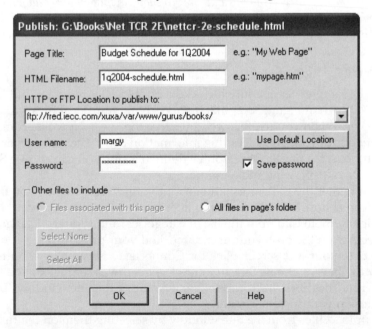

3. In the HTTP Or FTP Location To Publish To box, type the HTTP or FTP location to which you are publishing the page. Also enter the user name and password for your account on your web server.

4. In the Other Files To Include section of the dialog box, select the files that you want to transfer. You can transfer the current page and all files associated with it, which includes all the graphics and objects that you inserted in the file, or all files in the current folder. Composer displays a list of files to be transferred, and you can select or remove files from the list manually. If you are in doubt about which files to transfer, it is better to transfer too many files than to leave out a file that's needed for your page.

5. Click OK to start the file transfer. The names of files are displayed onscreen as the files are transferred, and you can monitor the progress of the transfer onscreen.

FrontPage 2002

If your web server supports FrontPage extensions, choose File | Publish Web in FrontPage 2002. The program uploads your entire site or recent changes. If you're working online with your web server, File | Save saves your changes directly to the web site.

If your web host does not support FrontPage extensions or if you aren't using the extensions, you need to use FTP to upload the files to your web site, as described in Chapter 33.

 If you have configured Windows Explorer to show all hidden files and folders, you may notice folders with filenames that begin with an underscore, like _vti_cnf. These folders hold file information used by FrontPage. Don't upload them to your web server.

Dreamweaver

Macromedia Dreamweaver not only includes a built-in FTP program, but it also has a Site window (shown in Figure 30-2) that displays both your local files and the files on your web server. When you create a web site, give the Site | New Site command to tell Dreamweaver about your site, including information about the web server to which you plan to upload the pages. Once you've defined a site, you can choose Site | Site Files or press F8 to display the Site window.

If you don't enter the FTP information about your web site when you first create the site, you can choose Site | Define Sites later; choose the site from your list of sites, click Edit, click Remote Info from the list of categories, and type the FTP host name, the base directory on the host, your user name, and your password.

To connect to your web server, click the Connects To Remote Host button on the Site window toolbar (or choose Site | Connect). Dreamweaver logs in and displays the list of web server files and directories on the left side of the Site window. The right side shows the files on your local computer.

You can upload files from the Site window by selecting them on the right (local computer) side and clicking the Put Files (up-arrow) button on the toolbar. When you

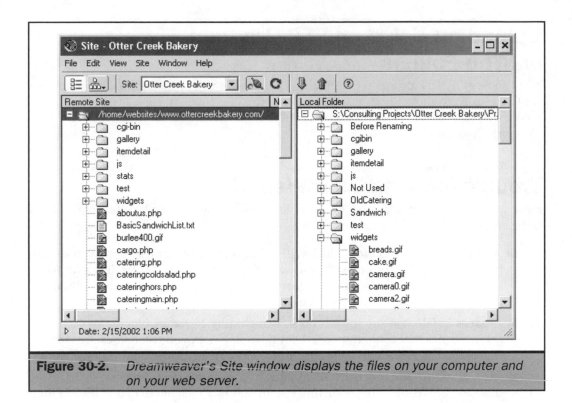

Figure 30-2. Dreamweaver's Site window displays the files on your computer and on your web server.

are editing a file, you can upload it from the editing window by clicking the File Management button on the toolbar and choosing Put from the menu that appears.

GoLive

GoLive contains its own FTP program. When you are ready to upload your site (or just a few pages), click the FTP Server Connect/Disconnect button on the toolbar. If you haven't entered or selected FTP settings yet, the Preference dialog box appears. After that, clicking the same button opens the Site window, taking you to the FTP tab as it connects to the FTP server for your web site.

To upload files, click the Incremental Upload button on the toolbar. GoLive compares the dates of the files in your Files tab with the files on the web server and shows you a list of updated files to upload (that is, web site files that you have edited on your computer since the last time you uploaded). Click OK and GoLive delivers your files to the web server. Alternatively, you can manually upload a page by dragging it from the Files tab over to the FTP tab.

Uploading Using an FTP Program or Web Folders

You can use any FTP program to upload web pages. Many FTP programs are available; see Chapter 33 for how to get, install, and use one. Windows XP comes with Web Folders, a built-in FTP program that enables you to add an FTP server to your My Network Places folder.

Troubleshooting Your Web Site

Here are the most common causes of trouble in uploading your web pages to a web server:

- **Capitalization problems**   Stick with all lowercase filenames. Most web servers run UNIX, which considers uppercase and lowercase letters to be different. Some FTP programs (including Dreamweaver's built-in file transfer) can automatically convert all filenames to lowercase.

- **Spaces in filenames**   Some browsers (including Netscape Navigator 4.*x*) balk at filenames that contain spaces. Don't use spaces in your filenames. Instead, make filenames readable by using dashes or dots to connect the parts of the name.

- **ASCII vs. binary**   Chapter 33 explains how FTP programs transfer text and nontext files differently, adjusting the line-ending characters in text files to meet the standards of Windows, Macs, and UNIX. Most of the files in a web site consist entirely of text, including web pages (with extensions .html and .htm) and cascading style sheets (with extension .css). Graphics files (GIF, JPEG, and JPG files) are nontext.

- **Files in the right folders**   When you transfer files, make sure to put them in the right folders. The easiest way to do this is to use the same folder structure on your own computer as on the web server and to use an FTP program that uploads the files to their corresponding folders. (GoLive and Dreamweaver both do this.)

- **Referring to files on your own computer**   When you create links, make sure that the URLs don't refer to the file location on your own computer. When the web pages are on your computer, a URL like **file:///D|/Web Pages/images/ mary.jpg** works fine, but once the pages are uploaded to a web server, **file:///** URLs don't work. (Yes, these URLs have three slashes.)

- **Relative pathnames**   Make sure that the names of files in links (<A HREF> tags) and images (<IMG> tags) are relative to the location of the web page. That is, if the linked file or graphics file is in the same folder as the web page that refers to it, type only the filename in the tag rather than the full pathname of the file. If the linked file or graphics file is in the parent folder of the folder that contains the web page, type **..\filename** to specify the file. References that are absolute (that start with "\" or "/" to indicate the root folder of your computer or the web server) can get you into trouble because your web site files may not be stored in what appears as the root folder of the web server.

- **HTM vs. HTML extensions**   Originally, web pages had the extension .html, but because Windows filenames used to be limited to three letters, many web pages were (and still are) named with the extension .htm. Both work on most web servers; just be consistent.

Chapter 31

Building Traffic to Your Web Site

There's one major trick to getting web site traffic—and it has nothing to do with banner ads, search engines, <META> tags, or promotions: *Have a good site.* Before you take step 1 to get people there, make sure your site is *ready* for prime time. Does it look nice? Is it easy to use? Are all the pages linked properly? And above all, *does it have enough content?*

Businesses who print their web site on their business cards and bags, only to direct people to a two-page site that announces "more coming soon!" or "under construction!" are shooting themselves in the foot. If you create a site that's updated weekly with great articles and snazzy pictures, a little promotion goes a long way.

Which is not to say that there aren't things you can do to get people there, as this chapter details, but we can only show you how to lead the horse to water. Getting him to drink is *your* task.

 As you probably know, people often enter a web site from pages other than the home page, so make sure that each page in your web site sells itself to a first-time visitor. This is especially true for people finding your site with a search engine.

How to Get Listed on Search Engines

Eighty-five percent of all web users find their sites through search engines and web directories like Google, Yahoo, AltaVista, Lycos, AOL Search, and Excite. (If you want to know the differences among search engines, check out Chapter 21.)

No matter what you call the tools, most people find your site by searching, and search engines are critical to the success of any web site.

The key to having search engines generate significant traffic to your web site is to understand both how people use search engines and how the search engines rank sites in their index. In general, most people don't know how to use search engines well; this means that when you craft your web pages, you have to anticipate that your audience members will only enter two to four words to describe what they are looking for.

After a user submits those few words to a search engine, the search engine software tries to select web pages that match the user's interests and needs. Although the exact formulas used by search engine software are highly confidential, specialists in search engine submissions conduct experiments on a regular basis to try to understand the formulas being used.

Most search engines look at a combination of attributes and apply different weightings to calculate rankings, which is one reason why different search engines provide different results when given the same search phrase. The attributes that are commonly used by search engines include

- <META> tags for both description and keywords
- The <TITLE> tag

- Content of the page
- Popularity of the web page

 Many search engines also sell positions in listings. That is, you can pay to be listed at or near the top. Other search sites display a list of "sponsored links" (that is, sites that paid a fee) to the right of the regular list of search results. Refer to each search engine's web site for specific information.

What Are <META> Tags?

<META> tags are HTML tags designed specifically to help search engines catalog your site—and they're critical to getting people to your site. (For more information on what HTML is and how it works, see Chapter 24.) The information inside the <META> tags goes in the HEAD section, meaning it doesn't show up on the page at all. You can put keywords and descriptions inside them to help automated search engines catalog your site.

Two <META> tags are important for helping people find your page: *description* and *keywords*. Each <META> tag looks like this:

```
<META name="type" content="text">
```

Replace *type* with either "description" or "keywords," and replace *text* with the information described in the next two sections.

The description <META> Tag

The *description* <META> tag enables you to describe your site in a few sentences—and aside from your site name, it's frequently the only description that search engines provide when someone finds your site during a search. (See Figure 31-1.) As such, the description tag needs to tell users everything they need to know about your site in a sentence or two.

A good description <META> section looks like this:

```
<META name="description" content="Bird feeders and bird nestboxes
for backyard and garden birds. ShelterHut is a modular birding
station with nature habitats for wrens, bluebirds, hummingbirds,
purple martins.">
```

In addition to providing a short summary of your site, the description <META> tag also needs to contain important, descriptive words because the text in the description <META> tag counts more than the <META> keywords and more than the same text within the body of the page when weighting search results.

Therefore, you need to write—and rewrite—the description <META> tag until it is as short as possible, yet still describes the essence of that page and uses all the important

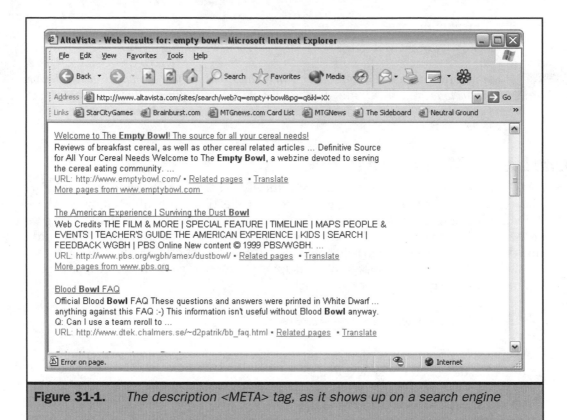

Figure 31-1.   *The description <META> tag, as it shows up on a search engine*

keywords. That's difficult to do, but it may be one of the most important things you *can* do for your site. The reason you need to keep the <META> tag short is so that the important words in the description represent the highest possible percentage of the total number of words in the description. For example, if an important keyword for you is "chocolate," and your description is 50 words long, then this keyword is only 2 percent of the description <META> tag. On the other hand, if your description is ten words long, the keyword "chocolate" represents 10 percent of the description.

Search engines compare the words in the description <META> tag to the words used in the body of the page, to make sure that the words in the description <META> tag are actually used on the page. The search engines do this because sleazy web site operators have tried inserting thousands of different (and unrelated) keywords in attempts to have their web pages appear on search results for which their sites are totally inappropriate.

The keywords <META> Tag

The *keywords* <META> tag contains keywords that may be used throughout the body of the web page. The list of keywords helps you to increase the weight applied to the ranking by the search engines, by indicating that certain words in the body are important. A keywords <META> tag looks like this, separating the keywords (and key phrases) with commas:

```
<META name="keywords" content="backyard, common birds, bird, bird
feeder, bird house, nesting box, birding, wild bird, nature,
songbirds, bluebird, purple martin">
```

Choosing keywords is important because you want to strike a balance between specific and general. After all, putting "Internet" as a keyword means that you'll be sharing that keyword with 109 million other web sites. On the other hand, choosing something too specific, like "antidisestablishmentarianism," means that people will have to be doing some pretty strange searches to stumble upon your site. Your best bet is to put in a bunch of general keywords, then put in more specific keywords that relate only to your site, and hope that people look for, say, "bluebird nesting box."

 After your site has been online for a while, look through your web site logs to see what keywords people are typing to find your site, and refine your list of keywords.

Because of the way search engines look at <META> tags changes periodically (and some engines won't look at <META> tags if they're formatted improperly), you can use an online automated service to analyze your web pages to help ensure that they are suitable to the majority of search engines. You can get some tutorials on current search engine philosophy at **www.siteowner.com**.

The <TITLE> Tag

The <TITLE> tag provides the words that show up when someone bookmarks your page and that show up in the title bar of the browser window. More important, search engines weight the text of the <TITLE> tag very heavily. Use page titles that describe what your site is—and ideally, titles that contain important words people search for.

One helpful trick is to use a different description in the <TITLE> tag for each page, which enables you to match the <TITLE> tag more closely with the exact content on that page. Not only does this improve the chances for that page to show up higher in the priority list for search results, but it also increases the number of different search words that will produce a listing for your site by the search engines.

Page Content

Although the <META> keyword tags help the search engines weight their results, the words in the body of the page are also cataloged. Even if the phrase "drosophilia melangaster" is nowhere in the <META> tags of your fruit-fly fan site, if your article on *drosophilia melangaster* reproduction mentions them 30 times, chances are search engines will still pick it up. Also, search engines tend to weight words that appear toward the top of the page a little more heavily than words that appear toward the bottom.

Popularity of Your Site

The methods that search engines use to rate popularity are, of course, highly confidential (search engining is a cutthroat business), but popularity has something to do with how many sites link to you and how many people click through on their search results to your page. If you're popular, you are ranked higher than a less-popular site.

Blocking a Page from Inclusion in Search Engines

Your web site may include pages that you don't want search engines to index. For example, if your site includes a message board with questions and notes from customers, it's usually a bad idea for these message board pages to be index. The pages change often, the questions and comments may not be positive, and people who post messages rarely want their names and e-mail addresses (which frequently appear in message board postings) included in search engine results.

Fortunately, there's a way to alert search engines that pages should be skipped. If you don't want a page to be indexed, include this <META> tag in the BODY element of each web page to be skipped:

```
<META name="robots" content="no index, no follow"
```

Submitting Your Site to Search Engines

If you've been on the Internet for more than just a few days, you know what "spam" is—advertising that you didn't request that arrives via e-mail—and you've probably received spam from people saying that they can make your site show up high in search engine results. Another frequent claim by these spammers is that they will submit your site to over 200 search engines.

These claims have two major flaws: no one can guarantee to make a site show up high in the search results of a search engine, and very few search engines generate significant amounts of traffic. In reality, most traffic comes from the top six to eight popular search engines—not from the specialized search engines and lists that these promoters talk about.

Although the Web truly has a site for everybody, most people using the Web don't use specialty search engines to find sites—probably because they don't know about them. (Also, the popular search engines do an adequate job of helping people find sites of interest.) You benefit most when you focus your search engine submission resources on the following search engines and directories. (According to several surveys, these are the most popular search engines as of mid-2002.)

- Google   **google.com**
- Yahoo   **www.yahoo.com**
- MSN   **www.msn.com**
- AOL Search   **search.aol.com**
- Ask Jeeves   **ask.com**
- LookSmart   **www.looksmart.com**
- InfoSpace   **infospace.com**
- Overture (formerly GoTo.com)   **www.overture.com**
- Lycos   **www.lycos.com**
- Netscape   **www.netscape.com**
- Excite   **www.excite.com**
- AltaVista   **www.altavista.com**
- ABC's GO.com   **go.com**

Each of these sites (some of which are described in Chapter 21) has a link that takes you to a form on which you can easily submit the URL of a web page for inclusion in the directory or search engine database. Because submitting a web page manually to each of these search engines takes less than ten minutes, submit your own pages manually instead of paying someone to submit them for you. In addition to the sites listed above, submit your site to any other search engines that you like to use, especially if you know of search engines that specialize in the type of information your site carries.

The sites listed above aren't necessarily the ones that we recommend when you are searching for information. They are the sites that the general public is most likely to use, so you want them to include information about your site. See Chapter 21 for our list of the best search engines.

Experienced webmasters review their search engine placement about once a month because search engines sometimes drop pages from their indexes. Some search engines take two to three months to list a site, so maintain a log showing the pages submitted, the search engines, and the date submitted. The log helps you to remember each month, as you review your placements, exactly how long it's been since you submitted your site.

**CREATING AND
MAINTAINING WEB SITES**

Yahoo in particular is known for being strangely picky about what sites they accept and what sites they do not. If you have a business site, being listed generally isn't a problem, but personal pages and fan sites may have some trouble. Keep submitting!

See the Search Engine Watch web site at **www.searchenginewatch.com** for more information about search engines and how to submit your site. They include listings of the current most popular search engines.

Getting Links to Your Site

The techniques for obtaining links to your site have changed a bit over the past few years, but the value of having links to your site has increased because search engines now include the popularity of web sites when they calculate the ranking of hits for their users. This means that links to your site not only bring traffic to your site, but they also help improve your ranking with the search engines.

Aside from being so good that people have to link to your site, there are two basic methods of getting others to link to you: getting listed on other sites and using web rings.

Requesting Links on Other Web Sites

Sites that sell products are reluctant to include links to other web sites, for fear of losing visitors to their own web site. On the other hand, many business-to-business and fan sites are designed to be information sources, so they'll frequently include a link list that includes noncompetitive companies that serve the same target market.

The process of obtaining links to your site requires research and monitoring. In addition, you'll probably need to maintain a links page on your own web site.

One of the best ways to identify candidates from which to request links is to use a search engine to identify web sites that are compatible with yours, then locate the links page within those sites. After you identify candidates from which to request links— and bookmark them—you are ready to begin your campaign of requesting links. Before you request a link from a site, add that site to *your* link list, so that you can demonstrate that you intend to link back.

To save time, you can save related pages in your Favorites or Bookmarks file, export your Favorites or Bookmarks to an HTML file, and paste the bookmarks and notes into an HTML template designed for your site, thus creating your links page. For information on favorites and bookmarks, see Chapter 19.

After you publish a links page on your web site, you are ready to e-mail the webmaster at each site to request that they link to your site from their links page. Be sure to describe why you think their audience will find your site beneficial. Give them the URL of your links page to demonstrate that you have already linked to their site.

For an example of how one site handles its link list, view the links page at the LABMED site, at **www.labmed.org/lnk_startingarescue.htm**l. (See Figure 31-2.) The page lists links, including the page title and the URL.

Joining Web Rings

One of the more innovative approaches to obtaining links to a web site is through *web rings*, groups of sites with similar audiences that agree to link to other sites in the ring. The concept targets visitors who are interested in the *topic* of a web site rather than the specific web site. The web managers in the ring let these visitors link to other sites in the ring and in return obtain reciprocal overflow traffic from the other sites in the ring.

Promoting your site through a web ring has several benefits, such as not having to research and continually maintain a links list. Most web rings use special software that directs users to the next web site in the ring, so that webmasters generally are assured that all the links in the ring are up to date. The potential downside to using a web ring is that sites in rings are generally less professional looking, which poses a potential

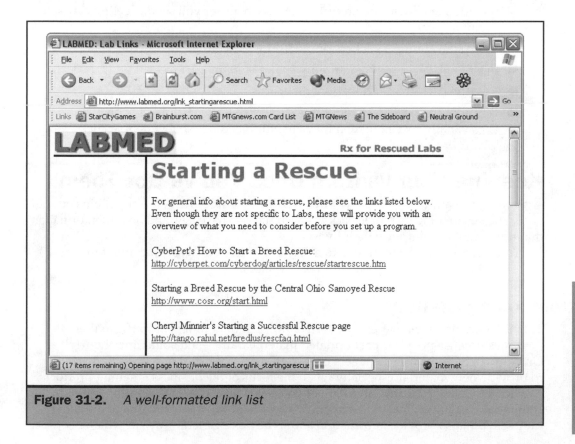

Figure 31-2.   *A well-formatted link list*

image problem. In addition, many web rings have very few members, so the amount of traffic generated may be low.

Here are two central clearinghouses for rings that you may want to investigate:

- WebRing **www.webring.org**
- The Rail **www.therail.com**

Other Ways of Publicizing Your Site

Aside from telling everyone you see that your site is on the Web, here are some other non-search-engine–related ways to let other people know about your site:

- Print the URL of your site on your business cards, stationery, and in your yellow pages ad.
- Add your URL to your signature block in e-mail and newsgroup messages.
- Include the URL in your return address whenever you send greeting cards or holiday cards.
- Have some bumper stickers printed showing your group or club's URL.
- Print the URL in your community group bulletin each week.
- Post the URL on all school bulletin boards.
- Buy advertising. (However, this is expensive—even banner ads on other web sites usually cost more than they are worth because so few people click them.)

Keeping Your Visitors Once You've Got Them

After you start attracting people to your web site, consider ways to keep them coming back. The key to bringing people back to a web site is to have new and helpful information that they can use to improve their lives.

You can do a number of things to achieve this, from the type of content that you place on your site to sending e-mail to past visitors.

Compelling Content

The big news organizations enjoy a tremendous amount of repeat traffic to their web sites because people expect updated material daily—and sometimes hourly! Unfortunately, most web managers cannot afford a large staff of writers and artists to provide new material, especially when the focus of the business is selling products.

However, being creative about what you sell is a good way of creating regular content. For example, many sites not only provide product information about what they sell, but also provide information about the more general ways in which people use their products. For example, if you have a site that sells birdhouses, you might want to create an interactive map that tells people what sorts of birds nest in their areas, and then explain which houses (and foods and environments) will attract the birds they want to see. You can then also have articles on standard problems people have with birdhouses—things like food-stealing squirrels and hungry cats. You can update seasonally, reminding customers and potential customers alike about what things look like from a bird's perspective as the summer ends and fall begins. And perhaps you can throw in a section where your customers relate their favorite bird stories…

As another example, StarCityGames (**www.starcitygames.com**) sells cards for an obscure card game called "Magic: The Gathering." How did they make their site into the #1 Magic online retailer? By getting fans of the game to write strategy articles for them, which encouraged Magic fans to check it out daily—and gave even Magic players who had no interest in buying cards a good reason to go there. Eventually, if they *do* buy cards, they'll think of StarCityGames.

Getting creative about what you put on your site can be inexpensive and profitable. Brainstorm with a few friends, and see what you can come up with!

E-mail Newsletters

People who want to return to a web site often forget to bookmark it. The best way to remind people to return is with an informative e-mail newsletter that contains short summaries of new articles on your web site and links to those articles.

Newsletters that promote a product web site should contain at least one moderately long summary of an article that is available on the web site and short summaries that contain links to new announcements on the web site. Alternately, newsletters can provide links to news articles found on other sites. By limiting the amount of content that has to be created specifically for the newsletter, you'll find it easier to maintain a regular publishing schedule.

If you are undecided on a format for your e-mail newsletter, take a look at the newsletters sent out by news organizations such as CNET (**www.cnet.com**), ZDNet (**www.zdnet.com**), and CMPnet (**www.cmpnet.com**). The strong interest in distributing e-mail newsletters has resulted in several companies that provide free or low-cost distribution to lists of people in return for placing advertising within the newsletter. (These sites also support discussion mailing lists and are described in Chapter 10.) For many purposes, accepting advertising by these newsletter services does not detract from the content, so you may want to investigate placing ads in these newsletters.

Companies that serve a wide range of customers should consider the use of a personalized e-mail product that can tailor the content to match the interests and needs of each subscriber. By adding special codes to a master newsletter template, the software can select which pieces of content to include for each person. For instance, if you sell golf products on your web site, you may have several different groups of customers—like novices, experienced players, and professionals. Even though members of each audience may look at the same product pages in your web catalog, they have different needs and buying motives that you can appeal to with a personalized e-mail newsletter.

To generate subscriptions to your newsletter, include a sign-up page on your web site. *Don't* send spam to publicize your newsletter! Make sure to send only appropriate information to visitors who have made inquiries, to avoid the appearance of being a spammer.

Some personalized e-mail products to review include

- UnityMail (Revnet)   **www.unitymail.com**
- Coravue (GuestTrack)   **www.coravue.com**

Analyzing Your Web Traffic

Getting your site on the Web is just the beginning. Good webmasters use their logs to fine-tune their site once it's up and running—changing page design to encourage more people to go to your dead (seldom visited) areas (or eliminating these areas), tracking promotions, and finding dead links (link to pages that are no longer there). Checking your web logs, discussed shortly, is critical to the long-term success of any site.

Hits, Page Views, Visits, and Other Miscellaneous Web Reporting

Web marketers frequently boast about the number of "hits" their web sites receive, but just what are they talking about, and what are they really saying?

The term that is most thrown around—and most abused—is *hits*. The following are a few commonly used terms and definitions used to describe web traffic:

- **Hit**   A hit is commonly thought of as the number of times a page on a web site is requested by a browser—but this is not accurate. Hits also includes the number of times all other files, including graphic images, are viewed. For example, if your home page has nine graphics on it, each time someone views your home page, the log file registers one hit for the HTML file and nine hits for the graphics, for a total of ten hits. Because the term "hits" has such an ambiguous meaning, most people are now measuring traffic in terms of *page views*.

- **Page view**   A page view is the viewing of one specific HTML file—without counting any graphics or other items on the page. If one person views a page, moves to another page, and then comes back to the page, only one page view is usually counted because the person's browser typically stores (caches) the page and doesn't request it again. Some ISPs and online services cache web pages on their own servers, so that if 100 America Online users see your page, your web server may experience only one page view.

■ **Visit**   A visit is all the pages viewed by a user within a continuous session, which can include anything from a single HTML file to a visit that encompasses the entire site and lasts for an hour or more. Standard web server logs include the IP (numeric) address (see Chapter 1 for more details) for each computer that requests files from the server, so traffic analysis programs use this identifier to determine the starting point and ending point for each visit or session. Because users don't "log out" from a web site, assumptions have to be made about when the user actually leaves the site.

■ **Visitor**   This term theoretically represents each unique individual who comes to a web site, which means that the total visitors to a site should be the unduplicated count of visitors. Unfortunately, IP addresses are reused by ISPs as different people dial into their networks. This means that two different people could visit a web site using the same IP address. Also, when an individual disconnects and reconnects to an ISP, the user is usually issued a different IP address, which appears in the log as a different visitor. The use of cookies (defined in Chapter 20) to identify when a particular computer returns to a site can help improve accuracy of these regulations, but that requires extra database programming (and not all users accept cookies).

■ **Organization**   An organization is represented in a web server's log as the domain name used by each visitor. Unfortunately, the number of domain names represented in a log file doesn't represent the actual number of different companies visiting a web site, for several reasons. With many people using ISPs and online services, there is no way to accurately count the number of different companies. One example is America Online, which has millions of people, all shown as coming from the same domain.

Things to Check in Your Web Log

Most professional (that is, paid) web hosting sites provide you with data about who is visiting your site. Some of them provide it in a rough dump of data called a *server log*, whereas others will provide a more professional *traffic analysis report.* In either case, you should sift through the data to check some important factors: referrers, errors, and browsers.

Where Your Visitors Come From

When looking through your web logs, keep a special eye on the *referrer* field, which contains the URL of the referring site and the page containing the link to your site. When people link to your site from a search engine, you can usually see the search phrase contained in the referring URL, which can help you determine how to better refine your <META> tags.

Error Codes

Users expect web servers to complete each request for a file that the browser requests from a server. As web users all know, sometimes things don't always work right, and the user receives an error message.

The status field contains a code that indicates whether the server successfully delivered the requested file or something happened to keep the file from being delivered. The typical status codes that appear in the log include

- **200**   Successful delivery of the file
- **302**   Redirect to another file
- **400**   Bad request
- **401**   Password required
- **403**   Forbidden to access the file
- **404**   File not found
- **500**   Server error

The redirect status code (302) indicates that the server has been directed to display one page in place of the requested page. Often you can use this feature to track hits from a particular source. For instance, you might have an ad elsewhere that directs people to a particular page—which, in turn, redirects users to your home page. By having the ad link people to the redirect page, you can easily track how many people clicked your ad.

The Browser Field

Generally, users are slow to upgrade, and the browser field shows you what visitors are using what browsers. If you're thinking about using some new technology that only works on recent browsers, check to see how much of your current viewer base you'll be alienating.

Site Paths and How to Use Them

Many traffic analysis programs can determine the order in which pages were accessed by each individual IP address. By understanding the various paths that people take through your web site, you can learn more about their interests and their decision-making during the visit. For instance, if most people go from the home page to the product summary page, then obviously your products are your big sell, but if more people go to the services page, then they probably want to learn about the support you offer before they read about what you sell.

Of course, this type of analysis requires a clear understanding of the content associated with each filename and of how pages are displayed to your users. Knowing how pages are displayed on various browsers and at different screen resolutions is important because the placement of links onscreen can affect what people click as much as their interests do. For example, if your page has the "products" link hidden where the user has to scroll down to see it, your customers may be clicking on services in a vain attempt to *find* the products.

You can also use paths to determine the level of interest an audience has in a topic. By breaking a long story or promotional page into multiple web pages that are linked from the first page through to the last page, you can determine how interest decreases as people move through the story. For instance, if a three-part article receives half as many hits on the second page as on the first page, you clearly are losing people very quickly. On the other hand, if the second page receives almost as many hits as the first page, then you know that people are interested through most of the story.

You can also use paths to scan for interesting synergies that you can exploit. For example, if you run a site that sells computer parts, you might discover that people move from the graphics card pages to the memory pages—indicating that people who are upgrading their video cards also want more RAM. You could then hold a promotion bundling the two to drive traffic and sales, or redesign your site so memory and video cards are on the same page.

Chapter 32

Web Commerce

No business can survive unless its potential customers know it exists. The Web offers you a unique opportunity to get the word out about your company, let your audience know what products and services you offer, and give them a way to order your goods over the Internet.

Doing business over the Web is like doing business in a physical store: you need to let folks know who you are, what you do, and where you can be found. Creating a web presence does have certain advantages over establishing a physical location, however. Instead of leasing a store, buying a sign, and printing marketing literature you'll have to live with for months, you can set up a presence that is reachable by anyone with web access, can be found through the search engines discussed in Chapter 31, can accept orders from web site visitors, and can be updated as often as you like.

Purposes of Commercial Web Sites

How much functionality you build into your web site depends on your goals for the site. For instance, if you expect visitors to make purchase decisions (and purchases!) based solely on the information on the site, you construct a very different site than if you see your site as an invitation for visitors to contact you by phone, fax, or in person.

A public relations (PR) site concentrates on providing information about your company, without getting into specifics about your products or services. A marketing site provides lots of information about products without trying to close a sale. A sales site does e-commerce: customers can actually buy from the site. You can think of these three types of sites as a logical progression. A PR site presents your company in its best light, a marketing site tells customers about your products, and a sales site lets them buy the perfect product from a company they respect. In addition to these types of sites, your commercial site might have the goal of providing technical support to your customers, or a way for your customers to interact with each other.

Of course, your site may have more than one purpose: PR, sales, and support, for example. If so, be sure to think about each of the purposes of the site, and make sure that there are pages that fulfill that purpose.

PR Sites

The goal of a PR web site is to make your business' best qualities known to anyone who visits the site. New product announcements, significant hires, expansions, web site redesigns, price changes, and alliances are all great candidates for inclusion on a PR web site. Although you should stay away from the "everything's news" mind set, whenever you make a change that affects your customers, you should announce it on your site. Figure 32-1 shows the corporate site of the McGraw-Hill publishing companies.

Create a special area on your web site that contains your press releases and, when possible, invite your visitors to receive the releases by e-mail. Running mailing lists is described later in this chapter (and general mailing list topics are discussed in Chapter 10), but for now bear in mind that most of your customers would appreciate monthly summaries of what's new with your company—not daily updates on every change you've made.

Figure 32-1. *A corporate PR site shows information about the company as a whole.*

Prominently display all of your company's contact information on your site, including an e-mail address so visitors can ask any questions that occur to them while they are at your site. Including your company's general contact e-mail address at the bottom of each page is a good idea—that way your potential customers won't need to dig through your site to find your e-mail address and can ask their question while it is fresh in their mind. You should also avoid making your press releases into sales documents. Remember, the object of a press release is to attract attention; nothing irritates editors, journalists, and potential customers like a sales pitch disguised as a news release. Get your potential customers to the site; then sell them your goods.

Note *Any time you include an e-mail address on a web site, the address will be "harvested" and used by spammers. Don't put the addresses of individuals on your site; instead, put "job" addresses like sales@sample.com. Most organizations use an info@ address for general inquiries. If you really want to avoid spam, display e-mail addresses as small pictures (GIF files) rather than as text.*

A number of sites offer advice on how to write a press release, though you should remember that many of the sites are maintained by marketing companies that would be happy to write your release for you. You could hire an outside firm to write your first few releases or more if you are happy with their work or don't have the time to write them yourself. Remember that you will be paying for a specialized service and, as when you hire any outside firm or individual contractor, you should ask to see samples of their work and to speak with some of their clients. A few firms to consider are

- Charles Kessler & Associates **www.net-market.com/howto.htm**
- Xpress Press **www.xpresspress.com/Writing_Service.html**
- Dr. Kevin Nunley **drnunley.com/release.htm**
- Media Works World Wide **www.mediaworksinternational.com/ press_release_service.html**

 A PR site, like all web sites, requires maintenance. Your organization looks foolish if the latest press release on your site is two years old. Be sure to include web site maintenance as part of the job of your PR department so that all PR activities are reflected on the site.

Marketing Sites

A marketing site goes beyond the basic Internet presence of a PR site by providing detailed information about your products and services, comparing your offerings to those of other companies, and listing prices.

The most important part of a marketing web site is the information about your products and services. Rather than focus on the glossy, newsworthy side of your company, your marketing information should be written like printed one-page *fact sheets.* Those fact sheets should list the name of the product or service and the specific function of the equipment (or the problem the service solves), as well the product's internal tracking code, stock number, dimensions, configuration options, and additional equipment (like cables, batteries, and toner) required to operate the product. Include photographs (and diagrams, if appropriate) of the product.

The next part of your web presentation for this product or service should describe your product's attributes and advantages. How you market your product depends on the type of product or service and how what you are selling is distinct from your competitors' offerings. One easy way to present your product is in a *feature/benefit format.* In a feature/benefit presentation, you list the qualities of your product and how the user will benefit from each of those features. For instance, if you build custom computer systems for businesses and home users, you could describe one or more of your typical designs, catalog the components that make up the system, and list the benefits of the components individually or as a part of the system.

You might also want to compare your products with those of your competitors in terms of features, performance, price, warranties, and so forth. If you're comparing your products and services with industry norms, you should list the feature, the average implementation of that feature in your area, and your implementation—then explain how your approach is superior. For instance, if custom computer builders in your area only include a 1.5-GHz chip in their $1,000 computers and you offer a 1.7-GHz chip (and similar or better components like RAM, storage, and video cards), you should point that out in your presentation.

If possible, include a tutorial about how to use the product, or an animated "tour" or walk-through of the product or service.

Sales Sites

A sales site extends the capabilities of a marketing site by allowing visitors to purchase your goods or services over the Web. Your site should include all the information visitors need to evaluate your products and the tools for them to purchase your products. Figure 32-2 shows a small web retailer's site.

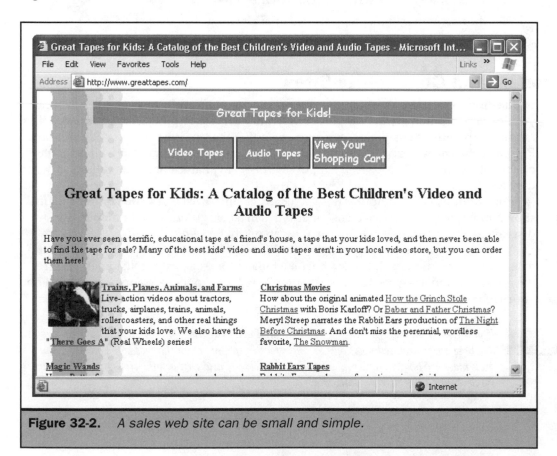

Figure 32-2.   *A sales web site can be small and simple.*

You have a number of options in setting up your sales site, though you should keep in mind that the security of transactions is extremely important. A customer's credit card number is far more likely to be stolen by a store clerk making minimum wage than by a hacker intercepting your e-mail, but you should still take every reasonable precaution to ensure that your customers' information is safe while in transit and when stored on your computers. Some customers refuse to order if the web site isn't secure. (They can tell by looking at the lock icon in their browser window.)

The easiest way to establish a sales site is to hire a web-hosting company to host the site for you. You'll need to provide the contents for the site and fulfill the orders yourself, but the hosting company takes care of your Internet security needs. In the following section, you'll learn enough about web security to evaluate a hosting company's services.

A number of software programs allow you to set up your stores with a minimum of original programming. Companies that offer this type of software include

- Alpha Software **www.onlinemerchant.com**
- Multiactive Technologies **www.ecbuilder.com**
- Storesonline **www.storesonline.com**

Support and Community Sites

In addition to selling, your web site can provide ongoing help to your customers. If your organization provides support or warranty service or otherwise has an ongoing relationship with its customers, consider providing that information on your web site. Putting technical information about your products on your site can help your customers during off-hours when your tech support staff isn't available and saves calls even when they are.

For example, Dell Computer hosts a technical support site at **support.dell.com** (as shown in Figure 32-3). When a customer types in a computer's serial number, the site displays support and upgrade information about that model.

You might want to host a message board for customers (or prospective customers) to ask questions and get answers. Other customers (or prospective customers) can read the questions and answers, too. See Chapter 29 for how to include a message board on your web site.

If you host a message board, monitor it constantly (at least once a day). You may need to delete spam, unrelated messages, or incorrect criticisms from the message board. Messages on a message board appear as part of your web site and can be embarrassing if they are incorrect or unrelated to your site

Figure 32-3. *The Web is an excellent medium for technical support.*

Selecting a Web Hosting Service

The most confusing step in selecting a web hosting service is finding one that offers secure services, shopping cart services, and other services that your e-commerce site might require. Fortunately, a number of easily accessible resources can help you find a web hosting service. Once you have a list of candidates, you can ask them pointed questions about what they will do for you.

Finding a Web Hosting Service

One place you can find web hosting services is on Yahoo: choose Business And Economy | Companies | Internet Services | Web Services | Hosting. From that starting point, you can search for hosting firms by region or get a complete list. Not all of the companies listed offer secure web sites, so visit each firm's web site, or contact the company in person to determine whether they offer the basic services you need to run your business on the Web. You can also find advertisements for hosting companies at the back of Internet industry publications. CNET reviews web hosting companies at **www.cnet.com/ internet/0-3799.html**.

Questions to Ask Potential Web Hosting Providers

Now that you have a list of companies that might host your sales site, ask the following questions to make sure they have sufficient resources to host your site.

- *Does the company offer a secure web server?* If not, move to the next company on your list.

- *How is the company connected to the Internet?* The best type of connection is a T3, an extremely high–capacity line, though multiple T1 lines are also acceptable. Choose a company with redundant connections, so if a line to one ISP goes down, plenty of bandwidth is still available from other sources.

- *Does the company have a Level Three digital certificate from a known certification authority?* A company needs a *digital certificate* to run a secure server. (See the section "Selling via Secure Servers" later in this chapter.) Well-established companies have a certificate from a certification authority. Not having one would not necessarily disqualify a firm from hosting your site, but it is better to find a company that does offer that extra level of assurance.

- *Does the company offer 24-hour live technical support?* Many smaller hosting companies do not have a live person answering phones around the clock, but your visitors may not always arrive during normal business hours. It is vital that your hosting company have someone on hand to receive calls informing them the site is unreachable or that something is broken.

- *What is the monthly fee?* The going rate for basic web hosting services is $20 to $40 per month. That price should include access to the secure web server, enough storage for your web site, and enough bandwidth so your visitors can browse your web site without your incurring additional charges.

- *How much storage is included?* The minimum amount of storage you should request for your site is 20MB, which should be enough for most smaller and medium-sized businesses. Additional storage can usually be purchased for a few dollars per month, so ask about that rate as well.

- *How much bandwidth is included?* In other words, what is the amount of data you can send and receive before the host starts charging extra? Most hosts allow from 3GB to 6GB of bandwidth usage, which should be plenty for the average business. If your site has lots of graphics or offers streaming audio or video, you can purchase more bandwidth. Web hosting companies usually charge extra for hosting streaming audio and video files.

■ *Can I use my own domain name?* If your firm has its own domain name (which it should), your web host provider should allow you to use it on your site. There may be a one-time setup fee to transfer your domain name to the Web hosting firm, but you should be able to negotiate it away.

■ *Can I update my site at any time?* You should be able to update your site at any time and as often as you like with no extra charge.

■ *How many e-mail addresses are included with the base price?* Many hosting firms provide ten or more e-mail addresses with your domain name, so you can receive mail as **info@***yourdomain***.com**, **sales@***yourdomain***.com**, and other addresses.

■ *Can I upgrade my account at any time?* Rather than your paying for extra bandwidth or storage, the hosting company should allow you to upgrade your account and reserve more storage and bandwidth for your site.

■ *How often is the site backed up?* Whether the site is backed up should not be an issue; the only question is how often. Many providers back up their sites every two or three days, though daily backups are preferable. Keep copies of everything you upload to your server.

■ *How are site statistics kept?* Your hosting company should make your site's visitor logs available to you, preferably in both raw and analyzed form. At the very least, your provider should tell you the number of times each file was accessed, the number of page views, and the number of visitors for a given day. These statistics should be updated every day. See Chapter 31 for information about web traffic logs.

■ *How long will it take to set up my site?* If you are uploading your own content, the site should be available the same day. If you are contracting with a firm to design and implement your site as well, the amount of time needed will depend on the complexity of your design.

■ *What CGI scripts are included? Can I run my own?* Most hosting companies have a library of CGI scripts, such as shopping carts and guest books, for you to use in your site. If you are confident you can write your own CGI scripts, ask if you will have the ability to augment your site with them.

■ *Can I use PHP or other server-side scripting?* See Chapter 28 for information on scripting languages, including PHP, that more advanced web sites may need to use.

Selling via Secure Servers

The best way to ensure that your web-based transactions are safe is to use a secure server.

What Is a Secure Server?

A *secure server* is a computer connected to the Internet with software that allows visitors to establish a secure (encrypted) link to your web server, safeguards user information on the server, and is difficult for even a determined attacker to break into. For a secure connection to be possible, both the user and the merchant must have the appropriate software in place.

The Internet and its transmission protocol, TCP/IP, were designed for efficiency and not security. Packets of information are sent "in the clear" and can be read by any computer, intended recipient or not. Web commerce entails sending sensitive financial information over a public network, so some care is required.

Enter cryptography. Using *public key encryption,* secure servers have built-in software to establish encrypted connections with other computers. The protocol used to establish these connections is the Secure Sockets Layer (SSL). The three major vendors of secure web servers are

- Microsoft Internet Information Services **www.microsoft.com/iis**
- AOL/Netscape Enterprise Server **enterprise.netscape.com**
- Apache **www.apache.org**

When someone visits your web site using Netscape Navigator or Internet Explorer, how do they establish an SSL connection? Fortunately, all recent versions of Netscape, Internet Explorer, Opera, iCab, and OmniWeb can establish SSL connections with secure web servers without the user needing to take any action.

Digital Certificates

As a user, however, you might want assurances that the people operating the secure server somewhere else on the Web and asking for your credit card number are who they say they are. Just as there's no foolproof way to guard against fraud in the real world, there's no 100 percent effective way to guard against fraud on the Web. To assure your visitors that you are a legitimate enterprise, you use digital certificates.

A *digital certificate* is a key pair created using public key cryptography. Unlike with PGP (Pretty Good Privacy, a widely used system for encrypting e-mail), which allows anyone to create a key pair, digital certificates can be created and issued only by *certification authorities,* bodies that verify the identity of the person or company requesting a digital certificate. Once generated, a digital certificate guarantees the identity of the certificate holder and is used like a key in the encryption process. The recipient can tell the message was signed by the certificate holder and can check the message against the public half of the key, maintained in a database by the certification authority.

Several levels of digital certificates are available, with the level depending on the amount of proof offered to establish the applicant's identity. One common scheme is as follows:

- **Level One** This level is a certificate tied to an e-mail address. The only check made is a return e-mail to that address to ensure it is valid. This level does not necessarily tie the e-mail address to an identifiable person or company.

- **Level Two** At this level, the certification authority asks for proof of an individual's identity, such as a driver's license, passport, or credit card. The information provided in the application is checked against common databases, such as those maintained by credit rating firms.

- **Level Three** This level is the highest level of assurance, normally reserved for companies and other permanent organizations. The applicant must supply three forms of identification to an authority such as a notary. Acceptable documents include a group's articles of incorporation and other public records.

If you are implementing your own web commerce site (rather than using a shopping cart service, described in the next section), you should seriously consider purchasing a Level Three certificate from a well-known certification authority. Having taken the time to register with a certification authority marks you as a serious company, not a fly-by-night organization. You should require the same of any company you hire to host your sales site for you.

A number of well-established certification authorities have web sites describing digital certificates in general and their products and services in particular. They include

- **VeriSign (www.verisign.com)** Generally considered to be the most ubiquitous certificate authority.

- **Thawte (www.thawte.com)** Thawte is owned by VeriSign, but they remain independent. They also offer a free e-mail certificate to anyone who wants one.

- **GTE CyberTrust (www.cybertrust.gte.com)** GTE's CyberTrust system is now only available by appointment, but if your needs are big, these guys are big enough to handle it.

Shopping Cart Systems

While your visitors shop at your web site, they may want to browse around and see everything before "checking out." Of course, if they see something they want to buy, they should be able to keep it on hand and purchase it when they leave. In other words, they need an electronic *shopping cart* to carry the items they want to purchase with them until they are ready to leave.

There are two ways to get a shopping cart on your site: installing software or using a service. Either way, you add code to the page on your web site, and you may experience some problems before getting it worked out entirely. Of course, the effort is worth it because eventually you will be able to offer your customers a convenience. Just think of the sites you've walked away from that required you to print, fill out, and mail an order form, and you'll see the major benefits of a shopping cart system.

The next two sections cover shopping cart services and software, respectively. Keep in mind that if you want to accept payment by credit card (the most common type of online payment), you will also need to get a *merchant account* with a bank or monetary services provider. If you already have a bank account and credit card, it should be easy. Most banks even provide Internet-based transaction services these days.

Shopping Cart Services

For smaller e-commerce sites, it's often easier to simply use a service provider, as opposed to getting, installing, and configuring your own shopping cart software. Once you set up an account with the shopping cart provider and meet their requirements for processing transactions (which are different for each provider), you can add the code to your web site and start selling securely. Each shopping cart service provides the HTML or other code that you need to add your web pages in order to use their service.

When choosing a shopping cart system, look for a system that can calculate various types of shipping (like USPS, UPS, and FedEx), provides SSL encryption, is easy to use (both for you and for your customers), supports your pricing schemes (whatever quantity discounts or other price breaks you want to offer), calculates sales tax by state (for U.S. orders), and e-mails you the orders using secure e-mail (because they contain customer and credit card information). You might also want to use a service that makes it easy for customers to pay using PayPal or other online payment systems. If you sell internationally, make sure that the system can handle international shipping and currencies. Prices for shopping cart systems vary: some charge a flat annual fee, whereas others charge by the number of orders you receive.

Here are some shopping cart services to consider:

■ AmeriCart   **www.americart.com**

■ VirtualCart   **www.vcart.com**

■ CoolCart   **www.coolcart.com**

For other services, start at the Google Web Directory (**directory.google.com**), and choose Business | E-Commerce | Services | Hosting | Shopping Carts.

Shopping Cart Software

Most secure web site hosting companies include shopping cart software in their web commerce packages, though you might need to provide your own software if you can't find a hosting company that meets all of your other needs and offers that software. A number of companies offer shopping cart software for web commerce, including these:

- **OsCommerce (www.oscommerce.com)** offers an open-source shopping cart system that works with the Apache web server, the PHP web scripting language, and the MySQL database server.

- **Mountain Networks (www.mountain-net.com)** offers a complete shopping cart system for a one-time fee of $499. This price includes one hour of installation support time.

- **AHG (www.ahg.com/software.htm)** offers several shopping cart packages ranging in price from $270 to $1,800.

When choosing shopping cart software, consider the factors about shopping cart services listed in the preceding section. Also make sure that the package runs on your web server, which may run the Windows 2000, Windows XP, UNIX, Linux, or other operating system.

Accepting Payments from Customers

To take payments for goods and services over the Web, you can ask customers to send you checks and money orders, or you can even have a credit card machine installed in your home or office. However, most people are either not willing to take the time to send you a check or money order or don't want to bother with having to call, possibly long distance. Your best bet is to arrange to accept credit cards by applying for a merchant account with a credit card service provider (or with your local bank). You may also want to accept payments with Internet-based payment systems like PayPal, described in the section "Alternative Payment Service Providers" later in this chapter.

Credit Card Service Providers

Most, but not all, consumers in the United States and Canada have some form of credit card. Your business can sign up for a credit card service, which processes credit card charges. These services charge you a 2 to 4 percent processing fee, depending on your charge volume and the average charge. (You pay a smaller percentage if your average charge is higher.) Most credit card servers are now online as well.

When choosing a credit card service, make sure that they accept all four common credit cards (Visa, MasterCard, American Express, or Discover), that their fees are fair, and that they can process charges from you over the Internet (so you don't have to install and pay for a separate phone line and credit card charge box). A good service will have a secure web site from which you can submit new charges and review your old charges.

Here are some credit card processing services that handle Visa, MasterCard, American Express, Discover, ATM/debit/check cards, and other credit cards over the Internet:

- **Authorize.Net (www.authorize.net)** also handles electronic checks.

- **Cardservice International (www.cardservice.com)** also offers electronic check services and web site shopping carts. These guys have been around the block a few times, have a strong reputation in the food service and retail markets, and are developing a good reputation on the Internet as well.

- **iBill (www.ibill.com)** refuses to process payments for certain items such as drugs, firearms, alcoholic beverages, pornography, phone cards, or airline tickets. (See details at their web site.) iBill does not handle electronic checks, but they do have a unique service, Web900, that allows customers to pay by calling a 900 number and being charged through their phone company.

> **Note** *All three of these services also offer foreign currency options for their merchant accounts.*

Alternative Payment Service Providers

For those customers who do not have credit cards, or who prefer not to use them on the Internet, here are other ways to pay online:

- **PayPal (www.paypal.com)**   This popular system claims that you can pay anyone who has an e-mail address. To use it, a customer signs up for a free PayPal personal account. To get money into your PayPal account (so that you can make payments from it), you provide checking account or credit card information. To make a payment, a customer goes to the PayPal web site, logs on, clicks Send Money, and fills out a form with the merchant's e-mail address and the amount to pay. The system works well. If you make payments that require PayPal to charge your credit card, you pay a fee (which makes sense because PayPal has to pay a small percentage to its credit card processing service to charge your card).

- **PayByCheck.com (www.paybycheck.com)**   This deceptively simple system allows you to take actual checks over the Web. The system uses a form that mimics the appearance of a check. You or your customer type in bank, routing, and amount information. PayByCheck verifies this information and uses it to create a paper check that it mails to its bank to debit funds from the purchaser's account. However, fees are much higher than PayPal's, including $10 per month and about $1 per check.

- **Web900 (www.ibill.com)**   iBill offers the unique Web900 service. They will bill people using their home phone for anything from $2 to $35 per call.

> | Note | *Be sure to read the user agreements when you sign up for these accounts. Make sure you know whether you will incur fees for making or accepting payments and whether restrictions exist on how you can use the account. If you are a merchant, expect reasonable fees—these services have to make money, too.*

Auction Sites

Auctions are popular on the Internet—just look at the success of eBay (**www.ebay.com**), the Internet's largest auction site. eBay and Yahoo Auctions (**auctions.yahoo.com**) are the largest sites, but there are many others. The vast majority are for specialty and niche sales.

How Auctions Work

What is an Internet auction? It's the same as an auction at Sotheby's or a county fair, except there's no person with a gavel shouting and pointing. Items are made available for bidding by sellers, with a date and time when the auction will end (usually from two to nine days after the start of the auction). Bidders can bid on items by telling the system how much they are willing to pay. Whoever has the high bid at the end of the auction wins the product. The seller and high bidder then arrange (usually by e-mail) for payment and shipping; the auction site usually doesn't get involved once the auction is over. Figure 32-4 shows an eBay auction in progress.

Some auction sites include *proxy bidding*. This system allows the bidder to tell the auction system the maximum amount that you plan to bid. The auction site software then automatically bids on your behalf, bidding only as much as required, and not going over your maximum. For example, if you specified a maximum bid of $10 for a used book, the bid increment was $1 (that is, each bid must be at least $1 above the last bid), and someone else bid $2 for the book, the auction software would place a bid of $3 in your name. Proxy bidding allows the auction to go on without requiring you to hover over the computer, waiting for others to bid. eBay and Yahoo Auctions both offer proxy bidding.

Some auction sites (including eBay) also offer online payments for auctions. That is, they accept credit card payments from buyers and remit the money (less a handling fee) to the seller. This service is useful for sellers who don't otherwise have a way of taking credit cards, although PayPal, described in the section "Alternative Payment Service Providers" earlier in this chapter, is a good alternative.

Internet auctions can have other variations. Some eBay auctions have a Buy It Now button that allows you to grab the item, ending the auction immediately, if you are willing to pay a price set by the seller. You may not get the lowest possible price, but if you really want the item, you don't have to wait, or take a chance on the price rising above the set price.

> | Note | *Most auction sites require verification by credit card—some to sell, some to buy, others both.*

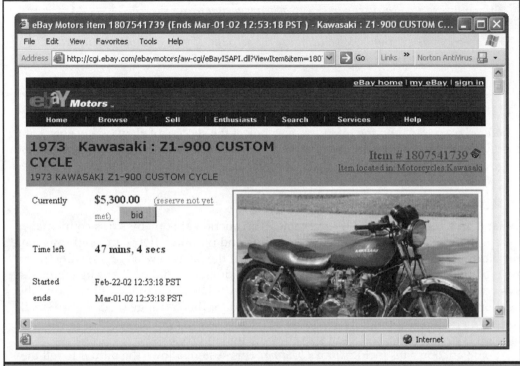

Figure 32-4. *You can bid on this motorcycle over the Web, but you only have 47 minutes left!*

Finding Internet Auction Sites

A good place to start looking for auctions is the Internet Auction List (**www.internetauctionlist.com**), which does its best to list all auction sites on the Internet. For auctions that specialize in a particular product, use a search engine like Google.com to search for "auction" and the type of product you are interested in.

Selling and Bidding

Before you can either list an item for sale, or bid on an item, most auction sites require you to sign up for an account, which is usually free. eBay pioneered a system of feedback ratings, so that the more successful auctions they complete, reliable buyers and sellers acquire higher and higher rating numbers.

To list an item in an auction, you sign in using your user name and password for the site, and provide information about the item you want to sell, including a description, minimum price, and (optionally) a picture.

To bid on an item, you sign in using your auction site user name and password and type your bid (or for systems with proxy bidding, your maximum bid).

Tips for Buying from Auction Sites

Here are some things to watch out for when bidding on items at online auction sites:

- *Check the seller's online rating.* If the auction site uses a system where buyers and sellers can rate each other, check the sellers rating, which should be overwhelmingly positive if you want to do business. Be wary of sellers with little or no selling history (for example, on eBay, sellers with only one or two buyer feedbacks).

- *Check shipping costs.* The price you got may be fair, but the shipping costs may be outrageous. The seller should explain the shipping charges in the item listing.

- *Check payment options.* If you buy much from online auctions, it pays to open a PayPal account, as described in the section "Alternative Payment Service Providers" earlier in this chapter. If the seller requires a money order, the money order fee (about $1) increases your cost. Some sellers wait until personal checks clear before shipping merchandise.

- *If someone doesn't come through, complain.* If a seller never ships the goods, or ships something that's substantially different from what was listed, complain first to the seller. (They may have made an honest mistake.) If the seller doesn't make things right, complain to the auction site, or give the seller a negative rating.

- *For expensive items, consider an escrow service.* Some auction sites offer an escrow service, in which the seller sends the item to the escrow service, the buyer sends the money to the escrow service, and only when both have been received does the escrow service send the money to the seller and the merchandise to the buyer. Escrow services cost money, though.

Consignment Sites

Consignment sites are more like online stores, except individuals interested in selling their stuff provide the merchandise. For example, you might want to sell an old Afghan windshield cozy you no longer use (you have a new chamois one), but you want a specific price for it and have no wish to haggle. You go to the consignment site, register, enter information about the windshield cozy with a picture, set some options including payment and shipping preferences, and click to add your item. The item now appears as part of the merchandise at the web site. Later, someone visits the web site in search of an Afghan windshield cozy and finds your item, as well as half a dozen others. If your item has the best price or the most appealing description, the visitor buys it.

Consignments are more like putting something up for sale, so most consignment sites are designed like web stores. You look around, select categories, and drop items into a shopping cart. When you are done, you check out. The consignment site collects the payment from the buyer (usually via credit card) and remits the money to the seller (usually by check, or by crediting the seller's bank account).

The following are a few large consignment sites:

- **half.com (www.half.com)** They offer books, videos, CDs, electronic equipment, and more. (See Figure 32-5.)

- **Yahoo Warehouse (warehouse.shopping.yahoo.com)** They sell books, computers, videos, electronics, CDs, and video games.

- **KinderCloset (www.kindercloset.com)** They offer children's clothing.

- **Amazon.com (www.amazon.com)** If you have a book you want to sell, you can list it on Amazon for free, and you pay a commission only when someone buys the book.

Tip *See the list of tips for buying from online auction sites in the previous section. Many apply to online consignment shops, too.*

Figure 32-5. *half.com* is a consignment site where you can buy and sell new and used items.

The Complete Reference

Internet

Part VI

File Transfer and Downloading

The Complete Reference

Internet

Chapter 33

File Transfer by Web, FTP, and Peer-to-Peer

Y ou transfer files all the time on the Internet, without even thinking about it. When you browse the Web, files are transferred to your web browser. When you send e-mail, files are transferred across the Internet to the message's recipient. Web and e-mail programs, however, are designed to handle a few particular file types, types that they know how to display or create. They also use special communications languages, called *protocols*, designed specifically for efficient transfer of those files.

Sometimes, however, you just want to get or send "any old file." It might be a word processor document, a spreadsheet, a photograph, or a program. To transfer the file across the Internet, you have several choices:

- Send the file as e-mail.

- Run your browser and click links on web pages to transfer the file.

- Run file transfer software specially designed to transfer "any old file." This software uses *File Transfer Protocol (FTP)*.

- Use a new feature of Windows XP called *Web Folders*. Web Folders provides access to files on web servers and on FTP servers from Windows Explorer.

- Run a peer-to-peer (P2P) file-sharing program like Gnutella to share files directly from your hard drive.

This chapter discusses how these different ways of transferring files work and the differences in using these methods. You'll also learn how to use telnet programs to log into a web or FTP server to manage your files. We also discuss some of the questions and issues that arise around file transfer on the Internet: ensuring proper transmission of files, avoiding viruses and other file contamination, and observing property rights.

Transferring Files by E-Mail

E-mail is a method of transferring files between individuals on the Internet or sending them to a specific list of people. E-mail is easy to use and well suited for smaller attachments, especially if you zip them first, but FTP or web transfer is better for larger attachments or for executable file types. Most e-mail programs make attaching files to messages very simple; you just need to attach the file and send.

Because e-mail was originally designed for text only, attachments need to be converted to a text-like data format before sending, using a process called *encoding*. All newer Windows e-mail programs handle the conversion automatically, and utilities exist to encode attachments for use with older e-mail programs. There are three different types of encoding, and both the sender and receiver must use the same method. Many Windows e-mail programs support all three methods, which are

- **Multipurpose Internet Mail Extensions (MIME)**   Increasingly, MIME is the Internet standard.

- **Uuencoding**   A method with roots in UNIX.
- **BinHex**   A method commonly used on Macintosh computers.

These methods are necessary because e-mail protocols were originally designed to handle only plain text messages. When a file is "attached" to an e-mail message, it is actually appended to the text message with a header that tells the receiving e-mail program how to decode it. The e-mail program trims off the remaining data and converts it to the appropriate file. If your e-mail program doesn't decode the message, the body of the message will contain large blocks of random text at the end.

If you use Outlook Express, you can see what an encoded attachment looks like. First select a message that has an attachment; then select File | Properties | Details tab and click the Message Source button. Scroll toward the end of the message until you see a block of random text like this:

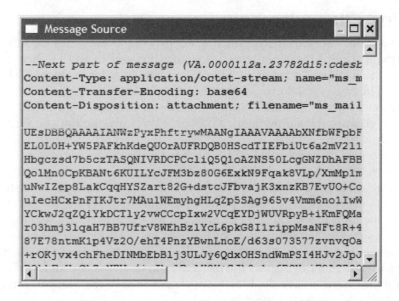

This sample shows a MIME-encoded attachment. However, attachments encoded with uuencode and BinHex have the same type of random text in the message source.

If you do receive such a file, examine the first few lines of text that follow the e-mail message for the words "uuencode" or "binhex" as a clue to the encoding method. Then check to see if your e-mail program allows you to choose that method. If not, ask the sender to resend the message using a different attachment encoding scheme. Another alternative is to download from the Web one of the uudecode or BinHex decoding utility programs available, such as WinCode. Save the e-mail message as a text file, open that text file in your decoding utility, and the utility will reconstruct the original file. For the full details of transferring files by e-mail, see Chapter 7.

Note
Many corporations and individuals block many types of e-mail attachments or delete messages containing attachments to reduce the risk of computer virus infections. Many e-mail mailing lists strip attachments from messages posted to the list. If you need to send attachments, it may be better to upload them to a web or FTP server and provide the URL so that others can download the file. AOL users can attach files to their messages to non-AOL users, and they usually arrive as MIME attachments, but AOL attachment support can be spotty.

Transferring Files via the Web

By far the most popular form of file transfer is to download files from the Web, especially free or trial software (described more fully in the next chapter).

Downloading Files with Your Browser

How does your browser handle this file transfer process? Sometimes the link you click to begin downloading a file actually redirects your browser to an FTP server, which is described in the section "Transferring Files Using File Transfer Protocol (FTP)" later in this chapter. The browser then turns over the job to its internal FTP client software (or to the operating system's FTP client utility) to transfer the file. You can browse other sites on the Web during the download, although your browsing may be slowed by the ongoing download process.

If the link you click to download a file does not redirect your browser to an FTP server, the web server delivers the file itself. When a web browser begins to receive a file from a web server, it examines the file's type. It either looks for information from the server as to the MIME type of the file (for example, text/HTML for web page files), or it looks at the file's extension (for example, .gif for pictures). Browsers focus on displaying files, not saving them, so if the browser knows how to display a given type of file, it does so. If it does not know how to display the file, it checks to see if it has any helper software that can display the file: a plug-in or a viewer program. Failing that, it asks you if you want to save the file. If you choose to save the file, you can proceed to browse other sites while the file downloads.

Browsers are increasingly clever about recognizing file types, however, so they attempt to display or play a file rather than simply save it. Some browsers can recognize a file as being a plug-in or other add-on component for the browser itself. They can then automatically install that component, given your approval, or they recognize that they are receiving a file that is executable (a program) on your computer and ask you if you want to run the program once it downloads. Some browsers can check with your computer about what program it associates with certain file types and run that program—even within the browser window itself. Increasingly, a browser, recognizing that it lacks the necessary viewer or plug-in to display a file, offers to download the required software.

For example, if you click a link that downloads a PDF (Adobe Portable Document Format) file, your browser may let you know that you need a plug-in (Adobe Acrobat Reader) to display the file and may help you download and install the plug-in.

Using a Web Server as a File Server

If you have a web server (or have the use of one), you can use it to distribute files. For instance, you can use it as a drop-box for other people to pick up files at their leisure, if they want them. To make the file available, you transfer the file to the Web server by using FTP (as described in the section "Transferring Files Using File Transfer Protocol (FTP)" later in this chapter). Then you can either link to the file from a web page or simply give people the URL for the file.

Windows XP Professional includes both a web and FTP server. To install it, choose Start | Control Panel | Add/Remove Programs | Add/Remove Windows Components. In the Windows Components Wizard window, select Internet Information Services (IIS), click the Details button, and select the File Transfer Protocol (FTP) Service and World Wide Web Service check boxes to install the FTP and web servers.

However, the terms of service for most broadband connections prohibit you from running servers, including FTP and web servers. If you use a dial-up line, you face the problem that your computer has a different IP address (described in Chapter 1) each time that you connect.

Transferring Files Using Windows XP Web Folders

Windows Explorer includes the ability to create locations in your My Network Places windows for FTP or web servers. These locations are called *Web Folders,* and they enable you to connect to FTP and web servers and to browse folders or files using Windows Explorer. The feature works on web servers that support the Web Extender Client (WEC) protocol and FrontPage extensions or use WebDAV protocol and Internet Information Services (IIS). It also works with most FTP servers. Once you are connected using Web Folders, the files on the FTP or web server appear in a Windows Explorer window, and you can copy, rename, and delete files as if they were on your own computer.

Note   *To connect to an FTP or web server using Web Folders, you need to have read and write access to the server.*

Several web servers, including MSN's, use the protocols needed to add a Web Folder to your My Network Places window. (Microsoft owns MSN, so this is hardly surprising.) In fact, Windows steers you toward MSN's servers, and you need to select Choose Another Network Location if you want to use any other server. If you use MSN and Windows XP, you may already have a My Web Sites On MSN Web Folder in your My Network Places window. Windows XP Pro users can also set up an IIS web server and share files using Web Folders from their computer.

To begin using Web Folders, you need to create a shortcut in My Network Places to a folder on an FTP web server.

1. Choose Start | My Network Places to see your My Network Places window. (If My Network Places isn't on your Start menu, choose Start | My Computer and click My Network Places under Other Places in the Task pane.)

2. Click Add A Network Place in the Network Tasks section of the Task pane. You see the Add Network Place Wizard. Click Next to move from screen to screen in the Wizard window. If you are not connected to the Internet at this time, Windows prompts you to connect.

3. The wizard asks, "Where do you want to create this network place?" (See Figure 33-1.) Your options are MSN Communities (Microsoft's MSN-based web server) or Choose Another Network Location, which can be either a web or FTP server.

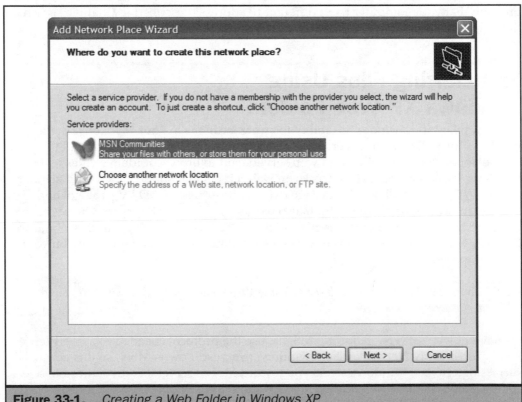

Figure 33-1. *Creating a Web Folder in Windows XP*

Note   *MSN Communities is a free service offered to MSN Passport users. In addition to the three megabytes of file storage space it provides, you can also use it to host a small personal web site and to create a mailing list. Additional storage space can be purchased.*

4. If you choose MSN Communities, you see a screen to create a new community or to use an existing community, if you created one previously. The next screens ask for a name and description for the community, and present options to keep the site private and unlisted in the community directory. Finally, the wizard asks if you want a shortcut in Favorites.

5. If you want to create a Web Folder on a network, web server, or FTP server, the process is just as easy. Type in the URL or browse to find the location and add a name for the Web Folder.

When the wizard finishes, you see an icon for your new shortcut in the My Network Places window. Figure 33-2 shows a shortcut for a user's MSN web sites and for several other web servers.

When you double-click the Web Folder shortcut, a window appears showing the files and folders (directories) on the web or FTP server, as shown in Figure 33-3.

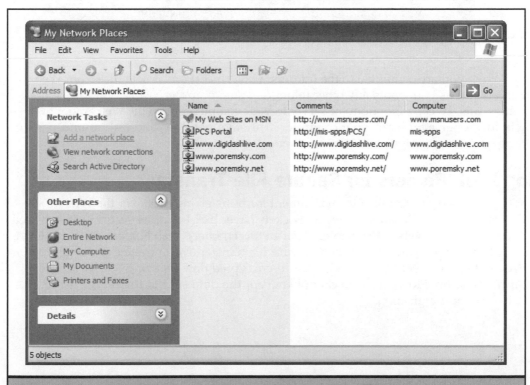

Figure 33-2.   *Web Folders can connect to web servers or FTP servers—either way, double-click to display the files on the server.*

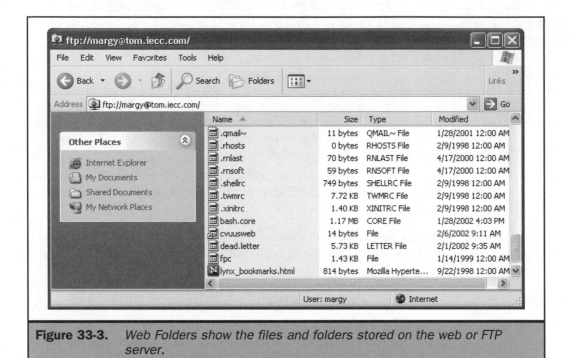

Figure 33-3. *Web Folders show the files and folders stored on the web or FTP server.*

When you are connected to the Internet, you can add and delete files from Web Folders just as you would any other folder on your computer, using Windows Explorer commands. To copy files from the server to your computer, open the Web Folder in one window, open a folder on your computer in another window, and use cut-and-paste or drag-and-drop to move files between them.

Using Web Folders for Secure File Transfer

Web Folders provide a secure environment for transferring files over the Web (few FTP clients or servers support Secure Sockets Layer [SSL] or other secure systems—see "Logging into a Web or FTP Server" later in this chapter). Web Folders, or WebDAV, is a file transfer protocol that supports secure file transfer over intranets and the Internet. Web Folders protects your password and encrypted data by using SSL or Windows authentication. However, you cannot encrypt the data sent to the server using Windows authentication.

On the other hand, because you are putting your web pages on a web server for all the world to see, file transfer security isn't usually a big issue. If it is, see the sidebar "Secure FTP" later in this chapter.

Transferring Files Using Peer-to-Peer File Sharing Utilities

Napster made file sharing popular and easy to do, using a technique known as *peer-to-peer* file transfer (often abbreviated as *P2P*). Although Napster, KaZaA, Morpheus, Gnutella, and other peer-to-peer systems are mainly for sharing MP3s (as described in the section on peer-to-peer music services in Chapter 22), other peer-to-peer services can be used for sharing any type of file.

When you use a peer-to-peer program, you don't need a web site to upload your files to. Instead, the peer-to-peer program on your computer connects to peer-to-peer programs running on other people's computers and transfers files directly, without passing through a server. As a result, peer-to-peer programs are very popular. However, most peer-to-peer programs do not provide secure access or the ability to control who downloads the files. For this reason, the use of these programs is best left for music, graphics, programs, and other files that don't contain personal or corporate information.

Popular P2P programs include BearShare and FileNavigator, which can be found at **www.gnuteliiums.com**. These are known as *Gnutella clients* because they use the Gnutella network to search for the file you want and use Gnutella's protocols for connecting to other Gnutella clients to transfer the files. Gnutella clients are like a mini search engine and file transfer system in one program. You use the same program both to search for and download file from other people's computers and to share your own files on the Gnutella Network. When you execute a search, the Gnutella client transmits your request to everyone in your Gnutella Network, and if any other Gnutella client has anything matching your search, you can download it. For example, Figure 33-4 shows a search using the keyword "vacation" that turned up songs, video clips, digital photos, documents, and web browser cookies with "vacation" in the title.

Note   *If you use a file sharing utility, be sure you set the options to share only specific file types and only files contained in specific folders. Otherwise, you may make every file on your hard drive available to anyone using a peer-to-peer program, including private or sensitive Word documents, checkbook files, tax returns, and other files. For this reason you should remove all file types from the share list except those you specifically want to share.*

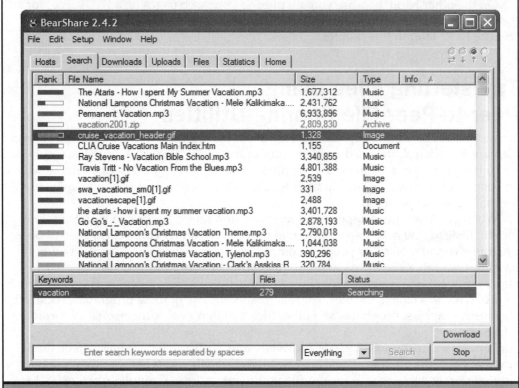

Figure 33-4.   *BearShare, a Gnutella client, searches for files on other people's computers.*

Transferring Files Using File Transfer Protocol (FTP)

FTP is designed for distributing files. Like the Web, it uses a *client-server* system, in which files are stored at a central computer and transferred between that computer and other computers. The central computer runs software called an *FTP server,* and the other computers run software called an *FTP client* (or *FTP program*). Using FTP, the client requests a file transfer (either an upload or a download), and then the client and server exchange data.

FTP communication is always between clients and servers, never between clients: just because two people have FTP client software doesn't mean they can exchange files with each other. One person might send a file to a server and the other person might then download that file, but a server must still be in the middle.

FTP Clients

FTP client software can be a separate, stand-alone program, such as Ipswich Software's popular WS_FTP (described in the section "Using Windows-Based FTP Clients Like WS_FTP" later in this chapter). FTP client software can also be built into other software. In fact, FTP client capability is incorporated in most popular web browsers, including Netscape Navigator, Internet Explorer, and others and is included as a command-line utility program in most operating systems (including Windows).

The FTP client incorporated into browsers provides basic FTP capabilities and works fine for downloading files from most FTP servers. You can also use browsers for uploading files to FTP servers if only basic FTP capabilities are needed.

Stand-alone FTP client software, whether a commercial program or an FTP utility provided as part of the operating system, generally offers more flexibility. Stand-alone FTP clients can help you deal with the less conventional configurations of FTP servers, with the various types of files, and with managing the files and directories at both ends of the transfer. FTP clients may rely on text commands (like the FTP program that comes with Windows) or may provide a graphical user interface with buttons and windows. Commercial programs sometimes also offer useful troubleshooting utilities.

FTP Servers

The Internet contains thousands of FTP servers. Many organizations that run web servers also run FTP servers to handle the distribution of various files: free programs, product documentation, or data files. Often, when visitors to a web site click a link to download something, the link actually redirects the visitor's browser to an FTP server. (You can tell that such a redirection has happened if you notice that the address your browser is using for the download begins with *ftp://* instead of *http://*.) For most Internet users today, such subtle redirections are their only exposure to FTP.

FTP servers supply other files besides those listed on web pages. In general, the other files on FTP servers support the needs of the more technical users of the Internet, such as UNIX users, network administrators, and software developers and testers.

Some files on FTP servers may be accessible to the general public, whereas others are accessible only by private users such as customers or members of the organization that runs the server. On many FTP servers at educational and nonprofit organizations, public access is a service due only to the generosity of that organization.

To separate the general public from the more private, privileged users, every user of an FTP server must log onto that server with a user name and password. If the server supports public access, members of the public log on using the login name *anonymous,* and either no password or the user's e-mail address as the password. For that reason, public servers are usually called *anonymous FTP servers.* Private users who log on using assigned names and passwords usually have access to additional folders (directories) that the public can't see. When you use a browser to access an FTP server, it automatically performs an anonymous login for you unless you direct it otherwise.

Most FTP servers run on variations of the UNIX operating system, which stores files in folders (like Windows and Macs). Unlike Windows and Macs, each file and folder has an owner and has permissions that control who can read, write, and change the file or folder. When you connect to a server, you see whichever folders your level of privilege permits you to see and use. Based on your user name and password, the FTP server allows you access to specific files and folders, and you may be able to see the files listed in a folder, download the files, put new files into the folder, or change existing files. Most FTP servers have a folder named pub (for *public*) that contains files for public downloading.

Transferring Files of Different Types

The FTP client and server don't need to know much about what type of file you are transferring. FTP has two modes of sending files, however: *ASCII mode* (or *Text mode*) and *Binary mode* (or *Image mode*):

- **ASCII (or Text) mode**   When transferring text files (including HTML files), use ASCII mode. Different computer systems use different characters to indicate the ends of lines. In ASCII mode, the FTP software automatically adjusts line endings for the system to which the file is transferred.

- **Binary (or Image) mode**   When transferring files that consist of anything but unformatted text, use Binary mode (also called Image mode). In Binary mode, the FTP software does not make any changes to the contents of the file during transfer. Use Binary mode when transferring graphics files, audio files, video files, programs, or any kind of file other than plain text.

Finding Files on FTP Servers

Many popular shareware and freeware FTP clients include a directory of public FTP sites from which you can download programs. Some include the capability to search those sites for files by name. However, you can also find files on FTP servers by using web search engines because of the links to FTP files now offered on web pages.

Running Your Own FTP Server

Most Internet users do not have a sufficiently broad audience for their files to need to run an FTP server of their own. Instead, they generally distribute their files by e-mail. Windows XP Professional includes an FTP server, and you can find FTP server software at many software sites, but unless you are permanently connected to the Internet, your users would have to know when you were connected. In addition, there are security issues with allowing other people access to your computer. To maintain security, an FTP server allows you to limit access to certain folders for certain users.

If you do need to be able to make files accessible to other people on demand, your ISP may allow you to maintain a folder on the ISP's FTP server. An alternative is to place files on your web site, if you have one. To understand the issues in distributing files from a web server, see the section "Downloading Files with Your Browser," earlier in this chapter.

Basic FTP Procedure

Whatever FTP client you use, you begin by running the FTP client and connecting to the FTP server. Then you transfer files and disconnect.

Connecting to the FTP Server

To connect to an FTP server, you tell your FTP client the host name of the server (for example, **rtfm.mit.edu**). The FTP client connects to the server and prompts you for a user name and password. You can log into an FTP server in one of two ways:

- If you have an account on the FTP server, you log in with a user name and password. You can access all the files that your user name gives you permission to use.

- If you don't have an account on the FTP server, you can log on anonymously. In anonymous FTP, you or your client program supplies **anonymous** as your user name and your e-mail address as your password (as a courtesy for the server's log records).

Once you have logged into an FTP server, the server may display welcoming and instructional text about using the server. You might see those messages, which start with three-digit numbers, or your client program may ignore them or intercept them and substitute its own messages or other indicators. For example, when you have transferred a file, you might see the message "226 Transfer Complete," or you may see a dialog box saying the same thing in other words.

Transferring Files

FTP servers typically contain many different directories (folders). Once you are connected to an FTP server, you select a particular folder, called the *current working directory,* from which you will download, or to which you will upload, files. If you have permission to do so, you may be able to create additional folders, rename folders, or delete them.

When you transfer a file—by either uploading or downloading—you use one of two modes, binary or text, as described in the section "Transferring Files of Different Types" earlier in this chapter. Your client program may choose the mode automatically, based on the file's extension, or you may need to choose the mode yourself.

Disconnecting from the Server

When you have finished using an FTP site, you disconnect from that site (or your FTP client disconnects when you exit the program). Some FTP clients allow you to connect to several FTP servers at once; disconnecting from one server doesn't affect your connection to other servers.

Updating Your Web Site

FTP is the usual means of transferring files from your personal computer to the web server that stores your own web site, or a web site on which you are a permitted contributor. Such transfers use private, rather than anonymous FTP: they require a user name and password.

Frequently, the FTP server to which you upload your web pages begins with *www*, not *ftp*. For example, if you are updating your web site at **www.gurus.com**, you may connect to the FTP server at **ftp.gurus.com**. You may be assigned a directory on the FTP server in which only you have the ability to add, delete, or rename files or folders. The web server may allow you to give other people permission to change the files in your directory.

Using Web Browsers as FTP Clients

Many browsers, including Netscape Navigator and Internet Explorer, include FTP client software that can be used for downloading files from most FTP servers. Some browsers can also upload files. Browsers provide only basic file management capabilities; their purpose is for fast and easy access to files via FTP.

Connecting to FTP Servers

To connect to an FTP server, type the URL of the FTP server into the browser's Location or Address box. To use anonymous FTP, you create the URL by prefixing the FTP server name with **ftp://**, like this:

```
ftp://rtfm.mit.edu
```

The browser supplies a user ID and password that satisfy the server's anonymous login requirements.

For private FTP servers, where you have a user name and password, type the URL into your browser in the following form:

```
ftp://userID:password@servername
```

Replace *userID* with your user name on the FTP server. Replace *password* with your password on the FTP server. Replace *servername* with the name of the FTP server. For instance, if you had private FTP privileges on **ftp.gurus.com**, your assigned user name was *reader*, and your password was *readit2u*, you would enter this URL:

```
ftp://reader:readit2u@ftp.gurus.com
```

*This entire URL, including your password, is stored in the browser's history file, so someone else using your computer could access your FTP site. To avoid placing your password in the URL, Netscape Navigator and some other browsers let you omit the password, as in **ftp://reader@ftp.gurus.com**, and prompt you for the password once the server is contacted.*

If you know the folder to which you want to connect at the server (whether you are using private or anonymous FTP), you can append the folder with a slash to the end of the URL. For instance, **ftp://rtfm.mit.edu/pub** connects you to the pub (public) folder of the anonymous **rtfm.mit.edu** FTP server, as shown in Figure 33-5.

Once you are connected, your browser displays directory names and filenames as a list of links. To open a directory, click its link.

*If you have an FTP program installed, typing an **ftp://** URL into Internet Explorer may cause Windows to run your FTP program to connect to the FTP server.*

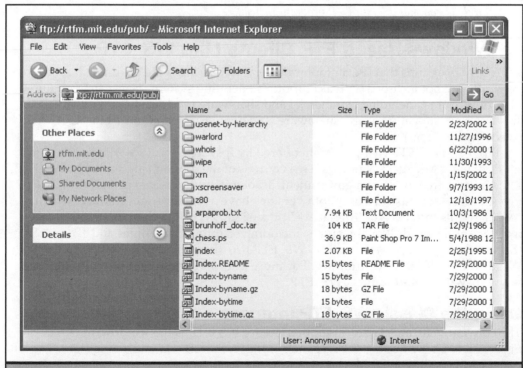

Figure 33-5.   *Your browser can connect to an anonymous FTP server.*

Downloading Files

To download a file, click or double-click it (depending on the browser). The browser may prompt you for a name and location on your computer. If, however, the file is a type normally displayed by the browser or any of the viewers or plug-ins with which it is configured, the browser downloads and displays the file, rather than prompting you for a filename and location. To store the file rather than display it, right-click the file and choose Copy To Folder or Save As to save the file.

Uploading Files

Internet Explorer can also upload files (assuming your user name on the FTP server gives you permission to do so). After you have opened the folder to which you want to copy a file, simply drag and drop the file into the browser window. IE may display a prompt asking you if you want to upload the files; click Yes and IE performs the operation.

Uploading files with browsers is rarely done; although browsers can upload files, few web sites use this feature. If you need to upload files, use Web Folders, your web editor's upload command, or an FTP program instead.

Using Windows-Based FTP Clients Like WS_FTP

FTP client programs that use a graphical user interface are quite common, but they generally are not included with a computer's operating system. They can be acquired in various forms, including commercial and shareware products from a variety of sources. You can get freeware, shareware, and demo FTP programs from TUCOWS (**www.tucows.com**).

WS_FTP is an FTP client program offered by Ipswitch, Inc. (**www.ipswitch.com**), for PCs under Microsoft Windows. Two versions of the program are available: WS_FTP LE, available free for certain government, academic, and personal users, and WS_FTP Pro (not free) for business use. Both versions have a similar user interface, which Ipswitch calls the "classic" interface. With version 7, WS_FTP Pro has a modernized interface and has additional features, including scripting capabilities and 128-bit SSL (Secure Sockets Layer) encryption. WS_FTP Pro also includes an option to use a Windows Explorer-style interface. For more information about both versions, see **www.ipswitch.com/Products/WS_FTP**.

Using the Classic WS_FTP Interface

The conventional, or "classic" user interface for WS_FTP is the window shown in Figure 33-6. The window has two panels—one on the left and one on the right. The left panel displays files and folders on your PC (the *local system*); the right panel displays files and folders on the FTP server (the *remote system*).

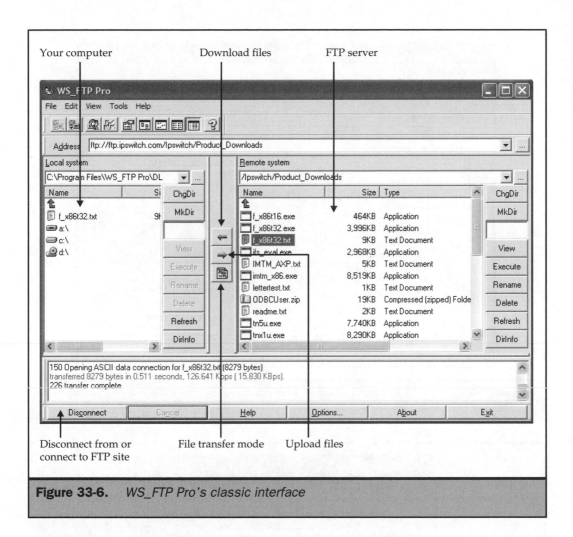

Your computer   Download files   FTP server

Figure 33-6.   *WS_FTP Pro's classic interface*

Launching and Connecting

To start WS_FTP, choose Start | Programs | WS_FTP Pro (or WS_FTP LE), unless you installed the program in a different folder. The main window appears. On top of the main window, you see the Connection dialog box (shown in Figure 33-7) or the Session Properties dialog box (shown in Figure 33-8), depending upon which version of WS_FTP you are using. Both dialog boxes perform the same functions: to allow you to choose which FTP server you wish to connect to or to add another server to WS_FTP's list. WS_FTP comes preconfigured with connections to a variety of FTP servers. If you want to connect to a different FTP server, see the next section, "Adding a New Site."

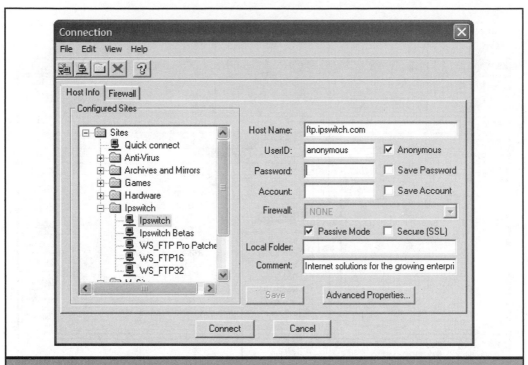

Figure 33-7.   *The Connection dialog box lets you choose an FTP server or specify a new server.*

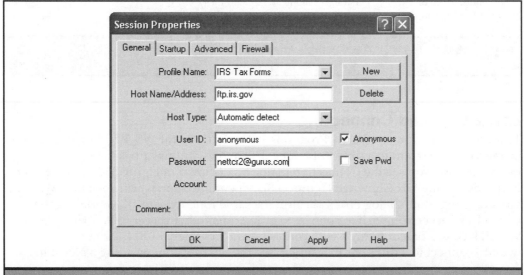

Figure 33-8.   *The Session Properties dialog box is used to choose FTP servers in WS_FTP LE.*

To connect to an FTP server from the Session Properties dialog box, set the Profile Name box to the server you want and click OK. From the Connection dialog box, first click to expand the Sites folder in the Configured Sites box, click the server's icon (such as Ipswitch in Figure 33-7), and click OK.

Whichever dialog box you use to make the connection, your PC dials up a connection to the Internet (if you aren't already connected), and WS_FTP logs you into your chosen server. You can watch the various command exchanges take place between client and server in the scrolling area at the bottom of the main WS_FTP window.

Once you are logged in, your computer's files appear on the left side of the window, and the FTP server's folders appear on the right (as shown in Figure 33-6). You can now do any of the following:

- To manage folders and files, see the upcoming section, "Choosing Folders, and Managing Folders and Files."

- To transfer files, see the upcoming section, "Transferring Folders and Files."

- To disconnect from the site, click the Disconnect button at the bottom left of the WS_FTP window.

- To disconnect from the site and exit WS_FTP, click the Exit button.

Adding a New Site

To add a site to WS_FTP's list of FTP servers, click the New button (in the Session Properties dialog box) or the New Site button (on the toolbar in Connection dialog box or choose File | New Site) and type in the information about the server:

- **Profile Name**   The name you plan to use for this FTP server, like My Web Site.

- **Host Name/Address**   The FTP server's host name, like **ftp.microsoft.com**.

- **Host Type**   Leave it set to Automatic Detect (the default). This setting tells WS_FTP what operating system the FTP server runs. WS_FTP can usually figure this out by itself.

- **User ID and Password**   Your user name and password on the FTP server (not the user name and password you use to connect to your ISP). For anonymous FTP, select the Anonymous check box and enter your e-mail address for the Password. Select the Save Pwd (Save Password) check box to avoid being prompted for a password when you log into this site.

- **Account**   Leave it blank unless you are told otherwise by the FTP server's manager.

If you are using the WS_FTP Pro Connection dialog box, a wizard steps you through the process.

Choosing Folders, and Managing Folders and Files

Once you have connected to an FTP server, before transferring files, you must open the source and destination folders you want to use on the FTP server (or "remote system" on the right side of the WS_FTP window) and on your PC (or "local system" on the left side). Each has its own column of buttons along its right side. Use the buttons as follows:

- **Move to a folder** either by double-clicking it or by clicking it once and then clicking the ChgDir button. To open the parent folder of the currently displayed folder, double-click the green up-arrow (which is followed by two dots). To return to a folder you have used previously (on either the local or remote system), click the down-arrow for the selection box at the very top of each panel. Choose the directory from the list that appears. In WS_FTP Pro, you may click in that same box, type a path into it, and press ENTER.

- **Move to a different disk drive** on the local system side by double-clicking the drive letter in the Local System box.

- **Create a new folder** by clicking the MkDir button (on either the local or remote system). Type a new folder name in the Input dialog box that appears and click OK.

- **Rename a folder or file** by clicking it and then clicking the Rename button. Enter a new name in the Input dialog box that appears and click OK.

- **Delete a folder or a file** by clicking it and then clicking the Delete button. To delete a folder on the server, however, the folder must first be empty.

Transferring Folders and Files

Transferring files, groups of files, or folders and their contents (including other folders) requires three steps, as follows:

1. Select the files or folders to be transferred. (To upload to a server, select files on the left side; to download, select files on the right.) Click a folder if you want to transfer the folder and its entire contents. To select multiple folders or files, drag across them.

2. Choose the transfer mode (ASCII or Binary). Use Binary for anything but plain ASCII text files. Choosing Auto causes WS_FTP to choose a mode based on the file extension—ASCII mode for .txt extensions, for instance. To program the Auto mode for certain extensions, click the Options button, then the Extensions tab of the WS_FTP Properties dialog box that appears. Follow the directions there.

3. Click one of the two arrow buttons between the Local (left) and Remote (right) panels. The arrow points in the direction of file transfer: left for downloads to your PC, right for uploads to the server. If you have selected a folder, WS_FTP displays a dialog box confirming that you want to transfer the folder (which it may describe as a "directory structure"), as well as the files; click Yes.

A dialog box appears during the transfer. When the files or folders are transferred, the destination display is updated. To update the display manually, click the Refresh button.

Secure FTP

FTP wasn't designed to be particularly secure: other than asking for a user name and password when you log into an FTP server, there's little verification and no encryption. If you need a more secure method of transferring files, two are available: FTP over SSH (secure shell, described in the section "Secure Telnet Using PuTTY" in this chapter) and SFTP (Secure FTP). Neither is widely used. If your FTP server uses FTP over SSH, get Secure iXplorer from the **i-tree.org/ ixplorer.htm** web site. Secure iXplorer is freeware and open source and supports FTP over SSH. If your FTP server requires SFTP, get SecureFX, a commercial product from VanDyke Software (**www.vandyke.com/products/securefx**).

Using Command-Driven FTP Clients

UNIX and Windows come equipped with command-driven FTP clients, programs you control by typing command lines (like DOS, in the old days of the 1980s). For each command line, you type a command (word) that may be followed by additional information (called *arguments*) and then press ENTER. For example, once you are connected to a server and have opened a directory, to download a file, you type the **get** command, followed by the name of the file you want to download, and then press ENTER.

An Overview of the Session

Here's how to run FTP, connect, transfer files, and disconnect:

1. Get ready to run the FTP program. In Windows, choose Start | Run to display the Run dialog box. In a UNIX GUI environment, open a command shell window (for example, an xterm window).

2. Type **ftp**, followed by a space and the host name of the FTP server, and press ENTER. (In Windows, if you are not connected to the Internet, you see the Dial-Up Networking window; click Connect. When you are connected to the Internet, the program window appears, with a name like C:\Windows\ System\ftp.exe.) You see a message confirming that you are connected to the server, like this:

```
Connected to ftp.gurus.com.
220 ftp.gurus.com FTP server (BSDI Version 7.00LS) ready.
```

3. If your attempt to connect fails, you may instead see a message saying that the host name is unknown or that the maximum number of connections to this host is already in use. Public (anonymous) FTP servers usually limit the number of simultaneous users.

4. The FTP server prompts you for a user name. If you have an account on the server, type your user name when prompted and then press ENTER. If you don't have an account on the server, type **anonymous** to use anonymous FTP and then press ENTER.

5. The FTP server prompts you for a password. Type your password if you have one or type your e-mail address for anonymous FTP. Your typed characters may not appear, for security reasons. Press ENTER again. If your account and password are acceptable to the server, you see an introductory message, like this:

```
230- Welcome to ftp.gurus.com.
230-
230- All sessions are logged.
230-
230 User anonymous logged in.
ftp>
```

6. Some FTP servers display a long introductory message. At the bottom of the message (if any) the program displays the prompt ftp> to indicate that it is ready for you to type a command.

7. At the ftp> prompt you may type any of the FTP commands described in the remainder of this section. At a minimum, you type commands to specify the directories from which (or to which) you wish to transfer a file; then you give commands to download or upload files. Before each transfer, you may need to type commands to check or set the best transfer mode (ASCII or binary) for the kind of file you are transferring.

8. When you have finished transferring files, unless you want to connect with another server at this point, type **quit** or **bye**. This command disconnects you from the FTP server and closes your FTP client program. A message confirms that you have disconnected. (If you want to leave your FTP client open and connect to a different server, type **close** or **disconnect** instead of **quit** or **bye**, and then press ENTER. Next, type **open**, followed by a space and the host name of another FTP server, and then press ENTER to connect to the other server.)

Listing Files and Folders in the FTP Server's Current Directory

To see a list of files and subdirectories in the current directory on the FTP server, type the **dir** command for a full listing of all details, or **ls** command for a shorter listing. (Not all FTP servers support the **ls** command.) The exact appearance of the listing depends on the FTP server's operating system. Figure 33-9 shows a typical listing for the **dir** command.

y), followed by the name
when any FTP command
50 CWD command

rint working directory,
xample, you might see
he FTP server types

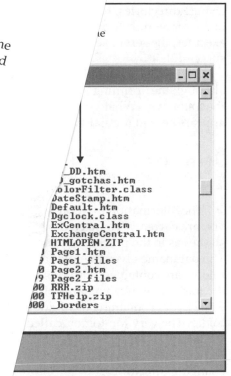

_DD.htm
)_gotchas.htm
olorFilter.class
DateStamp.htm
Default.htm
Dgclock.class
ExCentral.htm
ExchangeCentral.htm
HTMLOPEN.ZIP
Page1.htm
Page1_files
Page2.htm
Page2_files
RRR.zip
TFHelp.zip
_borders

(folder) to which
appear, separated by
ull name, or *pathname*.
he server: how
n this example) is
e, in this example)
der B, A is B's *parent*
initial slash (/).
c (anonymous) FTP
few tips for

e cd .. (that is,

(that is, the cd

e, starting at
irectory.

pitalization is
e correct

rently
older from
Often the
gram folder.
mes or
g a new
FTP client,

u can use wildcards to limit the files
haracter * matches any number of
ldcard character follow:

s that begin with C

contain helpful information about the

with "index," which is a name sometimes
about the FTP site

Lists compressed files for PC, UNIX, and

TP Server

you must move to the directory on the server
(or to which you want to upload a file). To

change directories, type **cd** (which stands for change director
of the server directory to which you want to move. (As it does
executes, the server sends a confirmation message, such as "2
successful.")

To find out the name of the current directory, type **pwd** (p
although the "printing" takes place only on your screen). For
the following. (What you type appears here in boldface; what
appears here in regular type.)

```
ftp> pwd
257 "/usr/home/george" is current directory.
```

The information in quotes gives the name of the file directory
you are currently connected at the server. Several names usually
slashes as in the preceding example, which give you the folder's f
The pathname gives the folder's place in the *directory structure* at t
folders are contained within other folders. The last name (george,
the folder to which you are connected. The name preceding it (hom
is the folder containing *that* folder, and so on. If folder A contains fol
folder. The very top folder, called the *root* folder, is indicated by the

Each FTP server has its own directory structure. On many publi
servers, the downloadable files are in a folder called pub. Here are a
changing directories:

- To change to the parent directory of the current directory, typ
  the **cd** command followed by two dots).

- To move to the top-level directory on the FTP server, type **cd /**
  command followed by a forward slash).

- You can move directly to a directory by typing its full pathnam
  the root; the full pathname starts with a / to represent the root c

- If the FTP server runs the UNIX operating system (most do), ca
  important. When typing directory or filenames, be sure to use th
  capitalization—most names use lowercase letters.

Selecting the Current Folder on Your Computer

Before you upload or download files, set the *current local directory*, the cu
selected folder on your computer (not the server's computer). This is the
which your FTP client can upload files and to which it can download files
FTP client is already set up to use a particular folder, usually within the pro

Note that some command-driven FTP clients do not accept folder n
filenames that include spaces. Consider renaming the local folder or creati
folder with a name that does not use spaces. If you are using the Windows

however, and the pathname of the folder contains spaces, the spaces will be okay if you enclose the pathname in quotes.

To change the current local directory, type **lcd** (local change directory), followed by the pathname of the folder on your computer. To move to the parent folder of the current folder, you may type **lcd ..** (the **lcd** command followed by two dots). (Using the dots is a way to avoid typing a parent folder name if it includes spaces.) To move to a subordinate (child) folder of the current folder, you may type **lcd**, a space, and then just the folder name.

For example, the command **lcd xfers** selects a subordinate folder (named xfers) of whatever the current folder is. Typing the command **lcd c:/myfiles** selects the folder myfiles on the C: drive of a PC.

You can't see what files or folders are in the current local directory by using FTP; you use your regular operating system commands or controls to browse that folder. On a PC, for instance, you would use Windows Explorer or a My Computer window.

Uploading Files

You can upload files to a folder on an FTP server if you have write permission in that folder. If you are replacing a previous version of a file, you also need permission to write to that file. Most anonymous FTP servers don't accept uploads, however, or they accept them into only one specific directory. Read the server's welcome message to find out the rules for the server you are using.

To upload a single file, use the **put** command. To upload a group of files, use the **mput** command. To upload a file, follow these steps:

1. Connect to the FTP server, change to the directory on the FTP server in which you want to store the file, and then set the current local directory to the folder on your computer that contains the files you want to upload.

2. If the file or files you want to upload contain anything but unformatted ASCII text, type **binary** to select Binary mode. To switch back to ASCII mode to transfer text files (including web pages, with the extension .html or .htm), type **ascii**.

3. Type **put**, followed by a space, followed by the filename on your computer, followed by a space, followed by the filename to use on the FTP server. Then press ENTER. For example, to upload a file named firstdraft.doc from the current local directory and call the uploaded version report.doc, the command is **put firstdraft.doc report.doc**.

4. You see a series of messages; the message "Transfer Complete" appears when the file transfer is done. Note that if a file with the name that you specify already exists on the FTP server, the **put** command may overwrite the existing file with the uploaded file.

If you want to check that the file is really on the FTP server, type **dir** to see a listing of files in the current directory.

You can copy a group of files to the FTP server by typing the **mput** (multiple put) command in place of the **put** command. Type **mput**, followed by a wildcard pattern that matches the names of the files you want to upload. (See the earlier section "Listing Files and Folders in the FTP Server's Current Directory" for examples of wildcard patterns.) The pattern * indicates that all files in the current directory on your computer should be copied.

For example, to upload all the files with the extension .html, type this command:

mput *.html

As it copies the files, the **mput** command asks you about each file. Type **y** to upload a file or **n** to skip it. If you don't want the **mput** command to ask you about each file before uploading it, type the command line **prompt** before typing the **mput** command line. The **prompt** command line turns off filename prompting (and if you type it again, turns prompting back on).

Downloading Files

To download files from the FTP server to your computer, follow these steps:

1. Connect to the FTP server, change to the directory on the FTP server that contains the file that you want to download, and then set the current local directory to the folder on your computer in which you want to store the files you download.

2. If the file or files you want to download contain anything but unformatted ASCII text, type **binary** to select Binary mode. To switch back to ASCII mode to transfer text files, type **ascii**. If, after downloading, you discover that a file you have downloaded is unusable, you probably forgot to issue the **binary** command before downloading the file.

3. Type **get**, followed by a space, followed by the filename on the FTP server, followed by a space, followed by the filename to use on your computer. Then press ENTER. (You can't use filenames with spaces.) For example, to download a file named bud04_12.doc and call the downloaded version budget_dec2004.doc, type the command line **get bud04_12.doc budget_dec2004.doc**.

4. You see a series of messages; the message "Transfer Complete" appears when the file transfer is done. To interrupt the file transfer, try pressing CTRL-C or CTRL-Z. Sometimes that doesn't work, and the only way to interrupt the transfer is to close the FTP window.

5. If you want to check that the file really is downloaded, don't try to use FTP. Browse the current local directory using the normal folder browsing features

of your computer. On a PC, for instance, use Windows Explorer or a My
Computer folder window to see a listing of files on your computer. On a
Macintosh computer, open the hard drive and navigate to the folder.

You can copy a group of files from the FTP server by typing **mget,** followed by a
wildcard pattern that matches the names of the files that you want to download. The
pattern * means that all files in the current directory on your computer should be
copied. For example, to download all the files with a file type of ZIP, you type **mget *.zip**.
As the **mget** command copies the files, it asks you about each file. Type **y** to download
a file or **n** to skip it. If you don't want the **mget** command to ask you about each file
before downloading it, type the command line **prompt** before typing the **mget**
command line.

Using Common FTP Commands

FTP clients and servers use a variety of commands, many of which have little use to
the casual user, and many of which are redundant (like **bye** and **quit**). Table 33-1 lists
commonly used FTP commands.

Function	Command	Description
Start FTP	FTP *hostname*	Starts FTP and connects to the FTP server named *hostname*.
Server connection	close	Disconnects from the FTP server, without exiting the FTP client software.
	disconnect	Disconnects from the FTP server, without exiting the FTP client software.
	bye	Disconnects from the FTP server and exits the FTP client software.
	quit	Disconnects from the FTP server and exits the FTP client software.
	user *name password*	Logs into the same FTP server using a different user name. If you omit *name* and *password*, FTP prompts you for them.
	open *hostname*	Used after disconnecting, connects to a new FTP server named *hostname*.

Table 33-1. *Common FTP Commands*

Function	Command	Description
Transfer mode (type)	ascii	Transfers files in ASCII mode (used for text files).
	binary	Transfers files in Binary or Image mode (used for all files except text files).
	type *transfertype*	Sets the transfer type. *Transfertype* must be ascii, binary, or image.
Directories	cd *dir*	Changes to the *dir* directory on the FTP server. If you omit the *dir*, FTP prompts Remote Directory and then waits for you to type the directory name and press ENTER.
	dir *pat*	Lists the files in the current directory on the FTP server that match the wildcard pattern *pat*, with full information about the files. Omit *pat* to list all the files.
	ls *pat*	Lists only the filenames of the files in the current directory on the FTP server that match the wildcard pattern *pat*. Omit *pat* to list all the files.
	lcd *dir*	Changes to the folder *dir* on your computer.
	mkdir *dir*	Creates a directory named *dir* on the FTP server (assuming that you have permission to do so).
	pwd	Displays the current directory on the FTP server.
	rmdir *dir*	Deletes the directory *dir* on the FTP server (assuming that you have permission to do so).
File transfer	get *old new*	Downloads the file *old* to your computer and names it *new*. Omit *new* to use the same name.
	mget *pat*	Downloads the files to your computer that match the wildcard pattern *pat*. Add **-i** at the end (preceded by a space) to turn off prompting during multifile transfers.

Table 33-1.   *Common FTP Commands* (continued)

Function	Command	Description
File transfer	put *old new*	Uploads the file *old* to the FTP server and names it *new*. Omit *new* to use the same name.
	mput *pat*	Uploads the files to the FTP server that match the wildcard pattern *pat*.
	append *file1 file2*	Uploads a file and appends it to an existing file. Type **append**, followed by the name of the file on your computer that you want to upload, and then the name of the file on the FTP server to which you want to append the file.
Feedback	verbose	Turns verbose mode on and off. When verbose mode is off, FTP displays fewer messages.
	?	Displays a list of the commands that the FTP client can perform.
	help	Displays a list of the commands that the FTP client can perform. Type the **help** command, followed by a space and a command name to get a short description of that command.
	remotehelp *command*	Displays the help information provided by the FTP server. Omit *command* to see a list of the commands the FTP server supports.
	status	Displays the status of the FTP client software, including the name of the FTP server to which you are connected, the file transfer mode (ASCII or Binary), and the bell mode.
	debug	Turns on and off debugging mode (which displays more information about what FTP is doing).

Table 33-1.   *Common FTP Commands* (continued)

Function	Command	Description
File management	delete *name*	Deletes the file *name* on the FTP server. If you omit the *name*, FTP says Remote File and then waits for you to type the filename and press ENTER. Most publicly accessible FTP servers don't let you delete files.
	mdelete *pat*	Deletes the files that match the wildcard pattern *pat* on the FTP server.
	rename *old new*	Renames the file named *old* on the FTP server, using the filename *new* (assuming that you have permission to do so).
	mls *dir filename*	Stores a listing of the contents of the *dir* directory on the FTP server, and all of its subdirectories, in the file *filename* on your computer. Type * as *dir* to list all files.
	prompt	Turns on or off filename prompting for **mput** and **mget** commands. When prompting is on, FTP asks before transferring each file.
Beyond FTP	trace	Turns Internet packet tracing on and off.
	!	Runs a DOS command shell and displays a DOS prompt. You can type DOS commands, such as **dir**, which displays the contents of a folder. To exit from DOS and see the ftp> prompt again, type **exit**.
	quote *command*	Sends a command to the FTP server that the FTP client software doesn't support. Type **quote**, followed by a space and the command you want to send.

Table 33-1. *Common FTP Commands* (continued)

Logging into a Web or FTP Server

Once you've uploaded files to an FTP or web server (or any Internet host that runs UNIX or Linux), you may want to do some file management—rename files, create folders, or make other changes. Some of these changes are convenient to do with an

FTP program, but some require you to log in and give UNIX commands. Telnet is an Internet service that allows you to log into other computers over the Internet and give commands, including file management commands.

To log into a host computer using telnet, you first connect to the Internet using your regular account. Then you run a telnet program (or secure telnet, or SSH program) and tell it to connect to the host computer (which may be your web or FTP server). The dialog box with the host computer appears in the telnet window, and you log into the host computer. When you are done, you disconnect from the host computer, usually by logging off. Then you exit from the telnet program, and (if you want) disconnect from the Internet. You (almost invariably) need to have a user name and password to log in using telnet. This section describes HyperTerminal (a telnet program that comes with Windows) and PuTTY (a secure telnet program).

Once you are connected, you need to know what commands to type to the remote computer. We describe some basic UNIX/Linux commands, which you can use on most FTP and web servers.

Telnetting with HyperTerminal

Windows XP (along with Windows 2000 and Windows Me) comes with two telnet programs: telnet (a very basic program) and HyperTerminal (a telnet program with more features).

Running HyperTerminal the First Time

To run HyperTerminal, choose Start | All Programs | Accessories | Communications | HyperTerminal. The first time, Windows may ask you whether to make HyperTerminal your default telnet program—if it does, click Yes. If you see a window titled C:\ Program Files\Accessories\HyperTerminal, run the Hypertrm.exe icon. You see the Connection Description dialog box:

Tell the Connection Description dialog box about the computer to which you want to connect (that is, the web server on which you want to manage files). Follow these steps:

1. Type the name that you want to use for the connection, choose an icon, and then click OK. You see the Connect To dialog box, asking for information about how to connect to the computer.

2. Set the Connect Using box to TCP/IP (Winsock) rather than your modem. (HyperTerminal can also be used as a terminal program for dialing into computers by phone.) The Connect To dialog box changes to display telnet settings (rather than settings for dialing in):

3. Type the host name or IP address into the Host Address box; for example, the host name of the U.S. Library of Congress is **locis.loc.gov**.

4. The standard *port number* (a number that tells an Internet host computer whether you are connecting for e-mail, the Web, telnet, or another Internet service) is 23. Leave the Port Number box set to 23, unless you were told to use another port.

5. Click OK. HyperTerminal tries to connect to the computer using telnet (If your computer isn't online with the Internet, you need to connect before this can work.) When you connect, you see a HyperTerminal window like the one shown in Figure 33-10.

6. Log in and use the remote computer by typing whatever commands it expects. You can use the scroll bar along the right side of the HyperTerminal window to see the backscroll buffer, which stores the last 500 lines of text that have scrolled up off the top of the terminal window. See the section "Logging In, Typing Commands, and Logging Out" later in this chapter for commands.

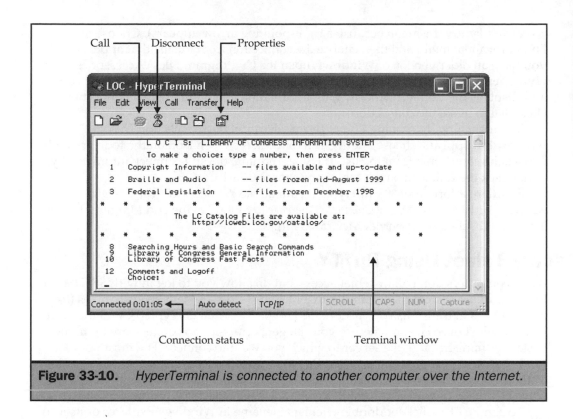

Figure 33-10.   *HyperTerminal is connected to another computer over the Internet.*

7. When you are done using the remote computer, log out, either by typing the log out command that the computer expects and clicking the Disconnect icon on the HyperTerminal toolbar or choosing Call | Disconnect from the menu.

8. When you exit from HyperTerminal, it asks whether you want to save the session (connection) that you just created. Click Yes. (If you never plan to connect to this computer again, click No to throw away the connection information that you previously typed.) HyperTerminal creates an icon for the connection on the Start | All Programs | Accessories | Communications | HyperTerminal menu (in Windows XP) or in the C:\Program Files\Accessories\HyperTerminal window (in previous versions of Windows).

Note   *Connection information is stored in a file with the connection name and the extension .ht.*

Reconnecting with HyperTerminal

To connect to a computer for which you've already created a HyperTerminal connection, choose Start | All Programs | Accessories | Communications. HyperTerminal appears twice on the menu: once as a program (to create a new connection) and once as a menu (you can identify the menu because a right-pointing arrow appears). Choose the HyperTerminal menu and then choose the connection from the list that appears. If you have an older version of Windows, open the C:\Program Files\Accessories\ HyperTerminal window and choose a connection. Either way, HyperTerminal runs and displays the Connect window with information about the existing connection; click Dial to make the connection.

If you are already running HyperTerminal, cancel the Connection Description window if it appears, choose File | Open (or click the Open icon on the toolbar), and choose the connection from the list. If HyperTerminal doesn't connect automatically, either click the Call icon on the toolbar or choose Call | Call.

For more information about HyperTerminal, see *Windows XP: The Complete Reference* or *Windows Me: The Complete Reference* (by John Levine and Margaret Levine Young, published by Osborne/McGraw-Hill).

Secure Telnet Using PuTTY

Some computers don't allow telnet access, but do allow you to log in with *SSH* (Secure Shell), a secure system that is similar to telnet. SSH closes telnet's security holes (for example, telnet transmits your user name and password unencrypted). Whether you can use telnet or SSH, and whether you can get permission to connect, are up to the system administrator of the server to which you want to connect. The most popular (and cheapest) SSH program is called PuTTY, which is a free implementation by Simon Tatham. You can download it from **www.chiark.greenend.org.uk/~sgtatham/putty** or from TUCOWS **(www.tucows.com)**. Versions are available for Windows 95 through XP.

To run PuTTY, click (or double-click) its filename in Windows Explorer or its icon. You see the PuTTY Configuration dialog box, shown here:

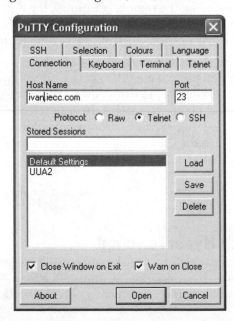

Type the host name or IP address in the Host Name box. For the Protocol setting, select Telnet if you want to use telnet (the same protocol that HyperTerminal uses) or SSH (for a secure connection). If you want to save these settings, type a name in the Stored Sessions box and click the Save button. If you want to use saved settings, click the connection name and click Load.

To connect, click the Open button. If PuTTY asks whether to save the host's key in your computer's Registry, click Yes. The PuTTY window looks like Figure 33-11—a simple window with no menus, toolbars, or buttons. Log in and use the remote computer by typing whatever commands it expects, as explained in the next section.

Logging In, Typing Commands, and Logging Out

When you connect to a computer using telnet or SSH, you must usually connect and log in before you can type commands. What commands you type depends on which operating system the remote computer runs. Many web servers run UNIX (or Linux, an open source version of UNIX). When you are done using the remote computer, you log out.

Logging In

When you connect, UNIX asks for your user name and password. Type each followed by pressing ENTER (or RETURN). UNIX is case sensitive, so be sure to capitalize your user name and password correctly. (User names are usually lowercase.) If the system

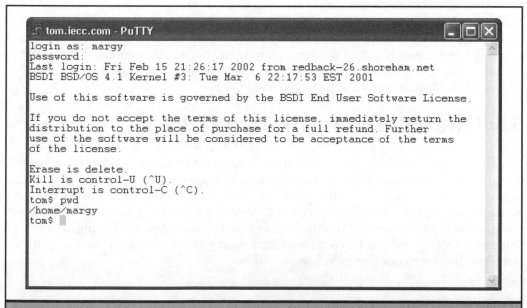

```
tom.iecc.com - PuTTY
login as: margy
password:
Last login: Fri Feb 15 21:26:17 2002 from redback-26.shoreham.net
BSDI BSD/OS 4.1 Kernel #3: Tue Mar  6 22:17:53 EST 2001

Use of this software is governed by the BSDI End User Software License.

If you do not accept the terms of this license, immediately return the
distribution to the place of purchase for a full refund. Further
use of the software will be considered to be acceptance of the terms
of the license.

Erase is delete.
Kill is control-U (^U).
Interrupt is control-C (^C).
tom$ pwd
/home/margy
tom$
```

Figure 33-11.   *The PuTTY windows contains your conversation with the remote computer.*

says that your password is no good, check that you spelled your user name correctly, too. Entering an incorrect user name or password three times in a row may cause the system to disconnect (to deter hackers).

Typing UNIX Commands

After you log in, you see a welcome message and the UNIX *shell prompt*, the symbol that means that UNIX is ready for you to type a command. The prompt varies from system to system, but it's frequently a dollar sign ($) or a percent sign (%). At the shell prompt, when you type a command and press ENTER, UNIX executes the command.

UNIX commands are single words, usually lowercase. They may be followed by additional information, which is separated from the command by a space. For example, you might type **ls -l** to run the **ls** command (which lists filenames, as explained later in this chapter) with the further specification that you want a detailed listing.

Here are some additional tips for typing UNIX commands:

- *Capitalization matters to UNIX.* Type commands as they appear here (or whatever other UNIX book you refer to), usually all lowercase. If the instructions say to type **ls** and you type **LS**, you'll see an error message.

- *If you make a mistake typing, press BACKSPACE, DELETE, or CTRL-H.* To cancel the entire command line before you press ENTER, press CTRL-U or CTRL-K. Misspelling a command usually results in a "command not found" error message.

- *Don't type any extra spaces or punctuation.* Separate commands from other information on the command line by a single space.

Logging Out

When you are done using the Internet, log out from your UNIX account. Type **exit** or **logout**, or press CTRL-D. The UNIX system logs you off, and if you are connected on a dial-up phone line, it hangs up the phone connection.

Working with Files on Your Web or FTP Server

UNIX systems have hierarchical (tree-structured) directories (folders) like Windows and Mac systems. One directory is the *current directory,* the directory where you are working. All commands refer to that directory unless you specify otherwise by including other information on the command line after the command. When you log into your account, in the current directory is your home (starting) directory and you can give commands to move to other directories (as described in "Changing the Current Directory" later in this section). Check your web server instructions to find out what directory your web pages are stored in.

Listing Your Files

To see a list of the files in the current directory, type **ls** and press ENTER. You see a
listing like this one:

```
Mail              cheeselist      guruweb
Mailbox           fpc             internet101
Mailbox.lock      fpcweb          mail
News              greattapesweb   net101
```

The items—files and other directories that are contained in the current directory—
are in alphabetical order down each column. (UNIX feels that capital letters come
before lowercase letters.) To see more information about the items in the current
directory, add the **-l** option to the ls command, like this:

```
ls -l
```

You get a more detailed listing like this one:

```
drwx------    2 margy   book        512 Feb  9  1998 Mail
-rw-------    1 margy   book     119487 Aug 31 21:35 Mailbox
-rw-rw-rw-    1 margy   book          0 Aug 20 14:55 Mailbox.lock
drwxr-xr-x    2 margy   book        512 Feb  9  1998 images
-rw-r--r--    1 margy   book       1538 Jun  6 11:20 index.html
-rw-r--r--    1 margy   book       1538 Jun  6 11:20 orderform.html
drwxr-xr-x    2 margy   book        512 Mar  3 14:28 net101
```

For each item, you see

- **Permissions**   For example, *drwxrwxr-x.* If the first character is *d,* the item is
  a directory; otherwise it is a file. The rest of the characters indicate who has
  permission to read, write, and execute the file. See the section "Changing File
  Permissions" later in this chapter.

- **Owner**   For example, *margy.* Each file and directory has one individual
  owner, usually the person who created the file.

- **Group owner**   For example, *book.* Each file and directory is also owned by
  a group. See the section "Changing File Permissions" later in this chapter.

- **Size**   For example, 512. The file size is shown in bytes.

- **Date and time**   For example, *Mar 3 14:28.* The date and time this file was
  last modified.

■ **File (or directory) name**   For example, *net101*. File and directory names are case-sensitive and cannot contain spaces.

Changing the Current Directory

To move to a directory (perhaps one you notice listed by the ls command), type **chdir** or **cd,** followed by a space and the name of the directory to move to. For example, to move to a directory named web, you'd type **cd web**. To move back to your home directory, type **chdir** or **cd** with no directory name. To find out the full name of the current directory, type **pwd** (print working directory).

Renaming, Copying, and Deleting Files

To rename a file in the current directory, type **mv** (short for "move"), followed by a space, the current filename, another space, and the new filename. For example, to rename *budget.html* as *budget.2004.html,* you'd type

```
mv budget.html budget.2004.html
```

If you want to make a copy of a file in a directory, use the **cp** (copy) command, specifying the name of the file you want to copy and the name to give the new file. For example, to copy *budget.jan04.html* as *budget.feb04.html,* you'd type

```
cp budget.jan04.html budget.feb04.html
```

Caution   *If there is already a file with the name that you want to use for the copy, you can inadvertently delete the file by that name. Before copying, make sure that there is no file with the name you want to use for the copy.*

To delete a file you never want to see again, use the **rm** (remove) command. Type **rm** followed by a space and the name of the file you want to delete. UNIX doesn't confirm the deletion; UNIX just does it, so watch out.

Caution   *Once you delete a file, there is no way to get it back. Very few UNIX systems have recycle bins or other methods of retrieving deleted files. The command to avoid is **rm .** (which deletes all the files in the current directory).*

To see what's in a file, you can use the more command. The more command works only for text files: if the file contains nontext information, you'll see garbage. To display a text file on the screen, type **more**, a space, and the filename. UNIX displays one screenful of information and then pauses. To see the next screenful, press SPACEBAR. To cancel the rest of the listing, press **q** (lowercase).

Making and Removing Directories

You can create a new directory (folder) by typing **mkdir,** followed by a space and the name for the new directory. UNIX creates your new directory in the current directory. To delete a directory and all the files and directories it contains, type **rmdir,** followed by a space and the name of the directory. UNIX doesn't display any confirmation that these commands worked: you just see another prompt. Use the **ls** command to check your work.

Displaying File Permissions

If you run a web site (especially if you run it with other people), you may need to work with UNIX files permissions. *Permissions* are settings that control who can do what with each file or directory. Permissions come in three types:

- *Read permission* lets you look at the contents of a file or directory. Read permission for a file lets you use the UNIX more command to read text files. Read permission for a directory lets you list the contents of the directory using the **ls** command.

- *Write permission* lets you make changes to a file or directory. Although you can edit the file, you can't delete or rename it unless you also have write permission for the directory that contains the file. Write permission for a directory lets you create new files, delete files, and rename files in the directory.

- *Execute permission* lets you run the program contained in a file. If the file doesn't contain a program, execute permission is useless. Execute permission for directories lets you open files in the directory as well as letting you use the **cd** command to make the directory your current working directory.

Each file and directory belongs to a user and to a group. Each user belongs to one or more groups, too. To find out which groups you belong to, type the command **id.** You see something like this:

```
uid=112(margy) gid=10(users) groups=10(users), 20(staff), 30(LISTS)
```

The *uid* and *gid* are your user and group ID number and name, which you might need to tell your system administrator someday if you have a problem. Your user name is the same name you use to log into your account. Your group is the one that the system administrator assigned you to when your account was created. Following that information is a list of the group names and numbers to which you belong. When you use the **ls -l** command for a detailed listing of files (shown in the section "Listing Your Files" earlier in this chapter), you see the name of the user and the group that own each file, as well as the permissions.

The permissions shown by the **ls -l** command (the first item on each line of the listing) work like this:

- The first character is *d* if the item is a directory, and - (a dash) if it's a file.

- The next three characters show the read, write, and execute permissions for the user who owns the file. The first of the three characters is *r* if the owner has read permission and - otherwise. The second character is *w* if the owner has write permission and - otherwise. The third character is *x* if the owner has execute permission and - otherwise.

- The next three characters show the read, write, and execute permissions for the people who belong to the group that owns the file.

- The last three characters show the read, write, and execute permissions for everyone else.

For example, the permissions *-rwxr-x--x* mean that the item is a file (not a directory); that the owner can read, write, and execute the file; that members of the group that owns the file can read and execute the file, but not write it; and that everyone else can only execute the file.

Changing File Permissions

If you own a file, you can change its permissions. For example, if you upload a web page to your UNIX-based web server and you want to let other members of your team edit the file, you may need to change the file's permissions.

To change a file's permissions, you use the **chmod** command, like this:

```
chmod permissions filename
```

Replace *filename* with the name of the file; replace *permissions* with code that specifies which permissions to change and what to change them to. Each code consists of three characters:

- *u* (user owner), *g* (group), *o* (other, or everyone else), or *a* (all) to specify whose permissions to change

- + or - to add or remove a permission

- *r* (read), *w* (write), or *x* (execute) to specify which permission to change

For example, the command

```
chmod g+w index.html
```

gives members of the group that owns the file permission to write (edit) the file.

If you own a file, you can also change which group owns it. Type the command

```
chgrp groupname filename
```

Replace *groupname* with the name of the group that should own the file and *filename* with the name of the file. (This command doesn't work on all versions of UNIX: if you get an error message, ask your system administrator or ISP to change the group.)

Quality, Security, and Ownership Issues

The ability to transfer files across the Internet raises a number of technical and other issues. Among them are ensuring the quality and integrity of the file, maintaining security of your computer, and observing copyright ownership rights.

Ensuring File Quality and Integrity

In nearly all circumstances, if a file has downloaded in its entirety, it is error free. Various schemes in file-transfer software detect any errors that occur during transmission. When problems occur, they are usually the result of sending a binary file as a text file, or vice versa, in FTP. The best way to check for those problems is to obtain from the original source exactly what size the file is supposed to be and make sure the file you downloaded is exactly that size.

Ensuring Security

Security has been a major concern the past few years and rightly so. Every day, several new viruses, worms, Trojan horses, or security vulnerabilities are discovered. With the increased popularity of broadband connections and computers maintaining an always-on connection to the Internet, you need to take security seriously. A worm or Trojan horse can be introduced directly to any insecure computer while it's connected to the Internet.

Note	*A* virus *or* worm *is an unauthorized program that is slipped into your computer, usually with malicious or mischievous intent, often deleting or damaging files on your computer. Such programs often reproduce and spread themselves to other computers. A* Trojan horse *is a program that is likewise copied to your computer by stealth, but its intent is to allow further access to your computer at a later time.*

Someone may intentionally or accidentally infect a file or create a file that is not what it appears to be and distribute it by posting it on an FTP or web server, e-mailing it, or submitting it to a newsgroup.

Although reading e-mail messages is fairly safe, someone could knowingly or unknowingly send you a file containing a virus as an e-mail attachment. If you open an infected file, your computer may be infected. To avoid problems, get and install virus scanning software, let that software examine any files you receive as e-mail attachments, and only open attachments you request. To be safe, resist the temptation to open the joke files Aunt Bea sends—if one is carrying a virus, worm, or Trojan, cleaning up after it isn't worth a few laughs now.

The best steps to take to avoid downloading corrupted programs or macro viruses are the following:

- Avoid downloading programs, any executable file type, or files containing macros from anyone but reliable sources, the trusted originator of a file, or any responsible organization that is likely to have the expertise and a sufficient vested interest in your security to avoid posting a corrupted file. A list of executable, and therefore potentially dangerous, file types is available at most antivirus vendor web sites.

- Check the file's exact length in bytes against published file length, if available. If the file you download is not the size it is supposed to be, do not use it. You either downloaded it incorrectly, had transmission problems during download, or it is corrupted. Note that some computers normally display file size rounded off to the nearest 1K. In Windows, for instance, you must right-click a file and choose Properties to see the exact file size.

- Scan the file for known viruses, using commercial virus-scanning software that has up-to-date virus definitions or signatures installed.

See the section on security issues on the Internet in Chapter 1 for more information, as well as Chapter 34.

Observing Property Rights

Copyright ownership and property rights are issues that arise because it is so easy to copy and distribute computer files. Though it may be easy to send a copy of a computer file to a friend, you may have no right to do so. Copyrights apply to any and all kinds of materials that can be sent as a file on the Internet: images, programs, data, text, scripts, applets, movies, sounds, and animations. That includes all the components of a web page, from the cute graphical bullets and bars to the hidden JavaScript that makes the page sing and dance. Even if you don't copy the material but instead link to the original file from your web page (for example, making a picture appear on your web page by linking to a graphics file on another web site), you may be violating copyright.

Creators of text and graphical materials retain their rights, whether or not someone else scanned the work from a magazine or other publication into a computer file. Just because someone e-mailed you an article and the author is unknown, you don't have the right to distribute the article. The same is true of cartoons, drawings, and photographs.

Even if a file appears to be free, the material that file contains can have any number of constraints on how, when, where, and how often it is used. You may be required to give credit on the page where you use it, for instance, or to abstain from using it in print. Finally, even if a file appears to be offered for free on a web or FTP site, it may not have been acquired legally. Some amateurs have been known to collect other people's image files and offer them (usually out of ignorance) for downloading on the Web. To avoid property rights issues, make sure that you have an explicit agreement with the actual author or authorized distributor of the work before using or copying a work.

 Use Google or another search engine to search for information about a file before deciding that you have the right to distribute it.

The Complete Reference

Internet

Chapter 34

Downloading and Installing Software

No matter how obscure it is, it's out there, and generally for free or at low cost. Nervous about shelling out $200 for Dreamweaver and want to try before you buy? Download a free demo. Play Dungeons and Dragons and want a free character generator? You got it. Concerned that your version of Windows isn't up to speed? Download the patch to update it to Microsoft freshness. Want to see the blooper reels from your favorite television shows? Go for it.

And if you want a security program, a virus scanner, and a spyware stopper to guard your new PC from hard-drive crunching attacks, it's all out there—for free or close to it.

Types of Downloadable Software

Of course, the quality of freeware items isn't always as good as full-priced software—but you'd be surprised at how often it is. You'll find five types of programs on the Internet:

- **Freeware**   Freeware software costs you nothing, and the publishers ask for no money. In some cases, freeware is actually free only for personal use—the companies make their money by selling licenses of their software to large corporations, and in that case the freeware version is as good as what you could buy in a store. In other cases, the software is created by a person who needs something, writes a program to fix that need, and then decides that others might have the same problems that he did and sends it out. Other times, it's some weirdo who slaps together a program just for the fun of it. The good thing is that no matter what the quality, it costs you nada.

> **Tip**   *Although freeware is, well, free, some of them ask for donations if you like the product. If you want to keep these people updating their software, think about sending them a small donation of $5 or so to keep their spirits up. Some freeware displays ads (it's known as* adware) *for which the author gets revenue from the program.*

- **Shareware**   Much like freeware, shareware programs cost you nothing to use, but they *do* expect payment if you use it regularly. Unlike freeware, shareware programs often have "nag screens"—reminders of payment that pop up every time you start the program (some people call this type of program *guiltware*). If you pay, the nag screen goes away.

- **Trialware**   Many large companies, like Adobe, Jasc Software, and Macromedia, offer trial versions of their products. These generally come in two flavors: time-limited and feature-limited. *Time-limited* versions let you do everything, but stop working after a set number of days—usually 30. (You can unlock it by paying for the program.) *Feature-limited* programs don't expire, but they are purposely "broken" in some way—for example, you're not allowed to save your file, or you don't have access to the advanced features. You can change this by ponying up the cash.

■ **Patches**   These are updates to programs you already own, and they fix bugs and close security holes. Patches are vital, especially for Microsoft software.

Particularly if you own Microsoft products, make sure all of your programs are fully up-to-date! Many malicious hackers rely on flaws in old versions to destroy computers and infect them with viruses.

■ **Media files**   Movies, MP3s, WAV files, and other multimedia goodness are files that people love to have on their hard drives.

The Web is usually your best source for finding the files you want, although peer-to-peer networks are becoming more popular for finding media files. (See Chapter 33 for information on peer-to-peer networking.)

Nearly every commercial Internet site (and many casual ones) offers a public downloads section. Within these download sections, if you are seeking software, you must find the subsection for your particular system. Documents, images, and other media files are generally not system-specific. The next section lists places to look for downloadable software.

Most Internet users download files from the Web today, but FTP servers (described in Chapter 33) are a less-common source. Many people also receive files by e-mail. Although the process by which files are downloaded to your computer using the Web, FTP, or e-mail is complex, the more recent your Internet software (and the more conventional your requirements), the more this complexity is hidden from you. If you are using the latest web browsers and are downloading popular software, for instance, the process may be fully automated.

Just because someone sent you a program by e-mail doesn't mean it's safe! Many viruses are spread via e-mail programs. See the section on viruses in Chapter 1 for more details. (Yes, we mention this again in a paragraph or two, but it's that important.)

If you are downloading something other than a program, however, or a file that originated on (or is principally intended for) a different kind of computer than you use, the underlying complexities can become very apparent. This chapter can help you surmount the difficulties involved.

No matter how you download files, however, the security of your computer system must be maintained. Computer viruses, *Trojan horses* (programs that contain "features" that you don't know about and that cause your computer to do things you may not have in mind), and other forms of malicious software are rare, especially when a file is downloaded from a software vendor, but are a finite risk for anyone who downloads files. Files received by e-mail from an unknown source (or forwarded by a well-intentioned friend), in particular, should *always* be checked for viruses before they are opened or otherwise used. See "Scanning for Viruses" at the end of this chapter.

Where Can You Find Files?

Here are some good places to look for the programs and files you need:

- **At the company's web site** Particularly if you're looking for a trial version of a program or a patch, the official site will have everything you need, as up-to-date as it gets.

- **At a shareware site** Many sites simply store large numbers of files; you can search through the files by operating system, function, shareware/freeware, and many other options, and then download the ones you like. If you don't know what the company's name is but know it's a popular program—or you're just browsing to see what you *can* download—these sites are invaluable. CNET's Download.com (**www.download.com**) and TUCOWS (**www.tucows.com**) are the two most popular shareware sites (one is shown in Figure 34-1). Other useful sites are CNET's Shareware.com (**shareware.cnet.com** or **www.shareware.com**) and ZDNet Downloads (**www.zdnet.com/downloads**).

Figure 34-1.   *Download.com allows you to search for software by type and operating system and lets you browse through categories.*

- **Via a web search**   If you can't find it on a shareware site, plug a couple of key words into Google (**www.google.com**) or Yahoo (**www.yahoo.com**) and take a gander. Searching is a way to find obscure programs, like a statistical calculator, an out-of-date DOS database program, or a searchable database of all episodes of *Buffy the Vampire Slayer*.

- **Ask a mailing list**   Particularly if it's a specialty program that interests you and if you're on a mailing list, why not ask the group if they have any suggestions? If your passion is constructing model railroads, and you want an electronic railroad layout program, asking a railroad mailing list is likely to find you not only all the programs that are out there, but also the ones RR fanatics *recommend*.

- **Use a peer-to-peer client**   Especially if you're looking for multimedia files, peer-to-peer networks are invaluable. Peer-to-peer networking is, essentially, people sharing what's on their hard drive with the world—and devoted fans have hard drives packed with pictures, sounds, and video waiting for you. At this writing, Morpheus was the most popular program for accessing the Gnutella P2P network, which lets you download any number of files and documents— not all of them legal. Needless to say, the lawyers of media companies are very leery of allowing electronic versions of their hard-bought movies and music to be passed around for free, so by the time you read this, Morpheus may be shut down. However, for good or for evil, the peer-to-peer model is popular—so if Morpheus is shut down, some other file-sharing client will become popular. It's simply a matter of finding it—see Chapter 33 for more information.

Tip   *To see whether you have the latest version of a program, visit the www.versiontracker.com site.*

Programs Everyone Should Have

What files do we think are critical for the well-being and enjoyment of every PC user? Try these:

- **ZoneAlarm (www.zonealarm.com)**   The finest firewall software around, it's absolutely free as long as you're a single user—and it stops hackers cold. If you have a high-speed connection (DSL, cable, ISDN), you *need* to have this on your computer. You may not want to run it all the time, but it's great when you think a virus or Trojan might have infected your computer. See the "Security Issues on the Internet" section in Chapter 1 for more information.

- **Pop-Up Stopper (www.panicware.com)**   If you're tired of annoying web sites constantly opening new windows on you every time you browse, Pop-Up Stopper is just the thing you need, opening new windows only when you press CTRL. Unfortunately, it seems to have some trouble stopping pop-up windows in

Internet Explorer 6 and above. Still, even if it doesn't stop *all* the windows on newer versions of IE, it still stops enough of them (and is small enough) to be well worth it.

- **Window Washer (www.webroot.com)**   If you value privacy and don't want people knowing where you've been surfing, Window Washer cleans your cache, your viewing history, and your cookies.

- **AdAware (www.lavasoftusa.com)**   A delightful new trend in the computer industry is *spyware*—otherwise-useful programs that have the nasty habit of secretly transferring private information from your hard drive (like your web browsing habits and e-mail addresses) back to their company to be used and sold as demographic information. AdAware scans your programs and cookies and deletes the spying portion.

- **WinZip (www.winzip.com) or ZipMagic (www.zipmagic.com)**   The majority of compressed files (files squeezed down to be smaller so they can be downloaded faster) are in the ZIP format. WinZip and ZipMagic are the two easiest ways of creating and unzipping compressed files. WinZip is shareware, ZipMagic is trialware, and both offer advantages over even Windows XP's built-in ZIP-handling abilities.

- **WinAmp (www.winamp.com)**   Sure, most operating systems come with a program that will play MP3 audio files for you—but if you have large numbers of music files (or plan to), nothing's as easy and compact as WinAmp.

- **Adobe Acrobat (www.adobe.com)**   You'll need this to read a lot of the documents on the Internet because Acrobat allows publishers to create book-perfect layouts that look the same no matter what platform they're viewed on.

- **RealPlayer (www.real.com)**   If you're going to be watching any sort of streaming media (see Chapter 22), eventually you'll need RealMedia's free player. Download it now and save yourself the inconvenience later.

- **ICQ (www.icq.com), AIM (www.aim.com), or Yahoo Messenger (messenger.yahoo.com)**   If you want to chat with your friends on the Net—and you will—any of these programs will do the job. Ask your friends what they have, and get whatever the majority of them use, or get them all. (For more information, see Chapter 14.)

- **WS_FTP LE (www.ftpplanet.com/download.htm)**   If you plan to upload files over the Web, WS_FTP LE is a "light" shareware version of the full-powered WS_FTP Pro, which allows you to transfer files via FTP with ease. See Chapter 33 for more information about FTP.

- **StuffIt Expander (www.aladdinsys.com)**   If you're a Mac user, eventually you're going to need to decompress a file. This is the gold standard of decompression programs for Mac users.

Downloading Files from the Web

In most instances, to download software from a web site, you simply click a link on a web page. Take note of any description provided for the file, such as self-extracting, StuffIt, or ZIP—because you may need that information in order to know what to do after the file downloads.

You can click web page links to download and save other types of files, too. If you are downloading a file other than a program file, however, simply clicking a link to that file may cause the browser to display the file's contents rather than saving it on your system. For instance, if a link takes you to an Adobe Acrobat PDF file, and your browser is equipped with an Acrobat reader, your computer downloads and displays the file rather than allowing you to save it. To ensure that the browser downloads a file, right-click the link (or, on the Macintosh, press OPTION and click) and look for a "Save *something* As" menu choice, where *something* depends on the browser and on what you are clicking. In Internet Explorer, look for Save Target As; in Netscape products, look for Save Link As. Select that choice.

> **Tip**   *This command works to save pictures embedded in web pages as well. Right-click on the file and select "Save Picture As" (or "Save Image" in Netscape) to download it to your hard drive, as shown in Figure 34-2. In Internet Explorer 6, if you hover your pointer over the picture for a moment, a small picture menu appears in the upper-left corner, allowing you to save it, print it, e-mail it, or open your "My Pictures" folder.*

If you do not have a link to click, but you do know the Internet address (URL) of a file, you may type that URL (or copy and paste it) directly into your web browser. For example, if you read that **ftp://ftp.randomserver.org/random.exe** is the URL of a program you want, type that address into the Location, Netsite, or Address box of the browser.

When downloading certain software, some browsers (notably Internet Explorer) display a dialog box giving you the option of running the software, rather than downloading it. If you trust the source of the software completely or do not intend to virus-check the software, you can choose that option. In general, however, it is best to download the file instead, so you can virus-check it before you start it. (Also, on slower connections, you can sometimes restart the download if it gets interrupted. If you're opening the file online, that hardly ever works.)

The browser may also display a dialog box that gives you the option of clicking a check box if you wish to always trust the source of the software you are currently downloading. Click that check box if you don't want to be asked again if you download

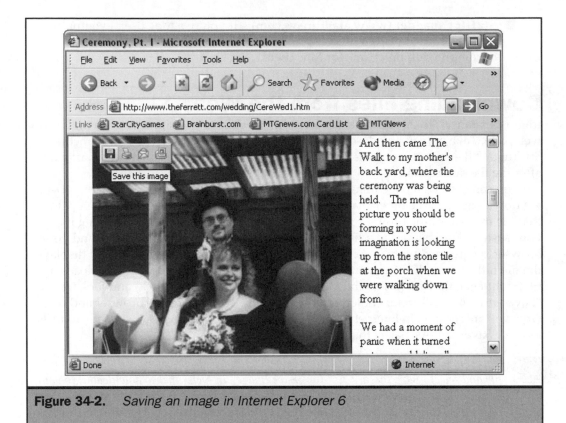

Figure 34-2. *Saving an image in Internet Explorer 6*

or install software from this vendor (which is useful for patches, which you're downloading from the software publisher's web site).

On most systems and browsers, a dialog box prompts you for the filename and folder you wish to use for storing the program on your computer. (On some early systems and browsers, the file is immediately downloaded to a particular folder or to your desktop, as defined in the Preferences or Options settings of the browser.) You can choose any folder you like to save it in.

We suggest creating a "My Downloads" folder that you always save your programs to because it's easier to find them when your downloaded files are always in the same place. Just be sure to clean out the old programs from your "My Downloads" folder once in a while to save hard drive space!

You can save the downloaded program under any name you like, but many downloaded files will not work if you change the filename. Do *not* change the file extension unless you are *quite* sure what you are doing. Note the chosen folder so you can find the file later, and note its filename and extension (a period and several letters). Click the Save button in that dialog box when you are ready. You see a dialog box that displays the progress of the download.

The time required for downloading large files can be quite long, especially on dial-up connections. (One of the joys of high-speed connections is downloading 5MB files in three minutes.) Depending on the server that supplies the file, your browser may be able to estimate the download time and to display it in the dialog box that appears during downloading. Otherwise, if the web page that describes the file gives the file's size, you can calculate download time. Most browsers, in the dialog box that appears during downloading, display the rate at which data is being received once downloading begins. Wait 30 seconds or so for the data rate to appear, and divide the file size by the data rate (being careful to recognize that megabytes are millions of bytes, and kilobytes are thousands of bytes). For example, a 6-megabyte (6MB or 6Mbyte) file received at a data rate of two kilobytes per second (2 Kbps) will take 3,000 seconds (about 50 minutes) to download.

Most browsers allow you to continue browsing the Web (or even to exit the browser) while a file is downloading. Pages appear much more slowly, however, while the download continues, and continuing to browse may slow the download further.

Finding Files on Your Computer After Downloading

When some programs download files, they don't always tell you where they put the files; nor do they ask you where you would prefer them to be stored on your computer. This problem is especially true for files you receive by e-mail.

One solution is to use your computer's find capability to search either for the filename or for a file with a recent creation date. In Windows 95 or 98, for instance, choose Start | Find | Files Or Folders, choose the Date Modified tab in the Find dialog box that appears, click During The Previous 1 Day(s), and then click the Find Now button. In Windows Me, it's Start | Search | For Files Or Folders.

For Windows XP, select Start | Search and click All Files And Folders when it asks you what to search for. Then click the When Was It Modified button, click the Specify Dates radio button, select Created Date from the drop-down list, and change the From and To dates to today. These settings give you a list of all files saved to your hard drive for the first time that day. (See Figure 34-3.) This may be a scarily large number of files, especially if you've been surfing or installing other programs previously, so remembering the name and location of your downloaded file is the best way to go.

Another solution is to check your program to see what location it is configured to use for attachments or downloads. The Eudora e-mail program, for instance, stores attachments in a folder named Attach within the Eudora program folder (unless you have configured it otherwise). Under Windows and using Microsoft's Outlook Express, shown in Figure 34-4, you'll generally have to save the attached file manually before you can access it on your hard drive. You can do this by opening the e-mail, right-clicking on the attachment, and selecting Save As.

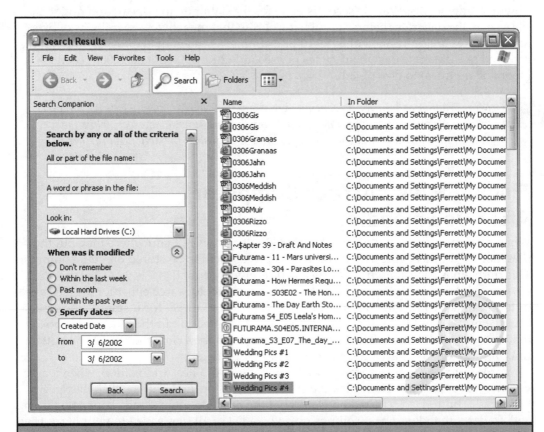

Figure 34-3.   *Searching for recent files in Windows XP is a lot easier to show than it is to write about!*

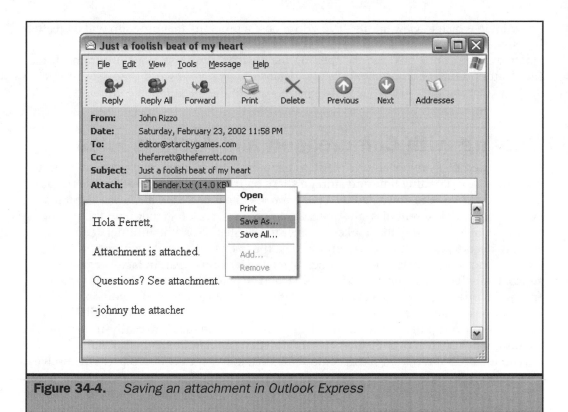

Figure 34-4.   *Saving an attachment in Outlook Express*

Determining What to Do with Downloaded Files

Usually, you know what you have downloaded and therefore know what to do with it—run it, open it with your word processor, view it in a graphics program, or whatever. However, before you do anything, make *sure* your computer has checked the downloaded file for viruses, even if the file is only a document. (See the section "Scanning for Viruses" later in this chapter.)

Sometimes, though, files are compressed to make them faster to download. To get them to work, you'll have to decompress them. See the following section, "Dealing with Compressed and Archive Files."

If, after consulting the following section, you still don't know what to do with the file, your computer may know what to do. In a Windows, Macintosh, or UNIX windowing environment, after you virus-check the file, try simply double-clicking the file; your computer might launch a program that can open the file. If no program is currently associated with that type of file on your computer, your computer might instead display a dialog box listing all the programs you have installed and then ask you to choose a program in which to view the file. If you do choose a program, that program will thereafter be associated with that file type—so it's better to try experimenting with it first. Press ESC to exit the dialog box, and try opening the file from within various programs. If the file is supposed to be a document file, for instance, launch your word processor program, and try opening the file in your word processor with the File | Open command.

Dealing with Compressed and Archive Files

Downloaded files are not always ready to be used. A file is often *compressed* in order to minimize downloading time and storage space on the computer where the file resides. In addition, if you are downloading a program, the file is probably an *archive file*: it may contain several different files, all squeezed down, that work together. Finally, the file may be *encoded* in a way that makes it easier to transfer across the Internet. You may have to decode, decompress, and unbundle a file in order to use its contents.

It sounds complicated, but the process gets easier every year; in fact, because Zip functionality has been built into Windows XP and 90 percent of all compressed Windows files are Zipped, you may not even need another program at all—and if you do, WinZip and ZipMagic can take care of the rest. In addition, many of the newer e-mail, FTP, and web browser programs either automatically process these files into ready-to-use files, or automatically turn over the task to software that can handle the task. Finally, there is a trend toward *self-extracting* files, program files that automatically decompress themselves once you click on them.

Compressed file formats are often referred to as *archive* formats—because most web hosts either have a space limit for how much you can store on their server or charge by the megabyte. Thus, shrinking the files makes things run smoother on the server end. Another reason they are called archive formats is because, in most instances, they allow compressing multiple files into one file. An entire folder of program and program documentation files, for instance, can be compressed into a single archive file.

Table 34-1 lists the archive and compression file types most commonly found on the Internet, by file extension (the ending characters in the file's name, preceded by a period). File extension is the best indicator of what kind of file you have, although you should also pay attention to descriptions found on the web site or in the readme.txt or index.txt files of an FTP site's folder.

Some files may have two extensions, such as *.tar.z.* Multiple extensions usually imply that the contents have undergone two or more steps in creating the file: perhaps an initial process to create a single archive from multiple files, and then another to compress the archive file.

Compressed Files for Different Computers

Dozens of different file types (file *formats*) exist for compressed files, but they all serve one purpose: to make files smaller in order to save storage space and downloading time.

File Extension	File Type	Explanatory Section in This Chapter
BIN	Binary file, usually referring to a Macintosh MacBinary file if downloaded from a Macintosh folder	"Decoding and Decompressing Macintosh Files"
EXE	PC program or self-extracting file (binary file)	"Using Self-Extracting Files" and "Installing Programs"
HQX	BinHex-encoded Macintosh file (text file)	"Decoding and Decompressing Macintosh Files"
SEA	Macintosh Self-Extracting Archive (binary file)	"Using Self-Extracting Files" and "Decoding and Decompressing Macintosh Files"
SIT	Macintosh compressed file (StuffIt) (binary file)	"Decoding and Decompressing Macintosh Files"
TAR	UNIX TAR archive (binary file)	"Unpacking TAR Archive Files"
UUE	Uuencoded UNIX or PC file (text file)	"Unzipping ZIP Files"
Z, GZ, Z, GZ	UNIX or gzip compressed (binary file)	"Unzipping ZIP Files"
ZIP	PC compressed file (ZIP) (binary file)	"Unzipping ZIP Files"

Table 34-1.   *Types of Files Most Commonly Downloaded*

Fortunately, in each of the most popular operating systems, only one or two formats are commonly used:

- **Windows**   The ZIP format predominates; files end in .zip or (if self-extracting), .exe. The format is so popular that, starting with Windows XP, Microsoft has not only built ZIP support right into the operating system, but also allows you to compress entire folders down into zipped folders. If you don't have native ZIP support (or if you're looking for more depth in your ZIP tools), the two tools most commonly used to both create and decompress ZIP files are Nico Mak's WinZip program, available in evaluation form at **www.winzip.com**, and Ontrack's ZipMagic, available at **www.zipmagic.com**. (The ZIP format should not be confused with files stored on Iomega's Zip disks, which are not in ZIP format.) Other tools exist for PCs, Macintosh computers, and UNIX workstations that can also decompress (unzip) ZIP files. Not all programs that use the ZIP format are entirely compatible; some decompression software is limited to earlier versions of the ZIP format, or else cannot handle certain advanced features.

- **Macintosh**   StuffIt format predominates; files end in .sit or (if self-extracting), .sea. The tool most commonly used to decompress files in SIT format is Aladdin's StuffIt Expander, and other tools are available free or as evaluation software at **www.aladdinsys.com**. PC versions are also offered.

- **UNIX workstations**   Predominant formats are the standard UNIX **compress** format, with the .z extension; or gzip format, with the extension .gz. To uncompress Z files, use the UNIX **uncompress** command, which takes the form **uncompress** *filename***.z**, where *filename*.z is your downloaded file. Another format commonly used in UNIX is gzip (GNU zip, not to be confused with the Windows ZIP format), designed to replace the UNIX compress utility. Files in the gzip format end in .gz. GZ software can be obtained from **www.gzip.org**. WinZip decompresses GZ files for PCs, and Aladdin Expander decompresses GZ files for Macintoshes or PCs. Tar, an archiver, is also widely used in combination with compress or gzip to make TAR.Z (or TAZ) and TAR.GZ (or TGZ) files.

Although you cannot use program files that are intended for a system other than yours, you can often use document, image, or other files. For that reason, you may need to decode a file in a format other than the predominant format for your system: ZIP files may contain useful files for Macintosh users, for instance.

Using Self-Extracting Files

Today, much of the software and other material available on the Web for downloading is in the form of self-extracting files. A *self-extracting file* is a combination of an extraction program and a compressed archive; when you run the program file, it extracts its own data into ready-to-use files. For the PC, self-extracting files have the extension .exe, and for the Macintosh they end in .sea. (The .exe file extension is used for nearly all programs on the PC, not just for self-extracting files, so you must rely on the site's documentation from which you downloaded the file to tell you that the file is self-extracting.) Self-extracting files are created by tools such as Nico Mak's WinZip and Aladdin tools. To use self-extracting files, do the following:

1. Virus-check the file you have downloaded, unless you are absolutely certain it does not contain a virus. (See "Scanning for Viruses" later in this chapter.)

2. Create a new folder for the file, and move the file into it if it's not already in one.

3. Double-click the file. The self-extracting file creates a series of files; it may ask you to tell it where to put the files, or it may just place the files in the same folder as the self-extracting file. (If the file contains a program and is both self-extracting *and self-installing,* it may ask you where you want to install the program. Extracting simply unpacks the files; installing informs your operating system that you have the program.)

4. Virus-check the extracted (or installed) files unless you are absolutely certain they do not contain a virus.

If this file is supposed to contain a program, and in step 3 nothing indicated to you that the program was installed, you may now have to install that program. See the section "Installing Programs" later in this chapter. If the file contains a document, multimedia, or something other than a program (or program enhancement), it is now ready to be used.

Unzipping ZIP Files

The most common compression format for files originating on the PC is the ZIP format. As mentioned earlier, Windows XP now allows you to open zipped files without resorting to any other programs, using its built-in Compressed Folders feature. A variety of other tools are available for decompressing the ZIP format, but the most commonly used program on earlier, zipless versions of Windows is WinZip. Other popular tools include ZipMagic for the PC, and PKUNZIP for Macintosh, UNIX, and other computers.

If you receive a UUE (uuencoded file, which are uncommon these days), most ZIP programs can open them.

Windows XP and ZIP Files

You can save space on your PC by using Windows XP to compress folders that you don't use often, squeezing them down so they occupy less space on your hard drive. These are called *compressed folders* or *zipped folders,* but they are actually ZIP files. You can access these folders just like you would any other folders in Windows XP, and you can open files from within them. Windows XP also allows you to extract files from any ZIP file as if it were a zipped folder, using Windows' Compressed (Zipped) Folders Extraction Wizard.

If you install another ZIP program on your computer under Windows XP (like ZipMagic and WinZip, discussed later), those programs replace Windows XP's ability to compress and extract files. If you install any ZIP program and decide you don't like it, you'll have to uninstall it and then reboot in order to get Windows XP's ZIP handling abilities back.

Advances in computing always come at a cost, though, and Windows XP's zipped folders feature has several disadvantages:

■ Many executable programs (EXEs) don't work if they're in a zipped folder because they need access to special files (called *dynamic link libraries*) that need to be untouched.

■ Your PC needs to use computing power to unzip everything on-the-fly when you open it, which can slow down your PC.

■ Many programs can't read or write files to or from zipped folders. For example, if you want to open a document, you need to move or copy it from a zipped folder to a regular folder before you can open it in most programs. WinZip and ZipMagic don't have this disadvantage, which is why we prefer them.

Still, if you have a bunch of old files that you don't use often (or a lot of large files that you want to send to someone else), this may be for you.

Extracting Files from a ZIP file or Zipped Folder in Windows XP   A slightly confusing thing for novices is that Windows XP does not draw a distinction between *zipped folders* (folders on your hard drive that you chose to compress) and *ZIP files* (which are generally downloaded from the Internet). The process for decompressing them is the same because they are the same thing.

All ZIP files and zipped folders in Windows have a little zipper on them (see Figure 34-5) to indicate that they're compressed.

To uncompress them, follow these steps:

1. Right-click on the zipped folder (ZIP file) and select Extract All. The Compressed (Zipped) Folders Extraction Wizard starts up, as shown in Figure 34-6. Click Next.

2. Select the folder you want to put the uncompressed files in. If this is a zipped program that you downloaded from the Internet, create a new folder to hold all the files so you can keep track of them (and can delete them all in one fell swoop if you don't like the program). If you haven't created a folder for the program already, you can do so now by clicking Browse, browsing to the place you'd like to create the folder in, and then clicking Make New Folder. Windows creates a subfolder for you, and you can type in the name of the folder that will hold all your programs. Click OK.

3. Click Next. The Wizard extracts the files and places them in the folder you've specified. If you would accidentally overwrite a file in the target folder with a file that you're decompressing (if, for example, you're unzipping a newer version of a program to a folder in order to update it), Windows asks you whether you'd like to replace the file with the ZIP file version, keep the older version that was already there, or cancel the extraction altogether.

4. When it's done, Windows offers to show you a list of the files you've extracted from the ZIP folder. Select the Show Extracted Files check box, and Windows will take you to the decompressed folder to look at the now full-sized files.

Figure 34-5.   *Zipped folders in Windows XP*

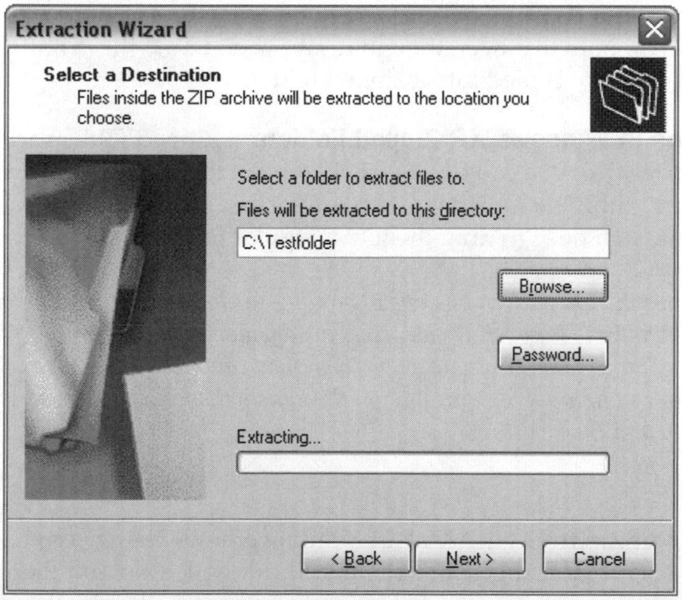

Figure 34-6.   *The Windows XP Compressed (Zipped) Folders Extraction Wizard*

Another way to extract files from a zipped folder is to open the folder in Windows Explorer by double-clicking it and then drag the files to another folder.

Zipping a Folder in Windows XP   You can't compress an existing folder, but WinXP gives you two options to turn folders full of files into tightly packed zipped folders:

- You can create a new zipped folder and drag files into it.
- You can select a bunch of files and send them to a zipped folder.

To create a new zipped folder in Windows XP, choose Start | My Computer to run Windows Explorer, and browse to wherever you'd like to create the new zipped folder. Then select File | New | Compressed (Zipped) Folder. Windows creates a zipped folder with the default name of New Compressed (Zipped) Folder; type in a new name for it and press ENTER. You can then drag whatever files you'd like into the new folder, and Windows automatically compresses them for you.

Dragging a file into a compressed folder creates a compressed copy of that file; the original file will still be wherever you had it.

Alternatively, you can select a number of files at once (either by CTRL-clicking individual files or by clicking the first file in a list, SHIFT-clicking the last in that list to select a range of files), right-clicking, and then selecting Send To | Compressed (Zipped) Folder. Windows then creates a folder for you and automatically names it after the oldest file in the folder. If that's not the name you wanted, you'll have to track it down and rename it. Also note that even though it says "Send To," the original files stay where they are; they are copied into a zipped folder.

Accessing Files in Windows XP Zipped Folders   Zipped folders act like any other folders in Windows XP; you can double-click to open them and double-click to open (some) programs within them. However, many programs can't read files directly out of zipped folders; you need to drag them to a regular folder first.

You can use the Up or Back buttons to browse—as long as you're only on the first level of a zipped folder. However, if you access a subfolder within a zipped folder, using the Up or Back buttons to browse through them may cause error messages. To safely get back to your nonzipped folders, click on the folders themselves to go forward and back, not the Up and Back buttons.

WinZip

You can obtain WinZip from Nico Mak Computing at **www.winzip.com**. (The program itself comes as a self-extracting, self-installing file; download it and then double-click it. The installation program inquires whether you wish to use the classic or wizard interface. Choose the classic interface if you intend to follow the steps in this section.) Once you have installed WinZip, to extract files from a ZIP file using WinZip (release 8.1), double-click a ZIP file or zipped folder. You see the WinZip window, as shown in Figure 34-7, listing the files in the ZIP file. Click the Extract button on the toolbar to extract files.

Compressing a bunch of files into a single ZIP file that you can send to other people is handy when you're sending out, say, extremely large and detailed pictures of your new child to all of your friends. Just click the New button on the toolbar, name the new ZIP file (zipped folder), select the files you'd like to add to the archive to be compressed (to select more than one file at a time, CTRL-click them), and click Add.

ZipMagic

ZipMagic, from Ontrack Data International, is particularly useful if you use a *lot* of ZIP files. ZipMagic runs continuously in the background, where it causes ZIP files to be displayed as folders in nearly all windows, not just in Windows Explorer. You open the ZIP "folders" to display and use the files (and folders) contained within, exactly as you would any other file or folder on your PC. That's what makes ZipMagic better than Windows XP's built-in Compressed Folders feature.

ZipMagic also has the benefit of being an almost one-stop decompression program, handling uuencoding, TAR files, and almost everything else discussed in this chapter (except for Mac compressed files, natch). Double-click a folder (zipped or otherwise),

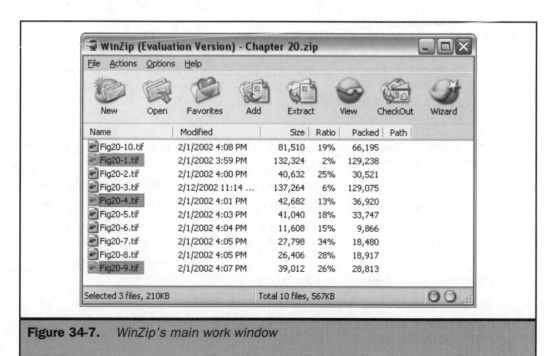

Figure 34-7. *WinZip's main work window*

and you see the contents of that folder (ZIP file). Note that each window is equipped with a tiny Zip button at the upper right; clicking that button allows you to disable the ZipMagic display in that window or to change ZipMagic's properties.

You can download ZipMagic from **www.zipmagic.com**. The program comes as a self-extracting, self-installing file. Download it and double-click it to begin the installation process. Once ZipMagic is installed, you may control it by double-clicking the Zip icon ZipMagic places on the Windows taskbar. ZipMagic appears within your browser window when you download archive files, and after the file is downloaded, gives you a choice of saving, installing, or (if the file is a document) viewing it.

PKUNZIP and UnZip

PKUNZIP (which comes with a companion program, PKZIP) and UnZip are two programs for unzipping ZIP files on a very broad variety of computers and operating systems. Both programs allow you to view and extract TAR, GZIP, BinHex, and uuencoded files, as well as ZIP files. A number of other programs for the ZIP format are also distributed on the Internet (mostly on FTP sites), with varying abilities to handle the full variety of ZIP file variants. Both PKUNZIP and UnZip are DOS programs that also run with Windows.

PKZIP and PKUNZIP are available from **www.pkware.com**, and UnZip is available at many sites worldwide, such as the FTP site **ftp.cdrom.com** in the United States and **www.mirror.ac.uk** in the United Kingdom. You must download the correct binary (program) for your computer and operating system; look for a folder or links named after your type of system at these sites.

PKZIP for Windows is Pkware's version for PCs running Windows, and it both zips and unzips. The program downloads as a self-extracting, self-installing file. Download the file and double-click it to both decompress and install the program. You can then launch PKZIP for Windows by choosing Start | All Programs | Pkware | PKZIP for Windows. To extract files from a ZIP file (or self-extracting ZIP EXE file) in PKZIP 4.5 for Windows, take the following steps:

1. Choose File | Open and, in the Open dialog box that appears, choose the ZIP file from which you want to extract files.

2. If you want to extract only selected files, CTRL-click them; otherwise, go to step 3.

3. Choose Extract | Extract Files from the menu bar. The Extract menu appears.

4. Click the Browse button in the Extract dialog box and in the Browse dialog box that appears, select a disk drive and folder for your files. Click OK in the Browse dialog box.

5. Click the Extract button to extract the files.

6. Click the Done button after the last file is extracted.

For DOS PCs and UNIX workstations, most versions of PKZIP and UnZip use command lines, rather than windowed interfaces. To run those programs, change to the directory where the program file UNZIP (or UNZIP.EXE) is stored, copy your ZIP file to the same directory, and then type the command **unzip** *filename*.**zip**, where *filename*.zip represents the name of your ZIP file.

Unpacking TAR Archive Files

In the UNIX operating system, archiving and compression are handled separately. In UNIX the term *archive* most commonly refers to files in the TAR format, which are created by the **tar** program. (TAR stands for Tape ARchive, but "tape" in this context is irrelevant.) The TAR format simply allows a group of files to be combined into one file, which ends in .tar.

If you use a UNIX workstation, the command to extract files from a TAR file in UNIX may vary with the particular operating system. The following form, however, works with most systems:

> **tar xvf** *filename*.**tar**

A TAR file may be compressed (using the UNIX compress command or gzip) into a Z or GZ file, and usually has the extension .tar.z, .tar-z, .tar.gz, .tar-gz, or .tgz. To obtain the files contained in such a compressed archive file, you first decompress the TAR file and then extract its files.

If you use a PC or Macintosh, the program you use to decompress ZIP or SIT files may be able to perform both operations: decompression of the Z file into a TAR file, and unpacking of the TAR file into individual files. That program may require you to know (or guess) what file or files are contained in the Z file. For example, if you open a compressed TAR file (TAR.Z, TAR-Z, TAR.GZ, TAR-GZ, TAZ, or TGZ) with WinZip, WinZip asks for the filename you wish to extract. The safest choice is to keep the name WinZip suggests, but to change the file extension to .tar. WinZip then offers to unpack the TAR file into the final, ready-to-use files.

 Keep in mind that the files contained in a TAR file are most likely intended for use on a UNIX system. If so, you will be unable to use any program files that are unpacked, although you may be able to read the documentation.

Decoding and Decompressing Macintosh Files

For most Macintosh users, files download, decode, and decompress without much fuss. Macintosh files are unique, however, which can occasionally complicate the downloading process. Macintosh files have a two-part (or *two-forked*) file format comprised of a *resource fork* and a *data fork*. UNIX and PC systems do not support such a file format, and most servers of downloadable files are UNIX or PC systems. Therefore, when Macintosh communications software transmits a file to a non-Macintosh system or across the Internet, it uses one of two schemes to preserve the full Macintosh file structure: MacBinary or BinHex.

When a binary file is placed on the Internet, the Macintosh software handling the transfer generally attaches a *MacBinary header* to the file, which contains the resource fork information. Such files are often denoted by a .bin extension attached to the file.

An alternative approach is to encode the binary file in *BinHex* format, which not only preserves the resource fork, but also stores the file as ASCII (text) characters. BinHex files carry an extension of .hqx. BinHex format, like UUE format, was intended to allow binary files to be carried by simple Internet programs, such as UNIX mail, that could handle only text. Even though most contemporary e-mail, web browser, and other programs can now handle binary files through the use of MIME, HQX files are still very common on the Internet.

Decoding BIN and HQX Macintosh Files

Files in either MacBinary (BIN) or BinHex (HQX) format cannot be executed directly on the Macintosh; they must be decoded first. Software to decode these formats is available on the Internet, but because that software itself must be in either MacBinary or BinHex, Macintosh users faced a "chicken-and-egg" dilemma. The dilemma is today solved by the built-in capability of most web browsers and other Internet programs for the Macintosh.

Many contemporary Internet programs for the Macintosh, including browsers from Netscape and Microsoft, and the popular Fetch FTP client program, handle MacBinary and HQX decoding automatically. A few, such as Netscape Navigator, rely on auxiliary "helper" software on the Mac, generally StuffIt Expander or one of Aladdin's other products. Netscape products currently come with StuffIt Expander.

When Macintosh Internet software downloads a file from the Internet and decodes it, you generally (by default) end up with two (or more) files on your desktop: the original file and the decoded file(s). You may discard the HQX and SIT or SEA files once you have a usable file. You can set many programs to delete the compressed file automatically, but you risk unpacking virus files.

If your copy of Netscape Navigator does not decode HQX files, it may be attempting to refer the job to a helper application that is not present. Take the following steps in your Netscape browser to decode the HQX file:

1. Choose Options | General Preferences; a Preferences dialog box appears.

2. Click the Helpers tab, and a Helpers card is displayed.

3. Scroll down the list on the Helpers card until you see Macintosh BinHex Archive in the leftmost column.

4. Double-click Macintosh BinHex Archive, and an Edit Type window appears.

5. At the bottom of the Edit Type window, change the Handled By preference from Application to Navigator (or Communicator, if you are using Netscape Communicator).

6. Click OK.

If you receive a downloaded file (say, from another Internet user) that is supposed to be a valid Macintosh file, but you cannot open or run the file, it is probably still in MacBinary or BinHex format. You can convert the file into a valid Mac file by using StuffIt Expander, by choosing Extract | MacBinary | Decode (for a BIN file) or Extract | BinHex | Decode (for an HQX file). A standard Open dialog box allows you to select the file: do so, and then click Open. You will find the decoded file in the same folder as the original.

Decompressing (Expanding) SIT and SEA Macintosh Files

The process of decoding a Macintosh file may involve several steps, including decompression. If you download and decode an HQX (BinHex) file, for instance, it may yield a compressed SIT (StuffIt) file, which must then be decompressed into a valid Macintosh file. Such files are sometimes indicated by a filename ending in *.sit.hqx*. In some instances, your software both decodes and decompresses the file automatically. If your Macintosh is equipped with StuffIt Expander, for instance, it both decodes and decompresses SIT files that are encoded in HQX format, leaving you with the original file HQX file, the SIT file, and the final, ready-to-use file.

StuffIt or SIT is the most common compression format used on the Macintosh. Aladdin Systems makes the expansion software for SIT files available for free on its web site at **www.aladdinsys.com**, in both HQX and MacBinary format. Aladdin's software can also decode a variety of other formats, including ZIP files.

Another common format, especially for program downloads, is the SEA format, the Self-Expanding (or -Extracting) Archive format. Downloaded files in SEA format require no special software to expand. They can be used as described in the earlier section of this chapter, "Using Self-Extracting Files." Files in SEA format are binary files, so they come with a MacBinary header. Fortunately, most contemporary browsers can decode the MacBinary header, leaving you with an executable SEA file. If, however, you obtain a SEA file from another source (such as on a floppy disk, downloaded by a PC user), you need to convert it to a valid Macintosh file, as described in the preceding section.

Using StuffIt Expander

If your Macintosh uses System 7.0 or higher, you may decode and expand files by selecting them and dragging them on top of the StuffIt Expander icon. Otherwise, to use StuffIt Expander to open a file that has been downloaded to your desktop:

1. In StuffIt Expander, choose File | Expand.

2. In the dialog box that opens, click the Desktop button, highlight your saved file, and click Expand. One or more new files appear on your desktop.

3. Choose File | Quit.

For PCs using Aladdin software, the process is similar. If a PC (or UNIX workstation) receives a BinHex or MacBinary file, however, the resource fork is discarded, saved as a separate file, or used by the program to construct an appropriate file extension. Usually, the lost information is not crucial, but some Macintosh file types (certain QuickTime movies and Macintosh sound files) put important information in the resource fork. These files generally do not work on a PC or UNIX workstation. Instead, you must find the QuickTime movie in a format called *flattened,* or the audio file in a format recognized by your computer.

Installing Programs

Once you have obtained a program file, either by decompressing or extracting the file from an archive (as the preceding section describes) or by downloading it in a ready-to-use form, you take the following steps.

First, on any system, unless you *completely* trust the source from which you downloaded the file, virus-check the file or files you downloaded or extracted from an archive file. Perform the virus check even if you already virus-checked the archive file from which the files were extracted. (Many virus scanners cannot examine the files within an archive.) See "Scanning for Viruses" in the next section.

If you are using a Windows system, unless the software arrived in a self-extracting, self-installing form and has already been installed, look for an Install.exe or Setup.exe file among the files you have downloaded or extracted from an archive. If you find such a file, double-click it. An installation program launches and steps you through the process of installing the software. After the installation finishes, it is important to virus-check your entire computer before running the new application. To run a newly installed program under Windows, choose Start | All Programs (Start | Programs on pre-XP Windows), and look for a new command with the name of your installed software.

On a Macintosh system, after virus-checking the program file or files, double-click the program file. The program launches and in most cases steps you through an installation process. Follow the installation process as you normally would for a new application installed from any other source. If an installation does not take place, simply move the program file and its associated files to a new folder in the Applications folder on your hard disk drive. To use the program, double-click it.

On a UNIX system, copy the program file to your bin directory. To run the program, type its name, followed by any switches or arguments the documentation directs you to use, and press ENTER.

Scanning for Viruses

It is important that all downloaded files, unless they come from an absolutely trustworthy source, be checked (*scanned*) for viruses before they are used in any way or stored anywhere but in a separate folder on your system. You should check all files, even document files, because of the possibility of *macro viruses*—viruses that make use of a word processor's or spreadsheet program's ability to execute instructions (macros), as well as display a file.

Here are a few warnings:

■ Never, *ever* open a program sent to you via e-mail without checking it—even if it's from a friend. New strains of viruses take advantage of security holes in e-mail programs to appear as innocent programs, but when you click them, they take over your e-mail client and send themselves out to everyone on your address list with an innocuous header like "Hi there" or "The file you requested." Just because your Mom sent it to you doesn't mean that it's safe.

■ *Never* follow any instructions sent to you via e-mail that tell you how to remove a virus. Sadistic hackers take advantage of people's ignorance by sending out e-mails telling people to search their computers for system files that are supposed to be there (and that are critical for the continued well-being of your computer), claiming these files are evidence of "infection." They then helpfully show you how to "fix" the virus by deleting those critical files, crashing your computer. (Also, AOL and Microsoft have never—and probably will never—issue a statement claiming that "There's nothing they can do about" any virus; after all, would *you* admit you were utterly clueless in a national press release?)

■ If you're ever in doubt about whether a virus is real or not, **www.antivirus.com/vinfo** has solid information regarding real (and current) viruses.

■ If you are browsing the Web and a dialog box pops up asking you to confirm downloading a program, click No unless you are sure you know what the program is. If you are visiting a reputable site for which you need a widely-used plug-in program (like Adobe Acrobat or RealPlayer), click Yes. Otherwise, be suspicious that the web server wants to download and install a virus or other malicious code.

For the most complete virus checking, obtain commercial virus-checking software, such as McAfee VirusScan (available from **www.mcafee.com**). Any good virus software comes with an online service that automatically briefs the software with the latest virus developments—you need to update your virus scanner at least once a week because hackers are developing new viruses all the time. Besides detecting viruses, antivirus software should also help you remove the viral infection from a file, although some files are too hopelessly infected to clean. See the section on viruses in Chapter 1 for more information.

Viruses are not common in downloaded files, especially if you stick to popular and reputable software libraries, but when you do get one, it can blow up months of work. Be sure to not only download new virus definitions weekly, but to also back up your important files to ensure that if something *does* slip by the immense net of virus protection, it won't be fatal.

Watch for Scams

Viruses are not the only malevolent programs lurking on the Internet. For example, several years ago, a pornography site in Moldova (a former Soviet republic) required users to download a special viewer program. Unbeknownst to those who downloaded the program, the "viewer" also reconfigured their computers to connect to the Internet via a long-distance call to Moldova! Presumably, the perpetrators arranged with the Moldovan phone company to receive a cut of the astronomical phone charges. AT&T noticed the strange increase in calls to Moldova and contacted the authorities. The moral of the story: download software only from reputable software libraries.

There aren't many viruses that run on the Macintosh (thankfully). You can have StuffIt Expander or some other Aladdin program automatically launch your virus-scanning program. You can find the control for doing so by choosing Edit | Preferences in the Aladdin program. The best protection is to download from known sites and to read news sites like MacInTouch (**www.macintouch.com**), the Macintosh News Network (**www.macnn.com**), and MacSlash (**www.macslash.com**).

Index

Symbols and Numbers

H

M

N

using, 373–381, 374
using directory server with, 376–377
using text chat feature with, 378
using voice chat feature with, 378–379
video conferencing with, 379
Nets
purpose of, 308–309
web site for, 309
Netscape 6 Mail program
avoiding viruses with, 215–216
basic commands for, 163–164
configuring, 165–166
configuring to work with AOL 7.0, 173
displaying complete headers for messages with, 166
downloading, 161
filtering e-mail messages in, 214–215
formatting e-mail for, 166
opening, 162
usage of, 161–166
Netscape browsers, downloading, 406
Netscape Composer 4.x, uploading web pages through, 699–700
Netscape Composer web editor. *See also* FrontPage web editor, web pages
adding horizontal lines to web pages with, 572
adding links to web pages with, 578–579
adding pictures to web pages with, 572–574
changing HTML source code with, 579
choosing backgrounds for web pages with, 570
choosing views for web pages with, 567–568
creating web pages with, 565
description of, 518
displaying HTML source code with, 568
displaying tags with, 568
downloading, 565
editing tables in web pages with, 576
editing web pages with, 566–567
entering and formatting text for web pages with, 571–572
formatting cells in web-page tables with, 577–578
formatting lists on web pages with, 572
formatting tables in web pages with, 576–578
inserting special characters in web pages with, 572

previewing web pages with, 568
saving web pages with, 579
setting colors for web pages with, 568–570
setting hyperlink colors with, 569
setting page titles and properties with, 570–571
starting, 565
using to format web pages with tables, 574–578
Netscape Mail & Newsgroups 6
canceling messages with, 294
downloading and reading messages with, 292–293
finding and subscribing to newsgroups with, 291–292
opening for newsreading, 290
printing messages with, 294
replying to messages with, 294
saving messages with, 294–295
selecting news servers for, 290
sending messages with, 294
starting new threads with, 294
unsubscribing from newsgroups with, 295
Netscape Messenger 4.7 e-mail client
avoiding viruses with, 215–216
basic commands for, 168–169
canceling newsgroup messages with, 300
configuring, 167–170
downloading, 166
filtering e-mail messages in, 214–215
finding and subscribing to newsgroups with, 295–297
newsreading with, 295–300
opening, 167
opening for newsreading, 295–300
printing newsgroup messages with, 300
reading and selecting newsgroup messages with, 298–299
reading newsgroup messages online and offline with, 298
receiving attached files with, 188
replying to newsgroup messages with, 299
saving newsgroup messages with, 300
sending attached files with, 187–188
sending newsgroup messages with, 299–300
starting new threads with, 299–300
threading messages with, 299
unsubscribing from newsgroups with, 300
usage of, 166–170

S

V

W

INTERNATIONAL CONTACT INFORMATION

AUSTRALIA
McGraw-Hill Book Company Australia Pty. Ltd.
TEL +61-2-9417-9899
FAX +61-2-9417-5687
http://www.mcgraw-hill.com.au
books-it_sydney@mcgraw-hill.com

CANADA
McGraw-Hill Ryerson Ltd.
TEL +905-430-5000
FAX +905-430-5020
http://www.mcgrawhill.ca

**GREECE, MIDDLE EAST,
NORTHERN AFRICA**
McGraw-Hill Hellas
TEL +30-1-656-0990-3-4
FAX +30-1-654-5525

MEXICO (Also serving Latin America)
McGraw-Hill Interamericana Editores S.A. de C.V.
TEL +525-117-1583
FAX +525-117-1589
http://www.mcgraw-hill.com.mx
fernando_castellanos@mcgraw-hill.com

SINGAPORE (Serving Asia)
McGraw-Hill Book Company
TEL +65-863-1580
FAX +65-862-3354
http://www.mcgraw-hill.com.sg
mghasia@mcgraw-hill.com

SOUTH AFRICA
McGraw-Hill South Africa
TEL +27-11-622-7512
FAX +27-11-622-9045
robyn_swanepoel@mcgraw-hill.com

**UNITED KINGDOM & EUROPE
(Excluding Southern Europe)**
McGraw-Hill Education Europe
TEL +44-1-628-502500
FAX +44-1-628-770224
http://www.mcgraw-hill.co.uk
computing_neurope@mcgraw-hill.com

ALL OTHER INQUIRIES Contact:
Osborne/McGraw-Hill
TEL +1-510-549-6600
FAX +1-510-883-7600
http://www.osborne.com
omg_international@mcgraw-hill.com